Reclaiming the Future

New Zealand and the Global Economy

Reclaiming the Future

JANE KELSEY

BRIDGET WILLIAMS BOOKS

First published in New Zealand in 1999
by Bridget Williams Books Ltd,
PO Box 5482, Wellington

© 1999 Jane Kelsey

This book is copyright. Apart from fair dealing for
the purpose of private study, research, criticism,
or review, as permitted under the Copyright Act,
no part may be reproduced by any process without
the prior permission of the publishers.

Acknowledgements
The publisher is grateful to the following for
permission to reproduce copyright material:
Craig Potton Publishing, for the cover photograph,
from *Moment and Memory: Photography in the
New Zealand Landscape*, 1998.
For the graphs: OECD Economic Surveys, New Zealand;
S. Chatterjee and N. Podder; Statistics New Zealand.

Cover photograph, 'Rising tide, Pakawau, Golden Bay' by Craig Potton
Internal Design by Afineline
Typeset in Sabon by Archetype
Printed by Astra Print Group, Wellington
Cover design by Mission Hall Design Group

ISBN 1-877 242 012

to Joy and Rua

with love and thanks

▲ Contents

Preface	*ix*
Introduction	*1*
1 ▲ Putting Globalisation in Perspective	*26*
2 ▲ Constructing Orthodoxy	*56*
3 ▲ Leading the World	*90*
4 ▲ 'Free' Investment	*121*
5 ▲ Transnational Enterprise	*161*
6 ▲ 'Free' Trade	*200*
7 ▲ The World Trade Organisation	*239*
8 ▲ Asia Pacific Economic Cooperation	*279*
9 ▲ The Multilateral Agreement on Investment	*315*
10 ▲ Reclaiming the Future	*353*
Appendix: Figures 1–6	*386*
References	*389*
Select Bibliography	*417*
Index	*425*

▲ List of Abbreviations

ABAC	APEC Business Advisory Council
ADB	Asian Development Bank
ACT	Association of Consumers and Taxpayers
APEC	Asia Pacific Economic Cooperation
APLN	Asia Pacific Labour Network
ASEAN	Association of South East Asian Nations
CER	Australia New Zealand Closer Economic Relations Trade Agreement
EU	European Union
FDI	foreign direct investment
GATS	General Agreement on Trade in Services
GATT	General Agreement on Tariffs and Trade
GDP	gross domestic product
GST	goods and services tax
ICFTU	International Confederation of Free Trade Unions
ILO	International Labour Organisation
IMF	International Monetary Fund
MAI	Multilateral Agreement on Investment
MFAT	Ministry of Foreign Affairs and Trade
MMP	mixed member proportional (representation)
NAFTA	North American Free Trade Agreement
NBR	*National Business Review*
NGO	non-government organisation
NZCTU	New Zealand Council of Trade Unions
NZIER	New Zealand Institute of Economic Research
NZPD	New Zealand Parliamentary Debates
NZTUF	New Zealand Trade Union Federation
OECD	Organisation for Economic Cooperation and Development
OIC	Overseas Investment Commission
PBEC	Pacific Business Economic Council
PECC	Pacific Economic Cooperation Council
TNE	transnational enterprise
TWI	trade weighted index
UN	United Nations
UNCTAD	United Nations Conference on Trade and Development
WTO	World Trade Organisation

▲ Preface

This book sets out to test the orthodoxy of the 1990s – that globalisation is irresistible, inevitable and desirable. It challenges the policies, laws and international agreements that have deeply exposed New Zealand to the global economy, and the belief that New Zealand is leading the world towards some global free market nirvana.

The book was started in 1993, but writing *The New Zealand Experiment* intervened. The delay proved fortuitous. I had a strong sense that the nature and benefits of globalisation were being overplayed, but it was difficult to prove at that time. By the end of the 1990s, the same belief was being expressed by commentators in many countries, backed by substantial statistical and empirical evidence.

This is not a book about the global economy. It is about the choices that have been made on behalf of New Zealanders since 1984, sometimes without our knowledge and often without our consent. It also sets out some of the issues that confront us as we seek alternative ways forward. Its conclusions are optimistic: they celebrate the emergence of New Zealanders from a state of grumbling acquiescence to the point where economic and social policies are (belatedly) subject to a contest of ideas.

Many people have contributed to this project along the way. Groups such as Corso, GATT Watchdog, Campaign Against Foreign Control of Aotearoa (CAFCA), Christian World Service, the Aotearoa New Zealand APEC Monitoring Group and the Trade Union Federation have raised awareness of international economic issues, and created a pool of alternative information and analysis on which I have drawn. Bill Rosenberg has been especially generous in sharing his time and knowledge of foreign investment issues. I am also indebted to my friend Bruce Jesson for his intellectual inspiration and personal friendship over the years. As always, my mother and my friends have been quietly supportive – especially Joy and Rua Rakena, to whom this book is dedicated, and without whose love and care it and much else could not have been achieved.

Further thanks go to the University of Auckland for its ongoing support, and to the University of Warwick School of Law which provided a space in which to write. Professor Upendra Baxi generously shared his home and his insights during my stay, and along with other colleagues around the world helped to stimulate the ideas that comprise the book's central theme.

Numerous officials at the World Bank, IMF, OECD, World Trade Organisation and Commonwealth Secretariat, diplomats at various embassies, and staff of think-tanks have provided frank and insightful interviews. Most have not been identified by name, but I trust I have faithfully represented their views. New Zealand government officials have provided detailed responses to requests under the Official Information Act on a wide range of subjects. The Ministry of Foreign Affairs and Trade also arranged for me to access the early files on APEC, which was of major assistance.

This is my fourth book in which Bridget Williams has invested her valued time, energy and friendship, and her consummate professionalism. Bridget, editor Alison Carew and a team of others have worked hard to make a detailed script accessible to readers, and to produce the book on a very tight schedule. Special thanks to my research assistant, Alison Greenaway, for her generous support, and for checking of innumerable footnotes in the later stages of production. A number of other people have read and commented on aspects of the book at various stages. I am grateful to them all for their corrections, criticisms and suggestions. While I have tried to address the issues they raised, the responsibility for whatever errors or omissions remain is solely mine.

Jane Kelsey
July 1999

▲ Introduction

'Globalisation' has been the buzz-word of the 1990s. Some commentators eagerly predicted the advent of a 'borderless world'.[1] US sociologist Frank Fukuyama talked of 'the end of history' as we know it. The global integration of technology and production was opening the door to a limitless accumulation of wealth and the satisfaction of people's ever-expanding desires – and to the embrace of liberal democracy throughout the world. 'This process guarantees an increasing homogenisation of all human societies, regardless of their historical origins of cultural heritages.'[2]

Others, such as David Korten, warned that the voracious expansion of global capital would see corporations come to 'rule the world'.[3] 'Healthy societies depend on healthy, empowered local communities that build caring relationships among people and help to connect to a particular piece of the living earth with which our lives are intertwined. ... Yet we have created an institutional and cultural context that disempowers the local and makes such action difficult, if not impossible.'[4]

Robert Reich, brought to New Zealand by the Labour Party in 1998, foresaw a twenty-first century devoid of national products, corporations and industries: 'There will no longer be national economies, at least as we have come to understand that concept. All that will remain within national borders are the people who comprise a nation ... .'[5] State-centred economies, governance and regulation would, it seemed, be transcended by a new global order.

For most of the decade, the vision of a global economy built on 'free' markets and 'free' trade and investment seemed invincible. Enthusiasts sought to advance the process more swiftly. 'Realistic' critics suggested ways to mitigate the adverse effects of globalisation, especially on labour and the environment. 'Unrealistic' critics denounced the growing inequalities and poverty, and warned of the erosion of democracy and the potential for unregulated capitalism to implode.

Free-marketeers have a vested interest in promoting the belief that globalisation is invincible. Critics can be summarily dismissed; there *are* no alternatives; resistance is futile. This book tells a different story. It insists that globalisation is neither inevitable nor irresistible; instead, it is complex, contradictory and open to contest.

'Globalisation' is used in this book in two different senses. *Globalisation as ideology* is the grand vision, a meta-narrative that imagines an interdependent and self-regulating global economy where goods, capital and ideas flow freely, irrespective of national borders, social formations, cultures or politics. *Globalisation in practice* describes a highly contested process where the competing interests of people, companies, tribes, governments and other groupings overlap and collide; alliances form; accommodations and more drastic revisions are made; and new contradictions arise. The process is dynamic, and the outcome is far from certain.

Globalisation as ideology should not be confused with globalisation as a description of economic, social or cultural life. Since 1984, however, true believers in the vision of an unfettered global market-place have sought to make that a reality in New Zealand. Partly as a consequence, New Zealanders' perceptions of the world, and our relationship to it, have changed. There is a sense of being more connected to the world. McDonald's and KFC now vie for custom with the ubiquitous fish and chips and meat pie. The difference goes beyond the food – New Zealanders have a more cosmopolitan self-image. Mum's hand-knitted jumpers have been replaced by sweatshirts with the 'Nike swoosh', and canvas sandshoes by Reeboks. Video recorders and pay-TV bring us blockbuster movies in the comfort of our living-rooms. Sky TV beams in sport from anywhere in the world – even the All Blacks have become a trade-marked commodity. New Zealanders fly to Sydney for the weekend or to Fiji for the week, and draw foreign money out of their home account through an automatic teller machine. Letters are almost passé for the computer-literate PC-owner. Corner hardware shops, greengrocers and bakeries have been replaced by foreign-owned supermarket chains which sell almost anything at almost any time of the day. Franchised retail stores sell cheap clothes from China or Fiji to families struggling to make ends meet, while local textile factories are forced to close and lay off their staff. Cars are cheaper too, thanks to Japanese imports, even if their odometers are wound back. All the local car assembly plants have gone. Telecommunications, buses, trains, planes, electricity companies, radio and television, newspapers, banks, forests and who-knows-what-else are owned by faceless transnational corporations, most of whose shareholders live offshore. The nightly television news carries the latest shifts in 'the market', assuming that ordinary viewers understand what they mean. Ministers hail the latest international trade agreement as the key to prosperity. Economic recovery is proverbially 'just around the corner'. The 'national interest' has been redefined to mean making business more competitive in the international market-place. For people with money, all this can be liberating. For many ordinary New Zealanders it represents a threat to identity, jobs, communities, and the right to control their own lives.

'Free' markets may make perfect sense in economic theory, although many economists would dispute that.[6] But as the philosophical foundation for human society, such markets are fundamentally flawed. The economy is not some self-regulating market-place detached from the society in which it operates. Pretending that economic and social reality can be reconstructed to fit the free market model creates practical problems for the productive economy, and social costs that become unacceptable. People, faced with governance by the market, demand an effective voice in the decisions that affect them, and new forms of intervention, regulation and support that re-embed economic policy in social life.

After a decade of radical, theory-driven change, it is hardly surprising that New Zealanders in the 1990s began to reassert the relevance of their social and political world in government decisions. It was clear that New Zealand could not simply go back to what existed prior to 1984, even if people wanted to. Society had changed; the new generation of 'children of the market' has known nothing else. Agriculture, industry and services have been restructured to reflect the free market economy. The capacity and functions of the state have been fundamentally altered. Different groups have become empowered, and there are new communities of poor and dispossessed. Maori have reasserted their role in political and economic life, variously supporting aspects of deregulation, suffering disproportionately from its impacts, and continuing to confront Pakeha (or non-Maori) society with its failure to redress the wrongs of the colonial past.

The free market revolution began in 1984 with a clear blueprint and a committed team of politicians, officials and private players who shared some common goals. In 1999 there are growing signs of resistance, but demands for a new direction have been, by contrast, unsystematic and unorganised. There is no alternative template, no coherent vision of the kind of society in which people want to live, or the kind of state they wish to empower. These challenges have been resisted by those in business, politics, the public service, academia and the media who have an economic interest in, and/or an ideological commitment to, the free market agenda. They reassert the inherent validity of their economic model, and blame the failures on a refusal to 'finish the business'. But the model of a self-regulating economy and society has become politically untenable. The state cannot permanently abdicate its responsibility for the country's economic and social well-being by leaving those outcomes to be determined by competitive markets. Just as governments are the vehicles through which deregulation is pursued, they also retain the authority to reassert some control. As New Zealand enters a new millennium, the critical questions are: how much room do New Zealanders, and future governments, have to choose a different path? And have the policies implemented since 1984 so foreclosed the options that change can take place only within the existing market-driven paradigm?

▲ LESSONS FROM HISTORY

In treating globalisation as inevitable, its champions in New Zealand and elsewhere have ignored the lessons of history. The starting point for this book is Karl Polanyi's account of the rise and collapse of the laissez-faire economy in Europe in the late nineteenth and early twentieth centuries, which he called *The Great Transformation*.

Free-marketeers of the nineteenth century insisted that they could judge social events solely from the economic viewpoint. This was a novel approach: 'Normally, the economic order is merely a function of the social, in which it is contained. ... Nineteenth century society, in which economic activity was isolated and imputed to a distinctive economic motive, was ... a singular departure.'[7] Although this new idea of a self-regulating market system tried to separate economic activity from society and politics, social relations did not disappear. Unregulated markets produced socially unacceptable outcomes, which in turn had political consequences. This created pressures to re-regulate. A determined attempt to revive free markets following the First World War failed. The economy became embedded in social relations once more, although the new society that emerged in the 1930s was quite different from the one that existed before.

Polanyi distinguished the idea that markets are self-regulating (in the sense that they tend to reach a price equilibrium) from 'a self-regulating market *system*', which 'implies markets for the elements of production – labor, land, and money', operating through free trade, a free labour market and a freely exchangeable currency.[8] In such a system, nature and human society were transformed into mere commodities. Social relations between families, communities, workers and businesses existed only within markets. The backlash this created intensified from the time of the First World War and 'was more than the usual defensive behaviour of a society faced with change; it was a reaction against a dislocation which attacked the fabric of society'.[9] It occurred in all three markets ('labor, land, and money'): 'Paradoxically enough, not human beings and natural resources only but also the organization of capitalistic production itself had to be sheltered from the devastating effects of a self-regulating market'.[10] Polanyi described this as a 'double movement': 'The market expanded continuously but this movement was met by a countermovement checking the expansion in definite directions. Vital though such a countermovement was for the protection of society, in the last analysis it was incompatible with the self-regulation of the market, and thus with the market system itself.'[11]

Polanyi described the breakdown of the market system from 1916 on. Pressures to re-regulate reflected ad hoc responses to specific situations faced by workers, farmers and manufacturers and were supported by pragmatic alliances of those affected in each instance. Opposition to the free market was not based on ideology, but on practicality. Significant new players had emerged, especially workers and women. Those whose ideological, political or economic interests were challenged insisted, unsuccessfully, that the interventions had caused the problem, and that the answer lay in further deregulation.[12]

In time, and against the backdrop of the 1929 Wall Street crash and the Depression, new forms of regulation, policy and law were introduced. Economies were rebuilt from within, nurtured by governments through financial assistance and active regulation, and protected from external competition through border controls. New social structures emerged. In some countries, these embodied a crude form of national interest and identity that laid the foundations for fascism. In other places, social reconstruction created new roles for working classes and women who had previously been excluded, new political dynamics and parties, and a more interventionist role for the state. The rise of extreme forms of economic protectionism and nationalism erupted as a collision of national political and economic interests in the Second World War.

Out of this turmoil and transformation emerged the era of welfare interventionism, in different forms across the countries of industrial capitalism. States secured their legitimacy through a domestic compromise: capitalism required an environment conducive to profitability, while people demanded policies of redistribution and welfare to mitigate the harshest effects of capitalism, and democratic participation in determining those policies.[13] Over time, this compromise created new contradictions. The expanding menu of government services, state support for the domestic economy and social welfare provision meant that the size of public administration and demands on government revenue continued to grow. But domestic capital had a limited capacity to absorb these costs, especially when it could expand only within its borders.

While governments intervened to build their domestic economy and deliver full employment, they also moved internationally to restore stability. Following the Bretton Woods Conference in 1944, the International Monetary Fund (IMF) was established to restore stability to the international monetary system and the General Agreement on Tariffs and Trade (GATT) to re-open the world's trading system. Both were subject to manipulation by the major powers. They also reflected the tension between the state's sovereign authority to set its national priorities and the requirements of international capital. The IMF had the power to disallow currency devaluation above a certain level and impose policy conditions on countries seeking balance of payments support. The GATT sought to balance multilateral trade rules and the need to maintain domestic stability. The compromise was an international trade regime that was multilateral in character, but predicated on domestic interventionism and a shared commitment by member countries to a set of social objectives (the most important of which was full employment). The rise of protectionism during the 1970s was a move by governments to minimise the social costs that resulted from making domestic adjustments to changing international economic conditions. Writing in 1982, international relations specialist John Gerard Ruggie argued that this rebalancing of international and domestic goals was consistent with the original GATT compromise, and predicted that the greatest threat to the compromise regime came not from protectionism, but from 'the resurgent ethos of neo-*laissez-faire*'.[14]

From the 1970s, capital in North America, Europe and Japan (and to a lesser extent in countries such as New Zealand and Australia) actively searched beyond its national boundaries for new markets, lower production costs and new synergies. Economic activity focused increasingly on regional and other international markets. Corporations restructured their production and distribution on a transnational basis. Financiers created new opportunities for investment in this more fluid and complex environment. To facilitate these developments, barriers to the efficient international operation of capital needed to be reduced, and preferably removed. Demands from business and supportive governments for economic liberalisation at a global level saw the rapid expansion of international agreements and agencies such as the World Trade Organisation (WTO), the North American Free Trade Agreement (NAFTA), Asia Pacific Economic Cooperation (APEC), and the ill-fated Multilateral Agreement on Investment (MAI). Intergovernmental financial institutions, notably the IMF and World Bank, promoted structural adjustment of poor countries, often as conditions attached to loans. At the domestic level, the promotion of the global free market meant rolling back the size, cost and regulatory role of the nation-state. Gaining the consent of the populace to do so was difficult; hence the opening of markets tended to coincide with 'strong government', which circumvented the democratic process and sought to insulate key economic activities from political intervention.

In the 1990s, these changes were implemented in the name of 'globalisation'. Neo-liberal economists, business media, international economic agencies and think-tanks hailed the progression towards a self-regulating global market-place as irresistible and irreversible. Yet this vision contained all the contradictions Polanyi had identified in the previous century. Its economic landscape was devoid of social and political relations, and of cultural and national identity. The social consequences of free markets in labour, natural resources and capital were therefore ignored, creating social conditions and political pressures that made the vision unsustainable at the national level. The self-regulating market began to fail. The institutional vehicles for global economic policy-making, driven by the same neo-liberal theories, were equally detached from the requirements of real economies; they too experienced challenges, from both member governments and popular unrest.

Governments who turned their back on these realities and imposed a pure free market agenda without popular consent put the legitimacy of their political systems at risk. For most Western industrialised countries, the Keynesian era had fostered a deep integration of economic, social and political life. Few governments could put the ideology of global free markets into practice for a sustained period of time, even if they wanted to. Some governments did make radical moves to deregulate, notably those of Margaret Thatcher in the UK and Ronald Reagan in the US – although their rhetoric was often purer than their practice. But these moves were superseded by a new compromise. It remains to be seen how successfully these compromises will defuse the pressures that brought them about.

'Globalisation' posed different challenges for non-OECD countries. Many were former colonies with fragile economies, heavy debt burdens, thin constitutional systems and often corrupt leadership. This left their governments vulnerable to pressure from foreign investors and international agencies such as the IMF to deregulate. Yet these governments already confronted the domestic realities of poverty, social disorder and political survival. Radical deregulation carried enormous additional social and political costs, and met with diverse forms of resistance from governments and their peoples.

▲ NEW ZEALAND AT THE CROSSROADS

Against this background, New Zealand appears an enigma. The aim of successive governments and their supporters was to put 'globalisation as ideology' into practice. 'The New Zealand experiment'[15] – the relentless pursuit of free market principles that began in 1984 – exposed a small, remote country of 3.8 million people to the full impact of international market forces. The theoretical template on which it was based treated the country's colonial history and the contemporary reality of its social and political life as irrelevant.

New Zealand never experienced the 'great transformation' described by Polanyi. Government intervention had driven the New Zealand economy from the earliest days of colonisation, and was deeply embedded in its social structure well before the emergence of the Keynesian welfare state. In 1984, agricultural production still depended on a system of family farms. Industry was supported by domestic intervention and border protection, while training was subsidised through apprenticeships in government departments and free education. Government commitments to regional development, social welfare and universal provision of core public services, such as health and education, had shaped the structure and values of the society. Most people were complacent and conservative. Party politics largely reflected those attitudes. There was little inclination to recognise the limited capacity of the domestic economy to carry the burden of a large interventionist welfare state, or to respond to the international reorganisation of capital and the need to find new markets as Britain abandoned its former colonies. Change was slow. Something had to give. But the decision to embark on a radical neo-liberal restructuring of New Zealand's economy in 1984 was based on a serious long-term miscalculation. Reconceptualising the society in terms of markets, and subjecting them to rapid deregulation, would not make the social, cultural and political foundations of the society disappear. The contradictions this created were bound to emerge as challenges to the new regime.

Architects of New Zealand's experiment behaved like their nineteenth century counterparts – described by Polanyi as 'the secular spokesmen of the divine providence which governed the economic world as a separate entity'.[16] Pre-eminent among them was the New Zealand Treasury, whose briefing paper to the incoming government in 1984, *Economic Management*, set the agenda for the market-driven economy. It began with an unexceptional survey of the international economic situation and outlook, painting a picture of uncertainty and change which could have drawn a range of responses. However, Part Two blamed the country's 'lacklustre' economic performance on two main factors: 'serious structural difficulties', which impeded international competitiveness; and an unwillingness to adjust to changing external conditions.[17] These problems were exemplified by a heavy reliance on government intervention, including industry subsidies and border protections such as tariffs; price restrictions on services; state monopolies on communications and energy; the protected position of the public service and of state sector activities such as health and education; the under-pricing of state-supplied goods and services; and the protected position of unions.

Treasury argued for policies that allowed the market to adjust faster, so that changes in international prices would be reflected in the domestic economy. This would ensure that the country's resources were continually reallocated to achieve the highest national income possible.[18] Treasury's answer to New Zealand's 'serious macroeconomic policy imbalances' was a textbook application of neo-liberal economic theory. Government should adopt a monetarist approach to controlling inflation, and float the currency. The labour market had to be deregulated, and protections removed from industry and agriculture. Tighter controls on government spending were required, accompanied by a shift towards indirect taxation and commercialisation of the public sector and social policy.

The international economy was little more than a backdrop to this domestic policy agenda. This was even more apparent in Treasury's 1987 briefing paper, *Government Management,* a 470-page ideological treatise on the need to limit the size and role of the state; the international outlook was confined to three pages in an appendix.[19] By contrast, Treasury's 1990 briefing papers invoked the spectre of globalisation to justify taking these policies further.

> We cannot escape the effects of changes taking place elsewhere in the world. We need to adapt and exploit the opportunities offered by these changes. Government policies should encourage New Zealand firms to adopt this international focus. Policies should avoid creating insular attitudes or imposing unnecessary risks or costs on activities that compete with the rest of the world.[20]

Barriers to international competitiveness had to be removed. For a relatively insignificant economy to attract investment and compete internationally, the overall stability and quality of its policies was critical: 'In an increasingly interdependent world poor policies can be quickly "punished" as investors shift their funds and their managerial skills elsewhere. This underlines the importance of New Zealand establishing policies broadly in line with *or better than* those in other countries.'[21] Treasury insisted that New Zealand had to be more than a passive bystander in the globalisation process; it was in the 'national interest' that globalisation be positively embraced. New Zealand could and should adopt policies that other countries eschewed, and present itself as a model for the world.

Successive New Zealand governments implemented this agenda almost without demur. The fourth Labour government of 1984–1990 was committed to 'opening up' the economy. It lifted exchange controls, deregulated the financial markets, and floated the dollar. Price stability was made the Reserve Bank's sole objective. Foreign investment rules were relaxed, and state assets (notably telecommunications, forests, and the Post Office Savings Bank) were sold to foreign companies. Domestic subsidies were withdrawn and domestic markets deregulated. Tariffs were reduced, and other trade protections were removed. Internationally, the Labour government pursued a vigorous free trade position in the Uruguay Round negotiations on the GATT, the extension of the Closer Economic Relations Trade Agreement with Australia (CER), and the birth of APEC.

The National government displayed equal fervour when it came to power in late 1990. International competitiveness became a justification for changing labour laws and imposing fiscal restraint. More central and local government assets were sold offshore. Public and social services were contracted out, with foreign suppliers and insurers claiming their share of the business. Rules governing foreign investment were further relaxed. Commitments to the new World Trade Organisation and APEC promised that future governments would continue to liberalise international trade and investment, or at least not reinstate restrictions. Accolades from the Organisation for Economic Cooperation and Development (OECD), credit rating agencies, the financial media and well-connected international think-tanks allowed the cheer-leaders to claim that the New Zealand experiment was both internationally orthodox and leading the world.

During the early 1990s, the justification for free market policies shifted from the need to address domestic inefficiencies to meeting the challenges of globalisation. While this was consistent with international trends, it was also politically expedient. Globalisation and domestic restructuring were flip sides of the same coin. TINA – 'there is no alternative' – applied to both. During the 1980s the ascendancy of neo-liberal economics, often described as the New Right, in a number of OECD countries also had a largely domestic focus. By the early 1990s there was evidence of unease, verging on a backlash, in many countries including New Zealand, although other governments, such as Ontario and Alberta in Canada, were only just heading down the neo-liberal path. While globalisation had the same policy agenda, it was portrayed as an inescapable development rather than a domestic policy choice. Once the Cold War ended, global capitalism assumed an almost complete hegemony. The process of international economic policy-making gained further momentum through the conclusion of multilateral negotiations in the GATT Uruguay Round (1993), agreements to extend regional economic integration through NAFTA (1992) and the European Union (1992), and the commitment to free trade and investment in APEC (1994). These arrangements provided new political mechanisms for committing current and future governments to global free market policies, external to – and in New Zealand's case completely bypassing – the domestic polity.

Globalisation assumed an aura of virtual omnipotence. It was unfashionable, almost unpatriotic, for New Zealanders to question the benefits it might bring. Its advocacy by corporate leaders, politicians and officials went largely unchallenged, despite a paucity of empirical evidence to support their arguments. Dissenting voices struggled to be heard. Critics drew parallels between the economic and social consequences of the global agenda and the New Zealand experiment, both of which sacrificed the well-being of poor people (and poor countries) to the self-interest of big business and wealthy élites. Globalisation was challenged as a second wave of colonisation, with transnational capital playing the role of imperial powers. A network of non-government groups and individuals, including the Campaign Against Foreign Control of Aotearoa (CAFCA), Christian World Service, CORSO and GATT Watchdog, worked to build an information and education base on international economic issues. Conservation groups focused more specifically on resource laws, the operations of transnational corporations, and international initiatives on environmental issues from global warming to toxic waste.

In 1993 the New Zealand Trade Union Federation (TUF), set up as the alternative union body to the Council of Trade Unions, began to raise the concerns of workers they represented in industries most directly affected by trade liberalisation, including clothing, textiles, footwear and forestry.

> We hear a lot about 'globalisation' these days, being told that we live in a global world, that the global economy offers us the way forward. ... Throughout these claims, there is very little that tells us what is being globalised, what effects it might have or where the changes are being felt. Tariff cuts and other moves to free trade are one aspect of policies that encourage 'globalisation'. The New Zealand government is continuing to liberalise trade and investment restrictions at the expense of New Zealand workers and New Zealand jobs. We are the losers while the winners are the members of the global elite.[22]

The Federation, which had strong links with activist workers' organisations in Asia, condemned the globalisation agenda as having 'introduced a new morality where the new god is the dollar and a failure to maximise profit is a mortal sin. Concepts of love, fairness, equality and social justice are given no value ... .'[23]

Among the few economists who took a critical stance were those working with the Alliance,[24] and members of the 'old school' such as retired academic Wolfgang Rosenberg, an economic nationalist of the post-war era.[25] In other disciplines, the author's own work linked global economic policy-making to New Zealand's neo-liberalism, and highlighted attempts to embed the new regime through foreign investment and international agreements.[26] This included a warning that anti-globalisation rhetoric tended to reinforce the TINA syndrome, and advised New Zealanders to 'maintain a healthy scepticism about claims that transnational capital, international institutions and agencies now control our lives and there's nothing we can do'.[27]

The dissenters had their own international networks – overlapping groups of activists in many countries who exchanged information and analysis, either in person or via the Internet, and sometimes coordinated their campaigns. Within these networks there were difficult debates over whether to engage with the international economic policy-making machine: some sought to influence it from within, while others saw no prospect of change, and the serious risk of co-option.

At the parliamentary level, NewLabour (and later the Alliance) actively campaigned against the globalisation package, especially the reduction of tariffs and industry support, the absence of any requirement for major foreign investment (except in land) to meet a 'national interest' test, and the sale of state assets into foreign hands. The party identified the Reserve Bank's monetary strategy as increasing New Zealand's exposure to speculative foreign capital and external financial crises; attempts to tie future governments to the free market agenda through international agreements such as the WTO and APEC were condemned.

From 1992, Winston Peters and his New Zealand First party also campaigned on 'economic sovereignty', often appealing to nationalist – and sometimes racist – sentiment. Peters tapped into an undercurrent of unease among many New Zealanders who remained deeply insecure about their colonial-based identity in a world that was rapidly changing around them. Opinion surveys, political polls and radio talkback shows recorded fears that the country's sovereignty was under threat from foreign companies and their parent governments. These fears were manifest in an outbreak of populist racism directed at Asian immigrants and investors from 1993 to 1996, and (rather ironically) in ongoing hostility to the settlement of Maori land claims by the Waitangi Tribunal.

By the mid-1990s, these critiques had gained more currency and the vision of a self-regulating 'free' economy was becoming socially and politically unsustainable. The New Zealand experiment had not delivered the promised prosperity, with only three years of significant growth since 1984. Successive governments had adopted a Darwinist attitude to the real economy. There was minimal investment in local production, and no positive government support for struggling industries. The export sector was now burdened by a grossly overvalued exchange rate. Unemployment was rising. Short-term speculators were cashing in on excessively high real interest rates, driven up by the Reserve Bank's monetary policy, and foreign owners were milking privatised assets. The balance of payments was deteriorating rapidly, and overseas debt continued to rise. The credibility of the neo-liberal model declined further in 1998, as unemployment, foreign debt and the current account deficit worsened and the economy moved into recession. These problems pre-dated the 'Asian crisis', which contributed to the severity of the economic downturn, but did not cause it.

Equally, there was no sign of improvement in the quality of life, for which many New Zealanders had endured considerable hardship. Inequalities continued to grow, and the gap between Maori and non-Maori on key indicators such as health, education and income had widened.[28] For many New Zealanders, short-term pain had become permanent. Core public services, especially health and education, were severely run down. Basic infrastructure such as roading had deteriorated; the electricity supply to Auckland's central business district collapsed; and the fire and ambulance services suffered sometimes life-threatening breakdowns.

The political legitimacy of the system of government was also damaged. There was a strong sense that the monopoly enjoyed by the National and Labour parties under the first-past-the-post electoral system had been abused by successive governments as they implemented their neo-liberal policy agenda. Demands for greater accountability and broader representation resulted in an indicative referendum in 1992 which supported changes to the electoral system. This was followed a year later by a binding vote in favour of a system of mixed member proportional representation (MMP), to take effect at the next election in 1996. MMP failed to provide the 'quick fix' the voters were looking for. A messy period of coalition between National and New Zealand First was followed in 1998-99 by a minority National government, backed by the free-market ACT party (the Association of Consumers and Taxpayers) and several independent (mainly Maori) MPs. The popular legitimacy of the political system remained low. But the combination of MMP and public rejection of the free market approach meant that politics re-entered some arenas of economic policy-making that the agents of change had sought to quarantine, including international negotiations on trade and investment.

As these pressures emerged, the Labour opposition softened the hardline approach it had taken in government. It remained committed to the 'fundamentals' of the free market economic policies it had introduced (while conceding that some may have been taken too far), but rejected the application of those principles to social policy (as had occurred with education, health and welfare benefits under National). Labour's official position on globalisation was difficult to distinguish from the views of its enigmatic spokesperson, former Minister of Overseas Trade Mike Moore. In 1997 Moore said that he supported 'internationalism' (the term he preferred) with 'all my heart and soul', not just as an economic and social good, but as an opportunity to provide a better world. He viewed internationalisation as evolutionary:

> We evolved from families, to tribes to the city state, to the Nation state and now to global and regional economic and political arrangements. ... These economic arrangements vary in their political intensity, but their historic thrust is profound. Just as the creation of a United States in North America, and the economic unification of jealous provinces created the economic powerhouse of Germany, these new arrangements are providing economic growth, security and common political values which is a matter of enormous economic, political and military significance.[29]

Moore argued that the state still had a role in specific areas such as environmental laws, educational expenditure, and research and development, but never explained how far globalisation might constrain a government's ability to act autonomously on these issues. A genuine free market evangelist, Moore contemptuously dismissed the critics of free trade and investment as 'wacko conspiracy types',[30] 'grumpy geriatric communists', and 'a mutant strain of the Left in New Zealand and weirdos from the Alliance-Social Credit types who tuck their shirts into their underpants [sic]'.[31] More temperate policy statements from other Labour leaders used globalisation to justify their stance that governments could not exercise effective control over the domestic economy, but could only seek to mitigate the effects of globalisation by providing support for local businesses and people. This reflected the Robert Reich line that economic globalisation was inevitable, but uneven in its effect.[32] Governments therefore needed to concern themselves with 'the future of national *societies* as distinct from economies, and the fate of the majority of citizens who are losing out in global competition'.[33]

Labour's union ally, the New Zealand Council of Trade Unions (CTU), maintained an active pro-globalisation stance, consistent with the position of the International Confederation of Free Trade Unions (ICFTU) to which it belonged. In his address to the Labour Party conference in 1995, CTU president Ken Douglas portrayed globalisation as potentially beneficial, and sought a role for the 'world trade union movement' in the process. He welcomed the decline in the central role of the nation-state as an opportunity for the 'collective pursuit of mutual self interest' to reassert itself.

> Globalisation is a real process. Finance, capital, trade, and even labour are increasingly mobile across borders. That has reduced the degree of control that governments can exercise. Technology is and will continue [sic] to accelerate this process. The sovereignty of the nation state is now much diminished. But the need for a new role for the government is not only, and possibly not even primarily, economic. There is less value in, and indeed less need for, the national entity. ...
>
> My own view is that we need to reject the narrow confines of nostalgic nationalism because the economic challenges of the next century are international. But equally we must reject them for positive reasons. Economic integration creates more space for New Zealand to play a positive role in building and encouraging collaboration for regional growth, expansion and stabilisation among Pacific Island nations, of which we are but one, even if an important one in terms of size and wealth.[34]

For Douglas, the government had a residual role as conciliator between conflicting interests in a market economy that assumed the contestants were equals when they were not. Hence, the tripartite politics of government, capital and labour should be played out on both the domestic and international stages.

The National government was also forced to respond to mounting challenges to globalisation. It remained committed to the goal of 'free' markets at the domestic and international level, but its references to globalisation began to acknowledge that the goal was now vulnerable. While Minister of Foreign Affairs and Trade Don McKinnon hailed New Zealand's embrace of the global economy, he acknowledged that failure to deliver positive benefits could put the whole neo-liberal project at risk:

> ... let us be optimistic. There is much to look forward to. Increasing interdependence does not mean a loss of freedom and individuality. It does not mean we cease to have choices about our future. However, increasing interdependence must give people results, if not they find an external force to blame and the events of the past twenty years will be reversed.[35]

The government and its supporters found they could no longer make radical changes almost at will. Numerous policy initiatives came unstuck. In 1998 National pushed through legislation to remove tariff protection for local car assembly, but had to defer similar moves for clothing and textiles after employers, unions and local communities jointly mobilised.

Farmers who traditionally supported National turned against 'their own' government during 1998, refusing to support the effective privatisation of the statutory producer and marketing boards. In 1997 and 1998, negotiations for a Multilateral Agreement on Investment at the OECD (which would have given foreign investors powerful new rights) drew protests from such diverse quarters as Maori, Grey Power, radio talkback callers and city councils; the government eventually supported a moratorium before negotiations broke down completely. At the local level, the corporatisation of water services faced a sustained challenge from within the Auckland City Council, and through an organised campaign of civil disobedience as consumers refused to pay their bills. Such campaigns suggested a backlash against the neo-liberal revolution. The opposition was mainly ad hoc, in response to specific proposals, and brought together pragmatic coalitions of business people, unions, farmers, local communities, the elderly and Maori.

Throughout this period, free market activists outside government warned that any retreat from the current line would have dire consequences. As Andrew Meehan (an executive director of Brierley Investments Ltd, member of the Asia 2000 board of trustees, and former chair of the government advisory group on foreign direct investment) wrote in the *Asia 2000 Foundation* magazine in 1995:

> Nations face a very simple choice – to accept the reality of globalisation – or to attempt to fight against it. Those who accept globalisation will reap the benefits of technology transfer, skills transfer, diversity of choice, capital for adding value and ultimately an increased level of national income.
>
> Those that fight globalisation will forego such benefits and be increasingly marginalised, leading ultimately to a reduced level of national income.
>
> New Zealand is currently faced with this choice. Over the past ten years, we epitomised the nation willing to recognise and accommodate globalisation. It would indeed be a tragedy to turn away from this universally acknowledged leadership role.[36]

In 1997 Bob Matthew (chair of both the New Zealand Business Roundtable and Brierley's) argued that globalisation, by way of international trade, financial flows and foreign direct investment, 'may not be unprecedented or inevitable'. But 'the sheer number of diverse peoples linked into the global economy and sharing in the prosperity' offered by open market systems was both.[37] He claimed that globalisation had not undermined national sovereignty. Rather, world economies had become more integrated because national governments had chosen that path, believing it would lead to economic growth and improved national well-being – just as New Zealanders had freely chosen not to remain in their fortress and become the 'Albania of the South Pacific'.[38] Matthew warned that a future government was fully capable of reversing trends towards greater globalisation – if it was short-sighted enough to want to do so.

In a re-run of the 1920s, the Business Roundtable's executive director, Roger Kerr, blamed the country's economic malaise in 1998 on the loss of momentum for change. He accused Cabinet ministers and other commentators of being 'in denial about the departure from a sound economic framework and the gathering economic problems', and commented:

> New Zealand was starting to become an internationally attractive economy after a decade of difficult structural reforms, but it lost the plot. Inward migration has slumped and the lower exchange rate suggests interest in it has waned on the investment world's radar screens. Belatedly, the Government may be realising the extent of the damage, but it is failing dismally to explain the economic realities to the community and to adopt a coherent strategy to correct the mistakes.[39]

But the influence of the Business Roundtable, which had dominated economic debate for over a decade, was waning. It had failed to see, or was ideologically incapable of seeing, that the contradictions of the self-regulating economy had created pressures that required accommodation if the fundamentals of a market-driven economy were to survive. The tension between the purists and the pragmatists was captured in an exchange between Kerr and the business editor of the *New Zealand Herald*, Rod Oram, in May 1999. Oram wrote:

> In a speech last week, [Kerr] said the *Business Herald* believed that the economic agenda of the past 15 years was 'increasingly irrelevant', taking that quote from this column. In fact, it was a misquote. The *Business Herald* is as committed to that agenda as the Business Roundtable. ... It is not that agenda which is increasingly irrelevant but the Business Roundtable itself, because of its refusal to join a broader economic debate and its failure to communicate well with the nation at large.[40]

The *Herald* argued that the government had focused too much on the macroeconomic level (for example, on monetary and fiscal policy) and not enough on the micro level. In some cases government should get further out of the way (for example, by reducing the cost of regulation); elsewhere it should become more activist, by helping to promote research and development or providing venture capital.[41]

Oram had indicated the beginnings of a contest of ideas over the economic direction of the country, really for the first time since 1984. Self-regulating markets had failed New Zealand capital. Some of its leaders in business and industry began reasserting the responsibility of government to support the domestic economy actively. There was no single 'alternative' voice of capital, and no single solution. One of the most influential voices was that of Hugh Fletcher, the recently retired chief executive of Fletcher Challenge, one of New Zealand's first home-grown transnational companies. In a widely quoted speech on globalisation in August 1998, Fletcher declared it was time to 'stop seeking refuge in denial and transfer of fault, such as to blame Asia, and have a more balanced contest of ideas as to how New Zealand can prosper in a globalised economy'. He urged a more pragmatic response to global trends:

> In the 15 years since the Lange government was elected and New Zealand opened up to the forces of globalisation, we have performed dismally, both economically and socially. ... Prospering in an age of globalisation requires us to determine simply and clearly what is really important to us, and then to focus on insightful and unconventional strategies which will deliver success on these matters.
>
> That requires us to exploit not only the spirit and drive of competitive individual entrepreneurship but also the power of co-operative endeavour. Both must be harnessed to make New Zealand residents the 'owners' of unique capabilities, so that overseas customers and capital are dependent on us.[42]

This vision could be realised, he said, only in a healthy society that was prepared to support people in need and resolve deep-seated grievances, such as claims under the Treaty of Waitangi. In effect, Fletcher was urging the government to restore the link between economic policy and the realities of New Zealand's economic, social and political life.

A variation on Fletcher's approach came from New Zealand Businesses for Social Responsibility, which included local entrepreneurs whose business ethos expressly included a commitment to their workers, consumers and local communities. One such member, Gilbert Ullrich, managing director of Ullrich Aluminium and deputy director of the Exporters' Institute, urged the government to focus on the promotion of export-driven industries 'rather than blaming beneficiaries for draining national income and workers for failing to save – something that is impossible for many families in a user-pays driven economy'.[43]

The form and extent of policy changes being sought were not yet clear. However, all were premised on the need to enhance New Zealand's role as an export-driven and internationalised economy, through a re-energised and more strategically focused domestic economy. Other economic commentators urged a more fundamental shift in focus, towards rebuilding the domestic economy so it could better service domestic needs. In

Taking New Zealand Seriously (1998), economist Tim Hazledine insisted that:

> We need government to stick up for our interests in the world; to tell the IMF and the OECD and the Americans politely but firmly where to get off: 'Thanks for your advice, but we are running our own show now.' Above all, New Zealand governments should be protecting and fostering our economic sovereignty, giving us the space within which we can sort out our own affairs. This certainly doesn't mean supplanting the market, but it means saying firmly that our own markets are more important to us than other people's markets. Those bonds of empathy and sympathy, of knowing and wanting to do unto others according to their tastes – the social capital – are best built up by people of fairly homogeneous experiences and aspirations – in our case the people of New Zealand – being able to deal repeatedly with each other in a secure economic setting. That is why I have urged that we import and export less, and develop production for the domestic market; and why we should not hesitate to exercise controls over foreign investment in our economy. This is not xenophobia or isolationism; it is just getting the proportions more aligned with our own best interests. Other countries should do it too – we will all be happier as a result.[44]

Both approaches sought to reconnect New Zealand business to New Zealanders' lives, reflecting concern for jobs, local communities and social well-being. The exporters' proposals sought to adapt the traditional role of New Zealand industrial capital to the more integrated international economy. Hazledine sought to alter this relationship by deepening the dependence of business on its domestic markets and communities, and reducing its dependence on the international economy. Either approach would require a significant rethinking of existing economic policy, and a realistic assessment of the extent to which any such shift was possible, given the pressures of the global economy and the economic and legal barriers set in place to prevent New Zealand changing tack.

▲ CONFRONTING COLONISATION

One further factor complicated the globalisation agenda in New Zealand. The wealth of New Zealand's colonial society was founded on the marginalisation and dispossession of Maori – a situation the welfare state modified, but never sought to change fundamentally. For a century and a half, Maori resistance to colonisation took different forms, and has continued to the present day. As Fletcher had astutely observed, any attempt to reconstruct a New Zealand economy within a healthy New Zealand society had to address the grievances of Maori. Yet the market model could never accommodate the cultural and spiritual relationships in Maori society between the human and natural worlds. Recognition of those connections is fundamental to any acknowledgement of Maori claims.

In February 1984, against a backdrop of widespread Maori protest over land claims, the Labour Party made a commitment to redress past grievances arising from the Treaty of Waitangi, dating back to 1840. Labour was aware that this would involve claims to resources held by the Crown, but was probably less cognisant of the constitutional implications of the Treaty's recognition of the tino rangatiratanga (self-determination) of the tribes.[45] Treasury's *Economic Management* ignored the existence of the Treaty of Waitangi and of Maori. By 1987, the Labour government was facing litigation by Maori to prevent the corporatisation of government holdings in land, forest and coal that were the subject of Treaty claims, and challenges to the privatisation of fisheries. In 1987, Treasury's *Government Management* sought to resolve the issue by reconceptualising Maori society in economic terms. Complex cultural and social relations were reduced to individual transactions within self-regulating markets, while the entire spiritual life-world of Maori was redefined as commodities governed by private property rights.[46]

Nonetheless, the globalisation-cum-deregulation agenda posed a conundrum for Maori. On the one hand, it weakened the grip of the colonial nation-state, opening up new political spaces, new ways of defining identity outside state-centred nationalism, and new opportunities for alliances. On the other hand, it would transfer some of the colonial state's power to the more distant hands of international capital, reduce the leverage over the Crown provided by the Treaty of Waitangi, and remove the buffer that the welfare state provided for the Maori working class and unemployed poor.

Consequently, Maori responses varied. Entrepreneurs positively welcomed the decline of the nation-based economy, and sought to advance their interests by embracing free market capitalism and supporting economic deregulation. Some Maori leaders with access to a large natural resource base and financial settlements from their Treaty claims believed they could now bypass the national economy and operate independently on the world stage. Cultural difference would be a positive asset in dealings with non-European investors and trading partners.[47] Tipene O'Regan argued this point strongly in relation to Ngai Tahu. Defining tino rangatiratanga as 'an iwi [tribe] in control of themselves and their assets in their own rohe [territory]', he rejected nationalist models that sought to confine Ngai Tahu's development to their traditional territory within a pan-Maori economic and political regime. O'Regan argued that the next generation would want to travel and take advantage of opportunities in other places. 'It seems fatuous to me to say we are going to ... have this separate physical area with its own administration and legal system and all the trappings of sovereignty. ... The only way for Maori to live in the new century is in the whole world.'[48] Ngai Tahu would choose their own trading partners, including international joint ventures. O'Regan had already helped to arrange the joint purchase of the Sealord fishing company by the Treaty of Waitangi Fisheries Commission and Brierley Investments Ltd, which was the centre-piece of the controversial settlement of Treaty fisheries claims in 1992. The profits would be distributed through a variety of education, cultural and development programmes for Ngai Tahu beneficiaries.

Robert Mahuta of Tainui, the other negotiator to secure a major Treaty settlement with the Crown, believed that the powerlessness of Maori stemmed primarily from a lack of capital. This meant that cultural nationalism had to take a back seat to economic nationalism.

> We want to establish an economic base, to be able to develop our own economic programmes to expand that base, to enhance the opportunities for our people and to play a much more significant role in the development of this country. The main thing about a capitalist system is that you have to have capital to produce the profit in order to be able to utilise it.[49]

The language of the future for Tainui would be economic. The corporate wing of the tribe would conduct its business activities, while a newly established Kauhanganui, comprising 183 representatives from 61 marae in the Tainui region, would decide how to distribute the benefits. Mahuta argued that, by becoming major players in fisheries, forestry and other sectors, the tribe could exercise greater control over its future. Assets such as Sealord, for example, could be worth a billion dollars: 'We don't have to stay in the company. We can take a profit and invest it in other parts of the economy.'[50] In his view, 'The only way we are going to beat the white man is at his own game. We could allow ourselves to come out thinking as white men, but ideally we will come out thinking as international people.'[51] Mahuta believed this strategy would not mean abdicating control to overseas interests or becoming submerged in the global economy. Indeed, he warned overseas buyers that 'if the dangers [of foreign ownership] become too great ... the solution at the end of the day for any sovereign government is to nationalise ... everything reverts to the state again'.[52] However, the feasibility of nationalisation, and his grounds for assuming that the interests of Tainui would coincide with those of the state in exercising that power, were not explained.

A further significant voice came from urban Maori – notably the

Waipareira Trust in West Auckland – who saw deregulation as a means to advance pan-Maori socio-economic well-being. Trust chief executive John Tamihere defined Maori sovereignty as

> ... marking out our share of the action and going for it. ... I see the dire state we are in and my job is to ensure that our children have more opportunity and quality of life than their parents. At this stage we are actually falling deeper and deeper into the quagmire. ... We've got to maximise our assets right now – in case the Asians, the Pacific Islanders and the Pakeha take over completely.[53]

This meant turning the Waipareira Trust and other Maori organisations into multi-million-dollar commercial enterprises, based on the belief that 'numbers and economy of scale equal power'.[54] Deregulation and globalisation allowed this transformation to occur; joint ventures with international companies added capital and expertise.

These Maori entrepreneurs had different visions and strategies, which sometimes clashed. Their conflicts fuelled a costly competition for power and resources, in which ordinary Maori had no real say. But they shared a belief that Maori could retain control over their resources and kaupapa (plans) in a deregulated global economy, build their economic base through commercial activities, and distribute the trickle-down benefits to their constituencies. None of them explained convincingly how they would guarantee to retain control over private sector partners whose objectives were purely market-driven – nor how they would reconcile the traditional spiritual and cultural foundations for Maori development with the workings of a free global market based on profoundly different values (assuming that those traditional foundations had not been abandoned).

Other Maori believed that such accommodations were not possible. Nationalists such as Mike Smith insisted that the long-term survival of Maori, and the world, depended on remaining true to the fundamental principles of mana atua (cosmic principles that explain the existence of the world), mana tangata (politics based on the value of people), and mana whenua (the enduring relationship between people and nature that ensures their mutual survival).[55] These principles formed an integrated whole, not a hierarchy where economic priorities dictated the shape of the political and social world. The market model destroyed these essential values and principles. It was not possible, for example, to reconcile the ethos of whanaungatanga (collective obligations among those with common ancestry), and the responsibilities of Maori as kaitiaki or guardians of their natural world, with the pursuit of individual self-interest and exploitation of resources that are integral to neo-liberal capitalism. Smith argued that Maori entrepreneurs, in embracing that model, had been seduced by government offers of commercial Treaty settlements in a classic display of 'divide and rule', and had betrayed past, present and future generations.

The Maori nationalist position was, at heart, a reassertion of both power and responsibility. The right to exercise tino rangatiratanga was less an issue of who had the ability to rule Aotearoa than one of who was its guardian. Smith commented, sympathetically, that many Pakeha now saw themselves 'being dispossessed of things they thought were theirs'.[56] But he insisted that responsibility for restoring the principles of people-centred development ultimately lies with the tangata whenua (people of the land):

> ... if we are seriously going to assert ourselves in our own country and take responsibility for the welfare of our land and of all the people here. We are the last line of defence. The Pakeha have blown it. So we have to step in and say, 'You aren't allowed to do that! This country is not for sale. You can't do that!' We never thought we owned these things but we knew that no one else owned them either. Once [privatised assets and resources] have gone from the control of the New Zealand government, they are further out of reach and harder to restore to Maori control.[57]

Smith believed that this required a pan-Maori approach. Others, notably activists from Tuhoe and Whanganui, described themselves as iwi nationalists, and viewed their occupation of disputed lands as the exercise of tribal sovereignty.

Most Maori belonged to none of these 'camps'. Many of the hapu who continued to press their Treaty claims through negotiations with the Waitangi Tribunal and the courts adopted a messy combination of entrepreneurism, traditional values and political pragmatism, which generated deep debate over what were acceptable outcomes. A vast number of Maori simply struggled to survive in urban or rural poverty; some were dislocated from their past, while others participated in local marae activities. Maori small businesses struggled too, especially when larger employers around them closed down. The positions adopted by Maori MPs reflected this diversity, as well as the paradox of operating in a liberal democratic parliamentary system based on individual franchise and majority rule. Their stances often appeared inconsistent – for example, opposing the removal of tariffs on the clothing industry, in which many Maori worked, but supporting the privatisation of the producer boards, from which Maori farmers had effectively been excluded. Yet these contradictions made more sense when viewed in light of the complexity of colonisation, class and the demand for self-determination.

▲ THE CHALLENGE

As the new millennium approached, globalisation seemed more a problem for New Zealand's future than a solution. The quest for a pure self-regulating market had created major contradictions. Despite the frustration of the Business Roundtable and ACT, the period of radical restructuring was nearing its end. Yet there was no sign that a significantly new policy agenda was about to emerge from the major political parties. Leading into the 1999 election, both National and Labour responded to public weariness of radical change by offering a less extreme version of the market model. Labour endorsed a localised version of Tony Blair's 'third way' which remained committed to globalisation, but focused on popular concerns about education and health, a halt to further deregulation, economic pragmatism, and building a future based on 'knowledge, skill and technology'.[58] A new generation of ministers in the National government, led by Finance Minister Bill English, also eschewed the blunt and brutal approach of the zealots in favour of a 'more mature and constructive use of the policy process and market mechanisms' to create a 'knowledge economy'. This meant focusing on middle-class concerns about a balance between tax cuts and maintaining social services, redirecting existing government support towards 'enterprise and innovation', and taking a more activist approach to fostering competitive markets.[59] Both parties sought to restore some stability by inserting a social and political dimension into the market model they had successively implemented since 1984. TINA still applied; these were variations within the market-centred paradigm.

The burning question is whether this new compromise will sufficiently address the contradictions the free market policies have set up; and if not, how much room exists for a more fundamental review. The answer rests partly on popular and political will. But it also depends on the extent to which the radical changes since 1984 have been irreversibly embedded. That is the subject of this book.

Chapter 1 takes issue with the belief that globalisation is inevitable, and highlights the tensions between globalisation and long-held concepts of sovereignty, democracy and tino rangatiratanga. Chapter 2 describes how the idea of global free markets as 'international orthodoxy' has been constructed in recent years; it concludes that the orthodoxy claimed for New Zealand is in fact fragmented and contested. Chapter 3 describes attempts to export New Zealand's model to other parts of the world. Chapter 4 examines the impact of unfettered foreign direct investment and deregulated finance flows since 1984. Chapter 5 explores the extent to which transnational enterprises have penetrated the New Zealand economy, and the ways in which their activities have created pressure to re-regulate. Chapter 6 covers 'free trade' policy, and its social and political contradictions. Chapters 7, 8 and 9 assess how far New Zealand's international commitments under the WTO, APEC and (potentially) the MAI prevent a reconsideration of these policies from taking place. Chapter 10 describes the impacts of these changes on New Zealand's economic and social life, and the apparent unwillingness of New Zealanders to adjust their values to the new market-centred vision of New Zealand. It concludes that New Zealanders are already beginning to exercise their choice to pursue an alternative path in the coming century.

1 ▲ Putting Globalisation in Perspective

The architects of New Zealand's free market experiment set out to ensure that the changes they made were difficult, preferably impossible, to undo. This chapter examines the way in which the radical transformation from a welfare state to a society organised around markets has been consolidated through an apparent consensus of New Zealand's political, economic and social élite. It challenges the underlying premise that, in the era of globalisation, New Zealand has no choice but to continue down this path. It then explores the tensions between globalisation and the central notions around which nation-states are organised – state sovereignty and democracy. A further tension for New Zealand is the relationship of globalisation to tino rangatiratanga – that is the sovereignty of the indigenous people of the country, affirmed in the Maori text of the Treaty of Waitangi signed by representatives of the British Crown and over 500 rangatira (chiefs) in 1840.

▲ THE POLITICS OF EMBEDDING CHANGE

Neo-liberal restructuring, or 'structural adjustment', aims to reduce the role of government in the economy and empower capital to regulate itself through markets. It is often described as a two-stage process. Political economists Stephen Haggard and Robert Kaufman suggest that the *initiation* phase of structural adjustment is most successful 'where and when political institutions insulate politicians and their technocratic allies from particular interest group constraints, at least in the short run'.[1]

The process of structural adjustment in New Zealand since 1984 has followed this path, as *The New Zealand Experiment* explained.[2] Through an ideological consensus amongst some key players, the policy norm of a deregulated, internationalised economy came to replace Keynesian interventionism. Committed individuals and agencies maintained effective control of economic decision-making in the Cabinet and throughout the machinery of government, deliberately pursuing what Brian Easton called a 'blitzkrieg' approach: 'In each case the "lightning strike" involved a policy goal radically different from the existing configuration, to be attained in a short period, following a surprise announcement and a very rapid implementation.'[3] Critics and opponents were continually on the back foot, and condemned as 'vested interests' or 'dinosaurs'. Any public consultation was limited to the detail of decisions already made. Economist Alan Bollard suggested in 1993 that even faster implementation was constrained by the speed at which the change agents could work, not 'by any self-imposed requirements to consult with industry, or other groups, or by major concerns about correct sequencing'.[4] Both major political parties were deeply implicated in the process.

Some champions of the free market believe that *consolidation* follows naturally from successful initiation. Once the changes have been made, social consensus and ideological convergence should emerge.[5] Roger Douglas, the driving force behind the 'reforms' of the fourth Labour government of 1984, shared this view. In his book *Unfinished Business*, he commented: 'Consensus among interest groups on quality decisions rarely, if ever, arises before they are made and implemented. It develops after they are taken, as the decisions deliver satisfactory results to the public.'[6] His ideological successor in the National government, Ruth Richardson, took a similar approach (see Chapter 3). So did others in the National government and ACT, senior Treasury officials, the chief executives of many other government agencies, and the Business Roundtable. There was never any question but that benefits would ultimately flow, and no suggestion that, left to themselves, these policies might cause such damage that a fundamental reconsideration was called for.

The theorists, Haggard and Kaufman, by contrast suggest that insulating economic policy from adverse political influences requires some effort; considerable sophistication and skill are necessary, along with social engagement. They highlight the importance of

> ... stabilising expectations around a new set of incentives and convincing economic agents that they cannot be reversed at the discretion of individual decision makers. Consolidation is most likely where governments have constructed relatively stable coalitions of political support that encompass major private sector beneficiaries, and have secured at least the acquiescence of the major political forces competing within the political system. Without such tacit or explicit alliances between politicians, technocratic elites, and those gaining from the policy change, reform attempts will necessarily falter.[7]

This 'embedded autonomy' expects a prosperous élite of beneficiaries in the private sector, such as financiers and wealthy entrepreneurs, to operate as a 'fire alarm' and mobilise resistance if a new government or its agencies look like changing course.[8] The restructured government bureaucracy appoints like-minded individuals who maintain control over policy advice and implementation, and relationships between the state and external pressure groups.[9] Embedded autonomy has an ideological dimension, too. Haggard and Kaufman talk about a process of 'social learning', which involves the

> ... evolution of a broader ideational consensus among leaders, interest groups, party elites and attentive publics [and] sets some boundaries on the range of economic debate. Such a consensus does not imply stasis or the absence of conflict; distributive struggles will always arise over policy. Nonetheless, it is possible that the long-term sustainability of policy choices will depend on a convergence of thinking about fundamental means-ends relationships in the economy. If so, then the formation of elite preferences, ideas, and ideology, as well as the evolution of public opinion, are potentially important... .[10]

In this process, a consensus among the élite is complemented by a broader adjustment of popular expectations. Citizens and firms are encouraged to lower their expectations and make individual, non-political adjustments to their more difficult circumstances. This may involve families sending more of their members into the workforce, selecting which children should receive costly education, and reducing consumption. Even if opposition develops and people become politicised, their demands are more likely to be directed at the government in power than at the system as a whole.[11]

To the proponents of structural adjustment, neutralising popular opposition stops short of requiring popular endorsement. Mere acquiescence is enough – although that does require a positive effort, and contains some risks. Development economist Joan Nelson notes that, where economic changes are slow to produce widespread benefits, or international conditions remain difficult, people may become restive. Assuming that outright coercion is not an option, the change agents are likely to seek support from new groups, to co-opt some prominent leaders of the disaffected, or to bring some popular elements on-side by creating a belief that they will share in future gains. Nelson comments: 'Ordinary people must be able to see some positive returns from adjustment, if they are to convert what is at best initial skepticism into more durable grumbling acquiescence.'[12]

According to the literature on structural adjustment, then, the new order will survive if it enjoys the active support of major political parties, the bureaucracy and private élites; if it appears to respond to popular concerns; and if the likely sources of opposition are co-opted, pacified or diffused. On one level, that seems an accurate description of New Zealand as it headed into the 1999 general election. Both Labour and National had abandoned the crude approach they took during the initiation phase, and each was repositioning to appear more responsive to concerns about economic stagnation and core public services, especially health. Most of the powerful voices of the business sector, the Council of Trade Unions leadership and Maori entrepreneurs seemed content to seek accommodations within the market paradigm. Yet the sequence of policy rejections and reversals suffered by the government in recent years, described throughout this book, suggests a level of unrest that has the potential to move beyond 'grumbling acquiescence' to demands for a more fundamental reconsideration of New Zealand's future direction.

The process of embedding the new regime in New Zealand was not just a political exercise. Changes were implemented through policies and laws whose substance and effects were intended to act as a bulwark against potentially hostile future governments. The 'fundamentals' of the New Zealand experiment – a deregulated labour market, a minimalist government, a strict monetarist policy, the liberalisation of trade, investment and markets, and fiscal restraint – comprise an ideologically coherent package that is premised on unfettered market forces and a limited state. Their collective impact on the workplace, the public service, core social services, business and the financial system has been profound.

Each 'fundamental' has been backed by legislation designed to implement and then maintain that policy. The Employment Contracts Act 1991 replaced an industrial relations system steered by government, employers and unions with an individualised relationship between employers and their largely de-unionised workforce. The State-owned Enterprises Act 1986 provided a transitional mechanism to prepare government operations for privatisation (similar legislation created local authority trading enterprises). Legislation governing health and housing brought extensive private sector participation into state-funded services. The State Sector Act 1988 and the Public Finance Act 1989 converted a public service that ran the welfare state into a corporate bureaucracy capable of delivering policy and services to a market template. The arms-length relationship between ministers and chief executives gave top officials far-reaching authority over policy formation, staff and operations. The Commerce Act 1986 emphasised efficiency in determining whether commercial players enjoyed a dominant position in a market, while the Overseas Investment Act 1986 said that the only foreign investments requiring a 'national interest' test were those involving land. The Reserve Bank Act 1989 made price stability the primary objective of the Reserve Bank, and guaranteed its independence from ministerial interference, subject to the monetary policy target set by government. The Fiscal Responsibility Act 1994 set standards for fiscal policy (such as an on-average budget surplus, low public debt and stable tax rates) which future governments are required to pursue.

None of this legislation is entrenched; it could all be changed by a simple majority of Parliament. Yet these Acts are unusual in that they impose statutory norms on government policy. The Reserve Bank Act and the Fiscal Responsibility Act in particular are explicit about one particular approach to monetary and fiscal policy. This approach constrains future governments on matters of political choice, which could previously have been changed without extensive parliamentary debate or select committee deliberation. By making any policy deviation subject to intensive scrutiny, the legislation ensures that future governments will be more effectively exposed to the 'fire alarms' inside and outside Parliament, and more vulnerable to scare-mongering about how 'the markets' would respond. A similar outcry would be expected if a government moved to amend the Employment Contracts or Public Finance Acts, or to raise taxes significantly.

A number of binding international economic agreements to which New Zealand is a party, notably the CER and WTO agreements, have a similar normative intent. But they are also coercive, in that commitments to maintain and enhance liberalisation policies are enforceable. Those obligations are technically much more difficult to change than those imposed by domestic legislation and breaches of the international rules may attract crippling sanctions. Although their terms are often opaque and a government can invoke legitimate exceptions or limit its new commitments, doing so is often cited as evidence of weak policy, and damaging to investor confidence.

This suggests that the *fear* of how foreign investors or local vested interests might respond to changes in domestic law or policy is a major element of embedding the free market regime, even when a government has a strong popular mandate for change. The deep penetration of international capital into New Zealand's economy and the economy's increased exposure to international markets have heightened this 'fear factor'. Since 1984, the boundaries between public and private, local and foreign, have eroded and in some cases disappeared. Core state operations have been privatised, often into foreign hands. The largest 'New Zealand' companies are now transnational and (except for the Dairy Board) are in legal terms foreign-owned. They control the country's key economic and productive infrastructure, which they run according to their global corporate priorities, exporting large portions of their profits overseas. Deregulated financial markets and the free floating dollar have reinforced this exposure to foreign markets, with large potential for short-term currency speculation provoking instability and capital flight.

This degree of exposure in the New Zealand economy was intended to have an embedding effect. As far back as 1987, economists David Harper and Girol Karacaoglu suggested that, once the process of financial deregulation was under way, it would be very difficult to turn back because the 'fungibility' of financial capital would frustrate any attempt to re-regulate: 'By deregulating the financial sector first and so quickly, the [Labour] government (maybe deliberately) has forced all future administrations into a very tight corner.'[13] Alan Bollard expressed the similar view that 'many of the reforms in New Zealand are likely to be long term. Removal of import protection is essentially irreversible because of New Zealand's undertakings through GATT, CER and other international agreements ... However, individual industries are always subject to ad hoc reregulation under lobbying pressure.'[14] Neither commentator said that governments *cannot* act; indeed, Bollard explicitly stated that political factors could still intervene.

There appear to be two main barriers to a future government changing direction: the formal constraints imposed through domestic and international law; and the assumption that capital will respond in a way that has catastrophic consequences for the country. Both are used to reinforce the TINA principle. This book seeks to explore the question from the opposite angle. It asks how real these barriers are, and whether the consequences of breaching them would be as dire as predicted, especially when balanced against the social, cultural, economic and political benefits that might ensue. But first, one further 'obstacle' needs to be laid to rest: the belief that globalisation, as an inevitable and irresistible process, makes these questions irrelevant.

▲ CHALLENGING THE MYTHS OF GLOBALISATION

Globalisation is a powerful ideal. It claims to be founded on economic science and accepted as international orthodoxy; it seems overwhelming and omnipotent. Yet this image is built on exaggeration and myth.

▲ *There are always alternatives*

Assertions that the policy changes made since 1984 were based on economic science have enjoyed little credibility, but claims of an international consensus have given them legitimacy. In one sense, those claims were true. From the 1980s to the mid-1990s, neo-liberal economics enjoyed a virtual hegemony among economic commentators, policy-makers and business leaders. This was enhanced in the late 1980s by Gorbachev's policies of perestroika and glasnost, the fall of the Berlin Wall, the tentative opening of China's economy, and the commitment to capitalism by former communist satellites in Indo-China. Once the Cold War was over, global capitalism seemed invincible. But consensus is an ideological construct, not an economic fact, and it changes over time.

The policy template for neo-liberalism is known as the 'Washington consensus' or 'Washington view'. This is because, as US economist Paul Krugman has explained, Washington is where the major economic institutions and the US government are located, and where important people in international economic affairs meet most often. What became conventional wisdom was, as a consequence, 'based more on the circular process of important people reinforcing each other's current dogma than on really solid evidence'.[15] Krugman concluded there was no quantitative assessment that showed this process of macroeconomic policy coordination had produced any significant gains.[16] Nevertheless, it was elevated to the status of economic truth.

British development economist John Toye refers to the construction of this international orthodoxy as the 'empowering myth'. He observed in 1993 that the process of consensus-mongering among economists conflates 'what economists believe with what is economic truth'.[17] No one feels the need to test the model empirically because they feel the facts are too obvious, and no one really wants to delve into alternatives, such as welfare economics, because the results 'are vulnerable to a whole raft of academic quibbles'.[18] An obsession with the 'economically correct' serves to freeze ideas. The learning process stops, so people continue to believe there is no possibility of change, even when neo-liberal policies have failed. In this climate of ideological closure, the TINA principle prevails.

In its most radical form, the Washington consensus is 'the New Zealand experiment' writ large. It requires the removal of trade restrictions and barriers to foreign investment, the deregulation of financial markets, and the lifting of exchange controls to allow the free flow of capital and conversion of currency. Monetary policy is focused primarily (or exclusively) on maintaining low inflation, and often made the responsibility of an independent central bank. This means that the government cannot use credit to boost jobs and growth. State support for domestic industry is withdrawn. Income tax scales are flattened and tax rates reduced; the emphasis on income redistribution through progressive taxation is replaced by an emphasis on flat-rate indirect taxes, especially on consumption. State activities and enterprises are commercialised and privatised, and users are required to pay for those services the state still provides. Government spending is cut, with income support and welfare provision reduced to a minimal safety-net. Private property assumes a greater importance, with property rights guaranteed.[19]

The Washington consensus, otherwise known as 'structural adjustment', is routinely imposed as a condition of debt financing by the IMF and World Bank. The reach of the Washington consensus has not been confined to poorer countries, however. The same agenda was championed by Ronald Reagan and Margaret Thatcher, and endorsed *in theory* across most of the OECD. Backed by a network of international institutions and agreements, as well as private sector supporters, think-tanks and the financial media, this policy agenda held sway for some fifteen years. But 'orthodoxies' cannot survive when the counter-evidence becomes too great. By the mid-1990s, the economic results of the largely market-driven approach in OECD countries had proved far from spectacular, especially when compared to the more state-supported approach of Asian capitalism. The Japanese later maintained that the Asian financial crisis did not negate that comparison (see Chapter 3). In 1997, Krugman observed that the Washington consensus was on the wane:

> A few years ago the conventional wisdom of free markets and sound money was treated by many people as revealed truth, even though there was actually a lot of contrary evidence. And policymakers are extremely reluctant to change their collective minds or admit that they themselves had been wrong. Nonetheless, in both the United States and Europe, the 'Washington view' has been badly eroded recently, at least insofar as it applies to advanced countries.[20]

Its credibility was weak in poorer nations too. Problems of debt and poverty continued to plague many of the countries subjected to structural adjustment programmes. When the IMF's orthodoxy was blamed for deepening the financial crisis in Indonesia in 1997, even the World Bank's chief economist, Joseph Stiglitz, felt the need to distance himself. In a landmark speech in January 1998, he reflected on the deepening crisis and poverty in Asia, and declared that the Washington consensus was neither adequate nor appropriate for the time.[21]

The belief that 'there is no alternative' has been one of globalisation's most powerful props. But the champions of globalisation tend to forget that the policy consensus on which they draw is not immutable. It was formed, and is being reformed, as part of a contest of ideas. The opening up of debate on New Zealand's economic policies in the late 1990s reflects that international trend. It shows that no ideas are set in concrete; there are *always* alternatives.

▲ Globalisation as evolution

Globalisation is also represented as an evolutionary process. At first glance there appears to be plenty of evidence for this. For most of the twentieth century investors had concentrated on long-term investment in their own company, or at least their own country. By the mid-1980s, however, that form of productive investment had been overtaken by short-term movements of capital. People and institutions rapidly invest and disinvest in shares, bonds or speculative financial products such as futures, irrespective of the kind of business and often irrespective of the country. As investment in companies becomes more fluid, foreign investors demand lower barriers to entering countries and fewer restrictions on how they operate there. This includes a range of deregulatory measures: easy movement of money, lower transaction costs, cheaper production techniques, low taxes, flexible labour practices, cheap wages and fewer environmental constraints. They also seek security for their investments beyond that given to domestic investors, including government commitments not to re-regulate or nationalise, and protection against claims by indigenous peoples. The rapidly expanding knowledge industries demand that their products are protected by intellectual property laws and made accessible only to those who pay. Technology and 'cyberspace' facilitate these cross-border flows of money, services and information, making them more difficult to monitor and control.

Corporate power has become much more concentrated in wealthy transnational enterprises (TNEs). These range from old-style multinationals that operate through branches or subsidiaries of a parent company, such as New Zealand's Fletcher Challenge, to firms that integrate their production across different countries, as Nike does, and franchised outlets such as the Body Shop or KFC.[22] In the late 1990s there is almost as much international trade within firms as there is between nation-states. The form of international trade has also changed. It used to involve the physical movement of goods manufactured in one country to another country. A large volume of trade now involves services – sometimes described as 'things you can buy and sell but can't drop on your foot'. These often require the producer or consumer to be mobile, as with tourism or consultancies, or they may be delivered transnationally through sophisticated technology, as with satellite television.

However, claims that these changes reflect a process of economic evolution ignore the historical precedent. The current degree of economic integration and interdependency is far greater than during the Keynesian era (roughly from the 1930s to the 1970s). But statistically, international trade, foreign investment and immigration are at comparable levels to those in the early twentieth century.[23] There are even historical parallels to today's technological revolution. Norman Angell, writing in 1912, described 'rapid post, the instantaneous dissemination of financial and commercial information by means of telegraphy, and generally the incredible progress of rapidity in communication' as creating

> ... a financial interdependence of the capitals of the world, so complex that disturbance in New York involves financial and commercial disturbance in London, and, if sufficiently grave, compels financiers of London to co-operate with those of New York to put an end to the crisis, not as a matter of altruism, but as a matter of commercial self-protection.[24]

That era of laissez-faire had a sense of evolution and inevitability, too. But history proved otherwise.

This is not to suggest that the world's economies have reverted in some cyclical way to an earlier pattern. There are qualitative differences between global economic integration then and now. Flows of finance capital are larger, more technologically integrated and less territorialised. They often operate through 'derivatives' and myriad other financial products which have become detached from, yet impact on, the real value of the currency in the trading economy. Transnational production is more widespread, with different aspects of the production process dispersed across a number of countries. Transnational enterprises adopt a wider range of organisational and legal forms. Patterns of trade, demand for specific products, and the comparative importance of goods to services have changed significantly. There are new forms of consumption and new modes of generating, transmitting and controlling knowledge. There are also new ecological and socio-economic 'externalities'. Above all, the rapid development of information technology is displacing traditional methods of communication. These shifts suggest that the modern dynamic has parallels with the previous era, but has taken a different form.

The 'evolution' argument also makes claims about the *extent* of globalisation that are not supported by the evidence. In most countries, the mass of economic activity still centres on small businesses that are locally based and serve the local market. In New Zealand, for example, some 90 percent of businesses employ ten people or less. They remain deeply integrated with their local and national communities. In a study of the importance of national boundaries, Canadian economist John Helliwell suggested that the economic linkages within nations are much stronger than those between them. He concluded that 'as long as national institutions, populations, trust, and tastes differ as much as they do ... transaction costs will remain much lower within than among national economies, even in the absence of any border taxes or regulations affecting the movements of goods and services.'[25] Economist Tim Hazledine comments on the economic value of cultural and social cohesion:

> Belatedly economists are coming to appreciate the value of the 'social capital', the empathy and sympathy found in relationships between people (including relationships within geographically defined communities such as countries, towns and neighbourhoods, and the cultural communities of kinship, class, hapu and iwi) and also in the broader sense of shared attitudes and goals. Neither democratic government nor 'free' markets can thrive without these relationships.[26]

The emergence of New Zealand Businesses for Social Responsibility reflects this shift in economic thinking (see Chapter 10).

Even transnational enterprises are rarely detached from their parent country. Political economist Robert Wade observes that most major transnationals maintain those operations that add greatest value to their products within their home countries, which are almost always within the OECD. They rely on synergies of social organisation, language, education and mutual expectations to improve efficiencies and the quality of the product or service. These characteristics are often organised within a national or sub-national community. Wade comments: 'Knowledge and information are not ... completely fungible [interchangeable] between places; trust and reputation are even less so.'[27] The relationship of transnational enterprises to home and host states is examined further in Chapter 5.

In OECD countries at least, the degree of exposure to the global economy remains a matter of choice. Economic integration can be a gradual process, as people and companies build linkages that take advantage of organisational synergies, economies of scale and new technologies; alternatively, governments can take a more radical approach. But most OECD governments have embraced neo-liberalism selectively and pragmatically. Yale political scientist Geoffrey Garrett observes that this policy choice has been heavily influenced by partisan politics. Governments in countries where left-wing parties and trade unions remained strong chose to mitigate the impact of global economic integration by increasing public spending, especially on welfare and income support. This is borne out by the fact that, while economic policies in the OECD are somewhat less interventionist than they were twenty years ago, the state's share of economic activity has on average grown. *The Economist* has pointed out that average government expenditure as a proportion of national income in OECD countries increased from 36 percent to 40 percent between 1980 and 1995.[28] Despite claims that credit rating agencies would downgrade such governments for their 'fiscal laxity', there was no lack of lenders willing to finance their public spending. By contrast, Garrett notes that OECD governments who were less influenced by left-wing politics and unions (as in New Zealand from 1984) chose to embrace neo-liberalism more enthusiastically, and in doing so deepened the social impacts of market forces. He concludes:

> Rather than becoming increasingly irrelevant, domestic political factors such as the partisan balance of political power and the strength of organized labor movements are at least as important today as they have ever been to the course of economic policy. Moreover, there is little evidence that countries which have chosen to expand their public economies in the era of global markets have suffered the dire macroeconomic consequences predicted by most analysts.[29]

▲ Assertions about global governance

Whatever the arguments for or against globalisation, it is often suggested that some forms of global control and intervention are now essential, on the grounds that international economic integration has made it difficult for the nation-state to govern the economic lives of its citizens.[30] International relations specialist John Gerard Ruggie describes global finance as flowing through a non-territorial 'region' which operates alongside territorially defined national economies, but which cannot be effectively controlled by those nation-states.[31] This means that short-term speculation can decimate the value of a country's currency, causing havoc to its domestic economy and international trade. Stock-markets have become so integrated that a crash in one has a domino effect around the world. The rapid growth of foreign investment has transferred decisions about strategic interests and assets into offshore hands. Many transnational enterprises are larger and more powerful than the national economies in which they operate; they can and do manipulate their commercial and legal operations to place themselves beyond the control of individual governments.[32]

Other international relations theorists, including James Rosenau, argue that the nation-state is becoming redundant as a source of economic regulation, and that national governments are being displaced by a more pluralist, less structured system of global governance. A variety of rules, agreements and organisations now transcend the territorial boundaries of the state. Each element is developing at a different pace and operates through a unique form.[33] Yet their shared commitment to principles, norms and procedures that promote the expansion of global markets means they act in a regular and patterned way. This provides coherence and the sense of an organic global whole.[34]

The growing array of bilateral, regional and multilateral arrangements that tie member governments to international policy frameworks will be discussed in more detail in later chapters. Briefly, the WTO, with its agreements on trade, services and intellectual property, is the most powerful of the multilateral bodies. Regional arrangements vary from supra-national federations, such as the European Union, to binding regional agreements such as NAFTA and voluntary commitments as in the APEC forum. Bilateral arrangements can provide for more intensive economic integration, as with the CER agreement between New Zealand and Australia, or address specific economic activities, such as bilateral investment treaties.

Other formal organisations, such as the OECD, and informal groupings of governments, like the Group of Seven (G-7), promote the convergence of global economic politics, policies and ideology. Internationally linked networks and think-tanks reinforce that process, without the need for formal diplomatic mandates or ratification. Officials often take part 'in their private capacity'. International economic lawyer Sol Picciotto observes that 'substantial decisions are frequently taken by unaccountable officials acting in arcane and secretive international forums which exert strong pressure on, even if they do not formally bind, national decision-making processes'.[35]

This overview suggests that international economic integration, backed by formal and informal agreements, poses real external constraints on the ability of governments to control economic activity within their country and to determine their policies independently. But this does not mean that a supra-national system of global economic policy-making has displaced national governments. This 'system' is neither coherent nor cohesive. Each of its elements – foreign investment, trade, finance capital, transnational enterprises, information technology transfers, regional agreements, networks and think-tanks – has its own characteristics and dynamics. For example, the anti-democratic leverage the IMF, World Bank and Asian Development Bank can exercise over borrowing governments poses quite different issues from the power and unaccountability of transnational enterprise. Unregulated capital flows, in turn, raise other questions, about whether governments can and should re-regulate. The way that think-tanks, consultancies and international media connect to construct an ideological 'orthodoxy' gives rise to specific concerns about the control of information. Each element of the international system of global governance exhibits its own degree of autonomy from states; each provokes a distinct response from states and institutions, and creates different forms of resistance. Each raises its own possibilities for contest.

Most governments do now attempt to nudge, rather than steer, their country's economic development, as a result of this system of external influences. But it is wrong to claim that states have been rendered powerless. Markets are never self-regulating. Capital needs a legal framework that sets and polices the rules for the markets in which it operates. It also requires a sound physical, technological and intellectual infrastructure, which markets do not reliably provide. Whether capital also needs a stable and well-developed social infrastructure depends on the form of investment (for example, short-term financial speculation or longer-term foreign direct investment), the economic activity involved, and the reason for choosing that location.

The state is the vehicle that provides regulation. It must therefore retain sufficient power to implement the kind of regulation the market requires. Drawing on numerous empirical studies, political scientists Robert Bates and Anne Krueger conclude that structural adjustment paradoxically requires the state to become stronger. Neo-liberal theorists

> ... pit the market against the state; expansion of the role of one implies, in their conception, a reduction in the scope of the other, as through privatization, cutbacks in public spending, and a reduction in regulatory powers. And yet ... economic policy reforms are not 'anti-state'; rather, they appear to strengthen the powers of the core of the state, the executive branch, and to enhance its control over key economic policy variables which affect the outcome of economic activity ... the expansion of the role of markets requires a strengthening of the state and especially of its financial bureaucracy.[36]

Political economist Robert Cox reaches a similar conclusion from a more critical perspective. When capitalism functioned through the national economy, the state actively supported it with policies of welfare interventionism. Today, the state is responding to the needs of capital in a different way. Domestically, it oversees the transition from state-centred to neo-liberal policies. Internationally, it helps build the raft of state-sponsored economic agreements, organisations and arrangements that maintain global capitalism.[37] This encourages a broad coherence between the restructured state and the private sector, and across the government's domestic and international agendas. However, for the state to carry out these roles it must maintain a sufficient degree of legitimacy among those from whom it derives its political mandate – that is, the country's citizens. When faced with contradictions between maintaining legitimacy and responding to the demands of international capital, it will not inevitably choose the latter path.

▲ International treaty-making

One way to limit the state's autonomy is through international economic agreements that commit present and future governments to ongoing liberalisation. These economic agreements share a number of core principles, although their details vary. 'National treatment' means that a government cannot give its domestic producers or investors more favourable treatment than it gives those from another signatory country. 'Most favoured nation' (MFN) status prevents a government from discriminating among the various signatories, so that the best treatment it gives to one has to be given to all.[38] 'Transparency' requires full disclosure to other parties of the rules, policies, practices, procedures and decisions that relate to the subject of the agreement. In many instances a government will enter 'reservations', which withhold coverage of part or all of the agreement. Because almost all agreements are committed to ongoing liberalisation, reservations will usually be subject to 'standstill', which means they cannot be added to, and a rule or expectation that they will be 'rolled back' and eventually eliminated. Many agreements also make provision for international dispute resolution;[39] in rare instances, an organisation may establish its own bodies for settling disputes. Most provide rules for exit, although in practice the cost to reputation, payment of compensation, and the risks of retaliation and international exile make that almost unthinkable.

Canadian constitutional lawyer David Schneiderman has described these treaties as a 'new constitutionalism', which in form and substance mirrors many features of existing national constitutions.[40] Most commit future generations of citizens to certain predetermined institutional forms and policies. They are difficult to amend, and often include binding enforcement mechanisms. Yet they serve a different constituency, conferring privileged rights of citizenship on corporate capital, while constraining the power of the nation-state and the democratic rights of its citizens. These agreements may defer to national laws, supplement them, or require them to be changed. The tension between old national constitutions and new global rules was exemplified when members of the Philippine Senate challenged their government's accession to the WTO. They claimed (unsuccessfully) that the binding commitments in WTO agreements not to discriminate against foreign providers of goods and services breached the core principles of the Philippine Constitution, which gave primacy to local workers, businesses and investors.[41]

Such agreements are explicitly intended to restrict the policy choices of future governments. For example, World Bank economist Bernard Hoekman and co-author Michel Kostecki describe the WTO as:

... somewhat analogous to a mast to which governments can tie themselves so as to escape the siren-like calls of various pressure groups. It is a mechanism through which the political market failure[42] that is inherent in many societies, both industrialized and developing, can be corrected, at least in part, because reneging on liberalization commitments requires the compensation of affected trading partners. This increases both the cost and the visibility of adopting inefficient trade policies to placate domestic interest-groups.[43]

Likewise, the extension of the GATT agreement on trade in goods to new sectors such as services was meant to 'both increase the credibility of initial reform and help governments resist demands from politically influential interest-groups for altering policies in the future.'[44] The General Agreement on Trade in Services was intended to impose costs on 'backsliding'. Hoekman and Kostecki note that this strategy will succeed only if governments are willing to tie themselves to the mast and the agreements do not offer escape routes. (As Chapter 7 explains, these conditions are often not met.)

Drafting these agreements is the exclusive domain of nation-states. Negotiations are limited to government representatives and those they invite to join them. Participation is coordinated by key ministries at the national level. Officials from the same agencies, working to consistent instructions, operate across the range of international forums and networks. Their continual interaction creates a basis for mutual understanding and consistency between negotiators. Politicians play a secondary, often symbolic role.

The text of an agreement (or treaty) usually becomes public only after negotiations are complete – for reasons that are overtly anti-democratic. The negative impacts of an agreement to deregulate and liberalise will immediately be visible, and the groups directly affected will often mobilise to resist. The benefits, however, are alleged to be longer term and more diffuse, and the beneficiaries will rarely organise in support.[45] Hence, as international relations specialist Robert Putnam explains, 'most professional diplomats emphasize the value of secrecy to successful negotiations'.[46] Indeed, they may go further, manipulating the flow of information to create a receptive environment, and actively constructing constituencies of beneficiaries who will seek to discredit the critics of 'reform'.

This rationale seems ironic, given that the best resourced and most readily heard voices are the major beneficiaries – big business, especially the transnationals. The Japanese government seeks a broad consensus of major business interests before deciding its stance in international economic negotiations, and meets regularly with the major corporate leaders. In the US, trade advisory committees have been created by legislation to provide public input into the US negotiating position on trade treaties. This 'public' is almost exclusively drawn from the business community, who gain privileged access to information, documents and key officials. In New Zealand, the business lobbies of Federated Farmers, the Employers' Federation, the Manufacturers' Federation, the Chambers of Commerce and the Business Roundtable have been the major non-government influences on the government's international negotiating position.

Governments involved in economic treaty negotiations have widely varying objectives. The major players tend to shop around for the international forum whose decision-making processes, agenda and status best serve their interests. International agencies also have their own agendas and legitimacy requirements, which lead to turf battles over issues, strategies and choice of forums. Given these tensions, it is relevant to ask 'what and why particular issues are left off the agenda of inter-state politics, who sets the rules of the bargaining game (meta-rules), and whence come the norms and ideas which are used to define issues and within which bargaining takes place'.[47]

When assessing New Zealand's options, it is important to consider the benefits and down-sides of these arrangements. A government has far more choice in deciding whether to enter an agreement, and if so on what terms, than it has about changing those commitments or deciding not to comply with them once they are made. In theory, a parliament can still implement policies and laws that conflict with an international treaty entered into by a previous government. But it would come under heavy diplomatic and economic pressure to step back into line. Withdrawing from an economic treaty altogether would result in denial of 'most favoured nation' treatment and open the country's international economic activities to discrimination by other countries.

However, there are options that stop short of withdrawal. Even agreements that are described as 'binding' contain many escape routes so that governments can alleviate serious domestic concerns. This provision is a double-edged sword. If all countries take advantage of it, the rule-based system breaks down. But if many other countries are already exploiting the loopholes, remaining 'pure' can put a country at a serious disadvantage. The threat of sanctions against those who breach an agreement is not a guaranteed disincentive. Penalties are usually restorative rather than punitive, and arise long after the benefits from the breach have been secured. As Chapter 7 shows, rich countries frequently deviate from the rules; poor ones have less leeway, although many still adopt a creative approach.

The international agreements also stop short of replacing national laws with global ones. Treaties, and sanctions awarded in international forums, are generally not enforceable in domestic courts unless national legislation specifically says so. That has been done, for example for international arbitration awards in disputes between governments and foreign investors at the International Centre for the Settlement of Investment Disputes at the World Bank;[48] incorporation of that mechanism into the proposed Multilateral Agreement on Investment (MAI) was one reason why the MAI became so controversial. International treaties may also be used by the courts as an aid to interpretation, although New Zealand courts have been conservative about doing so.[49]

▲ SOVEREIGNTY AND DEMOCRACY

These notions of inevitability, evolution, global governance and all-powerful economic institutions sustain the imagery of globalisation. The cumulative effect is deeply disempowering. Once people believe that overwhelming economic forces are integrated in some space outside the nation-state and beyond the influence of governments or citizens, there seems little point in trying to influence it – even when they feel it is destroying their lives.

But that idea of globalisation directly challenges the historical notions around which people organise their political lives: the sovereign authority of the nation-state to regulate economic activities that occur within, or impact on, its realm; the democratic mechanisms through which governments are supposedly held to account; and the power of self-determination that vests in indigenous peoples.

The fundamental tensions between the historical sovereignty of the nation state and the global economy cannot be dismissed as quickly or as lightly as the advocates of globalisation would have us believe. Sovereignty is defined in *Black's Law Dictionary* as including:

> The supreme, absolute and uncontrollable power by which any independent state is governed; supreme political authority; the supreme will; paramount control of the constitution and frame of government and its administration; the self-sufficient source of political power, from which all specific political powers are derived; the international independence of a state, combined with the right and power of regulating its internal affairs without foreign dictation; also a political society, or state, which is sovereign and independent.[50]

This definition condenses the diverse and contrasting elements of internal and external sovereignty, and equates the state's legal sovereignty with its actual capacity or power. Internal sovereignty implies a central, supreme political authority with the exclusive right to make laws and the power to require compliance, if necessary by coercion, from those within its territorial boundaries. A permanent relationship exists between the state and a clearly defined geographical space. There is a population of citizens who owe allegiance and enjoy rights, and of non-citizens such as guest workers or refugees whose territorial presence renders them subject to state authority. The state has the ability to transform national institutions and regulate the disposition of economic resources by legislative and administrative means.

External sovereignty depicts a world that is partitioned into sovereign states of equal authority, each of which recognises the internal sovereignty of the others. This recognition includes the independence of sovereign states in all matters of domestic politics, and the right to defend their territory against invasion. In the exercise of external sovereignty, states are the only actors. All are formally autonomous, equal and self-determining. Each has the authority to confer on other actors or agencies the right to exercise some of its powers. There are countless situations where the state has subordinated its legal authority to some external institution, set of rules, dispute resolution process or predesignated sanction, through the voluntary exercise of its sovereignty. Under international law, states are ultimately self-determining. Just as they can delegate some of their powers to an international body, so can they withdraw that delegation. Hence, the state can (in theory) decline to negotiate a treaty, renege on international obligations, refuse to implement international rulings, and withdraw from any agreement or organisation at any time and on its own terms.

These definitions reveal a stark contrast between an internal world of order, cohesion and government, and an almost anarchic international sphere which is fragmented and devoid of central authority. The two are brought together under the rubric of *legal* sovereignty to depict the supreme authority of the state and the legal order, conferred internally by a written or unwritten constitution, and recognised externally (or limited by consent) in international law and legal instruments. In New Zealand that authority rests with the Governor-General in Council, which in practice means the Cabinet. So long as the global economy is conducted according to international law, the state's formal legal sovereignty remains undiminished.

This image of sovereignty assumes the legitimacy of New Zealand's colonial state. Once a state has been recognised at international law, it is irrelevant how that state secured its power. Some of the New Zealand government's staunchest defenders concede that the English Crown embarked on 'a revolutionary seizure of power' when it unilaterally declared British sovereignty over New Zealand in May 1840.[51] Ever since, the Crown's authority has been challenged by Maori asserting their tino rangatiratanga (sovereign authority), which was confirmed by the Declaration of Independence in 1835 and the Treaty of Waitangi in 1840, and never given away. However, there are differing views among Maori as to what constitutional changes would be required in practice to guarantee their tino rangatiratanga in Aotearoa New Zealand today (see below).

The legal definition of 'sovereignty' is also far more refined than the meaning commonly given to it by New Zealanders. In popular discourse, sovereignty generally implies a world of territorial and self-contained nation-states which are inviolate and enduring. Each has a national economy, national identity, national polity and national legal system. It is this idea of nationhood which many Pakeha (or non-Maori New Zealanders) in particular feel is now under threat. People fear losing control over the decisions that affect their lives, decisions they believe belong to the democratically elected government. Technically, they are concerned not about the loss of legal sovereignty, but about the erosion of the state's 'capacity to act independently in the articulation and pursuit of domestic and international policy objectives'.[52] This often assumes a level of power that the colonial state never really had. But people fear its loss quite desperately, all the same.

The extent to which any state's capacity to act is under threat depends on the depth of its integration into the international economy, the leverage it can exercise in that environment, and the costs and benefits of the action proposed. When a country is vulnerable to the actions of foreign corporations, governments or financiers, the state's legal sovereignty remains intact, but the demands of these external forces can shape the direction of policy and law. Areas of influence extend beyond economic matters to decisions affecting indigenous rights, the environment, labour, social policy and human rights. Appeasing powerful international players and 'the markets' may assume greater importance for a government than the democratic choices and economic, social and cultural needs of its citizens – often on the basis of assumptions, rather than empirical assessment.

The distinction between sovereignty and the state's capacity to act is encapsulated in an exchange between Reserve Bank Governor Don Brash and economist Wolfgang Rosenberg in 1996. Brash argued that all companies owned abroad

> ... are obliged to comply with New Zealand's laws and regulations, obliged to pay New Zealand's taxes and tariffs, and obliged to pay wages and salaries sufficiently generous to attract staff from New Zealand-owned companies. ... No matter how many companies are owned abroad, ultimate authority resides with the New Zealand Government, *subject of course to the right of foreign investors to take their capital to more hospitable climes if the New Zealand authorities make unreasonable demands.* There is no loss of sovereignty.[53] [Emphasis added.]

Brash went on to suggest that the 'greatest threat to our ability to control our destiny arises not from foreign investment but rather from poor economic policy – which leads to rising public sector debt, slow growth in real incomes, inflation and all the rest'.[54] In other words, sovereignty remained intact; so did the state's power to act independently, *provided* it did not impose unreasonable demands on foreign investors or deviate from the current economic path. Rosenberg replied that, in practice, this meant the state's capacity to act had been severely constrained:

> True, there may be little difference between the pro-profitability and anti-social welfare attitudes of foreign and domestic business. However, the central position of foreign investors, especially in the fields of finance and media ownership, the threat of possible withdrawal of foreign investment from New Zealand, and the size of foreign-controlled enterprise in New Zealand combine to make a so-called 'leftward' swing of governmental policies and strategies unlikely, if not impossible.[55]

In other words, the sovereign state could not exercise its power to move to the left. Later chapters will suggest that this overstates the case, although the constraints Rosenberg points to are very real. Democratic participation in decisions about the extent of a country's exposure to the international economy is therefore critical. Failure to provide this has provoked complaints internationally of a 'democratic deficit', especially in relation to international economic policy-making, and the treaties that seek to lock these policies in.

In some countries, the treaty-making process is subjected to intense political scrutiny at every stage. In the US, this is required by the Constitution. The President can make treaties, with the concurrence of two-thirds of the Senate. Congress has the constitutional power to determine whether international treaties are incorporated into US law. Congress can also grant the President what is called 'fast track' authority to negotiate an international trade agreement, which they undertake to accept or reject in its entirety and not attempt to amend.

In preparation for negotiations, the President must take advice from the International Trade Commission and from public hearings,[56] and 'seek information and advice from representative elements of the private sector with respect to negotiating objectives and bargaining positions before entering into a trade agreement ... and with respect to other matters arising in connection with the administration of trade policy'.[57] This is provided by the Advisory Committee for Trade Negotiations, comprising up to 45 individuals from 'government, labor, industry, agriculture, small business, service industries, consumer interests and the general public'. Once negotiations are complete, the committee reports on 'whether and to what extent the agreement promotes the economic interests of the United

States'.[58] There are numerous other opportunities for informal and formal input from the private sector. Before entering an international trade agreement, the President must consult with the major Senate and Congressional committees as to whether the move is feasible and desirable, and give Congress 90 days prior warning of an intention to sign. Ratification occurs only after the President has informed Congress of how the agreement serves US interests, and it has approved any implementing legislation. Despite this elaborate machinery, public interest groups in the US complain that almost all the advisory bodies are dominated by big business interests, and that they often cannot secure access to information until negotiations are virtually concluded – let alone influence the negotiations, except through lobbying and public pressure.

By contrast, governments in the UK, Australia and New Zealand have traditionally deemed treaty-making (in theory by the Queen or Governor-General, but in practice by the Cabinet) to be either an act of state or an exercise of Crown prerogative.[59] This relies on the distinction, described earlier, between internal and external sovereignty: the authority to make domestic law rests with Parliament, while the authority to enter binding international treaties is effectively the prerogative of the Cabinet. In 1996, Minister of Foreign Affairs and Trade Don McKinnon explained the rationale. Participation in the international community is mediated through the state's exercise of 'external sovereignty', whereby the government, on behalf of New Zealanders, determines and protects New Zealand's interests abroad: 'We work externally to protect interests and values important to us (and to many other countries).' McKinnon contrasted this with 'internal sovereignty', which is about 'operating with the consent of the people', and includes public debate, consultation and parliamentary processes.[60]

The disjuncture between internal and external sovereignty allows the government to quarantine the exercise of treaty-making within the global community, away from domestic participation and scrutiny. Its origins lie with the Treaty of Westphalia in 1648, which recognised the state as the supreme power within its borders, thus laying to rest the church's transnational claims to political authority.[61] For the next three centuries, international treaties dealt mainly with military and strategic matters. Today, as global economic policy-making reaches deep into Parliament's traditional domain, the distinction between internal and external sovereignty has become untenable.

Both Australia and Britain have introduced some new measures for parliamentary oversight of executive treaty-making.[62] In Australia this was sparked by controversies over the federal government's international commitments on human rights, environmental and labour laws. After an extensive consultation process in 1995, the Senate Legal and Constitutional References Committee identified several key concerns.[63] Little information was publicly available on treaties to which Australia was bound. There was insufficient consultation with industry, community groups, states and territories before Australia was committed to a treaty. There was no forum where members of the public could express their views before a treaty was ratified. Finally, there was no parliamentary involvement in the treaty-making process.[64]

Based largely on the Senate committee's recommendations, the Liberal government implemented a number of changes which increase formal democratic participation, but deliver little effective democratic control. A treaty must now be tabled in Parliament at least fifteen days before the government takes definitive action to become a full party to it (with some exceptions for 'urgent and sensitive' agreements). A national interest analysis must accompany each treaty, setting out the major provisions and the obligations the treaty imposes, an assessment of its advantages and disadvantages, and a description of any changes required to make Australian law comply. Any such legislation must be passed before a treaty can be ratified. The new Joint Standing Committee on Treaties is empowered to inquire into matters arising from treaties and national interest analyses, and matters referred to it by the House or minister. A Treaty Council was established to provide for consultation with the states, and a treaty database created. A list of treaties under negotiation, and all national interest analyses of recently signed treaties, are posted on the Internet.[65] However, the decision on whether to sign and ratify a treaty still rests exclusively with the Executive.

In New Zealand, pressure for greater democratic scrutiny of the treaty-making process grew during the 1990s, led by international jurist Kenneth Keith and the Law Commission,[66] and supported by interventions from Clerk of the House David McGee,[67] and the Ministry of Justice.[68] The Law Commission's report in 1996 observed that:

> New Zealand's international obligations have implications well beyond the technical law-making process. They have major consequences for approaches to law and public power ... for law reform agencies, for legal practitioners, and for the courts. They are also reflected in the growing debate about 'sovereignty'. ... A better understanding of our international obligations requires better education and information for the [legal] profession at large, and for the public. But it also has a profound influence on the democratic process and popular participation in national law-making.[69]

Recognising that effective participation required public input during the negotiation stage, the Commission recommended that: 'Where possible, there should be early notification of matters subject to negotiation and extensive consultation with interested parties such as Maori, women's groups, environmental groups, and the business sector.'[70]

Demands for greater government accountability on international issues gained momentum during the controversy over the proposed MAI in 1997. All of New Zealand's opposition parties expressed support for greater parliamentary participation in the treaty-making process.[71] The Coalition government's response was minimal. In May 1998, following a report from the Select Committee on Foreign Affairs, Defence and Trade,[72] the Deputy Prime Minister tabled a notice of motion that required all treaties subject to ratification to be presented to Parliament beforehand, accompanied by a national interest analysis prepared by the government. Both documents would then be referred to the select committee. The government could not sign the treaty until the select committee had reported back or 35 calendar days had expired.[73]

These changes were introduced for a trial period under Parliament's sessional orders, and applied only to international treaties where Cabinet's decision to ratify was taken after 17 December 1997. Non-treaty commitments such as APEC were therefore excluded, even though they were intended to constrain future policy decisions on trade and investment, and played a significant role in the international circuitry of economic policy-making.

The national interest analysis would outline the obligations the treaty imposed, the costs of compliance, the measures required to implement it, and the consultation process that had been followed. But the government rejected the select committee's suggestion that the analysis should also address the advantages *and disadvantages*, and any economic, social, cultural and environmental effects, of entering *or not entering* the treaty.[74] The select committee retained full discretion on whether to hold an inquiry, and if so, whether to call for submissions.

Parliament would still not discuss the text of a treaty until negotiations were complete and the content finalised. Even then, Parliament had no right to vote on the treaty, and could not impose constraints on the Executive. There was no prior requirement for the Cabinet to secure a parliamentary mandate to negotiate, nor to engage in public discussion at any stage. The Official Information Act still gave the government conclusive grounds for withholding information provided in confidence by another government or international organisation,[75] and information considered likely to seriously damage the New Zealand economy by premature disclosure of a decision 'to change or continue Government economic policies ... relating to entering into of overseas trade agreements'.[76] There was no attempt to address the objections from Maori that the colonial government had no authority under the Treaty of Waitangi to make international commitments unilaterally, and that iwi (Maori tribal groups) had a constitutional right to be fully involved.

The sessional orders fell well short of the scrutiny given to domestic legislation and regulations, and they had little effect. They were introduced mainly to defuse pressures over the proposed MAI, but because negotiations on the MAI were suspended in late 1998, the agreement was never concluded and thus never debated in Parliament. A number of national interest analyses were tabled in 1998 and 1999. Only one involved an international economic treaty (related to the financial services agreement at the WTO). The select committee decided not to seek submissions, and its report was never debated in Parliament. The sessional orders were due to lapse at the end of the 1999 session. A review by the select committee would then recommend whether they should be renewed.

The new process failed to meet concerns about the 'democratic deficit' in relation to the signing of international economic treaties. Claims of a 'democratic deficit' are compounded by the secrecy of negotiations at the international level, and by the unbalanced commitment in the agreements to the expansion of global capitalism. In the late 1990s there was pressure for greater involvement of 'civil society' in the international treaty-making process. 'Civil society' is a politically neutral term that refers to any person, organisation or entity other than the state itself, and can thus include transnational corporations and neo-liberal lobby groups such as the Business Roundtable.[77] Many of the international institutions responded by offering selected representatives of so-called 'civil society' an opportunity for dialogue, on the institutions' terms. The WTO organised special forums on development and the environment. OECD officials held informal meetings with non-government organisations (NGOs) in Paris to hear their objections to the MAI, and to complement input to the negotiations from the International Confederation of Free Trade Unions (ICFTU), whose advisory role at the OECD was already institutionalised. Government-approved union representatives and environmentalists were allowed to participate in the bottom-rung working groups of APEC, while the regional grouping of the ICFTU was granted informal meetings with APEC's chair. The World Bank agreed to work with a coalition of NGOs to assess the impact of some of its programmes, while the Asian Development Bank approved (minimalist) policies for consultation with indigenous peoples and NGOs.

This kind of engagement was actively sought by the ICFTU and by Western environmental NGOs who believed that globalisation was inevitable and therefore sought to give it a 'green' or 'social' face. The ICFTU eschewed the notion of a national labour market, and positively welcomed globalisation as the basis for a new form of international corporatism between government, business and organised labour. It suggested that representatives of these three interests could fashion a new consensus on the relationship between economic and social policy, and national and international responsibilities. The ICFTU aimed to secure commitment to the International Labour Organisation (ILO) Declaration of Fundamental Principles and Rights at Work,[78] within a liberalised global economy where 'all countries should aim if not for totally free trade, [then] for progressively more and more open trade with no obvious stopping point'.[79] The ICFTU saw unilateral commitment to both goals as preferable: 'just as it is in the interests of countries to liberalise trade even if others do not, it is also in the interests of countries to implement basic labour standards even if others do not'.[80] The US and the European Union generally supported such demands, as did the New Zealand Labour Party. By contrast, the negotiating position of the National government and its lead officials was to oppose any substantive reference to social, labour and environmental goals in international economic treaties, insisting that there were other, more appropriate forums where they could be pursued.

Not all unions supported the 'social clause' approach. Members of the New Zealand Trade Union Federation objected that these agreements could not be made worker- or environment-friendly. Free markets, by definition, created conditions that maximised the exploitation of people and resources for profit. They argued that unfettered international competition was all about the deregulation of labour markets, less stringent health and safety requirements, the erosion (or elimination) of minimum wages and conditions, the loss of job security, and the reduction of the social wage – as experienced in New Zealand since 1984. Human needs were subordinated to the 'national interest', which was redefined as economic growth through free markets. When representatives of labour were co-opted into such a paradigm, they delegitimised those who continued to resist it.

Some activists have proposed an alternative approach to countering globalisation at the international level – what US international lawyer Richard Falk calls 'globalisation-from-below'. Progressive social forces should develop a coherent counter-ideology, with a common theoretical framework, political language and programme to challenge both the state-centred and market-oriented paradigms.[81] But this raises the question: who determines the common framework, language and programme? Most 'international' NGOs who challenge the impact of globalisation, especially on development and the environment, are Western-dominated and have little contact with grass-roots movements in other countries. There has been some increase in information sharing and the coordination of campaigns among different countries, including through the Internet for those who can access it. But effective opposition to globalisation remains largely a local response to its impact on people's daily lives. Attempts to coordinate opposition under some international umbrella could therefore prove as disempowering as globalisation itself.

▲ DECOLONISATION

For many Maori (as for other indigenous peoples) there is a further dimension to globalisation. Tino rangatiratanga remains the central objective of most Maori political discourse. The notion that the nation-state is in decline has widespread appeal, because it suggests that new configurations of political power are possible. In a speech on globalisation in 1995, the chair of the Waitangi Tribunal, Judge Eddie Durie, observed: 'a global society shifts our thinking beyond territoriality'.[82] He pointed out that indigenous cultures pre-date national states, which are largely modern innovations. States come and go, or change, but cultures endure. They are not creations of the state; their rights of autonomy are inherent. Nor do they depend on the maintenance of territorial integrity. They transcend the state, crossing geographical boundaries. Durie suggested that the time was right to embrace a 'deliberative democracy' at the domestic level which would value the reconciliation of peoples in a climate of mutual respect and interdependence, and mediate cultural conflicts through agreed processes. Internationally, the system of unitary and exclusive national states had to be rethought, because it forced colonised indigenous peoples to stand outside the accepted framework for international law.[83]

Maori have widely divergent views on what powers would be exercised under any new constitutional arrangements, by whom, through what processes, and in what relationship to the colonial state. But as Mason Durie explains, these views are underpinned by shared goals and principles:[84]

> Structural arrangements for self-determination are important and the promotion of absolute Maori independence (as if it were a possibility) has been seized upon by the media to illustrate how unrealistic Maori can be. A media image of Maori bent only on separate development and anti-Pakeha sentiment is as misleading as the picture of a racially harmonious nation within which Maori are happy to blend with an otherwise colourless society. Central to the debate is whether Maori aspirations for fairness and the chance to remain Maori can be fostered within a single nation-state or whether other arrangements are necessary. Views change. ...
>
> But tino rangatiratanga, mana motuhake, Maori self-determination, cannot

be measured simply by the constitutional arrangements for governance or the level of Maori autonomy. More important is whether the goals of self-determination are being realised. The broad aims of self-determination are the advancement of Maori people as Maori and the protection of the environment for future generations. Economic self-sufficiency, social equity, cultural affirmation and political power, stand alongside a firm Maori identity strengthened by access to whanau, hapu and iwi and confirmation that future generations of Maori will be able to enjoy their lands and forests, rivers and lakes, harbours and the sea and the air. Those goals underlie the significance of Maori self-determination.[85]

The positions Maori espouse on constitutional change often correspond to their attitudes to globalisation. Maori entrepreneurs, in both iwi and urban authorities, tend to identify tino rangatiratanga with economic security. They support new economic arrangements that will free them from colonial government control over their decisions and economic activities. Rather than seeking a new constitutional framework, they maintain or establish their own arrangements for internal governance (although the status of urban Maori authorities as iwi, and their entitlements under the Treaty of Waitangi, have been strongly contested by traditional iwi). Their relationship with the colonial government is pragmatic, negotiating compromise financial settlements for Treaty claims, cooperating with government initiatives, and accepting contracts to deliver government services. All this implies self-management rather than self-government.

Maori nationalists, however, usually seek a new constitutional arrangement that challenges the supremacy of the colonial state. For those who derive their tino rangatiratanga solely from their iwi, the recognition of the state is irrelevant. For them, constitutional change involves reconceptualising and reasserting their sovereignty on a unilateral basis. Those who promote a pan-Maori approach to tino rangatiratanga advocate a new political arrangement that reconciles tribal and urban, traditional and contemporary perspectives – one that is based on traditional values, yet can effectively engage with the issues posed by a colonial capitalist society. This position has a strong Treaty focus. The colonial state is the 'Crown' from which Maori can claim Treaty obligations; it is also a more easily accessible target for political pressure than international capital. That means it is better for economic and political power to remain within the colonial state than for it to be further diffused offshore. Hence the position of Maori nationalists often appears contradictory: the need to hold firm against further erosion of their tino rangatiratanga leads them simultaneously to attack state sovereignty and defend the colonial state's power against the encroachments of globalisation.

The intensity of Maori commitment to tino rangatiratanga cannot be underestimated. The state's acknowledgement of the issue waxed and waned during the 1990s. A significant debate occurred in 1995, prompted by a series of constitutional hui under the auspices of rangatira Hepi te Heuheu and also by a number of high-profile land occupations. The National government response to tino rangatiratanga was minimal, and widely rejected by Maori; it successfully used the settlement of several major Treaty claims to sideline the sovereignty debate once again. But even that token response caused problems for National with its non-Maori constituency and many MPs.

The debate on domestic constitutional arrangements resurfaced in response to international treaties that impacted on Maori concerns. In 1993 a landmark claim was lodged with the Waitangi Tribunal to protect Maori control of indigenous knowledge – a move that was widely supported by Maori, and focused attention on the intellectual property agreement at the WTO.[86] Maori nationalists ran education programmes linking globalisation to colonisation, and highlighting the threat that foreign investment posed to Maori control of their resources. Responding to their constituency, Maori MPs became increasingly aware of international treaty issues and worked across party lines on some of them, notably the MAI. Underpinning Maori arguments were dual concerns: the constitutional right of Maori to participate as equal partners with the Crown in the international arena; and the substantive risks that globalisation posed to the Maori life-world. These were challenges that would not go away, and had much wider implications than the negotiation of international treaties.

▲ REFLECTIONS

The claims made for globalisation are difficult to sustain. Globalisation is not an evolutionary process; history shows that attempts to create a global self-regulating market-place have fallen apart before under the weight of economic, social and political contradictions. The international orthodoxy and policy consensus that sustain the belief in global free markets are transitory, the products of a particular time, and are already being revised through an ongoing contest of ideas. Governments (at least in the OECD) are neither shrinking nor powerless. They remain the vehicles through which deregulation – and re-regulation – are pursued. To maintain their political legitimacy, they need relative autonomy from the interests of capital. Attempts to tie their hands through international agreements that supplant national constitutions can only work if a government is willing, and there are no escape routes – conditions that rarely occur in practice and often create local controversy when they do. In sum, there are no grounds for believing that New Zealand is being swept along some linear and evolutionary path that will lead inevitably to a global free market in a borderless world.

Globalisation as ideology also sows the seeds of its own political destruction. Its claims to inevitability and orthodoxy deter people from thinking about, let alone pursuing, alternatives. The notion allows no prospect of change. This creates its own contradictions, however, as people reassert their right to influence the decisions that affect their lives. In doing so, they invoke notions of sovereignty, democracy and tino rangatiratanga. The tension between the two sets of ideals remains unaddressed. *Globalisation in practice* raises different questions about the extent to which a state's capacity to act is constrained, but these are essentially matters of politics and economics, not of evolution.

2 ▲ Constructing Orthodoxy

The mythology of globalisation is enormously powerful. It allows governments to abdicate responsibility for the consequences of their own policies, laws and practices; it justifies a refusal to consider alternative policies that might cause less harm to people, communities, and their environment.

The New Zealand model of structural adjustment has attracted attention internationally because of its audacity in attempting to convert global free market ideology into economic reality. However, its curiosity value has been backed by a sufficient degree of international policy consensus for New Zealand to be taken seriously. New Zealand's image as being part of a global orthodoxy, and yet leading that agenda, has provided crucial legitimacy to policies that were frequently unprecedented and deeply unpopular. The claim to 'world-leading orthodoxy' is not as contradictory as it sounds. New Zealand's approach has been 'orthodox' in the sense that it pursued the *ideal* of globalisation. It has been 'world-leading' (at least among countries of the OECD), because other countries have not chosen *in practice* to follow that path. This chapter examines the process of constructing what John Toye calls the 'empowering myth', at both national and international levels; it identifies New Zealand's claims to economic orthodoxy and world leadership as artificially created and self-perpetuating.

▲ SHAPING THE CONSENSUS

Every historical era has a body of intellectuals who give it cohesion and self-identity. When a major transformation occurs, they act as 'constructor, organiser, "permanent persuader"', helping to build a new hegemony around a particular economic system and accompanying set of ideas.[1] These are not primarily the traditional intellectuals found in universities and other hallowed halls (although such people make some contribution).

Rather, they are the activists who generate and disseminate new ideas in diverse arenas, such as the media, business, politics, and the professional conference circuit. Their ideas are rarely new. Often they reorder existing concepts, or revive and re-articulate those that have fallen from favour in recent years, adapting them to suit the new circumstances. In describing this process, Italian theorist Antonio Gramsci notes: 'What was previously secondary and subordinate, or even incidental, is now taken to be primary – becomes the nucleus of a new ideological and theoretical complex.'[2] The language, concepts and 'experts' of the outgoing regime are marginalised, and the ideology and assumptions of the new intellectuals are elevated in their place. This helps to explain why certain agents and ideas emerge at a particular economic, social and political conjuncture and appear to act collectively in pursuit of a consensus. The process also allows for challenges from those whose pre-eminence is displaced, and from those who wish to generate new alternatives.

'Globalisation' has drawn upon and reworked economic and philosophical theories that date back several centuries; although discredited in the early twentieth century, their time has come again. These theories have powerful advocates within academia – names such as Milton Friedman, Robert Nozick and Friedrich von Hayek – whose influence must not be underestimated. But notions of the global free market are also articulated, refined and rationalised in a range of other influential arenas. Institutions such as the IMF, World Bank and WTO are not simply economic agencies; they also construct an intellectual framework for their approach. Transnational corporations advance their cause internationally through groups such as the US Council for International Business or the Business and Industry Advisory Committee at the OECD, generally locating their self-interest in a theoretical justification.

Political parties from different countries have created international networks to exchange information and ideas about policies, strategies and structures to enhance free market capitalism, such as the International Democratic Union of conservative parties inaugurated by Margaret Thatcher in 1983.[3] Other networks extend this web. 'Independent' thinktanks, heavily sponsored by vested interests, play an important complementary role in generating reports, ideas and debate which are too politically sensitive for officials to explore, and would be dismissed as self-interested coming directly from the corporate sector. The business press and electronic media package information and analysis in an ideologically consistent way, supported by selected 'experts' whom they vest with authority. Servicing such networks and assisting the implementation of their programmes is a new breed of policy 'consultants'. These are often retired or recycled officials and politicians contracted by international financial agencies and 'reforming' governments to replicate similar strategies and models across the globe.

This is *not* to suggest a global conspiracy. As globalisation critic David Korten notes, shaping the agenda 'works much more like any networking or shared culture building process out of which alliances among individuals and groups emerge and evolve. There is no conspiracy, though in practical terms, the consequences are much as if there were'.[4]

▲ International networks

It is hardly surprising that the world's major economic players seek to advance their long-term interests in a systematic and organised way. Some of these forums for discussion date back to the period following the Second World War. For example, the informal and little-known Bilderberg Group first met in 1954 in Holland, and brought together powerful (and unnamed) business and political leaders from the US and Europe; the group's purpose was to develop strategies for rebuilding and strengthening industrial capitalism.[5]

A more formal grouping known as the Trilateral Commission was established by the chair of Chase Manhattan Bank, David Rockefeller, and others in 1973. By 1998 it comprised some 325 'distinguished citizens' from the political, corporate and intellectual communities of North America, Western Europe and Japan. It provides a private forum for information and published reports on issues affecting the global economy. A major focus of these reports has been the need to strengthen the capacity of governments to restructure their economies and to negotiate international agreements that will service the needs of international capital. One report in 1975 described governability and democracy as 'warring concepts. An excess of democracy means a deficit in governability; easy governability suggests faulty democracy. At times in the history of democratic government the pendulum has swung too far in one direction or the other.' The authors concluded that the pendulum had already swung too far towards 'an excess of democracy' in the US and Europe, and was in danger of doing so in Japan.[6] Canadian sociologist Pat Marchak notes that 'the arguments of the Trilateralists and those of monetarists, supply-side economists, and fanatical libertarians dovetailed in certain crucial respects'. But unlike the libertarians, who advocated the withering away of the state, the Trilateralists 'assumed that governments were essential to economic growth, provided that [they] were not stopped by popular pressure from taking corrective action as the world economy was restructured'.[7]

Other groupings have assumed a more public and activist role in constructing an international consensus over recent years. The Geneva-based

World Economic Forum (WEF) has as its mission simply 'to improve the state of the world'.[8] Established as the European Management Forum in 1971, it sought initially to increase the competitiveness of European business by sponsoring dialogue among European corporate leaders on management issues. Its agenda later expanded to addressing political, economic, social and environmental concerns. Participants from other rich nations were added, and then from 'developing' and 'emerging' countries. Renamed the World Economic Forum in 1987, its membership comprises 1,000 of the world's largest corporations. To qualify, a company must have a minimum turnover of US$1 billion, a global outlook and 'strong management'. Membership is by invitation and is secret. When the initial quota of 1,000 companies was filled, the Forum established a second tier of 'global growth companies'. Members pay a subscription, but the main funding comes from transnationals who are also 'institutional partners', such as Nestlé, Coca Cola, Hewlett Packard, Volkswagen, Audi, Price Waterhouse, Booz-Allen & Hamilton, Deloitte Touche Tohmatsu and DHL.[9]

The Forum's public affairs officer describes it as a 'giant dating agency' for transnational corporations and governments.[10] Each year it organises an invitation-only, six-day meeting in the Swiss resort of Davos, which it calls 'the summit that defines the global agenda'. The real influence of the meeting on global or national economic policies and decisions is hard to gauge. Attendance is limited to one person per company. Informal meetings of chief executives in each sector (for example, automotive, financial services, communications and entertainment) aim to identify major strategic issues and form industry-wide alliances. World political leaders are also invited to Davos. The presence of 200 top news editors, and 400 reporting press, promises them plenty of media exposure. Attending without minders, politicians such as Nelson Mandela, F.W. De Klerk and Chief Mangosuthu Buthelezi have engaged in backroom dialogue, as well as interfacing with the corporate meeting. A select group called Global Leaders for Tomorrow (for those under 45) is invited. Other clusters include a Club of Media Leaders (editors-in-chief of the world's largest media corporations) and the Club of Mayors of Megacities. Regional meetings facilitate similar dialogue between global corporations and governments.

In 1997 the World Economic Forum launched an Intranet service for subscribers called WELCOM (World Economic Community), which brings together companies, governments and academic experts on request. Virtual Knowledge Integration Centres were also planned on topics such as global competitiveness or 'geo-political, geo-economic and geo-societal affairs', serviced by 300 leading academics called 'Forum Fellows'. The

Forum aims to 'create a hotline among the world's financial decision-makers including chief executives of major banks, finance ministers, heads of central banks, heads of the World Bank/IMF, [and] BIS. Our ultimate objective is to make WELCOM the "Intranet" of the 10,000 top global decision-makers.'[11]

New Zealand's Fletcher Construction was a Forum member for some years; while it saw benefits in the opportunity for strategic dialogue with non-competitors in that sector, the company was not a major player in the meeting, or in wider Forum activities. The company's chief executive at the time, John Hood, was named a Global Leader for Tomorrow, as was Maori executive Whaimutu Dewes. National's Jim Bolger is the only New Zealand politician to have spoken at Davos; as Prime Minister, he addressed the conference on 'global governance' in 1994. Reserve Bank Governor Don Brash has attended regional meetings of the Forum.

New Zealand's role in the Forum and other international networks has been marginal. Their significance to New Zealand lies in the contribution they make to framing the international environment that has elevated global free market policies to the status of international orthodoxy.

▲ National think-tanks

The international networks are complemented at the national level by 'independent' think-tanks. The New Zealand Business Roundtable is a typical example.[12] A detailed study of the Roundtable, published in 1998, documents its success in pushing the boundaries of what was thought possible, to a point where the previously inconceivable was embraced as government policy.[13] The Roundtable began aggressively setting New Zealand's policy agenda in 1985. In the following years it commissioned a plethora of reports from 'experts' (often self-styled) on topics ranging from privatisation, fiscal policy and labour markets to MMP, crime and the Treaty of Waitangi. Its high-profile media presence, especially in sympathetic forums such as the *National Business Review*, was bolstered by sponsored lecture tours by foreign 'experts' and published speeches by prominent Roundtable members. Executive Director Roger Kerr maintained strong links with the policy process through his former Treasury colleagues, other officials, politicians and private sector consultants. Despite an apparent decline in its influence during the late 1990s, the Roundtable has undoubtedly been the dominant external influence on the policy agenda of successive New Zealand governments since 1984.

Leading members of the Business Roundtable and other key New Zealand supporters of the free market have active links to an international network of think-tanks committed to a common cause. Roger Douglas has maintained especially strong contacts with Canadian organisations such as the Fraser Institute in British Columbia, established by self-styled 'visionaries' in 1974. The Institute's objective is to redirect 'public attention to the role of competitive markets in providing for the well-being of Canadians'.[14] In 1993, one of its monthly bulletins was dedicated to Roger Douglas. It described him as a 'heroic figure' who, despite his 'missionary work' in explaining how 'socialist governments could achieve socialist goals with capitalist means', was only just being recognised by policy-makers in Canada.[15]

A five-year plan produced by the Fraser Institute in 1997 offers interesting insights into how such think-tanks operate.[16] The Institute's successes were identified as those programmes that 'defined and occupied a certain niche in the public policy process'. The most effective had focused on empirical issues, including surveys of hospital waiting lists, 'government spending facts', a 'fiscal performance index', and 'poverty line estimates'. Of doubtful authenticity and lacking in intellectual rigour, these programmes were useful gimmicks to help the Institute set the agenda on key issues and create a media presence. A fax broadcasting system, supported by a private foundation, flooded the country's talkback radio shows with the Institute's perspective. Public service television gave extensive air-time to Institute conferences, especially when the topics were controversial.

The five-year plan proposed an increase to their annual budget of C$2.7 million to enable the Institute to target health care, the legal system, environmental regulation, labour markets and debt. New indexes of family distress and crime would address 'the decay of civic virtue and the apparent collapse of social order in school-aged children'. More resources would be committed to penetration of the national media and 'other second hand dealers in ideas'. The 'lead product' would be a series of 'Economic Freedom' initiatives, centred on the Index of Economic Freedom co-produced at the time by the Washington-based Heritage Foundation and the *Wall Street Journal* (discussed below).

These initiatives linked the Fraser Institute with one of the most prominent US think-tanks. Established in 1973, the Heritage Foundation was credited with being 'the collective brain behind [Ronald] Reagan and George Bush'.[17] Its mission was 'to formulate and promote conservative public policies based on the principles of free enterprise, limited government, individual freedom, traditional American values, and a strong national defense'.[18] Funded by donations, subscriptions and its own revenue, the Heritage Foundation's main focus was on research and publications aimed at key politicians, policy-makers, academics and the media. In 1997 it produced some 200 documents and spent one-third of its US$18 million budget on marketing. An annual guide offered journalists a ready-reference list of 1,500 (sympathetic) public policy experts in 70 different areas. Mini-Heritage Foundations operated across the US.

The Business Roundtable also maintained strong links with one of the original neo-liberal think-tanks, the London-based Institute of Economic Affairs (IEA). Founded in 1957 by Antony Fisher, the Institute was supported strongly by Friedrich von Hayek, the iconic author of *The Road to Serfdom,* and a major intellectual influence on the New Zealand strand of neo-liberalism.[19] Ideologically, the Institute is more sophisticated than the Roundtable or its other counterparts. Director of its Health and Welfare Unit, David Green, believes that capitalism must be firmly rooted in a bourgeois culture and moral order, with a strong emphasis on the role of 'civil' (that is, non-state) society. He also believes that people's life situation is a matter of choice. The Institute has subscribers, not members, and operates through networks of people who know each other. Its programmes follow a familiar pattern – running seminars for postgraduate students, commissioning research on key issues, organising conferences, and facilitating less formal dialogue among influential figures from government, business and academia. For decades, the Institute operated on the fringe of British intellectual and political life, but under Thatcher it entered the mainstream. Years of investment paid off as the Institute became a reference point for the new intellectual élite.

Green distinguishes between corporate lobbies, which have members and engage in political activity, and the think-tanks, which exist to propagate ideas. With some organisations, such as the Heritage Foundation and the New Zealand Business Roundtable, this distinction is blurred. Think-tanks also vary from conservative to libertarian, within broad free market parameters. Their international links, including cross-referenced websites, are systematically constructed. The Institute's founder, Antony Fisher, created the Atlas Foundation in the late 1970s with the explicit goal of populating the world with mini-Institutes. According to Green, Atlas played a part in establishing some 100 free market think-tanks, many in Latin America, but extending to India and Ghana. When Australian Greg Lindsay set up the Centres for Independent Studies in Australia and New Zealand, he sought advice directly from Ralph Harris, then Director of the Institute.

The Institute's major connection with New Zealand was the Mont Pelerin society, founded by Hayek in 1947. Membership is by invitation and is not disclosed, but it numbered around 400 when the society had its annual meeting in Vienna in 1996. In the early 1980s, Roger Kerr and Alan Gibbs began participating regularly in Mont Pelerin meetings, and recounted the 'successes' of New Zealand's restructuring as they unfolded.

The 1989 Mont Pelerin meeting, held in Christchurch, was attended by Gibbs, Rod Deane, Douglas Myers and Peter Troughton, along with Roger Douglas and Ruth Richardson. Also attending were National's Simon Upton (who won a Mont Pelerin prize in 1986 for an essay entitled 'The Withering of the State'), and Donna Awatere Huata and Rodney Hide (both later to become ACT MPs).[20] It was at the 1989 meeting that Douglas delivered his 'blitzkrieg' speech on how to implement radical change.[21]

The relationship between the Business Roundtable and the British Institute of Economic Affairs became more visible in the 1990s, as the Roundtable expanded its focus on social issues such as the welfare system and the family. Stuart Sexton of the Institute's Education Unit was commissioned in 1990 to write an evaluation of the New Zealand education policy known as 'Tomorrow's Schools';[22] David Green produced *From Welfare State to Civil Society* in 1993.[23] Green was not uncritical of the New Zealand approach. In 1987 he had been a consultant to the controversial Gibbs Taskforce that produced *Unshackling the Hospitals*.[24] While committed to the same objectives, Green believed that the market model Gibbs proposed was too crude. When interviewed in 1998, Green cited the Coalition government's ill-fated Code of Social Responsibility as an example of a crude and inappropriate moral crusade, and observed that neither the New Zealand government nor the Business Roundtable seemed to understand properly the need for a strong civil society if free market capitalism was to succeed.

Probably the most active Roundtable connection has been with Australia, through the Tasman Institute, the Centre for Independent Studies and the HR Nicholls Society. The Institute was founded in 1990 by Michael Porter (not the Harvard-based Michael Porter who co-authored the 1991 report *New Zealand's International Competitiveness*). An interview in March 1998 offered an extraordinary insight into how such players see the importance of their contribution to changing the agenda of countries, and collectively of the world. Porter viewed the shift in economic orthodoxy as the product of events and an influential network of strategically placed individuals, which operated through 'mates – it's always mates'.[25]

As Porter tells it, high-flying economics graduates from élite US universities such as Stanford, Harvard and Chicago found the academic job market closed during the early 1970s. So they moved into government, and quickly became senior advisors in countries such as the UK, the US and Chile. Porter himself went to the IMF, then to the Reserve Bank of Australia, and was seconded from there to Prime Minister Gough Whitlam's office; he later moved to the Australian National University and then became a professor at Monash University. 'Government at that time became very exciting. Because the political parties were basically doing nothing very well, so the think tanks were able to fill the breach.' Well-resourced special units were attached to the offices of political leaders in many of these countries, feeding new ideas into government. In Australia under Whitlam, they did not get far.

Using seed money from the Ford Foundation, Porter then established the Centre for Policy Studies at Monash in 1979. The Centre became a magnet for people keen to discuss neo-liberal ideas, and international gurus were eager to visit, often without payment. Backing from mining companies, plus a large government 'Centre of Excellence' award, allowed the Centre to carry out research and to publish reports on what became hot agenda items, such as privatisation and the construction of competitive markets in electricity and telecommunications.

The New Zealand connection began in 1983, when Prime Minister Robert Muldoon imposed a freeze on prices, wages and interest rates. The deputy governor of the Reserve Bank, Rod Deane, was by then working actively with others to promote neo-liberal alternatives; they invited Michael Porter and the editor of the *Australian Financial Review* to a conference in Wellington to 'give a talk on the evils of what Muldoon had done'. According to Porter, the conference and media coverage were carefully managed, and prompted media speculation that some officials and government agencies wanted to bring down the government, which from his perspective 'was true, perfectly true'. Porter's visit laid the foundation for a strong relationship with Treasury officials, especially Roger Kerr, whose team was by then working on the 1984 post-election briefing paper, *Economic Management*.[26] Porter also became 'mates' with Roger Douglas, Labour's finance spokesperson.

Back in Australia, Monash University had become uneasy about Porter's activities. He refocused his attention on New Zealand, with its new radical Labour government. A steady flow of Treasury people – Kerr, Bryce Wilkinson, Rob Cameron, and about 30 others – visited Monash, but Porter mainly came to New Zealand, as a ready publicist for Treasury's ideas. This interaction saw the New Zealanders copy several Australian initiatives, notably by establishing the Centre for Independent Studies in 1986, spearheaded by Australian Greg Lindsay. With the likes of Rod Deane and entrepreneurs Alan Gibbs, Ron Trotter, Douglas Myers, David Richwhite and John Fernyhough as board members or trustees, the Centre promoted neo-liberal policies with variable success during the 1980s. Even though the Roundtable supported its creation, New Zealand was too small for two such organisations, and the Centre effectively disappeared.

A particularly ambitious joint project, launched in 1987, involved establishing the Tasman University in Auckland with a franchise operation in Melbourne (a legal device to circumvent problems of establishing a private stand-alone university in Australia). The rationale was explicitly ideological. Tasman aimed to be in the forefront of applied business, microeconomics and computing, and to 'create a network of graduates and research relationships which will foster intellectual growth and development, political reform and economic growth and innovation in the region'.[27] The list of adjunct professors reads like a 'who's who' of neo-liberal scholars from the US and UK. Porter claimed that the initiative was facilitated by Roger Douglas, and had Prime Minister David Lange's support. It was to be funded by a share issue, underwritten according to Porter by Alan Gibbs and key Australian individuals including Rupert Murdoch. Sponsors of the feasibility study included Gibbs and Ron Trotter, other prominent free-marketeers such as Michael Friedlander, Douglas Myers, John Elliott and Michael Fay. Porter's company, Economic Concepts Ltd, acted as consultants, with law firm Russell McVeagh as the legal advisors.[28] According to Porter, a team of top academics from the US and New Zealand was ready to join. Then the share-market collapsed. Together with ongoing opposition from the Australian government, this eventually scuttled the project, but not the idea. Porter commented: 'My real agenda was to get the universities here to change so we could then get a competitive franchise and that's still a goal.'

In 1990 the Tasman Institute was formed instead, with Roger Douglas as one of three founding directors. It was funded by equity contributions of A$50,000 each from six companies (including Electricorp, whose chief executive by then was Rod Deane), plus A$100,000 from Porter. The early focus was the emerging and commercially attractive area of environmental economics. The Institute worked closely with the Business Roundtable, and together they brought the US law and economics evangelist, Richard Epstein, to Australia and New Zealand. Kerr was awarded the first Tasman Medal by the Institute for 'services to economic reform'.

The Tasman Institute formed part of an interlocking Australian network which had its foundations in Crossroads, a group Porter referred to as a widely respected 'secret society'. Begun in the late 1970s, it brought together 'dry' Liberal MPs, officials and people like Porter and Wolfgang Kasper (who wrote a report on immigration for the Roundtable in 1990).[29] Crossroads met about every six months until at least 1997. It never produced documents, just talk. The Tasman Institute brought some New Zealanders into the group – mainly Roundtable members but also politicians, including National Party President Sue Woods, and Ruth Richardson, who was 'very much in the loop'.

One Crossroads strategy was to create 'front' organisations, a technique

Porter said was borrowed from the left. For example, 'all of a sudden there were huge ads from the Car Owners' Association complaining about tariffs', although the Association had only two members at the time. Such activities fuelled allegations of a conspiracy. Porter refuted these, but went on to observe: 'It was quite secret anyway and it was certainly plotting and scheming. But only for the benefit of the country and not for self-benefit. Nobody was gaining any money out of it. ... It wasn't a conspiracy, but it was a network and it still exists and it's very powerful.' A later 'front' group, called Project Victoria, appeared to be an association of all the business groups in the state. With Tasman Asia-Pacific (the consulting arm of the Tasman Institute) as its principal consultant, it set about preparing a privatisation strategy in anticipation of the election of the pro-market Liberal government of Jeff Kennett in 1992. The National Priorities Project was a similar group formed earlier to promote changes to taxation laws, such as flatter tax rates.

Crossroads spawned other pressure groups that focused on specific issues. The most significant was the HR Nicholls Society, formed in 1985 by a number of key Australian free-marketeers, including Porter and Peter Costello (subsequently Treasurer in the Liberal government). The main object was to destroy Australia's trade unions and secure a labour market based on individual contracts. Porter later became its vice-president. He also wrote a paper for the New Zealand Business Roundtable promoting radical labour market deregulation.[30] Both Roger Kerr and former Roundtable chair Douglas Myers were invited to address HR Nicholls conferences.

The interaction with New Zealand was strengthened further when the Kennett government in Victoria began its privatisation programme. Porter noted a deep connection between the Treasuries of New Zealand and Victoria. Queenslander Wayne Gilbert, a leading member of the HR Nicholls Society (and subsequently chief executive of Auckland's electricity supply company, Mercury Energy),[31] was recruited to chair the state electricity group. Peter Troughton (who was head-hunted from the UK to run New Zealand's corporatised Telecom) had moved to become chief executive of Transgrid, and would later oversee the privatisation of Victoria's electricity.[32] Roger Kerr was on the board of Transgrid, and Tasman Asia-Pacific were advisors to the Victorian Treasury on the electricity privatisation process.

Once privatisation had become more orthodox in Australia, Porter moved the focus of his operations to Asia. Tasman Asia-Pacific secured projects from the World Bank, Ausaid, the Asian Development Bank and Vietnam Southern Masterplan, mainly for water privatisation in countries including Vietnam, Fiji, Indonesia, the Philippines and India. In 1996 the

Tasman Institute became formally affiliated with Melbourne University, which by then was more entrepreneurial. In 1998, 25 percent of shares in Tasman Asia-Pacific were bought by Macquarie Bank. The strong personal involvement of New Zealanders in the Institute and in Tasman Asia-Pacific continued. Roger Douglas and John Fernyhough were on the boards of both.[33] The Institute's advisory council included Douglas, Rod Deane and Ron Trotter (as well as Rupert Murdoch).

Think-tanks exist to push one ideological position. They do so single-mindedly, but to varying effect. They cannot, by themselves, construct a new orthodoxy. Whether their ideas take root will depend on the extent to which they cross-fertilise with other intellectual, political, social and economic conditions. Some, like the Institute for Economic Affairs, will see their long-term investment in propagating their ideas eventually pay dividends. Others will fail to find a market niche, as with the New Zealand Centre for Independent Studies. Their influence will vary according to the state of the policy debate in individual countries and in the international funding agencies. But just as they gain ascendancy in propitious times, the influence of neo-liberal think-tanks will decline along with the fortunes of that regime. Because their ideological commitment makes it impossible for them to adjust to the changing environment, they are likely to become less relevant and influential over time.

In the late 1990s the Business Roundtable began to show that pathology. Statements by Executive Director Roger Kerr bemoaning the loss of commitment to ongoing market 'reforms' have been quoted elsewhere. This frustration extended to other key actors who had helped build and sustain the momentum for over a decade. When Douglas Myers, part of the Roundtable's inner circle and the richest man in the country,[34] retired in November 1997, he gave an embittered valedictory interview to the *New Zealand Herald*. He complained that 'middle New Zealand' was in danger of rejecting the internationally competitive economy which he and others had worked so hard to establish, before it was complete. When people criticised the wealth of individuals like himself, they overlooked the contribution big business had made to the country's economic recovery – jobs and wealth creation, sports sponsorship (including around $25 million to yachting), and scores of speeches on behalf of the Business Roundtable. People had demonstrated their anti-business sentiments in the way they applauded the departure of financiers Michael Fay and David Richwhite to live in Geneva. Other corporate leaders, including Alan Gibbs, had left the country in despair. People, said Myers, just did not understand.[35]

▲ INTERNATIONAL INSTITUTIONS

The international economic networks offer opportunities for major businesses to develop their plans for the global economy; the think-tanks are more overt propagandists, with widely varying credibility. However, intergovernmental agencies such as the IMF, WTO and OECD have an intrinsic legitimacy as voices of economic orthodoxy.

That their separate statements of economic philosophy converge to form a coherent economic policy agenda is hardly surprising, for the same governments play key roles in each of these institutions (and the US is dominant in all of them). Their ideological positions are also a product of the times; since the late 1970s they have reflected the neo-liberal preference for international rules and domestic policies that promote self-regulating markets. New Zealand's textbook approach to structural adjustment is hailed as exemplary, and endorsements from these organisations are, in turn, celebrated as evidence that the country is a model for the world. Given the strong influence that member governments have on what the international agencies say about their policies, the New Zealand government's interpretation of economic performance and proposals for future policies are frequently mirrored in the institutional reports.

▲ The OECD

The Organisation for Economic Cooperation and Development was established by the major industrialised countries in 1961 as an expanded version of the Organisation for European Economic Cooperation, formed in 1948. New Zealand joined in 1973. Designed to undertake economic research and analysis, the OECD became increasingly important during the 1970s as a counter-force to pressure at the UN from newly decolonised poor countries for a New International Economic Order. The OECD's Articles of Agreement are agnostic in ideological terms. Its mandate includes policies that

- 'achieve the highest sustainable economic growth and employment and a rising standard of living in Member countries, while maintaining financial stability, and thus ... contribute to the development of the world economy';
- 'contribute to sound economic expansion in Member as well as non-member countries in the process of economic development'; and
- 'contribute to the expansion of world trade on a multilateral, non-discriminatory basis in accordance with international obligations'.[36]

Since the Reagan and Thatcher period, however, the OECD has adopted a more-market approach.

The OECD's public image is one of an independent and authoritative economic agency. Yet the organisation is heavily influenced by its individual member governments on matters that directly affect them. Many key officials come from (and sometimes return to) member governments. The Economics Department is the core of the OECD. It publishes a semi-annual *Economic Outlook* for all OECD countries. Desk officers assigned to a particular country also produce draft annual or bi-annual surveys on that country's economic performance, but the final versions are negotiated with, and signed off by, the government concerned. If criticisms by OECD economists survive, they may be relegated to footnotes, while the major policies that the government wants to plug are generally (but not always) included in the report. Where the policy prescriptions of the OECD and the government coincide, there is relatively little dispute.

One official described how the process would work in relation to New Zealand:

> ... at Economic Development Review Committee meetings, the OECD staff present a paper which gives their view on New Zealand's policies, what they've done and what they should be doing, and New Zealand responds, and there's a diplomatic toing and froing ... a lot of word crafting and drafting. ... That is actually just the tip of the iceberg in terms of the OECD's work. It gets a lot of attention of course because the OECD's scorecard in a sense is taken quite seriously, but a lot of what comes out there is a result of some compromise stuff.[37]

Another described how one New Zealand Treasury official handled this situation in practice:

> The Economics Department likes what New Zealand is doing, but they put in a few qualifications and a bit of concern about increasing inequality of income. Is the safety net adequate? So [the Treasury official] comes along and says things like, well, we don't understand this. If nobody's falling through the safety net, then the safety net's too high. Then he says things like, you should realize that beggars on the streets are a European phenomenon ... there's this hushed silence, a breathtaking silence ... there is a lot of hypocritical pontificating from Europeans about social exclusion and all that sort of stuff, and they've got dreadful social problems. ... But when New Zealanders are a bit too direct, that doesn't go down well ... .[38]

This process means that the annual OECD surveys of the New Zealand economy reflect the broad harmony of OECD philosophy and the New Zealand government's policy position. Some downsides are reported, but they receive the best possible spin. Minor qualifications and concerns may be expressed, along with occasional strong criticism of peripheral matters, such as New Zealand's second-to-lowest OECD ranking for spending on overseas development assistance.

When the reports are released publicly, the New Zealand media regularly portray them as objective assessments of how well the country is doing, and the government perpetuates the illusion. External praise of this kind became important in the later 1980s as the Labour government pushed through policies that were increasingly unpopular and failed to deliver the promised economic benefits. When the Secretary-General of the OECD visited in June 1988, he recounted how New Zealand had been singled out in the communiqué of the OECD ministerial meeting in May for its efforts and speed in effecting structural change:

> This country to some extent is setting the pace, showing the way on structural improvement. Of course things are not all perfect – there are on the economic landscape clouds of concern. This is the normal trough countries go through when implementing far-sighted policies. I have the impression that things are moving rather fast in a very bold and very resolute structural adjustment which of course means some pain but will pay off in the future and is already beginning to pay off. ... Coming from Europe, to see a Labour government undertaking such a program of reform is rather astonishing.[39]

In December 1988, with the economy in recession, the *New Zealand Herald* reported the OECD's half-yearly *Economic Outlook* under the headline: 'OECD likes look of NZ'.[40] In 1989, as the economy continued to stagnate, OECD statements remained upbeat. *Reuter* headlined its story on the annual survey of New Zealand: 'NZ economy set for strong growth OECD believes'. According to the survey, it said, New Zealand's

> ... economic reforms and adjustment policies have created the conditions for stronger, sustainable economic growth. ... Maintaining the momentum of micro-economic reform ... would enhance New Zealand's economic prospects. ... It would be particularly unfortunate if confidence in the government's economic strategy were to be undermined at this stage.[41]

Finance Minister David Caygill hailed the survey as showing that the reorientation of New Zealand's economy had been an 'outstanding achievement'. New Zealand 'could fairly claim to have scored almost straight "A"s in its latest report card'.[42] Attending the OECD ministerial meeting in Paris in June 1989, Labour's Peter Neilson claimed that the government's economic policy programme had been praised 'as an example of what other governments can achieve if they are really committed'.[43] In December, as the economy again headed towards recession, the OECD *Economic Outlook* predicted that 'export growth and increased private investment could bring steady but unspectacular growth for New Zealand in the next two years'.[44] These partly self-scripted accolades offered important external validation of Labour's economic programme.

As the 1990 election approached, a special OECD report on progress in structural adjustment, released in June 1990, suggested that New Zealand 'finish the fiscal job'. Special reports like this are informed by the views of officials and politicians, but unlike the annual country surveys are not subject to an informal veto by the government. This report cited the Labour government's failure to implement labour market flexibility, reduce protection, reform the tax-benefit system and cut government expenditure as the reasons 'why the broader economic benefits of the comprehensive reforms adopted since 1984 have been slow to appear'.[45]

The congruence between OECD commentaries and New Zealand government policy continued after the election of the National government, reflecting the central role of the Treasury as the advisor to both. The OECD's *Economic Outlook* was released within days of the government's December 1990 package of fiscal austerity and benefit cuts. Under the headline 'National changes fit in with OECD views', the *National Business Review* commented: 'Ruth Richardson's slash and rebuild economic policies may not impress those being slashed, but the latest OECD report suggests it fits with that organisation's view of how to rebuild'.[46] When the next official New Zealand country report was released in March 1991, the *New Zealand Herald* hinted more directly at a connection, with the headline: 'Government and OECD – Did they read the same book?'. It went on: 'The scorecard of the December 19 Government financial package is pretty much the checksheet of the latest report of the [OECD] released yesterday.' It also reflected the direction of Treasury's 1990 post-election briefing to the incoming government.[47] The OECD committee had apparently received the draft report on 10 December. Final clearance was given on 17 December, 'after revisions in the light of discussions during the review', which involved the Treasury, Reserve Bank and 'New Zealand authorities'. As the *Herald* noted, it 'would be strange if the Government did not know what thrust the OECD report would have when it sent its December statement to the printers'.[48]

As the country began to emerge from a traumatic recession in early 1992, the visiting Secretary-General of the OECD was reported as assuring New Zealanders once more that the benefits of the reforms were beginning to show: 'The fact is that New Zealand has done more than most of the OECD countries, quicker than most of the OECD countries, in the direction of policies which have the consensus of all the OECD countries.'[49] This time there *was* an economic upturn. The government continued to cite OECD approval to bolster its legitimacy. In 1994, Prime Minister Jim Bolger said that the recommendations of an OECD report on unemployment and job creation read

> ... like a list of the economic reforms carried out in New Zealand over the past 10 years. ... We have been used in the discussions as an example of what you can do – face some big reform decisions, but you do get jobs, investment and ongoing growth in the economy. So we are the good boys on the block. ... It is a vindication of 10 years of reform in New Zealand.[50]

The OECD's 1995/96 survey recognised that the New Zealand economy again faced problems – but the (government-sanctioned) solution was 'more of the same'. The *Evening Post* noted that the OECD prescription for more liberalisation of the New Zealand economy echoed the policies pushed 'by the Business Roundtable, conservative politicians and ACT'. Although the economy had been substantially liberalised, the report said, 'more remains to be done'.[51] Problems were deftly side-stepped: the health 'reforms', for example, which had plunged the hospital system into chaos, were described as a 'promising way of responding to patient demands while containing costs', whose potential had yet to be realised.[52]

A print media search covering 1986 to 1997 found only one serious critique of the OECD process, and that was in the *National Business Review* in May 1989. Noting that 'Roger Douglas would have been over the moon' at the OECD report for 1988/89, the *NBR* suggested that readers should consider 'just how independent that review really is'. While the statistics were gathered throughout the year by the OECD, they came from various New Zealand government agencies. The review involved an OECD team visiting the country and talking to officials, politicians from both sides, and prominent business people. The draft report went to a meeting where New Zealand officials had a chance to thrash out the findings, cull any factual errors, and 'temper any issues mentioned that might be politically sensitive'. Significant changes could result – as shown by a leaked draft report in 1979 that was critical of the Muldoon government's economic policy, and differed substantially from the final published document.[53]

Other divisions of the OECD, such as Education and Social Affairs, are less central, and governments exercise less direct control over them. While these divisions are pro-market, they will at times disagree with governments and the Economics Department on issues such as pensions and education policy. A 1997 OECD report on tertiary education in New Zealand was amended after discussions with the government, but it still questioned the lack of evidence to support a radical market-driven approach, and noted the disruption and discord caused by 'the pace and particularly the presentation of the processes of change'. The government was advised to 'build on dialogue and involvement of the stakeholders' to produce '"fine tuning" rather than further deep reforms'.[54] Within months, the National government released a Green Paper proposing even more extreme changes to the tertiary education system.[55]

OECD staff see a large part of their work as educating governments to adopt more 'orthodox' economic positions. However, one OECD official described the New Zealand government's attitude to the organisation's work as that of a 'contributor', not a 'learner': 'By and large they regard themselves as coming over here to contribute to what other countries can learn, rather than to learn about countries. ... That's very much a Treasury attitude anyway.' Yet New Zealand's actual influence in the OECD is limited. In comparative public management, for example, 'New Zealand is much studied, but not much copied. ... I think the attitude here to New Zealand is one of interest and to a certain extent admiration in terms of the comprehensiveness of what they've done, but a fair degree of healthy skepticism.'[56] In fact, very few OECD countries have imitated specific New Zealand policies, and none (other than Mexico) have gone to such extremes; nor, despite glowing endorsements from their political leaders on occasional visits to New Zealand, do they seem likely to do so.

▲ WTO trade policy reviews

New Zealand's efforts were also praised by the GATT and WTO. The Trade Policy Review Mechanism, introduced in 1976 and carried over into the WTO in 1994, provides for routine surveillance of each member's trade policies in terms of WTO objectives.[57] The process involves the relevant government and the WTO secretariat each submitting a report to the General Council for discussion. The European Union, the US, Japan and Canada are reviewed every two years, but most reviews are every six years.

New Zealand was reviewed in 1990 and 1996, and received glowing reports for its textbook application of GATT/WTO-consistent policies. The 1990 report downplayed the stagnant state of the economy by emphasising its future prospects.[58] In 1996 New Zealand was hailed as exemplary. The government's own ten-page report had a smug, evangelical tone: 'New Zealand has continued to make considerable progress towards the goal of free and open trade and investment which it advocates for all economies at the multilateral level'.[59] The report described the government's four-tier approach: unilateral domestic policy initiatives to create an 'open and outward-looking' economy; bilateral commitments through CER ('one of the most far reaching bilateral free trade arrangements in the world'); regional economic groupings such as APEC, which the government required to be 'outward-looking, open-ended, trade-enhancing, Asia-Pacific friendly, comprehensive in sectoral coverage and not compromising of New Zealand's unilateral reforms'; and the WTO, where multilateral free trade was the 'first-best' outcome.[60] Endorsements from the OECD and 'World Competitiveness Reports' (discussed below) were cited in support of this assessment.

The WTO secretariat's report described New Zealand's results as 'remarkable'. The secretariat was especially impressed by the government's disciplined adherence to its liberalisation programme. This had established economic credibility and removed doubts about political backsliding. The report noted with approval that the rising current and trade account deficits, rising exchange rate and declining export competitiveness 'may actually be creating additional support for reform, rather than calling it into question'. Export industries were pressing government to maintain substantial budget surpluses as a source of domestic savings, while export and import-competing lobbies urged the removal of remaining import protections for other industries. 'The authorities are determined to pursue import policy reforms to their logical conclusion ... the elimination of tariffs on [a most favoured nation] basis.'[61]

The WTO report drew solely on accounts by New Zealand officials or sympathetic commentators, who portrayed New Zealand prior to 1984 as a 'basket-case' economy which had been successfully transformed.[62] More critical analyses by economists such as Brian Easton were ignored.[63] The report recited the official projections of gains from the GATT, claiming that 'most studies' saw New Zealand as one of the Uruguay Round's greatest beneficiaries.[64] The potential increase in real economic growth was estimated at about one percent a year: 'New Zealanders can now expect a 50 percent increase in real per capita income each 14 years rather than each 21 years.'[65] Treasury's economic projections were taken at face value. Tax cuts were going to stimulate consumption growth, and exports of non-commodity manufactures would increase, sparking renewed growth in private investment. The current account deficit would remain at about 5 percent of GDP, then narrow slightly. Unemployment was expected to fall to between 5 and 6 percent. Real GDP growth would be between 3 and 4 percent.[66] (By December 1998 the Treasury was projecting a GDP growth rate of minus 0.9 percent, an unemployment rate of 8.7 percent, and a current account deficit of 6.5 percent for the 1998/99 year.)[67]

Other economic indicators, such as increased inequality and poverty, were not remotely relevant to the review; they were domestic distributional issues that had nothing to do with free trade. The only criticism of official policy acknowledged in the report was the Business Roundtable's claim that the government had not gone far enough, notably in the privatisation of producer boards.[68] The release of the 1996 WTO report was accompanied by a half-page press release from the government, hailing New Zealand's status as a free-trader *extraordinaire*. The story was carried uncritically by the business and general media.[69] New Zealand's next review in 2002 looks set to present a challenge to the WTO, given the serious deterioration in the external current account and trade deficits and in the foreign debt, the stagnant and at times recessionary state of the economy, and an anticipated rise in unemployment. (See Appendix.)

▲ *IMF annual reviews*

The IMF's annual reports on New Zealand are not public documents. However, summaries are released which governments are able to use to strategic advantage. The IMF's mandate is to oversee the stability of the international monetary system through ongoing surveillance and loans to member governments faced with balance of payments emergencies; such loans are conditional on their implementation of rigorous structural adjustment policies. Periodic threats of IMF intervention in New Zealand's affairs have been used to bolster 'more market' positions in economic debate. The demise of the Muldoon government was arguably hastened by a leaked IMF report in July 1984, which said that New Zealand would need IMF support if existing economic policies continued.[70] Once New Zealand's neo-liberal experiment was under way, the IMF's approval helped to feed the 'good news' machine. When newly appointed IMF chief Michel Camdessus visited New Zealand on a familiarisation tour in 1988, the media reported his full support for the government's economic restructuring.[71] He said that the 'ambitious restructuring programme' had achieved 'remarkable results', with reduced balance of payments and budget deficits, and lower inflation. While New Zealand might have to accept some negative side-effects of monetary policy on interest and exchange rates, especially as they affected exports, slowing the programme would make recovery even more difficult. In 1992, the IMF was again used for political scaremongering. Minister of Health Simon Upton argued that if the country switched to MMP, governments would be afraid to take difficult decisions; this, he claimed, would produce such policy paralysis, instability, uncertainty and huge debt that the IMF would have to step in and run the economy.[72]

As part of its surveillance responsibilities, the IMF produces an annual review of the New Zealand economy. This, too, has been a regular source of 'good news' for the free-marketeers. The process involves a visit by an IMF staff team, who collect economic and financial information and discuss the country's policies with officials. The team prepare a report, which is discussed by the IMF's executive board; a summary of the Board's discussions is forwarded to the government. The process is secretive. The working papers prepared by IMF staff and (with the government's permission) the summary of the final report are made publicly available, but the full documentation remains confidential. This makes it difficult to assess the data used, and to challenge the assumptions, causal explanations, conclusions or policy prescriptions.

The common philosophy of the IMF and the New Zealand government shines through the annual reports. The 1996 staff report, for example, praised New Zealand for its 'bold and impressive reforms', and applauded the 'vigor and broadly-based nature of the current economic upswing, and the accompanying remarkable drop in unemployment'. It gave the credit for a potential one percent rise in the output growth rate (to 3.5 to 4 percent per year) to a substantial increase in private sector investment, and better resource allocation following deregulation.[73] In January 1997 the *Evening Post* reported on another IMF staff working paper under the headline: 'IMF Praises "Sweeping" Reforms'.[74] These glowing testimonials contrasted with a more reserved internal IMF report which noted that New Zealand's growth rate from 1978 to 1996 was similar to that of other OECD economies, although it had been more impressive in the past five years. Because 'it is not clear yet if this recent performance is a temporary or a permanent phenomenon, it is extremely difficult to assess the prospects of the New Zealand economy in the future. Some crude calculations suggest that the potential growth rate of the economy is in the range of 1.7–4.1 percent'; that is a fairly broad spectrum.[75]

The IMF report of November 1997 again saw the Executive Board praise the 'rigorous macroeconomic policies and innovative reforms ... that had transformed the economy into one that is outward-oriented and dynamic'. For several years, New Zealand had been 'reaping the benefits of reforms' with robust economic expansion, low unemployment and low inflation.[76] But the Board warned that a 'sizable external imbalance posed risks, given New Zealand's already high stock of external liabilities and its vulnerability to external shocks'. The current account deficit had 'widened markedly' to 6 percent of GDP in the June 1997 year.[77] Real short-term interest rates remained comparatively high, and the fiscal surplus had narrowed as a percentage of GDP. The IMF's staff and directors were apparently divided about the Reserve Bank's approach to monetary policy.

Having recognised these deficiencies, the IMF Executive Board endorsed a number of recommendations which read like a Treasury/Business Roundtable manifesto. It supported moves to deregulate the economy further, and reduce medium-term expenditure to allow monetary policy to ease. Health care restructuring should be speeded up, with greater competition between the public and private sectors. The future cost of pensions needed to be reduced, given that privatisation of the pension system had been rejected in the 1997 referendum.[78] Eligibility for benefits should be tightened, and work incentives enhanced. Deregulation of the producer boards would improve export competitiveness, along with the liberalisation of agricultural trade by other countries. These broad-ranging recommendations were made under the guise of restoring the country's balance of payments equilibrium.

The OECD, WTO and IMF present a public image of united and uncompromising commitment to the globalisation agenda, which has helped sustain the New Zealand 'success story' in good times and in bad. Yet, as subsequent chapters show, all these institutions face internal conflicts and external challenges that render their current version of institutional orthodoxy very insecure.

▲ THE APPROVAL OF 'THE MARKET'

Perhaps the most powerful barrier to deviating from the free market path – indeed, to even talking about deviation – is the fear of how 'the markets' would respond. The prospect of a downgrade in New Zealand's credit rating or a negative story in the *Economist* has politicians, policy-makers and commentators transfixed, like possums caught in a car's headlights. Often they also 'play possum', using these fears to justify holding firm on a policy that is singularly unsuccessful or deeply unpopular. This has allowed the voices of international capital to exert an enormous influence on government policy.

▲ *The credit rating agencies*

In February 1990 the *National Business Review* observed:

> In the financial world, rating agencies are the guys you love to hate. Chiefs of tottering and over-leveraged companies blame the agencies for pushing them into bankruptcy by lowering their ratings. Banks, jealous of their in-house credit analysts, say the ratings aren't much use. But the media and general public view ratings as near oracular pronouncements of corporate health or malaise. Whatever one's opinion, all agree the agencies wield great power.[79]

The article was about the credit rating of companies. How much more powerful, then, are these agencies when they rate a government's 'sovereign debt'? Such ratings have come to enjoy a similarly exalted status and mystique. During the 1980s, the globalisation of capital and the deregulation of financial markets meant that investors demanded credible and consistent assessments of risk, including the risk on public debt. Newly corporatised and privatised state-owned enterprises required commercial ratings. Financing the growing levels of public sector debt also became a serious issue, and governments needed a credit rating to sell their bonds in international markets, especially where private investment funds faced legal restrictions on the level of investment risk they could take.

A government's 'sovereign' rating provides a ceiling for all that country's domestic borrowing, both public and private. It may vary for short- and long-term, foreign and domestic debt. If the sovereign rating falls, so does that of private companies registered in its jurisdiction. In theory, the higher the credit rating, the more secure the debt for overseas lenders, and the lower the interest rate that the government and major private corporations have to pay when borrowing overseas. Thus a high rating is seen to enhance the country's competitiveness and potential to attract investment. A fall in credit rating can, in theory, raise the cost of borrowing money offshore – assuming that interest rates are actually influenced by the rating change. But despite the hype, a credit rating downgrade may not significantly influence the final interest rate a government or corporation is charged. When Standard and Poor's downgraded New Zealand's sovereign rating in 1991 from the 'AA' it received in 1986 to 'AA-', one economist noted that the financial markets had already discounted the re-rating.[80] New Zealand still had a good name among overseas financial institutions, and an abrupt change in the cost of financing was not expected. Interest costs could rise slightly. But the government was not planning to borrow overseas in the coming year, so any rise would apply only to any refinancing of existing debt.

Credit ratings are frequently treated by governments, the media and economic commentators as objective facts. Yet credit rating is a commercial business, which exists to service the international investment community by assessing the extent to which government policies serve that community's interests. It is dominated by two competing private firms, both based in New York: Standard and Poor's Corporation, and Moody's Investors Service. Standard and Poor's has been owned by publishers McGraw-Hill since 1966. In addition to its rating business, it runs a range of subscription services and publications, and provides a major stock index and related information services for equity markets. Moody's has been owned by the financial information company Dun and Bradstreet since 1960, and also produces research reports. Both companies follow the same basic process and use very similar criteria, although they differentiate their 'brands' by using slightly different designations. Until the mid-1980s they mainly provided ratings on private companies for borrowers on the New York market. As demand grew, both began expanding their services and locations. By the late 1980s each had operations in Australia, which also monitored New Zealand. Their extensive information base, brand-name recognition and reputation (whether deserved or otherwise) give these firms an effective 'duopoly'. Some say this provides stability, consistency and credibility, which would be difficult under aggressively competitive conditions. Others question the power that this gives two privately owned, profit-driven American corporations over the affairs of companies *and countries* throughout the world.

Governments pay the rating agencies a fee to assess their creditworthiness. The rating is updated annually, after an on-site inspection. The agencies may place a government on a watch-list for regrading up or down, depending on certain policy commitments or economic outcomes. There is nothing objective about the rating process. A study by Australians David Hayward and Mike Salvaris in 1993 pointed to major inconsistencies in the ratings that the same agency gave to different Australian state governments, and that different agencies gave the same governments. They asked: 'Does anyone seriously believe that Victoria is less likely to repay its debts than NSW? Does anyone seriously believe that Victoria is less financially sound than South Australia? Yet according to the ratings, this is indeed the case.'[81] They found equally striking inconsistencies in the ratings of different countries, and a lack of objective criteria to support them.

> Compare Australia with the UK. Australia's general government public debt and deficits are both less than half the size of the UK's. On these indicators, it would surely be safe to assume that Australia would have the higher credit rating. In fact the opposite is the case, and by quite a margin, for whereas the UK enjoys a AAA rating, Australia is rated a full two notches below this level.[82]

Because both agencies take account of political stability, as well as wider economic strength, in assessing perceived investor risk, sovereign ratings are political exercises. They effectively become commentators on the health of the economy, the responsibility of the government, and the policy agenda it needs to pursue. Governments are expected to avoid potential downgrades or respond to negative rating reviews by implementing policies of further liberalisation, deregulation and privatisation – the kind of policies that will be viewed positively by the foreign investors who subscribe to the rating agencies. As illustrated below, threats of rating downgrades are used by investors to pressure reluctant governments and by politicians to justify unpopular policies. The rating agencies generally play along, publicity being good for business, although the Standard and

Poor's analyst responsible for New Zealand since the early 1980s seems genuinely bemused by the ability of the New Zealand media to make even 'no comment' from the rating agency into big news.[83]

Sovereign ratings were not an issue in New Zealand until its 'AAA' credit rating was downgraded to 'AA+' in April 1983. This was blamed on growing fiscal and current account deficits and the economic rigidity of policies under Prime Minister Robert Muldoon. Public debt had increased from $4.2 billion in 1975 to $21.9 billion in March 1984, to finance sectoral assistance, the 'Think Big' energy projects and the managed exchange rate. Debt continued to grow after 1984 as a result of exchange rate movements, continuing deficits and refinancing the 'Think Big' debt. Both agencies downgraded New Zealand's sovereign rating again in 1986. By 1987 public debt had reached $42 billion.

Sovereign ratings began to play a more significant role in political debate during the period following the share-market crash.

> The government's policies have won praise from Moody's Investors Service, a US-based credit-rating agency. While expressing concern about the debt level, it says in its April [1988] report that the country is politically stable, has realistic policies and successful micro-economic reforms and is improving its fiscal and external accounts. It says New Zealand is in a recession. But it adds that the government's reforms 'stand a good chance of eventually placing the economy on a course of sustained growth'.[84]

The mere suggestion of a rating review quickly became a justification for keeping the neo-liberal programme on track. In 1989, the *New Zealand Herald* warned:

> ... the comments of credit-rating watchers show how little room the Government has to move on its spending. ... For all the New Zealand Government's economic policy consistency ... the American rating agency Standard and Poor's, while retaining its present rating, has talked about policy drift. Drift in economic or other waters – including those of electoral politics – brings risks.[85]

Affirmation from the agencies provided the carrot to balance the stick. Following David Lange's resignation as Prime Minister, Finance Minister David Caygill toured major international financial centres in September 1989. The media reported that bankers and credit rating agencies were increasingly optimistic about the country's economy and attributed this to the end of political instability. Caygill complained that New Zealanders were 'a little slower to display the optimism about their economy that is so evident from the outside', and claimed that the historically high level of unemployment was the only 'black spot' still on the horizon.[86]

Over the next three years of stagnation and recession, speculation about a credit downgrade was ever-present. Immediately following the 1990 election, commentators predicted a double downgrade. The new Minister of Finance, Ruth Richardson, used the situation to dramatic effect, taking off for New York to convince the agencies otherwise. She said they had invited her; Standard and Poor's said the new government had suggested the meeting. The Opposition was refused the material that Richardson supplied to the rating agencies – an Official Information Act request made in June 1991 remained unanswered in November. Labour leader Mike Moore speculated that Richardson had briefed the agencies on proposed policies that would 'change New Zealand in a way that would please financial institutions lending money to the Government. The public has a right to know what the Government told those agencies and why the minister is not prepared to trust New Zealanders with the same information.'[87] In January 1991 Standard and Poor's reduced their rating one notch to 'AA-', bringing it into line with Moody's. Richardson claimed a victory, saying that if New Zealand had fallen below the 'AA' category, 'a lot of sovereign lenders to this country would have had to shut the door on that lending. When you get to a certain threshold, the answer is no-no. It's sort of yellow-card (warning) stuff. We need to be able to hold on to the credit rating we've got now because it puts us in the league of countries who are getting to grips with their problems.'[88]

In August 1991 Standard and Poor's endorsed Richardson's 'mother of all budgets', which slashed government spending, as a move in the right direction. It noted that the country 'still faced problems', but also acknowledged that in a deregulated economy the government's ability to alter conditions was 'significantly reduced. You can create the environment but unless the private sector takes advantage of that environment there's very little a government can do.'[89] By this time, commercial responses to comments by credit agencies seemed to have lost all sense of proportion, especially in the fickle financial markets. In November 1991 *Reuter* reported that the New Zealand dollar had suddenly plummeted after Moody's expressed concern about the government's fiscal stance, following its back-down on changes to pensions. This followed a warning from Moody's in June that New Zealand's rating 'was in jeopardy if the government did not reform its policies'.[90]

Good news from the agencies continued to reinforce the government's policy direction. A triple-A grading from Moody's for a government medium-term note programme in September 1991 was seen as evidence of 'the revival of the restructuring process under the National government, especially in social welfare and labour markets'.[91]

Scaremongering about the rating agencies resurfaced in the lead-up to the 1993 election and electoral reform campaigns. Peter Shirtcliffe, the spokesperson for the Coalition for Better Government, warned that MMP could destabilise economic policy-making and trigger a credit rating review, putting at risk New Zealand's reputation among US investors as a bond-buyers' haven.[92] The agencies seemed more interested in the impact of the election on future policies than in the accompanying referendum on the electoral system. In April 1993 Standard and Poor's expressed concern about the National government's 'possible reaction to its weak standing in the opinion polls and the impact of the election later this year on policy direction'.[93] A few months later, just before the election, Standard and Poor's hinted at an upgrade in one to three years – provided that policy settings remained unchanged and external debt continued to fall. It now believed that the political risk lay with 'an indecisive election result, rather than a change in Government', as Labour was not expected to shift the policy settings significantly.[94] Moody's agreed that ratings would be affected only 'if we saw a fundamental shift in the direction in which a country was moving. ... Both of the major political forces have been largely moving in a similar direction.'[95] National was even prepared to promote the view that Labour and National policies were in harmony, once the election was over. As Finance Minister Bill Birch prepared for a post-election trip to New York, he said 'he would tell the ratings agencies he was confident no political party or group of parties would threaten the foundations of the country's recovery'.[96]

Not a lot was heard from the agencies during National's second term, as the economy enjoyed a rare period of strong growth. But as the first MMP election loomed, the rating agencies became more interested in its impact. Moody's linked a possible upgrade directly to the political situation, announcing in January 1996: 'We are going to examine what effects, if any, an MMP system would have on New Zealand's medium-term economic outlook'.[97] Birch welcomed the review, presumably because it would offer National some pre-election ammunition to use against Opposition parties who questioned the 'fundamentals' that the rating agencies considered pivotal, notably the Reserve Bank and Fiscal Responsibility Acts. The upgrade came in February 1996. It meant that New Zealand was now supposedly more creditworthy than Australia, and could demand a lower premium from foreign investors – notions that were patently absurd. With Labour determined to retain its appeal to 'the markets', finance spokesperson Michael Cullen tried to claim that the upgrade 'was a sign of the long-term success of the structural reforms undertaken by the fourth Labour government'.[98] Other commentators questioned what an upgrade actually signified. Bryan Gould, Vice-Chancellor of Waikato University and a former British Labour MP, pointed to the real state of the economy and of society, and warned against self-delusion.[99] Even a *National Business Review* columnist pointed to the 'piteous' returns on the stock-market, the 'pathetic' export performance and poor productivity, and concluded that 'the reform process has been oversold'.[100]

As the Coalition government formed by National and New Zealand First became unstable in 1998, credit agencies made yet another appearance. Moody's placed New Zealand on 'credit watch' because of the serious current account deficit.[101] As Treasurer, New Zealand First leader Winston Peters had the task of convincing the agency not to downgrade. By August the Coalition was collapsing. Moody's commented: 'we really need to look at ... what effect political developments have on economic policy and clearly there are all different kinds of scenarios that one could build ... that would have an effect on any potential rating action.'[102] While other media reported the issue uncritically, an editorial in the Manawatu *Evening Standard* put it into perspective:

> International credit agencies might view developments here with concern, but New Zealanders have to make political and economic decisions that make sense to them, and not necessarily those that will make sense to the international agencies. New Zealanders will accept the need ... for government spending to be prudent, but they will not accept that New Zealand economic policy must be designed to satisfy international formulas and opinions.[103]

Credit rating is not a neutral activity. The rating agencies will endorse policies that favour international investors and criticise those that reduce their returns: that is the nature of their business. They do not provide an independent assessment of the health of the New Zealand economy. Yet New Zealand governments have made themselves willing captives of the credit rating agencies, partly because they appear mesmerised, but also because the ratings offer another means to legitimise their policy position, secure a political advantage, and resist demands for change.

▲ Competitiveness rankings

Whereas credit ratings reflect an interplay between the interests of governments and international investors mediated through the rating agencies, rankings of international competitiveness appear to be little more than propaganda. The annual Global Competitiveness Report is produced by the World Economic Forum, discussed earlier. The report's authors describe international competitiveness as 'the ability of a nation's economy to make rapid and sustained gains in living standards' on a five to ten year horizon.[104] According to the report's core theory, a country's growth prospects depend on its initial income level, plus other characteristics such as government policies, geography and the educational base. Yet the report focuses exclusively on government policies. Its ideal government would maintain open markets and flexible labour practices; spending would be lean, with low tax rates; there would be an effective judiciary, and a stable political system.

The four factors given most weight in the survey are the openness of the economy to international trade and finance; the role of the government budget and regulation; the development of financial markets; and the flexibility of the labour market. These factors are rated according to quantitative data. The assessment of the remaining factors – the quality of the infrastructure, technology, business management, and judicial and political institutions – is based on surveys of chief executives. It is significant that Harvard professor Jeffrey Sachs, who chairs the advisory board for the report, acknowledges that the choice of factors is debatable and somewhat arbitrary, and that the measurement 'is imperfect, to say the least'.[105] He believes the report's index, which ranks countries according to their competitiveness rating, has considerable value as a 'shorthand' guide for business and government, *as long as it is interpreted with the caveats in mind*'.[106]

When citing the competitiveness ratings, New Zealand's free-market champions have systematically ignored these important caveats. The rankings regularly appear as objective fact in government speeches and Budget statements,[107] promotional materials,[108] and the media. They first became 'news' in 1986, when New Zealand was ranked eleventh; reporting continued despite a fall to thirteenth in 1987 and seventeenth in 1989. By 1996, however, National's restructuring policies saw New Zealand rocket into third place. The report claimed that:

> New Zealand is the new star, ranking third in the world, and heading the Anglo-Saxon economies in the ranking. New Zealand's high ranking is a tribute to a decade of structural and policy reforms, including opening of the economy; scaling back of government spending; widespread privatization; and significant innovations in many areas of governmental action, from fiscal policies, to pensions, to central banking. New Zealand's reforms will be widely studied, and emulated, in future years.[109]

The following year New Zealand dropped to fifth, the report noting that the country 'faces the test of consolidating the decade-long fiscal and structural reforms and translating these into solid economic growth'.[110] By 1998 New Zealand was down to thirteenth again, no longer warranting specific mention in the text of the report.

This posed problems for the government's 'good news' machine. The

Ministry of Foreign Affairs and Trade deftly adapted its 1998 version of the glossy booklet, *Invest in New Zealand,* changing the reference to New Zealand as 'the *fifth* most competitive nation in the world in 1997' to '*one* of the most competitive' in 1999. But it retained the reference to its third ranking in 1996 for 'receptivity towards foreign investment'.[111] The booklet also drew support from the opposition World Competitiveness Yearbook and other ranking exercises, presumably selecting statistics that made New Zealand look 'best' in the eyes of foreign investors.

Prominent among these other reports was the Heritage Foundation's Index of Economic Freedom. In 1997, New Zealand was ranked fourth (behind Hong Kong, Singapore and Bahrain), and was praised for implementing what the OECD had called 'the most comprehensive economic liberalization program ever undertaken in a developed country'.[112] The Heritage Foundation claims that the Index is objective: 'Economic freedom may sound like a vague term that is open to interpretation. It is not.' The Foundation defines 'economic freedom' as the 'absence of government coercion or constraint on the production, distribution, or consumption of goods and services'.[113] The Index assesses the extent to which government policies maximise or restrict 'personal economic choices', grading them on a scale of one to five according to 50 'independent economic factors'. The factors are grouped under ten headings, with descriptions that equate neoliberal ideology with economic fact:[114]

Trade Policy: 'The degree to which a government hinders the free flow of foreign commerce has a direct bearing on economic growth.'

Taxation Policy: 'All taxes are harmful to economic activity. A tax is essentially a government-imposed disincentive to perform the activity being taxed.'

Government Intervention in the Economy: 'The greater the degree to which the government intrudes in the economy, the less individuals are free to engage in their own economic activities.'

Monetary Policy: 'If a government maintains a "tight" monetary policy ... individuals have the economic freedom to engage in productive and profitable economic activities. If the government maintains a "loose" monetary policy ... money loses its value and individuals are less free ... .'

Capital Flows and Foreign Investment: 'Restrictions on foreign investment hamper economic freedom and thus limit the inflow of foreign capital.'

Banking Policy: '... banks provide the economy with the financial means to operate ... . The more government controls banks, the less they are free to engage in these activities.'

Wage and Price Controls: 'A free economy is one that allows individuals to set not only the prices on the goods and services they sell, but also the wages they pay to the workers they employ.'

Property Rights: 'The accumulation of private property is the main motivating force in a market economy. ... This factor examines the extent to which private property is protected by the government and how safe it is from expropriation.'

Regulation Policy: 'Although there are many regulations that hinder business, the most important ones are those associated with licensing new companies and businesses.'

Black Market: 'Black markets are a direct result of government intervention in the market. ... The smaller the black market, the higher the economic freedom.'

The Index is interested only in policy 'inputs', not in their results. The benefits are assumed. So is the universal distribution of economic freedom (despite the definition of 'wage freedom' as the right of employers to set workers' wages).

The Index was regularly cited in the government's speeches and promotional materials, including *Invest in New Zealand*.[115] It was also drawn on heavily as independent supporting evidence in a Business Roundtable report, *New Zealand in an International Perspective*, which concluded: 'It is clear from the evidence, both qualitative and quantitative, that the extent of liberalisation over the last 12 years places New Zealand in a class of its own within the OECD area. People all over the world have come to consider New Zealand a special case, and they are right.'[116]

Both the World Competitiveness Reports and the Index of Economic Freedom are no more than assessments of New Zealand's conformity with 'globalisation as ideology'. Their shoddy methodology make them questionable as measures even of that.

▲ The international media

The other significant voice of the market has been the media. For most of the period since 1984, the media seemed to rely mainly on economists,[117] often drawn from the banking and investment agencies who profited most from the liberalisation of the economy. Their warnings of dire consequences should government deviate from the chosen path were taken and repeated as objective truth. The occasional dissenting voice, for example that of independent economist Brian Easton, were reportedly banned from use in some publications or were lost in the chorus of praise that was conveyed by generally uncritical business journalists.[118]

The international media joined the refrain. A report commissioned by the *Economist* in 1985 hailed the New Zealand government's 'exhilarating dash for economic freedom':

> Delighted progressive businessmen hardly dare believe that a Labour government is doing these things, while bewildered old trade union leaders loyally pretend that it isn't. ... During his 36 years as a newspaperman your correspondent has visited most major countries, but he can remember no economic experiment that he has been more eager to see succeed than that of this brave New Zealand Labour government.[119]

Subsequent reports in the *Economist* included such phrases as 'the sort of socialism of which millionaires approve', 'out-Thatchering Mrs Thatcher', 'an international model for economic reform', 'a paradise for free-marketeers – if not for those New Zealanders who have lost their jobs', and 'the most thoroughgoing economic reform in the OECD'.[120] In the lead-up to the 1993 election, the *Economist* observed: 'During the past decade New Zealand has implemented free-market reforms more radical than any other industrial country's. ... On November 6th New Zealanders will decide whether they want the experiment to continue. Their verdict will send an important signal to the rest of the world's economic reformers.'[121] After National failed to secure a majority at the 1996 election, the *Economist* pronounced 'the end of radical reform in New Zealand':

> New Zealand might have lost its appetite for further reform, but its economy is still a model for others. Why on earth, you might well ask, does *The Economist* devote so much more space to New Zealand, a tiny country of only 3.5m people, than to other nations of similar size, such as Albania or Uruguay? The answer, quite simply, is that the country merits it. Over the past decade or so, New Zealand has embraced more of the free-market reforms that this newspaper espouses than any other industrial country. The problem is that although the ruling National Party convinced us that it was on the right track, it apparently failed to convince enough New Zealand voters.[122]

In 1997 the Coalition government was described as 'wobbly', with a 'feeling that other countries ... are now reforming more vigorously than New Zealand – heresy considering the country's reputation as a laboratory for free-market ideas.'[123] There were occasional criticisms. One article linked New Zealand's economic policies to an increase in inequality (see Chapter 10).[124] Another before the 1996 election observed that 'after one of the world's boldest experiments in economic reform ... the voters are restless and distrustful of politicians. ... Though all these reforms were necessary, the manner in which they were carried out had served to undermine faith in politicians'.[125] A somewhat alarmed piece in 1998 compared the current account deficit to the levels in collapsed East Asian economies:

'A sudden outflow of capital, as in East Asia, is unlikely so long as the government maintains its prudent policies. But the OECD and the IMF have warned that New Zealand's net foreign debt of more than 80% of GDP (the highest in any rich economy) leaves the country vulnerable.'[126] Overall, the *Economist* remained strongly supportive of New Zealand's 'brave' experiment – and regretful about the loss of momentum from the mid-1990s.

The *Times*, the *Financial Times*, Toronto's *Globe and Mail* and the *Wall Street Journal*, among others, echoed the *Economist*'s applause.[127] Alternative versions of New Zealand's 'success' story were initially rare. Some Canadian journalists raised questions,[128] and the Canadian Broadcasting Corporation carried several documentaries that highlighted the downside of the New Zealand experiment.[129] In the UK, a full-page feature in the *Independent* in March 1994 detailed the social costs of New Zealand's structural adjustment programme. Headlined 'What happens when you scrap the welfare state?', the story began: 'New Zealand has, and its economy is stronger. But there is a dark side: one in seven below [the] poverty line; record numbers of people in jail; armed police on the streets; queues at charity "food banks".' After cataloguing the social distress and decay in poorer New Zealand communities, it concluded: 'there is the feeling that something irreplaceable has already been lost. For 40 years, New Zealand tried to build a civil society in which all its people were free from fear or want. That project has now lapsed. In its place is only a vague exhortation for individuals to go and get rich.'[130] An article in *Le Monde Diplomatique*, translated into four languages and distributed across Europe in April 1997, was scathing:

> New Zealand is a model – but not the kind it imagines itself to be. Looked at closely, its economic results are far from spectacular. ... Not much scope there for giving lessons to the rest of the world. ... But if what you want to know is how best to revolutionise a society from top to bottom so that the market is given priority more or less throughout; how to make systematic use of political voluntarism and ideological warfare; how to convert renegades from the left before going on to reject or corrupt them; how to turn to your own advantage the confusion of militant socialists and trade unionists and the tendency of intellectuals to abandon the economy and the people, and focus on 'civil society' and 'minorities' – then, yes, New Zealand is an example to us all.[131]

The Australian press was frequently diffident, and sometimes caustic, about what New Zealand had to offer. The Australian Liberal Party at federal and state levels embraced aspects of the New Zealand model, promising labour market deregulation during the Victoria state election in

1992, and a universal goods-and-services expenditure tax in the federal election of 1993. The media countered with horror stories about the 'New Zealand disease'. While the *Australian Financial Review* was often positive, it also preferred the more pragmatic approach that Australian governments had taken to market restructuring since 1983.

Media criticism of the New Zealand experiment increased in the later 1990s, both abroad and at home. New Zealanders became more assertive in questioning and opposing official policy, and in putting forward alternatives. Some newspapers began to publish dissenting views in opinion pieces and stories, although television remained a lost cause for current affairs unless it could be conveyed as a human interest story. The *Listener* re-emerged as a weekly magazine prepared to present a left-wing point of view. The *Independent* consistently provided a more balanced analysis than the myopic *National Business Review*. Doubts about the 'economic miracle' deepened as the economy moved back into recession in 1998 and unemployment began to rise. As negative critiques of the international agreements, notably APEC and the Multilateral Agreement on Investment, became more popularly accepted, coverage of such views in the media became almost mainstream. After more than a decade of portraying New Zealand's great success story, the media appeared to have recognised, however belatedly, its role in promoting a contest of ideas.

▲ REFLECTIONS

New Zealand's free-marketeers fostered the image of being orthodox and leading the world. For much of the 1980s and 1990s they were justified in making that claim. Their policies mirrored the ideological line promoted by informal international networks and think-tanks, by the commercial rating agencies and financial media, and by the major international economic institutions. Successive governments received accolades from these sources for leading the world, and this provided an important source of legitimacy for often unpopular domestic policies.

But the implications of a world-leading orthodoxy were rarely explored. Had other countries just not seen the light yet? Were they just slower than New Zealand, and the evolutionary forces of globalisation would eventually see them follow down the same path? Or was there a gap between ideology and practice which meant that New Zealand served an important symbolic role, while other governments attended to their domestic economic and social needs? The next chapter explores these questions further, as it documents attempts to export the New Zealand model to the rest of the world.

3 ▲ Leading the World

In January 1998, Minister of International Trade Lockwood Smith told the Orewa Rotary Club: 'When I travel overseas they know about the All Blacks, sheep, Anchor brand and they know of the success of New Zealand's economic reforms.'[1] An enormous effort has gone into selling the New Zealand model offshore. While a lot of ego is involved, and often lucrative consultancies, there is also a missionary zeal. The sales pitch is selective in its evidence, sometimes seems disingenuous, and always carries a favourable spin. It almost never mentions the downside – the huge increase in inequality and poverty, a deteriorating social service infrastructure that is near collapse in places, a real economy battered by government policies, and Maori struggling to survive (see Chapter 10).

Most overseas interest in New Zealand centres on the techniques used to initiate such massive changes, and the policies applied to the restructuring of the state: corporatisation, financial accountability and the public sector management regime. Staff within the World Bank have been the most energetic in creating opportunities to export the model, through seminars and speaking tours, consultancies, commissioned reports or exposure trips to New Zealand. Other agencies such as the Asian Development Bank (ADB) and Commonwealth Secretariat have also been involved in this evangelism. On occasion, overseas governments have invited key architects of the experiment to visit their country. The New Zealand government has created outlets of its own through the overseas speeches of its diplomats and politicians, by directing aid funding into technical assistance for restructuring programmes in poorer countries, and by funding initiatives at the Commonwealth Secretariat.

The investment pays dividends. Stories of emulation reflect a positive image of the 'reforms' back home, reinforce claims to world-leading orthodoxy, raise New Zealand's profile internationally, and generate further accolades. Despite the country's economic and social malaise, the perception that New Zealand's restructuring was a success story prevails internationally. Yet the 'good news' machine has also met with scepticism, and prompted a search for counter-evidence by critics concerned that the New Zealand model might be applied to their country. The future fortunes of the model may ultimately depend less on people's understanding of what is really happening in New Zealand than on the outcome of the current debate on the desirability of the global free market paradigm. This chapter describes some of the ways in which the New Zealand 'success story' has been promoted internationally, and to what effect; it also locates these proselytising activities in the debate on the role of states and markets, which will shape the future direction of international economic orthodoxy.

▲ THE INSTITUTIONAL OUTLETS

Word spread rapidly about the remarkable New Zealand experiment. From the early 1990s, individual governments, from Alberta and Iceland to Latvia and Mongolia, looked to it as a model. International agencies promoted specific New Zealand policies as a template for member countries; the Commonwealth Secretariat, for example, focused on public sector management. By far the most important vehicles for transmitting the New Zealand model were the international financial institutions – the IMF, World Bank and Asian Development Bank. To understand their interest in New Zealand, it is necessary to provide a short history.

The World Bank and IMF trace their origins to a conference of 44 countries (including New Zealand) held at Bretton Woods in New Hampshire from 1 to 22 July 1944. The goal was to reconstruct war-torn Europe and restore Western industrial capitalism. The IMF was intended to oversee the international monetary system by maintaining short-term currency stability and addressing any balance of payments emergencies. The International Bank for Reconstruction and Development (generally called the World Bank) would focus on longer-term economic development and structural issues. (Plans for a third institution, the International Trade Organisation, fell foul of the US Congress.) Although nominally under the UN umbrella, the so-called 'Bretton Woods institutions' quickly assumed a virtual autonomy. The US, as major shareholder, calls the shots in both. Their decision-making structures are almost identical. They hold joint annual meetings. Their buildings are even in the same block in Washington. Over time, a number of 'baby banks' (including the African Development Bank, the Asian Development Bank, the Intra-American Development Bank, and the European Bank for Reconstruction and Development) also emerged.

By the late 1970s, the Bretton Woods institutions appeared to be redundant. But the Third World debt crisis gave them a new lease of life. For the next two decades, the IMF and World Bank became the major conduits for structural adjustment policies backed by far-reaching 'conditionalities', which debtor governments had to comply with. The institutions had real power, which they did not hesitate to use. Although they appeared to speak with a single voice, there were tensions between them, especially when some more pragmatic elements in the World Bank challenged the IMF's more rigid approach.

In 1994 the IMF's managing director, Michel Camdessus, described the 'interim committee' that advised the Fund as

> ... not merely a committee of 24 finance ministers: it is the only forum where finance ministers representing virtually the whole world meet on a regular basis. Its work has already become more clearly focused – better targeted on the challenges of globalization. ... For those who want global and more effective economic policy cooperation at ministerial level, there is no need to look any further.[2]

Despite an appalling track record in solving the debt problems of poor countries,[3] the IMF acted as if it were invincible. Camdessus asked the joint annual meeting in 1994:

> Why are we so sure that we're on the right track here, and so assertive about our mission for the future? Part of the reason, certainly, is that the Fund's work in developing and transition economies in balance of payments difficulties is called for by our Articles, but another is that it is relied upon not only by those countries themselves, but also by bilateral, multilateral, and commercial creditors and donors. They rely on the Fund for its analysis, for its 'green light' for the phasing in of their contributions, and frequently for taking the initial risk. In this field, the Fund's partnership with our members and with the international financial community at large is of the closest kind.[4]

The World Bank (actually a group of five agencies)[5] has a complementary mandate to that of the IMF, but a distinct culture and approach. Its website describes the Bank as 'a partner in strengthening economies and expanding markets to improve the quality of life for people everywhere, especially the poorest'.[6] The Asian Development Bank shares this market-based approach to economic development. Its president, Mitsuo Sato, speaking at the ADB's 1995 annual meeting, said: 'We all know that economic growth contributes immensely to poverty reduction'.[7] Yet the loan record of both Banks was no better than that of the IMF.[8] In the mid-1990s, under its new president, James Wolfensohn, the World Bank promised a more efficient and socially responsive approach to implementing its market-based economic development model. Its critics remained unconvinced.[9]

The IMF and the World Bank have responded differently to criticism. The IMF maintained its austere macroeconomic strategies with minimal reference to a social dimension, although it began stressing the importance of 'good governance' to successful markets. The mandate and organisation of the World Bank and its regional variants gave them more room to move. Recognising the inappropriateness of a self-regulating free market for Eastern Europe, especially after the collapse of the Russian economy, the World Bank resurrected the role of the state, and stressed the participation of 'civil society' in building a free market economy. This was still structural adjustment, but with a more transparent, social face.

At the end of the century, however, both institutions have again been the subject of fierce attack. Progressive social movements held them jointly responsible for causing the destitution and powerlessness of poor people and poor countries, while expanding the wealth of corporate and corrupt élites. Trenchant critic David Korten, for example, described the World Bank as an export-financing facility for transnational corporations, the IMF as the debt collector for rich countries' financial institutions, and the GATT as the creator and enforcer of a corporate Bill of Rights.[10] Political conservatives, especially in the US, were equally vocal, alleging gross inefficiency and lack of accountability, and challenging the pretensions of these supra-national structures to run a command economy on a global scale. The Asian crisis intensified the differences between and within the institutions. The IMF (and the US government) struggled to maintain control in the region, amid accusations that they were making the situation worse. The World Bank seemed more ambivalent: while its president lined up alongside the IMF, its chief economist turned his back on the 'Washington consensus' to which both institutions adhered.[11]

So how are the IMF and World Bank relevant to New Zealand? New Zealand is a very small shareholder in each, and a minor contributor in times of crisis. Yet both institutions have a huge influence on the global economic environment to which New Zealand is so heavily exposed. More specifically, New Zealand governments since 1984 have adhered to the same 'Washington consensus'. As discussed earlier, the IMF's annual reports on the New Zealand economy have bolstered the image of international orthodoxy, while scare tactics about IMF intervention have been used to keep free-market policies on track. There is also a more direct relationship. Some of New Zealand's key change agents have worked for the Fund, either on secondment or through consultancies. Even more New Zealanders work for the World Bank; most are former government officials, and describe themselves as 'true believers in the New Zealand reforms'. They (and others) promote New Zealand as a model for their clients to follow. Former New Zealand politicians and officials are employed by the Bank as consultants, with support from the Tradenz office in Washington. Exposure tours are organised for policy-makers from poor countries and Bank staff to see New Zealand's 'miracle' for themselves. New Zealand universities and individual academics offer training programmes on restructuring. The 1995 annual meeting of the Asian Development Bank in Auckland provided a further opportunity to promote the New Zealand approach.

Although both institutions are committed to the 'Washington consensus', the World Bank is much more supportive of New Zealand as a role model than the IMF is. The IMF's mandate centres on balance of payments and economic stabilisation concerns. While the conditions it sets on loans often include privatisation and fiscal restraints, it has tended to leave the detail of state restructuring to the World Bank. The IMF's culture differs markedly from the World Bank's: it is hierarchical, and speaks with a single voice, adhering strictly to economic 'orthodoxy'. In 1998 there were 2,600 staff in 110 countries; people working at the IMF are constantly in touch with each other, and know what is expected; they are unlikely to put forward a paper that would be voted down. IMF officials actively foster an external constituency for change, tapping into networks which cultivate policy-makers in client governments, and often include former staff members. As international relations specialist Miles Kahler observes:

> By far the most significant coalition-building by the IMF is the construction of transnational alliances with technocrats in government ministries that share IMF policy preferences, typically the finance ministry and central bank. These ministries, responsible for macroeconomic and budgetary oversight, are often in agreement with the prescriptions of the IMF, whose programs provide them with valuable ammunition. The career paths of these technocrats have also predisposed them toward transnational alignment with the [international financial institutions], since many have spent time as staff members at one of them. The Fund and the Bank also attempt to *create* such interlocutors and allies in the longer run through programs of technical assistance, ensuring that this critical transnational link is sustained over time.[12]

New Zealanders in this network include key change agent Rod Deane (who was alternate executive director at the IMF in 1974–76), the Reserve Bank's Grant Spencer (seconded to the IMF in 1981–84), and Alexander Sundakov, a former Treasury official who was with the IMF in Kiev before returning in 1998 to run the New Zealand Institute of Economic

Research. Aside from these networks and formal meetings, New Zealand's direct influence on IMF policies has been comparatively muted. Former Treasury head Graham Scott was a visiting scholar at the IMF in 1996; his paper 'Government Reform in New Zealand' set out lessons for countries seeking to follow a similar path.[13] Ruth Richardson gave a seminar at the Fund. But IMF officials seemed circumspect about New Zealand's relevance to debtor countries undergoing structural adjustment. One suggested that New Zealand had more to offer OECD countries: 'I think sending out a lot of New Zealanders without a great deal of experience in developing [economies] or economies in transition is dangerous and could rebound unfavourably.'[14]

The World Bank's approach is less organised. The Bank has more than 7,000 staff, mostly based in Washington. A major restructuring in 1987 failed to sustain cuts to staff numbers or costs. Continued attacks on the Bank's profligacy and inefficiency prompted another major restructuring in 1997. Some staff enthusiastically supported the new 'flatter, faster and more decentralized structure';[15] other people inside and outside the Bank were sceptical that it would make much difference.[16]

There is a *relative* plurality of views in the Bank, both between and within country teams and specialist divisions (but rarely among the powerful senior economists). While staff are constrained by World Bank policies and shareholders' decisions, and have limited exposure to dissenting views, interviews about the New Zealand model revealed a diversity of opinion. Bank officials readily identified themselves as either 'true believers' or 'sceptics', although the latter were reluctant to criticise New Zealand *per se*. Many argued that the New Zealand model was inappropriate for countries that lacked the institutional infrastructure to operate through market-based (especially contractual) mechanisms. Others felt there was insufficient discussion of other models, notably in Europe. Some (but not many) expressed concern about the social costs of New Zealand's restructuring. These were individual views, however. There was no evidence of any contest of ideas on an institutional level.

The New Zealand model enjoyed enough support at the Bank to have an influence disproportionate to the country's size or strategic importance. One official suggested that New Zealand appealed to World Bank staff and client governments because the package was neat and simple: 'for busy people, you know, it's like "ahah, there's a paradigm there"'. He called it 'intellectually a kind of economists' dream'. Countries that were over-regulated and wanting an honest professional government were 'looking for quick fixes and magic bullets ... a contractual model in which you're freed of all those petty constraints, and they're replaced by a contract, and you fulfil it or you don't, and you're punished if you don't and you're rewarded if you do. They think it's going to short cut their problems.'[17]

Support for the New Zealand model was often based on slight information. Bank officials had little time to read detailed research. They relied on the media, circulating papers, seminars by visiting New Zealanders, and word of mouth. There were many energetic proselytisers on the staff; Ruth Richardson and Graham Scott were invited to give seminars. Talks by US academic Allen Schick (see below) and the author have been among the few counter-voices.

▲ GOOD GOVERNANCE

The interest shown by the World Bank and Asian Development Bank in the New Zealand model also reflected their shift of focus in the 1990s away from funding infrastructure projects and broader programmes to promoting markets and private sector investment. Many traditional debtor countries lacked the prerequisites for a market-driven economy, including a strong legal system and public administration, and private sector institutions such as a stock-market. The desire to bring Eastern Europe and Indo-China into the global market economy reinforced the importance of building a strong and competent state that could create and sustain such a market.

'Good governance' and 'capacity building' became the new buzz-words, and were absorbed into the broader structural adjustment programmes. 'Capacity building' meant creating the administrative infrastructure to support the free market economy (discussed further below). 'Good governance' was shorthand for a limited government whose role was to facilitate markets, Western-style rule of law, individual liberty, private property rights, and passive forms of electoral democracy. A government that lacked these features could legitimately be required to adopt them as a condition of financial assistance. Hence, the 'conditionalities' attached to IMF and World Bank loans extended beyond the implementation of macroeconomic and microeconomic policies to include policies relating to governance, sustainable development, human rights and democracy.[18] Non-debtors were encouraged to undertake these changes voluntarily.

Most borrowing countries found such pressure hard to resist. Some of these governments *were* corrupt and had appalling records in human rights. But the motives behind the new conditionalities were not humanitarian; they were promoted as the necessary conditions for free markets to operate. The effects could be perverse. Pressure on a government from foreign investors to deregulate could conflict with World Bank demands that it improve its environmental or labour standards. A loan condition that required a government to democratise its political system might clash with requirements that it implement economic policies so unpopular they would cause the government to collapse. Support for 'good governance' was also selective. Repressive and corrupt regimes, such as those of Salinas in Mexico and Suharto in Indonesia, attracted little adverse comment until they became a liability for the major powers and economic institutions. Indeed, the World Bank's World Development Report in 1997 reported that: 'In Indonesia the Ministry of Finance and the planning agency Bapennas have been the guardians of the purse and the brains of the civil service. These central agencies are staffed by professional and capable employees recruited on the basis of merit.'[19] Some countries, such as China and Russia, enjoyed considerable autonomy in negotiating loan conditions because of their strategic position.

In 1995 the Asian Development Bank says it was the first of the international financial institutions to adopt an official policy on governance. The founding principles were *accountability* of public officials for delivering specific results, *transparency, predictability,* and *participation* of key stakeholders.[20] Three aspects of government were targeted. First, the management of public sector (including quasi-state) agencies should be strengthened, and the way governments make and implement policy and deliver services should be changed. Second, governments needed to improve their capacity to create and foster an 'enabling environment for private sector growth'. Third, the role of 'civil society' should be enhanced, including the 'participation of stakeholders and beneficiaries in development policies and projects and a growing role of NGOs in delivering certain services' (but not in setting the agenda).[21] By May 1997, three Asian Development Bank loans totalling US$290 million and over twenty technical assistance grants had been directed towards restructuring core administrative systems. Two-thirds of the remaining loans and over 80 percent of the technical assistance grants had some component of strengthening institutional capacity.

The World Bank signalled its own formal repositioning in the 1997 World Development Report, *The State in a Changing World*. The ideal of self-regulating markets, promoted in the Bank's 1996 report, *From Plan to Market*,[22] sank with the ignominious collapse of the Russian economy. The 1997 report resurrected a role for the market-friendly state. Government and market were now seen as complementary, with the state being 'essential for putting in place the appropriate institutional foundations for markets'.[23] This meant the currently limited capacity of client states should be expanded over time to create an efficient and competitive market economy and harness the innovative participation of businesses, labour, households and community groups. In Eastern Europe especially, this gradual approach made more sense than instant deregulation and privatisation, which corrupt élites could exploit as easily as they could the old command economy. The role of the 'capable state' was: to provide a non-distortionary policy environment, including macroeconomic stability; to invest in basic social services and infrastructure; to protect the vulnerable; to protect the environment; and to establish a foundation of law.[24] In policy terms there was no deviation from the 'Washington consensus' model. Specific policy prescriptions included liberalising trade, lowering entry barriers for private industry, competitive privatisation, and reforming the civil service. It was simply stated that monopoly public providers of infrastructure and services should be privatised: 'A carefully managed privatization process brings very positive economic and fiscal benefits'.[25] Likewise, social services should be targeted, devolved and community-based. Environmental policy should be flexible, and operate through self-regulation and market-based instruments. All these policies required a sound framework of market-based regulation and law. This was standard New Zealand restructuring.

The report suggested that development assistance should be channelled 'to poor countries with good policies and a strong commitment to institutional reinvigoration'.[26] The Bank should offer technical advice to these countries, backed by local expertise, and promote the sharing of experiences by using advisors from different countries and backgrounds. Financial assistance should be made available to help ease the early pain of transition. The Bank should also 'provide a mechanism for countries to make external commitments, making it more difficult to back-track on reforms',[27] presumably through the combination of loan conditionalities, binding commitments to international economic agreements, and dependence on foreign capital.

The report's vision was of a strong but limited state with effective rules and restraints, market-based competition, and 'increased citizen voice and partnership'.[28] Globalisation and democracy were co-requisites: 'global integration of economies and the spread of democracy have narrowed the scope for arbitrary and capricious behavior'.[29] But this was a very specific form of democracy that ensured cooperation with and consolidation of the structural adjustment programme. It was *not* a vision of a strong participatory democracy. Indeed, formal constitutional restraints, such as a balance of powers between the executive, legislature and judiciary, and strong local and central government, were described as multiple veto points that would make 'reform' difficult. Because the 'capable state' would also require public sector restructuring, strong leadership was considered vital. Changing macroeconomic policy quickly by using 'a small group of competent technocrats' was not so hard, because such policies did not require an institutional overhaul.[30] But establishing 'good' microeconomic policies, and more capable state institutions to implement them, would be resisted more strongly by those who stood to lose from the changes, and would thus take longer. The report observed that far-sighted and reform-oriented leaders and élites had 'transformed the options for their people through decisive reform'. In the process, 'they made the benefits of change clear to all, and built coalitions that gave greater voice to often-silent beneficiaries'. These change agents succeeded because they 'spelled out a longer-term vision for their society, allowing people to see beyond the immediate pain of adjustment'. Effective leaders gave their people 'a sense of owning the reforms – a sense that reform is not something imposed from without'.[31] They did not, however, give their people a choice about whether or not to pursue the policy path.

Most of the report's list of leadership strategies were consistent with the structural adjustment literature referred to in Chapter 1, and familiar to New Zealanders.[32] Changes were to be initiated during periods of actual or perceived crisis, or a new government's 'honeymoon' period; working through strong political leaders, supplemented by committed technocrats in key government agencies; constructing a political and intellectual climate of support, backed by vocal beneficiaries; ensuring transparency and certainty of policy commitments to boost (business) confidence in government; and consulting and co-opting key private firms, labour unions and 'civil society'. The report suggested that states with weaker institutions might need 'self-restricting rules, which precisely specify the content of policy and lock it into mechanisms that are costly to reverse'.[33] Where the list of strategies diverged from New Zealand's approach was in its suggestion that losers be compensated, and its stress on developing consensus.[34]

There were a number of favourable references to New Zealand in the report,[35] although support for the New Zealand model had been toned down from earlier drafts. One author noted that his original enthusiasm, based on a study trip to New Zealand in 1995, had been tempered by reflection. On the very first page there was a 'strong cautionary note' that what worked in countries like New Zealand might not work in countries at very different stages of development, such as Nepal.[36] The report expressed more explicit reservations about applying the approach adopted in New Zealand to public sector management:

> The so-called new public management reforms in industrial countries have sought to move delivery away from the core public sector ... primarily by using market mechanisms and formal contracting. New Zealand provides

the most dramatic example. ... Several developing countries are now emulating these reforms. But what is feasible in New Zealand may be unworkable in many developing countries. ... Countries with little capacity to enforce complex contracts, and weak bureaucratic controls to restrain arbitrary behavior under more flexible management regimes, need to proceed with caution.[37]

▲ EXPORTING THE NEW ZEALAND EXPERIMENT

The staff of the international financial institutions, especially the World Bank and Asian Development Bank, drew on the New Zealand experience for two distinct purposes. The first was to advise governments on strategies for implementing structural adjustment programmes. The second was to promote New Zealand's innovative approaches to state sector restructuring and public sector management, and to a lesser degree to education and labour market policies.

▲ *Selling the strategies*

Former Finance Ministers Roger Douglas and Ruth Richardson were employed by World Bank staff to inspire client governments to pursue radical restructuring programmes and advise them on how politically to implement them. One Bank official described how, in 1990, the new Brazilian government was seriously considering privatisations. The president of the National Bank of Development asked the World Bank for a visit from a 'core of people who have gone through it, who have done it and can discuss what in their experience has worked and hasn't worked'. The team included Roger Douglas, who had recently left the Labour Cabinet. Douglas reportedly emphasised

> ... the transition, all the information, all the experience, that he himself had gathered from the years he was a minister and maybe afterwards in the effort to reduce the size of government. And it was very important because (a) he was unquestionably one who had done a lot of that and (b) there was no question at that time that the transformation had not stopped, so there was a lot of steam in the process. So he was persuasive both because he was talking about an experiment which was highly valued abroad for those who believe in it, plus he was the one who did it. It was extraordinary. It made a hell of a difference for Brazil, according to the Brazilians.[38]

The same economist used Douglas again in Peru, where the Minister of Transport had asked the World Bank for advice on 'how to do it':

And again the themes were why and how, and it was an extraordinarily successful conference. ... [He was useful] to impart the message of how you start, what are the conditions, what is the mood, what are those things that make the initial steps.[39]

Ruth Richardson was seen to be more helpful about how to maintain the momentum. A different official observed: 'Ruth doesn't talk a whole lot of substance. You would probably call her a cheer leader, and people use her that way. I think she's quite good also at strategy. ... The bank is in a deficit position on political matters ... so the Ruths and Rogers of this world have been useful in terms of communicating some of these ideas to policy makers.' This was especially so for Latin American ministers, who tended to be academics and 'don't usually have the political nous that people like Roger and Ruth have'.[40] Another official working in the same region was more sceptical:

> ... we organised a big conference on the international experience of public sector reform and had Ruth Richardson perform, and she's a wonderful performer, she had the congressmen dancing in the aisles ... the whole country, at least in a limited body, wanted to become New Zealand the next day, and it was from that moment on I kind of realised I committed a grave error, not only for Peru but for Latin America. I like Ruth and I very much admire her but Peru turned out to be the beachhead ... for her particular assault on Latin America.[41]

His main concern was 'the unreflective invasion of these kinds of ideas of the Bank [into] Latin America'.[42]

Interest in these strategies was not confined to the World Bank and debtor countries. New Zealand's experience was actively sought out by some OECD governments, notably in small countries such as Iceland or provinces within a federal system, as with Alberta in Canada, wanting to introduce radical market-based programmes. Douglas enthusiastically shared his 'blitzkrieg' strategy with political parties and governments in various countries, especially Canada. In 1990 he reportedly told the Reform Party convention in Saskatoon that 'consensus for "quality decisions" is achieved after they are made. He advised them not to reveal their program – but, if elected, to implement it as quickly as possible to overwhelm the opposition.'[43] The Canadian Taxpayers Federation (a group with similar views to those of Douglas's own Association of Consumers and Taxpayers) distributed large numbers of his book, *Unfinished Business*, to politicians, policy-makers and journalists. Ironically, the Canadians used New Zealand not as a success story, but as an example of how bad things could get if governments failed to tackle debt early enough. The myth that 'New Zealand hit the debt wall in 1984' was central to the story. (In fact, the problem in 1984 was a short-term liquidity crisis caused by a speculative outflow in anticipation of a post-election devaluation.) The fiction was perpetuated in a notorious documentary made by Channel W5 in 1993, which illustrated the consequent disintegration of New Zealand's caring welfare society with a story about the shooting of a baby hippo at the cash-strapped Auckland Zoo.

Canadian interest in New Zealand coincided with the election in 1993 of a Conservative government in Alberta, with an explicit mandate to cut public spending in response to a perceived fiscal and debt 'crisis' (although critics say that the province's net debt was negligible at the time).[44] According to the communications director for Premier Ralph Klein, the selection of a new party leader and the election had 'created such impetus and consensus that the only issue then was how to get it done. Which allowed blitzkrieg to happen, to use your context. ... And that's where tactically Roger Douglas's advice helped us.'[45] Alberta's neo-liberal restructuring was driven by political and commercial self-interest rather than ideology, but Douglas's strategy was equally applicable. *Unfinished Business* was photocopied and circulated among politicians and advisors. The W5 documentary was screened for the governing caucus. At the invitation of Treasurer Jim Dinning (who was also a senior executive of Transalta, later a major player in New Zealand's privatised electricity market), Douglas addressed the caucus en route to a Taxpayers Federation conference in 1993. His advice was reflected in the Klein team's subsequent strategy:

> A lot of my specific job is to deal with the news media here and we do a lot of what our local media call carpet-bombing. Which is you dump so much on them in one day that they can't possibly keep up with the criticism of it. It's part of what Roger Douglas had taught us. The faster you go in that context too the less time and potential the interest groups have for being able to make specific one-issue cases.[46]

Alberta journalist Lorne Gunter suggests that Douglas had credibility because of his claim that governments could make these changes and remain politically popular, as evidenced by the election of 'reforming' governments in New Zealand throughout the decade.[47] His audience was probably not interested in alternative explanations for New Zealand's electoral results, and certainly would not have been offered any.[48]

Ruth Richardson was equally active on the international stage. In addition to consulting work for the World Bank, Asian Development Bank and Commonwealth Secretariat, she too lectured to foreign governments. Among her clients were the governments of Argentina, South Africa, Iceland, Germany and Vietnam. Her advice mirrored the contempt for democratic participation she showed when Minister of Finance. Public service unionists from Iceland had just returned from a study tour of New Zealand when Richardson visited Reykjavik in 1996. One of them sent the author the following account:

> Our finance minister invited Ruth Richardson to speak to the 'opinion builders' of Iceland (as she herself said), i.e. the heads of departments and companies in the state sector, members of parliament and prominent men from the private sector. Richardson seemed to me quite desperate in her argumentation. But I am sorry to say that it did not affect the 'opinion builders' as they were obviously willing to believe all she said and were quite fascinated by her rude way of argument. ... In her finishing words she said she had 4 things to recommend to the Icelandic government:
> 1. Make all the changes they were going to do fast, and as many at the same time as possible.
> 2. Don't discuss them with the labour movement.
> 3. Don't listen to any protests made by the labour movement or others.
> 4. Make the changes as soon as possible as there are nearly 4 years to the next election.
>
> This sounded quite grotesque when she said it, but I am sorry to say that the government has done just this. During February, we have seen the birth of 4 bills concerning the rights of public workers, public workers' pensions, the rules in the labour market, and turning the Post and teleservices into state owned enterprises.[49]

Other reports suggest that this dogmatism could also be counter-productive. One Richardson admirer told of 'the problems she had in Switzerland ... [when] Arthur Anderson took her on as a consultant there and trotted her around and sold her as part of their team and her explanations went down very well, people loved it, but when she came to the part where she said "and this is what you must do" ... it went down like a lead balloon.'[50] Such negative responses were not reflected in the public relations stories back home. It clearly riled Richardson, who was by now an avid ACT supporter, that New Zealanders were not interested in what she had to say. In March 1998 she told the *New Zealand Herald* that she could not understand 'why many New Zealanders do not see the urgent need to strip back the role of the state'. She had spoken to the Mongolians the week before, 'and they couldn't wait to get stuck in'. Here was 'a newly transformed socialist state that is embracing the New Zealand model with alacrity ... sometimes outsiders can see things more clearly than we can.'[51] There were alternative explanations for such enthusiasm: perhaps the outsiders were themselves fervent ideologues; or perhaps they had been exposed to only one version of the New Zealand model. Possibly they were less enthusiastic than Richardson liked to believe.

As a political technique, New Zealand's blitzkrieg approach generated a great deal of interest among supporters and critics of structural adjustment programmes. But that approach was feasible primarily because of New Zealand's exceptionally 'thin' political system. A single house of parliament, a government elected in a first-past-the-post system, and no written constitution meant that those who steered through the changes faced no effective political or legal barriers. Few OECD countries had such thin democracies, although those governments that showed an interest, such as Iceland and Alberta, had some similarities with New Zealand. Some World Bank clients had equally thin democracies, but encouraging them to adopt the blitzkrieg approach made a nonsense of claims that good governance was concerned with promoting genuine democracy. It was also rare for audiences to be told about the negative impact these strategies had on the political legitimacy of government, as evidenced in New Zealand by the two referenda that led to the introduction of MMP, pressure for greater transparency in negotiating international treaties, and Maori demands for effective participation in economic policy-making at both national and international level. Blitzkrieg may have succeeded in the short term, but it had left a negative long-term legacy.

▲ Selling the policies

At the level of substantive policy, international institutions were most interested in New Zealand's state sector restructuring and public sector management programmes. Policy consultancy became an export industry. Former New Zealand officials were the major purveyors. Graham Scott and Tony Dale (both ex-Treasury) and Rob Laking (formerly at the State Services Commission) worked on World Bank or IMF projects in Eastern Europe, Latin America and Asia. One Bank official commented: 'Quite a few New Zealanders are on a circuit and I bump into Graham Scott in Russia or I hear that he's been to Mongolia. So he's ... a great purveyor of the message.'[52] Other New Zealand consultants were also involved. The Tradenz office in Washington facilitated contracts with the Bank, mainly for consultants who paid Tradenz a retainer or commission.[53]

Because the IMF relied primarily on staff and local contacts, it drew on a limited panel of consultants with specific expertise. Few New Zealanders were on the panel. The World Bank funded a broader range of projects, and had a policy to increase private sector involvement, so it made more extensive use of consultants. The hiring process was decentralised, and operated through word of mouth. While there were systematic reviews of project portfolios, there seemed to be no institution-wide performance evaluation of the consultants used by Bank staff – according to one official, 'the true test is the market test, do you ever use them again?'.[54] Bank staff tended to employ and recommend consultants who shared their views. Some were personal contacts. Former politicians and officials might be employed because of what they did when in government. Others actively touted for work. This explains the uneven but extensive role played by New Zealand consultants in the Bank, but not in the Fund.

The Asian Development Bank's approach to consultants seemed more systematic, with easily accessible guidelines on their procurement and use. *ADB Business Opportunities* provides monthly information on new projects in the pipeline, procurement opportunities and contracts being awarded. This is big business: the ADB's technical assistance projects in 1997 involved 384 individual consultants and 169 teams from consulting firms. Most involved giving advice, formulating policies, programmes and projects, carrying out studies or providing training. Others ran regional conferences and workshops. The US secured almost one quarter of the 1998 contracts, worth US$33 million; Australia secured 12 percent.[55]

In 1998, New Zealand's technical assistance contracts with the ADB were worth just over US$9 million.[56] Much of this work involved expertise in restructuring. According to *ADB Business Opportunities* in April 1998, New Zealand consulting firms were short-listed for the following contracts: monitoring the implementation of education reform in Uzbekistan;[57] teacher training in Vietnam;[58] capacity building for social reform in Thailand;[59] policy and regulatory frameworks for the gas sector in the Philippines;[60] retraining legal professionals in a market economy for Mongolia;[61] pension reform in Kyrgyz;[62] implementing a gas regulatory framework in Indonesia;[63] and implementing a ports policy in India.[64]

One of the most intensive projects involving New Zealand was in Mongolia. In 1989 that country faced mass demonstrations demanding the Soviet-style command economy be replaced by free markets and democracy. The initial radical free market government was replaced in 1992 by a more pragmatic one, which gave way in 1996 to a return of the free marketeers. This turbulence reflected huge problems: economic disarray, unemployment, cuts to government subsidies and pensions, and the collapse of social services in a traditionally strong welfare state. By 1997 the government was 'back on track' under a standard three-year IMF programme. Policy dialogue involved the Asian Development Bank, the World Bank, the IMF and other agencies. According to one Soros Foundation commentator, Mongolian officials treated 'the mantra of privatisation and a free market as a panacea for economic problems'.[65] They had decided that New Zealand would be their model. The Asian Development Bank sponsored a delegation of parliamentarians and officials to New Zealand, and then to Victoria, Australia to 'see how the

New Zealand model was adapted to a different set of circumstances'.[66] Later, the Mongolian government asked the Asian Development Bank for technical assistance to help restructure its public service along New Zealand lines. The New Zealand government also offered bilateral assistance under its overseas development and aid programme. This included advice from Graham Scott on public sector restructuring. Academics also became involved, with staff from Auckland University contracted to train officials on corporatisation and privatisation.

According to one World Bank official, the Mongolian leaders faced political difficulties in making across-the-board cuts to the civil service, and saw the New Zealand approach as a solution. By redefining the purpose of government, they could say that they needed only a fraction of the staff. With Scott's assistance, legislation was drafted that included the equivalent of the State Sector Act, Public Finance Act and Fiscal Responsibility Act. But it met strong political resistance. The 1998 report of the New Zealand Overseas Development Assistance Programme (NZODA) noted: 'Progress on the reforms was severely limited in Mongolia which meant that legislation due for passage in early 1998 had still not been passed by the end of the year'.[67]

The changes also carried a high social cost. The Mongolian education union reported in May 1998 that, on the advice of the Asian Development Bank, the government was laying off 7,500 education workers at all levels in order to reduce spending on public education. Deep budget cuts had already affected school facilities and teacher salaries.[68] The ADB claimed it was sensitive to rising unemployment and poverty levels, and the deterioration of health, education and other services. But while it acknowledged the risk of further deterioration in the quality of life, and hence in public support for change, it promised only that: '*Within the framework of the strategy* necessary alignments will be made to the operational program to accommodate these shifting development emphases and priorities as economic recovery progresses'.[69] New Zealand apparently supported those priorities: between 1997 and 1999, NZODA budgeted $777,000 for advice to the Mongolian government on government restructuring, but only $158,000 'to address poverty arising from re-structuring the Mongolian economy'.[70]

The New Zealand government cooperated with the World Bank on other projects. Graham Scott was engaged by the Thai government and the Bank 'to provide a strategic overview of the reform process', and helped establish the mechanisms through which officials could develop and implement 'strategic reform'.[71] He reported that the Thai Prime Minister had an agenda of change he wanted to pursue, and that the head of the Civil Service Commission had attended a two-week course in New Zealand on restructuring. Scott recommended a set of programmes for NZODA funding, including technical advice on policy in such key areas as corporatisation and integrating budget and financial management. Reserve Bank Governor Don Brash was also assisting Thailand to restructure its central bank.

The World Bank also worked closely with the Commonwealth Secretariat to promote New Zealand's public sector management programme. The two organisations co-sponsored a seminar on privatisation, along with Ernst & Young, in Wellington in December 1996. The intention was 'to expose senior officials from Latin America and Asia to the systematic nature of the New Zealand programme and to witness the process and outcomes by visits to selected enterprises'.[72] Participants were offered the chance to interact with senior officials, government advisors, business leaders of privatised firms, and officials from other countries.[73] The seminar was largely the initiative of individual Bank staff. Feedback indicated that not all the participants believed everything they were told.

The Commonwealth Secretariat ran its own public sector management programme, with New Zealand as its model. In the early 1990s the Secretariat's management and training division had begun sponsoring dialogue among Commonwealth countries on public sector restructuring. At the Commonwealth Heads of Government Meeting (CHOGM) in Auckland in 1995, the official communiqué, heavily influenced by the New Zealand government, endorsed the initiative; in addition, New Zealand announced a special $1.5 million technical assistance fund, called the Programme on Good Governance. A senior official of the State Services Commission was seconded to help run the Secretariat's public sector management programme. Although a broad UN definition of 'good governance' was adopted, the focus was on public sector restructuring, capacity building, media training, and support for human rights activities and institutions.

The Commonwealth Secretariat offered to help its members to build their 'institutional capacity', and to access technical assistance and resources from other agencies, including the Asian Development Bank and World Bank. The programme provided 'integrated packages of assistance ... incorporating advice, training and policy analysis, through the provision of experts, consultancy services, workshops, exchange and specialised programmes, professional collaboration and project management'.[74] A loose-leaf portfolio of best practice was developed, along with a series of country profiles. New Zealand's profile, written by the State Services Commission and released in 1995, was one of the first. It told a familiar story. The country's economic position in 1984 had required 'dynamic solutions for major problems'.[75] The state cost too much, contributed too little to generating wealth, and was a dead weight on the society. It had to be exposed to market rigours. Overseas readers were reminded that New Zealand governments had set their sights very high: 'State sector reform in New Zealand has been part of a much wider endeavour to turn around a weak and over-protected economy, by changing the very character of the country.'[76]

Unlike most other official commentaries, the profile conceded that the results of the 1993 election and electoral referendum 'indicated that New Zealanders were close to, or perhaps had reached their tolerance for large scale reforms, for the time being at least'. Nevertheless, governments could not stand still; further changes would be needed to meet a rapidly changing world economy. While some initial expectations may have been unrealistic, there were major successes: greater transparency in state activities and processes, the 'liberation' of management from central controls, and new financial management and accounting systems. The public service had 'shed the stodgy, unadventurous and in some respects secretive character it had for many years'.[77] The report acknowledged the wider impact on the lives and careers of thousands of state employees: 'There is no doubt that the scale and significance of these impacts were underestimated ... Maori people experienced quite disproportionately the negative effects.'[78] It also admitted there was only anecdotal evidence of the effectiveness of the changes, but said this was usually positive. The analysis it presented of the economy was relentlessly upbeat, claiming consistent economic and employment growth. The credit rating agencies, Global Competitiveness Reports and international commentators such as the *Economist* had all praised New Zealand's achievements. Although there had been costs and mistakes, a gentler approach would not have delivered the changes that were necessary.

The report confidently concluded: 'All this indicates that New Zealand is very clearly better off for having comprehensively reformed its state sector'.[79] It identified seven key elements in this success, which reflected the Douglas/Richardson/World Bank approach to implementing structural adjustment programmes. They were:
- unflinching political determination;
- very clear objectives, agreed at the highest levels, and based on an intelligent appreciation of the community's tolerances;
- a set of comprehensive and well-integrated principles;
- sound legal architecture that re-defines the rules outright;
- a demanding but realistic timetable;
- a core of unified, highly motivated, experienced and imaginative senior public servants, provided with sufficient resources and discretion to manage implementation; and
- very effective information and public relations systems.

Prospective readers of the report – primarily officials, advisors and politicians from poorer Commonwealth countries – were assured that 'any proposed reform programme that includes all these features will almost certainly succeed and that a programme that lacks any one of them will almost certainly not'.[80]

The Secretariat also organised annual ten-day residential seminars for Commonwealth ministers and senior officials on public sector restructuring. These were sponsored by the Secretariat and the Ministry of Foreign Affairs and Trade, and run through the Graduate School of Business and Government Management at Victoria University of Wellington.[81] The New Zealand model was examined in detail, with other countries covered more briefly. The speakers were a formidable array of former and current ministers and officials who had spearheaded New Zealand's structural adjustment programme.[82] One participant in the 1997 seminar observed: 'Most of those we heard were talking the same language. Everyone was saying "my god this sounds too good, we're not hearing anybody about [the downside]". There was some criticism ... but that was very, very rare and limited'.[83]

As a more entrepreneurial initiative, special study tours of New Zealand were instigated in the mid-1990s by a New Zealand economist at the World Bank. These were run mainly on contract through the Bank's Learning Leadership Centre. Described as a 'non-traditional way of encouraging policy reform', the tours were usually initiated by a client government or by World Bank staff.[84] They came from places such as Peru, Argentina, Brazil, Mexico, Eastern Europe, Costa Rica and Bangladesh, and involved government officials, politicians, Bank staff, journalists, unionists and business leaders. Some tours specialised in areas such as agriculture, public sector management or education, although participants were told that micro-level changes worked only in the context of comprehensive macro-level change. There was no pretence at balance, in the tour programmes.[85] One background briefing paper for tour participants described the New Zealand model as 'conventional Washington consensus reforms', with four special characteristics: first, the changes had been comprehensive across all sectors, including the public sector; second, without exception, the best possible policies were implemented; third, the approach was 'non-ideological, initiated by a left-of-centre government'; and fourth, the separation of desired general outcomes from specific outputs, with performance contracting of civil servants, was novel. The paper represented New Zealand as 'a living and working example of what is possible and the economic outcomes that result from such policy and institutional reforms'.[86] The tour organiser explained:

> ... we're not necessarily selling the New Zealand model, but we're using the New Zealand experience to stimulate them to make some policy change in their country. ... And one of the big lessons that comes out of New Zealand is that change can be done, reforms can be done. ... We are satisfied if they just come away with that message ... invigorated by seeing a few examples of some things they could do. So we have found that if the policy discussion is bogged down, if a particular minister cannot get enough of his colleagues to go along with something, or he's at a loss to know what to do with something ... [the tour] will act as a catalyst to motivate and spring things to the next step.[87]

Some World Bank officials were uncomfortable with these initiatives, and the flow-on effects for the countries they worked with. One expressed concern at the organisers' lack of responsibility for how the knowledge would be applied, and the fact that tours were arranged without the full involvement of the country's programme team at the Bank:

> ... we're getting dangerously close to promoting the business of some private sector consultants who have an interest in selling the reforms rather than an interest in people reaching a measured judgement about them. I suppose in New Zealand this is giving the impression that the World Bank thinks the New Zealand model is wonderful and it's sponsoring it all over the place. But this is a private effort [from within the Bank], this is not bank policy.[88]

Other Bank staff sought to dampen their clients' enthusiasm for New Zealand, stimulated by these excursions. For example, the Latvian Prime Minister (apparently relying mainly on newspaper articles) and his finance minister (who had done a brief exposure tour arranged through the Bank) were converts to the New Zealand model. The Bank's economist responsible for Latvia, New Zealander Helen Sutch, did not believe the model was appropriate for that country as it struggled from the shackles of Soviet rule with almost no functioning government infrastructure. At the Latvian Prime Minister's request, the World Bank and the New Zealand ambassador in Moscow arranged a high-level seminar in Riga in July 1997. The ambassador presented the standard 'good news' line. Allen Schick, a public sector management specialist who had written a cautious report on New Zealand's state sector restructuring in 1996,[89] insisted that Latvia was not New Zealand, and that it needed to build its internal capacity before thinking of handing responsibility for regulation over to the market. Alexander Sundakov, the IMF's representative in Kiev, strongly disagreed. He said Latvia could and should leapfrog straight from a command economy to a deregulated economy. Sutch presented the World Bank's 1997 report on the role of the state, diplomatically stressing the importance of building the state's legal and administrative capacity in order to minimise corruption. Unusually for a World Bank seminar, the author was invited to contribute an analysis of the social impacts of the restructuring in New Zealand (under the auspices of the United Nations Development Programme).

The New Zealand government also created its own outlets for selling the New Zealand model offshore. Thailand's Mekong Institute in Khon Kaen has been described as 'New Zealand's biggest project in the region by far'.[90] Set up in 1996 with a five-year budget of NZ$12.5 million, it provides officials from the Greater Mekong Region (Cambodia, Laos, Burma, Thailand, Vietnam and the Yunnan Province of China) with 'the training necessary to confront the challenges and opportunities of moving toward more open economies and greater regional integration'.[91] In a speech to the Institute in late 1997, Minister of Foreign Affairs Don McKinnon gave 'New Zealand's experience of, and expertise in, economic and public sector reform' as one of three reasons for the government's involvement. New Zealand universities secured contracts at the Mekong Institute to run courses on public sector restructuring and 'economic transition', drawing heavily on the New Zealand experience.[92] There appeared to be little attempt to provide balance through critical perspectives on the economic and social impact of New Zealand's 'reforms'. As with previous seminars, feedback suggested that the sales pitch was not always successful. Participants in these programmes brought their own individual and shared experiences and cultural perspectives from which to assess what they were told. Doubtless they went away with new ideas, but there was no wholesale acceptance of the New Zealand approach.

Most of these activities occurred offshore. Sometimes they were reported at home, but mainly they fed the belief of New Zealand politicians, policy-makers and consultants in what they were doing. Hosting the annual meeting of the Asian Development Bank in May 1995 offered a rare opportunity to promote New Zealand in an international forum and capture some of the glory at home. In contrast to the austerity the international institutions demand of debtor governments and their people, these meetings are lavish affairs for the official participants and their accredited fellow travellers. The annual meetings of the Asian Development Bank attract around 3,000 delegates, officials and 'invited observers' – mainly financiers, consultants and contractors touting for business from Bank officials, governments and each other. Everything is scripted in advance. Governors present set pieces in plenary sessions, mainly for media and domestic political consumption. Opportunities to speak more frankly behind closed doors are limited, although most governments hold bilateral discussions. 'Observers' are treated to parallel seminars given by politicians, academics, financial analysts and agency officials on current international issues – as well as to the cocktails.

The National government eagerly used the 1995 annual meeting to showcase New Zealand's 'success story' to the international financial community and fellow governments through a series of speeches, seminars and displays. Offering to share New Zealand's expertise and the lessons of the past decade, Prime Minister Jim Bolger invited 'others of like mind to join us in the most exciting small economy anywhere'.[93] Some delegates were enthusiastic; others were sceptical. The meeting will be remembered by most New Zealanders and the bored international media for two other events. Students, human rights NGOs and unemployed workers' groups took to the streets, protesting against New Zealand's economic policies and abuses by foreign governments. The police over-reacted in full view of the television cameras. The foreign media were also fascinated by several high-profile land occupations, including that of Pakaitore (Moutua Gardens) in Wanganui. At a press conference called by Maori nationalists to condemn unregulated foreign investment and the Asian Development Bank, Maori lawyer Annette Sykes warned visiting financiers:

> ... it's about time you sat down and talked to us because the present illegal government has no warrant to deal with resources, neither for the past, nor the present, and certainly not for the future. ... If they do not acknowledge the status that we enjoy nationally and internationally within law, then they will be facing extreme acts of terrorism and activism amongst us, and it is about time they changed.[94]

The press conference brought threats of sedition charges against Sykes and fellow activist Mike Smith,[95] although the government wisely retreated. Both episodes showed the potential such meetings create for heated confrontation and international embarrassment. With even greater fanfare, New Zealand hosted the Commonwealth Heads of Government Meeting later that year, at which the government's Good Governance initiative to operate through the Commonwealth Secretariat was announced.

▲ *'Structural adjustment' diplomacy*

These promotional activities have been complemented by the overseas speeches of politicians and diplomats. They tend to follow a standard format. Each begins with the image of a moribund economy teetering close to bankruptcy in 1984, then describes the government's key policy 'reforms' and commitment to the so-called 'fundamentals': an open economy, limited government, fiscal prudence and labour market flexibility. Some speakers treat these as self-evident virtues, and make sweeping but unsubstantiated claims about economic growth and recovery. Others cite economic indicators, although the statistics are crafted to bolster the image of 'success'. Negative indicators, such as the level of foreign debt, the current account deficit, and prolonged periods of stagnation and recession, are almost always ignored. There is no mention of the serious deterioration of parts of the country's social and physical infrastructure, nor of the accompanying social distress, widening inequality (especially for Maori) and deepening poverty.

A typical example is John Wood's speech to the Wisconsin Forum in February 1997, when he was New Zealand's ambassador to Washington.[96] Entitled 'New Zealand: First to See the Light?', it began: 'New Zealand now has one of the most open and competitive economies in the world. ... To me, the benefits of this common openness are self-evident. Thirteen years on there are few New Zealanders who would want our country to go back to the way things were.' After outlining the background and the major policy changes, Wood set out his version of the results. As shown below, these were either so selective as to be misleading, or simply wrong:

- *The country was now enjoying a period of sustained economic growth.* GDP growth for 1996/97 was only 2.4 percent,[97] and during the first quarter of 1997 (when Wood was speaking) the economy actually contracted by 0.2 percent.[98]
- *Actual and projected real GDP growth for mid-1993 to 1999 was an average 4.1 percent, whereas in the period 1976 to 1990 it averaged 1.4 percent.* The six-year period 1993-99 combined the short-lived recovery with Treasury's optimistic future projections; was compared to a fourteen-year period from 1976-90 that included the six years of Rogernomics; and omitted the inconvenient recession from 1990 to mid-1992. (See Appendix: Figure 1.)
- *Underlying inflation had levelled at around 2 percent since 1991.* Excluded from this account is the huge hike in inflation during the mid-1980s; the recessionary impact of bringing it rapidly to below one percent in late 1991; the huge speculative financial flows that resulted from the Reserve Bank's monetary policy in the mid-1990s; and the ongoing damage to exporters from a seriously overvalued exchange rate.
- *Unemployment had fallen from 11 percent when the decade began to 5.9 percent.* The official rate for 1996/97 was actually 6.5 percent and predicted to rise to 7.0 percent in the following year;[99] unemployment had peaked at 11.1 percent in March 1992 under National; and even the low 5.9 percent was still 50 percent higher than in 1987, when the Household Labour Force Survey began.
- *New jobs were being created at a rate of 5 percent a year.* These new jobs were predominantly part time; New Zealand still had no more full-time jobs in 1997 than it had ten years before.

- *For the first time in 20 years the government achieved a budget surplus, representing 3.3 percent of GDP, and projected a surplus of 5.9 percent in the year ending June 2000.* This was correct, but such projections are notoriously unreliable; the Budget Policy Statement 1999 projected a *deficit* of 1.3 percent for the year to June 2000.
- *Public debt had been reduced from 52 percent to 30 percent of GDP.* Again, the debt had peaked in 1992 under National, after seven years of radical restructuring; much of the reduction had come from the sale of assets.
- *All foreign currency debt will be repaid this year.* Government was repaying only *official net* foreign currency debt; private overseas debt and net foreign equity ownership had materially increased. (See Appendix: Figure 3.)

Wood offered further evidence of New Zealand's 'success': credit rating upgrades from Moody's and Standard and Poor's; top placing in the World Competitiveness Report (sic) for 'government policies most supportive of business'; fourth ranking in the Heritage Foundation's Index of Economic Freedom; and 'least corrupt country' in the Transparency International survey. As noted in Chapter 2, the *raison d'être* of all these agencies is to promote precisely the policies New Zealand has implemented, so their endorsement lacks any semblance of objectivity.

Politicians have been equally cavalier in what they say overseas (as well as at home) about the New Zealand experiment. The *New Straits Times*, for example, reported in June 1998 that Trade Negotiations Minister Lockwood Smith had advised the Malaysia New Zealand Business Council (Sarawak Chapter) to 'use New Zealand's experience in reviving its ailing economy in the 1970s and early 1980s as a guide to make the necessary reforms for economic recovery. "Our experience shows that it is the country which makes the reforms fastest that will get the biggest returns the earliest".'[100] Smith apparently omitted to tell his audience that the New Zealand economy was then in a period of negative growth, with rising unemployment, foreign debt at over 100 percent of GDP, and the current account deficit matching the deficits of the East Asian economies that had recently collapsed – or that Australia, which had taken a more pragmatic approach to restructuring, had produced more sustained economic growth since 1984 (see Chapter 10).

It is not surprising that citizens who opposed their governments making such changes began to seek out alternative sources of information. Groups of trade unionists from a number of OECD countries came to see for themselves the impact of deregulation on unions and on workers' lives. Senior officials responsible for social services in Swedish regional governments visited twice, producing lengthy reports that warned against adopting similar measures in Sweden.[101] Groups of Japanese from regional government, state enterprises and business sought a cross-section of views, and frequently went away unconvinced of the benefits to Japan of the New Zealand model. New Zealand critics of the approach were invited to give lecture tours in countries where the New Zealand model was being sold – in 1997 and 1998, for example, the author spoke at specially arranged conferences or undertook lecture tours in Australia, Canada, the UK, Iceland, Guyana, Japan, Latvia, Lithuania, Norway, Sweden and the Philippines.

▲ COMPETING PARADIGMS

Overseas interest in New Zealand's restructuring needs to be seen in the broader context of debates about the role of states and markets. New Zealand governments had assumed an extreme position, which they then sought to implement. Those who shared their views were eager to seize on evidence from New Zealand that this could be done. Others, however, were sceptical, not simply because the model was not appropriate to the circumstances of certain countries, but because they disagreed with the paradigm of self-regulating markets.

Once the Cold War was over, and the battle between capitalism and socialism appeared to have been won, a new conflict over the appropriate model of capitalism took its place, fought out mainly between the US and Japan. For the 40 years after the Second World War, the US had easily dominated the international economic arena, including the international financial institutions. By the mid-1980s, however, Japan had become the second biggest shareholder in the World Bank's two main lending bodies, and the main co-financier of its loans; by 1992 it was the second biggest shareholder in the IMF. Despite this prominence, Japan was consistently criticised by the US for undermining World Bank and IMF policies. International relations specialist Robert Gilpin suggested that the US viewed Japan as a special threat 'because it is the first non-Western and non-liberal society to outcompete them. Whereas Western economies are based on belief in the superior efficiency of the free market and individualism, the market and the individual in Japan are not relatively autonomous but are deeply embedded in a powerful nonliberal culture and social system.'[102]

Robert Wade has documented the growing tension between the ideological commitment of the US to free markets, with extensive liberalisation and privatisation, and Japan's support for the market-guiding role of the state (especially in industrial policy) which involved subsidised and targeted loans as part of a regional strategy of industrialisation. Japan insisted on its economic strategy being taken seriously in the World Bank, and eventually secured reluctant approval for a study of the East Asian Model. This was published in September 1993 as *The East Asian Miracle: Economic Growth and Public Policy.*[103] Employing what Wade considered a skewed approach to the evidence, the report attributed Asia's economic success to fiscal and market discipline, rather than industrial policy and government intervention. Wade described the final document as 'heavily weighted towards the Bank's continuing advice to low-income countries to follow the "market-friendly" policies apparently vindicated by East Asia's success.' But there were enough concessions to Japan's pro-active approach for him to conclude that, while 'the Bank emerged with its traditional paradigm largely unscathed, this particular episode may even be looked back on as an early landmark in the intellectual ascendancy ... of Japanese views about the role of the state'.[104]

Parallel battles were fought out in the Asian Development Bank, where Japan held the presidency. At a special seminar on 'good governance' during the Bank's annual meeting in 1997, these competing paradigms were centre-stage. Ruth Richardson was the keynote speaker.[105] She argued that sound economic policy and implementation were more important than a country's natural resources or endowments, and vital if the country was to realise the potential of such cultural factors as a commitment to the capitalist ethic. New Zealand had learned this lesson. Its new public sector management model of transparency, accountability and private sector disciplines had 'brought world acclaim'. The government's role as economic participant had been reduced to setting the legal framework within which open and competitive markets could operate. Services were delivered through the private sector. Privatisation within deregulated markets had been designed to prevent 'policy slippage' if political fashions changed, while the government had bound itself by law to continue 'sound' fiscal and monetary policy. Free and open financial markets could be relied on to pressure governments to change any policies that were 'misaligned'. The Ombudsman and the Official Information Act provided transparency. Political commitment, a clear strategy and high-quality implementation by a core of people had been the key to success, alongside effective communication and a sense of urgency. The failures had been in health and education, where coherence and boldness had given way to powerful vested interests that made progress difficult. In support of her case, Richardson cited endorsements of New Zealand by the OECD, the World Economic Forum's competitiveness reports, the *Economist*, Transparency International and the *Financial Times*. Other governments, she said, should follow suit.

In a strong rejoinder, the director-general of Japan's finance ministry, Isao Kubota, warned: 'so long as we base our analysis on false assumptions

– that the government is a necessary evil, that the government and private sector are enemies by nature, and that the smaller the government, the better – we may not be able to realize the full potentialities of the country.'[106] He argued that markets sometimes failed because of unequal access to information, lack of expertise, irrationality and short-term motives. They produced externalities that required governments to intervene for the benefit of society. Beyond that, successful economic development required an active state. Governments also had a legitimate, albeit difficult, role in building strategically important industries that had a potential comparative advantage. Governments could help create conditions for development by changing people's ideas, behaviour and savings patterns, and by fostering debate on policy aims and measures. A government also had to maintain economic, social and political stability. Kubota insisted that the different conditions in rich and poorer countries required tolerance of diversity. He concluded: 'Because policy measures largely hinge on cultural, economic, and social structures of the country, successfully reflecting the will of the people is important, and the government can play a vital role'.[107]

These tensions came to the fore again in 1998 in the debate over who should take responsibility for addressing the Asian financial crisis, and how. The stakes were high: the future of the 'Washington consensus' and of global free market orthodoxy. The IMF was accused of failing to recognise that speculative investment in Asian countries, supported by the corrupt practices of some governments, was creating unsustainable current account deficits and private sector debt. Indeed, the Fund's annual report on South Korea in 1997 praised its continued impressive macroeconomic performance and enviable fiscal record.[108] The Asian bubble burst so spectacularly that the market's 'self-correction' became a crash. The IMF put together a series of rescue packages for the Thai, Indonesian and South Korean economies. The World Bank, the Asian Development Bank and individual governments (including that of New Zealand) played a role. The rescue effort required a replenishment of IMF funds. Asked to contribute US$18.5 billion, the US Congress demanded committee hearings on the functioning, financing, accountability and effectiveness of the IMF. Opponents of the IMF ranged from the right-wing Heritage Foundation and American Enterprise Institute to progressives such as Ralph Nader's Public Citizen group and Walden Bello from the Centre for the Global South in Bangkok.[109] All objected to the secrecy and lack of accountability of the Fund and of US Treasury officials. The Fund was portrayed as serving giant banks, global corporations, wealthy investors and corrupt local tyrants; the progressive voices also condemned the IMF's policies for causing further economic damage and human misery.

This sense of outrage was fuelled by the IMF's approach to the Asian crisis. The rescue packages had imposed requirements of fiscal austerity, high interest rates, depreciation, deregulation of the financial sector, and removal of restrictions on capital flows. But the formula was designed to deal with excessive government debt and high inflation; the problem in Asia was speculative local and foreign investment, private debt, and the imminent collapse of the internal economy. The IMF's intervention made the crisis worse, and provoked a deepening recession.[110] An internal memorandum admitted that the directive to shut sixteen insolvent banks in Indonesia had caused the run on the currency that plunged the country's financial system into crisis.[111] In January 1999 the Fund conceded that it had 'badly misgauged' the severity of the collapse.[112]

The rescue packages had a perverse impact. Financiers and speculators who had fed the Asian frenzy, and knew the risks they were taking, largely escaped the consequences. As with the IMF bail-out of the Mexican economy in 1994, and the debt crises in the 1980s, money was recycled from mainly US taxpayers via IMF loans to debtor governments to international commercial banks.[113] The foreign loans of private companies became the liability of the debtor government; every loan to those governments had to be repaid on pain of losing the IMF's stamp of approval. Bello condemned this as 'socialism for the global financial elite'.[114] The restructuring packages were designed to attract foreign investors back under even less restraint than before. Yet nothing required them to engage in sound investments, and there was no reason for them to enter such unstable and recessionary countries except to benefit from 'fire sales' of government assets or collapsed companies.[115] The US Trade Representative told Congress in February 1998 that she expected the changes to create new opportunities for US firms.[116]

The IMF's demand that the borrowing governments reduce subsidies on basics such as food and fuel fell most harshly on the poor, who already faced rising prices and unemployment. Higher interest rates made it impossible for many solvent local firms to keep afloat as the economy contracted, export returns fell and import costs increased. South Korea's media coined the term 'IMF suicides' for those who could not survive psychologically or financially. Sixty percent of the population of Indonesia, the world's third most populous country, were suddenly plunged into poverty. Riots and political instability threatened the viability of governments there and elsewhere.[117] Under pressure, the IMF slightly relaxed its fiscal demands. But new economic crises emerged. Russia defaulted on its IMF repayments in September 1998, and had no prospect of repaying its long-term debt. In 1999, financial instability spread to Latin America. The Brazilian currency collapsed, requiring another huge bail-out.[118] But Fund officials could not concede there was any basic problem with their economic model. Indeed, Managing Director Michel Camdessus called for a stronger IMF role in coordinating macroeconomic policies, and developing and implementing monetary reform. This would require more money and extended powers.[119]

As the largest individual contributor to the rescue package, Japan wanted to build on the existing strengths of the East Asian economies – high savings, high standards of education, active technology transfer and export-oriented trade. Japan's proposal for an Asian Monetary Fund, as a more flexible and less deflationary alternative to the IMF's approach, was opposed by both the US and the IMF because it would undermine the latter's ability to demand significant policy changes. The *Financial Times* reported US officials as saying they would 'use the opportunity provided by the crisis to force radical structural reform on other countries that would amount to what some critics see as an Americanization of the world economy'.[120] Meanwhile, the US blamed Japan's domestic policies for intensifying the global economic downturn, and insisted that it liberalise its finance sector and accept more US exports. The Japanese maintained pressure for a regional approach to the crisis, and announced their own Miyazawa Plan (named after the Japanese finance minister) in late 1998, which an unhappy US belatedly joined.[121] They also provided the funds for a Tokyo-based Asian Development Bank Institute that began promoting alternative approaches to the IMF's prescriptions.[122] The IMF remained in charge overall, but the US was visibly losing its grip on the international financial institutions as a vehicle for advancing its interests and ideological preferences.

Meanwhile, the US faced dissent within its own ranks. In January 1998, the World Bank's chief economist, former Clinton advisor Joseph Stiglitz, publicly criticised the IMF's approach to the Asian crisis. He described the Washington consensus as 'neither necessary nor sufficient, either for macro-stability or longer-term development', and implicitly attacked the IMF's approach in East Asia.[123] His speech was quickly contradicted by the Bank's president, James Wolfensohn, who issued a firm endorsement of the IMF's policy programme and promised that the Bank would do its share to see it implemented.[124] In questioning the Washington consensus, Stiglitz was challenging the international orthodoxy that had prevailed for almost twenty years. The champions of the orthodoxy fought back, but there was no guarantee that they would win.

▲ REFLECTIONS

Exporting the New Zealand model has helped to embed it in a number of ways. First, it confirmed the belief among its adherents that they were indeed leading the world, and fuelled their determination to remain true to the cause. Second, it conferred an aura of international authority which enabled them to disregard the challenges and lack of support at home. Prime Minister Jenny Shipley's address to the Global Forum on Reinventing Government, chaired by US Vice-President Al Gore in Washington in January 1999, concluded: 'While the majority of politicians in each of these [Labour and National] governments have grasped the need for reform, we have not always succeeded in capturing the imagination of voters in terms of the need for and benefits of reform. This will be a never-ending challenge for all governments.'[125]

Third, it created a cadre of serving politicians and diplomats, former politicians and officials, consulting firms, university departments and international agencies who had a vested interest in promoting and sustaining the 'good news' story. Collectively, they formed the kind of élite which the structural adjustment theorists suggested would sound the alarm at any hint of deviation from the policy model.[126]

At the same time, however, many within that cadre were supplicants to external agencies whose patronage was not secure. New Zealand-style structural adjustment was a fashion. By 1999 it still enjoyed an extensive following, partly as a result of attempts to export the 'success story', including through New Zealand's overseas aid programmes, and largely through a concerted promotion by some World Bank staff to their poor country clientele. But its core principles faced a determined challenge from Japan, and were even under fire from within the World Bank. The alternatives being offered were variations on a theme. But because New Zealand's position was so extreme, any such shift in economic orthodoxy would be enough to deprive the New Zealand model of its external legitimacy.

4 ▲ 'Free' Investment

The goal of a global free market is to create a self-regulating system where goods, capital and ideas – but only selected people – move freely around the world. A 'free' investment regime means that owners of money have the right to move it as, when and where they please. In practice, most countries still actively regulate foreign investment. Not so New Zealand. Successive governments since 1984 have committed themselves to establishing an unfettered foreign direct investment (FDI) regime, deregulated the financial markets, lifted exchange controls and floated the currency. This regime was founded on a belief that unrestricted movements of capital would see investment flow to the most profitable locations, ensuring the efficient allocation of the world's scarce resources. More investment would, in turn, enhance economic growth, consumer choice, jobs and living standards for all.

This is the orthodox international line. According to the OECD, 'Governments welcome FDI as a source of capital and innovation and as a means to promote competition and economic efficiency.'[1] The theory says that imposing restrictions on – or offering incentives to – foreign investors will distort the equilibrium of capital markets. So New Zealand opted for an effectively free investment regime, backed by 'sound fundamentals' of minimal regulation, open competition, low inflation and taxes, flexible labour markets and free trade. While New Zealand governments put the theory into practice, those with whom New Zealand was competing for investment generally did not.

International investment can take different forms. Some investors specialise in short-term speculative investment, often betting on changes in the value of a currency and, if their fund is big enough, causing such changes to occur. Alternatively, institutional investors such as insurance or pension funds spread their investments across the share-markets of many countries, quitting their portfolio in one company or country when they anticipate better returns elsewhere. Other investors, usually transnational enterprises, engage in foreign direct investment by taking a controlling stake in an existing corporation or asset;[2] privatisations are especially appealing. The goal is often to expand their international business, but not always. Predatory investment companies take over undervalued or poorly managed firms, strip them of their assets and move on. It is relatively rare these days for a foreign investor to enter any country with a long-term commitment and build something from scratch.

The changes introduced since 1984 have made New Zealand a playground for all these kinds of investment. New Zealand companies have also set forth to make their fortunes in the world. For the champions of globalisation within government and business there are no downsides to foreign investment. Opening the doors, they insist, will bring new investment, more jobs, access to technology, and greater integration into the global economy. By the end of the 1990s, however, there is no evidence that unregulated foreign investment has brought those promised benefits – or that it ever will. In the process, ownership of much of New Zealand's infrastructure and natural resource base (other than land), has passed into foreign hands, often those of major transnational enterprises. In 1999, overseas companies control key areas of the country's economic, social and cultural life – daily newspapers and radio, petrol, airlines, railways, supermarkets, computer hardware and software, telecommunications, office supplies and equipment, the book trade, pharmaceuticals, biscuits, flour production, brewing. All the major banks and eight of the ten top insurance companies are overseas-owned.

International financiers have also taken advantage of the floating exchange rate and finance market deregulation to speculate on the currency and in share and property markets, fuelling a 'get rich quick' mentality which diverts capital from longer-term productive investment. The country has been left with a massive overseas debt, foreign dominance of the share-market, and a burgeoning external current account deficit. There are some clear lessons for New Zealand from elsewhere in the world. The collapse of the East Asian economies, for example, confirmed the dangers of unrestricted foreign investment and unregulated flows of speculative finance. International commentators have reluctantly conceded the folly of letting capital run free, and begun talking of the need to re-regulate. New Zealand's economic policy-makers have not.

This chapter examines New Zealand's open investment policy, questions its sustainability, and discusses proposals for the re-regulation of foreign investment, equity markets and short-term capital flows.

▲ FOREIGN DIRECT INVESTMENT

Foreign capital has historically played a large role in the New Zealand economy. As a settlement colony, New Zealand initially attracted absentee investors, especially from Britain, who speculated in land. Other capital inflows went mainly to finance the colonial government's debt. By 1886 this stood at £71 million. The government had to continue borrowing to service the interest and repayments on the debt.[3] Further foreign investment, often from Australia using English money, centred on the finance and insurance sector. After the advent of refrigerated shipping in the 1880s, British interests began investing in New Zealand's primary industries. The country's focus on agricultural exports meant there was minimal foreign investment in domestic industry. Government was the primary funder of infrastructural development, which was financed by more borrowing from overseas.

Even so, the ratio of private foreign investment to 'national income' (gross national product) in 1948/49 was still just 10.9 percent.[4] The growth of domestic protection in the 1950s attracted new investors, especially from the US, who sought to circumvent New Zealand's trade barriers by producing locally. These investors faced major constraints. The state reserved to itself many areas of economic endeavour. The exchange rate was fixed, and individuals and companies needed Reserve Bank approval to move money in and out of the country. Overseas investors had to meet a 'national interest' test, and there were controls on foreign investment in strategic industries. Regulations restricted who could be a bank, what banks could do, and even the interest they could charge. These controls were later condemned for preventing local companies from expanding offshore, and for limiting foreign investment in New Zealand. They were also a nuisance for travellers, and restricted consumer choice. But the economy was stable and growing, and the policy reflected the prevailing international orthodoxy.

Some economists still viewed the level of foreign investment as dangerously high. In his 1971 book *Takeover New Zealand*, former Secretary of Trade and Industry Bill Sutch expressed concern that 'in the last decade, foreign finance, now coupled at the supranational level with international industry has vastly expanded its power in New Zealand'.[5] The foreign-influenced finance sector especially had the capacity to frustrate a government's credit policies, upset the balance of payments, and exercise control over industry by threatening to disinvest.

In the late 1970s the shape of New Zealand business had begun to change.[6] The traditional oligarchy, including companies such as Fletcher Holdings and Wright Stephenson, had begun reorganising and was eager to expand. Local investment opportunities were limited. More lucrative opportunities offshore required the Muldoon government's permission. This did happen; for example, Fletchers was given approval to buy Crown Zellerbach Canada, a major British Columbian forest company, in 1982. But the constraints were frustrating for an increasingly aggressive corporate sector, including the new breed of investment firm epitomised by Brierley Investments Ltd.

The fourth Labour government (1984–1990) began 'opening the economy' by removing restrictions on outward investment. Major companies took the opportunity to list offshore, initially in Australia but later further afield. Fletcher Challenge claimed it had to raise equity overseas because the domestic capital market was too small, and prudential requirements meant that major investors and fund managers had to spread their exposure. Foreign direct investment by Kiwi businesses became a source of national pride. Like our yachties in the America's Cup, New Zealand companies were showing they could foot it with the world.

Sometimes their international operations raised eyebrows. In 1988 a *Frontline* television documentary exposed the Chilean operations of the Dairy Board, Carter Holt Harvey and Fletcher Challenge to public scrutiny.[7] Fletcher Challenge forestry workers were shown axing trees while wearing open-toed sandals, and living in rat-infested huts. Carter Holt chairman Richard Carter said he did not believe that torture was still taking place under the Pinochet regime, 'in a government-condoned sense'. Carter and Ron Trotter (chair of Fletcher Challenge and the Business Roundtable) both argued that Chilean-style labour laws were needed at home. These overseas investments assisted the Business Roundtable's agenda in other ways: Fletchers was able to supply customers from its Canadian operations during a prolonged lockout of 600 workers at Kawerau in late 1985, in an early assault by Roundtable companies on the militant unions.

Major manufacturers moved offshore too. Treasury thought this was 'quite sensible' if their goods could be produced more efficiently elsewhere. Its officials argued that the manufacturing sector needed to respond to changing international conditions, and that traditional manufacturing was being replaced in most OECD countries by the rapidly expanding service industries.[8]

The Labour government began reducing restrictions on inward investment in mid-1987 by raising the threshold at which investments required Overseas Investment Commission approval, from $500,000 to $2 million in value; in 1989 it was lifted again to $10 million. The Commission, located in the Reserve Bank, operated on the presumption that investment applications should be granted and compliance costs minimised. Approval requirements became perfunctory, except in the areas of broadcasting, commercial fishing within the exclusive economic zone, and rural land. Despite the loosening of restrictions, investment hardly flooded in. Indeed, there was a net capital outflow in late 1987 through 1988 (following the share-market crash) which averaged 1.7 percent of GDP. Most of that outflow was to Australia, whose exporters now had easier access to New Zealand through tariff reductions and CER.

The privatisation of some of the country's largest companies, beginning in 1988, gave foreign investment a boost.[9] Minister of Finance Roger Douglas and Treasury officials saw no logical reason for excluding foreign buyers; indeed, the sales were structured in ways that made overseas participation inevitable. The Labour Cabinet was initially somewhat hesitant about selling to foreigners. Following a public outcry, the proposed sale of Petrocorp to British Gas in early 1988 was abandoned for allegedly technical legal reasons, and a sale immediately announced to a Fletcher Challenge subsidiary. Such sensitivities dissipated as the Post Office Bank, Development Finance Corporation, Tourist Hotel Corporation and cutting rights to state forests went partly or wholly into foreign ownership. Telecom was sold to a consortium led by US companies Bell Atlantic and Ameritech just before the 1990 election. Many of these state assets were sold cheaply in a depressed market while the exchange rate was falling.

Coming to power in October 1990, National enthusiastically picked up where Labour left off. In mid-1991 Cabinet approved a strategic framework that would 'proclaim that New Zealand unambiguously welcomes foreign investment'.[10] Overseas missions would target banks and corporations with a generic promotion campaign, complemented by investment seminars and ministerial tours. A series of promotions was planned for Minister of Finance Ruth Richardson to Japan, Korea, Hong Kong and Singapore. National continued the pure free market line that investors wanted a deregulated economy based on the fundamentals of price stability, low tax, fiscal restraint and flexible labour markets. It rejected active investment incentives. Minister of Foreign Affairs Don McKinnon confidently told Tokyo investors: 'Our greatest incentive to investment is an economy that has taken the process of regulatory reform further than any other.'[11] A 1992 Cabinet document told the Prime Minister a different story: there was a global perception that New Zealand was not a competitive investment destination without explicit investment incentives.[12] Such suggestions, which emerged periodically in investment surveys, were anathema to officials and ministers alike. The Cabinet document also noted the reluctance of some business sectors to recognise the benefits from foreign direct investment.

If business was ambivalent, the public was becoming quite hostile.

Antipathy was fuelled by a further round of asset sales to overseas buyers, notably the Bank of New Zealand and New Zealand Rail, and the Asian buy-up of prime commercial and residential property. Local firms were seen as easy targets for foreign takeovers, and there were fears that foreigners were acquiring rural land. In a *National Business Review* poll in 1992, 34 percent of those surveyed felt foreign investment was already too high.[13] These attitudes hardened as the government embraced Asia. Its eight-year strategic plan, Asia 2000, was intended to excite local firms about business opportunities in East and South-east Asia, and redirect the country's culture and identity towards a new economic destiny. While McKinnon proposed 'a giant, dramatic leap into Asia',[14] Prime Minister Jim Bolger talked of developing a 'true Asia consciousness', and even called New Zealand an 'Asian nation'.[15] A hostile public reaction forced a rapid revamping of the vision, to one of an Asia Pacific community whose member states maintained their own identity, values and social norms.

Part of this new direction was an immigration policy that targeted wealthy Asians. Maori nationalists objected to being further marginalised by another influx of immigrants, and criticised the government for failing to involve them in major policy decisions that directly affected them.[16] Asian immigration was equally unpopular with non-Maori. In a *National Business Review* poll in April 1992, just under half the respondents felt there were too many Asian immigrants in the country, even though two-thirds thought they made a positive contribution. Opposition was strongest among women, young people and low income earners.[17] Acknowledging the underlying concerns about economic control, McKinnon promised a 'better understanding [of] what we as a nation want' – but not a change of direction. He insisted that a strategic framework (such as Asia 2000) would enable New Zealanders to 'retain clear and focused control of our national goals in the Asia Pacific region'.[18]

Fears of an Asian economic takeover had a strong element of racism, reminiscent of the hostility shown by white settlers to Chinese and Indian immigrants since last century, and to Pacific Islanders from the 1970s.[19] They were also unsubstantiated. Asian investment centred on commercial property; the bulk of this had been purchased after 1987, and amounted to around $1.5 billion up to 1992 and over $1 billion in 1993.[20] In the 1993/94 year, around three-quarters of property deals worth more than $5 million in the central business districts were to offshore purchasers. Buyers from Singapore and Hong Kong accounted for almost half of this.[21] But most foreign investment in New Zealand still came from Australia and the US. The *Financial Times* reported in August 1993 that: 'US investment [in New Zealand] has risen sharply following publicity there about the success New Zealand has had in implementing policies favoured by the so-called Chicago monetarist school of economics.'[22] It pointed out that Bell Atlantic and Ameritech now controlled Telecom, International Paper managed (and later majority-owned) Carter Holt Harvey, Wisconsin Central managed and part-owned the national railway, and other US companies had substantial interests in plantation forestry and manufacturing.

The populist backlash against Asian investors diverted the debate on foreign investment from more serious issues. Between 1989/90 and 1993/94 – primarily during National's term of office – overseas ownership of New Zealand companies (defined as 25 percent equity or more) increased 145 percent, from $13.7 billion to $33.6 billion. This was three quarters of the estimated value of all the assets of the Crown as at 1994, which were then valued at $43.4 billion.[23] The pace of foreign investment was quickening. The inflow of direct investment in 1992/93 had been $4.4 billion, more than twice the previous year's figure. There was another surge in investment approvals by the Overseas Investment Commission in 1993, up 37 percent on 1992. The main target areas were manufacturing ($3 billion), communication and telecommunications ($1.9 billion) and commercial leasing ($1.8 billion). Approvals for rural land sales into full foreign ownership increased from $44 million to $138 million, reflecting a growth in purchases by US and Asian buyers, mainly for conversion to forestry. There was also a noticeable shift to foreign-owned firms employing fewer than 50 people, and a marked increase in the capital to labour ratio. Few foreigners applied to invest in new businesses that created real jobs. The vast majority of approvals related to the takeover of existing companies or the acquisition of assets.[24] It should be noted that these approvals were for proposed investments only. How many of them led to actual purchases is not known, as the Commission does not keep such figures.[25]

Applications for approvals were not scrutinised in depth by the Commission. In response to an inquiry from the Ombudsman, the Minister of Finance said this was not due to a lack of adequate resources. It reflected the Overseas Investment Commission's role in the wider context of government policy, which was 'to foster the development of strong international linkages'.[26] In fact the Commission did not decline a single application between 1991 and 1995. (It declined one in 1996, and six, all land-related, in 1997.)

By 1994, the top ten companies by turnover (excluding four that were cooperatives, statutory marketing boards or state-owned enterprises) were between 30 and 100 percent overseas-owned.[27] Foreign shareholdings in all three of the largest 'New Zealand' companies were well above 40 percent. The massive profits secured by foreign investors in 1993/94 fed the public perception that the country was being used. *Foreign Control Watchdog* reported in December 1994 that:

> Wisconsin Central picked up New Zealand Rail for next to nothing, after decades of the taxpayer shouldering its losses, and promptly started reaping profits. The cutting rights to the publicly owned State forests were sold for a song to both local and international Big Business. Now New Zealand pinus radiata is flavour of the month and prices have rocketed. Carter Holt Harvey, New Zealand's biggest forest owner, is now American-owned. It announced a $325 million record profit for 1993/94. Seven TNCs between them reported a 1993/94 profit of $1 billion. Fletcher Challenge, which is over 40% foreign owned, set a NZ record with its 1993/94 $675 million profit (of which it paid all of $13 million in tax). ... Telecom NZ ... has announced a record profit every year. For 1993/94 it was $528 million. ... Those are examples of huge sums of money leaving New Zealand, money made from taking over productive New Zealand enterprises.[28]

In 1995 the National government moved to assist foreign investors further by streamlining the process. Without public consultation, it introduced an amendment to the Overseas Investment Act 1973 which specified the criteria for consent to applications from foreign investors. Previously the criteria had been administrative, and could be varied relatively easily. This amendment allowed investors in assets other than land to invest as of right, provided they showed business experience and acumen, were financially committed to the investment, and were of good character. No criterion of national interest applied. It also eased the remaining restrictions on the sale of rural land and offshore islands. For those applications, the relevant ministers were required to consider whether the investment would, or was likely to, create new job opportunities or retain existing jobs otherwise under threat; introduce new business skills or technology; develop new export markets or increase New Zealand's market access; increase market competition, efficiency or productivity; introduce additional investment for development; or increase the processing of primary products. The ministers could consider any other matters they saw fit. Where land was being used for agricultural purposes, they were also required to consider whether experimental research would be carried out, who controlled the company, and what use would be made of the land. It was never explained why these factors were relevant to land sales but not to other types of investment.

The media were outraged when the 1995 Amendment Bill came back from the select committee containing draconian new secrecy provisions. These would allow all information connected with an investment application to the Overseas Investment Commission that was not otherwise in the public domain, including the fact of the application, to be kept secret, possibly forever. Publication would attract a maximum fine of $30,000 or twelve months' imprisonment for individuals or a $100,000 fine for companies. As confidentiality powers under the Official Information Act were already widely used by the Commission to prevent disclosure, the secrecy provisions would have made it almost impossible to monitor foreign investment. Under pressure, the government deleted them.

The 1995 amendment to the Overseas Investment Act also hit a raw nerve with the public. In a *National Business Review* poll, half of those surveyed did not want land sold to foreigners, and would support a law to ban foreign ownership of land in New Zealand. Opposition was strongest among women, students, retired people and the unemployed. But even 37 percent of professionals, managers and technicians said that foreign land ownership should not be allowed, and 44 percent wanted it banned. Over 40 percent of National voters were opposed to such sales.[29] Maori opposition to foreign control was also becoming more vocal, among both pan-Maori groups and tribes. Government was selling off resources that were subject to claims against the Crown for breaches of the Treaty of Waitangi. These resources were hard enough to recover when held by the Crown. Once ownership moved offshore, they were likely to be lost forever. Maori claimants insisted that government should settle its internal obligations to them before selling the country's treasures overseas and repaying its foreign creditors. At the Asian Development Bank's annual meeting in May 1995, foreign investors were warned that failure to consult with the tangata whenua (people of the land) could see dams blown up and forests burnt down.[30]

Both the Alliance and New Zealand First began campaigning aggressively on the issue. New Zealand First leader Winston Peters declared: 'We are fighting for the future of New Zealand to ensure that our children can say, with every certainty, "New Zealand is ours".'[31] He did not oppose foreign investment, only foreign control. The Alliance supported genuine foreign investment, but opposed the transfer of assets to foreigners who neither created nor extended the country's productive base. The Alliance initially reaped most of the political benefit of this campaign. Peters subsequently picked up support with his allegations of corrupt practices by the corporate élite, centred on the Cook Islands tax schemes.[32] Labour sat uncomfortably on the fence, welcoming foreign investment generally but drawing the line at foreign ownership of rural land.

In October 1995, the New Zealand branch of the American Chamber of Commerce came to the government's defence with a report that stressed the importance of foreign investment to the New Zealand economy. This was circulated to political parties, government departments and business groups, along with a leaflet from Minister of Finance Bill Birch defending the Overseas Investment Amendment Bill. Based on interviews with senior management from eleven large overseas companies in New Zealand, the report could hardly pass muster as a reliable and objective analysis of the issues.[33] The Chamber also commissioned a survey directed more at the government; this was equally unconvincing, with only 100 of the 430 US-owned or associated companies providing returns. It advised the government that among the impediments affecting decisions to invest in New Zealand were the Resource Management Act (53 percent of respondents), the non-resident withholding tax (62 percent), relatively light criminal penalties for copyright infringement (78 percent), and the permission required from the Overseas Investment Commission for investments over $10 million (52 percent). Not surprisingly, respondents supported the Employment Contracts Act (90 percent), the Reserve Bank Act (81 percent) and the reduction of trade barriers (98 percent). Interestingly, 58 percent of the companies surveyed also criticised the absence of a takeovers code, which government had recently decided not to pursue.[34]

Foreign investment was now an election year issue. In a *National Business Review* poll in March 1996, 59 percent of respondents thought that foreign investment was good (slightly down from 64 percent in 1992); but 43 percent now said that current levels were too high (up from 34 percent in 1992). The latter response was strongest among pensioners and those earning under $35,000. Australia was the most acceptable investor (85 percent approval), followed by the US (67 percent), Japan (56 percent) and Hong Kong (51 percent).[35] The Alliance rode the issue hard, but its support fell away mid-year. New Zealand First hit a 29 percent high in the May polls on an anti-foreign investment, anti-immigration, anti-privatisation platform. Peters promised a mix of constraints on foreign purchases of land and shares, and limits on the stake foreigners could hold in local companies. This would be complemented by a national savings scheme.

Bolger warned voters there would be a 'Sunday, bloody Sunday' if a Labour-led government was elected with the Alliance or New Zealand First as its coalition partner.[36] Japanese investors were said to be nervous, which was damaging the country.[37] This was pure scaremongering, as Labour showed no intention of tightening existing laws. National's ultimate provocation was to sell the Forestry Corporation to a consortium of Fletcher Challenge, Brierley Investments and a Chinese state-owned enterprise (ironic in itself) two months before the election. Affected Maori tribes were furious that the sale had proceeded while their claims over the forest land were still before the Waitangi Tribunal or under negotiation with the Crown. Peters promised that New Zealand First would return the cheque the day after the election.[38] The Alliance organised a petition for a citizens' referendum to reserve the sale (but discontinued it after the election).

When the votes were counted, New Zealand First held the balance of power, and chose to form a coalition government with its arch-enemy, National. In the Coalition Agreement, the guiding principle on foreign investment was highly opaque: 'While recognising the need for overseas capital and the need to maintain investor confidence and without eroding any existing ownership rights the Coalition agrees that as a statement of general principle it is desirable that the control and ownership of important New Zealand assets and resources be held by New Zealanders.'[39]

Despite Peters' pre-election promises, the detail of the agreement contained few changes to the immigration and foreign investment regimes. A minor tightening of controls on foreign ownership of farm land was suggested, and there was a commitment to the 'New Zealandisation' of commercial fisheries.[40] Immigration would stay at current levels, pending a Population Conference in May 1997. The strongest point was a prohibition on the privatisation of certain 'strategic' state assets and businesses – notably Electricorp and Transpower, public radio, TV1 and New Zealand Post – and restrictions on sales of local authority-owned power and gas utilities, airports and ports. However, there was no mention of other state assets (including Landcorp, Coalcorp, state houses, hospitals, Crown Research Institutes and universities), new developments (such as private prisons) and local infrastructural services (for example, contracting out rubbish, transport and water). Nor was there any reference to buying back rights over the state forests. The privatisers in National soon made it clear that they would exploit any loopholes, pointing out that privatisation was not defined in the agreement.[41] Once the Coalition broke down in August 1998, the agreement became meaningless anyway.

In a supposed concession to New Zealand First, the Coalition government introduced a new amendment to the Overseas Investment Act in December 1997. The explanatory note expressed 'the Coalition Government's desire to ensure that overseas investments demonstrate a commitment to New Zealand'. Yet the criteria for assessing applications for foreign investment, other than in farm land, were unchanged. The definition of farm land still did not include land that was currently planted in trees. It was claimed that the 1997 Amendment Bill strengthened the criteria in the principal Act by ensuring that overseas investments involving farm land could be approved only if they would result in 'substantial and identifiable benefits to New Zealand'. Yet the minister had only to 'consider' whether that was the case in assessing whether the investment was in the national interest. Indeed, changes to the wording of the Act appeared to remove any residual ministerial discretion to refuse an application: the provision that the minister '*shall grant* that approval, consent, or permission *only if satisfied that*: ... .' became the Minister '*must* grant the approval ... *if satisfied that*: ... .' The Bill contained none of the changes relating to farm land promised in the Coalition Agreement, and nothing that dealt with foreign investment in strategic assets.

During this period, the government also became embroiled in a furore over negotiations in the OECD for a Multilateral Agreement on Investment (MAI) (see Chapter 9). The agreement aimed to remove virtually all restrictions on foreign investment, and was described by its critics as a Magna Carta for transnational corporations. For most of 1997, ministers and officials treated concerns about the MAI with disdain. So did Labour's Mike Moore, who accused 'the left in New Zealand' of borrowing their materials and arguments from extreme right-wing militia in the US who believed in a one-world conspiracy.[42] Both the Coalition government and Labour failed to read the signs, and found themselves confronted by an angry anti-MAI campaign that brought together Maori, activist unions, students, anti-free trade groups, local mayors and Grey Power, as well as Alliance and New Zealand First MPs. Ministers reluctantly acknowledged the potential of the MAI to constrain a range of policy options, which they had previously denied. The government embarked on a damage control exercise to sell the benefits of foreign investment to opposition caucuses and the country. A disastrous hearing before the Maori Affairs select committee was followed by a series of government-run hui, which failed to convince Maori that foreign investment was good for them. New Zealand First, especially its Maori members, rediscovered its economic nationalism. Labour again sat uneasily on the fence. The Alliance had a field-day, until negotiations on the MAI were suspended in April 1998, and officially abandoned in November.

None of this dented National's commitment to attracting foreign investment through 'sound fundamentals'. In January 1999 it released the latest version of its promotional brochure, *Invest in New Zealand: The Right Choice*.[43] This extolled the benefits of an open economy – 'the result of a decade of far-reaching and comprehensive economic reform'. The country's 'positive economic environment' was based on price stability, controlled government expenditure, tax reform, deregulation, privatisation of state enterprises, removal of subsidies, reduced trade barriers, and labour market reform. Potential investors were offered a 'broad-base, low-rate tax regime', with low set-up costs. They were assured that 'minimal and transparent regulations make investing in New Zealand a straightforward process', and that the country's 'flexible and negotiable labour costs are among the lowest in the OECD'. There were endorsements from the chief executives of foreign-owned Tranz Rail, Air New Zealand and Independent Newspapers (although no mention that the latter's Tony

O'Reilly believed the government should offer incentives such as tax breaks to foreign investors).[44] Although the government remained committed to its purist line, it was short on empirical evidence. Indeed, a 1997 *Business Herald*/University of Auckland survey of international business suggested that the main barriers to operating in New Zealand were the local availability of senior management (54.5 percent), overseas travel demands (70.5 percent), societal attitudes to business (43.2 percent), and keeping up with global trends (31.8 percent).[45] The government's liberalisation strategy did nothing to address these concerns.

Attempts to track the officials' advice to government during this period suggest they were complacent and out of touch with the political debate. In 1991 ministers had established a Foreign Direct Investment Advisory Group of five private sector leaders. Its task included educating New Zealanders about the positive attributes of foreign investment, and promoting measures that would create a favourable investment environment.[46] Apart from a few promotional initiatives, the advisory group made a minimal contribution to the public debate. From mid-1994 to mid-1995 it was in limbo. A review in May 1995 reported that there was little cooperation and no common policy objectives on foreign direct investment among government agencies, and equally little coordination between the public and private sectors.[47] The group had few resources (the result largely of resistance from Treasury) and no full-time staff. Ministers agreed to establish a better-resourced group, again led from the private sector, to focus on education, dialogue, promotion and public policy.[48] The revised version was just as ineffectual. In December 1997, Treasury officials advised their ministers that the advisory group should be disestablished, because of 'the maturing of New Zealand's investment environment, the ongoing work of other government departments, and the greater role now being played by the business community in public debate'. A media strategy was suggested to ensure that disestablishing the group was not seen as government 'withdrawing from its stance on foreign investment'.[49] But some specialised promotion of foreign investment was still apparently deemed necessary. In 1999, responsibility for the task was transferred to Tradenz.

▲ WHO OWNS NEW ZEALAND?

By 1998 New Zealand's level of foreign direct investment was twice that of Australia or Canada. A large amount of it had been in privatised businesses and resources. Trends in foreign direct investment had remained relatively consistent throughout the 1990s.[50] Between 1993 and 1997, the main approvals from the Overseas Investment Commission (viewed by country and by value) went to Australia (28 percent), the US (25 percent), Canada (11.5 percent), the UK (8.8 percent), Hong Kong (7.5 percent) and Singapore (5.4 percent). Some 40 percent of land sale approvals (by area) went to the US, and 25 percent to Malaysia. In 1997 most investment applications still came from Australia. The Commission's figures suggest there was also significant disinvestment in 1997, reflecting New Zealand's economic decline and the Asian crisis: Singapore withdrew a net $51 million, Japan $40 million, Sweden $58 million and Brunei $18 million.[51]

When applications from 1993 to 1997 are categorised by activity, banks and financial services made up about 14.2 percent of investments, manufacturing 17.3 percent and commercial leasing 13.2 percent. Three-quarters of land sale approvals (by area) were for forestry, 6 percent for sheep-farming and 5 percent for dairy.[52]

TABLE 1: OVERSEAS INVESTMENT COMMISSION ACTIVITY: FIVE-YEAR OVERVIEW

All Transactions	1993	1994	1995	1996	1997	1993–97
Total Invest. Consents Granted	382	362	444	339	281	1808
Total Invest. Consents Refused	–	–	–	1	6	7
Total Consideration ($m)	9409	5226	4877	6821	5175	31,508
New Invest. Consents Granted #	N/a	264	332	285	198	
% of Total (by number)		73%	75%	84%	70%	
Total Consideration ($m)		2593	2871	5349*	2147	
% of Total (by value)		50%	59%	78%	41%	

Source: Overseas Investment Commission Figures 1997, www.oic.govt.nz, Attach. 1.
* includes Trustbank, $1.3 billion
# excludes transactions between overseas investors and corporate restructurings

A large number of investment applications involved the transfer of ownership from New Zealand to overseas owners, or 'new' foreign investment (see Table 1). From 1994 to 1997, these accounted for almost 60 percent of investments (by value). The proportion increased in the first half of 1998. In that period, 127 applications (some multiple) led to 131 consents, worth $3.1 billion, and to six refusals (all land-related). Four-fifths of the consents (by value) were transfers from New Zealand to foreign owners, a huge increase over the second half of 1997. Some transfers were very large: Kirin Brewery's purchase of 51 percent of Lion Nathan was over half the total new investment,[53] while Capital Properties' purchase of the privatised Government Property Services accounted for 8 percent. Some 86 consents related to land and involved 33,158 hectares (including the 5,899 ha of Glenburn Station in the Wairarapa). Most of it was freehold; only 260 hectares was leasehold and forestry rights. The main purposes for investment in land were agriculture, forestry and mining, with the US taking the largest share.

As at March 1998, total foreign direct investment in New Zealand – the value of overseas controlling interests in local companies – was $64.5 billion, the highest since the Statistics New Zealand series began in 1989. The largest component and growth area was equity investments, where growth mainly reflected the increased market value of some investments and retained earnings.[54] Some 68 percent of all foreign direct investment in New Zealand was held by Australia ($19.2 billion), the US ($15.9 billion) and the UK ($8.5 billion). Outward direct investment over the same period provides a stark contrast.[55] In the year to March 1997, New Zealand investors had *dis*invested a net $2.4 billion offshore. That was reversed in 1998 with net investments of $0.7 billion, mainly as New Zealand parent companies repaid long-term borrowings and lent more to their overseas subsidiaries. Most of these investments were in OECD countries (where New Zealand companies had disinvested $4.4 billion in 1997). Total direct investment overseas by New Zealanders as at March 1998 was $10.4 billion (down from the high of $13.2 billion in 1996), of which 70 percent was in Australia. The country's net international investment (total New Zealand investment abroad minus total foreign investment in New Zealand) as at March 1998 was negative $89.5 billion (see Table 2).[56] This figure was some $9.6 billion worse than in 1997, which itself was $9 billion worse than in 1996.

TABLE 2: NEW ZEALAND'S INTERNATIONAL INVESTMENT POSITION 1994–1998
NZ$M

	1994	1995	1996	1997	1998
Total NZ Investment Abroad*	23,471	24,927	34,738	33,094	35,186
Total Foreign Investment in NZ*	90,843	95,986	105,598	112,964	124,691
Net International Investment Position	-67,371	-71,060	-70,860	-79,870	-89,505

Source: Statistics New Zealand, *International Investment Position, 31 March 1998*, Table 1.

* Includes Direct Investment Abroad, Portfolio Investment Abroad, Other Capital Investment Abroad, and Other Reserve Assets.

▲ FOREIGN DIRECT INVESTMENT: THE KEY TO THE FUTURE?[57]

The open investment regime was premised on the belief that New Zealand's future economic growth depended on a significant ongoing flow of foreign investment. In 1998 the government estimated that New Zealand would need $75 to $100 billion in investment in the next five years to maintain strong growth, an amount it said was clearly beyond the savings of fewer than 4 million people.[58] Bob Edlin, writing in the *Independent*, took issue with the assumption that much of this investment would have to come from offshore. A mid-point of around $90 billion over five years meant $18 billion of new investment a year. This was about the level of gross capital formation in 1994/95, much of which came from the domestic economy.[59] Assuming the local contribution was, or could be, around three-quarters of what was required, the need for foreign investment would be minimal. Instead of relying on more overseas investment, he urged the government to work on increasing the level of domestic savings which could provide this pool of capital. A similar position was taken by leading businessman Hugh Fletcher, who advocated a compulsory superannuation scheme.[60] To achieve the investment objective, some mechanism would be needed to ensure that a significant proportion of those domestically generated funds were invested locally.

If the country did rely on more investment from overseas, there was no guarantee that it would be the kind of investment required. Investment applications were not subject to any national interest criteria, except in the case of land. Only so-called 'greenfield' investment created *new* productive capacity; investment that merely transferred existing companies and resources to new owners made very little positive contribution to the economy. Bill Rosenberg, the investment analyst for *Foreign Control Watchdog*, estimated that only half of the investment applications approved by the Overseas Investment Commission in 1995 (and one quarter by value) involved greenfield activity. Most were in forestry; yet the downstream benefits to New Zealand from forestry investment are limited, because under the GATT the government cannot require investors to process the logs locally. The remaining 76 percent of applications (by value) involved takeovers or restructuring of existing investments. While these may introduce new technology, most research and development in New Zealand by foreign investors tends to involve adapting existing products to local conditions. This still may be useful, but there is no guarantee that it will include the transfer of technology and skills. Again, this cannot be required under the GATT. What appears in the statistics as 'new' foreign investment must also be examined carefully. Increased foreign direct investment in a company may reflect a change in the book value of the shareholding (which is very high in the case of some privatised assets), rather than actual investment in the company.

It cannot therefore be assumed that more foreign investment will create significant new production or growth. Nor is there any guarantee that investors will return their profits to the local and national economy. The government has claimed that in 1996, 90 percent of the value added by foreign-owned companies remained in New Zealand; only 10 percent of profits were remitted overseas.[61] This claim is based on a KPMG survey, the methodology of which is unsound. The survey polled 700 New Zealand-registered companies with more than 25 percent foreign ownership, but only 130 (19 percent) replied. A further 59 companies were included in the analysis of some questions, based on public information. There is no indication of how representative the sample is. Rosenberg notes that the sectoral distribution is quite different from the Statistics New Zealand survey of all economically significant enterprises. The questionnaire is undated, and both it and the methodology remain unpublished.

The government's statement confuses 'value added' (which includes salaries, depreciation and interest) with 'profit'. In fact the KPMG data indicates that only 37 percent of *net profits* were retained in the specific companies surveyed, and 47 percent were retained within New Zealand. Statistics New Zealand data suggests that the average annual retention from 1989 to 1995 was 40 percent, although it was *minus* 41 percent between 1989 and 1991 (in other words, earnings remitted overseas were greater than profits made). Major companies such as Telecom have paid out between 70 and 90 percent of their profit as dividend. Investment analyst Brian Gaynor notes that in the year to June 1997, foreign-owned companies reinvested only 17 percent of their earnings in New Zealand companies, with the remainder being paid as dividend to their overseas owners. By contrast, New Zealand companies operating offshore reinvested 83 percent of their earnings and took only 17 percent as dividend.[62] The situation was even worse in the year to December 1998; foreign direct investors in New Zealand earned $2.79 billion in profit, all of which, *plus* another $11 million, was taken as dividend – there was *no* net reinvestment. In the three years from 1996 to 1998, accumulated profit on foreign direct investment was $10.6 billion, only $844 million of which went back into the local companies; $9.8 billion, or 92 percent, was paid to the owners as dividend. This compares with a 62 percent reinvestment of profits from 1992 to 1994.[63]

In addition, it appears that foreign investors pay less tax than their domestic counterparts. In 1995, the average tax rate paid by overseas companies in *Management* magazine's Top 200 was 24.8 percent, compared to 29.9 percent for local companies. They also paid more in (tax-deductable) interest, a possible indication of tax-avoiding arrangements between parent companies and their subsidiaries. This has significant revenue implications, given that foreign-owned companies are estimated to make half of the operating surplus in the country.

One of the strongest arguments in favour of foreign investment is that it creates more employment. The government often claims that one-third of working New Zealanders rely on jobs that are directly or indirectly created by foreign investment.[64] Labour's Mike Moore has condensed this into 'one third of employees in New Zealand owe their jobs to foreign investment'.[65] According to Statistics New Zealand, the number of New Zealanders employed in overseas companies in 1995 was only 17.6 percent. The 'one third' presumably includes an estimate of the number of people working for suppliers to such companies – a number that will vary widely according to the kind of operation. It could equally be said that the majority of locally, sometimes publicly owned businesses provide work for the minority of overseas firms and their employees (for example, transnational cleaning companies or electronic data services contracted to government agencies). If a foreign investor decides to exit the business, those jobs do not simply disappear; someone else, possibly local, is likely to buy the company. By contrast, where foreign investment involves a merger or takeover, there may be a serious loss of local jobs, as occurred in the banking industry and in most of the privatisations.

Whether an increase in foreign investment would provide new jobs is a matter for speculation, and depends largely on whether it is greenfield investment. But examples given by politicians of sectors where these benefits might occur are not convincing. Minister of Overseas Trade Lockwood Smith has repeatedly claimed that, given more foreign investment, forestry can create an extra 30,000 jobs and up to $5 billion a year in extra foreign exchange receipts. In late 1998 he admitted that such claims made him an 'optimist'.[66] During the previous decade, the traditional forestry giants Fletcher Challenge and Carter Holt Harvey, both now majority foreign-owned, and other forestry majors had laid off large numbers of staff.[67] The Asian downturn promised further cuts. In 1998 Fletcher Forests announced that its problem with servicing the debt on the purchase of the state forests in 1996 required another $60 million a year in new revenue, or comparable savings through cuts to staff, lower pay to contractors and asset sales.[68] Carter Holt Harvey (the third-ranked company in *Management* magazine's Top 200 in 1998) adopted an especially aggressive approach. Its majority owner, International Paper, which employed over 80,000 people in 31 countries, was severely affected by the Asian crisis and planned a massive asset sale. Net profits from the local company fell dramatically. It had already sold non-core businesses and stopped pruning its trees. Contractors were forced into new deals which drove some small operators out of business. A further strategy, dubbed 'the Genesis initiative', involved cutting administrative and support staff and closing plants; this was on top of planned lay-offs following the $300 million upgrade and expansion of the Kinleith pulp and paper mill. A leaked document showed that the company intended to break an industrial agreement (which the Employment Tribunal had ruled prevented compulsory redundancies) so it could lay off 70 additional Kinleith workers and introduce individual contracts.[69] Redundancies were expected ultimately to save $42 million a year. The document complained that 'Kinleith mill workers are just in it for the money and live in a mini social-welfare state called Tokoroa'. The existing collective contract was described as encouraging an 'income maximisation mentality rather than promoting efficiency'.[70] Resistance to change was blamed on the union. The company's answer was to individualise, de-unionise and cut staff. By March 1999 some 2,200 fewer New Zealanders would be working for Carter Holt Harvey than three years previously.[71] The employment record of New Zealand's foreign-owned forestry sector gave Lockwood Smith *no* grounds for optimism.

Other employment-related arguments are sometimes made. It is claimed that foreign-owned companies employ mainly local people, and that many of their chief executives are New Zealanders.[72] This may be true, as employment practices in some of these firms are probably better than those of local businesses, especially in high-value activities. The government also claims that on average, foreign-owned companies pay their employees 28 percent above the average wage.[73] This is apparently based on the KPMG survey. But the survey has a sample bias away from low-wage sectors such as wholesale and retail. Its findings seem inconsistent with low pay levels in service sectors such as cleaning and security, where foreign firms are prominent – although competition from transnationals may be forcing local companies in those sectors to pay even less. The suggestion that foreign investments secure higher labour productivity is also problematic. This may be true of communications, business and finance, as a result of large-scale redundancies and new technology. But the overall rate of labour productivity growth in New Zealand has fallen since 1989, which is when foreign investment began to increase rapidly.

A final argument is that an open investment regime benefits domestic investors in foreign-owned companies, both within New Zealand and overseas.[74] Yet New Zealand investment overseas has not been a success. Domestic companies have borrowed heavily to invest offshore, but the majority earned well-below-expected returns. In the year to June 1997, only $149 million was earned from direct investment overseas. Brian Gaynor blames New Zealand companies for continuing the 'Brierley tradition' of buying major shareholdings in poorly performing and badly managed companies which could be turned around easily and capitalised on. This was no longer appropriate to the corporate environment of the

1990s. By contrast, overseas investors believed in buying into excellent companies at the quality end of the market, something that few New Zealand investors could afford to do.[75]

The government is correct in claiming that thousands of ordinary New Zealanders are shareholders in foreign companies based in New Zealand. However, the number of non-controlling shares held by individuals in locally listed companies has been declining; reports suggest that only 12 percent of the population are shareholders.[76] Those who invest individually rather than through large funds are powerless, given the government's refusal to impose a takeovers code, the country's weak securities and insider trading laws, and minimal corporate governance and disclosure requirements.

The proponents of foreign investment regularly leave the economic downside of foreign investment out of their equation. While the government was repaying official overseas debt, the private sector filled the vacuum left by the state, and local and transnational businesses borrowed offshore. New Zealand has built up an extremely high level of foreign debt (see Appendix: Figure 3). Foreign debt is the total amount the country owes offshore. The private sector component of this includes debt owed by companies, financial institutions and producer boards. In the decade to 1994, the debt ballooned from around $12 billion to over $67 billion, as the private sector filled the vacuum left by the state, and local and transnational businesses borrowed offshore. The government made repaying its public overseas debt a major policy plank and reduced the level from a high of $47.3 billion in 1993 to $29 billion by 1996. When he announced the sale of the Forestry Corporation in August 1996, Minister of Finance Bill Birch said the government would use the proceeds to 'move the Government to *zero net foreign currency debt*' (emphasis added). This referred to the *net* level of overseas debt denominated in *foreign currency*, which then stood around $1.1 billion. Some media, notably the *National Business Review*, enthusiastically converted this into repayment of *all* the government's remaining overseas debt.[77] Most public foreign debt was in fact denominated in New Zealand dollars, and totalled around $15.1 billion net. Bill Rosenberg likened Birch's announcement to 'boasting that you've paid off your credit card, "forgetting" to mention that you still owe ten times as much on your BMW'.[78] Meanwhile, the growth in New Zealand's private overseas debt showed no signs of abating. The annual Statistics New Zealand survey of the country's overseas debt showed that the total debt had increased by $2.4 billion in the year to March 1999. Official overseas debt was reduced overall by $2.6 billion; local companies had continued to borrow offshore ($5.0 billion in 1999). The debt level had reached a staggering 103 percent of GDP, over three times the value of annual exports of goods and services (see Chapter 10).[79] This debt had to be serviced and repaid.

The debt problem was compounded by New Zealand's serious current account deficit (see Appendix: Figure 2). A deficit in the current account of the balance of payments means the country earned less from exports and income from its investments overseas than it paid for imports and income from foreign investment in New Zealand (including interest and profits remittable on loans and investments). To fund this deficit, the government and local firms have to borrow, sell assets or reduce the country's foreign exchange reserves. But increased foreign ownership meant even more profits were exported, putting an even greater burden on the balance of payments. Wolfgang Rosenberg observes that mortgaging the country's assets to foreign investors effectively means the value added to goods and services produced in New Zealand goes overseas. The official remedy is to 'reduce our imports for which we can pay no longer, since the foreign exchange earned by exports must be used to pay the profits and interest due to foreign investors'.[80] It also means providing the conditions that keep foreign investors sweet.

Annual current account deficits are nothing new. By 1994 the country had run one for 27 of the last 30 years. The annual deficit fell from an extremely high 9 percent of GDP in 1985 to 1.7 percent in June 1994. But by mid-1995, the high exchange rate meant imports were cheap and exporters were really suffering. The current account deteriorated significantly to a deficit of $3.3 billion. Whereas in the 1980s current account deficits had been covered by overseas borrowing, they were now being met by overseas purchases of government stock and the sale of New Zealand resources to foreign buyers, which added little to the productive base of the economy. By September 1996 the deficit was back up to 4.6 percent of GDP. In March 1998 it reached 7.3 percent.[81] After falling in the second half of 1998 it deteriorated again to 6.4 percent of GDP in the March 1999 quarter (see Chapter 10).

A major cause of the ongoing balance of payments problem was the continued decline in manufacturing exports. However, a second difficulty was the comparatively poor performance by domestic investors overseas. Gaynor estimated that, had they performed as well as foreign investors in New Zealand, the deficit would have been reduced by about $2 billion.[82] He compared this with the situation in Australia, where the deficit had risen to 4.7 percent of GDP during 1998 (but GDP growth remained strong). Gaynor identified three major differences.[83] Australia's problem was a fall in export growth, with 54 percent of its exports going to Asia in 1998 (compared to 35 percent of New Zealand's), while imports had increased. New Zealand's export figures had recovered somewhat during the year, as a result of currency depreciation and diversified markets. A second difference was in the services deficit. New Zealanders spent more when travelling overseas than the local tourism industry earned; the Australians did not. But the biggest difference was in investment. Australia's investment deficit was only 3.4 percent of GDP, whereas New Zealand's was 7.3 percent. There were two main reasons for this. First, a larger share of New Zealand companies were foreign-owned, and the overseas investors had remitted all their earnings out of New Zealand, with a negative impact on the dollar. In part, this reflected the New Zealand bias towards overseas owners in privatisations, whereas Australia encouraged local shareholding. Australia's foreign investment regime was also more tightly regulated. Second, Australian investors were more successful overseas. They had a positive return, over one-third of which was remitted back home. Offshore investments by New Zealanders showed a negative return, with the interest costs on their borrowings being greater than their offshore earnings (or losses).

In a speech in June 1998, Reserve Bank Governor Don Brash partially acknowledged the situation. He was previously on record as having no problems with the country's assets becoming entirely foreign-owned; he had now revised that position, in light of concerns about a political backlash against large-scale foreign ownership, and the 'considerable social and economic cost' if foreign investors became concerned about the current account deficit and decided to quit.[84] His solution, however, was to have the public sector continue to run budget surpluses as a contribution to national savings. There was still no suggestion, however, that he would address the fundamental causes of the problem: unrestricted foreign direct investment and the export of profits offshore, low domestic savings, incentives to engage in speculative rather than productive investment, and an economy which was dependent on an export sector which the government's economic and monetary policies continually undermined.

▲ FINANCIAL MARKETS: THE CASINO ECONOMY

Foreign direct investment has a reasonably visible impact; the second major form of foreign investment is less obvious, but potentially much more unstable and difficult to control. In this category are transactions involving foreign currency, bonds and a range of other financial instruments, and portfolio equity investments, which are often small, shorter-term shareholdings in local companies.

International flows of finance capital are the epitome of globalisation, seeming to operate beyond the reach and understanding of mere mortals.

Unimaginably large numbers, which in theory represent money, flit between computer screens located in different parts of the world. 'Traders' engage in a game designed to make these numbers grow, independently of any changes in the real economy. They create an illusion of wealth, which can collapse as rapidly as it expands. The game requires speed and stealth, rewarding investors who outguess their competitors. Those who play wield enormous power but carry almost no personal risk. Huge financial exposure can be built up with almost no cash outlay. When the bubble bursts, the economies of whole countries, regions, and potentially the world, fall too. Panics, driven by herd instinct, create runs on currencies. These affect the viability of exports, the value of debt and interest owed, the cost of imports and the availability of credit. Local communities suffer, with businesses closing and jobs being lost. Inflation escalates, forcing up prices for essentials such as food and imported fuel. Interest rates are hiked to retain investors or attract them back, while viable businesses go under and banks collapse. The more deregulated an economy, the greater its exposure to such risks.

These risks are not new. Nor are arguments about whether they can and should be regulated, and if so by whom and how. History is a great teacher. In October 1929 the Wall Street crash almost brought the world economy to its knees. Writing back in 1936, British economist John Maynard Keynes reflected on the shift from a norm of owner-run businesses, which were established as a way of life rather than in calculation of expected profit, to one where ownership was separated from management and organised through investment markets driven by short-term self-interest. While investments were 'fixed' from the viewpoint of workers and local communities, they were 'liquid' for the individual investor. Companies became owned by people with no special knowledge or commitment to the long-term development needs of the business. This increased the instability of the economic system.[85] Even in normal times, the value of shares 'established as the outcome of the mass psychology of a large number of ignorant individuals is liable to change violently as a result of a sudden fluctuation of opinion due to factors which do not really make much difference to the prospective yield'. In abnormal times, 'the market will be subjected to waves of optimistic and pessimistic sentiment, which are unreasoning and yet in a sense legitimate where no solid basis exists for a reasonable calculation.'[86] Professional investors and speculators try to identify these trends ahead of others, and profit from them:

> ... when he purchases an investment, the [investor] is attaching his hopes, not so much to its prospective yield, as to a favourable change in the conventional basis of valuation, i.e. he is, in the above sense, a speculator. Speculators may

do no harm as bubbles on a steady stream of enterprise. But the position is serious when enterprise becomes the bubble on a whirlpool of speculation. When the capital development of a country becomes a by-product of the activities of a casino, the job is likely to be ill-done. The measure of success attained by Wall Street, regarded as an institution of which the proper social purpose is to direct new investment into the most profitable channels in terms of future yield, cannot be claimed as one of the outstanding triumphs of *laissez-faire* capitalism.[87]

Keynes concluded that the state was in the best position to take a long-term view of the general needs of the society, and should assume 'an ever greater responsibility for directly organising investment'.[88]

Keynes was talking about speculative investment in shares. Karl Polanyi provided a parallel analysis of concerns about currency trading under the old laissez-faire system, where currency values were set by international movements in the price of gold. This system collapsed during the First World War, but was revived with a vengeance in the 1920s. Polanyi reflected that:

> In retrospect our age will be credited with having seen the end of the self-regulating market. The 1920's saw the prestige of economic liberalism at its height ... . Stabilization of currencies became the focal point in the political thought of peoples and governments; the restoration of the gold standard became the supreme aim of all organized effort in the economic field. The repayment of foreign loans and the return to stable currencies were recognized as the touchstones of rationality in politics; and no private suffering, no infringement of sovereignty, was deemed too great a sacrifice for the recovery of monetary integrity. ...The thirties lived to see the absolutes of the twenties called into question ... .[89]

Attempts to maintain the gold-exchange standard collapsed in 1931 as the US and Britain, facing financial difficulties, began to manage their own currencies. Many other governments followed suit, imposing national controls on currency values and movements, mainly through their central banks, and by domestic regulation of corporate activity. Fragmentation replaced integration in the international monetary order.

The creation of the International Monetary Fund in 1944 was an attempt to restore stability to the international monetary system after the Second World War. How this should be done was the subject of controversy from the start. In 1943, Keynes proposed a scheme to promote monetary stability through an international clearing union (which would operate like a national banking system) and an international currency (initially, but not permanently, defined in terms of gold). But the Bretton Woods conference adopted a US proposal to link currency values to either gold or US dollars, and make them freely convertible. Emergency balance of payments assistance would be provided from a subscribed fund, an approach that allowed the US to limit its liability, and to exercise strong influence on the IMF's policy direction as its largest shareholder.

In New Zealand, the debate over whether to join the IMF raged for years. The vocal supporters of Social Credit raised three main concerns, reflecting common fears about external control of a country's currency.[90] The first was the suggestion that the US government intended using Bretton Woods as a way of opening markets to US goods. The second was the impact of membership on national sovereignty. IMF members were required to report to (and in some cases gain consent from) the Fund before making any formal change in their currency value. This removed the right of the state to make key decisions on domestic finances and economic policies. The third concern (from Royalists) was the erosion of links to the pound sterling and hence the British Empire. Economist Wolfgang Rosenberg was more concerned about the impact on the country's economic priorities. Joining the IMF would mean that 'the Government of New Zealand will in the future carry out a logical policy of private enterprise in a world of fluctuating economic conditions'.[91] In particular, it would give the freedom to convert currencies precedence over domestic economic policies designed to maintain full employment.

In late 1960 the National Party became the government. Faced with a serious shortage of foreign exchange, it viewed the IMF as a potential source of funds. (The IMF provides temporary balance of payments support to a member country by allowing it to 'draw' on a multiple of its paid-up quota.)[92] In 1961, Minister of Finance Harry Lake issued a White Paper justifying the government's decision to join the Fund.[93] The International Finance Agreements Act was passed after a lengthy parliamentary debate. Labour MPs opposed the move on grounds similar to Rosenberg's; in particular, they feared the IMF would insist on corrective policies that reduced demand and economic activity generally, resulting in stagnation or recession, and unemployment. The debate in New Zealand continued through the 1960s as the National government twice drew on the Fund.[94] Labour leader Norman Kirk accused the government of signing away sovereignty over economic activity and 'tying New Zealand so tightly to international institutions that even when a change of government takes place, the area for that Government to initiate new policy will be severely restricted'.[95]

The potential for a global financial crisis re-emerged in the 1970s, as the world's financial systems began to change. The IMF's arrangements were designed to serve a system of fixed exchange rates. In 1971 this system collapsed when the US announced that its dollar was no longer freely convertible into gold. Numerous countries then chose to float their currencies. In 1976 an IMF meeting decided to accept floating exchange rates as the official basis for valuing currencies, which meant the financial markets largely determined their value. This decision recognised a process that had begun three years earlier. But floating exchange rates created new risks and uncertainties for importers, exporters and investors. As banks moved to mediate that risk, trading in foreign exchange became an important new source of profit, and the traditional business of lending money became less significant. Foreign relations expert Ethan Kapstein observes:

> The macroshocks of the 1970s did not bring an end to global finance; on the contrary they provided a fillip. With the wild fluctuations in foreign exchange values, corporations looked to banks to help in managing their currency exposure. The banks themselves saw speculation as a road to new profits, and foreign exchange trading floors expanded in all the major financial institutions.[96]

Under Ronald Reagan's presidency from 1980, US economic policy encouraged major financial players to engage in speculation and risk. Finance markets were deregulated, monetary policy kept interest rates high, and competition became cut-throat. The US government effectively guaranteed many of its financial institutions, creating a recipe for recklessness known as 'moral hazard'. Massive personal fortunes were made by bankers and investment brokers who, by takeovers and leveraged buy-outs, merely rearranged the ownership of existing firms and shifted risk from equity holdings to debt. This became common practice internationally. Its defenders claimed that the disciplines imposed by takeovers and debt-servicing costs improved corporate efficiency, and justified the massively increased share price, profits and dividends. Having compared the economic growth figures of the 1980s with periods when these disciplines were not present, US economist Paul Krugman concludes that there is no evidence to support this claim. Most of the increased value of companies came from redistributing income and jobs of workers to the earnings of shareholders and managers, not from the creation of new wealth.[97]

Other factors contributed to change. Inflation created uncertainty, which in turn prompted innovation. Milton Friedman's monetarist approach to controlling inflation, which was adopted internationally to varying degrees, produced unstable interest and exchange rates. Governments moved to liberalise rules on capital flows and deregulate commercial banking. Share-markets became larger, more sophisticated and interconnected. New technologies made complex international transactions cheap and simple. A bewildering array of financial products emerged onto the markets. 'Financial arbitrage' (which aims to buy a product in a market where the price is low and sell it where the price is high) prompted speculation on price changes in commodities, currency, interest rates, bonds and equities. 'Derivatives' allowed real producers, or speculative investors, to insure against such changes in value. 'Securitisation' turned financial assets into marketable commodities for which someone else assumed responsibility.

Perhaps the most controversial new product was the 'hedge fund'.[98] Such funds engage in high-risk speculation on currencies, bonds, derivatives and other short-term financial instruments. Often based in tax havens, they involve small clubs of wealthy private investors who play with very high stakes, yet have virtually no say in how the fund is managed. A typical operation involves short-selling a currency; for example, speculators enter into a contract to sell currency at a certain date, but do not buy that currency themselves until the date when the contract falls due; they profit if the purchase price they pay is lower than the sale price, and lose if the currency has appreciated.[99] When large amounts are involved, these deals can create a run on a currency from which the funds generally benefit. Hedge funds are 'highly leveraged', borrowing many times their original investment.[100] Hence, a hedge fund of US$11 billion (the estimated value of George Soros's Quantum Fund in 1995) could have control over as much as US$110 billion.[101] Lenders' exposure to these funds becomes difficult to assess because their operations are secretive and many appear as 'off balance sheet' transactions. The funds can exercise greater influence on foreign exchange and interest rate movements than interventions by central banks. As for their ethics, Paul Krugman describes some of the hedge fund investors he knows as being 'about as moral as great white sharks'.[102]

Most of the world's international financial transactions now involve short-term speculation on financial instruments, shares or property. In 1998 the world's imports and exports accounted for only 2 to 3 percent of global foreign exchange trading. As well as creating instability, this diverts investment funds from genuinely productive enterprises where generating profits takes time. The banking industry has changed accordingly. The deregulation of commercial banking, lower barriers to foreign investment, and the privatisation of state banks saw control of the global banking system concentrated in a few intensely competitive hands. David Korten comments on the results: 'Financial institutions that were once dedicated to mobilizing funds for productive investment have transmogrified into a predatory, risk-creating, speculation-driven global financial system engaged in the unproductive extraction of wealth from taxpayers and the productive economy.'[103]

▲ NEW ZEALAND'S FINANCIAL DEREGULATION

The fourth Labour government wanted to be part of this world. It would have been unrealistic for it to ignore the rapidly changing financial environment. Characteristically, however, the new government chose to go further and faster than most other countries. The short-term liquidity crisis that accompanied the snap election in July 1984 was fortuitous. In 'crisis' mode, Labour had an excuse to move rapidly. The scope and speed of its financial policy changes have been described as unequalled in the OECD or the Pacific region over the previous two decades.[104] According to the Reserve Bank, the financial sector went 'in short order, from among the most regulated of the OECD countries to probably the least regulated'.[105] Controls on capital leaving the country were removed almost immediately. Within two years, Labour had lifted all price regulations in the financial sector and controls on the balance sheets of financial institutions. It promised to increase competition in financial markets through a largely self-regulatory system of prudential oversight, which was supposed to minimise the systemic effects if individual institutions failed. Monetary policy was pursued through the open market.

The deregulation of financial markets and the floating of the dollar coincided with the Reserve Bank's embrace of monetarism. High inflation and an expectation that the value of the dollar would fall meant interest rates were kept high (see Appendix: Figure 5). Money flooded into the country, pushing the dollar up; between mid-June and mid-November 1985 it appreciated about 22 percent. While there was some easing of monetary policy, the government tightened its fiscal policy and interest rates increased; the trade-weighted exchange rate index (TWI) rose again between September 1986 and June 1988 by 20 percent, and the dollar appreciated 56 percent against its US counterpart.[106] The focus on maintaining low inflation through interest (and exchange) rates, irrespective of the impact on production or employment, provided a virtual guarantee for foreign investors at the time.

The influx of capital fuelled a frenetic spiral of share-market and property speculation. Cowboy investors with paper companies plundered sturdy local firms, commonly paying with their worthless shares and backed by grossly overvalued security. Merchant and investment bankers such as Fay Richwhite became intermediaries in internationalised capital markets. Major firms, and subsequently state-owned enterprises, developed their own treasury operations. Huge sums were raised through Eurokiwi bonds, whereby New Zealand debt was sold to foreign buyers in offshore markets. Complex international transactions, some involving offshore tax havens, provided new vehicles for tax avoidance and fraud, many of which were not discovered until the corporate entities collapsed. The 1994–1997 Cook Islands tax inquiry (the 'Winebox inquiry') later put the transactions of several major New Zealand corporations under the microscope.[107]

As competition squeezed the profits from traditional transactions, financial institutions diversified. New products and niche markets were created. Financial information services expanded to service investors. Banks lent recklessly. The speculative futures market developed a life of its own. Property trusts provided opportunities for real estate investment, while unit trusts serviced consortiums of small investors and investment funds. Complex tax avoidance schemes and insider trading were applauded as clever practice. Sharebrokers fed the frenzy, taking their profits, while professional ethics often seemed to go by the board.

The share-price index rose by 140 percent from 1984 to 1987. Market capitalisation increased from $17.6 billion at the end of 1985 to $42.4 billion a year later, and reached $42.8 billion by September 1987. The bubble burst spectacularly a month later. New Zealand was hit more harshly than almost any other country. By December, the share-market value had almost halved, to $24.2 billion.[108] This speculative spree gutted the productive base of the country, ruining many solid businesses that had fallen prey to the corporate raiders. Other companies were burdened with debt. Some closed. Many were sold cheap, mainly to offshore buyers because there was no local capital. Investors were left with worthless shares, and often with big debts. Unemployment spiralled.

Five years of stagnation and recession followed. A period of significant recovery began in 1992. However, the combination of financial deregulation and the Reserve Bank's tight monetary policy set the scene for another round of speculation in 1996. Domestic investors, still wary of the share-market, had opted for property instead. This, and a rapid influx of immigrants into Auckland, caused property prices to escalate. The Reserve Bank responded by talking up the interest and exchange rates. Short-term speculative investment, known as 'hot' money, again flowed into the country to take advantage of the highest real interest rates in the OECD and a seemingly guaranteed exchange rate. In October 1996 alone, $2 billion was invested in New Zealand dollar securities from Europe and Japan.[109] The TWI peaked at over 70 points. The tradeable sector, which was not the cause of the inflation, was devastated once again by a heavily overvalued dollar. From mid-1997, as the economy declined and real interest rates fell, speculative capital left as rapidly as it had come. The exchange rate plummeted, destabilising the economy once more.

Over this time, the ownership of corporate New Zealand changed dramatically. Foreign equity investment grew from $9.8 billion in the year to March 1989 to $28 billion in the year to March 1994 (almost all of this was foreign direct investment in New Zealand companies, approved by the Overseas Investment Commission). Foreign control of publicly listed companies went from around 17 percent in 1985 to nearly 40 percent in 1993. By 1998, foreign investors held 60 percent of the share-market by value, and the majority of local stockbroking firms were now owned by transnational companies.[110]

A study of the shift in ownership of the Stock Exchange's top 40 listed companies between 1989 and 1996 reveals that foreign institutional investors were increasingly important (see Table 3).[111] While local institutions reduced their investment in the top 40 companies, participation by overseas institutions grew, attracted by high yields (especially from privatised businesses) and growth prospects with little exchange rate risk. The share of total assets owned by corporations also increased; but again, the local share fell while foreign investment grew. The share (by value) of the top 40 companies held by overseas institutions and corporations trebled, from 19 to 58 percent. Despite these transactions, the New Zealand share-market never regained its 1987 high, unlike those in other countries. Global share-markets soared by 37.8 percent in 1998; the local market fell by 3.2 percent.[112] While New Zealand shares failed to reflect the 'bull' markets overseas, they were guaranteed to share in any crash when that bubble burst.

TABLE 3: TOP 40 COMPANIES, 1989-96 OWNERSHIP (BY TYPE, AS % OF THE TOTAL)

Type of Investor	Dec '89	Dec '92	Nov '94	Mar '96
Local investment institutions	16	14	14	11
Overseas investment institutions	10	24	31	32
Local corporates	21	10	9	8
Employee share ownership plans	4	4	3	3
Overseas corporates	9	20	23	26
Other	40	28	23	20

Source: 'Ownership Structure of New Zealand Stockmarket', Doyle Paterson Brown Ltd, 1996, reported in National Business Review, *12 April 1996*

Currency and stock-market speculation carried different risks. Reports from several government committees had suggested changes to the stock exchange's structure and rules after the 1987 crash, but basically their substantive recommendations were ignored.[113] By the late 1990s, New Zealand's light-handed approach to regulating the stock-market, competition, corporate governance and ownership was widely criticised.[114] The Stock Exchange operated a system of self-regulating surveillance that largely relied on feedback from brokers about unusual price movements and inadequate information.[115] Brian Gaynor accused the Market Surveillance Panel, which is responsible for enforcement, of 'snap[ping] its teeth at the little companies but when it comes to bigger boys it purrs and sneaks away'.[116] For example, the requirement to prepare an independent report on a merger of Macraes Mining with Australian company GRD was waived in 1998 because the Australian Stock Exchange would require a meeting of minority shareholders and a report. But the Australian report failed to address many issues of concern to Macraes shareholders. The West Australia Supreme Court subsequently ruled that GRD did not have to hold a meeting at which it could not vote. The merger went ahead. Minority Macraes shareholders were left holding shares whose value fell from 70 cents to 30 cents.[117]

Intensive lobbying by the Business Roundtable and other corporate interests kept New Zealand's insider trading laws weak.[118] The Securities Commission is required to investigate an allegation of insider trading, but leaves it to the shareholder to prosecute, which few small holders can afford. Ten years after the legislation was passed, no one had successfully sued, although several cases were settled out of court. A Securities Commission report in December 1998 censured high-flier Eric Watson for share dealings during the purchase of McCollam Print by Blue Star (bought by US Office Products in 1996 from Watson, who remained the chief executive); but the report stopped short of concluding that insider trading had occurred. The Commission had to rely on an investigation by the Securities and Exchange Commission in the US, where insider trading is treated as a serious criminal offence.[119] The tactics of Doug Myers in maximising the personal returns to himself and fellow directors in the sale of Lion Nathan to Kirin Brewery (Japan) also provoked outrage in many quarters. One major US portfolio investor warned that foreign investors would be scared out of the New Zealand market by 'the higher risk premium attached to New Zealand shares because of the Third World corporate standards'.[120] Compounding the Securities Commission's lack of powers was its limited budget; it received only $2.38 million from the government for 1997/98, whereas the Australian Securities Commission operated with a government grant equivalent to NZ$148 million. Companies with the financial resources to launch long and costly court cases could quickly exhaust the New Zealand Commission's budget. Responding (inadequately) to criticism, the 1999 Budget allocated the Commission a further $500,000 for enforcement, a review of securities regulations, and participation in international discussions on regulation of securities markets.

The 1995 Cabinet decision not to impose a takeovers code represented another success for the Business Roundtable lobby, whose argument that major shareholders were entitled to a premium prevailed over the right of all shareholders to be treated equally.[121] In this, the Roundtable's ideologically driven position was apparently at variance with the US-based transnationals, who viewed the weak local regulation as a major disincentive to investment.[122]

New Zealand's direct regulation of banking is also weak by international standards. The Bank of International Settlements places responsibility for monitoring a bank's solvency on its home government, while the host country checks the bank's liquidity. Convergence of banking policies is fostered through dialogue. Most banks remain quite heavily regulated, being told by individual governments how much capital they must hold, where they can operate, what products they can sell and how much they can lend a single customer. Such regulation recognises that depositors lack adequate information, and that new banking products carry serious risks, with dangers of contagion from a run or collapse. But the sheer power of financial institutions poses a dilemma. No bank would be able to meet its contingent liabilities if they all fell due at the same time. Equally, governments cannot afford to keep bailing the banks out, and would encourage reckless behaviour if they did. Yet sometimes the government cannot afford to do nothing – hence the US Federal Reserve Board's role in the US$4 billion rescue of hedge fund Long-Term Capital Management in October 1998, because its collapse 'could paralyse the global financial system'.[123]

The Reserve Bank of New Zealand's light-handed approach to regulation is based on a system of disclosures from banks and market surveillance. It relies heavily on home-based regulation of the banks by their mainly Australian owners, and assumes that the parent company will rescue any New Zealand bank at risk of collapse.[124] While the Labour and National governments intervened to bail out the Bank of New Zealand, in 1989 and 1990 respectively, Labour did not rescue the privatised Development Finance Corporation in 1989 – a decision that was highly controversial. Whether it would stand aside again if the parent of a major bank failed to step in is uncertain, given the potentially severe social, economic and political ramifications of doing so (see Chapter 5).

Greater regulation of corporate transactions is clearly possible, although some question whether it is even worth New Zealand maintaining an independent share-market; they suggest that, in light of the extensive cross-ownership of companies, it may be sensible to merge with the Australians.[125] In the eyes of many, including major investors, stronger regulations are also desirable. While the Business Roundtable maintains its ideological purity, transnational investors indicate a desire for rules that provide certainty and stability, and small investors demand greater protection of their interests. The needs of workers and local communities, as Keynes noted, remain irrelevant to the corporate ownership system, even though its outcomes dramatically affect their lives.

▲ REGULATING SHORT-TERM CAPITAL FLOWS

The regulation of capital flows is more difficult and more controversial. Unfettered flows of finance capital are considered, even by those who profit from them, to pose a major threat to international economic stability. In early 1997, before the Asian collapse, leading hedge fund operator George Soros said: 'Although I have made a fortune in the financial markets, I now fear that the untrammelled intensification of laissez-faire capitalism and the spread of market values into all areas of life is endangering our open and democratic society. The main enemy of the open society, I believe, is no longer the communist but the capitalist threat.'[126]

Global currency trading is estimated to involve US$2 trillion a day. These rapid and often speculative flows of finance capital are highly volatile. In a deregulated global financial market, profits are high. So are the risks, especially in the hands of inexperienced or reckless traders. Speculation has individual winners and losers. But the cost can include economic disruption and potentially the meltdown of entire economies. As international interdependence grows, so does the domino effect of collapse. Speculation may not create a country's financial crisis, but it feeds off it, speeding the meltdown and deepening its impact. In some countries it may push vulnerable currencies over the edge.

As economist Brian Easton notes, crises take various forms, which often converge.[127] A *currency* crisis results from the sudden selling of the country's currency, which is fed by and feeds speculative trading. It can be caused by rational assessments of risk, or reflect a herd mentality. Governments respond in various ways: intervening through the central bank to try to hold the value of the currency; increasing interest rates to attract buyers back; and allowing the currency to devalue (formally, if there is a fixed exchange rate, or through the market if the currency is floating). A *banking* crisis arises when the banking system has too few assets to cover its liabilities, either because banks do not have enough liquidity to meet immediate demands (especially if there is a run of withdrawals) or because they are insolvent (that is, the value of their assets does not cover their liabilities). The latter often results from lending on highly overvalued assets, such as property or shares, whose value suddenly falls, or from a currency depreciation that increases their liability for debt held in a foreign currency. A *debt* crisis occurs when a country's inability to repay its foreign debt (private and public) forces its government to go to lenders and seek new terms.[128] The crisis may be due to external shocks beyond the government's control, overlending by foreign banks, government failure to adjust policies to prevent the default, or a combination of all three.

The consequences of these crises for the country and its people are often devastating. But that is not why the major international actors get involved. A serious currency, banking or debt crisis can potentially dry up trade, investment and financial flows, and choke the world economy, especially if it spreads to other countries. It also threatens the solvency and stability of the international banking system, which is dominated by North American, European and Japanese institutions whose own imprudent practices may have exposed them to serious financial risk. In a growing number of cases, their governments and the international financial institutions those governments control have designed bail-out packages aimed primarily at rescuing the banks and restoring the debtor country's ability to pay its creditors. The packages are effectively an advance from major powers to their own financial institutions. The cost of this 'corporate welfare' falls on taxpayers in the home country and local communities in the debtor country, who never went near the casino. Producers in the real economy – workers, shopkeepers, exporters, families – all pay.

Crises within richer countries have been largely self-contained, notably the collapse of the European Exchange Rate Mechanism in 1992,[129] and various bank bail-outs in the US in the 1980s and 1990s.[130] The Mexican financial crisis in 1994 and the East Asian crisis in 1997 had wider ramifications, as they signalled to investors the potential for the new high-growth economies to fail. In July 1997 the governments of Thailand, Indonesia and Malaysia watched as their currencies were devalued and two decades of growth vanished in two weeks. The run on their stockmarkets wiped out hundreds of billions of dollars in capital. Property prices plummeted, industries closed, consumption slowed, unemployment spiralled and infrastructure projects came to a standstill. Thailand and Indonesia arranged unprecedented bail-out packages with the IMF, supported by other institutions and the major powers. The shock was compounded when the South Korean economy collapsed in November 1997. Banking scandals in Japan intensified the sense of crisis. In 1998 Russia followed, then Brazil in early 1999.

Official explanations and responses sought to keep the legitimacy of deregulated global markets intact. The East Asian situation was blamed on 'weak fundamentals' and 'bad governance' – specifically the lack of regulatory capacity, ineffective monitoring of financial institutions, and corruption in the affected countries. The solution was therefore to strengthen institutional capacity and systems for financial prudency, and to install 'good governance'. In a symposium on capital account convertibility, US trade economist Dani Rodrik reflected on the inadequacy of this response:

> A sad commentary on our understanding of what drives capital flows is that every crisis spawns a new generation of economic models. When a new crisis hits, it turns out that the previous generation of models was hardly adequate. Hence, the earliest models of currency crises were based on the incompatibility of monetary and fiscal policies with fixed exchange rates. These seemed to account well for the myriad balance-of-payments crises experienced through the 1970s. The debt crisis of 1982 unleashed an entire literature on over-borrowing in developing countries, placing the blame squarely on expansionary fiscal policies (and, in some countries, on inappropriate sequencing of liberalization). But crises did not go away when governments became better behaved on the monetary and fiscal front. For example, the [European Exchange Rate Mechanism] crisis in 1992 could not be blamed on lax monetary and fiscal policies in Europe, and therefore led to a new set of models with multiple equilibria. The peso crisis of 1994–95 [in Mexico] did not fit very well either, so economists came up with yet other explanations – this time focusing on the role of real exchange rate overvaluations and the need for more timely and accurate information on government policies. In the Asian crisis, neither the real exchange rate nor inadequate information seems to have played a major role, so attention has shifted to moral hazard and crony capitalism in these countries.
>
> The moral of this twisted story is twofold: (a) financial crises will always be with us; and (b) there is no magic bullet to stop them. These conclusions are important because they should make us appropriately wary about statements of the form, 'we can make free capital flows safe for the world if we do x at the same time,' where x is the currently fashionable antidote to crisis. Today's x is 'strengthening the domestic financial system and improving prudential standards.' Tomorrow's is anybody's guess. If we are forced to look for a new series of policy errors each time a crisis hits, we should be extremely cautious about our ability to prescribe a policy regime that will sustain a stable system of capital flows.[131]

Walden Bello, a Filipino academic and Director of the Centre for the Global South in Bangkok, has offered an alternative to the official view of the Asian crisis. Domestic governments sought to fast-track capitalist development by relying heavily on short-term investment. International agencies and voices of 'orthodoxy' encouraged them to deregulate their financial markets, offer high domestic interest rates and provide security through fixed exchange rates. As foreigners chased lucrative returns in the 'tiger cub' economies, they paid little heed to the quality of investment. Foreign and local finance was diverted into short-term and highly inflated property, equity and bond markets. When it became clear that domestic borrowers would default on interest and loans, local and foreign investors withdrew. A run on the currency ensued. Speculators moved in for a quick return. Acting like a herd, investors created chaos in the Thai, Indonesian, Malaysian and Philippine financial markets. Bello notes the irony that these countries were then blamed by the institutional creditors whose advice they had followed.[132]

South Korea and Thailand complied, to varying degrees, with the IMF template which focused on rebuilding foreign investor confidence. Indonesia descended into anarchy, and its loan conditions were constantly revised. Malaysia escaped the IMF net, and therefore had much more room to move. Prime Minister Mahathir bin Mohamed accused speculators of deliberately dumping the Malaysian ringgit to provoke a rapid devaluation and short-sell the currency and shares. (Most commentators argue that domestic disinvestment began the slide, and speculators then made it worse.) Mahathir was bitterly ironic about Western insistence that the markets should be left to readjust and reallocate resources more efficiently:

> The proponents of market forces say it will take time. A lot of people will suffer. Countries will lose their independence. The strong will overcome the weak. They, the strong, will then consolidate and give better service. The people must surely want better service and better goods from those most capable of delivering these than to have their independence and the shoddy goods and services their own people and government provided.[133]

Determined not to concede Malaysia's independence to the IMF, Mahathir imposed controls on capital movements. All ringgit held overseas had to be repatriated. Movement of money in or out of the country was controlled, and the exchange rate was fixed against the US dollar. International fund managers and speculators lost badly. But interest rates fell and the economy stabilised. Questions remained about the sustainability of this approach. Sceptics noted Mahathir's failure to address internal economic problems, especially nepotism. Others argued that investors would circumvent the regulations, given time.[134] Yet Mahathir's actions showed that the unorthodox was possible, and forced open the debate about financial regulation.

Most governments and commentators subsequently conceded the need for regulation of short-term capital flows. Many zeroed in on the hedge funds. The financial interests on Wall Street offered a minimalist concession, agreeing that some soft reporting disciplines on hedge funds were justified, but not regulation.[135] Other regulators sought more active intervention, based on experience. The Governor of the Reserve Bank of Australia, for example, condemned the hedge funds as 'the privileged children of the international financial scene', entitled to the benefits of free markets with none of the responsibilities.[136] This followed an attack on the Australian dollar in June 1998 which forced the Reserve Bank to intervene to stabilise the currency.[137] The Governor suggested that the Basle capital requirements (operated by the Bank of International Settlements) were 'excessively generous' in their treatment of financial markets, and supported the right of poorer countries to impose temporary controls. On 23 March 1999 the Canadian Federal Parliament voted by 164 to 83 'that the government should enact a tax on financial transactions in concert with the international community'.[138]

Various regulatory options were being considered. India had maintained traditional controls on foreign exchange movements, and was among the least seriously affected by the East Asian crisis. A more innovative approach was the proposed Tobin tax, a small uniform tax on all currency transactions anywhere in the world. This would provide a disincentive to short-term speculative investments (which often have very small profit margins), but would have minimal impact on long-term investment and the commodity trade. The idea was opposed by investors and the major powers as ineffective unless there was universal adherence, which seemed unlikely. But it was still open to individual governments to impose the tax, however imperfectly. Chile used a different approach of reserve requirements to limit the impact of short-term investment flows on its currency. This required any foreign investor or local company borrowing abroad to hold 30 percent (later 10 percent) of the foreign capital inflow in a non-interest bearing deposit at the central bank for the first year, after which it was released to them.[139] It was basically a tax on capital inflows. Ironically, just when people were looking to Chile's example, it reduced the reserve requirement to zero; by April 1999, however, it was talking of imposing it again.[140] Voices of the finance sector, notably the *Wall Street Journal*, attacked the Chilean reserve requirements as ineffective because investors found ways around them; they insisted that the best solution was sound regulation of domestic financial institutions and continued market 'reform'.[141]

Other interested parties promoted institutional responses that combined global rules with investor guarantees. George Soros defended open capital markets as economically and politically desirable, but conceded that they were unstable, imperfectly informed, and lacked collective rationality.[142] His proposed solution was an International Credit Insurance Corporation, presumably within the IMF, which would explicitly guarantee loans and credits to the limit defined for each country. Once that limit was reached, investors would take their own risk. While there would be problems in deciding how that credit should be distributed within the country, Soros said, no scheme was going to be perfect. At the same time, he opposed the free entry of foreign banks into domestic markets, arguing that they creamed off the wholesale market and left less profitable clients under-served; they also gave priority to the interests of their home country when a crisis occurred. He proposed that banks should have to meet strict reporting requirements on their currency position and that of their clients, possibly with limits imposed.[143]

The IMF offered its own solution. In late 1997 it announced plans to amend the Articles of Association to include power over the liberalisation of member countries' capital accounts.[144] The Fund already had authority to monitor and supervise financial flows connected with trade in goods and services, exchange rate movements, credit flows and debt servicing. It now sought power to do the same with direct and portfolio investment. The change would require all IMF members to make a commitment to liberalise their capital flows fully over time. Meanwhile, countries would need to follow IMF advice and targets in pursuing sound macroeconomic policies and strengthening their domestic financial system. The IMF's new power would also carry an expanded surveillance function. Critics accused the IMF of asking governments to do more of what created the problem in the first place.[145] The result would be huge capital inflows when there was confidence in the economy, and unimpeded outflows when, rationally or otherwise, capital took fright.

So, despite a growing recognition of the need to re-regulate, there was no agreement on how and to what degree. The most powerful voices remained those with direct financial interest in short-term profitability, and hence in mobility of global capital, and they trenchantly opposed attempts to establish an effective international regime. It was left to individual governments to decide whether and how to move. Some were already doing so.

The guardians of New Zealand's financial system believed there was no need. Reserve Bank Governor Don Brash insisted that the market should be left to self-correct.[146] Justifying New Zealand's minimalist approach, he commented in late 1998:

> Those who ask why nobody is coming up with a plan to protect New Zealand from the Asian crisis are asking the wrong question. New Zealand already has a plan. It was set in the mid-eighties, when we as a nation set about reforming our economy to be more flexible, more open, and more adaptable. In effect we decided that rapidly adapting to international shocks was better than trying to pretend we could resist or avoid them.[147]

The unwillingness even to explore the options threatens to leave New Zealand exposed as an outpost of purity in a world where more pragmatic governments are seeking to protect their economies from speculative capital flows. Once more, New Zealand's ideologues have ignored the lessons of history. As Keynes observed in 1936: 'To suppose that there exists some smoothly functioning automatic mechanism of adjustment which preserves equilibrium if only we trust to methods of laissez-faire is a doctrinaire delusion which disregards the lessons of historical experience without having behind it the support of sound theory.'[148]

▲ REFLECTIONS

The certainty of successive New Zealand governments (and their advisers) about the benefits of unrestricted flows of finance capital and foreign direct investment has been based on theory, backed by little empirical evidence. In Bruce Jesson's words, New Zealand has become a country run for the benefit of rentiers.[149]

Unrestricted flows of short-term capital have created the potential for a major financial crisis to hit New Zealand. It is possible to lessen the risk of an internally generated share-market crisis through stronger regulation of the Stock Exchange and corporate activities; but nothing will stop a local meltdown if the US share market crashes. Protecting the currency from a crisis caused by speculative forays or contagion is more difficult. Yet governments elsewhere are exploring, and using, a range of regulatory strategies. These warrant greater consideration than the New Zealand government's financial advisers seem prepared to give.

The risks posed by short-term capital are beyond the purview of most New Zealanders. They are more concerned about foreign direct investment. Successive governments, in opting for a policy that seeks indiscriminately to attract as much foreign investment as possible, have aroused deep-seated emotions. Even in 1992, many New Zealanders believed that too many of the country's assets were already controlled from offshore. While the opinion polls may reflect elements of xenophobia and racism, there is a widespread sense that New Zealanders are losing control of important aspects of their lives. For Maori this feeling runs deep, and compounds historical experiences of alienation and dispossession in their own land. Business leaders and economic commentators have added their voices to the populist concern. The government's response has been to insist on the benefits foreign investment will bring. Yet there has been no convincing evidence of the significant gains in employment, new productive investment, or benefits for small investors that have been promised.

Instead, foreign investment has been a major cause of the country's chronic problems with the balance of payments and foreign debt.

There *are* alternatives – notably, higher levels of domestic savings, complemented by strategic injections of foreign capital into productive enterprise, and a stronger regulatory regime. This may not be consistent with the 'international orthodoxy', but it is what many other OECD countries do. Fears of a backlash by foreign investors must be weighed against the lack of proven benefits of foreign investment. There is no need for New Zealand to be committed forever to a free investment regime.

5 ▲ Transnational Enterprise

The major beneficiaries of 'free' investment are the transnational enterprises (TNEs) that currently dominate world markets in every strategic activity – electronics, telecommunications, banking and insurance, food production, textiles, media and entertainment, mining, chemicals, armaments and many others. According to the United Nations Conference on Trade and Development (UNCTAD), the 100 largest transnational corporations in 1995 (ranked on the size of foreign assets) owned US$1.7 trillion worth of assets in their overseas companies – around one-fifth of the world's foreign-owned assets. They had foreign sales of US$2 trillion and employed close to 6 million people in their offshore operations.[1] Some had total revenues larger than the gross domestic product of countries in which they were operating. Almost nine-tenths of the top 100 were based in the US, the European Union (EU) or Japan.[2] While New Zealand can name its own – Fletcher Challenge, Carter Holt Harvey, the Dairy Board, Brierley Investments, Fernz Corporation, among others – most of these are now legally foreign-owned, and none made *Fortune* magazine's Global Top 500 in 1998.

Transnational enterprises are enormously powerful. Some even suggest they have made nation-states redundant. In 1995 globalisation guru Kenichi Ohmae, the former managing director of McKinsey and Co Japan, described nation-states as 'unnatural – even dysfunctional – actors in a global economy'.[3] Others say that this, at least, is their intent: 'The men who run the global corporations are the first in history with the organization, technology, money, and ideology to make a credible try at managing the world as an integrated economic unit. ... What they are demanding in essence is the right to transcend the nation-state, and in the process, transform it.'[4]

Transnationals epitomise globalisation. The popular stereotype is of free-ranging mega-corporations which operate in a borderless market-place and act in ways that nation-states cannot control; their sole motivation is to make money for their shareholders (and top-tier management); what happens to workers, indigenous nations, consumers, or the environment is not their concern, except as it affects financial return. This stereotype is true in many respects. Yet, as Chapter 1 explained, transnationals behave selectively: while many take a ruthless approach to their operations offshore, most have a strong home identification, and behave differently in their own country. Nor do transnationals always have their way. States still can, and do, regulate corporate activities, to varying extents and with varying success. Above all, people are not impotent – consumers, local communities, indigenous nations, trade unions, and environmental groups resist and innovate when confronted by the power of transnationals. This chapter examines the issues raised by a range of transnational enterprises in New Zealand, and the responses of those who are most directly affected.

▲ THE NATURE OF TRANSNATIONAL ENTERPRISE

Transnational firms are not new. In the seventeenth, eighteenth and nineteenth centuries, chartered corporations such as the Dutch East India Company and Hudson's Bay Company were notorious for their exploitation of actual or potential colonies, supported by their parent governments. Twentieth-century industrialisation saw the expansion of firms such as Ford, General Electric and Royal Dutch Shell, which operated mainly through subsidiaries in a number of countries. Their goal was either to circumvent border protections and gain entry to local markets, or to exploit natural resources and cheap labour in order to minimise production costs and maximise profits. By the 1970s rapid changes were occurring in production, information and communications technology, and international transportation systems had improved. It became easier to locate different parts of an integrated production process in different countries to take advantage of their particular attributes, including raw materials, technology, low labour costs or proximity to markets. Integrated production meant that trade within firms greatly expanded, which in turn meant new opportunities to minimise tax and legal liability. Competition focused less on price than on the range and quality of products. As competition increased, transnationals sought to improve their efficiency by relying more on technology and building strategic alliances with former competitors. The rise of regional free trade areas such as the European Community and later the North American Free Trade Agreement (NAFTA) gave a new impetus to mergers, takeovers and alliances that would provide privileged access to these markets. The financial sector developed innovative ways to service the offshore needs of domestic companies, and increasingly followed their own transnationals offshore. Governments came under pressure to ease restrictions on the mobility of capital and to open their countries to foreign investment. The free market agenda led politically by Margaret Thatcher and Ronald Reagan helped to fashion a more congenial environment for transnational enterprise. Firms, and many governments, began operate at a regional level, then globally.

By 1994, global sales by some 280,000 foreign affiliates of companies were around US$6.4 trillion annually, and their share of world output was about 6 percent.[5] Not all these firms were huge conglomerates. Transnational enterprise takes myriad forms – subsidiaries, branches, partnerships, joint ventures, franchises, licences and subcontracting. Small and medium-sized businesses have also become transnational. Firms with a similar focus, such as high-tech industries, often cluster in one location – for example, Silicon Valley in the US or special free trade zones in poorer countries.

Paradoxically, transnationals now seem to be shrinking in size, in terms of the number of employees and locations in which they operate, yet their incomes are often huge and growing. This may reflect an increase in 'network' firms, where a small team of highly paid executives and specialists runs the core management, design, sales and promotion operations in-house, while other activities are contracted out, often to low-wage countries. Some say that this kind of subcontracting provides more flexible work opportunities, especially for women, who disproportionately provide the labour. This can, in turn, alter the way women, households, labour and the state interact within the society. Decentralisation of production and supply can also open up new opportunities to build alliances and networks on local and global scales. These opportunities may extend to some indigenous peoples and marginalised communities. More frequently, however, transnational subcontracting on the 'periphery' is associated with child labour, appalling health and safety conditions, slave wages, the banning of unions, and human rights abuses. The textile trade is especially notorious in this regard.[6]

Supply networks have also changed. Increased computerisation allows importers to use 'just in time' inventories. This enables producers to target production and reduce stockpiles, and suppliers to avoid holding large inventories. But 'just in time' production and ordering also mean 'just in time' work for contractors and employees. For customers dependent on imports, ordering short in hard times can mean long and costly delays. Many local producers and retailers now depend on supply contracts with large foreign-owned companies, whose requirements limit their options and offer little security. The remaining independent producers must find unique product ranges and niche markets. New small businesses emerge locally to service transnational operations, but they have far less autonomy and are more vulnerable than the independent small businesses that directly service local communities and domestic economies. Professional services have also changed. The major legal and accounting firms play a central role in designing transnational business operations.[7] Technology allows long-distance servicing, frequently from offshore. Local lawyers and accountants are often displaced by, or reorganise into, national and transnational partnerships.

Transnationals are often portrayed as global, yet the big firms maintain the bulk of their operations within the OECD. Most inward and outward investment is also concentrated there. The US is the largest exporter and importer of investment. In 1995, around two-fifths of investment from the US went to the European Union.[8] Despite this, political economist Robert Wade notes that overseas investment is still quite a small proportion of net domestic business investment in the US and Europe. He concludes that there is no huge 'transnationalisation' of the US economy, and even less in Germany and Japan.[9] Although transnationals invest much less in poor countries, they often hold strategic economic positions there, such as control over the marketing of a country's main export crops. Their impact relative to the size of the country's economy can be enormous.[10]

The world of transnationals is full of paradox. They are the key players in a global economic policy framework that assumes that competition drives efficiency. Yet they also act as large corporate combinations, using their economic power to demand national laws and international agreements that protect their market share and enhance their dominance. In his bestseller *When Corporations Rule the World,* David Korten remarks that transnationals 'espouse a theory that assumes small firms but advocate policies that strengthen monopoly'.[11] Their advantages of market dominance, scale, mass marketing, brand identity, access to funds and international networks make it very hard for smaller players to compete. This crowds out many domestic companies, who tend to be more committed to the particular industry, workforce and community – and less likely to evade local controls. The business culture changes; so does the relationship between company and staff. No longer valued as an asset to the business, employees are usually the first victims of the transnational drive to increase profits. As a result, the spread of transnational business is often seen as a threat to local businesses and jobs, and sometimes to local culture and identity.

The dominant position of transnationals has been strengthened through alliances of mega-firms. These are designed to create economies of scale and expenditure, especially in high-technology research and development, and to build market share by combining their complementary strengths within the global market. New cross-border arrangements between firms almost trebled between 1990 and 1995, to around 4,600; three-quarters of these were within the OECD.[12] Major corporations also entered informal alliances, funding joint research and development programmes and sharing their technology and facilities. Mergers and takeovers almost inevitably mean 'rationalisation' and redundancies in the constituent companies, wherever they are based. In January 1999 Selwyn Parker described the impact of recent 'mega-mergers' on New Zealand. Most of the top ten mergers in 1998 had substantial New Zealand investment, including Compaq with Digital, SBC Communications with Ameritech, Bell Atlantic with GTE, British Petroleum with AMOCO, Deutsche Bank with Bankers Trust. He concluded: 'In head offices' endless quest for synergies, reduced costs – often through redundancies, closure of duplicate operations and economies of scale – the New Zealand outpost can be jerked around like the ball on the end of a long chain'.[13]

The impact of these changes on people's lives can be huge. Micro-level studies show how shifts in business ownership affect the social structure and dynamics of local communities. For example, a team of geographers from the University of Auckland has studied the effects of substantial changes in the local commercial balance of power on the Northland town of Kaikohe. In 1987 the town had a number of locally owned firms with strong connections to the regional economy, and a few larger, externally owned businesses that were mostly sourced and controlled from outside the area. By 1994 many local businesses had shut down or were planning to do so. There were a larger number of firms with external connections, whose strategic and operational decisions were likely to be influenced from elsewhere in New Zealand and overseas. Their turnover and staff numbers were much higher than local independent firms, giving them greater control over the local business community. Local independent businesses showed a higher degree of loyalty to local services. Business with outside affiliations increasingly used services from elsewhere. More owners and managers lived outside the community, which eroded their commitment to Kaikohe and contributed to the loss of local economic control. The researchers noted that 'external connectedness' is a double-edged sword for such towns: 'While consumers benefit from access to a wider range of goods, external ownership and control may inhibit local economic linkages'.[14] These effects are felt even when capital reorganises nationally to seek economies of scale; they are far more severe when the locus of control for key decisions shifts offshore.

When things go wrong, the transnational's political leverage, a morass of legal complexities and the 'corporate veil' help shield it from liability.

Union Carbide, for example, escaped any formal liability for the deaths of hundreds and the maiming of thousands in the Bhopal gas disaster of 1985.[15] The locally incorporated Union Carbide India had minimal capitalisation, which meant it could close with relatively little cost, while the parent company denied any responsibility. Because Union Carbide India was a joint venture with the Indian government, the politicians faced a conflict of interest in holding the company to account. India's desire to attract more foreign investment gave threats of capital flight and non-investment added potency. The transnational location of key actors allowed them to shop around for the most favourable jurisdictions. The difficulty of proving that the gas leak had caused people's illness or death, the weakness of Indian negligence laws, problems of enforceability, and political pressures on the judiciary meant that litigation was unlikely to succeed. Ultimately, the poverty of the victims left them powerless against the giant transnational enterprise, self-interested politicians, and mercenary lawyers chasing contingency fees.

Transnational operations, especially in resource-intensive activities such as forestry and mining, often clash head-on with indigenous sovereignty. In Canada, Chile, Mexico, Papua New Guinea and New Zealand, resistance to transnationals and the governments that support them has ranged from legal claims to land occupations to civil war. In New Zealand, iwi such as Tuwharetoa ki Kawerau have long-running Treaty claims over land leased in the late 1960s to Tarawera Forests, then part-owned by the Crown to Fletcher Challenge, on very poor terms. (Despite hearings on the Tuwharetoa claim before the Waitangi Tribunal in 1995, there was still no report from the Waitangi Tribunal in June 1999.)[16] The same iwi, and others, have long battled against the desecration of the Tarawera River by Fletcher's Kawerau pulp and paper mill, and the creation of what is called the 'black drain' where it enters the sea.[17] Nearby, Tuhoe activists ran a successful campaign to secure a moratorium on the clearance of native forest on tapu Taiarahia mountain, near Ruatoki, which Fletchers wanted to plant in pine.[18] These struggles were mirrored by First Nations campaigns in Canada against Fletcher's then subsidiary, TimberWest, and other major forestry companies in British Columbia, where most logging takes place on Crown-owned land, a significant part of which is under claim.[19] The Mapuche people in Chile have been tied up in protracted legal cases which failed to restore control of 80,000 hectares of ancestral land, much of which is in forests owned and milled by the Carter Holt Harvey subsidiary, Bosques Arauco. In October 1998 the company allegedly ignored a court order not to fell the forest, and brought in private security personnel to deal with Mapuche who tried to prevent them from doing so. A number of Mapuche were seriously injured, and charges were laid against several of their leaders under Chile's internal security laws. Mapuche leaders likened the government's response to 'the darkest years of the military dictatorship. ... In addition, forestry companies are employing armed men, establishing vigilante brigades and collaborating with police forces in order to protect the companies' interests.'[20]

Sometimes these conflicts lead to war. The unrestrained exploitation of the Panguna mine in Bougainville by Rio Tinto, without the consent of traditional landowners and payment of fair royalties, largely triggered the independence war in 1988.[21] The Bougainville Revolutionary Army shut down the mine, but the Papua New Guinea government was determined to reopen it. In 1997 the government hired South African mercenaries, Executive Outcomes, to pursue the war and maintain the blockade of the island. After that arrangement was exposed, the government cancelled the contract and the Prime Minister was forced to resign. The mercenary company had previously taken mining concessions as part-payment for similar operations, prompting speculation that this was also part of the Bougainville deal.[22]

These conflicts with indigenous peoples have their roots in colonisation; to some degree transnationals are just new actors in a long-running struggle for self-determination. Yet power is also being transferred from the colonial state, which can be challenged at the very least on moral grounds (and in the case of New Zealand, on the basis of the Treaty of Waitangi), to more remote international corporations whose sole responsibility is to their shareholders. This is literally a struggle for survival. The corporations can come and go; but the relationship between indigenous peoples and their land is forever.

▲ TRANSNATIONAL RIGHTS AND RESPONSIBILITIES

Individually and collectively, transnationals demand that host states provide regulatory and policy settings that serve their interests. Their parent states have been willing to sponsor formal and informal agreements to enhance the operations (and profitability) of transnationals, usually taking care to limit any impact on their own economy. Since the 1960s the OECD, whose members include the major capital exporters, has developed investment codes and a Declaration on International Investment and Multinational Enterprises to promote the liberalisation of investment and non-discrimination between local and foreign investors. The 1980s and 1990s have seen a rapid growth in the number and coverage of bilateral investment treaties, regional trade agreements and multilateral agreements, notably under the WTO. The IMF and World Bank impose conditions on loans that require debtors to relax their foreign investment rules, and to privatise and deregulate. The World Bank coordinates and guarantees private sector loans, and operates a facility to resolve disputes between governments and investors. The transnationals have developed their own instruments and facilities through the International Chamber of Commerce.

The corporations are strong on their rights, but have an aversion to responsibilities. Their home governments usually defend the lack of effective constraint – except on labour and environmental matters, where richer countries face domestic pressure to maintain high standards, and often seek to impose those same standards on their competitors. Many poor countries face a dilemma. They recognise the need for – or inevitability of – foreign investment, and actively compete for it, often with limited success. Yet most of them share a deep-seated concern about the power this gives transnational companies over their economies.

Attempts within the United Nations to balance the growing power of transnationals with the right of states to regulate their economic activities met strenuous resistance. In 1974 the UN created a Commission and a Centre on transnational corporations, and work began on a Code of Conduct for transnationals and a Code on Technology Transfer. These codes would not have been binding or enforceable without state action, and lacked effective sanctions. Even so, rich countries resisted and negotiations broke down. Work on the codes was suspended, and effectively abandoned, in 1991.[23]

To forestall other developments, the OECD developed its own voluntary Guidelines for Multinational Enterprises in 1976.[24] These are minimalist, being designed to encourage (rather than enforce) socially and politically acceptable behaviour by enterprises operating away from home. Corporations are urged to cooperate with the development goals of the host countries and to respect their policies. They should refrain from anticompetitive practices and avoid improper political activities. They are also 'encouraged' to maintain good industrial relations and safe procedures, and to supply information on health and environmental hazards to their host governments and subsidiaries. The section on employment states that enterprises 'should' recognise the right to trade union representation; ensure constructive negotiations with managers who have authority to make decisions; maintain labour standards at least comparable to those of similar employers in the host country; upgrade the skills of workers as practicable; give reasonable notice of operational changes that would severely affect workers; and not threaten to shift part or all of the business in order to unfairly influence negotiations on the right to organise.[25] OECD governments are, in turn, 'encouraged' to promote the guidelines.

The OECD's guidelines for transnationals are non-binding: they contain no sanctions, and no obligatory mechanisms for dispute resolution. There is no attempt to make parent corporations responsible for the default of their subsidiaries. The transnationals reluctantly accepted the concept of guidelines, but successfully argued that host states should be required to take corporate interests into account when changing their laws.[26] The guidelines were reviewed in 1991, when the main addition was an exhortation that transnationals 'take due account of the need to protect the environment and avoid creating environmentally related health problems'.[27] A further review began in late 1998.

Under pressure in the late 1990s, some large transnationals took steps to develop their own customer charters and ethical rules on child labour and eco-labelling. These were voluntary, and of varying sincerity. Other moves have government support. An example is the Ethical Trading Initiative on labour standards that is being developed jointly by the British government, transnationals such as Tesco Stores, The Body Shop, Boots the Chemist and British Telecom, numerous development NGOs, British unions and the ICFTU.[28] Its proposals would combine codes of conduct, monitoring and transparency, adapted to particular companies' conditions. The terms of any commitments would be voluntary – the fundamental obligation of transnationals is still to maximise the value of their shareholders' investments.

▲ TRANSNATIONALS AS POLITICAL ACTORS

As noted in Chapter 1, transnationals have an ambiguous relationship with location and with the state. What presents as a globally integrated, market-driven firm still has to be incorporated somewhere. Its legal home may be a tax haven, such as Bermuda or the Cook Islands. But most transnationals also want a political home, with a government that will advance their interests at national and international levels. Transnationals also rely on host governments to provide a legal, physical and technical infrastructure. This then subjects them to the local laws on labour, taxation, indigenous rights, the environment, safety, consumer protection, monopolies and pricing.

Transnationals need the state. At the same time, globalisation makes it difficult for states to regulate the flow of money across national borders and to control transnationals' activities through domestic regulation. Actual or threatened capital flight or investment boycotts can have a dramatic impact on countries that depend heavily on foreign direct investment. Systematic tax avoidance restricts the ability of home and host governments to gather revenue and maintain their country's physical and social infrastructure. In the 1997/98 financial year, for example, Rupert Murdoch's News Corp and its subsidiaries paid only A$325 million in corporate taxes worldwide, on profits of A$5.4 billion; the group had paid no tax in Britain since 1987, on accumulated profit of £1.4 billion.[29] These factors give the more powerful transnationals considerable leverage over government policy. Political economist Razeen Sally observes that transnational enterprise is 'not only the key economic and commercial actor in structures of international production', but is also 'implanted in the institutional arrangements of nation-states, as well as subnational and supranational regions'.[30] These linkages invest the enterprise with a political identity. Logically, it seeks to minimise constraints at national levels and secure international rules that require governments to liberalise. Political leaders are warned that they must embrace – and be embraced by – the deregulated global economy, or be left behind. The more open a country's economy, the more vulnerable it becomes to a loss of credibility in the eyes of international investors and to demands from the transnationals to liberalise further.

Transnationals lobby hard to achieve these ends. At the international level they collaborate actively with each other to promote their common cause. They help create and fund seemingly autonomous voices to promote their international agenda, such as the World Economic Forum based in Geneva (Chapter 2). The voice of transnational capital is institutionalised in leading international economic agencies; for example, the Business and Industry Advisory Committee at the OECD was a key player in pushing the Multilateral Agreement on Investment as a 'high quality' charter of investor rights (see Chapter 9). Transnationals also form ad hoc coalitions around particular negotiations or issues, such as the energy companies' lobby during international talks to reduce ozone-depleting CFCs.[31]

Transnationals lobby home and host governments just as aggressively. The most powerful corporate lobby is the United States Council for International Business (USCIB), comprising 300 transnationals, service companies, law firms and business associations. Its mission is to 'advance the global interests of American business both at home and abroad'.[32] The Council is allied to the International Chamber of Commerce and the International Organization of Employers, and officially represents US business positions in the main intergovernmental bodies. The International Chamber of Commerce calls itself the world business organisation for promoting the global market economy. It claims 7,000 member companies from 130 countries, and was chaired in 1998 by a senior executive from Nestlé.[33]

The American Chamber of Commerce operates in numerous countries, producing reports and submissions that seek to influence the policies of the host government. The New Zealand affiliate (known as AMCHAM) represents many of the US-related transnationals operating in New Zealand, and adopts a non-ideological approach when advocating their interests. In 1995 and 1998, it commissioned surveys of its members to counter growing opposition to foreign investment in New Zealand, and to promote its members' policy demands (see Chapter 4);[34] in late 1997 it produced a survey critical of the Resource Management Act (discussed below).

The most effective corporate lobby in New Zealand is the Business Roundtable, 80 percent of whose members are either foreign-owned or local transnationals. Its ability to influence political decision-making was discussed in Chapter 2.[35] Individual business leaders have played a complementary role, including in defence of the 'thin' political system that allowed New Zealand's free market revolution to occur. In 1993 Peter Shirtcliffe, a Roundtable member and chair of US-controlled Telecom, fronted an intensive, well-funded campaign against the introduction of mixed member proportional representation (MMP), claiming it would provoke an outflow of foreign investment and hinder rational (that is, neo-liberal) economic policy.[36] He reiterated these fears before the first MMP election in 1996.[37] A pre-election commentary in the *National Business Review* supported his stance, citing a survey of the top 500 companies, conducted prior to the 1993 referendum on the electoral system. Some 13 percent said they would consider relocation if MMP were introduced, 25 percent would consider partial relocation, and 34 percent would consider reduced capital expenditure. The columnist concluded: 'the situation need not be gloomy if the voting public is made aware of the likely consequences of an economic nationalist victory in the elections.'[38]

The 1998 survey by the American Chamber of Commerce was interpreted as evidence of anti-MMP sentiments among big business. Those surveyed ranked 'political instability' as the least attractive feature of New Zealand's business environment. The *New Zealand Herald* reported that just over half the responding firms had considered quitting the country, and cited MMP as the main adverse change.[39] Ironically, many of the specific policies they mentioned as unfavourable were examples of the conflict between the government's pure market approach and transnational self-interest, such as parallel importing, the electricity restructuring, and zero tariffs on vehicle assembly. The passage of these measures had coincided with the breakdown of the Coalition government in 1998. But those policies and their implementation reflected the idiosyncrasies of the National ministers responsible for them, more than the political system of MMP.

In the 1980s and 1990s, the economic power and mobility of transnational investors put strong competitive pressures on governments seeking to attract and retain them to liberalise their laws on taxation, resource management, labour, product standards, competition, foreign investment and so on. Critics say there is no logical end-point to this process of competitive deregulation, which they term a 'race to the bottom'. As a blanket statement, this is an oversimplification. Regulations and laws cannot be produced or enforced at either the national or international level without the cooperation of the state. Governments are subject to their own constraints and influences – historical, social, cultural and political – which often challenge the erosion of economic and political controls. Whether a government can resist demands from international investors will depend heavily on whether the country has retained a sufficiently viable domestic economy to survive a loss of foreign investment and to service its foreign debt commitments. Equally, a relentless 'race to the bottom' is not in the interests of capital globally. A single peripheral country such as Guyana or Nauru can be exploited to the hilt. But when capital secures rapid deregulation in a number of dynamic countries with integrated economies which then collapse (as occurred in Latin America in the 1980s and East Asia in the late 1990s), there is a danger of systemic economic crisis.

The risks of 'capital flight' can also be overstated. For the transnationals, there are benefits to long-term profitability from having social stability, a sustainable pool of natural resources, and an appropriately skilled (but preferably non-unionised) workforce.[40] The investment they sink into starting up, learning about an environment, and gaining acceptance among local stakeholders also means they are often reluctant to relocate. Again, this applies differentially. Transnationals tend to maintain strong involvement with their home country. Most of their assets and employees are usually located there, and a large majority of their shares are held by local individuals and legal entities. Top management and governance are also based in the home country. The bulk of research and development is carried out at head office. Research undertaken abroad mainly adapts technology to local conditions or 'listens in' to local research. So the activities that add greatest value to a transnational's operations are still concentrated within the home country.

Poorer countries, and smaller ones with open economies and few transnationals of their own, tend to host more activities with low added-value. For them, competitive deregulation is a serious issue, and threats of capital flight are real. Transnational lobbies in New Zealand, including the Business Roundtable and the American Chamber of Commerce, have argued this point forcibly. But while some foreign direct investors may withdraw when countries refuse to deregulate, they also leave highly deregulated countries for other reasons – for example, Fernz Corporation decided to shift to Australia in 1999 because its ownership, markets and operations were now mainly overseas.[41] Other New Zealand companies have shifted to Australia because of its investment incentives and more activist economic environment (see Chapter 6).

Successive New Zealand governments have been keen to respond where the deregulatory demands of transnationals fit their own objectives. Their justifications usually include the irresistibility of competitive pressures, the equally irresistible demands of foreign investors, the futility of attempting to regulate transnational activity, and the benefits of deregulating unilaterally.

▲ Taxation

Taxation is a major focus of pressure from transnationals. The effectiveness of such pressure is illustrated by the international tax legislation passed by the New Zealand Parliament on 12 December 1995, the final form of which was strongly influenced by lobbying from the American Chamber of Commerce.[42] Non-resident companies previously paid 38 percent income tax, while local companies paid 33 percent; under the new tax-credit regime, foreign and domestic investors paid the same levels of tax.[43] Officials estimated that this would cut the annual tax take by around $140 million.

The new regime was presented to Parliament as part of a fiscally neutral package. Lower income taxes for overseas companies would be balanced by new rules to limit tax avoidance (although the American Chamber of Commerce warned that these should not be a disincentive to foreign investment). One aspect of these new rules addressed the common practice of 'transfer pricing', whereby transnationals vary their taxable profits in different countries by manipulating the price of transactions between different parts of the firm; this allows them to record profits in the location where taxes are lowest. Foreign taxpayers would now be required to make a 'conscientious effort' to establish and document 'arm's length' prices for cross-border transactions. It was up to Inland Revenue to prove those prices were wrong.[44] Such a liberal regime was justified as limiting compliance costs on investors. A second tax reduction strategy covered in the legislation was 'thin capitalisation', whereby corporations fund their local operations from excessive levels of debt, and claim interest repayments as tax deductions instead of paying tax on those earnings as profits. The legislation restricted interest deductibility to companies with a worldwide debt-to-asset ratio below 75 percent (and in some cases up to 110 percent) – very high in international terms.

The Labour opposition gave its support 'more in a spirit of resignation than of wild enthusiasm', and asked: 'Why is the Government so soft on multinational and transnational tax dodgers ... when [it] is so hard on the little battlers here in New Zealand?' It agreed with the government that the measures were required 'to prevent the more aggressive behaviour of other jurisdictions from collaring more than their share of income that has been earned within our shores' – a reference to the transnationals' practice of structuring profits so that they paid enough tax in the US to reduce the risks of being audited by powerful US tax agencies.[45] However, the time lag in securing revenue from the amendments on transfer pricing and thin capitalisation would mean 'we give money away before we get any back'. Officials admitted there was a wide margin of error in their figures.[46]

In mid-1998, Minister of Finance Bill Birch floated the possibility of reducing the tax burden on transnationals even further; he suggested that the company income tax rate might be reduced below that for personal income tax if Australia reduced its levels: 'If we are not going to be lost in a bidding round with countries like, say, Australia to attract business, we are going to have to match what they have done or are thinking of doing in terms of corporate taxation.'[47] This assumed that even slightly higher corporate taxes (or stricter laws on transfer pricing and thin capitalisation) would significantly affect investment decisions. No methodologically sound evidence was presented to demonstrate that tax levels were more important than other attractions that required taxpayer investment, such as an educated workforce, research and development, and quality infrastructure. It also assumed that the loss of actual or potential foreign investment would be disastrous for New Zealand – a view challenged in Chapter 4. The connection between lower tax rates and actual investment levels was yet another article of faith. But once tax cuts were made, they became psychologically embedded. Any policy that included raising corporate (or other) taxes again would set off the alarms bells, making the policy a political liability.

▲ Environment

A second focus for transnational pressure is the environment. The term 'environmental dumping' has become a common phrase in transnational commerce. Poor countries desperate for foreign investment are the major dumping grounds. Larry Summers, who served as Secretary to the US Treasury under President Clinton, offered the chilling rationale that poor people in poor countries have shorter life spans and less earning potential than wealthy people in rich countries. In a memorandum to colleagues he asked: 'shouldn't the World Bank be encouraging more migration of the dirty industries to the LDC's . ... I think the economic logic behind dumping a load of toxic waste in the lowest-wage country is impeccable and we should face up to that.'[48] When industries that produce such wastes occur in rich countries, they are most often located in poor and non-white areas where people lack political and economic influence, and have no choice about where they live.[49]

Waste disposal has become a lucrative transnational business. US company Waste Management is the world's largest waste disposal corporation, with revenues exceeding US$10 billion by 1995. It has a history of siting dumps and incinerators in poor, non-white communities, and has been repeatedly fined for environmental and anti-monopoly violations in the US.[50] Waste Management's New Zealand operations have been built on the contracting out of local government services in Auckland and North Shore cities, Hamilton, Hutt Valley, Wellington, Wanganui and New Plymouth. In May 1999, the Commerce Commission refused the company permission to proceed with a $115 million takeover of its major competitor Waste Care, whose French parent company Suez Lyonnaise des Eaux had decided to quit New Zealand. Because the takeover would result in Waste Management owning the only two landfill sites in Auckland after 2003, the Commission concluded that the barriers to new entrants would be too high. In a second application later that month, Waste Management promised to divest some assets, but required the details to be kept confidential.[51] Further privatisations could see Waste Management increase its ability to underbid competitors and dictate terms. One solution is to resist the privatisation of services, but strong competition laws and environmental regulation also become imperative.

Transnational (and local) businesses often complain about the compliance cost of seeking approvals for resource use and meeting the conditions imposed. These costs have risen with greater environmental awareness and stronger NGO and community lobbies. In 1997 the Business Roundtable stepped up its campaign to weaken the Resource Management Act 1991, itself a more-market version of the Bill introduced by the Labour government in 1989. The American Chamber of Commerce added its voice with a survey on the impediments to investment posed by the Act.[52] This survey, like others from the Chamber, was seriously flawed, drawing conclusions from only 42 responses to 680 questionnaires. Yet it contributed to the pressure on government to endorse business-friendly changes to the legislation. In 1998 Minister for the Environment Simon Upton commissioned a report on changes to the legislation, including a 'think piece' from Owen McShane (who was known to support a radical market approach to resource law reform) and two more moderate commentaries.[53] The government produced a formal proposal for amendments to the Act in November 1998. These would open up the processing of resource consents to the private sector; limit rights of appeal on resource consent applications; limit public notification of such applications; remove the requirement to make all decisions subject to the sustainability principles of the Act; and restrict the ability of councils to put in place mechanisms to protect the environment.[54] The Minister claimed that there was not enough time to test out all the proposals[55] – this was, in other words, yet another experiment. The legislation was supposed to be introduced in March 1999; it finally appeared in July. Submissions were called for, but there seemed no chance the Bill would be passed before the election.

An equally volatile issue has been transnational liability for hazardous activities such as mining. One example is the Coeur Gold (NZ) Golden Cross Mine in the Waitekauri Valley, near Waihi.[56] This was a 'shelf' company with little paid up capital; 80 percent of it was owned by a complex four-tier company structure which, through two intermediate US companies, led to Coeur D'Alene Mines Corp in Idaho. The previous owners until 1993, Cyprus Amax of Denver and Viking Mining (locally owned by the Todd Group), had sited a tailings dump containing cyanide and heavy metals on a deep-seated, 1.5 kilometre landslide. The 'toe' of the 3 million tonne slide is believed to be in the bed of the Waitekauri River. Tailings dams are meant to hold toxins so they will never escape.

For years, local people and Coromandel Watchdog warned that the dam could eventually rupture, or toxic contents could seep through cracks and slow leaks – by which time the foreign owners would be long gone. By mid-1995 Coeur Gold knew that the tailings dam was sliding downhill, but continued mining and adding toxic waste for another three years. It spent $27 million trying to stop the slide, but this failed.[57] In April 1996 the Waikato Regional Council decided that 'the long term continuance of the mine tailings on a site of known instability is high risk which could result in contingent liabilities for future generations'.[58] The Council required the tailings to be moved and stored at a site with greater security, when or before the mine closed. In February 1997 the company admitted that 500,000 tonnes of buttressing rock designed to slow the slide was in the wrong place and may have worsened the situation.[59] Coeur Gold (NZ) complained about the cost of resource management objections by Coromandel Watchdog,[60] and threatened the group with bankruptcy if they did not immediately pay $20,000 costs awarded against them.[61] But the company's real financial problems stemmed from the falling international price of gold and the cost of remedial work on the tailings dam.

The estimated cost of moving the dam was over $100 million.[62] Coeur Gold (NZ) had signed environmental bonds for just $11.5 million.[63] The US parent company wrote off the entire value of the mine – US$53 million (then equivalent to NZ$75 million) – and shut it down in December 1997, four years earlier than predicted. With no local assets to be called on, the company would avoid liability for any future clean-up costs.[64] The same company was being sued by the US government for its share of an estimated US$980 million clean-up of mining pollution in Idaho.[65] It also faced litigation over Coeur Gold (NZ) from disgruntled shareholders, and investigation by the American Securities and Exchange Commission.[66]

Concern about the hazards posed by tailings dams prompted several reports from the Parliamentary Commissioner for the Environment which urged more effective legislation. Licences for the existing open-pit mines were granted under the Mining Act 1971, but imposed no liability once the company ceased its operations and restored the site as required. If it abandoned the site, the land eventually revested in the Crown, which was left carrying the risk. In 1988 the Commissioner said there was an urgent need to establish legal responsibility for dam safety, arrangements for bonds or trust funds that would survive the project, and a special fund to cover the management of environmental hazards in perpetuity.[67] The new mining and resource management laws passed in 1991 did little to improve the situation. The government received the royalties from mining, but had no legal responsibility for any environmental effects. Local authorities were responsible for monitoring those effects and compliance by the companies, and dealing with any long-term damage; but they could not ultimately recover the costs from the company. In Coeur Gold's case, the Waikato Regional Council had the power to increase the company's environmental bonds and make it shift the waste, but was reluctant to scare the company away. Meanwhile, Kiwi Blue, a 'clean' local business involved in exporting bottled water, relocated from nearby Paeroa to avoid the risk of water contamination, depriving that town of a sustainable industry.

A further report from the Parliamentary Commissioner in 1997 concluded that the economic benefits from mining – the profit to the mining company, government royalties, employment, and contracts for local services – were 'short-lived compared to the potential long-term environmental risks and restrictions on future uses of land'.[68] Dangers included catastrophic failure of dams and gradual contamination by leakage. There were also risks to the traditional relationships of the tangata whenua with their ancestral lands, waterways and other taonga (treasures), and their role as kaitiaki (guardians).[69] Drawing on international precedents, including a US federal law passed in 1997, the Commissioner recommended legislative changes that would allow local authorities to require mining licence-holders to establish trust funds or bonds to pay for the long-term management of tailings dams once a mine had closed.[70] The changes were included in the 1998 proposal to amend the resource management laws, but were dropped from the 1999 Bill. They were considered unnecessary by the industry because of the voluntary initiatives taken by existing mines and Coeur Gold following the Coromandel Watchdog campaign.[71]

The settlement of indigenous claims to resources, stronger environmental protection, and the regulation of 'dirty' industries are all possible if the political will is there. The costs of losing foreign investors need to be weighed against the social and environmental benefits, the longer-term savings on clean-up operations, and the impetus to develop more sustainable use of resources locally. The onus should fall on those who promote resource-intensive and dirty industries to prove their worth.

▲ Privatised monopolies

A third area of controversy arises from privatisation, especially of former state monopolies. As competition for new markets intensified during the 1970s, transnational enterprises around the world focused on an uncharted and highly lucrative terrain – the enterprises and activities owned or run by the state. With government expenditure sometimes comprising half a country's gross domestic product, private ownership of state assets and access to government contracts for procuring goods and services was a prize worth fighting for.

The belief that the state was inherently inefficient and the market intrinsically superior became an article of faith in the 1980s. OECD governments rolled back the state to varying degrees. Poor countries were required to privatise as a condition of debt financing. The neo-liberal 'orthodoxy' meant there was no need for any objective cost-benefit analysis, nor any assessment of how the state might perform better.

New Zealand's free-marketeers attacked the state with particular fervour.[72] Beginning in 1986, any potentially commercial government operations were corporatised and most were prepared for sale. Staffing levels were reduced, social obligations removed and unprofitable activities terminated. The decision to privatise by tender, rather than by share floats, made transnational investment inevitable. State railways went to Wisconsin; telecommunications to US companies Bell Atlantic and Ameritech; most of the major banks passed into Australian hands; steel ended up with Australian mining giant BHP; state forests were shared among the US, China, Japan and Malaysia, as well as New Zealand-based but foreign-owned transnationals; electricity supply companies drew in firms from Alberta and Kansas.

Other forms of privatisation, especially contracting out, attracted transnationals to health care services (Aetna Health), information processing (EDS), and utilities such as waste disposal (Waste Management and Onyx) and water supply (Vivendi and Thames Water). In 1999 a US desk operation called Cyberuni even touted itself as the world's first university without any buildings, offering degrees to New Zealanders through the Internet.[73] Other education transnationals were predicted to enter the tertiary 'market' to take advantage of neutral funding for approved public and private 'providers' from 2000. Transnational security firms and corrections corporations such as Serco and Group 4 secured a foothold in policing and prison services; these areas have historically been confined to the state because they curtailed people's liberty, yet commercially confidential contracts now prevent effective public accountability.

All state operations and assets were sold as quickly as possible, irrespective of the economic returns. Alan Gibbs, a leading free-marketeer and former chair of Forestcorp, reportedly believed 'that public ownership should be liquidated at any cost and that the benefits to the country were much greater than any discount in price. He would have given the forests away to have got them out of public hands.'[74] Over the next decade, some 39 assets were sold for about $19 billion. There was never any independent audit of the economic (let alone the social) costs and benefits of the privatisation programme.[75]

Privatisation saw a massive transfer of wealth from government and taxpayers to a few companies and individuals. The project was steered through by a combination of government officials, politicians, corporate lobbyists, and private sector advisors. Key players among the latter were a select group of merchant bankers and consultants for whom privatisation was especially lucrative. They collected a transaction fee for advising on potential privatisations; there were brokerage and underwriting fees if the sale proceeded (which they invariably recommended); and afterwards, the buyer would need financial and other investment services, which the broker would often provide. Sometimes they blurred the boundaries by advising the government and also acting as buyers.

The big accounting, legal and consultancy firms, such as PriceWaterhouseCoopers, Ernst & Young and Credit Suisse First Boston, were part of a global network whose annual earnings from privatisation ran into hundreds of millions of dollars. In 1996, PriceWaterhouse alone advised governments (not buyers) on 336 major privatisations with a total value of US$35 billion.[76] Local niche players were an equally important part of the privatisation industry, acting as brokers for foreign investors and short-term financiers. Pre-eminent among them was Fay Richwhite. In various public and private forms, Fay Richwhite/Capital Markets acted as adviser and/or purchaser in the privatisation of Telecom, Development Finance Corporation, Housing Corporation mortgages and Tranz Rail.[77] It was central to devising and delivering the Cook Islands tax deals that were the subject of the Winebox inquiry.

A rare parliamentary investigation was held in 1991 into the sale of the Government Printing Office. Initially valued by Fay Richwhite at $70 million, it was sold to entrepreneur Graeme Hart's Rank Group for $23 million, with a further $10.6 million from property sales. A twelve-month delay in settlement cost the government an estimated $700,000 to $1 million in interest on debt. Fay Richwhite complained that the process had taken much longer than anticipated. Treasury agreed to vary the terms of the written contract, and the government paid out $270,000 more than it was legally liable for. Fay Richwhite's fee was calculated on the expected sale price of $43 million, as valued by the merchant bank itself, rather than the actual return from the sale.[78] The purchase provided the launching pad for Hart's subsequent capture of the New Zealand retail book trade. He later sold the company that had grown from the initial purchase of GP Print to the US transnational, Blue Star.

A more notorious example was Fay Richwhite's exceptionally favourable treatment by the Labour and National governments in successive bail-outs of the Bank of New Zealand. Fay Richwhite received a 30.5 percent stake in the BNZ as part of the $600 million rescue package in 1989, for which it paid only around $300 million. The government repurchased 85.7 million of these shares in the second ($720 million) bail-out in 1990 at 70 cents a share, well above the independent valuation of 55 to 60 cents.[79] Fay Richwhite also received convertible shares that were valued even higher and delivering above market returns. BNZ minority shareholders were not offered the same opportunities. In November 1992, the BNZ was sold to National Australia Bank in a deal brokered by the New Zealand government and Fay Richwhite. Minority shareholders unsuccessfully campaigned for a better deal. The BNZ's reported net profits of $302 million and $318 million in the next two years were twice the projected level. Business journalist Brian Gaynor asks the obvious (but unanswered) question: 'why did the Government offer special deals to only one BNZ shareholder in 1989 and 1990, particularly when that shareholder was an active promoter of tax schemes which deprived the Crown of tax revenue?'[80] With the slowing of privatisation and stiffer competition, both Michael Fay and David Richwhite left for Geneva in 1998.

Some state activities were targets for privatisation everywhere in the world. Telecommunications, for example, seems to have almost limitless potential to expand.[81] Telecom New Zealand was the jewel in the government's crown. Created as a state-owned enterprise when the Post Office was dismembered in 1986, the government turned it into a profitable business by removing its social obligations, and absorbing the costs of staff cuts and new technology. It was sold to Bell Atlantic and Ameritech in

1990 for $4.25 billion. Local corporates Fay Richwhite and Freightways took 5 percent each. No single foreign shareholder or consortium was allowed to hold more than 49.9 percent of shares after three years, although the date was extended a year in 1993. A large part of the share sell-down went to overseas buyers.

Telecom proved a bonanza for its new owners. Profits rose from $257 million in March 1990 to $528 million in 1994 and $620 million in 1995 (a return on equity of 30 percent). *Foreign Control Watchdog* complained that: 'Most companies pay out about 50% [in dividend]; Telecom has averaged 70% since it started and in 1994 announced that it was increasing that to about 90%'.[82] Under foreign ownership, most of this was likely to leave the country, depriving the company of investment and the local economy of flow-on benefits, and increasing the external current account deficit. Telecom's profits rose another $100 million to $716 million in 1996; but 1997 was a bad year, with profit only $581 million. Telecom more than recovered in 1998, with a new record profit of $845 million. Meanwhile, staff had been cut from 16,263 in September 1989 to 9,257 in 1994 and 8,136 in 1998. A rash of telephone exchange problems and slipping service standards in 1995 were widely attributed to the loss of experienced staff. Telecom, in turn, blamed increased complaints about its services on bad weather and longstanding industrial action by its workers (whose pay rates had increased only 5 percent since 1991).[83]

By November 1996, Bell Atlantic and Ameritech had realised an estimated $3.1 billion on their original investment through selling down their shareholding and a 1994 share cancellation.[84] Their combined net investment of $1.15 billion for a 49.5 percent share was worth $7 billion at the current market price. A further buy-back of shares by the company, announced in late 1996, meant they had recovered 85 percent of their original investment – without taking into account their substantial dividends over the six years. At the end of 1998, Bell Atlantic and Ameritech announced they were selling all their shares and moving on to new pastures. When Rod Deane (former deputy governor of the Reserve Bank, head of the State Services Commission, and chief executive of Electricorp) retired as chief executive of Telecom in 1999, he would leave behind an annual salary of $1.78 million, and become the (well paid) chair of the Telecom board.

Telecom maintained an effective monopoly over local services. Long-running legal and political battles over access by competitors to the local call network prompted the Ministry of Commerce in 1998 to suggest greater disclosure of costs and profits on such services. Telecom opposed this as being too costly. While BellSouth left the country in frustration, Clear Communications settled legal proceedings launched in 1997 against the government for failing to enforce Telecom's undertakings, ahead of deregulation, to set up six local telephone companies.[85] Other allegations that Telecom was abusing its dominant market position centred on the portability of telephone numbers when subscribers changed suppliers, and consolidated billing of accounts for customers supplied by other companies.[86] Perhaps the most stark example was Telecom's decision to match, street by street, the price for residential services offered to Lower Hutt customers by US cable television company Saturn Communications. Yet the Commerce Commission found this was not an abuse of Telecom's market power.[87]

Such disputes prompted a major review in 1999 of the Commerce Act 1986.[88] That Act was one of the Labour government's earliest moves towards light-handed regulation. The goal of the previous 1973 Act was 'to assist in the orderly development of industry and commerce and to promote its efficiency, and the welfare of consumers, through the regulation, where desirable in the public interest,' of trade practices, monopolies, takeovers and the prices of goods and services. The 1986 Act sought to 'promote competition in markets' – but allowed companies to secure dominance in a market where efficiency gains were seen to outweigh detriments from the loss of competition. Increased economic efficiency would 'enable the economy to produce more output with the same level of resources and thereby enhance the welfare of New Zealanders'.[89]

Competition law in New Zealand was significantly weaker than in most OECD countries.[90] The discussion paper on the 1999 review of the Commerce Act noted that the small size of New Zealand's economy meant there would be high levels of concentration within particular domestic markets. It observed that 'an overly permissive policy may entrench monopolistic and oligopolistic elements in the market'. Because New Zealand did have a permissive merger and acquisition regime, it needed a robust mechanism to prohibit anti-competitive behaviour. The report concluded that this was lacking, and suggested a more competition-focused test for acquisitions similar to the Australian legislation – a move that would also enhance integration under CER. This was significant: not only was policy failure being acknowledged, but the solution was to bring New Zealand more into line with other OECD countries. Submissions were evenly split between those who said that a higher concentration of market share had to be tolerated in a small economy in order to achieve efficiency gains and economies of scale and scope, and those who said that small size meant stricter controls were required.[91] Introduction of the amendment was reportedly delayed after high-level lobbying by Telecom's Rod Deane. The proposed change was minimalist; it would not affect the bulk of mergers and would still give priority to considerations of efficiency. And because the proposed controls rested on competition, rather than regulating prices and behaviour, they meant increased transnational investment was almost inevitable. Nevertheless, such measures could bring some strategic activities, including deregulated and privatised utilities, under closer scrutiny.

The privatisation of local electricity supply companies and state-owned generators was also very lucrative and open to abuse of market power by transnationals. Driven by theory, governments had progressively dismantled the integrated state electricity system since 1986.[92] This involved separating transmission from generation, splitting the state-owned generator into competing companies, and converting the elected non-profit power boards into profit-driven electricity supply companies. The Labour government began the process by corporatising the electricity department in 1986. The local power boards were transformed into electric power companies in 1990, and into commercial electricity supply companies with diverse ownership structures in 1993. A rash of hostile takeover bids and friendly mergers followed; during this time, supplying electricity seemed almost a sideline. The main foreign-owned players were Alberta-based TransAlta and Utilicorp from Kansas. The companies raised their electricity prices to cover debt servicing and profit requirements. The government expressed concern that electricity companies were abusing their monopoly over the power-lines and supply contracts to block the entry of competitors. The Electricity Industry Reform Act 1998, passed in July under urgency, prohibited any company from owning both electricity line businesses and retail or generation businesses from 1 May 1999. Labour opposed the move, claiming the government had taken 'an electricity industry that was working pretty well in practice and ripped it to bits, because it was not working well in theory'.[93] The existing companies, supported by ACT, complained that the split reduced their value and amounted to expropriation.[94] TransAlta threatened to pull out of the country if the government proceeded with the plan. At the same time, the change created new opportunities for mergers and takeovers (at grossly inflated prices), consolidating control of electricity into fewer, and increasingly transnational, hands.

The government also split the state-owned generator into two companies, Contact Energy and ECNZ; ECNZ was later split into three companies. Contact Energy was publicly floated in March 1999. Some 175,000 local investors applied for priority registration. But the government had decided there had to be a 40 percent 'cornerstone' shareholder. Only two companies were in the final bidding – TransAlta and US-based Edison Mission Energy. TransAlta was already the country's largest energy retailer, with 530,000 customers, and was returning a dividend of around

6 percent. In October 1998 the Ministry of Consumer Affairs condemned its customer contracts as 'onerous and harsh on consumers'.[95] The Commerce Commission cleared TransAlta to take up to 50 percent of shares in Contact Energy. That would have given the company one million of the country's 1.6 million electricity customers, control over two-fifths of New Zealand's generating capacity, and rights to nearly half its gas production. The strategic stake went instead to Edison, for $1.21 billion. Among Edison's US$48 billion international operations was Indonesia's first private power venture, awarded in a non-competitive process after the personal intervention of President Suharto and with support from highly placed US lobbyists (including former Secretaries of State Warren Christopher and Henry Kissinger).[96] Following the collapse of the Indonesian economy, the company faced demands to renegotiate the excessive electricity tariff the company had been guaranteed for 30 years.

Contact Energy ended up nearly 62 percent overseas-owned. In addition to Edison's 40 percent, another 18 percent of shares were reserved for offshore institutions, 14.4 percent for New Zealand/Australian institutions and 27.6 percent for the New Zealand public. Investment analyst Brian Gaynor calculated that half the shares issued to offshore institutions were sold for instant profit in the first three days. He partly attributed the priority given to offshore buyers to 'broker self-interest', estimating that they earned $7.6 million on the 109 million shares issued to northern hemisphere institutions (much higher than the proportionate income from Australasian sales).[97] Gaynor questioned why government officials put so much effort into selling the country's assets to foreign interests, thus worsening the balance of payments, instead of working to stimulate export growth.[98]

The government insisted that the changes would lower electricity prices to consumers (although Commerce Minister John Luxton said 'it was not promised that householders would necessarily get cheaper power'). But they failed to do so, as the companies sought to recoup their excessive spending. In anticipation of winning the Contact Energy bid, TransAlta had paid $171 million for the retail business of Orion, owned by the Christchurch City Council; the operation was independently valued in 1997 at around $13 million. In March 1999 TransAlta announced price rises of between 5 and 15 percent for its 530,000 customers. Energy Minister Max Bradford blamed the line companies for abusing their monopoly and not passing on savings from the transfer of metering costs to the retail companies. Orion backed off its suggested price increase. TransAlta did not. Bradford insisted that competition among the supply companies would eventually force prices down, so only the monopoly line businesses needed regulation.[99]

Back in December 1998, Bradford had proposed only light-handed regulation: 'to enhance the credibility of the threat of price control', the Commerce Commission would be given power to limit prices, where it was efficient to do so, and after a lengthy period of review.[100] By May 1999 he had been forced to introduce legislation that could regulate monopolies generally, with specific provisions for line companies. The Commerce Commission would be required to authorise a price for line company charges by 31 December 1999 for the largest companies, and dates in 2000 for the rest.[101] If the price was lower than that being charged by line companies, they would have to refund customers back to 1 April 1999. The government also announced it would build a special information base so consumers could participate in the market 'at little or no cost'.[102] But it refused to address the myriad other transaction costs and charges that would inhibit even informed customers from changing supplier. The government's discussion paper on the Commerce Act (discussed above) insisted that 'these proposals do not signal any change to the Government's approach to price control generally'.[103] However, ACT warned that 'regulation begets more regulation', and wanted everything left to the market.[104] Labour demanded regulation of retail company pricing as well, but not direct price controls (which the Commerce Act still allowed).[105] The minority government did not have the numbers on its own to push the legislation through.

The model of the electricity market was premised on consumer sovereignty. But this was no level playing-field. Resource-intensive companies had long used their influence to secure special, often secret deals on electricity. Their lobby, the Major Electricity Users Group, actively sought out better deals for commercial customers. For years, Comalco NZ had been supplied with cheap electricity for its aluminium smelter at Bluff. Comalco's ultimate parent was Rio Tinto of the UK. When Comalco renegotiated its contract in late 1993, the company secured exclusive access to around one-sixth of the country's current total electricity output. This guaranteed it supply for twenty years. Although the price would almost double by 2010, it would increase only 10 percent in the first decade.[106] In 1994/95 the price Comalco paid for power was 2.5 cents a kilowatt/hour; the average retail price paid by consumers was 10.22 cents, and 7.7 cents for industry. Hence Comalco was paying less than a quarter of what householders paid.[107] The company claimed this preferential treatment was justified by its steady demand and good custom. It was also a good corporate citizen: in return for the $1.5 million a week subsidy from electricity consumers in 1993, Comalco had donated $1 million to save the kakapo.[108] Its chief executive, Kerry McDonald, was an active member of the Business Roundtable and a government nominee on the APEC Business

Advisory Council in 1997–98. The electricity market ensured that the likes of Comalco would continue to secure power at prices far below those paid by households and small businesses.

Just as the government conceded the need to regulate electricity prices and proposed changes in order to control Telecom's virtual monopoly in telecommunications, so it could apply those measures to other aspects of transnational activity.

▲ WORKER AND PUBLIC WELFARE

Labour markets are prime candidates for competitive deregulation. Transnationals take advantage of low-cost, non-unionised labour in many poor countries. In 1994, for example, Prime Minister Jim Bolger praised a horticultural plant in Thailand operated by Brierley Investments Ltd, where the workers earned 40 percent of the average Thai wage, or about 40 cents an hour.[109] Competitive pressures generate demands for 'labour market flexibility' in richer countries. New Zealand's Employment Contracts Act 1991 was designed to force down wages and conditions by individualising employment relationships and de-unionising the workforce. Cutting labour costs and increasing productivity also meant reducing the workforce. Sometimes this was compensated for by labour-saving technology. Often it meant workers doing more for less. As corners were cut and safety standards undermined, workers, customers and the public were all potential casualties, as the operations of two transport transnationals, Tranz Rail and Stagecoach, illustrate.

During the first wave of corporatisation in late 1986, New Zealand Rail was relieved of its social responsibilities, 9,000 jobs were cut, and it was made profitable. In 1992 the company was sold for $328 million to a consortium led by Wisconsin Central Transportation Corp, and including Fay Richwhite and controversial businessman Alex van Heeren. In just eight years, Wisconsin had risen from a small player in the US, hauling bulk cargo in the upper Mid-West, to become the largest American regional railway and a predatory transnational. Eager to join the rail privatisation boom, it was also buying companies in Britain and Tasmania.

In 1996 Wisconsin's shareholding was restructured through a share issue which left Tranz Rail's assets worth $500 million more on paper than three years previously.[110] Local institutions reportedly received only about 5 percent of the 27 million new shares issued, with most trading going through the US. The 18.8 percent stake held by a Fay Richwhite subsidiary was now valued at $146.9 million, a gain of around $140 million on its equity investment. Brian Gaynor commented: 'Tranz Rail is another example of how a small group can obtain rich pickings at the public trough. The company's prospectus reveals how the current owners have made huge profits since the assets were bought from the Government nearly three years ago.'[111] After the lucrative restructuring, Wisconsin began selling off its revalued shares.

Tranz Rail's operating profits had varied. Transport writer Robert Miles noted that its gains came less from expanding the business and more from 'share market manoeuvres, further lay-offs, and sidelining the safety of shunters'.[112] Revenue per employee increased by around 14 percent between 1993 and 1995; personnel costs fell 4.6 percent in 1994 and 6.6 percent in 1995. By 1996, staff levels had been reduced by 11 percent since 1993. By then, the managing director's salary package exceeded $500,000.[113] In 1999 Tranz Rail employed 4,533 staff, around 700 fewer than in 1993. The major staff layoffs had occurred prior to privatisation, falling from 14,900 to 5,900 between 1987 and 1991; further marginal reductions had a disproportionate impact.[114]

Falling staff numbers and threats of redundancy put pressure on Tranz Rail workers to take jobs for which they were poorly trained. Tranz Rail continued using shunting practices that US railroad authorities had ordered Wisconsin to stop using in the US.[115] In November 1996 the company was convicted of failing to take all practicable steps to ensure the safety of employee Jack Neha, who died in a shunting operation. The judge held that the accident was a direct result of a business decision to cut costs by reducing staff numbers; inadequate training and monitoring; and pressure on workers to accept jobs from fear of redundancy.[116] Other deaths followed.[117]

Tranz Rail's practices also endangered public safety. In 1996 the Transport Accident Investigation Commission suggested that a near miss between the Northerner and a Wellington commuter train may have been caused by a train controller's lack of sleep, associated with work-related stress and, possibly, irregular shifts.[118] The company also proved reluctant to fund safety barriers at level crossings, despite a number of fatalities.[119] But the greatest public outrage was provoked by Tranz Rail's attitude to six-year-old Morgan Jones, who lost his sight and a leg after falling from a train in 1994. The company admitted that a faulty hand-rail hook had caused the fall, but refused to concede its legal liability. This attitude permeated from the top – Wisconsin's chief executive confessed he was a 'little bewildered by why so much has been made' of the Morgan Jones case.[120] It is perhaps not surprising that the parent company was reported to have the worst railroad safety record in the US.[121]

The Scottish-based transport company Stagecoach was an equally adversarial employer. In 1997, the UK magazine *Management Today* described the company's style as 'aggression more redolent of America's raw, frontier capitalism, echoed in the company's name'.[122] Stagecoach was started in 1980 as a family business, and publicly floated in 1993. By 1998 it had over 30,000 staff, 4,000 rail units and 12,000 buses operating in the UK, Sweden, Kenya, Portugal, Australia, Finland and New Zealand. Offshore expansion and aggressive practices saw its turnover increase from £148 million in 1993 to £501 million in 1996 and £1,381 million in 1998; pre-tax profits grew from £18 million to £216 million over the same period.[123] The company's success in the UK was built on privatisation of the bus, regional train and rolling stock companies, often with generous subsidies, and a 'voracious' appetite for taking over competitors. The Monopolies and Mergers Commission in the UK described its behaviour in one situation as 'predatory, deplorable and against the public interest'. It was openly hostile to unions and adversarial with its workers. In mid-1997 an embarrassing shortage of drivers meant it had to cancel 39 trains a day on the Southwest line, incurring a £900,000 penalty.[124] The company's pre-tax profit in the year to March 1999 was $660 million, up 39 percent on the year before.[125]

Stagecoach moved into New Zealand in 1992. It secured three-quarters of the Wellington and Hutt Valley bus service market, with promises to hold fares (which it did). In August 1998 Stagecoach bought the Yellow Bus Company (which ran two-thirds of the Auckland region's bus routes) and Auckland ferry operator Fullers, as part of a plan to develop and expand the Auckland public transport system. The company promised major investment, more services and new stock.[126] Between 1992 and early 1999 it invested $15 million in 60 new buses. The combined fleet of 1,000 buses had an annual turnover of $130 million.[127]

Stagecoach's profits came mainly from screwing its staff. In January 1999, Auckland drivers were presented with new contracts which offered a one-off payment in return for abolishing lunch-breaks. This could require them to work long hours without a break and to spread their eight-hour work day over twelve hours. The offer was made before the existing contract expired, so the workers could not legally strike. When drivers in the Hutt Valley rejected contracts that cut conditions on work hours, union rights, leave and overtime, they were locked out over Christmas and strike-breakers were hired.[128] During January 1999 the company was running only 85 percent of its services.[129] The dispute ended in a significant victory for the workers.

Not long before this, Stagecoach had been served notice by the Occupational Safety and Health Service to take 'reasonable steps' to improve driver safety, after the drivers' union complained that many buses had no two-way radios, despite repeated assaults, vandalism and attempted robberies.[130] A prolonged dispute over disabled access to Wellington buses under the Human Rights Act saw Stagecoach eventually agree to run buses fitted with wheelchair access on specified routes, and to order more.[131] The Human Rights Commission noted the importance of regional councils setting requirements for urban buses, as the Canterbury Regional Council had done on several routes it subsidised.[132]

The combination of structural unemployment, de-unionisation and individualised contracts gave transnationals a licence to exploit their workers. Unsafe practices were the result of a market environment that encouraged short-term cost-cutting, imposed only light-handed occupational health and safety laws, and was dismantling the state-run accident compensation system once designed to protect victims and their families. Few of these changes could simply be reversed. But, as Stagecoach's drivers had shown, active unions could still win disputes. Regional councils could still dictate requirements to public transport operators. And more severe penalties could still be imposed for breaches, alongside better protections for the safety of workers, customers and the public, as governments managed to do in other parts of the world.

▲ ACCESS TO BANKS

Consumers are often portrayed as the major beneficiaries of globalisation. But not all consumers are equal. The consolidation of the banking sector since the 1970s has left some 150 of the world's 65,000 banks in control of about half the world's banking assets.[133] The high returns are in commercial and investment banking. Traditional banking services for small businesses and local communities are a costly nuisance, and such customers are often deliberately deterred.

Financial deregulation in New Zealand brought intense competition to the banking sector, as evidenced by mergers and constant cutting of costs. The larger institutions streamlined their operations, reduced staff and demanded increased productivity. Branches closed, and unprofitable retail services to individual customers were dispensed with, while new services to the corporate and wholesale sectors expanded. As the number of financial institutions was whittled down, foreign companies began to dominate. By 1995, fourteen of New Zealand's sixteen registered banks were entirely or substantially foreign-owned. By 1999 only the relatively small Taranaki Trustee Savings Bank (TSB) was locally owned. The banking system was effectively controlled by four Australian banks and one British: the Bank of New Zealand was owned by National Australia Bank; the ANZ included the former Postbank; the Commonwealth Bank of Australia owned three-quarters of the ASB; Westpac had bought Trustbank; and the British-owned National Bank had bought Countrywide.[134] The returns were enormous. In the 1997/98 year the New Zealand operations of the big four Australian banks earned them A$750 million.[135]

It is hard for a small country to resist surrendering to bigger players in the cut-throat market-place of international finance. But foreign control of the banking system carries real risks. The BNZ's reckless lending practices, under a board of private sector entrepreneurs, led to government bail-outs in 1989 and 1990 amounting to $1.3 billion.[136] The situation was blamed on the 'moral hazard' of continued government ownership, where directors lacked the disciplinary effects of going bust. But Westpac showed that the same could happen in the private sector.[137] Formed in 1982 when the Bank of New South Wales and Commercial Bank of Australia merged, Westpac rapidly expanded through a series of (often unwise) mergers and takeovers. One subsidiary began making unhedged loans that had to be repaid in foreign currency; when the Australian dollar fell, many small investors were caught unawares. In 1987 a major fraud was discovered in its foreign exchange section. The New Zealand Court of Appeal held Westpac liable in 1993 for losses incurred after a Napier sharebroker collapsed during the 1987 crash, because the bank had allowed him to continue operating.[138] A series of bad loans in the late 1980s, especially on property, left Westpac with A$5.4 billion in shareholders' funds but A$6.2 billion in problem loans by 1991. A failed share issue saw the major shareholder, AMP, inject A$300 million, leaving the underwriters covering A$883 million. A new chief executive was brought in from the US to restructure. Closures, asset sales and several thousand lost jobs brought Westpac back from the brink. In 1996 it bought Trustbank NZ for NZ$1.27 billion. By 1996 Westpac's after-tax earnings were over A$1 billion.

Martin Gimpl in the Christchurch *Press* asked what would have happened if the bank had failed: 'With all of our trading banks now foreign owned a failure by an overseas parent would have dire consequences for New Zealand account holders. There would be no protection like that offered when the Government-owned BNZ got into difficulties for many similar reasons.'[139] His solution was diversification; yet ownership continued to consolidate. Australian Prime Minister John Howard insisted that their 'big four' would not be allowed to merge, despite the recommendations of an inquiry into the financial system.[140] But the industry continued to press for deregulation. Mergers have potential benefits of economies of scale and reduced transaction costs for banks and clients. But banking expert David Tripe warned the smaller number of competitors also reduced consumer choice with potential to increase charges and cut services.[141] Meanwhile, the Australian banks' commercial priorities would determine the shape of New Zealand's banking system. Indeed, on-line banking meant that much of it could be run directly from Australia.

The costs and benefits of financial deregulation were unevenly spread. In 1997 the Consumers' Institute conducted a survey of banks, and rated the ANZ and BNZ below average on overall performance, service and charges; locally-owned TSB was the only bank to rate above average on all three.[142] A major concern was the singular focus on commercial and wealthy customers at the expense of small and poor account-holders. A 1995 inquiry into bank fees by the Australian Price Surveillance Authority had been strongly critical of high monthly account-keeping fees and discriminatory charges based on the size of account balances. These hit mainly low-income earners, while better-off customers could escape them.[143] Similar fees were introduced in New Zealand (except by the TSB), and were then increased. ANZ/Postbank – once 'the people's' Post Office Savings Bank – lifted the minimum balance before waiving fees from $300 to $1,000 in late 1998.[144] Other banks refused to open accounts for people with 'adverse credit histories'. The ASB required a $500 opening deposit. Income Support insisted it would only pay welfare benefits into a bank account. Charities such as the Methodist Mission began operating accounts for single parents, psychiatric survivors and those left in debt after marriage breakdowns. The Banking Ombudsman reported a flood of complaints, but the issue was outside her jurisdiction. The banks responded that their fees were less than those charged in some other countries.[145]

The transnationals were generally not interested in the needs of small account-holders, be they businesses, beneficiaries or even well-paid individuals. Rural areas were often left without access to a bank. In June 1999 a local community trust in the small North Island town of Maungatoroto opened a Community Money Exchange, following the closure of the town's last bank.[146] The exchange operated as an intermediary, conveying transactions to customers' banks outside the town, even though those banks declined to be involved. The fee was cheaper for the customer than driving to the nearest bank, and the profits went back to the community. Meanwhile, Taranaki TSB capitalised on its status as the country's sole New Zealand-owned bank, expanding in 1998 outside its local area through low-cost telephone banking. The PSIS, formerly a public service credit union, also remained successful, with a local niche and loyal customer base which received a high level of personal service.[147] On a small scale, these were viable local alternatives to the transnational juggernauts, but they depended on popular support to survive.

▲ THE KNOWLEDGE INDUSTRIES

Among the most powerful transnationals are those that dominate the knowledge and information technology industries. UNCTAD estimates that 70 percent of global payments of royalties and fees are transactions between parent firms and their foreign subsidiaries. IBM ranked as the seventh largest transnational in 1995, with total assets of US$80 billion, global sales of US$71.9 billion and 225,000 employees.[148] With information technology (IT) the growth business of the future, moves by Microsoft to lock Internet access into its Windows operating systems led to anti-trust (anti-monopoly) charges in the US courts – probably the only forum that could call such a company to account.[149] There have been no New Zealand competitors in the mass software markets dominated by Microsoft, but some small local producers of 'niche' software have done well. Locally owned assemblers of 'clone' IBM-compatible computers have also had varying success in a cut-throat market led by transnational brand names. The most successful, such as PC Direct, have been bought out by transnationals, as have most of the larger computer retail chains.

Control of information technology is a major source of power. Information once kept in filing cabinets and safes is now held in machines. As technology becomes more sophisticated and expensive, and skills more specialised, these databases have been centralised. Creating and operating such systems has become a transnational enterprise in itself. The economies of scale enjoyed by the huge IT companies allow them to undercut almost any local company bidding for large government or private contracts. As a result, governments and businesses have entrusted sensitive personal information and core operations to profit-driven foreign corporations, and become dependent on one company's system. The risks are exemplified by the debacle with the police computer system, 'INCIS'. When Cabinet approved the tailor-made system in 1994, it was to cost $97.8 million and be completed in 1997. By 1999 the cost was around $127 million, plus $50 million that was absorbed by its developer, IBM. Phase One was still not finished, and it seemed unlikely that the second and third phases would ever be commissioned. Meanwhile, police numbers were being cut in anticipation of reduced staffing needs and to pay for the cost overruns. Despite these problems, the police were committed beyond the point of return, something Information Technology Minister Maurice Williamson had warned about at the start: 'Should the chosen operating environment and applications not continue to be developed and supported into the future, the police would encounter extensive costs, not just in the purchase of new software, but in the considerable retraining of all staff, not to mention the loss of momentum and subsequent time delay.'[150]

Perhaps the most powerful transnational information systems operator in New Zealand is Texas-based Electronic Data Systems (EDS), which specialises in outsourcing, business process management and systems integration. EDS was started by Ross Perot in 1962 and sold to General Motors in 1984. By 1998 it was the second largest computer services company in the US, operating in more than 40 countries, with 100,000 employees. Despite earnings of US$15.2 billion in 1997, falling profits prompted plans to save around US$750 million by eliminating some 8,500 jobs worldwide.[151] According to the company's website in 1999, its New Zealand activities span finance/insurance, government, energy, health and communications. It describes itself as 'New Zealand's largest supplier of outsourcing services', with more than 1,000 employees.

Its New Zealand operations began in November 1994 when EDS bought GCS, formerly the government computing service. In July 1995 it acquired Databank, a collective set up by the major banks to provide core data processing services. Databank gave EDS control over the IT services of the banking system, and a platform to promote future options for electronic business through on-line and Internet banking. Major systems breakdowns in 1997 and 1998 locked customers out of their bank accounts or failed to process welfare benefits,[152] although it is difficult to know whether such incidents have become more frequent or serious under EDS ownership.

EDS also secured control over key parts of the government's information technology, running systems for Treasury, Inland Revenue, Social Welfare, Police, Courts, Corrections, Land Information, and Education, the Land Transport Safety Authority, the Serious Fraud Office, Health Support Services, the Qualifications Authority and various local health authorities. In 1997 the company signed a multi-million dollar contract with the Department of Social Welfare for the three-year redevelopment of the SWIFTT benefit processing system, plus outsourcing (including assets and staff) of Social Welfare's IT unit, Tritec. The desktop management arm of EDS was also contracted to manage over 6,000 desktop computers in Social Welfare and the Department of Corrections. By 1997 EDS held contracts with the emergency services, including for disaster recovery processing, and administered the student loan scheme for the Ministry of Education.[153] EDS also established Inland Revenue's new system whereby large employers were required to file monthly tax schedules electronically. When the system worked more slowly than anticipated, thousands of employers missed the first deadline for electronic filing, and had to be exempted the penalty.[154] Because the system was not designed to work on Macintosh computers, businesses totally dependent on 'Macs' were given a one-year exemption, but told they would then have to change their computer systems at their own cost.[155]

Securing government contracts has been part of a global strategy for EDS. According to one senior executive in 1993, the company spent a lot of time in the late 1970s and early 1980s 'shaping the [US] federal government marketplace and promoting the notion that outsourcing or systems integration was a smart move. We started doing that in the United Kingdom a few years ago, and now, as in the United States, the contracts are beginning to come in. Europe is just further behind.'[156] Part of its UK strategy was the controversial hiring of Mark Thatcher as a consultant. In New Zealand, government was already on-side. Significantly, EDS was a major sponsor of the Coalition government's controversial 'Beyond Dependency' conference in 1997; it also ran the Wisconsin state contract for the work-for-the-dole scheme on which the New Zealand policy was being modelled. The extent of government dependency on EDS raised issues already confronted by managers of the UK's Inland Revenue Department. In 1998, they acknowledged that, when the ten-year contract with EDS to run the department's IT system expired, there would 'not be the competence within the department to ask the right questions about IT, let alone come up with its own answers'.[157]

Companies such as EDS expand by creating demand for their services. For example, in a joint project with the Ministry of Health, EDS promoted an 'integrated system of information management' across primary and secondary health care. This would allow information to be readily accessed by the entire public and private health sector.[158] In late 1998 an ad hoc project was already under way with Capital Coast Health and several Auckland Crown Health Enterprises. Total integration would require participation by primary health providers, especially the country's 2,500 GPs. Complementing a Ministry of Health awareness campaign, EDS said it was 'helping sponsor awareness among GPs through independent practitioners associations (IPAs), which provide the critical mass for a commercial focus in the primary sector'.[159] It also co-sponsored the GPs' conference in 1998. A key element of its campaign was the marketing of common technology through the IPAs, so that individual practitioners did not buy incompatible computer systems.

The health information initiative was globally unprecedented, and offered EDS a new product to market internationally. New Zealand was seen as small enough to experiment in. It already had a numbering system for patients through the 'national health index', alongside 'reasonably sophisticated' privacy laws. A steering group from all parts of the health sector, called the Health Information Council, was set up to promote the initiative – another familiar strategy of transnationals. As a public health tool, the system had the potential to identify populations at greatest health risk, such as Maori. But the idea proved hard to sell to up-market GPs who had a comfortable contractual relationship with their funders and did not need access to a database. It was unlikely to provide the detailed information GPs with small practices would need for it to be useful to them. There were also serious privacy concerns. The autonomy enjoyed by health funding agencies and hospitals to enter such deals suggested there was the potential to repeat the INCIS debacle on a similar scale.

By 1999 EDS controls a massive amount of New Zealand's commercial and government information. An outcry at the time GCS (the Government Computing Service) was sold prompted the Privacy Commissioner to issue a transitional Information Privacy Code specifically covering the information EDS took over.[160] In addition to the government's general principles on privacy, EDS was prohibited from transferring any 'identified information' out of New Zealand, except with the written authority of the government agency concerned, and after telling the Commissioner where it was being transferred and what safeguards would apply. Public accountability beyond that would run into problems of commercial confidentiality.

The other major conduits of the 'knowledge society' are the media empires.[161] They have the power to shape people's view of the world, whether or not that power is used. In New Zealand, foreign ownership and commercialisation of the media also threaten the transmission and hence the survival of Maori language and culture.[162] In June 1999 the Waitangi Tribunal found the lack of Maori involvement in radio spectrum allocation was extremely damaging to the language, and called for Maori participation in further auctions, plus compensation.[163]

New Zealand's print media are controlled by two transnational companies, Independent Newspapers Ltd (INL) and Wilson and Horton. In 1998 they owned 81 percent (by circulation) of New Zealand's main provincial daily newspapers and 92 percent of the daily metropolitan papers. INL was 49 percent owned and controlled by Rupert Murdoch's Australian/US News Ltd, and controlled 48 percent of daily newspaper circulation in New Zealand. This included all the newspapers with a circulation over 25,000, except the *New Zealand Herald* and *Otago Daily Times*. It published around 70 percent of the country's newspapers, magazines and sports publications, as well as weeklies and both Sunday papers, and owned major magazine distributors.

Murdoch runs the world's biggest media empire. He strongly defends his right to interfere in editorial matters, and claims it is his responsibility sometimes to do so.[164] Having secured control of several major UK papers (including *The Times* and the *Sun*), he moved aggressively in 1969 to take them out of Fleet Street and de-unionise the staff. In 1998 Murdoch stopped his company HarperCollins from publishing Christopher Patten's book on the hand-over of Hong Kong, reportedly to protect his investment in China.[165] Predictably, he is a fan of the New Zealand experiment. According to Bill Rosenberg: 'A few months after the 1996 election of the conservative Howard-led government in Australia, Murdoch criticised it for not carrying out radical reforms, saying New Zealand was the model to follow'.[166] Murdoch also knows how to cultivate connections. In 1992 New Zealand's Minister of Broadcasting, Maurice Williamson, accepted an invitation to visit Murdoch at his home in Los Angeles. That same year, Murdoch's subsidiary expressed an interest in buying TV2. During a visit to New Zealand in October 1995, Murdoch hosted Prime Minister Jim Bolger to dinner.[167] In 1996 and 1997, his chief executive expressed an interest in TVNZ if it was privatised.

Wilson and Horton was locally owned until 1995, when Brierley Investments raided its shares and sold a controlling 28 percent interest to an Irish group, Independent Newspapers Plc (INP). By the end of 1995, INP owned 45 percent, by September 1996 85 percent, and by 1998 all of it. Independent Newspapers is controlled by the O'Reilly family, headed by Tony O'Reilly, chairman of US-owned H.J. Heinz (which owns Watties). In 1998 INP owned the *New Zealand Herald* plus ten provincial newspapers, and had two-fifths of daily newspaper circulation in New Zealand. Rosenberg notes that, while O'Reilly does not have the same reputation for interference in politics and editorial policy as Murdoch, and his *New Zealand Herald* has been publishing a broader range of opinion than INL's newspapers, he is no left-winger. In March 1998, Wilson and Horton co-sponsored the élitist 'Williamsburg' conference on Asia in Queenstown, at which O'Reilly offered 'an investor's view' of New Zealand. He praised a 20 percent return on capital, describing the country as 'the top destination for multinational corporations which wish to locate in a fair, free and friendly enterprise for all of South-east Asia'. He concluded:

> Looking at and participating in the miracle of New Zealand in commerce, I have no doubt whatsoever that the next century will confirm what we already know – that New Zealand has found the economic way of fairness and transparency and a real return on capital; and that because of this, many others are in the process of finding the way to invest in this extraordinary country.[168]

Unlike the big daily newspapers, the specialist business press is locally owned. Liberty Press, which runs the *National Business Review* (*NBR*) and a number of business magazines, was formed by the Colman brothers in 1997. The *NBR* is an unashamed propagandist for neo-liberalism, and since 1997 has served as a party broadsheet for ACT. Barry Colman is a member of the Business Roundtable. Its more balanced competitor, *The Independent,* is co-owned by its editors, Warren Berryman and Jenni McManus.

Television New Zealand remains state-owned, although its sale is periodically proposed. It is run as a purely commercial enterprise, but still has the potential to be a genuine public broadcaster. In most countries public broadcasters are legally required to promote national identity and culture. New Zealand relies on competitive bidding by programme makers through New Zealand on Air. A survey of 11 OECD countries in 1999 showed New Zealand had the lowest local content on television, with 24 percent; the most comparable country, Ireland, had 41 percent.[169] Privately owned TV3 is controlled by CanWest Global Communications Corporation, a part-owner of the Ten Network in Australia and with links in Chile and the UK. Canadian Izzy Asper, who holds 90 percent of the voting power and 65 percent of the equity in CanWest, is also a fan of New Zealand's neo-liberalism. He was reported in 1995 as saying: 'Since the reformation in New Zealand in the 80s, you've become the experimental laboratory for the entire world. Sir Roger [Douglas] has travelled to Canada and is revered ... the fact is, New Zealand is one of the most professionally managed countries in the world.'[170] Pay television broadcaster Sky Network Television Ltd is 41 percent owned by INL. Other shareholders include TVNZ (sale announced in June 1999), Craig Heatley (reputedly the financial backer of ACT) and Tappenden Construction (headed by fellow free market evangelists Alan Gibbs and Trevor Farmer).

Public radio has a knife-edge existence. The government began privatising the radio frequencies in 1990,[171] and corporatised Radio New Zealand's assets in 1992. In April 1996 it sold the 41 commercial stations of state-owned Radio New Zealand, the Radio Bureau (an advertising production studio) and Radio New Zealand Sport to the New Zealand Radio Network Ltd for $89 million. The buyer was owned equally by Wilson and Horton (now 100 percent INP-owned), Australian Provincial Newspapers (over 42 percent INP-owned)[172] and Clear Channel Communications (the latter two being joint owners of the eight-station Australian Radio Network). Later that year Radio Network Ltd bought the Prospect radio network, giving it control of 53 stations and 60 percent of radio advertising in New Zealand. With its new stable, the company declined to renew its supply contract with Radio New Zealand's news service in April 1997. This left public radio $1 million short on its budget, further squeezing its spending on news. The Commerce Commission twice declined a Radio Network application to buy more stations and frequencies in the north of the South Island, because this would give it dominance in the market for radio advertising. The company has increased its stations elsewhere. The Network's major private competitor is New Zealand-owned Radio Pacific, which owns 80 frequencies and broadcasts to over 95 percent of the country's population. Radio Pacific is a ratings-driven talkback network, with hosts in 1998 ranging from progressive liberal Jenny Anderson to libertarian Lindsay Perigo ('The Politically Incorrect Show').

Foreign media ownership does not automatically mean foreign control of the news. Media commentator Tom Frewen suggests that the 'softness' of newspaper reporting in New Zealand is due more to the lack of competition among metropolitan papers than to who owns them.[173] Others blame it on commercialism, and overworked self-censoring journalists concerned to protect their jobs and wary of litigious public figures.[174] But the *potential* for editorial direction is there. Some want it to be exercised more readily. Executive director of the Business Roundtable, Roger Kerr, complained in May 1995 that the Christchurch *Press* was being far too negative:

> It was either a critic or, more latterly, a supporter of official policy, but rarely a catalyst with a positive agenda of its own … . Some of our other newspapers are more like their counterparts around the world in encouraging governments and the community to raise their sights. The Auckland based *National Business Review* and *The Herald*, for example, between them argue for privatisation of government businesses, more competition in health and education, producer board reform, the removal of the ACC monopoly, deregulation of postal services, and fire service reform, all of which would move New Zealand closer to Asian levels of economic performance. *The Dominion* last year said that this was 'No time for a breather'. The South Island papers seem mainly content with the status quo. … If New Zealand is to avoid an MMP siesta, more organisations and individuals are going to have to do the hard work of understanding economic and social issues, be prepared to debate them and create an environment where politicians are able to implement further changes – or indeed are unable to resist a consensus that change should occur.[175]

Other countries counter threats to the media's 'fourth estate' role by maintaining a strong public broadcasting system and a culture of debate that supports genuine investigative journalism in news and current affairs programmes. That remains an option in New Zealand so long as TVNZ and the remnants of public radio are not privatised. Most other countries also restrict foreign investment in the media; New Zealand could still impose 'national interest' requirements and limits on foreign ownership in future transactions. A stronger commitment to quality local programming and the imposition of quotas for good local content (especially current affairs) are both perfectly possible.

▲ REFLECTIONS

The power of transnational enterprises intensifies the impact of large-scale foreign direct investment. The stronger their foothold in a country, the greater their potential to constrain a state's capacity to act. Yet even when they seem entrenched, transnationals are not omnipotent. Like all economic actors, they remain subject to the laws of the states in which they operate, and require the cooperation of workers and local communities. One solution is to control their entry in the first place. Sometimes that is not possible; often it is too late. Even then, a range of regulatory tools are still available. Implementing these is largely a matter of political will. But as this chapter shows, market failure and social costs can also make it a necessity. Other tensions arise. Indigenous peoples have inherent rights, and treaties carry obligations. Environmental hazards, if not prevented, require remedies which someone has to pay for. Workers, consumers and local communities are not inevitable casualties; they deserve protection for their safety and well-being. Knowledge is not a mere commodity; it is the conduit of culture, a foundation of democracy, and a source of power with the potential to be abused. Transnational enterprise increases the risk in all these areas. Yet unions continue to defend their workers. Indigenous peoples resist, and reassert their right to self-determination. Environmental groups document, expose and confront those who abuse the lifeworld. Communities innovate and survive.

6 ▲ 'Free' Trade

The companion to free investment is the unfettered movement of goods and services across all national boundaries known as 'free trade'. Most governments and trade theorists treat this as an ideal to be advanced through reciprocal negotiations, where each country agrees to make the playing-field more level over time. In New Zealand since 1984, Labour and National governments have set out to dismantle all barriers to trade ahead of other countries, believing the others would see the benefits and follow suit. In 1998 National's Trade Minister Lockwood Smith proclaimed: 'we will gain nothing from being behind the trade liberalisation race, and trying to play poker at the international table. ... Influence for a country as small as New Zealand can only come from moral leadership.'[1]

Even if other countries failed to follow, the free-traders insisted that New Zealand would still benefit. The country's domestic producers would become more efficient, productive resources would be reallocated to their most profitable use, and the economic well-being of New Zealanders would be improved. They were not alone in such beliefs, which were part of the prevailing international economic orthodoxy. But, as noted in earlier chapters, orthodoxies change. The irony of the early 1990s was that, while New Zealand's policy-makers were firmly adhering to neo-classical theory, even those trained in that tradition were observing 'a growing trend in economic analysis towards models in which markets get it wrong'.[2] As US economist Paul Krugman pointed out: 'If policy could be made without politics, the new trade theory and related developments elsewhere in economics would point quite clearly to a broad-based program of government intervention in the economy.'[3]

By the end of the century, it seemed clear to most people that the world was not going to follow New Zealand's example. Powerful governments were pursuing managed approaches to trade, and using their economic strength over countries that could do little to retaliate or resist. The

Americans continued to make their own rules when they felt their domestic economic interests were threatened. Japan's commercial culture remained impenetrable to many outsiders, and its government was committed to protecting politically important sectors such as agriculture and fisheries. Even the Australians, under pressure from unions and business in 1997, imposed a moratorium on tariff cuts after 2000, and became lukewarm about extending the CER agreement with New Zealand.

As the New Zealand government stuck resolutely to its free trade position, it faced a concerted backlash from local manufacturers, unions, local communities, and even farmers. Although the car industry was effectively wiped out by the elimination of tariffs in 1997, a pragmatic coalition of unions, small manufacturers and local communities managed to contain tariff reduction in the textile, clothing and footwear industries. Farmers, the traditional supporters of National and, for a decade, of free trade, took to the streets in 1998 and turned back the government's proposal to deregulate the monopoly producer and marketing boards. While sheep farmers were protesting in June 1999 against the threatened imposition of safeguard measures by the US government to protect its local producers from lamb imports, the New Zealand pork industry was urging the government to provide it with similar protection. At the same time, the marketing and testing of genetically modified food provoked an outcry from doctors, 'green' activists, consumer advocates, Maori, academics and concerned citizens; this was heightened by the government's partial abdication of control over food safety and labelling to the Australians under CER. Maori generally supported initiatives that sought to break down those monopolies that denied them self-determination, especially the producer boards; yet they opposed liberalisation measures such as the removal of tariffs which hurt them as workers, small business owners and provincial communities.

The Coalition government was forced to back down on a number of key policies, as the free trade ideal became as politically untenable in New Zealand as it had become elsewhere – although the minority National government sought to revive some of these policies close to the 1999 election. This chapter examines the arguments for a more strategic approach to international trade, and the degree to which trade policy and the CER agreement would constrain a future government's capacity to adopt such an approach.

▲ TRADE THEORY AND INTERNATIONAL REALITY

Successive Labour and National governments claimed they were applying orthodox neo-classical trade theory, based on notions of comparative advantage, global allocative efficiency and aggregate economic welfare.

The argument runs thus. When resources are invested in producing one thing, something else will not be produced. This creates an 'opportunity cost'. It makes economic sense for a country to focus its resources on producing the goods and services it is best at – in which it has a *comparative advantage*. This applies even if there are other products it can also produce more efficiently than other countries can. The country's resources will be better used by producing a limited range of goods and importing the rest, than by producing everything for itself and cutting itself off from trade. Hence the government must ensure that its policies do not distort the flow of capital to where it will be most efficiently (that is, profitably) used. If all countries specialise in producing what they do best, and provided they can freely trade those products with one another, each country's resources, and the world's resources, will be allocated most efficiently. Because more efficient production generates greater income and increased opportunity to buy goods and services from other countries, free trade will enhance global economic welfare.

There is, however, a gaping chasm between neo-classical trade theory and international trade practice. The theory assumes a perfect global market, yet international commerce takes place within grossly imperfect and politicised markets. Most small and poor countries seek to protect their key industries and producers, and to retain a modicum of economic self-sufficiency. The biggest players – the US, the European Union and Japan – are actively interventionist. They all accuse each other of breaking the agreed multilateral trade rules, while making up their own.

The US, in particular, insists on the right to threaten or use unilateral sanctions against what it considers to be unfair trade practices, based on the 'section 301' and 'super 301' provisions of the US Trade Act.[4] The US Trade Representative creates an inventory of 'unfair' practices in other countries, selects priority targets, and restricts imports from those countries if the practices are not eliminated. New Zealand has been threatened with such action for maintaining its statutory producer board monopolies. 'Special 301' powers take a similar approach to intellectual property. The US threatened to use them when New Zealand introduced laws for parallel importing of brand-name goods, passed under urgency during the 1998 Budget debate.[5] US law therefore puts its government outside the rules-based system it requires everyone else to obey. Not surprisingly, the US has consistently resisted moves to reduce its own protections in politically sensitive sectors, such as its domestic agricultural subsidies.

Paul Krugman suggests that the importance of trade in the US is more political than economic. With exports accounting for about one-eighth of US output, domestic production is still predominantly for domestic consumption.[6] The defence of free trade has become a major issue in the US because ideologically it provides 'an important touchstone for advocates of free-market economics', and politically it 'is important as a counterweight to crude economic nationalism'.[7] Pitted against the US free-traders are equally determined, and politically influential, producers who demand domestic protection; US unions have taken a similar position. Krugman argues that the opponents of this position overstate the costs of protectionism: 'The real harm done ... is much more modest and mundane: It reduces the efficiency of the world economy.'[8] The standard estimates of these global efficiency costs are also very low. Other problems, such as traffic congestion or wasteful defence contracts, cause greater losses to the US economy. From this, Krugman concludes: 'There is a better intellectual case for protection than there used to be, and the case for free trade is often overstated'. While the argument for free trade is still strong – 'not as an absolute ideal, but as a reasonable rule of thumb'[9] – it is an unrealistic goal, given the belief of US producers and politicians that other countries, especially Japan, are following different rules.

Out of these political realities, new approaches to trade policy have emerged. 'Managed' trade is the favoured approach of the Clinton administration. This involves negotiating quantitative trade targets with another country, without specifying the rules or policies by which they are to be achieved. Hence it allows national differences to be accommodated and governments to manage their domestic pressures. Defenders of a rule-based approach to international trade condemn this approach as 'bureaucrats allocating trade according to what domestic lobbying pressures and foreign political muscle dictate'.[10] They also claim that the results of managed trade reflect the uneven bargaining power of the parties, even between Japan and the US. For these two countries and others like them, it does offer a politically tenable solution. But relying primarily on managed trade through bilateral negotiations would leave a small country like New Zealand extremely vulnerable.

A second approach is termed 'strategic trade policy'.[11] This concludes that comparative advantage does not depend solely on a country's natural attributes, but can be built up and change over time. Historical circumstances will be important, and so will the knowledge base that results from research and development and cumulative experience. Countries can also gain short-term advantages from investing in innovation, and maintaining a certain scale of production. An activist trade policy, based on strategic government support for certain activities, can help strengthen a country's competitive position. Producing goods or services onshore also generates valuable spill-overs to the local economy and community. Critics of this approach say that governments are not good at 'picking winners', and that their interventions distort the efficient allocation of productive resources through the market, which in turn costs jobs. These theoretical arguments, common in New Zealand, are debatable, especially given the poor returns from an increasingly self-regulating market since 1984 (see Chapter 10).

Other trade theorists support a more activist approach that embraces a range of non-trade considerations. Orthodox trade theory assumes that any financial, psychological and social costs associated with free trade – costs of disruption, resettlement, rehousing, retraining and periods of unemployment – will be outweighed by the aggregate benefits to the world economy. Dealing with these downstream costs is not the concern of trade policy.[12] Nor does it address the distribution of these costs and benefits. As trade economist Paul Streeten observes:

> When the lion's share of the gains go to ... higher income groups, the poorer are worse off. It is then possible that the countries with large gains from trade fail to benefit because their internal inequalities are great, and those with small or no gains do not benefit because international inequalities are great. [Alternatively, the] gainers from trade may be people who represent one set of values, for example, those of speculative financial gains, whereas the remainder represent other values, such as hard work with its rewards. They may judge the costs of free trade to be too high.[13]

In the period following the Second World War, there was an attempt to provide some balance through a two-pronged approach. This aimed to reduce the very high levels of trade protection through multilateral trade negotiations, and to mitigate the distributional and social side-effects at the national level through a combination of welfare and public services and the responsible use of short-term trade safeguards.[14] In the era of neoliberalism, the 'Washington consensus' insists that trade is liberalised *and* domestic supports are reduced or withdrawn (see Chapter 1). The social costs of free trade are left starkly exposed.

The most obvious casualty is employment. The lower cost of imports and the removal of government support impact disproportionately on workers in manufacturing. Most new jobs created by the reallocation of capital tend to benefit higher-skilled workers in niche-market manufacture or technology, or in the expanding services sector. In that sector too, differentials have grown. International 'trade' in services means that high-skilled, mobile service providers (for example, consultants, executives, airline pilots) can command internationally competitive payment, high status and attractive conditions. Yet the services sector of the home economy (for example, entertainment, food, cleaning, childcare, education and health care) involves mainly low-paid and insecure work. It disproportionately employs women, indigenous people and migrants, who are constantly under pressure to accept reduced pay or conditions, and frequently at risk of losing their jobs.

The social instability this creates is bad for people and bad for the economy. Because social harmony and cohesion contribute to efficiency and growth, it is a legitimate goal of economic policy to preserve a particular way of life, set of values, community, and culture; for example, by supporting small farmers or economically depressed regions. This requires trade policy to make conscious trade-offs. As Paul Streeten argues:

> In an international environment in which comparative advantage changes rapidly, trade policy can become a policy for tramps: it imposes the imperative to move from one occupation to another, from one residence to another. The citizens of an already fairly rich country, or a like-minded group of such countries, may say: We already enjoy many earthly goods. We wish to forgo some extra income from international trade for the sake of a quieter life, for not having to learn a new trade, for not being uprooted from our community. There is nothing irrational or 'noneconomic' in such a choice.[15]

Equally, commitments to self-determination for indigenous peoples, genuine ecological sustainability, full employment and a fairer distribution of wealth and resources are available as political and economic choices. The extent and economic cost of such choices will vary according to the strength of the country's internal economy, its dependence on international trade, and the influence of domestic political and cultural considerations on government policy; none of these factors is fixed. There will be less choice for many poor countries and for trade-dependent smaller countries like New Zealand. But there are choices, nonetheless.

New Zealand governments since 1984 have never conceded this possibility. They opted instead for a Darwinist approach to the tradeable sectors of the domestic economy, in the certainty that their theory was right. The trade policy briefing to the incoming Minister of Foreign Affairs and Trade in 1993 explained: 'New Zealand did not adopt open policies to enhance our trade negotiating stance. Those policies were adopted because the governments of the day considered they were in the best interests of New Zealand.'[16]

The strategy for exposing 'fortress New Zealand' to the international market-place focused on withdrawing border protection and domestic assistance from local producers. In 1984 almost every part of the economy was heavily regulated. A complex system of trade protections – mainly tariffs, import licensing, and export incentives and subsidies – had been built up over the years in response to various balance of payments, employment and industry needs. There had been some moves towards industry deregulation and the reduction of import licensing under the National government in the early 1980s. The Closer Economic Relations Trade Agreement with Australia (CER) was signed in 1983. But these changes were too slow for many of Prime Minister Robert Muldoon's caucus critics. When the new Labour government quickened the pace of deregulation in 1984, there was little partisan dispute. Traditional productive sectors were subjected to a 'scorched earth' regime where only the most internationally competitive would survive. The adjustment costs as resources shifted from protecting inefficient activities to expanding more efficient ones were considered temporary and unavoidable. Treasury advised that the net benefits were best secured through an integrated and accelerated process of change.[17]

Formal responsibility for trade policy was split when the old Department of Trade and Industry ceased to exist in 1988. Domestic aspects such as tariff levels and trade remedies went to a new Ministry of Commerce (which was later headed by ex-Treasury officials).[18] International trade became the responsibility of the Ministry of External Relations and Trade (formerly the Ministry of Foreign Affairs), which later became the Ministry of Foreign Affairs and Trade. Once foreign affairs and trade were merged, trade issues came to dominate the government's foreign policy positions. This coincided with the rapid expansion of international economic negotiations, notably the Uruguay Round of the GATT from 1986 to 1994, and the emergence of the APEC forum in 1989. These eclipsed the earlier focus on negotiating annual quotas for agricultural products with the European Community (an example of 'managed' trade) and periodic reviews and extensions of CER. As the negotiations assumed a higher profile both internationally and at home, the Ministry of Foreign Affairs and Trade took a more activist policy role. Treasury was always close by.

▲ INDUSTRY

Treasury's 1984 briefing paper to the incoming government, *Economic Management,* identified two main targets for trade liberalisation: agriculture and industry. The Manufacturers' Federation had already agreed reluctantly, in the context of signing CER in 1983, to the progressive conversion of import licensing to tariffs, and the reduction of domestic protection. But it stalled on the implementation, prompting retaliatory sanctions from the US. *Economic Management* insisted that removing trade barriers and export incentives was essential to improve domestic efficiency and achieve trade liberalisation through the GATT and CER. The

Labour government decided to move quickly, largely bypassing the Manufacturers' Federation in the process.[19] By late 1986 the government had announced that most import licensing would end within two years, and a programme of tariff cuts. Export incentives were to go by April 1990. Progress towards a free trade area with Australia would be stepped up. Director of the New Zealand Institute of Economic Research (NZIER) Alan Bollard described this transition as 'multidimensional in its nature and radical in its impact, moving many industrial sectors from a high degree of external regulation to regulation by markets and other contractual arrangements within only three years'.[20]

In 1987, around 30 percent of manufactured output was still covered by plans for the phasing-out of protection in specific industries. Import licensing and tariffs continued to offer some support for industry, with most directed to the sensitive areas of motor vehicles, apparel and footwear. Treasury wanted the removal of protection to go further, faster. It insisted that the problems the export sector faced as a result of the impact of monetary policy on the exchange rate were temporary, while the distortions caused by regulatory control were long-term.[21] Treasury's 1987 post-election briefing paper urged the government to speed up the pace of change: 'on the basis of experience to date we conclude that the reform programme for assistance to import substituting industries in particular could be significantly accelerated without imposing excessive adjustment costs on the economy, and that accelerating that programme would bring significant benefits'.[22]

Treasury warned that taking a piecemeal approach would increase the risk of politicians capitulating to industry lobbies and making decisions based on particular industries' needs, rather than on (theoretical) economy-wide costs and gains. It wanted all industry assistance reduced, with the highest levels cut the most. Treasury argued that a 'more even-handed policy' would produce a more effective pattern of investment throughout the economy, stronger economic growth and higher living standards. Faster progress would bring these benefits more quickly.[23]

Transitional costs and employment and equity considerations were deflected. Treasury argued that industry protection benefited workers in one industry at the expense of those in another. It also prevented labour from moving into new, more productive industries that would benefit all. The best way to promote employment was to make wages and labour respond to market forces in a vibrant, internationally competitive economy.[24] While there were risks that reducing assistance too rapidly would provoke more intensive producer lobbying, and certain kinds of labour and capital might find it hard to relocate, Treasury believed that a 'reasonable' period of adjustment would allow people to 'search and if necessary to retrain for a new job [and] minimise the extent to which people are unemployed and production falls as a short term response to the new assistance regime.'[25]

The 1987 briefing paper made no attempt to examine the impact of deregulation to date, beyond a passing reference to a study by the NZIER which found that increased market competition had tended to reduce prices to the consumer and increase product differentiation. The study also reported that some consumers, workers and firms were worse off.[26] Alan Bollard subsequently remarked on how little work had been done 'to establish the relative gains and costs borne by consumers and producers, and downstream distributional consequences. In fact the whole question of the magnitude of net benefits to the economy, and indeed whether they are positive, has been taken very much on faith.'[27]

By the end of its second term, the fourth Labour government had done largely as Treasury prescribed. The effective rate of assistance to manufacturing fell from around 37 percent in 1985/86 to around 19 percent in 1989/90. The targets for deregulating trade with Australia were met by 1990, five years ahead of schedule. Most import licensing was abolished, with the rest to be eliminated by 1992. Labour began a phased tariff reduction programme in 1985. A 1987 review aimed to halve higher levels of tariffs by 1992. In March 1990, Labour announced that more cuts, beginning in 1993, would reduce tariffs to a maximum of 10 percent by 1996, with higher protection for textiles, clothing and shoes, and vehicles.

However, National's Minister of Commerce Philip Burdon had told manufacturers before the 1990 election that 'the National Party is not making any further tariff reductions: you can hold us to account on those remarks'.[28] In July 1991 an officials' review said Labour's programme should proceed, with heaviest cuts in the most protected industries. A special caucus committee on tariffs advised moderation. Burdon agreed. He also deferred some cuts to specific tariffs for clothing 'as a safety net for the industry. I am not prepared to stand by and see the complete erosion of the industry's domestic base.'[29] This was a temporary hiatus. A further round of tariff cuts was announced in 1994, to begin in 1997. The government described the targets as 'tough but fair'. Tariffs would be reduced in the most protected industries – textiles, clothing and shoes, and motor vehicles – to 15 percent by 2000. With approximately 28,000 people still employed in those sectors, the government acknowledged that job losses would be heavy. However, it predicted that efficient industries would produce 40,000 new jobs a year in the following three years.[30]

A further review in 1998 was to focus on reducing all remaining tariffs to zero.[31] But when the time came, New Zealand had a Coalition government of National and New Zealand First. The Coalition Agreement negotiated in late 1996 said that the 1998 tariff review would 'proceed in line with current policy, *taking into account the policies and progress of other trading partners*'.[32] This was a concession to New Zealand First's pre-election policy, which was to impose additional tariffs on goods from protectionist countries or reduce tariffs on imports from countries with open trading practices. Its leader, Winston Peters, called for a trade policy that 'puts New Zealand first, just as [the Asian tigers'] policies put their people first'.[33]

This posed a dilemma for the Coalition government. New Zealand's largest trading partner was Australia. From 1983 to 1996, their Labor government had been fervent free-traders. The Liberal opposition initially sought to go one better, and promoted zero tariffs by 2000 in its 1992 election manifesto. By 1995 the political climate, and Liberal policy, had changed. Unilateral liberalisation gave way to a more managed approach to trade. Liberal politicians wanted to link tariff cuts to domestic cost-reductions for manufacturers and access for exporters to specific markets – a position supported by the Australian Chamber of Manufacturers and opposed by the Business Council of Australia.[34] The Liberals became the government in 1996. In June 1997, the Australian Industries Commission advised the government to cut tariffs unilaterally on imports of new cars, textiles, clothing and footwear to 5 percent by 2008. Job losses of up to 100,000 were predicted. The unions led a vigorous campaign against the proposal, and opinion polls showed massive support for retaining tariffs.[35] The government backed down, announcing that it would freeze tariffs in those sectors at 2000 levels (15 percent) until 2005. The policy would then be reviewed in light of other countries' trade policies.[36]

In New Zealand, Winston Peters was now the Treasurer. In the 1997 Budget he did a complete turnaround from his party's pre-election position. Foreshadowing an accelerated review of tariffs after 2000, he sidestepped the issue of what New Zealand's trading partners were doing by citing the APEC commitment to free trade by 2010 (failing to mention that it was, in fact, voluntary and non-binding):

> ... we don't intend taking a wait and see approach, but we intend to provide leadership in this area, whilst working to ensure that our trading partners follow suit. There are no prizes for coming last, so the 1998 Tariff Review will set a timetable to remove all remaining tariffs well within the 2010 deadline set by APEC.[37]

A ministerial briefing paper in July 1998 claimed that New Zealand was 'very much in the OECD mainstream' with its tariff policies. This was based on data up to 1996; since then New Zealand had further reduced tariffs while many other countries had not. It also cited the APEC goal as evidence of orthodoxy; yet the attached APEC schedule showed that very few countries had made commitments similar to New Zealand's. Contradicting its own argument, the paper then admitted that New Zealand had chosen a different and faster path than its trading partners, who were 'reducing tariffs at different rates, reflecting different assessments about the needs of their domestic economies'. Such wide variation meant New Zealand could not model itself on others. Moving more slowly would mean foregoing the benefits to the economy, with no offsetting gains. Indeed, by removing tariffs quickly, New Zealand might help shift the negotiating agenda for trade liberalisation onto non-tariff issues, such as competition law, investment and services. The impact on jobs was downplayed; the paper claimed there were adequate employment initiatives to improve the 'efficiency with which the labour market adjusts'.[38]

The 1998 tariff review, overseen by the Ministry of Commerce, focused on eliminating tariffs in those industries where levels would still be at 15 percent in 2000. The Ministry's review document provided no formal cost-benefit analysis of a move to zero tariffs, just the familiar assertions of a stronger, more competitive economy, lower costs and consumer savings.[39] The motor vehicle industry asked for a quick decision about its fate, so the review of imported motor vehicle tariffs was accelerated. The Ministry's terms of reference for that review proposed zero tariffs for cars and light commercial vehicles by 2002. There were few precedents for this. Australian exports to New Zealand were already duty-free under CER. Only Hong Kong, Singapore and Japan had no tariffs on cars. Australia's tariff on imported vehicles would be frozen at 15 percent until at least 2005.

Commerce Minister John Luxton claimed that existing car tariffs cost consumers about $300 million a year – a subsidy of $180,000 per job.[40] The Alliance pointed out that only one-third of car imports were new cars, and once the cuts already scheduled were completed in 2000, the total consumer subsidy would be only $85.3 million a year in 1996/97 dollars. Balanced against that, the Minister had ignored factors which meant the sudden removal of tariffs would be a net cost to the economy. Some $180 million would be lost in export earnings from vehicles and components. Increased vehicle imports would mean more overseas borrowing and, alongside lost exports, would lead to a further deterioration in New Zealand's trade balance and external current account (see Chapter 10). That was without considering the loss to local communities of production, jobs, incomes, skills training, regional development and a home market from which to launch exports. The $300 million in lost tariff revenue, plus taxes on wages and profits from the car industry, would have to be compensated by other taxes or spending cuts. Workers who were made redundant, and their families, would also need government support.[41]

The motor vehicle companies asked the government for a firm decision as soon as all submissions were in. Their industry was in decline, but not yet dead. Around 25,000 of the 65,000 new cars sold annually in New Zealand – and about 14 percent of all first-time registrations – were still locally assembled.[42] The first car assembly plant had been opened by General Motors in 1926, and by the early 1980s the industry employed around 8,000 workers. In 1997 the number of jobs was down to 1,500, with around 4,000 more in the components industry.[43] The US car-makers had all closed their New Zealand assembly plants. Four Japanese plants were still operating: Nissan at Wiri in Auckland (230 workers), Toyota in Thames (330), Honda in Nelson (220), and Mitsubishi in Porirua (360).[44]

Local feelings ran high. In Thames, the recently upgraded Toyota plant was the town's biggest employer, reportedly putting $14 million in wages into the local economy each year.[45] People took to the streets, wrote letters and signed petitions. Commerce Minister John Luxton was booed at a street meeting in late September.[46] Thames already had chronic unemployment, and the other major employer, a foundry, had an uncertain future.

The Coalition government was unmoved, and announced in December 1997 that it was accelerating the reduction of tariffs to zero by 2000. This meant sudden death for the local motor vehicle industry. The foreign firms chose not to stick around, as they could easily supply the local market from offshore, especially Australia. Mitsubishi stopped production in Porirua mid-year, and Honda ceased in Nelson in August 1998. The Nissan plant at Wiri closed in July 1998, and the Yazaki component assemblers in nearby Mangere had laid off all 400 workers (almost all women) by November. The Toyota factory in Thames closed in December 1998.

The May 1998 Budget announced the immediate removal of the remaining 15 percent tariff on motor vehicles. Luxton predicted that the cost of new cars would fall by $3,000 to $4,000.[47] The car companies began an aggressive advertising campaign to sell lower-priced new imports. But not all the tariff savings were passed on to the consumer. Market leader Toyota cut prices by only 5 percent, after increasing some of them a few months before the Budget.[48] A Nissan spokesperson said that their prices would depend on the exchange rate and on demand, and might even increase.[49] *New Zealand Herald* business editor Rod Oram warned that: 'consumers should not bet on benefiting from the misery of Thames, Nelson and other car-making communities. Exchange rates, the machinations of multinational production, the consolidation of dealer networks and other factors could deny them the savings.'[50]

The impact of factory closure on a town like Thames was devastating.

Toyota made the port of Thames the entry point for all its vehicles into the country, and the plant was adapted to process the imports, as well as refurbish fleet and rental cars. This operation employed around 60 of the 320 workforce. The Toyota Resource Centre remained open for six months; from an initial 120 workers seeking jobs, only 40 remained on their list, although some had moved away, taken early retirement or otherwise withdrawn from the workforce. The local economy remained fragile. Workers who had accumulated bonuses over the years were now on much lower rates of pay, so there was less money in circulation. The least skilled found it hardest to find jobs, especially Maori, the young and those nearing retirement age. With the local hospital under threat of closure, prospects for the town looked pretty bleak.

The local community was determined not to die. On the initiative of a local businessman, supported by a public meeting, the Thames Business Enterprise Project was established to attract outside businesses to the town.[51] The government had promised $400,000 in contestable funding to help the four communities affected by the closures to develop alternative industries. The Thames project was outside its terms of reference, but the government found $110,000 which was matched by local contributions from the Thames Community Board and private enterprise. Businesses that expressed an interest in moving to Thames wanted venture capital or incentives, which were not available. The project concentrated instead on initiatives that would strengthen the town's existing businesses and ensure that Thames as a town survived.

The government's moves to eliminate tariffs on textiles, clothing and footwear proved much more difficult. In August 1997, the Ministry of Commerce invited submissions on the plan for zero tariffs in these industries. There was no question that tariffs should be removed – it was just a matter of how and when. The review was to be completed by the end of March 1998, with a report to Cabinet in May. Free trade advocates in the Business Roundtable, Employers' Federation, Federated Farmers, downstream industries,[52] and private consultancies endorsed the proposal, saying that zero tariffs would provide certainty, consistency and efficiency, and benefit producers, importers and consumers. Their submissions offered little or no empirical evidence to support that view.

The submission from the National Council of Women pointed out that the Ministry's proposal itself lacked 'statistics, facts or evidence to support the statements and/or assumptions it contains'. Similar concerns were expressed by a former Deputy Secretary of Trade and Industry, Peter Donovan, who had participated in the Uruguay Round negotiations. He argued that, although there were sound arguments for shifting from a high-tariff to a low-tariff regime, the proposition of *zero* tariffs needed to be considered in its own right. The gains might be very small or non-existent. Low tariff levels were more likely to impact on the profit margins of individual companies than on industry- or economy-wide cost structures. The footwear industry supported Donovan's view, citing an Australian study of the motor vehicle supply industry which suggested that 98 percent of the benefit of tariff reduction was achieved when tariffs reached 15 percent, and only 2 percent by cutting them to zero.[53]

The textiles, clothing and footwear manufacturers said they did not oppose the goal of free trade, provided the transition was gradual and fair. Since 1987, when tariff reductions began, the industry had proved it was internationally competitive. Exports had expanded, as had markets beyond Australia. In 1998 there were still 1,500 plants operating, with sales of $2.4 billion, including exports of $0.5 billion. The industry paid $170 million annually in company taxes. It was also the major employer in many regional areas, employing 21,270 people directly, with some 5,000 more people dependent on the industry. This represented one in ten manufacturing jobs. Seventy-four percent of its workers were women; one-third were Maori, Polynesian or Asian. This skilled and experienced workforce was already insecure and underpaid. The number of full-time equivalent workers in the apparel and textile sector had dropped from 30,939 in 1985 to 16,710 in 1997.[54] The National Distribution Union noted that the fall in hours worked was even more severe. Wages were just 58 percent of comparable wages in Australia, and below the New Zealand average wage. The industry could still not compete with China, the source of 43 percent of imports by value. In the footwear industry, about one-third of production was exported, and local producers held 29 percent of the local market by value. A rapid move to zero tariffs would cost almost 1,500 jobs – again, predominantly of women, Maori and Pacific Island workers.[55]

The textiles, clothing and footwear industry argued that it could compete successfully in the future in small-run production that targeted niche markets overseas. But its small-business base meant it had to adjust to that strategy gradually. And it could reorient itself to exports only if it maintained a critical mass and a core domestic market. The precipitate removal of tariffs would threaten at least 50 percent of the industry. The resulting loss of confidence would also mean low investment in capital and training. Larger companies would either relocate offshore, meaning smaller firms would lose the support they provided, or become importers of goods made in Asia, as Bendon had done. Many small companies would close. Primary producers, for example of wool for carpets, would lose their guaranteed local outlets and have to depend on sales to less reliable overseas processors. Industry-funded research, with its ability to add value, would disappear. Trainees in the textile and clothing industry would be unable to use their skills; courses would close, and local designers would be unemployed or forced to move offshore.[56] There was no guarantee that consumers would benefit. A 15 percent tariff added only 15 cents to the cost of a pair of briefs or 55 cents to a t-shirt. If the tariff were removed, overseas exporters, local importers and retailers might not pass on the savings, and use the cuts to improve their profit margins instead.

The industry predicted that its workforce would halve, creating a huge demand for income support. Low morale among those laid off would flow on to their families. Nor would displaced workers find jobs easily in other industries. Although conditions across the Tasman were not identical, Australian research showed that only 47 percent of textile, clothing and footwear workers who had been made redundant had found employment within the next two years, and one-third of them had taken jobs that were lower paid.[57] The New Zealand government had done no equivalent research. Evidence to date showed that the so-called 'sunrise industries' of tourism and electronics had not delivered the promised jobs, even before the East Asian economies collapsed.

There was considerable cynicism in the industry about the government's claim that the APEC free trade agreement 'requires the removal of all tariffs between signatory countries by 2010 at the latest'.[58] As mentioned earlier, the commitment was voluntary and non-binding for all member governments. The carpet manufacturers asked: 'who is to say that APEC members will in fact meet these goals by 2010/2020?', especially as the high tariffs in some APEC countries had recently been increased.[59] In addition to tariffs in other countries, the industry faced a long list of non-tariff barriers. These included processing delays at customs, quarantine regulations, restrictive labelling requirements, statutory charges, arbitrary 'anti-dumping' duties, 'voluntary' export controls, local content and ownership requirements, and restrictive rules of origin (which specify the required proportion of local content).

LWR Industries (whose majority shareholder was Brierley Investments Ltd) was especially blunt: 'It seems to us that our politicians want us to win a race that no-one else is running in. This stance is not "leadership". It is abrogation at best and stupidity at worst. Standing up in world forums saying "we are the most free Western economy" does not achieve any measurable benefits for New Zealanders.'[60] The Employers and Manufacturers Association (Northern) insisted that the 'practicalities of the international market place need to be appreciated ... and don't always match up to "purist economic theory".'[61] Industry submissions urged the government to follow the Australian example and hold tariffs at the 2000 level until 2005, with any further reduction being contingent on parallel moves by New Zealand's international trading partners.

The Trade Union Federation, which represented most of the unions directly affected, also sought a freeze on tariffs in the industry until 2005. Its submission demanded a full assessment of the impact of tariff reductions before any further cuts were considered. The submission was supported by a report commissioned from economist Tim Hazledine, which concluded that, despite four decades of liberalisation of world trade, there was no systematic evidence that liberalisation had produced the predicted efficiency gains. All the serious studies were driven by theory, not fact. Forecasts of future efficiency gains used simulation models. There was no attempt to go back and ask whether previous forecasts had come true. Hazledine commented:

> ... it is rather as though, out there in the great economic jungle, there have been roaming (or believed to be roaming) large beasts called TREGs (Tariff Reduction Efficiency Gains). But, in nearly half a century, no intrepid explorer has ever gone into the jungle and captured a TREG and brought it back to the economic dissection table so that its weight and size can be actually measured. Could it be that the TREG is in fact a mythical beast, or perhaps just too tiny to be spotted in the jungle?[62]

In particular, there was no empirical evidence that tariffs in the textile, clothing and footwear industry prevented the profitable expansion of other industries. In a growing, high-wage, full-employment economy, it was possible that expanding industries might pull people and investment away from textiles and clothing by offering better-paid jobs and a more attractive return on investment. But that was very different from pushing people out of employment in textiles and clothing and expecting them to be easily and quickly redeployed elsewhere, especially in times of low growth and high unemployment and underemployment. Hazledine concluded:

> The theoretical case for unilateral tariff elimination is weak at best and most likely wrong, in the sense that middle-of-the-road assumptions show net efficiency gains, not losses from continued protection. The [textiles, clothing and footwear] sector generates jobs and profits and produces useful goods for New Zealanders. To risk tossing all this aside in the name of an ephemeral free-trade dogma seems almost incredibly foolhardy and irresponsible.[63]

The submission from the CTU, the other major trade union body, was brief. In two pages, it described its interests as 'somewhat remote', as it had few affiliates in the industries affected (although the National Distribution Union was one). It suggested that 'tariff policy should be less unilateral', and accompanied by an incomes policy.

The officials' report on the submissions in May 1998 explained that a number of them fell outside the terms of reference, because their primary purpose was to argue that government policy to remove all tariffs before 2010 was wrong. The report offered a fragmented description of the submissions, rather than an analysis. This prompted a further intervention from the industry, objecting to the failure to present the context and logic behind the submissions. At this late stage, the Ministry produced its own study, commissioned from the NZIER, to support its proposals. The report reiterated the expected benefits of lower costs to consumers, efficient reallocation of resources, increased competition, increased employment, and reduced public sector and company compliance costs. It noted potential problems and adjustment costs, including that capital might be stranded in redundant assets, and workers with industry-specific skills could find re-employment difficult. However, it reached the 'intuitive conclusion' that, while a short lead-time intensified the adjustment shock, the quicker tariffs were removed, the sooner benefits would accrue. In the present case, it believed, there had been ample prior warning of the government's intentions, so the adjustment costs should be minimal.[64] The Apparel and Textile Manufacturers commissioned the Infometrics agency to analyse the NZIER study. While disclaiming any definitive forecast, it concluded that 'with more realistic assumptions and inclusion of employment effects into the model, the argument for zero [textile, clothing and footwear] tariffs as soon as 2001 is reversed, or at least significantly undermined.'[65]

The government now faced the situation that Treasury had foreshadowed in 1987: proposals that were viewed by those affected as too extreme had provoked them to resist. The textile, clothing and footwear industry had more to fight for than the transnationals affected by the removal of tariffs on motor vehicles. Most of these firms were small. Almost all were locally owned, although the larger firms had expanded offshore. Many came under the Manufacturers' Federation, which over the years had become a convert to free trade; but the industry was determined to fight tariff removal and the Federation had to back them. The TUF unions and National Distribution Union were equally determined, and worked hard to build a united industry campaign. Local authorities mobilised to defend their communities, sending a delegation of seventeen mayors to meet with the Minister. The local backlash against car plant closures had strengthened public support, and encouraged sympathetic coverage in the media.

The campaign gradually secured political support. The Alliance had consistently opposed the tariff cuts. In April 1998 Labour announced that it supported a link to Australia's tariff levels, and later backed an APEC-related phasing-down of tariffs in textiles, clothing and footwear, starting in 2005 and ending in 2010.[66] New Zealand First MPs also saw the implications of tariff cuts, especially for Maori workers and communities, and put pressure on the Coalition Cabinet.[67] The officials were split. The 'free market' ministries of Commerce, Treasury, Labour, and Foreign Affairs and Trade proposed zero tariffs by July 2001; the more socially focused agencies of Women's, Maori and Pacific Islands Affairs suggested a three-stage process, ending in 2003.

The government refused to consider an Australian-style moratorium, saying it would postpone the flow-on benefits for up to a decade. But Minister for Enterprise and Commerce Max Bradford read the political signs. Going further than any of the officials had proposed, he negotiated a compromise with the manufacturers in September that would see tariffs removed on textiles by July 2004, and on clothing and footwear by July 2006. Bradford told the Cabinet:

> While it is not as ambitious a path as we would like, it nevertheless meets our target of getting tariffs down to zero well before 2010. I support its acceptance because I believe that we are already placing considerable reliance on businesses in New Zealand to help us ride the present economic conditions and they will appreciate the added certainty of an agreed tariff policy. Moreover, in the current political environment, I consider that the willing buy-in of those most affected by the changes is highly desirable.[68]

The government passed the Tariff (Zero Duty) Amendment Bill under urgency on 29 September 1998. This was only a partial victory for those in the industry; the cuts had merely been deferred. Meanwhile, the government had not given up. Their credibility as hosts of APEC required them to maintain the benefits of tariff cuts. An NZIER study in June 1999 of savings to consumers on cars, household goods, shoes and clothes claimed the average New Zealand household was $22 a week better off than if tariffs had remained in 1987 rates, and would be $42 better off by 2010. Economist Bryan Philpott noted that the terms of reference steered the researchers away from employment, wage and other effects, and dismissed the methodology of looking only at prices as 'rubbish'; a valid study needed to look at the whole community and changes to people's real welfare. [69]

The partial victory also came at a price to the industry and its workforce. Uncertainty about the future meant businesses had deferred investment, suppliers held off from signing contracts, banks withheld loans, factories closed and workers were laid off without redundancies.[70]

▲ AGRICULTURE

Agriculture was the other main target for trade liberalisation. In 1984, agriculture contributed 60 percent of New Zealand's exports and 7 percent of GDP.[71] It was still the major earner of foreign exchange. Farmers received input subsidies, including cheap finance and farm development incentives, and an easily exploited supplementary minimum price (SMP) for their products. Between 1984 and 1987 these supports were withdrawn. A 20 percent devaluation in 1984 was expected to help compensate for the phasing-out of SMPs, but the dollar rapidly appreciated after it was floated in March 1985. The deregulation of the financial sector and the withdrawal of subsidised credit raised farmers' interest rates to market levels. User-charges were imposed on a range of government research services, and from late 1996 state-owned enterprises charged commercial rates for services such as electricity and rail transport. Many farmers who had invested at inflated land prices or expanded production during the SMP-driven boom were over-exposed. As interest rates rose, farmers reduced their expenditure on fertiliser and maintenance, and cut stock numbers to service the debt. According to farmer Robert Bremer and historian Tom Brooking, the terms of trade at the farm gate for sheep farmers in the 1985/86 financial year fell to 56 percent of levels in 1974/75, which was not a particularly good year. The decline was such that 'by 1985 a great number of influential policy-makers, including the Minister of Finance, were looking upon New Zealand's traditional agriculture as a "sunset industry", although most of the propounded alternative industries found their own sunset after the 1987 financial crash'.[72]

The agricultural sector survived, but its structure began to change from the traditional family farm towards larger-scale operations, with farmers devoting more effort to financial management and marketing.[73] The new breed of farmer, whether survivors of restructuring or new entrants, proved to be stalwarts of the free market. Through the Federated Farmers lobby, they demanded that other sectors face similar disciplines to their own, and that burdens imposed by resource management and accident compensation legislation be reduced.

Agribusinesses began to emerge. The most prominent were corporate farmer Apple Fields and its offshoot, Dairy Brands New Zealand. Investment analyst Bill Rosenberg describes these companies as 'among the most unsuccessful businesses of the decade: they have failed in almost everything they set out to do, except generate hype'.[74] Apple Fields first listed in 1986 when it was a major apple producer and the country's biggest supplier of export apples. In 1994 it was subject to a Securities Commission report which attacked deficiencies in its accounts. In 1995 it received an exemption from the Overseas Investment Commission, despite being two-fifths overseas-owned. For a number of years Apple Fields spearheaded the campaign against the Apple and Pear Marketing Board, blaming its own successive huge losses on the board's refusal to grant it independent marketing rights. In late 1996, Apple Fields abandoned agribusiness and began subdividing its holding into large lifestyle blocks for the wealthy on the perimeter of Christchurch.[75] The company's shares traded at 10 cents in February 1999, down from 33 cents at the beginning of 1998 and 74 cents at the start of 1996.[76] In 1999 Dairy Brands (chaired by former Minister of Finance Ruth Richardson) still owned fifteen dairy farms and leased one in Canterbury.

The entrepreneurial fervour of the farming sector concealed two deep-seated contradictions. Most New Zealand farms were still small units with an integrated economic, social and cultural function. Farming practices were semi-feudal, relying on the unpaid labour of family members and cooperation within the rural community.[77] Conservative rural values and a colonial residue also fostered a strong sense of self-sufficiency. While farmers supported across-the-board deregulation once the initial impact on them had passed, there was also unease over the social impacts of the changes, and concern about the future of the family farm and the survival of rural communities. Bremer and Brooking commented in 1993 on the 'growing awareness among farmers of rural deprivation arising from [the] inexorable loss of rural services and amenities as economic restructuring ... gradually depopulated the countryside'.[78] As this threat became more acute, doubts began to set in.

The second contradiction related to Maori. Pakeha farms are the epitome of colonisation. The loss of their land through war, law, trickery and the individualisation of titles left Maori with around 3 million of the country's 66 million acres by the 1980s.[79] Many present-day farmers are descendants of those responsible for such practices, and have shown little concern about the ethics and consequences of what was done. Land that remained in Maori hands was often fragmented into individual shareholdings, held in blocks and run by Maori incorporations, or divided into small 'uneconomic' pieces which (by law) were re-aggregated into economic units and compulsorily managed by the Crown. Maori farming often struggled to survive in a rural community that was historically hostile; the larger units were also disadvantaged in a producer board system where control was based on one farm one vote. With the strong representation of Maori MPs in New Zealand First, the Coalition government formed in late 1996 faced demands from organised Maori farmers and growers for more say in their industries, although small Maori farmers remained invisible.

Both these tensions came to a head in 1997 with the battle over the deregulation/privatisation of the statutory producer and marketing boards. New Zealand farming was already facing serious economic pressures. The heavily overvalued dollar had strangled exports for two years. Then the dollar fell dramatically. The benefit of that was counter-acted by increased costs for imported goods, initially high interest rates, falling property values and a flat economy. The promised benefits from the Uruguay Round had not been delivered; subsidies and protection remained widespread in the US and Europe, even as those countries accused New Zealand of breaching the free trade rules.[80] The collapse of the Asian markets, on which exporters had been encouraged to refocus, fuelled a growing unease about the future prospects for farming. The Federated Farmers leadership, still fervently advocating the free market, seemed at odds with significant parts of their constituency.

In 1998 there were three producer boards with single-seller export monopolies: the Dairy Board, the Apple and Pear Marketing Board and the Kiwifruit Marketing Board. Four more – the Meat Board, Wool Board, Pork Industry Board and Game Industry Board – were non-trading producer boards, whose functions centred on marketing, regulating quality, and research and development. The Raspberry Marketing Committee and Hop Marketing Board covered small clusters of producers. The boards offered individual farmers and local cooperatives advantages of scale and investment in research, development and marketing which they themselves could not provide. In return, the boards had a statutory monopoly and the power to levy producers to finance their activities.

These structures were anathema in a self-regulating economy. But it was not easy to abolish a system of cooperative marketing that had been developed over some 80 years for social and political reasons as well as economic ones.[81] By the 1980s, the boards controlled around 80 percent of all agricultural and horticultural exports. They varied enormously in their size and powers, largely reflecting the influence of the relevant industry. The most prominent was the Dairy Board, a transnational enterprise which in 1998 was ranked first in *Management* magazine's top 200 local companies, with revenue of $7.6 billion, assets of $4.2 billion and 6,500 employees in seven different countries.[82] At the other end of the scale, the Hop Marketing Board covered a handful of producers in the Nelson area.

Treasury had launched the official assault on the statutory producer boards back in 1984, devoting a whole chapter in *Economic Management* to arguments for their deregulation.[83] Although the boards were owned by New Zealand farmers and growers, they enjoyed a statutory monopoly and were treated as state trading enterprises for GATT purposes. As such, the boards were automatically branded by Treasury as inefficient and lacking accountability. Their statutory monopoly posed obstacles to innovation, and distorted investment decisions. By protecting inefficient producers and erecting barriers to new entrants, they also imposed efficiency costs on the economy. Treasury urged the new government to remove the boards' statutory monopoly, withdraw their power to impose compulsory levies, and open the boards to competition. Treasury officials could see no downside to this proposal.

As part of the deregulation of agriculture, the Labour government removed the boards' access to cheap finance in 1985. In 1988 it gave the Dairy and Apple and Pear Marketing Boards a more commercial focus. Around the same time, corporate orchardist Apple Fields challenged the imposition of a levy by the Apple and Pear Marketing Board, claiming it had the effect of substantially lessening competition in the market and therefore breached the Commerce Act 1986. The Privy Council ruled in Apple Field's favour in late 1990.[84] Partly as an alternative, the Labour government passed the Commodity Levies Act in September 1990, enabling the Minister to impose levies on producers to fund research, marketing, promotion and quality assurance by bodies representing their views and interests. The National government later exempted the Apple and Pear Marketing Board from the relevant Commerce Act provisions from January 1994.[85]

The assault on the producer boards gained momentum in 1991, after the much-publicised Porter Report on New Zealand's international competitiveness criticised their focus on basic commodities and their limited objectives. Suggesting a role for 'vigorous domestic rivalry' in the dairy industry, the report proposed deregulating the highly successful Dairy Board.[86] The Business Roundtable and associated companies began a sustained campaign against the boards. The objections were partly ideological, focusing on the monopoly status of the boards and their ability to impose levies. But deregulation was also in the interests of the Roundtable's member companies (including Restaurant Brands, Progressive Enterprises and Woolworths), who stood to benefit from direct supply contracts between growers, processors and retailers. In 1992 the first of many Business Roundtable reports on the issue described the meat industry as the victim of political and vested interests, at the expense of commercial incentives and market outcomes.[87] This analysis was reputedly endorsed by the Minister of Agriculture and by Treasury.[88] Another report commissioned from former Minister of Finance Roger Douglas (now a consultant) promoted the privatisation of all the boards.[89] Apple Fields, an active member of the Business Roundtable, remained locked in combat with the Apple and Pear Marketing Board.[90]

The campaign was supported by attacks on the Dairy Board from within the US. The US Dairy Trade Coalition, a lobby of farmers and agribusinesses, complained that the New Zealand Dairy Board dominated the world dairy market through its 106 subsidiaries. The Coalition accused the Dairy Board of using aggressive sales and pricing strategies to undermine US competitiveness in foreign markets. These practices were also blamed for increased pressure on the US government to raise subsidies to its producers under the Dairy Export Incentive Program, so they could compete in 'Third World' markets. The Dairy Board's use of transfer pricing allegedly deprived the US government of revenue, and gave the Board competitive advantages over tax-paying US companies. The Coalition cited a legal opinion commissioned by Apple Fields from a US academic, warning of possible anti-trust action against the producer boards.[91] One cheese importer took the Dairy Board to court for operating as a cartel in breach of US anti-trust laws. The Dairy Board claimed that, as an instrument of the New Zealand government, it was exempt from such laws. The initial finding against the Board was reversed in 1997.[92] These accusations were full of ironies, given the global dominance of US agribusinesses, the 120 percent tariff on butter imports to the US, and the US government's generous export subsidies.[93] Any effective strategies to contest that dominance would apparently not be tolerated. The US government also made the deregulation of New Zealand's single-seller boards a key condition of any negotiation on a bilateral trade agreement – something the New Zealand government desperately wanted, although the prospects seemed almost fanciful.[94]

Maori entered the fray from another angle. In 1995 some Maori kiwifruit growers complained to the Waitangi Tribunal that the export monopoly exercised by the Kiwifruit Marketing Board deprived them of the opportunity to use their ancestral land to support themselves. They wanted a separate export licence for their company, Aotearoa Exports Ltd, to handle crops from Maori and non-Maori growers. Former Labour Prime Minister Geoffrey Palmer, acting as counsel for the Maori claimants, called former Finance Ministers Ruth Richardson and Roger Douglas as witnesses. The Business Roundtable reports on the producer boards were entered in evidence. The Tribunal found that the grievance was genuine, but that it was not a Treaty of Waitangi issue. It also noted that 'there was much argument, some of it ideological, about the supposed merits or otherwise of single desk selling of kiwifruit' – arguments it deemed irrelevant.[95] This conjuncture of positions highlighted the 'colonisation paradox'. Maori were pursuing their own agenda, genuinely concerned to use their land in ways that enhanced their self-determination and economic well-being. This led them into an alliance with zealous free-marketeers and transnational corporate interests whose world-view and agenda were far removed from, and inimical to, their own. None of these 'allies' showed any ongoing commitment to addressing the issues of Maori resource ownership and self-determination. Nor, equally, did the defenders of the producer boards.

This paradox continued following the formation of the Coalition government in late 1996. New Zealand First ministers Winston Peters (Treasurer) and Tuariki Delamere (Associate Treasurer) were determined to press the demands for deregulation, especially of the kiwifruit industry, being voiced by Maori and dissident growers (especially in Peters' Tauranga electorate). Treasury eagerly encouraged them. There was a minor problem. The Coalition Agreement promised to support the producer boards so long as they retained supplier support. Treasury suggested that 'a more commercial interpretation would render [the Agreement] consistent with liberalisation of kiwifruit exports' – meaning that votes would be weighted according to product volume, rather than the number of suppliers.[96]

Immediately after the Coalition was formed, Delamere asked Treasury to report on the ability of kiwifruit producers to export directly, rather than through the Kiwifruit Marketing Board. Treasury took the opportunity to push its standard arguments and proposals for removing the statutory export monopoly, corporatising the Board with a share giveaway to growers, and if necessary funding promotion through the Commodity Levies Act 1990. There was no specific reference to Maori.[97] A subsequent report indicated that the Federation of Maori Authorities was actively lobbying for the granting of independent export authority, using similar arguments to Treasury's, but expressed a preference for coordinated competition over complete deregulation.[98]

Treasury's advice to ministers made no pretence to neutrality; its officials argued relentlessly for deregulation, to apparently receptive ears. They also sought to influence the industry debate. Treasury helped to plan a government-supported 'Kiwifruit Summit' at Tauranga in October 1997 for 200 invited participants. Its title was unambiguous: 'Kiwifruit: Stage Three and Beyond – Transition Path to Corporatisation and Deregulation'. The Kiwifruit Marketing Board viewed the summit as unnecessary. Treasury told ministers it was an opportunity to move the debate forward and promote change as inevitable. As further leverage, ministers could point to threats of US anti-trust litigation, US preconditions for negotiations of a free trade agreement, and the need for concessions on state enterprises in future WTO negotiations. The strategies Treasury suggested included establishing an 'eminent persons group' to review the regulatory environment, with terms of reference that would largely predetermine the outcome.[99]

New Zealand First was leading the charge. National ministers were initially more reserved; this was their electoral heartland. Since 1991 National's agriculture ministers had pursued a path of dialogue and consensus building, and secured agreement from boards and farmers to consider options for greater competition. Change was piecemeal. The Apple and Pear and Hop Marketing boards had a statutory monopoly on imported and domestic sales of their fruit. Under the Uruguay Round agreement in 1993, the import monopoly had to be converted into tariffs; these would then be reduced. The government seized the opportunity to remove the monopolies on sales within the country as well.[100] The chair of the Hop Marketing Board objected that outside operators would get a free ride into an industry that producers had spent 40 years building up.[101]

After five years of consultation, National introduced a Producer Boards Act Reform Bill in 1996 to remove the compulsory purchase powers of the Meat, Wool and Pork Industry boards (which were no longer used), and to move the boards from a producer focus to an industry facilitation role. The 1996 election intervened. The Bill was revived and referred to select committee in March 1997, with one month for submissions.[102] Positions began to polarise. Demands for immediate deregulation came from processing companies, lobby groups such as Federated Farmers and the Business Roundtable, and ACT MPs.[103] They were supported by Commerce Minister John Luxton, but not by some rural National MPs and their constituents.[104] As a compromise, the government proposed that the boards should retain quality control powers, with industry agreement. Development plans prepared by the boards had to consider explicitly whether other entities could perform board functions more efficiently and effectively – a move that provided openings for both privatisation and judicial review.

Membership of the boards proved a major issue. The Federation of Maori Authorities lobbied hard over the question of representation. Maori producers comprised over 15 percent of producers; but because they were concentrated in large holdings, they had little voting power. New Zealand First MP Tu Wyllie described the existing boards as patronising and an impediment to Maori economic development. He claimed there had been no Maori on a producer board for twenty years. Voting based on stock numbers would give Maori incorporations a stronger collective voice.[105] The government was happy to support that position, which also favoured the largest corporate and private stockholders. Labour and the Alliance wanted 'one farm one vote', with special consideration for Maori and women. The Bill was reported back and passed in December 1997, with voting based on stock numbers.

In early 1998, the pace quickened. During discussions about the Kiwifruit Marketing Board, the Cabinet apparently agreed to support total deregulation of all the boards. Agriculture Minister Lockwood Smith began briefing the various producer boards, suggesting they prepare plans for the removal of their statutory protection. The intention was to make the boards responsible for planning their own demise, and thereby secure acceptance and ownership of the outcome. Delamere and New Zealand First wanted immediate deregulation of the Kiwifruit Marketing Board. Treasury noted 'the risk that, if the Government directly opened up the reform debate (by, for example, promoting rapid reform), the current Board/industry effort in moving towards deregulation could be re-directed into protecting the status quo'.[106] However, it insisted there had to be a fixed timetable to prevent slippage. Officials suggested the 'lower-risk' option of a firm date for submitting plans for the deregulation of all boards, except for the Kiwifruit Marketing Board, which should be deregulated straight away.

Winston Peters originally planned to use the 1998 Budget to announce the deregulation of the Kiwifruit Marketing Board as at 1 April 1999, and seek plans for the rest by October 1998. The industry, and apparently key government departments, had not been consulted about the proposal.[107] Agriculture Minister Lockwood Smith was against a fast-track approach on kiwifruit, believing it would divert other boards into opposing the government's approach. He also rejected the suggestion that the Budget should specify objectives to guide the preparation of plans, as those objectives would become the focus of attack, especially as they had been prepared without adequate consultation or analysis. Setting the boards a deadline that was before the end of 1998 would also be a breach of faith. Smith urged a third option: the Budget should deliver a strong message that reinforced the existing process.[108] Treasury considered this was unsatisfactory: 'The Boards currently control the public debate and can put public pressure on the Government to implement proposals which may be contrary to the public interest. ... Publicly stating objectives will show leadership and will allow the Government to manage communications with the public.'[109] Further delay would also mean that changes could not eventuate until 2000. Treasury again urged immediate action on the Kiwifruit Marketing Board, via regulation rather than legislation.

As a compromise, the May 1998 Budget gave the nine statutory producer and marketing boards until 15 November to develop plans for competitive, market-driven structures. The issue was how, not whether, 'they will operate without specific statutory backing'.[110] Boards were also required to produce a timeline for deregulation.

The executive director of the Business Roundtable, Roger Kerr, blamed the delay on the 'lingering attachment of farmers to the idea that the [producer] boards served their interests', having been fed a 'diet of rhetoric and misinformation'. He wanted the producer boards privatised, with farmers given tradeable shares. They could then choose whether to invest in their board's research and promotion activities or to cash up and invest elsewhere. As producers, they could access alternative market outlets through long-term contracts and corporate farming.[111] Lockwood Smith was initially cautious, but new Minister of Food, Fibre, Biosecurity and Border Control John Luxton – a free market zealot – rashly staked his political future on getting the changes through.[112] Farmers, he claimed, were 'outlawed by the current Dairy Board Act from making normal business choices'; they had 'no way to know whether the next dollar invested by coercion ... is going to give as good a return [as] if you used your money to reduce your overdraft or mortgage.'[113] Luxton's suggested remedies were very similar to Kerr's.

As Lockwood Smith predicted, the boards went on the offensive. The Dairy Board stated that its report to government would not prepare for deregulation. It insisted that small producers needed to retain a critical mass in the aggressive global market. The Board had already shown it was efficient, innovative and able to match international investment in research and development, product innovation and marketing. Because the industry was operating in a globally protected market, farmers needed to maintain the Board's collective powers and resources. The retiring Dairy Board chair, Dryden Spring (a National Party fundraiser and former government appointee to APEC's Eminent Persons Group), labelled the deregulation plans 'a gigantic economic hoax ... based on shallow ideology, not deep study', and warned that 'the stakes are very, very high'.[114] An analysis commissioned by the Dairy Board showed that the industry could lose $200 million a year under a multi-seller structure.[115] Nonetheless, the two largest dairy companies, which were producer-owned, formed a joint venture in preparation for taking over the Board if deregulation occurred. Further consolidation of the industry followed.[116]

The more recent origins of the Kiwifruit Marketing Board produced a different dynamic, but a similar outcome. The licensing of export companies began at grower request, in 1977. The single-seller Board was formed in 1988, after a cycle of 'boom and bust', to provide stability, marketing and leverage in an intensely competitive international market. In response to external pressure from dissident growers and concern about the Board's debt, the National government secured grower support in a 1995 referendum to split the Board's marketing and regulatory arms. The single-desk operation was required to consider applications for independent exporting, where they did not compete with board exports; however income from those exports would return to the pool. Surveys in 1998 suggested that 90 percent of industry participants supported the system.

Mobilised under the label 'United Kiwi', kiwifruit growers now challenged the view that deregulation was 'inevitable' and 'evolutionary'. In September 1998, they delivered an uncompromising message to the government:

> Growers do not function in an 'ideological' environment. ... We are the industry experts. We live in the communities that rely on the viability of the kiwifruit industry. And we know, from experience and from comprehensive research, that maintaining the single desk exporter is the best option for our businesses, communities and industry.[117]

Without the critical mass the Kiwifruit Marketing Board provided, it would be impossible for growers to avoid dependence on contract growing of fruit for offshore supermarkets and agribusinesses. Fragmented, growers would be at the mercy of global food companies that controlled produce volumes five to ten times the size of New Zealand's annual produce exports.[118]

United Kiwi and its pipfruit counterpart, United Fruit, commissioned reports on the social impacts of deregulating their boards. These highlighted the government's failure to understand the social costs of deregulation – increased dependency on state benefits, greater personal stress, family breakdown, and migration from the regions. Secondary impacts on retail and commercial interests, community organisations, schools and volunteer services had also been ignored.[119]

The pipfruit growers echoed the kiwifruit growers' concerns that a concentration of global market power would produce gains for overseas retailers and consumers at major cost to New Zealand growers and surrounding communities. The government was not proposing any transitional assistance to those affected by deregulation. The negative effects on incomes, employment and property values would flow through the regional economies that depended on the industry, notably in Hawke's Bay and Nelson, where three quarters of the country's pipfruit crop was produced. On tactics for resistance, the report suggested that 'well-researched public education campaigns can be very effective in mobilising opinion and electoral support for or against public policy issues', because they allow people to ask why the policy is being proposed, who is likely to benefit and how they will bear the costs.[120]

As the political battle intensified, Treasury was forced to release a report showing that single-seller marketing added considerably to export earnings. It subsequently criticised the report's failure to address 'deadweight' costs which stifled innovation, enterprise and investment. The government maintained that one-third of farmers, especially influential office-holders, believed that deregulation was the right path to follow; the

Meat and Wool Section of Federated Farmers, for example, had voted to deregulate both their boards.[121] But a Dairy Board poll suggested that a majority of ordinary farmers were opposed to it.[122] Their concern was about the potential end-point of the deregulation agenda – corporate control of the family farm.

National was losing vital support on the ground, and in the party and its caucus.[123] Prime Minister Jenny Shipley was confronted by angry growers and farmers in Hawke's Bay and Nelson. New groups of producers emerged to fight the deregulation agenda, and threatened to descend on Parliament. Within weeks of the 15 November deadline, the government backed off from its demand that the boards make a commitment to deregulate. Luxton still maintained that change was needed, but now said it could evolve. The boards allowed the government to back down gracefully. Ongoing management of the issue was spread between Luxton, now called the Minister of Food and Fibre, and a Producer Board Project Team of officials from Treasury, Commerce, Agriculture and Fisheries, and the Prime Minister's Department; a committee of six ministers, including the Prime Minister; and an advisory group of senior industry representatives. The Dairy, Meat and Wool boards continued their consultations with producers. The Apple and Pear and Kiwifruit marketing boards produced corporatisation proposals that would give growers non-tradeable shares. The Pork Industry, Hop and Raspberry boards agreed to deregulation, and were waiting for the government to act. While the producer boards would make some changes, these appeared to fall well short of what a self-regulating market required. Farmers and growers had won the battle, but not yet the war.

The government had not given up. A raft of pre-election Bills included new proposals to corporatise the Dairy, Apple and Pear and Kiwifruit Boards. All the Bills followed discussions with industry leaders and reputedly carried their approval. The Kiwifruit Marketing Board was to become a company, Zespri Group Ltd. The current Board had to prepare a plan by 1 December 1999 for allocating company shares to existing growers. The plan had to be approved by the minister and a referendum of 75 percent of votes cast (the voting formula to be determined by the board). However, if there was insufficient voter support the Minister would determine the share allocation plan: so the referendum was about the distribution of shares, not the corporatisation proposal itself. Shares were to be tradeable 'at least' among producers, opening the way for greater concentration of holdings by agribusinesses and potentially by non-growers. (The securitisation of shares could further alienate actual control from grower hands). The Bill provided for making regulations which *may* create a new board with powers to grant export authorities to

Zespri or other exporters, effectively relocating the single-seller monopoly to a new body. The Apple and Pear proposals were similar.

The Dairy Industry Restructuring Bill would replace the Dairy Board with a mega-corporation of major cooperative dairy companies. For six years the new corporation would retain the exclusive right to export to markets where dairy quotas applied. Quotas would then be gradually transferred to a new company, owned by shareholders in the existing dairy companies. Exports to markets not governed by quotas would be unrestricted. The restructuring would take effect from September 2000 provided the mega-company had been created by then and approved by the Commerce Commission. If not, the Act would expire. Unlike the fruit proposals, the change was not subject to direct farmer referendum; but mergers of individual cooperatives into the mega-company would require support from existing farmer shareholders.

The government was determined to get these Acts passed before the election. It created a special select committee on which ACT's Owen Jennings held the balance of power. The legislation would mean fruit growers retained a notional single seller monopoly, operating through diverse exporters; but they could still lose control of the corporatised boards if shares became openly tradeable. For dairy farmers it would mean the demise of the cooperative basis of the industry, the gradual loss of the single seller monopoly, and the possible emergence of a tradeable quota market. While the mega-corporation could compete against other transnational agribusinesses like Nestlé, it was possible that if shares became widely tradeable the corporation could become foreign controlled. The haste and political manipulation in these latest moves risked further alienating significant elements of the farming community from the free trade agenda.

▲ CLOSER ECONOMIC RELATIONS WITH AUSTRALIA

Policies on tariffs and producer boards, and other trade policies such as parallel importing, were driven by a neo-liberal commitment to increasing domestic economic efficiency, backed by neo-classical trade theory. International trade obligations played a minimal role. The CER agreement with Australia was the exception. An initial deal, called the New Zealand Australia Free Trade Agreement, had been reached back in January 1966. Its scope was limited; a long list of exemptions covered almost all goods not already traded between the two countries. In March 1980 the Australian and New Zealand Prime Ministers endorsed the concept of closer economic relations in a joint communiqué. Negotiations moved quickly, with limited public debate, and a formal agreement was signed in 1983.

CER provided a valuable tool for supporters of internal deregulation in both countries. Under the initial agreement, export incentives that affected trade in goods were to be eliminated by 1987, tariffs by 1990 and import licensing by 1995. In late 1987 the target date for free trade in goods was brought forward by five years to 1990. The parties agreed to extend CER by examining regulatory and restrictive trade practices. Their reasons were explicitly anti-protectionist, as both countries sought to improve their competitive trading position with third countries and take the lead in global liberalisation of trade. As Australian business consultant Geoff Allen observed: 'the hard bilateral talk going on between the United States and Israel, the United States and Canada, and Australia and New Zealand became a laboratory for the trading world'.[124]

This leadership extended to trade in services. Industries such as tourism and transport began pressing for inclusion in CER in the mid-1980s, bolstered by initiatives in the US, OECD and European Community. The CER Trade in Services Agreement took effect on 1 January 1989. It was described as 'full-blooded and comprehensive', even though the regime was subject to each country's foreign investment laws.[125] It went further than the only other bilateral services agreement of the time, that between the US and Canada.

The two economies became increasingly integrated through the private sector. Formal changes in the legal and regulatory environments came more slowly. Competition law, which traditionally dealt with controlling monopolies, applied on a trans-Tasman basis from July 1990, although the thresholds used in each country were different (see Chapter 5). Anti-dumping laws were repealed in relation to trans-Tasman trade. Both moves signalled a major shift away from traditional concerns about fairness in international trade towards promoting efficiency within a single market. Competition lawyer Jim Farmer notes that the benefits of harmonisation were assumed throughout. There was no clear assessment of the nature and extent of the existing barriers, nor of what harmonisation would mean for domestic producers or for international trade with other partners.[126]

Between 1983 and 1998, bilateral trade increased around 275 percent; although figures were clouded by the growth of trans-Tasman companies, the rate of increase appeared to decline in the later 1990s.[127] CER was always more important to New Zealand, given its trade dependence on Australia, although there were frequent arguments about which country benefited most. Australia maintained a larger number of exemptions from CER coverage, but contended that these were far outweighed by the benefits to New Zealand of access to a market five times the size of its own. New Zealand's trade deficit with Australia in the year to June 1998 was A$1.93 billion.[128]

Trans-Tasman investment also boomed, even though there was no free investment agreement. Relocation of New Zealand businesses across the Tasman had a major impact on jobs. In a matter of months in 1996, for example, the combination of a grossly overvalued exchange rate and incentives offered by Australian state governments saw Cedenco relocate its tomato processing plant from Gisborne to Victoria, with 400 seasonal and 90 permanent jobs lost. Other moves were Arnotts Biscuits from Auckland (290 jobs); Helene Curtis from Christchurch (118 jobs); S.C. Johnson Wax from South Auckland (45 jobs); Caroma Industries from Auckland (15 jobs); Corfu Jeans from Thames (25 jobs); Reckitt & Colman from Auckland (107 jobs); and Johnson & Johnson from Auckland (job losses unknown).[129] Conversely, some New Zealand firms picked up work from Australian contracts, such as the ANZAC frigates.

CER generated a certain degree of economic integration, especially in market access. But the theory of economic integration assumes first, that both countries are moving in the same direction at a similar pace, and second, that any political and social barriers can be quarantined. Ideologically driven New Zealand governments from 1984 had deregulated further and faster than the Australians, who remained more attentive to domestic political considerations and structural adjustment costs. In the early 1990s, the Labor government in Canberra became visibly less enthusiastic about extending CER, its sights being firmly fixed on the growing Asian markets. In 1994 Prime Minister Paul Keating said 'for us it's been all give, give, give and New Zealand's been all take'.[130]

These tensions were heightened in 1994 when Australia imposed visa requirements on visiting New Zealanders; it then informed the New Zealand government by fax that it was reneging on a deal to open its domestic aviation market to Air New Zealand, just days before the deal was to proceed. The New Zealand government chose not to take the issue to arbitration.[131] The annual review of CER in early 1998 showed that progress had stalled on most new issues. The Australians continued to reject an investment agreement that would prohibit discrimination against each other's investors, claiming there was no need, and it would conflict with Australia's existing treaty with Japan.[132] Nor would Australia reduce the 'rules of origin', which required 50 percent local content before goods could qualify under CER – a requirement New Zealand producers found increasingly difficult to meet. A common aviation market was agreed to, but the Australian government, protective of Qantas and nervous about public sentiment, refused to agree that airlines could pick up passengers in each other's country en route to a third.[133]

When Australian Prime Minister John Howard visited New Zealand in February 1999, following the latest annual review, local producers publicly aired their dissatisfaction with CER. They pointed out that Australian industry received tax breaks worth around NZ$1.4 billion a year, which put unsubsidised New Zealand manufacturers at a competitive disadvantage.[134] Some objected to blatant moves to protect Australian markets, such as the exclusion of New Zealand apples from Australia, supposedly to keep out fire blight. Howard's visit resulted in the establishment of a CER taskforce to make progress on outstanding issues, such as reducing the list of exemptions on services, social security and child support, and investment.[135]

CER appeared to be drifting. This partly reflected Australia's other priorities now that the easy gains had been made from CER. But it equally reflected the fact that CER had now become a domestic political issue in both countries. Australians' concerns surfaced in relation to local content for broadcasting. Back in 1994, the Australian Broadcasting Authority had suggested that New Zealand programmes should be considered local programmes under the CER services agreement. Following a public outcry, it reversed its position. New Zealand producers successfully challenged that decision in the Australian courts.[136] The Australian film and television industry waged a massive campaign, including a star-studded event at the Sydney Opera House, to defend their 'genuine' local content against 'cheap' New Zealand competitors such as *Shortland Street*. In April 1998 the Australian High Court upheld the initial ruling that New Zealand productions had to be given the same market access as Australian ones.[137] The decision was deeply unpopular. But in March 1999, the Australian government announced it would not seek to renegotiate that aspect of CER.[138]

In New Zealand, two issues emerged as politically controversial. The first involved the harmonisation of standards. A Trans-Tasman Mutual Recognition Arrangement was signed in July 1996, and finally came into force on 1 May 1998, after delays in passing the necessary law in Australia. Goods legally sold in Australia could now be legally sold in New Zealand and vice versa, and professionals securing qualifications in one country could practise the equivalent occupation in the other.[139] All decision-making processes in relation to goods and services had to be consistent with a set of principles of good regulatory practice developed by the Council of Australian Governments.

The harmonisation issue erupted in late 1998 over the vexed question of the testing and labelling of genetically modified food. In 1995 the two governments had signed an agreement establishing a system for the development of joint food standards, to become effective in July 1996.[140]

The objectives were to reduce unnecessary barriers to trade; to adopt a joint system to develop and promulgate food standards; to provide for the timely development and adoption of standards appropriate to members; and to facilitate the sharing of information on related matters. The agreement extended the food standards system operating in Australia since 1991 to New Zealand. This would involve the development of standards by the Australia New Zealand Food Standards Authority. This would have at least seven members, only two of whom would be nominated by the New Zealand government.[141] The Authority would take advice from the Australia New Zealand Food Authority Advisory Committee. Again, there were two New Zealand government nominees out of seven. In 1998 executives from Coca Cola and Nestlé were official coopted as 'independent experts' by the Committee. The Authority's recommendations would be considered by the Australia New Zealand Food Standards Council, made up of ministers from each Australian state and territory, and one New Zealand minister, who had a single vote. The New Zealand government could withdraw from the agreement by giving twelve months notice. A review was built in for 1999. There was no parliamentary debate in New Zealand on the adoption of this agreement; signing it was a matter for the Executive, in the exercise of its 'external sovereignty'. Subsequent amendments to the Food Act were required to bring New Zealand law into line. These were passed by Parliament in June 1996, after the agreement had been signed.[142]

The Food Authority was to develop, and the Food Council to approve, an Australia New Zealand Food Standards Code. This would cover food safety, composition, testing methods, production, containers, packaging and labelling, and other matters affecting consumer health. Article 5 required all member governments to ensure that the standards would be incorporated automatically into their domestic law, without amendment. Any New Zealand food standards coming within the scope of the agreement had to be approved by the Food Council, except in emergencies. Subsequent changes to those standards would require Council approval. The same standards would apply in both countries, unless exceptional health, safety or environmental reasons required otherwise. Where the New Zealand minister decided the standard was inappropriate because of 'exceptional health, safety, third country trade, environmental, or cultural factors', the Authority could be asked to prepare an alternative.

The process was to be run by the Food Authority. It would receive applications for the development or variation of standards, which would be assessed, then put out for public submission and possibly public hearings. The agreement required 'transparency, timeliness and accountability, including a commitment to consultation and public involvement'.

Consultation would involve 'industry and other interested parties'.[143] The food industry knew what it wanted. The bilateral food trade was big business, worth over $1 billion annually, and had a well organised lobby. Major companies, including transnationals operating in both countries, were eager to cut transaction costs and reduce regulatory requirements. The Business Roundtable and the Food and Beverage Exporters' Council co-sponsored a report from CS First Boston that criticised the costs of heavy regulation, and concluded that: 'Regulators cannot easily determine what level of product safety, quality or information consumers might value. Such preferences are best discovered through the market. Sellers find out what consumers prefer and determine how best to meet their diverse needs.'[144]

The first major test came in July 1998, when the Food Council accepted the recommendations of the Food Authority that 'substantially modified' foods that did not imitate natural foods should be labelled. Assessments of food safety would be based on tests by the manufacturers because of their 'commercial sensitivity'. The Authority's proposed labelling guidelines advised that 'claims should not arouse or exploit fear in the consumer'.[145] New Zealand critics claimed that most genetically modified food would escape labelling, including products that contained genetically modified soybeans or maize. The environmental working party of the Royal New Zealand College of General Practitioners challenged the Food Council as an inappropriate authority to decide what should be introduced into the human body.[146] The Council deferred a decision on the labelling of 'substantially equivalent' food (modified food that looked and tasted like conventional food) until December.[147]

The Food Authority subsequently recommended against mandatory labelling of such food, which was also the position of the Australian and New Zealand governments. Yet, presumably because of pressure on the Australian state health ministers, the Food Council voted by a majority of six to four to require the labelling of 'substantially equivalent' genetically modified food.[148] Officials were asked to draw up a definition of genetically modified food, and regulations for ministers to approve early in 1999. The New Zealand government was spared from having to decide whether to opt out when Prime Minister Jenny Shipley backed down from its hardline opposition to labelling. The food companies exercised their market power, and failed to submit applications for approval of genetically modified food for sale by the May 1999 deadline. Officials estimated that around 500 products on New Zealand shop shelves contained genetically modified ingredients, yet the Food Authority had issued only two companies with approvals by April 1999. In a major victory for the industry, the deadline was extended by over a year to June 2000.[149] The opponents of genetically modified food raised further concerns when one of the Food

Authority's first rulings was approval for the American biotechnology group Monsanto to market genetically altered soybeans and cottonseed, used in foods such as salad dressing and ice cream. Approval was based on information supplied by the company and not independently tested.[150]

Genetically modified food was now a hot issue in New Zealand, prompting several unsuccessful attempts by Alliance MP Phillida Bunkle, via successive private member's bills, to secure genetic food labelling and a Commission of Inquiry.[151] Labour sought to straddle consumer concerns and those of researchers and industry.[152] National struggled to balance its support for light-handed regulation with political pragmatism. Maori expressed opposition to any manipulation of genetic material as a violation of the inherent tapu of the natural world and its life-force.[153] The issue was not about to disappear. While approval to develop and test genetically modified foods was subject to domestic approval processes, decisions on food safety and labelling would be made in a trans-Tasman regulatory forum over which the New Zealand government, let alone Parliament or iwi, had no control. Consequently, the CER agreement was bound to come under fire, despite the paradox that it was the Australian health ministers, not the New Zealand government, who had demanded the labelling of 'substantially equivalent' food.

The second issue was potentially even more volatile. In March 1999, the New Zealand government admitted that the issue of a single currency was on the agenda of the CER taskforce established after Howard's visit in February. The possibility of such a move had received considerable media coverage in Australia prior to Howard's visit, but nothing was heard in New Zealand.[154] Prime Minister Shipley insisted that the talks would not be substantive. However, two months later a 40-page paper entitled 'Economic Integration and Monetary Union' appeared on Treasury's website.[155] It stated in bold type at the beginning: 'The consideration of monetary union is not on the Government's agenda'. This was simply a background paper produced in accordance with Treasury's 'responsibility to be at the forefront of economic thinking, and to anticipate and examine new issues'. It reflected the thoughts of the author, and was not proposing a course of action. Noting that papers prepared on the subject in the early 1990s had rejected the idea, this paper suggested the need to reassess the arguments. However, the tone was strongly supportive of the concept of monetary union, although agnostic on the form it should take, and with whom. The author frankly conceded there would be little practical difference for New Zealand between forming a monetary union and simply adopting the currency of another country, such as Australia or the US, given the limited weight New Zealand would have in any such union.

The main arguments in favour of an independent currency were the country's ability to choose its own inflation rate, and to stabilise output in the face of regionally specific economic shocks by revaluing the currency and altering relative wages and prices. The paper doubted the effectiveness of the latter, and suggested that greater economic integration and monetary union might reduce the likelihood of such shocks. On the subject of inflation, it offered a critical assessment of the Reserve Bank of New Zealand's monetary approach:

> New Zealand is the smallest OECD country to have a fully independent monetary policy. To continue to justify this stance on an economic basis, there should be evidence that monetary independence has been beneficial – or at least, of little cost. Over the last eight years, New Zealand has enjoyed very low rates of inflation, although its record is not dissimilar to that of most other OECD countries. Despite this low inflation, however, real short term interest rates have been higher than in our main trading partners; the New Zealand economy has not been noticeably more stable than other OECD economies and trade volumes have grown only slowly despite having a trade share substantially below that of almost all other small OECD economies. When the counterfactual is not available, there should be no presumption from these outcomes that monetary independence should be the natural option for the New Zealand economy.[156]

The writer expressed an economist's view of what was good for the New Zealand economy. That this would also be good for New Zealand's people was taken for granted. The paper did refer to the possible distributional impact of integration, noting that 'the benefits of integration will not necessarily flow to residents remaining in the country'.[157] A region could decline as resources migrated elsewhere or competition had a negative effect. Because economic integration placed priority on economies of scale and market access, production would tend to locate near large cities, although this might reverse over time as wages increased in those centres. In an integrated Australasian economy, 'it is reasonable to consider cities such as Sydney or Melbourne at the local "core", and smaller cities such as Brisbane, Auckland or New Plymouth as the periphery'. There was already considerable relocation of economic activity within New Zealand and with the rest of the world; this would be no different: 'Some New Zealand industries would move overseas, and some overseas industries would move to New Zealand.'[158] A footnote made the social and national implications even clearer: 'The distinction between residents and citizens is important. Even if people remaining in New Zealand were worse off after closer integration, it would not necessarily be a disadvantage to all New Zealanders, as some will migrate to take advantage of the higher wages in the benefiting regions'.[159]

This was much more than a social and economic issue. A national currency is perhaps the most potent symbol of a country's sovereignty. The adoption of the European Monetary Union was predicated on economic, political and social integration within the European Community. The decision to proceed had an historical and political motivation, not just an economic one. Neither Australia nor the US would be interested in deep integration with New Zealand, and any such suggestion would cause a furore in this country. Moves to a single Australasian currency would be seen by many New Zealanders as a precursor to political integration with Australia. Economic autonomy would be severely constrained, with a common currency requiring harmonisation of the monetary policy controlled by each country's central bank. (Some New Zealanders, however, might prefer the less doctrinaire approach of the Reserve Bank of Australia.) Shifts in currency value would be determined by the fortunes of the dominant economy, Australia. Maori from all perspectives were likely to see the loss of control over the currency as a threat to tino rangatiratanga. Even the politicians seemed to understand that this was one issue that could not be addressed in terms of economic theory.

▲ REFLECTIONS

'Free' trade policy in New Zealand since 1984 has been driven by theory, not by empirical economic or social analysis. It began to come adrift in the late 1990s, as threatened sectors mobilised to defer, if not defeat, the government's proposals.

The campaign against zero tariffs defended an earlier compromise between workers and national-based capital that New Zealand governments had helped construct during the Keynesian era. Workers in industries such as footwear and textiles had been protected through a national award system that guaranteed them relativity of pay and conditions with other sectors. Local business had been provided with domestic support and border protection to keep them viable, and hence provide jobs and foster regional development. The threat posed by zero tariffs brought workers, businesses and local communities together, at a time when other pressures (such as employers cutting costs in a deregulated labour market) also forced them into conflict. The government set down future tariff cuts in legislation. But the legislation is not immutable, and New Zealand is not yet committed to zero tariffs across the board. There is still room for manoeuvre.

The battle over the producer boards encapsulated the contradictions between the 'pure' free market and the country's historical and social structures. Farmers remained a powerful lobby, whose form of production was fundamentally incompatible with the free market they seemed to favour. By contrast, the desire of large Maori land-holders for self-determination led them into an unlikely alliance over producer board deregulation with free-marketeers from the Business Roundtable and Treasury, backed by Maori MPs in the Coalition Cabinet. The National government was caught between its free market principles and its political interests, which they attempted to reconcile in a chancy pre-election manoeuvre.

CER has perhaps been the most significant mechanism for 'bedding in' free trade policies through both economic integration and legal obligations. This occurred without debate about the non-economic implications. As those implications emerged in relation to the labelling of genetically modified food and a common currency, the process of further economic integration with Australia seemed set to encounter vigorous and intense challenge.

7 ▲ The World Trade Organisation

The primary vehicle for insulating free trade from social pressures and locking in commitments to trade liberalisation is the World Trade Organisation (WTO). The WTO had its origins in the General Agreement on Tariffs and Trade (GATT), which was negotiated in 1947 against the backdrop of an International Conference on Trade and Employment. The Agreement reflected the post-war compromise between a rules-based system to lower international trade barriers and the need to protect member nations' balance of payments and domestic social objectives.[1] Although the US sought to limit these domestic elements, the preamble of the Agreement included a commitment to 'raising standards of living, ensuring full employment and a large and steadily growing volume of real income and effective demand, developing the full use of the resources of the world and expanding the production and exchange of goods'.[2] A leading trade economist of the time, Jacob Viner, conveyed the prevailing orthodoxy: 'There are few free traders in the present-day world, no one pays any attention to their views, and no person anywhere advocates free trade'.[3]

Almost 40 years later, in 1986, the Uruguay Round of GATT negotiations began. The next seven years of negotiations were conducted against a very different backdrop – the collapse of the Soviet Union and the end of the Cold War, the rise of the Asian tiger economies, and the embrace of free market policies by many poor countries (both voluntarily and otherwise). With US hegemony in decline, the major capitalist powers had adopted aggressive trade practices, prompting fears that the world would split into three competing blocs: North America, Europe and Asia (Africa was economically invisible). The conclusion of the Uruguay Round negotiations in 1993 was therefore a 'success' in itself. In the process, the GATT was transformed. A relatively porous agreement centred on trade in goods was expanded to cover agriculture, the growth area of services, aspects of investment, and protection of intellectual property rights.

Equally significant was the decision to bring all the Uruguay Round agreements under a new World Trade Organisation, whose mission was to promote the self-regulating global economy. The Ministerial Declaration urged the IMF (overseeing international monetary stability), the World Bank (dealing with 'economic development') and the WTO (responsible for international trade) to follow 'consistent and mutually supportive policies ... with a view to achieving greater coherence in global economic policymaking'.[4] Globalisation was portrayed as evolutionary and inevitable. In December 1996 the WTO's first director-general, Renato Ruggiero, declared that global economic integration was 'beyond the point of no return'. He urged member governments to move beyond traditional sectors and assumptions, and show 'leadership rooted in the support of a knowledgeable and engaged global community'.[5]

The WTO's ideal of a single global market-place soon confronted political reality. Internal tensions within the organisation intensified as poor countries struggled to meet their Uruguay Round obligations, while rich countries demanded new negotiations and exploited exemptions to limit the impact of trade liberalisation on their own countries. Groups directly affected by the agreements, such as farmers, continued their protests; indigenous peoples condemned the WTO's market-centred vision as cultural anathema; NGOs challenged the democratic deficit of WTO decision-making at the domestic and international levels.

The significance of the Uruguay Round and the new WTO bypassed most New Zealanders. Generally people thought it had something to do with agriculture, and believed that the country's future depended on it. This was certainly the message promoted by successive governments. The 'successful' outcome of the Uruguay Round in 1994 offered further proof that the policies adopted so vigorously from 1984 onwards reflected international orthodoxy. The Uruguay Round also provided an opportunity to commit future governments to the changes of the previous decade. In 1994 the National government hailed the conclusion of the Uruguay Round as 'a key factor in shaping New Zealand's economy', ranking it alongside refrigerated shipping in the 1880s and the negotiation of the CER in the early 1980s.[6] Labour's Mike Moore, who had overseen the first four years of negotiations as Minister of Overseas Trade, dismissed those who criticised the GATT as 'a mutant strain of leftist thought'.[7]

New Zealand's position during the Uruguay Round was driven by neo-classical trade theory, unadulterated by other economic or social considerations. Because those who were driving the negotiations never doubted the benefits of free trade, they saw no need to debate its merits or the implications of the agreements they were signing. This was an exercise of 'external sovereignty'. Parliament's role was limited to approving the minimal changes required to bring New Zealand laws into line – after the agreements had been signed. The fact that future governments would be committed to maintaining existing free trade policies, on pain of economic retaliation, was not open to debate.

The potential results of the Uruguay Round for agriculture were seriously overstated, while the implications of the agreements on services and intellectual property were inadequately explained. By the late 1990s disillusionment had set in among free trade's strongest supporters, the farming sector. Critics of free trade, including Maori and some unions, continued to challenge the WTO's model of development; other unions and environmentalists sought to give the WTO a social face. As the free-traders in government and the bureaucracy prepared for a new 'millennium' round of negotiations in late 1999, New Zealanders seemed much more sceptical than in 1986. Other countries were reverting to, or continuing, pragmatic and often protectionist trade practices. Both of New Zealand's major political parties, National and Labour, remained enthusiastically committed to free trade, claiming that globalisation left a small country no alternative. This left New Zealand out on a free trade limb, with very few other countries alongside. The shifting international debate, combined with pressures at home, suggested that this position would be unsustainable.

▲ THE GATT: AN HISTORICAL OVERVIEW

The General Agreement on Tariffs and Trade was first negotiated in 1947 by the governments of 23 industrialised countries. New Zealand became a 'contracting party' (the technical term for GATT members) the following year. Initially the GATT dealt only with trade in goods, and its objectives were relatively uncontroversial.

Certain core provisions – 'national treatment' and 'most favoured nation' status – were critical to achieving the objective of a multilateral, non-discriminatory and rule-based approach to international trade. 'National treatment' required foreign products to receive no less favourable (but possibly better) treatment than domestic products. It applied unconditionally to all GATT parties. 'Most favoured nation' status required a contracting party to give all GATT members the best treatment it gave to any one of them. This applied unconditionally, except where a free trade area or customs agreement had been approved or where 'developing' countries had been granted preferential rights. The Agreement carried a commitment to progressive liberalisation. This meant that concessions made could not be withdrawn without full compensation, and countries were expected to reduce barriers further in the future. Existing commitments were enforced through the GATT's own dispute procedures. Governments were allowed to take emergency measures to safeguard their balance of payments, provided these were non-discriminatory, temporary and phased out. Certain exceptions existed to protect areas such as public morals, order, health, security, and conservation of exhaustible natural resources, provided they were not a disguised trade restriction. Emergency measures could be taken where imports unforeseeably posed a serious threat to domestic producers, and there were special provisions to impose countervailing duties where countries were accused of dumping underpriced goods.

The original Agreement was meant to operate under the umbrella of an International Trade Organisation that would stabilise and reopen the world's trading system following the Second World War. This was agreed to in the Havana Charter of 1948. However, the US Congress refused to ratify the creation of such an institution, believing it would impinge on US economic interests and autonomy. The idea was abandoned in 1950. Instead, GATT members engaged in a series of multilateral negotiating rounds, which aimed to reduce the large number of border protection measures (especially tariffs) that had recently emerged and were operating as barriers to trade.[8] The GATT was serviced by a secretariat in Geneva.

In theory, the GATT operated through negotiated consensus. In practice, it was dominated by the major powers of Europe and Japan, but more especially the US. American political scientist Margaret Karns described the GATT as a primary instrument of US international policy, which created the rules and negotiating processes for a liberal international trade regime compatible with American interests. The US used these rules to serve its own policy objectives, even when doing so compromised the GATT's stated goals. Over time, the GATT legitimated the open trading system, providing a forum to generate peer pressure and oppose policies that would close markets. US dominance was assured through the 'major interests' norm, which enabled the major suppliers and consumers of products to take the lead in negotiations and disputes. Karns also observed that 'over the years the United States has consistently attempted to use GATT dispute settlement machinery to promote its short- and long-term trade interests'.[9] Such bullying had an especially severe impact on small and poor countries, who were targeted by the US for formal complaints or unilateral retaliation (see below).

The first six negotiating rounds of the GATT, held between 1947 and 1967,[10] were relatively uncontroversial. They concentrated on reducing import protections, with governments 'binding' themselves not to raise tariffs above specified levels on certain products. The Tokyo Round, from

1973 to 1979, produced a further reduction in tariff levels. With fewer direct trade barriers, attention also turned to domestic rules and practices that allegedly discriminated against foreign traders. But the GATT's political dynamics had begun to change. In 1974 there were 99 contracting parties. Many new members were recently decolonised countries, especially from Africa, who were promoting a New International Economic Order within the UN. They had already secured the right to special and differential status in 1964 through a new Part IV of the GATT. This was further institutionalised through a General System of Preferences. The rich countries who had previously controlled the GATT could no longer command consensus support for their measures. They responded by negotiating a series of plurilateral agreements on non-tariff barriers (for example, subsidies and dumping), which only some GATT members were party to. These codes were linked to the GATT, but were not part of it.[11]

The Tokyo Round was predicted to take 27 months; it took six years. Trade negotiations had become more complicated and fractious. US hegemony was weakening under pressure from Asia and Europe. Trade tensions were threatening the authority of the multilateral trading system, with a record number of trade disputes being lodged with the GATT. As the world's economy entered a severe recession, the US blamed its economic woes on unfair competition and protectionism, especially from Japan, the newly industrialised countries and the European Community. The Reagan administration demanded an extensive new round of GATT negotiations to extend the core principles of liberalisation and non-discrimination into new areas, especially those of interest to American transnational enterprises. These ranged from services and investment to government procurement, intellectual property, and agriculture. But other governments were weary of multilateral negotiations. Japan preferred a bilateral approach to trading relationships. Western Europe was not keen to extend the GATT. The Group of 77 poorer countries (known as G-77), including India, Malaysia and Tanzania, wanted negotiations in a more sympathetic forum such as the United Nations Conference on Trade and Development (UNCTAD). As supplicants for special treatment, however, the bargaining position of poorer countries was weak. Those with huge debts faced accompanying pressures from the IMF and World Bank to undertake export-based structural adjustment, and threatened (or actual) unilateral attacks from the US for 'unfair' trade practices.

The US had strong allies in the GATT Secretariat and some member governments. The new GATT Director-General, Arthur Dunkel (a former Swiss chief negotiator), set about constructing a consensus in favour of a new round. The first meeting of GATT ministers since 1973 was held in August 1982 in an atmosphere of mutual mistrust and US aggression;

Australia even walked out. The final Ministerial Declaration warned that the multilateral trading system was in danger. The ongoing GATT work programme for reporting to the GATT annual session in late 1984 was an uneven compromise: agriculture was included, despite opposition from the European Community, and the programme fell short of US demands on services and investment; the G-77 had opposed almost everything it contained. When the GATT Council met in June 1985, however, the traditional rich/poor (North/South) split had broken down as the newly industrialised countries re-evaluated their positions.[12] India and Brazil, speaking on behalf of the harder-line poorer countries (known as the Group of 24, or G-24), opposed negotiations on anything but outstanding GATT issues. The ASEAN countries (Singapore, Malaysia, Indonesia, Thailand, the Philippines and Brunei) supported a new round, as did South Korea and Chile. The US side-stepped this lack of consensus with a procedural manoeuvre, and resistance fell away. A special session of the Contracting Parties agreed in October 1985 to prepare for a new round.

The Uruguay Round was officially launched by a ministerial meeting in Punta del Este on 20 September 1986. Its basic principles, objectives and agenda were set out in a lengthy Declaration. There would be fourteen separate groups negotiating on goods, as well as dispute settlement, trade-related aspects of intellectual property rights, and trade-related investment measures.[13] There would be separate but parallel negotiations on trade in services. A Trade Negotiation Group was given overall responsibility for the round.

Equal voting rights for all GATT members gave the round a veneer of democracy. In practice, the major players – the US, the European Community and, less visibly, Japan – made the critical decisions through a mixture of exclusionary dialogue and brinkmanship. Most poor countries had one representative, if any, available to service the GATT in Geneva; the sheer logistics of resourcing seven years of negotiations in fourteen working groups were beyond their reach. The US sent some 100 officials and 500 lobbyists to the ministerial meeting in Brussels in 1990 that was supposed to end the round. Some poor countries had one or no negotiator there. New Zealand had about seven in its official delegation. These inequalities were reinforced by the process known as 'green room' meetings, where senior negotiators from selected countries brokered deals that were then placed before the remainder of the delegates for comment. Poor countries complained that they were excluded, and subjected to the politics of 'divide and rule'.[14]

Small and poor countries had to choose where to put their resources and energies. New Zealand was a bit player, and its negotiators concentrated on influencing the agenda in areas of special interest and expertise, notably agriculture. New Zealand was an enthusiastic founding member of the Cairns Group of Free Trading Nations, an economically and geographically diverse grouping of agricultural exporting countries, which acted as a ginger group on liberalisation of agricultural trade.[15] The combined GDP of its members was a little less than Japan's. But their share of world agricultural exports, at 26 percent, was significantly larger than that of the US (14 percent) and not far below that of the European Community (31 percent). Their main target was European agricultural subsidies. The Cairns Group first met in August 1986, and played a critical role in ensuring that agriculture was included in the Punta del Este Declaration. While tensions between the US and European Community dominated the Uruguay Round, the Cairns Group was described as a bridge-builder. Australia provided the intellectual and political leadership.[16] The group had its own internal tensions, especially in convincing the hard-line free-traders to accept 'special and different treatment' for so-called 'developing' economies.

For seven years the Uruguay Round negotiations seemed to be in perpetual crisis.[17] Two major ministerial meetings broke down. President Clinton's fast-track negotiating authority, which prevented the US Congress from unpicking the details of international trade agreements, was due to expire in mid-1994; this meant that substantive negotiations would have to be completed in December 1993. Faced with this deadline, the US and Europe reached a compromise, which other GATT members had no choice but to accept. On 15 March 1994 at Marrakech, trade ministers signed the GATT Final Act and its accompanying agreements. The 1947 Agreement had been rewritten, with its coverage extended beyond trade in goods to agriculture and trade-related investment measures. New agreements dealt with services and intellectual property rights. Yet behind the hype, even sympathetic OECD and World Bank reports put global gains from the round at just one percent additional economic growth. Moreover, the distribution would be highly unequal – some 70 percent of the benefits would go to OECD countries, while Africa and Indonesia would be net losers.[18] The penalty of losing 'most favoured nation' status meant those poor countries could not afford to opt out if they wanted to. By the end of the round, the GATT had 128 contracting parties, and twenty more wanted to accede. The major outstanding question was the accession of China – in particular, whether it should be defined as a 'developing' country and attract the associated concessions, or be treated as a 'developed' country because of the size of its economy, as the US insisted.

▲ THE WORLD TRADE ORGANISATION

The creation of the WTO as an institutional umbrella for all the Uruguay Round agreements was a momentous development. In a scenario reminiscent of 1948, the US negotiators opposed the move almost to the end because of its potential to encroach on US autonomy. The Europeans insisted that the complex array of new agreements, and the programme for future negotiations built into those agreements, required a formal organisation. The Americans eventually conceded. But when the US Congress came to ratify the outcomes, it strongly reasserted the nation's domestic sovereignty. The Uruguay Round Trade Agreements Act 1994 made it clear that US law would prevail. It also required detailed annual reports on the implications for the US of WTO activities, and mandated five-yearly reviews of the costs and benefits of continued WTO membership.

The WTO was born on 1 January 1995. The organisation possesses an independent personality under international law, and has the power to approve retaliatory sanctions; it therefore constitutes a formal layer of authority beyond the nation-state, although its decisions are still ultimately controlled by the member governments. The organisation has four specific functions: first, to facilitate the implementation and operation of the agreements on trade in goods, trade in services, and intellectual property rights; second, to provide a forum for negotiations on existing or new issues; third, to administer the dispute settlement machinery and the trade policy review mechanism; and fourth, to cooperate with the World Bank and IMF to achieve greater coherence in global economic policy-making.

The WTO agreements provide the mechanism for ongoing negotiations, without the need for a formal new round (although this can still occur). They set dates for reviews and further negotiations on specific issues, notably services, agriculture and intellectual property. Ministerial meetings of all members are to be held at least biennially, to decide what new trade-related issues are put on the agenda and to conclude outstanding matters. Between meetings, the WTO operates through a General Council of officials, which doubles as a dispute settlement and trade policy review body (see below). Separate councils on trade in services, trade in goods, and trade-related intellectual property rights oversee those specific agreements, working through numerous committees. Consensus and democracy still, in theory, prevail. The US argued for a voting system weighted according to a country's trade, which would have given the major powers similar control to that they wield in the IMF and World Bank. The proposal was rejected. Funding for the WTO is determined by a member country's share of world trade, but all have the same voting power. Formal votes are rare; the preference for 'consensus' means the major powers still shape the outcome.[19] This is a vexed issue, which came to a head during the process of appointing a new Director-General of the WTO in 1999 (see below).

The WTO is an international *economic* institution. Even the GATT's historical reference to full employment and raising living standards was framed by economic objectives. The WTO's ideal of global free markets has no room for social considerations. The 1994 Declaration on the WTO observed that: 'Trade liberalisation forms an increasingly important component in the success of the adjustment programmes that many countries are undertaking'. Such programmes often involve 'significant transitional social costs'.[20] But because these are considered temporary, it would distort the equilibrium of world markets to promote trade policies that redistribute global wealth from rich to poor countries, or compensate for any inequalities in market power. Redress for transitional social impacts should be sought instead through the complementary structural adjustment programmes of the World Bank. This reasoning effectively quarantines the WTO from the social, cultural and environmental impacts of its economic policy agenda while strengthening the World Bank's role.

The WTO is equally insulated from external voices of dissent. Its status as an intergovernmental organisation makes it impossible for anyone, other than a member government or its chosen advisors, to participate in the WTO's official processes. Negotiations are confidential, with government commitments generally not disclosed until after the deals are signed. Most governments, however, maintain formal or informal relationships with corporate lobbies whose interests the WTO serves to promote. These groups are usually consulted before and during negotiations. Trade unions and public interest NGOs have much more difficulty just accessing information, even in democracies and even when they redefine their concerns in GATT-compatible terms. Those living under authoritarian governments are automatically excluded, and risk retaliation if they insist on airing their views. Indigenous peoples are consistently denied the right to an independent voice in the domestic or international negotiating arena; some governments, as in India, deny that they even exist.

The WTO's internal operations are also shrouded in secrecy. Formal documentation is almost never released until decisions are made, and not always then. Documents and arguments presented to disputes panels are not publicly available, although a non-confidential summary can be requested by a member government. Even the reports and recommendations of disputes panels are sometimes not released. This secrecy is rationalised as a standard and necessary element of inter-state diplomacy and a legitimate exercise of external sovereignty. World Bank economist Bernard Hoekman and co-author Michel Kostecki offer a more political explanation: WTO negotiations are meant to push governments further than they would otherwise go, and to counteract pressures to regress. Getting governments to tie themselves to the free trade mast is easiest when they can make the initial commitments and sign agreements without the interference of domestic pressure groups. Embedding these commitments increases the cost of a government subsequently placating domestic pressure groups by seeking to change direction. As noted in Chapter 1, the effectiveness of this strategy depends on the willingness of governments to tie their own hands, and on the absence of loopholes in the agreement.[21]

These socio-economic and democratic tensions have always been implicit in the GATT. When its scope was limited, and it took a less doctrinaire approach to trade liberalisation, the tensions were contained. The breadth and depth of the Uruguay Round agreements, the establishment of a formal institutional structure, and the WTO's ideological commitment to a self-regulating global market-place have vastly increased the potential for internal conflict and external challenge.

▲ BRINGING NEW ZEALANDERS ON BOARD

New Zealand's GATT negotiators took the country's commitments under the Uruguay Round further than those of most other countries. National, with Labour's support, locked future governments into low levels of trade protection for goods and agriculture, open access for foreign providers of key services, fewer restrictions on aspects of foreign investment, and tighter intellectual property laws. Officials of the Ministry of Foreign Affairs and Trade defended the right of every state, under international law, to agree to fetter its own authority in return for a future benefit: 'a government agrees to abide by certain rules in return for similar undertakings by other countries so that a common goal can be achieved. Treaty accession or ratification should thus be viewed as a positive exercise of sovereignty by a state rather than a diminution of it'.[22] However, the assessment of 'future benefit' to New Zealand was not based on empirical studies, public debate or parliamentary mandate. Politicians and officials truly believed that free trade and investment were so beneficial that future governments should not be permitted to retreat from present commitments. Any distributional, employment or regional development costs created by implementing the WTO agreements, or concerns about democracy and tino rangatiratanga, never seemed to enter their consideration.

The mainstream media decided that the GATT was a ratings killer – too difficult for audiences to grasp. The government and officials were able to claim almost anything they liked.[23] According to journalist Ian Wishart (press secretary to Trade Minister Mike Moore when the Uruguay Round began), the earliest prediction of a $400 million benefit for New Zealand was plucked out of the air.[24] At the end of the round in 1994, the National government's glossy publication, *Trading Ahead*, predicted that increased market access and export prices should boost export returns by $1 billion over the next decade.[25] It cites 'conservative' estimates that the GATT outcome *could* increase the country's GDP by an additional two to three percent over the next decade.[26] If correct, that meant $150 to $230 million more in national income annually for ten years. *Trading Ahead* also projected a *possible* 20,000 to 30,000 more jobs over the next decade.[27] Yet the testimonials in *Trading Ahead* from companies in various sectors were far from fulsome about the gains from the Uruguay Round: it 'will not ensure a fair deal overnight, but it sure will improve the odds for us' (the dairy industry); 'the gains will not necessarily be rapid' (meat exports); 'New Zealand exporters may not get all the gains ... but the reductions [in tariffs] will be useful' (fishing); 'it doesn't bring in major breakthroughs for us', but reduced tariffs in offshore markets would be 'helpful for business' (breweries); the 'result will not have any marked effect on New Zealand's competitive position in the Australian market' (exporters to Australia).[28]

The projected economic benefits, which were cited constantly in ministerial speeches, were speculation based on computer modelling; no studies at that time assessed the net effect of the agreements on employment.[29] The only detailed, independent New Zealand studies of the expected impact of the Uruguay Round were prepared by the New Zealand Institute of Economic Research (NZIER). One modelling exercise, based on the draft agreement in 1993, predicted annual gains for New Zealand agriculture of up to 0.7 percent of GDP for five years.[30] A follow-up study by the same authors in 1994 suggested that by 2000, meat and dairy production would be 2.4 and 5.1 percent higher, respectively, mainly as a result of increased market access. With a small spill-over effect into higher investment and productivity in agriculture and the rest of the economy, real GDP would be 2.3 percent higher. However, achieving this would depend on New Zealand securing the lion's share of the 'new freer markets', displacing competitors.[31]

A further NZIER report in June 1994 assessed the gains for agriculture from the final agreement. The report was comparatively subdued, noting that 'political forces associated with agriculture protection have been extremely hard to break down'.[32] The compromises needed to secure an agreement showed that 'the Cairns Group may have been over optimistic in their expectations of what a Uruguay settlement could mean for them and their farmers'.[33] Previous analyses had suggested significantly greater gains than now seemed likely. The study concluded that the most important achievement of the round was that agriculture was now firmly on the WTO's negotiating agenda.

All these studies were based on computer-modelled projections. As trade economist Ron Sandrey notes: 'Simplifying assumptions must be made and sectors and markets must be aggregated to make the model manageable even to a computer. ... Models are, by definition, an abstraction from reality.'[34] Social factors such as income distribution, regional development and employment were never built into these models. Because the models were based on historical trends, nor could they consider the two most significant variables affecting the eventual outcomes – international economic conditions, and domestic and international politics. The Ministry of Foreign Affairs and Trade has not subsequently undertaken any empirical cost/benefit analysis of what was actually achieved from the Uruguay Round.

It was virtually impossible for outsiders to evaluate the government's position while negotiations were taking place. Successive Labour and National governments saw no point in promoting public discussion during the Uruguay Round. In late 1992, officials claimed that the government had actively exchanged views with unspecified 'interest groups'. It had also distributed 'explanatory material' – a reference to a four-page paper setting out the officials' interpretation of the overall position.[35] According to that paper, most of the government's proposed commitments to the liberalisation of agriculture and industry were already in place, or would be by 1996, so there were no significant policy shifts or new measures that needed to be discussed. Certain trade restrictions, including non-tariff barriers such as the Apple and Pear Marketing Board's monopoly over importing apples and pears, would have to go.[36] The only tariff cuts, beyond those already scheduled, would affect beer, pharmaceuticals, and pulp and paper. Quantitative restrictions (import licensing), export subsidies and internal support measures that were inconsistent with GATT rules had already been removed and would not be reintroduced. The country's services regime was already so open that little change was needed. Pharmaceutical laws had to be amended to abolish compulsory licensing, as required by the intellectual property rights agreement; the government had already withdrawn plans for parallel importing or the use of generic (non-brand name) drugs.

Officials argued that opponents of the Uruguay Round's objectives had ample opportunity to participate in debate, and that the degree of secrecy was normal for international negotiations.[37] They refused a request from Gatt Watchdog under the Official Information Act for a copy of the draft text produced by Director-General Dunkel in 1992, claiming its release might 'damage seriously the economy of New Zealand by disclosing prematurely decisions to change or continue Government economic or financial policies in relation to ... the entering into of overseas trade agreements'.[38] Yet GATT Publication Services was selling the document in Geneva.[39] In October 1993, Trade Minister Philip Burdon used the same justification for refusing to release a copy of the New Zealand government's offer to the Uruguay Round. He claimed that the round had reached 'a critical phase, and therefore the release of details of the offer now could prejudice a successful outcome for New Zealand'; the details would, however, be made available when the final agreement was signed.[40] Presumably, the 'prejudice' would arise from people in GATT democracies, including New Zealand, lobbying their governments in support of a different position. According to the antiquated distinction between 'internal' and 'external' sovereignty, the public could only be entrusted to know and discuss the government's position once a binding agreement had been signed.[41]

This secrecy extended to Parliament. The Clerk of the House, David McGee, later observed that this was 'one of the most important international agreements that New Zealand has ever entered into'; yet Parliament was not allowed to vote on the country's accession.[42] The Alliance – the only party openly critical of the GATT – was refused information until the end. Because the government's commitments largely cemented in existing policies, Parliament's only role was to approve the minor amendments to New Zealand laws that were required to bring them into line. The agreement was tabled, with an explanatory paper, on 12 July 1994. The Uruguay Round Bill containing the necessary amendments was introduced the following day. Labour and National gave it their enthusiastic support. Only the Alliance raised serious concerns in the House.[43] Many of the 54 submissions to the select committee on the Bill raised constitutional issues about the Treaty of Waitangi, parliamentary scrutiny of treaties, and constraints on future economic policy-making. Others challenged the economic, social, cultural and environmental costs of the agreements, and questioned their benefits. Almost all the submissions were dismissed as irrelevant to the narrowly framed Bill, and no significant changes were made. The agreements themselves were not up for debate.

There had also been no attempt to inform or involve Maori, either during the negotiations or prior to ratification. When the National Maori Congress belatedly learned of the negotiations and sought a dialogue with government in early 1994, officials could see nothing in the agreements to disadvantage them. The Congress disagreed:

> The Crown has not only neglected its Treaty of Waitangi responsibilities to the iwi and Maori Treaty partners, but it has violated the very principles of democracy by not adequately informing the public of the pros and cons of the GATT agreement and by not seeking the consent of New Zealanders before signing and ratifying an international agreement which has such widespread and direct consequences on the lives and livelihoods of individuals and communities.[44]

Accordingly, the National Maori Congress said it did not consent to New Zealand's ratification of the WTO, and Congress members would consider themselves exempt from its provisions.

Since then, several additions to the WTO agreements have been ratified. Those on information technology and basic telecommunications were approved in 1997 with no parliamentary involvement. In 1998, a protocol to the services agreement dealing with financial services was subject to the new sessional orders. These required the agreement, with a National Interest Analysis, to be referred to the foreign affairs, defence and trade select committee for consideration. The analysis simply asserted the benefits the government expected from the agreement;[45] no submissions were sought by the select committee, and there was no subsequent parliamentary debate. So the sessional orders produced no greater transparency than before.

▲ THE WTO AGREEMENTS

The extreme approach of successive New Zealand governments to trade liberalisation in the traditional area of trade in goods, and the tensions that created, were examined in Chapter 6. The new agreements on agriculture, services and intellectual property negotiated in the Uruguay Round created their own contradictions, which involved different protagonists raising quite diverse concerns.[46]

▲ *Agriculture*

The priority for successive New Zealand governments and trade officials was to open up restricted markets (especially in the US and the European Community) to New Zealand's agricultural exports, and to 'bind' future governments of all GATT members to lower levels of protection for imported agricultural products.

Agriculture had been off the GATT negotiating agenda since the mid-1950s. The original GATT rules of 1947 were designed to accommodate

US insistence that the proposed International Trade Organisation should play no role in US agricultural policy. The rules negotiated in 1949 and 1950 permitted quantitative restrictions and export subsidies, subject to ineffectual caveats. In 1951 the US Congress imposed import quotas on agricultural goods, which were unlawful under the GATT, and in 1955 the US government sought, and received, a waiver from the GATT rules. The Ministerial Declarations from the Kennedy and Tokyo Rounds legitimated these deviations by giving agriculture a special status, and effectively removing it from the GATT's trade liberalisation programme.

While the US continued to protect its own agriculture, US producers wanted access to other major markets. The European Common Market and Japan, who both had strong farming lobbies of their own, insisted that agricultural self-sufficiency was unique as a source of security and way of life. In the 1970s, the European Community offered its farmers high prices and open-ended guarantees, creating an inevitable surplus which it sought to export. Its payment of agricultural export subsidies and restitutions became institutionalised through the Common Agricultural Policy. The US initially responded by securing agreement from individual countries to 'voluntary export restraints' and 'orderly market arrangements' for agricultural products, measures which again were inconsistent with the GATT. Later it launched a subsidised Export Enhancement Program which targeted the markets of other agricultural exporters, mainly the European Community. Mark Ritchie, an advocate for American small farmers, notes that the real beneficiaries of such farm support payments were the US agribusinesses, who secured an international competitive advantage by buying crops from US farmers at prices far below the costs of production.[47] International relations specialist Richard Higgott comments that:

> At the level of values, there continued to be fundamental differences between the rhetorical weight placed by the United States on a 'free market' and the emphasis placed by the EC on 'sovereignty' and the 'management' of international transactions. At the level of action, the [EC's] increasingly aggressive export approach promoted a backlash from the United States.[48]

With the European Community and the US accounting for some 40 percent of the world's trade in food, this conflict was set to dominate agricultural negotiations throughout the Uruguay Round. The European Community's attempt to keep agriculture off the agenda failed. The US took a hard line, demanding severe cuts to both agricultural subsidies and income support that was linked to production. The European Community urged a more gradual approach. Both governments were lobbied intensively by agribusinesses, who stood to benefit from access to new markets, but also to lose their domestic subsidies. Small farmers lobbied in their own way. Imaginative and often militant protests occurred across Europe. In Japan, pressure from local rice farmers saw their government support agricultural liberalisation and the phasing-out of export subsidies, but insist on the right to intervene for social and national security reasons, such as paying domestic subsidies to maintain a minimum level of self-sufficiency.

The Cairns Group generally supported the US, and played a significant activist role; its Latin American members twice threatened to quit negotiations unless progress towards an agreement was made. The group produced two documents: the declaration from the Cairns Group's 1986 meeting, and proposals tabled at the GATT agricultural meeting in November 1989.[49] Both documents sought improved market access and a reduction in subsidies and trade-distorting internal supports in the major markets – by first converting non-tariff barriers into tariffs, and then reducing those tariff levels. The Cairns Group insisted that unsubsidised farmers would respond to market forces and new opportunities by developing diverse and reliable sources of supply, thus increasing global food security; however, it did concede that very poor countries could still receive some special treatment.[50] The group's critics insisted that food security must also include 'the ability of a country to produce most of its basic food necessities, the survival and economic welfare of peasant producers, respect for the cultural preferences of consumers when it comes to grain and other foodstuffs, and the political stability of rural society'.[51] Malaysian commentator Aileen Kwa observed: 'When people have no purchasing power, they have no food, regardless of whether food prices might be cheaper than if food was locally produced. Net-food-importing countries ... are the most vulnerable'.[52] World Bank studies confirmed that the Uruguay Round's agriculture agreement would leave net food importers, especially the poorest countries, in a worse position.[53] Such concerns were raised throughout the negotiations. While those pressing for agricultural free trade were prepared to vary the extent of and timetable for liberalisation, they were not about to reconsider the free trade goal.

The original December 1990 deadline for the end of the Uruguay Round passed, with negotiations between the US and the European Community on agriculture, and hence the entire round, in stalemate. By 1993 political conditions had changed. In the US, President Bush was succeeded by Bill Clinton. In the European Community, the fiscal cost of subsidies, combined with the ideological climate in the UK and Germany, opened the way to a review of the Common Agricultural Policy (although France strenuously opposed the reduction of subsidies). The compromise between the US and the European Community, known as the Blair House Accord, was reached in November 1993. The accord, with refinements, was presented to the remaining GATT parties as a *fait accompli*.

The Agreement on Agriculture contained some commitments to improved market access which were of benefit to New Zealand exporters. A more controversial aspect related to both tariffs and non-tariff barriers, which were to be converted into tariff equivalents (a process known as 'tariffication'). The total average tariff level for the base period 1986–88 would then be calculated, and cut by 36 percent over six years, beginning in 1995. All countries, including poorer ones, would have to bind themselves not to raise tariffs beyond that level. Export subsidies would also be reduced, working from a 1986–90 base.[54] Government support for domestic production, calculated by an 'aggregate measure of support' over all agricultural commodities and programmes, would be cut by 20 percent by 2000, again using a 1986–88 base, and bound. However, the aggregate measure was selective. It covered domestic subsidies and price-support policies, such as administered prices. But it did not include direct transfers to farmers, income transfers unconnected to production, and direct payments for limiting production under certain conditions. Nor did it cover compensation paid to farmers in the European Community to take land out of production, or deficiency payments to US farmers. Poorer countries were required to match two-thirds of the cuts, and had ten years to implement them; but no base-line was set, effectively leaving those governments free to define their own initial levels. They were also exempted from the tariffication requirement for staple foods. Significantly for New Zealand, producer boards and marketing monopolies were prevented from imposing quantitative restrictions on imports, as the Apple and Pear Marketing Board did for pipfruit.

The New Zealand government offered to bind itself and future governments to a maximum agricultural tariff level of 7.1 percent, down from 17.8 percent. New Zealand was the only country to eliminate permanently all the agricultural export subsidies that existed during the base period; it also undertook not to reintroduce any subsidies linked to the export of specific agricultural products. Having built up expectations of a massive windfall to agriculture from the Uruguay Round, the government was eager to 'talk up' the outcome. Its 1994 publication *Trading Ahead* claimed that farm sector revenues would rise by between $1 billion and $1.5 billion over the next ten years.[55] A working paper prepared for the World Bank in 1995 offered a far more sober assessment. The agreement had not substantially decreased agricultural protectionism worldwide; in some cases it had actually increased.[56] Taking the example of agricultural tariffs, protection was much higher in 1986–88 (the base-line period agreed for tariff reductions) than at the end of the round. Governments were required to convert the value of their non-tariff protections, which affected many sensitive products, into tariff equivalents. The figure they arrived at was often excessively high. So-called 'dirty' tariffication enabled Canada, for example, to raise its base tariffs on dairy products to more than double its actual 1986–88 levels.[57] As a result, the maximum tariff levels that many governments bound themselves to in the Uruguay Round were significantly higher for most commodities than the average levels of protection that applied when the agreement was ratified in 1994; those governments could actually *increase* their current tariff levels. The working paper concluded that the effective exemption of agriculture from GATT disciplines over the years had fostered a strongly protectionist approach to agricultural policy in OECD countries, based on trade restrictions and domestic price support.[58] Very little or no liberalisation in highly protected commodities, including dairy products, could be expected from such countries by 2002.

Subsequent OECD figures confirmed this assessment. In 1994, subsidy transfers per farmer amounted to US$16,000 in the US and US$18,000 in the European Union; in 1995, the first year the Uruguay Round was implemented, overall subsidy transfers in both economies rose by 5 percent. Some 20 percent of the cost of US farm production was financed by government subsidies totalling US$25 billion. The United Nations Development Programme put the US *subsidy* per farmer even higher at US$29,000 – nearly 100 times the US$300 per capita *income* of corn producers in the Philippines.[59] In 1997 the European Union spent US$42 billion on farm supports, almost one-third of its overall budget.[60] Some 80 percent of these supports went to one-fifth of its farmers.[61] Far from there being a reduction in surpluses, the European Union's wheat surplus was predicted to rise dramatically by 2005. The solution proposed by its farm ministers was to intensify efforts to export grain. In these conditions, export-dependent farmers within highly liberalised economies would struggle to compete, unless they allied themselves to agricultural transnational enterprises. This would, in turn, exacerbate tensions between traditional agriculture based on family farms and the commercial interests and practices of agribusinesses. Increased exports of subsidised produce would make non-subsidised exports from these countries uncompetitive.

The Uruguay Round agreement required new negotiations on agriculture after five years. The Cairns Group wanted actual negotiations to begin in 1999.[62] The US was keen, provided it set the agenda. The Europeans were not, and said the preparatory work should not begin before 1999. The battle was shaping up to be as acrimonious as the Uruguay Round. In May 1998, Australian Trade Minister Tim Fischer talked of inter-governmental discussions, which included the US, on how to undermine support within Europe for the European Union's position.[63] Ultimately, the major powers seemed destined to set the pace and scope of any new agricultural negotiations, driven by the desire to protect their domestic producers and assist their agribusinesses to expand offshore. Any gains (or losses) to New Zealand farmers would be incidental.

The negotiating environment in 1999 was very different from the Uruguay Round. Romantic notions of globalisation had been deflated by the harsh realities of the East Asian and subsequent financial crises, the fair trade versus free trade debate in the US and elsewhere, and a pragmatic political approach to trade liberalisation in many countries. While talk about free trade continued, it seemed that few new doors were about to open for New Zealand farmers. They were already agitated by government moves to deregulate the producer boards. Prominent farming leaders, such as former Dairy Board chair Dryden Spring, commented on how little the Uruguay Round had achieved.[64]

Farmers' frustration turned to anger in March 1999 when the US International Trade Commission recommended that the President invoke 'safeguard' provisions in the GATT and impose additional tariffs on imports of New Zealand and Australian lamb to protect the fragile US sheepmeat industry.[65] New Zealand farmers protested about the hypocrisy of the US in preaching free trade while practising blatant protectionism. The Australian and New Zealand governments threatened to complain to the WTO that the US action was not justified.[66] In the same week, the Pork Industry Board asked the New Zealand government to impose short-term tariffs on imports of subsidised Canadian and Australian pork, claiming these had increased in volume and were undercutting the price of the local product.[67] Critics objected that even temporary safeguards would delay much needed restructuring in the pork industry. Economist Keith Rankin notes the difference between the two scenarios.[68] The US promoted free trade for nationalist economic purposes: it demanded that other countries open their markets to US exports, but imposed tariffs on imports to the US from unsubsidised producers in other countries, in order to protect struggling US farmers. This effective tax on imports was a cheaper option than paying its farmers subsidies. New Zealand's unsubsidised pork producers, on the other hand, were asking for protection from subsidised Canadian exports. Rankin concludes that the US action was not justified on economic criteria, whereas imposing tariffs to support New Zealand pork farmers could be.

Ironically, that option would have been foreclosed if Ministry of Commerce officials had succeeded with a proposal in 1998 to repeal New Zealand's anti-dumping and safeguard laws. These provisions had formed part of the original GATT compromise that allowed governments to ameliorate temporarily the impact of trade liberalisation on jobs and local industry. The agreement defined the conditions under which they could be used, and member governments provided for them in their domestic law.

Under New Zealand law, countervailing duties could be imposed where goods from other countries were subsidised or sold at below their production cost, and threatened to cause 'material injury' to a New Zealand industry that produced similar goods. 'Safeguard' action allowed temporary protections where a large and unforeseen increase in imported goods was causing 'serious injury' to a domestic industry.[69]

New Zealand's extreme policy environment in the 1990s could not tolerate even short-term protection, whatever benefits it might bring to businesses, workers and their families, regions and communities and however rarely it was used. In 1998 the Ministry of Commerce proposed to repeal those laws.[70] It suggested instead a 'net national benefit' test that would weigh the adverse effects of imports on local industry against expected benefits to consumers and other producers. All such decisions would be subject to domestic competition law, which gave primacy to economic efficiency.

The move was internationally unprecedented. The Business Roundtable and the Commerce Commission (which oversees competition law) supported the proposal. Most other submissions opposed it. A joint submission from seventeen major companies (including some members of the Business Roundtable), endorsed by the CTU, the Engineers' Union, the Manufacturers' Federation, and the Employers and Manufacturers Association (Northern), claimed that the theoretical arguments underlying the proposal were unproven and lacked supporting evidence; many of them were irrelevant in a market the size of New Zealand's. Any 'net national benefit' test would be highly subjective, and increase uncertainties. By diverging from internationally accepted rules, New Zealand would compromise its access to WTO dispute procedures. The submission argued that the move should be contingent on international acceptance, and the adoption of a similar approach by New Zealand's trading partners – which officials admitted was 'clearly unlikely' ever to occur.[71]

The Ministry of Commerce was undeterred. The government was committed to 'encouraging economic growth through the operation of open and competitive markets'.[72] In pursuing this goal, it was illogical to distinguish between domestic and international trade. Where the relevant policies were out of sync, New Zealand's international position should be harmonised with its domestic laws, which the government had already redesigned to meet efficiency goals. If New Zealand was out of step with other countries, it should use international trade negotiations to draw the other countries into line.[73] Those who had made submissions expressed outrage at the officials' shallow and predetermined analysis. The minister was forced to call for a further report. The reporting date slipped further, with no likelihood of legislation emerging before the 1999 election.

In the renewed negotiations on agriculture, the New Zealand government could retain its pure line and simply insist that others follow suit, collaborating with fellow free-traders (including the opportunist US) to seek more effective commitments to freeing up agricultural trade. But negotiations seemed likely to be prolonged, and the prospects of success slim. Meanwhile, New Zealand's highly efficient farmers would be seriously disadvantaged in export markets where their competitors remained subsidised. A prudent government would reconsider what support it could give to farmers to survive and diversify, and how to attract the next generation onto the farm. The alternative was to turn family farms over to agribusiness, which would lose the cost advantage of family labour, and have complex social impacts on rural communities. As the producer board controversy showed, any genuine exploration of alternatives would also need to address the position of large and small-scale Maori farmers, and the colonial foundations on which New Zealand agriculture is built.

▲ *General Agreement on Trade in Services (GATS)*

The New Zealand government's focus on agriculture deflected attention from other important aspects of the Uruguay Round, which carried their own potential for conflict. Since the 1970s, there had been a marked shift in OECD countries towards service-based economies. Information technology, telecommunications, media and entertainment, banking and consultancy, private education and health, security, transport and tourism were all growth areas in the international economy.[74] They were also areas in which the major transnationals, especially from the US, had a competitive advantage. Seeking to enhance this, they lobbied hard for freer access to foreign markets and more favourable rules.

The old GATT rules were designed for trade in goods across borders. The concept of trade in services is different. The service provider and the consumer often need to be in the same place. The consumer might come to the provider, as with tourism, or the provider could travel to the consumer, as most consultants do. Alternatively, the provider might set up in the consumer's country, running a university or a private prison. Sometimes technology allows supply across borders, as in Internet retailing or call-centre operations.[75] Barriers to trade in services will therefore differ from traditional barriers to trade in goods. Some governments do not allow foreigners to supply certain services, such as television, education and retail banking, because of their strategic nature. Sometimes governments impose special restrictions on foreign suppliers, in order to maintain prudential supervision, local content, self-sufficiency, employment, skills transfer or regional development. Free trade in services means removing any such barriers that discriminate against foreign service providers. It also means easing restrictions on the right to set up commercially, and to move both service personnel and money in and out of the country.

Moves to liberalise trade in services date back at least to 1972, when the OECD convened a high-level group of 'experts' to identify trade issues in the lead-up to the Tokyo Round. The group began recasting services as a trade matter, and exploring the policy options.[76] Their goal went beyond non-discrimination against and between foreign companies; they also wanted domestic service markets to be deregulated. This required a 'sea change' in attitudes to the regulation of services, from a focus on their social purposes to the narrow commercial criterion of whether regulations impeded trade.[77] A binding international agreement would mean that governments who tried to tighten restrictions on service industries would face demands for compensation and threats of retaliation from member countries whose service suppliers were adversely affected. The 'experts' recognised that there would be concerns about the 'implications for national sovereignty, economic welfare, legal autonomy, and cultural integrity', but treated these impacts as acceptable and inevitable.[78]

Work in the OECD on further liberalisation of trade in services reached a stalemate, and the US decided the issue should be included in the Uruguay Round. It sought a comprehensive, binding agreement. The European Union wanted the agreement to apply only to sectors that individual countries opted to have covered (known as a 'bottom-up' approach).[79] Many poorer countries opposed the inclusion of services altogether, because giving foreign service industries the right to establish themselves in those countries would increase the dominance of transnational corporations, and prevent governments from supporting their domestic service industries. Although they failed to block negotiations, the poorer countries did force services onto a separate track from the rest of the round.

The result was a separate WTO agreement known as the General Agreement on Trade in Services (GATS). The core GATT principles, procedures and rules now applied to services, with some variations. The 'most favoured nation' rule meant that a government could not discriminate between service suppliers from different signatory countries, unless it had reserved the right to do so when the GATS was signed. Because this led to a long list of country-specific reservations, the parties agreed to renegotiate them periodically, beginning in 1999. 'National treatment' allowed foreign and domestic services to be covered by different rules, provided their treatment was equivalent. Most importantly, the agreement was 'bottom-up' – that is, 'national treatment' applied only to those services a member country had opted to include; even then, the member could limit the extent of the agreement's application to those services. The schedules of reservations were subject to rules of 'standstill' (meaning that coverage of a service could not be withdrawn) and 'rollback' (meaning that each country's commitments were expected to be extended over time).[80]

GATS prevented governments from using specific measures that would restrict competition, and hence market access for foreigners, in the sectors covered, even if the same measures applied to domestic providers. For example, unless they had reserved the right to do so, governments could not restrict the number of suppliers of a service, dictate what legal form they must take or how many people they could employ, or limit their level of foreign shareholding. Equally, governments could not restrict international payments and transfers. Any requirements regarding qualifications, technical standards and licensing procedures had to be based on 'objective' and transparent criteria. Such requirements could not operate to restrict supply, and had to be kept to a minimum. Information about a member country's laws and practices had to be readily available. As with the GATT, there was limited provision for a country to deviate from the rules when faced with a balance of payments emergency or for certain public policy reasons. The WTO dispute settlement procedures applied, including the possibility of sanctions being imposed on trade in goods for a breach relating to trade in services.

The major transnational enterprises and the US government were disappointed that the lucrative areas of government procurement of services and competition policy were excluded from the agreement, and that foreign suppliers were denied access to government subsidies on the same terms as domestic suppliers. These omissions would be revisited during the built-in review in 1999. Negotiations continued on some of the controversial issues that were not concluded in 1994, notably basic telecommunications, financial services and maritime transport. Under strong pressure from the US, a basic telecommunications agreement was concluded in February 1997.[81] Negotiations on the liberalisation of financial services resumed in April 1997; the agreement was signed in December 1997 and came into effect, following ratification, on 1 March 1998.[82] Work on the mutual recognition of professional services began with accounting, and non-binding guidelines were agreed in May 1997. The completion of negotiations on maritime transport services was deferred until 1999.

As with agriculture, New Zealand went further in its GATS 'offer' than most countries. The government's commitments guaranteed non-discriminatory access for foreign companies in telecommunications, banking, professional services, tourism, audio-visual, construction, transport, and private education at primary, secondary and tertiary levels. There was a promise not to tighten the overseas investment regime. A future government that adopted a more restrictive regulatory approach to these services would invite retaliation, unless those regulations came within one of the limited and temporary GATS exceptions. The government could not, for example, prevent foreign operators from securing control of the New Zealand tourism industry and running it from offshore through their own networks of booking agents, hotels, souvenir retailers, restaurants and transport operators, provided they did not run foul of New Zealand's weak domestic competition laws. International consultancies and other megafirms could not be prevented from dominating the supply of professional services, especially where mutual recognition agreements applied. Changes to the tertiary education system announced in 1998 meant domestic and foreign private providers would be treated the same as public universities or polytechnics. This included equal access to tuition subsidies from 2000. Although the 1994 GATS provisions did not extend to state subsidies, the government decided to pay foreign suppliers the same, provided they were quality assured. If that policy remained unchanged, any extension of GATS to cover subsidies would *require* the government to do so, with limited benefits to the country in return.[83]

Maori had special concerns about the agreement. While the government reserved the right to give favourable treatment to Maori commercial interests, it was illegal under the GATS to discriminate on other grounds, such as recognition of Maori spiritual and cultural values, cultural requirements for professional training where mutual recognition agreements applied, or non-commercial measures to promote self-determination if they affected a foreign supplier's commercial interests.

The New Zealand government has done what the proponents of international trade in services prescribed: regulation driven by social purposes has been displaced by commercial imperatives within a competitive market-place. The government had to apply the agreement to the services already 'offered', on pain of retaliatory sanctions unless it could invoke one of the temporary exceptions. In the further negotiations that begin in 1999, governments will be under pressure to extend these commitments to such sensitive areas as health, broadcasting, prison management and security systems. But so long as GATS is a bottom-up agreement, there is no requirement to extend its scope or to 'offer' new services. Domestic policies can also limit the impact of the agreement, such as stopping the further privatisation and contracting out of central and local government services. As discussed in Chapter 5, it is also still possible to regulate the operations of foreign service suppliers, and to protect cultural, social, regional and consumer interests, once they are here; how that is done in the sectors covered by the GATS must be carefully framed to avoid being challenged as a disguised form of discrimination against foreign suppliers – unless the government feels the measure is important enough to pay compensation or risk a dispute hearing and retaliatory sanctions.

▲ *Agreement on Trade-related Aspects of Intellectual Property Rights (TRIPS)*

The inclusion of intellectual property rights in the Uruguay Round seemed incongruous. Its proponents argued that the protection of intellectual property was essential to ensure a free flow of goods and services, provided a vital incentive for innovation, and was a legitimate protection of property rights. Its critics saw it as protectionist, denying general access to knowledge and innovation, and impeding the development of poorer countries by requiring them to pay massive royalties to the transnationals.

International rules on intellectual property – the Paris Convention on patents and trade marks, the Berne Convention on copyright and the Rome Convention on 'neighbouring' rights – have been developed over a century. All are administered by the UN-based World Intellectual Property Organisation (WIPO). Poorer countries have consistently blocked the negotiation of tighter rules at WIPO, claiming that they need the same rights to access knowledge and technology that richer countries enjoyed when intellectual property laws were weak.

To break this deadlock the US insisted that intellectual property rights be included in the Uruguay Round. The Intellectual Property Committee (a coalition of thirteen major US companies, including IBM, Du Pont, General Motors, Merck & Co., and Pfizer) worked with the US Trade Representative on a proposal to standardise world intellectual property laws along US lines, and to make them binding and enforceable under the WTO. The companies wanted protection against the 'theft' of royalties from brand-name clothing, videos and music. They also sought 'proper' returns and incentives for investment in research and development in drugs and technology.[84] A number of poorer countries led resistance to the proposal. They insisted that WIPO was the appropriate forum for dealing with intellectual property; the Uruguay Round should address only the genuinely trade-related issue of counterfeiting. The stakes were high: payment of royalties under the US proposal would mean a massive transfer of wealth from the economies of poor countries to the corporations of rich countries. Based on the latter's assessments of lost earnings from royalties in 1987, the total cost to poor countries would be between US$100 billion and US$300 billion a year; the total export income of those countries was just US$500 billion.[85]

Tensions ran high. In 1988, the US Congress passed its 'special 301' laws, allowing unilateral retaliation against intellectual property practices the US deemed 'unfair' (see Chapter 6). It was clear that Congress would not approve the Uruguay Round agreements unless intellectual property rights were included. Poorer countries also faced mounting pressures from potential foreign investors to protect intellectual property, so they opted to trade off some of their objections for concessions in other areas, notably phasing out the grossly unfair multi-fibre agreement. OECD countries, especially France and Canada, had their own concerns about the 'cultural imperialism' of the US motion picture and entertainment industry. When the US refused to agree that audio-visual services had special cultural characteristics, the European Community announced it would make no offer on that sector, and other countries withdrew theirs.[86]

The Agreement on Trade-related Aspects of Intellectual Property Rights (TRIPS) covered a wide range of intellectual property: copyrights and related performance rights; layouts of integrated circuits; 'geographical origin' indicators (as in wine); trade marks, industrial designs and patents. Minimum lengths of protection were set down for each, and the basic rules of 'national treatment', 'most favoured nation' status and transparency were to apply. Compliance was to be subject to the general WTO dispute settlement process. Signatory governments were required to implement the agreement within a year, although poorer countries were given another four years to comply with all the rules except 'national treatment' and 'most favoured nation'; very poor countries were given ten years.

The agreement harmonised intellectual property laws at the minimum standard then applying across most of the OECD.[87] Countries that did not currently grant patents in certain areas, including chemicals and pharmaceuticals, were given some leeway for implementation. Parties were still allowed to 'adopt measures necessary to protect public health and nutrition, and to promote the public interest in sectors of vital importance to their socio-economic and technological development',[88] provided these were consistent with the agreement (meaning, basically, that they did not breach 'national treatment' or 'most favoured nation' rules). There were also exceptions for diagnostic, therapeutic and surgical methods for the treatment of humans and animals. However, patents over plants and animals (other than micro-organisms) and essential biotechnology processes were excluded only temporarily, with further negotiations scheduled for 1999.[89]

New Zealand's negotiators did not see intellectual property as a major issue. The Secretary for Commerce, John Belgrave, explained:

> Part of the emphasis on patent legislation comes from America ... . New Zealand had not been able to ignore the American position. We are strong compatriots in the GATT round on agriculture. We are relying on the United States in agriculture. It makes sense that we cannot ignore the United States when it comes to patent legislation in the GATT context.[90]

New Zealand needed to make only minor changes to its copyright and trade mark legislation to comply with the agreement.[91] The most substantial change extended the term of patents from sixteen to twenty years, and restricted the grounds on which an invention could be refused a patent; new measures were also applied to the importing of goods with trade marks registered in New Zealand.

The main controversy involved challenges from Maori to the very notion of intellectual property rights over taonga (such as flora and fauna, and traditional medicines) of which they were guardians. Intellectual property rights commodify and privatise knowledge, including products of nature, to enable its exclusive exploitation for private gain. For traditional societies, and for indigenous peoples, this presents a basic conflict of values and world-views. In India, hundreds of thousands of people took to the streets to defend their access to traditional seeds and medicines, which transnational enterprise was seeking to patent. In New Zealand, the National Maori Congress called a hui in February 1994 to discuss its opposition to the agreement and invited officials from the Ministry of Foreign Affairs and Trade. Lawyer Moana Jackson explained that for Maori, the agreement was irreconcilable with their role as kaitiaki or spiritual guardians of the life-world and with their tino rangatiratanga as recognised in the Treaty of Waitangi. Knowledge was created over time, not by a single author or inventor. It was the repository of culture and identity. The benefits were shared. It could neither be owned nor sold. Not all knowledge was available to everyone; its custodians had responsibilities for its protection and use.[92]

This message was supported by the Mataatua Declaration on Cultural and Intellectual Property Rights first endorsed by a hui (gathering) of indigenous nations in Tauranga in 1993. The Declaration affirmed that:

> Indigenous Peoples of the world have *the right to self-determination*: and in exercising that right must be recognised as the *exclusive owners of their cultural and intellectual property*. ... The first beneficiaries of indigenous knowledge (cultural and intellectual property rights) must be the direct indigenous descendants of such knowledge.[93]

The signatories demanded a moratorium on further commercialisation of indigenous medicinal plants and human genetic materials, until indigenous communities had developed appropriate protection mechanisms. The document was subsequently signed by over 80 indigenous nations and tabled at the UN.

Government officials had great difficulty in understanding that Maori objections to the agreement went beyond specific problems with the wording of the text to a rejection of its very essence. Subsequently, a claim was lodged with the Waitangi Tribunal that the Crown had violated the tino rangatiratanga of iwi over their indigenous knowledge and taonga in diverse ways, including through the intellectual property agreement.[94]

Maori actively opposed international and domestic moves to extend intellectual property rights to biodiversity, which the powerful biotechnology industry was demanding with US support. This extended beyond genetic engineering in agriculture to the manipulation of human organisms.[95] The US Patent Office already issued such patents, and US government agencies were major players in the Human Genome Project to map and sequence DNA in 100,000 human genes, at a cost of over US$3 billion. An extension, the Human Genome Diversity Project, sought to map genetic diversity across the world, especially targeting indigenous peoples. An international meeting of indigenous peoples in 1994 expressed outrage: 'Without consultation with the indigenous communities, several projects are now taking blood, hair, tissue and other samples which could be used for patenting or other purposes. These practices not only violate ethics and human rights, but also violate our spirituality and our knowledge of creation that connects us with all forms of life'.[96] Officials from the ministries of Commerce and Foreign Affairs and Trade held a series of consultations with Maori over biodiversity and bio-security initiatives, seeking to defuse the intensity of their opposition. But such consultations were always premised on the potential to commodify knowledge and the legitimate genetic manipulation of the life-world. Indigenous peoples remained dependent on decisions made by colonial governments and international forums in which they have no voice as of right.

In 1999 this debate led back to the WTO. The initial intellectual property agreement had required WTO members to protect plant varieties in their patent system, but had excluded coverage of biodiversity and the patenting of life-forms. A review was built into the provision, to begin in 1999. The US insisted the review was to discuss the implementation of patents on plant varieties and extending coverage to biodiversity. ASEAN and South Asian countries especially called instead for a reconsideration of the coverage of plant varieties.[97] Indigenous peoples shared these concerns, but had no role in the official proceedings. They were left to compete with the transnationals in lobbying their national governments, some of which refused to recognise their very existence, or to find alternative ways to express their dissent.[98] In New Zealand's case, any effective representation of Maori views would require the government to fundamentally rethink its approach to intellectual property rights. While this seemed most unlikely, the growing outcry against genetically modified foods suggested indigenous peoples might find potential allies at home and internationally.

▲ SURVEILLANCE AND ENFORCEMENT OF WTO AGREEMENTS

Each of these agreements potentially limits the capacity of a future New Zealand government to act independently. However, a government can invoke existing trade remedies (such as temporary safeguard and anti-dumping laws) or impose trade restrictions for emergency balance of payments reasons. Some measures are allowed for conservation or health reasons, provided they are not 'disguised trade sanctions'. The use of these powers is policed by the WTO's dispute settlement process. When the Uruguay Round agreements were signed in Marrakech in 1994, member governments promised 'to endeavour to take all necessary steps to make their domestic laws conform' with their provisions.[99] The WTO has the power to approve cross-retaliation and other trade sanctions against governments who breach the rules.

The WTO agreements are the product of complex negotiations and often unprincipled compromises. The resulting texts are opaque and leave ample room for disputes. Under the old system, a specially convened panel of trade experts heard complaints and reported to the GATT Council for a decision. Any one GATT member, including the transgressor, could veto the adoption of the panel's report, although disputes seldom got that far.[100] It was a long and costly process, which the major powers were able to manipulate. The WTO's Dispute Settlement Body, created in 1994, sought to improve the process. If initial consultation and mediation fail, an ad hoc panel, usually comprising former GATT or high-level trade officials, examines the evidence and presents recommendations to the parties and the Dispute Settlement Body. There is appeal beyond that to an Appellate Body. Where a signatory has breached an explicit commitment, it can be required to remove the non-conforming measure; where there is an 'effective' breach, it can be required to adjust its policy or law and provide compensation. Failure to comply within the required time leads to further negotiations on appropriate compensation. This can, if unresolved, result in a request by the injured party for approval to retaliate by suspending concessions or obligations to the offending country. The earlier power of veto has gone; a consensus is now required *not* to implement a recommendation.

The WTO relies mainly on embarrassment and peer persuasion, backed by awards of compensation, where a member fails to implement a decision. The aim is to restore the situation to what it should have been. This approach avoids a direct clash with state sovereignty. However, the capacity of governments to act can be severely constrained. A 1998 decision by the Appellate Body against India illustrates the dilemma. The intellectual property agreement gave poorer countries until 2000 or 2005 to comply with some aspects. Pharmaceutical transnationals and agribusinesses secured a special provision that required those governments to establish an interim system to receive applications for patents, known as a 'mailbox'. In 1995 the Indian government introduced a bill to provide that system, but it lapsed when Parliament was dissolved. The system subsequently operated under administrative direction.[101] In 1996 the US, later joined by the European Union, claimed that India had breached its obligations under the intellectual property agreement.[102] Both the WTO dispute panel and the Appellate Body agreed. The Indian government was required to comply within eighteen months, or face severe sanctions from the US and the European Union. It promised to do so, despite the domestic sensitivity of the issue. In March 1999 the Indian Parliament passed the necessary legislation, although it still did not go as far as the US and its transnationals wanted.[103]

The dispute process is frequently criticised for being non-transparent, undemocratic, and run by the major powers in the interests of their transnationals. The hearings are in secret. The evidence remains confidential unless parties choose to release it. They can veto proposed members of the panel. The panel can seek outside information. But third parties such as environmental NGOs (or companies) have no rights to participate, because only WTO member governments have legal standing. Trade disputes with an environmental dimension are especially controversial. The so-called 'Shrimp Turtle' case involved a US ban on imports of shrimps from countries whose boats were not fitted with turtle-excluder devices, as required on all US domestic shrimp boats. The dispute panel and Appellate Body upheld a complaint from Thailand, Malaysia and others that this was a discriminatory non-tariff barrier, and that its impact went beyond what was necessary to achieve the environmental objective.[104] The ruling created a furore in the US, which could no longer veto the acceptance of the dispute panel's recommendations. In March 1999 the US administration announced a new system for certifying shrimp fishing practices which it said would comply with the ruling without needing to amend the US environmental legislation under which the ban was imposed.[105] Environmental NGOs have called (unsuccessfully) for legal standing at such hearings, although there are controversial moves to allow them to lodge third party opinions to inform the trade experts on the panel about the environmental issues involved.

For small and poorer countries, the dispute settlement process offers some prospect of stemming arbitrary action by the major powers. They had hoped the 1994 revamp would strengthen the process, especially with the removal of the veto. But the 'major interests' norm means that the major powers still dominate almost every dispute hearing, either as complainant or as respondent. The ability of a country like New Zealand to enforce WTO agreements is therefore contingent. Its exposure to complaints also depends on whom it offends, and how the major powers decide to retaliate. In March 1999, for example, a WTO dispute panel upheld a complaint from the US and New Zealand that Canada's milk pricing system subsidised its dairy exports. Canada was expected to respond with a complaint about New Zealand's ban on foreign trout imports. Meanwhile, New Zealand threatened to take Australia to the WTO for refusing to allow the importation of New Zealand apples. The Australians claimed there was a risk of importing fire blight, but New Zealand officials said they were using this as an excuse to protect their domestic apple producers.

The rules-based system was also meant to provide a forum for resolving disputes between the major powers. In 1999 the dispute settlement process, and potentially the WTO, were plunged into crisis as the US and European Union struggled for power. Back in 1996, the New Zealand government had joined consultations (initiated by the US) with the European Union regarding the latter's ban on beef treated with growth hormones.[106] The European Union had opted not to use the Codex Alimentarius (recognised by the WTO as the international standard-setting body in food safety) and had set its own standards, on the basis that states had the right to set precautionary standards for health protection as they deemed necessary. A dispute panel in July 1997 found the ban was not supported by scientific evidence that proved actual harm would result from eating the beef. The European Union lost its appeal in January 1998, and said it wanted more time to conduct a risk assessment study to show that the ban was justified. In May 1999, the US announced it was seeking approval to impose sanctions worth US$202 million in retaliation for the European Union's failure to implement the WTO decision.[107]

A related crisis involved the unlikely issue of banana imports (which made up less than one percent of trade between the US and the European Union). In 1998 the US, plus Ecuador, Guatemala and Honduras, challenged European Union rules that gave preference to banana imports from former colonies in Caribbean and South Pacific countries, arguing that they locked out the banana exports of major American transnationals operating in Latin America (especially Chiquita). The complaint was upheld by the dispute panel and the Appellate Body. The European Union was ordered to open its market, and announced it would 'honour its obligations' by 1 January 1999. The way it proposed to do so was unacceptable to the US, which threatened to retaliate unilaterally. The matter was set down for arbitration. Meanwhile, the US announced in early March 1999 that it would impose tariffs on US$500 million worth of European exports, ranging from cashmere sweaters to cheese. The goods chosen for retaliatory sanctions came from locations the US considered were most supportive of the banana regime. The procedure used by the US was technically within the WTO rules. The European Union called an emergency session of the WTO Council. The Canadians criticised both sides for treating the WTO as if it belonged solely to them. India's representative warned that the WTO could not survive under the weight of US unilateralism.[108] The dispute panel subsequently approved retaliatory sanctions worth US$191 million for damages incurred; the European Union had until August 1999 to produce a new proposal. The US claimed victory, even though it does not produce bananas. The Caribbean countries, whose economies depend on such exports, saw themselves as the casualties of a battle over a much bigger prize – 'the question of hegemony in the WTO'.[109]

▲ POST-URUGUAY ROUND FRACTURES

The WTO faces the tensions and power plays of any intergovernmental forum; but these have been compounded by its commitment to globalisation. The WTO's first ministerial meeting, in Singapore in December 1996, confirmed its image as a 'club for the rich and powerful'. Each government delegation read its prepared statements in the plenary session, but the real work took place at informally convened meetings to which many poor countries were not invited. Some delegations had to rely on briefings from NGOs who were present. The more formal meetings of Heads of Delegation provided 'a sounding chamber to measure the degree of resistance to positions agreed behind closed doors'.[110] When several poorer countries complained, they were told that invitations were based on a country's region, size and development status, and the need to balance 'transparency' and 'efficiency'. Nor were all NGOs created equal. Business NGOs received special briefings and bilateral meetings, while public interest NGOs struggled to gain access to the building.

Many poorer countries claimed they were worse off under the Uruguay Round, and demanded a review of its implementation. They accused the major powers of complying with the letter, but not the spirit, of the agreements, especially the multi-fibre agreement relating to textiles. Meanwhile, the obligations on poorer countries were overwhelming. Very poor countries, called 'least developed countries' or LDCs, had not received the technical assistance promised to them. The meeting recognised that these countries had become further marginalised, and approved a 'comprehensive and integrated plan of action'. But the plan simply left it to individual governments to improve their concessions on market access for such countries.

Rich countries were in another world altogether. Most were eager to renew negotiations (already built into the agreements) on agriculture and services, and aspects of the intellectual property agreement. The Cairns Group complained about the manipulation of agricultural tariff levels, and the ineffective implementation of the Agreement on Agriculture, especially by the European Union and the US. The group wanted new negotiations forthwith; the Europeans were intent on delay. Some countries, notably Australia and the UK, were lobbying hard for a whole new 'millennium round' in which commitments in different sectors could be traded off. The US preferred rapid negotiations on selected topics, to provide an 'early harvest' on issues where there was agreement (and which benefited them). The model for this was the Information Technology Agreement (ITA), which had been concluded in just eighteen months and signed off in Singapore.[111]

The WTO's second ministerial meeting was held in Geneva in May 1998. The East Asian crisis, the expiry of President Clinton's fast-track negotiating authority, the suspension of MAI negotiations, growing opposition to 'free trade', and mounting external attacks on the anti-social and anti-democratic nature of the WTO all cast a pall over proceedings, even though they were rarely acknowledged. Poor countries again pleaded for a review of existing Uruguay Round commitments and unfair arrangements. Rich countries paid lip service to issues of poverty, inequality and debt, and to the desperate situation of the poorest countries, mainly in Africa. But their solution was to liberalise faster and more comprehensively. The Europeans, supported by many of their OECD allies, again promoted a comprehensive millennium round to move the WTO further. The US still wanted a sectoral approach that focused on the in-built agenda (including agriculture), the coverage of all services, the patenting of biodiversity, and government procurement. To allay the fears of poorer nations, the OECD countries insisted that any negotiating mandate and final agreements would require consensus. Given the experience of the Uruguay Round, that was hardly reassuring.

The Geneva meeting was called primarily to celebrate the GATT's 50th birthday; the only real achievement was setting the date for the next ministerial meeting. When President Clinton dropped in to Geneva for two hours to launch the celebrations, the price for his presence was an agreement on electronic commerce, cobbled together from a US draft in less than three months. Clinton's speech keynoted US demands, and offered US 'leadership' for the coming year. In practice, this meant the US would host the ministerial meeting that set the new negotiating agenda, and would chair the General Council for 1999. Delegates of many poor countries expressed their frustration privately, but were publicly subdued.

Only Cuba's Fidel Castro launched an unrestrained attack on the US. Proposing an alternative WTO agenda – 'Global Economic Crisis. What to do?' – he called on poor countries to take a stand as the majority in the WTO. Delegates rushed to shake his hand. But the WTO's global vision seemed more at risk from the major powers pushing it beyond the capacity of its poorer members than from the latter's resistance.

This tension was encapsulated in the battle over who would become the next WTO Director-General. To date, every chief of the GATT or WTO had been from an OECD country. Poor countries believed it was their turn. The process began in September 1998. By March 1999 it was a contest between New Zealand's Mike Moore, who was sponsored by the US, and Supachai Panitchpakdi, the deputy prime minister of Thailand. Three months later it had reached an acrimonious stalemate. Moore's supporters claimed he had enough support for a 'consensus' and refused to take a vote. Poorer countries backing Supachai accused the US of bullying, and condemned the process as an inauspicious omen for any new WTO round. The final outcome was a job-share arrangement in which Moore took first turn. Malaysian journalist Chakravarthi Raghavan observed: 'the power play and the process used to promote a consensus have demonstrated that the "rule-based" WTO is an undemocratic, non-transparent institution, with a manipulative decision-making process that makes the system an instrument of the powerful.'[112]

Outside pressure on the WTO was mounting as well. The GATT's 50th birthday party was guarded by riot police with tear gas and water cannons behind metal barricades. Thousands of farmers, unionists, students and unemployed people from throughout Europe had marched peacefully through Geneva. At night, the youth of the city rioted in the streets, something rarely seen before. The irony of the situation was not lost on the UN Secretary-General, Kofi Annan, a belated invitee to address the birthday party. His emissary observed: 'No one should be fooled by the festive atmosphere of these celebrations. Outside there is anguish and fear, insecurity about jobs and what Thoreau described as a "life of quiet desperation".'[113]

There was no global counter-revolution. Pockets of resistance had emerged where the new WTO agreements impacted directly on people's lives. Indigenous nations campaigned to protect their traditional knowledge from the latest form of colonisation and cultural genocide. People in Africa mobilised around issues of food security and access to technology. A coalition of Filipino senators and congressmen, unions and NGOs challenged the ratification of WTO agreements as violating the constitutional primacy given to national industry, workers and products. The subsequent judgement of the Philippines Supreme Court was an extraordinary exercise in judicial capitulation, beginning and ending with discourses on the desirability and inevitability of globalisation.[114] In India, hundreds of thousands of peasant farmers repeatedly took to the streets to protest against the power that the intellectual property agreement gave to foreign agribusiness. Family farmers in Europe and Japan rebelled against the threat to their survival from the liberalisation of agricultural trade. Despite some attempts to coordinate opposition to the WTO internationally, most of these movements remained nationally based.

International unions and some western NGOs focused more narrowly on labour and environmental issues. They faced an uphill struggle. As noted earlier, the WTO is an economic forum; discussions on social or environmental concerns could occur only if they were redefined in trade-related and pro-globalisation terms, and the member governments agreed. Accepting these conditions, ICFTU unions and environmental NGOs repeatedly called for the GATT, and later the WTO, to examine the relationship between trade liberalisation and labour and the environment, and to negotiate 'green' and 'social' clauses in the various agreements. Free-traders insisted that labour and environmental concerns should be accommodated only if they did not distort efficient and open trading. Sympathetic academics such as Michael Trebilcock and Robert Howse have warned that this rigid approach is threatening the WTO's legitimacy. They criticise the tendency of free-traders to dismiss advocates of 'fair trade' as 'charlatans (protectionists masquerading as ethicists)', and those seeking to link trade and the environment as 'irrational moral fanatics, prepared to sacrifice global economic welfare and the pressing needs of the developing countries for trivial, elusive or purely sentimental goals'.[115]

> [By] indiscriminately dismissing all fair trade claims and eliding those based on thinly disguised protectionism and claims legitimately based on international labour and environment standards, [free-traders] run the risk of being discredited as moral philistines and thus being marginalised in political debates that do indeed carry serious risks for a liberal international trading order.[116]

New Zealand's officials and ministers have taken a hard line on these issues. North American and European governments have been much more sympathetic, although their support is often attributed to self-interest. Effective domestic lobbies have forced those governments to maintain higher environmental and labour standards, making it hard for local companies to compete with producers in countries with less restrictive codes. Local NGOs, unions and producers pressure their governments to overcome this competitive disadvantage by demanding similarly high standards from all other countries.

The governments of most poor countries have opposed calls for 'social' and 'green' clauses in WTO agreements. They object to being told how to use their resources by rich countries who want to maintain their own living standards, jobs and lifestyles; they argue that such countries should have to take responsibility for their own excessive demands on natural resources by lowering their energy consumption and carbon dioxide emissions.[117] They should also deal with the problems of debt and structural inequality that create conditions for the exploitation of labour and the environment in poorer countries. At the same time, many of these governments are highly authoritarian, and suppress local unions and environmental activists when they demand that appalling domestic standards are improved.

The arguments in favour of linking trade and labour standards come mainly from the ICFTU unions. They explicitly seek to adapt, not to challenge, the free trade paradigm. The ICFTU lobbied unsuccessfully for the inclusion of a working group on labour standards in the Punta del Este Declaration in 1986. The US and France tried equally unsuccessfully to reintroduce the issue late in the Uruguay Round.[118] In the lead-up to the Singapore meeting in 1996, the ICFTU lobbied again.[119] It hoped that the 1996 OECD report on Trade and Labour Standards might offer support. The report did concede that market forces alone would not automatically improve 'core' standards, and that more direct measures were needed; but it found no consensus that the WTO was the appropriate or effective forum for achieving this.[120] Indeed, ASEAN governments threatened to boycott the 1996 WTO meeting if labour was discussed. When the US and Norway raised the issue, almost all the poorer countries, and New Zealand, were opposed to discussing it. The final Singapore Declaration rejected the WTO having any active role on labour standards, leaving them to the ILO. The Declaration reiterated the belief that trade liberalisation would foster economic growth and development, and thereby promote 'core' labour standards. At the same time, it criticised the motives of those who sought to impose high labour standards for protectionist purposes, and 'agreed that the comparative advantage of countries, particularly low-wage developing countries, must in no way be put into question'.[121]

Pressure on the ILO from the ICFTU and sympathetic governments produced a new declaration on labour standards just before the WTO ministerial meeting in 1998. The unions again urged stronger cooperation between the WTO and ILO, the inclusion of 'core' ILO labour standards and employment considerations in WTO trade policy reviews, and the establishment of a WTO working group on trade and labour standards. The ICFTU also called for a commitment to consultation with trade unions and other 'democratic representatives of civil society'.[122] While the US supported this position, other governments remained adamant that the

ILO was the only appropriate forum. This was the line taken by the New Zealand government – which was ironic, given its derisive attitude to the ILO when a complaint from the CTU resulted in an ILO report criticising the Employment Contracts Act in 1994.[123]

The WTO response to environmentalist demands was also slow and superficial. The GATT had set up a Working Group on Environmental Measures and International Trade in 1971. It never met. The group was revived in 1991, and later became the Committee on Trade and the Environment under the WTO. The document establishing the WTO minimally altered the 1947 GATT preamble by referring to the 'optimal' rather than 'full' use of the world's resources, and adding 'at sustainable levels'. Attempts by the US and by NGOs to highlight the environment at the WTO ministerial meeting in 1996 produced a limited discussion of the negative effects of eco-labelling on trade, and the relationship between the WTO's dispute settlement mechanism and international environmental agreements (such as the Convention on International Trade in Endangered Species (CITES) 1991). The Committee on Trade and the Environment was made a permanent WTO body, and secretariats responsible for international environmental agreements gained observer status at the committee. A database for trade-related environmental measures was approved.

The 1998 ministerial meeting also achieved little. That is not surprising, given the comment at the time by the WTO Director-General that imposing environmental standards was 'doomed to fail and could only damage the global trading system'.[124] Big business shared his view. The International Chamber of Commerce warned of the 'potential threat to the multilateral trading system if measures are not taken to avoid conflicts' with the multilateral environmental agreements, and national and regional eco-labelling schemes.[125] This meant subordinating environmental measures to the trade priorities of the WTO.

New Zealand officials took a similar approach. During the Uruguay Round negotiations, they told the Minister of Foreign Affairs and Trade that the round 'has had a bad press amongst environmentalists. ... It was almost as if there were an assumption that free trade is bad for the environment'. They believed there were few environmental issues that could not be adequately catered for in the existing GATT agreements. The officials suggested promoting the idea that international environmental negotiations should bear in mind the GATT's objectives and seek to minimise any trade distortions. Any work on trade and the environment in the GATT should not involve any major new initiatives.[126] By 1997 the government was prepared to see some agreed international rules. But it insisted that trade measures, such as sanctions, should only be used to advance environmental objectives where they were necessary (in other words, where the environmental benefits would outweigh any negative trade effects), had the least effect on trade of any option, and were not used for protectionist purposes. The burden of proof should rest with those proposing the measures. Disputes would be resolved within the WTO framework, effectively leaving non-environmental trade experts with the right to determine what environmental protection a country could legitimately impose.[127]

A special WTO symposium on Trade and the Environment in April 1999 saw little change.[128] The US and the European Commission were accused of using environmental concerns to promote their own agendas for the new WTO round, including the need to involve 'civil society' and NGOs. Director-General Ruggiero suggested establishing a new World Environment Organisation to deal with environmental questions and standards, instead of the WTO. Poorer countries stressed elements from the UN environmental summit in 1992 that recognised the need for better market access, transfer of technology and provision of new and additional resources to help them deal with environmental problems. There was nothing approaching consensus on the issue. A parallel forum on Trade and Development produced a similar stalemate on labour issues.

There seemed no prospect of labour becoming part of the WTO's mainstream agenda, and little for the environment except on the margins and subordinate to free trade goals. Other NGOs and people's organisations, including unions in poor countries, believed it was futile to try. Taking a less benign view of globalisation, they insisted that economic redistribution, genuine sustainability and just employment could not be achieved through an institution whose *raison d'être* was to increase the power and profitability of transnational capital through global free markets.

Added to these pressures were the challenges to the democratic deficit in WTO processes, referred to earlier. By the ministerial meeting in May 1998, the US and the WTO leadership had decided that the credibility of the WTO was sufficiently under threat that it needed to appear more open and sensitive to union and NGO concerns. The US Trade Representative, Charlene Barshefsky, described the 'failure of public trust in the system, public suspicion, public mistrust of secrecy' as the greatest threat to the multilateral trading system. She urged greater transparency to build public understanding, the recognition of core labour standards, and the reconciliation of trade and environmental goals. Barshefsky suggested that the WTO establish regular, ongoing and formal consultation with the private sector and NGOs.[129] President Clinton echoed this message in his address to the Geneva meeting: 'This dynamic, idea-based new global economy offers the possibility of lifting billions of people into a worldwide middle class. Yet it also contains within it the seeds of new disruptions, new instabilities, new inequalities, new threats to the global economy'. The WTO had to be more accountable, open its dispute hearings to the public eye, accept briefs from outside experts, including NGOs, and make its reports available. More broadly, it needed to listen to 'ordinary citizens':

> I propose the WTO, for the first time, provide a forum where business, labor, environmental and consumer groups can speak out and help guide the further evolution of the WTO. When this body convenes again, I believe that the world's trade ministers should sit down with representatives of the broad public to begin this discussion.[130]

Within the hour, an ICFTU press release hailed Clinton's speech as 'remarkable' and 'agenda-setting': 'We have been calling for globalisation with a human face, and are delighted that President Clinton has clearly been listening.'[131] Even Director-General Ruggiero talked of growing pressure from 'very real public concerns' over 'financial instability, development, marginalization, protection of the environment, social conditions, employment, public health, or cultural diversity'. But like Clinton, he was offering participation on the fringes of the WTO, on its terms, and consistent with its economic goals:

> We have to improve our ability to respond within our own rules and institutions to the interrelationships which undoubtedly exist, showing that the different policies required can be mutually supportive rather than contradictory. ... Progress in this direction clearly requires more information on our role and more dialogue ... with the civil society.[132]

Free-traders saw this as the thin end of the wedge. The *Financial Times* quoted one former WTO official as saying: 'This is the place where governments collude in private against their domestic pressure groups. Allowing NGOs in could open the doors to European farmers and all kinds of lobbyists opposed to free trade'.[133] He had little cause for concern. The 'dialogue' began with briefings for NGOs, initiated by the WTO in September 1998. The go-between, the International Centre for Trade and Sustainable Development, had been formed in 1996 to promote the harmonisation of these two elements. While its Programme Advisory Board was wide-ranging, and included some strongly critical NGOs from poor and rich countries, its Trade Advisory Council consisted almost entirely of government and institutional officials. Its main funders were governments and mainstream environmental organisations, who also provided the majority of the board's governors. The subsequent forums on the environment and development, mentioned earlier, failed to pacify those critics who wanted to engage with the WTO, and did nothing to convince the sceptics.[134]

▲ REFLECTIONS

Sustaining a regime for international trade based on agreed rules was difficult enough when it dealt only with the traditional trade agenda contained in the GATT. As the Uruguay Round and then the WTO expanded to include a grab-bag of more peripheral issues of importance to the major powers, the regime became more complex and controversial. The WTO's mission to promote a coherent global economic policy agenda reflected the fervour that surrounded globalisation. But the ideal of a single global market bore no relation to the political and economic realities of the WTO's member countries and their people. New Zealand governments opted to take a pure line, arguing that they were leading the way, but if others failed to follow the country would still be better off. This was something New Zealanders had little chance to debate at the time, and many subsequently came to doubt.

Despite attempts by New Zealand's trade negotiators to tie future governments to the WTO mast, there are still opportunities to make different policy choices if a government is prepared to use them. While these measures are open to abuse by the major powers to the detriment of other countries, other countries do use them too. It remains open to a New Zealand government to invoke the emergency balance of payments, temporary safeguard, anti-dumping and conservation provisions. It could also refuse to extend existing commitments, and back demands by poorer countries for a fairer approach to international trade. More fundamentally, it could support calls for a reconsideration of the basic economic development model on which the WTO (along with the IMF and World Bank) operates. The international fractures in the WTO are likely to make such a debate imperative – a move which its more powerful members will be determined to resist.

In the meantime, the level of scepticism about free trade and concern about the democratic deficit should force the government to debate any new WTO initiatives, and provide a detailed and broad-based assessment of the costs and benefits secured from the Uruguay Round, and any new negotiating stance. The Treaty of Waitangi requires the government to hold parallel dialogue with Maori about New Zealand's negotiating position and procedures, and provide a comprehensive Treaty of Waitangi Impact Assessment of any agreements which are subsequently proposed

Such debates would not produce consensus, but they would ensure a level of public awareness and political accountability that has not existed before. However, that seems unlikely to happen. Despite a cosmetic consultation with interested groups, and even a public advertisement seeking submissions, the government's basic negotiating stance was already determined well in advance of the Seattle meeting in late 1999. There was no inclination to debate, let alone rethink the free trade paradigm.

8 ▲ Asia Pacific Economic Cooperation

APEC – Asia Pacific Economic Cooperation – has been aptly described as 'four adjectives in search of a noun'.[1] It is avowedly not a defensive trade bloc. Operating under the rubric of 'open regionalism', APEC aims to advance the process of economic integration throughout the world, particularly within the World Trade Organisation. Its mission is to serve the needs of the market. One Canadian official described APEC as 'a product of the new era of globalisation, an era in which business does business in an increasingly borderless world'.[2] A senior US official explained in 1995 that: 'APEC is not for Governments. It is for business. Through APEC, we aim to get governments out of the way, opening the way for business to do business.'[3]

APEC is symbolically important, confirming New Zealand's economic orthodoxy. As a means of formally embedding neo-liberalism, however, it is relatively impotent. APEC has no binding agreements or enforcement mechanism. It relies instead on a mass of commitments, expectations, declarations, reports and 'norms' that are 'voluntary and non-binding' – although New Zealand governments usually fail to mention that fact. These are used to generate peer pressure and provide member governments with external justifications for implementing economic policies that face opposition at home. Vested interests who stand to benefit from APEC are expected to promote and defend its activities. APEC's non-institutionalised, informal process means there is no need for governments to secure formal negotiating mandates, disclosure or ratification, and no risk that legislatures will interfere. This allows for flexibility and diversity, within a broadly shared set of goals. In theory, APEC is an ideal vehicle to promote regional economic integration across countries with diverse cultural, social, political and legal systems, where formal legal agreement is extremely difficult. But it has not worked that way.

APEC is formally committed to three complementary goals: trade and investment liberalisation; trade and investment facilitation; and economic and technical cooperation. The first and second are usually merged to form a free trade and investment agenda that reflects the neo-liberal capitalism favoured by the US, Australia, Canada and New Zealand, and serves the need of those countries to break down entry barriers to Asian economies. The third goal, economic and technical cooperation (or 'ecotech'), reflects the more activist preference of Japan and other Asian countries whose economies are quite deeply integrated already.

In practice, the free-marketeers have driven APEC's agenda since 1994 through a formal commitment to free trade and investment across its richer members by 2010 and its poorer ones by 2020. Australian journalist Kenneth Davidson described the situation in 1995 as 'a struggle between contrasting ways of capitalist organization and the ideologies legitimizing them', in which the Anglo-American members were trying 'to get the Asian winners of the economic game to deny the cultural basis of their success in order to create the conditions where the losers can become winners'.[4]

In a decade, APEC has not progressed very far. It calls itself a community of 'economies'. But the key players are still governments, which have different and sometimes conflicting political, economic and social agendas. The real-life economies of APEC members remain rooted in diverse cultural, legal and social structures. These realities are reflected in APEC's founding commitments to flexibility, voluntarism and consensus as its *modus operandi*. That pragmatic accommodation became difficult to sustain as APEC sought agreement on concrete commitments to achieve the 2010/2020 liberalisation goal. Most Asian members continued to insist on voluntary economic cooperation within diversity. This clashed with the US preference for a rules-based free market approach, supported by Australia, Canada and New Zealand. Combined with the Asian crisis, these disagreements left APEC virtually paralysed.

This internal instability was accompanied by external challenges, as concern about the APEC agenda spread among those it affects but excludes. APEC defines its members as 'economies' – partly to get around the fact that both China and Taiwan are members, but also because it effectively excludes such 'non-economic' considerations as poverty, indigenous sovereignty and human rights, and the people associated with them. Some groupings, notably regional ICFTU unions, sought a seat at the APEC table in order to represent their sectoral concerns. A broader based network of workers' organisations, NGOs and human rights groups took a more oppositional approach. They challenged APEC's operations as exclusive, secretive and anti-democratic, and condemned its economic model as serving the interests of international capital and local élites, while it deepened injustice and inequality. Views expressed by meetings of indigenous peoples on APEC mirrored their rejection of the WTO as an assault on sovereignty, although to some indigenous entrepreneurs it promised welcome new opportunities.

By the time it was New Zealand's turn to take the chair in 1999, APEC was facing a crisis of credibility. Commitments to APEC's goals were few, voluntary and retractable. The Asian miracle – APEC's much-heralded economic platform for the new millennium – was shattered. Despite brave talk, the setback was far from temporary. References to consensus and flexibility could no longer hide the tensions between members over which economic model APEC should pursue. Big business expressed scepticism about APEC's lack of progress towards its objectives, while small business was treated as largely irrelevant. Popular opposition to the free market agenda in poor countries, especially those undergoing structural adjustment programmes, was complemented by a wind change in richer countries. The vision of APEC as the vanguard of globalisation was proving to be a mirage.

▲ A BRIEF HISTORY OF APEC[5]

The 'Asia-Pacific region' is an artificial construct. It has no natural geographical boundary, no common historical or cultural base, no coherent identity. It spans a diversity of small, middle-sized and major powers with conflicting domestic concerns and varying international allegiances. The US and Canada have no obvious non-economic link to Asia. Australia and New Zealand have geographical and cultural affinity with each other, and strong economic links through CER; but despite the occasional politician's fancy, the two countries are not credibly part of Asia. Some obvious participants such as China and South Pacific nations were originally omitted altogether; most of the latter still are. Russia, Peru and Vietnam, who became active members in 1998, were chosen for strategic reasons. The ASEAN countries, who are integral to Asia, have been the least enthusiastic about APEC. Indeed, Malaysia has actively promoted the formation of an East Asian Economic Caucus, which would exclude the non-Asian members of APEC (the US, Canada, Australia and New Zealand).[6] In early 1999, Prime Minister Mahathir bin Mohamed resurrected the idea as an alternative to APEC.

When APEC was formed in 1989, no one really knew what it was going to do. Countries in Asia and on the Pacific Rim – notably Japan, the Republic of Korea, ASEAN members, Australia and the US – had strong but differing motives for achieving a regional economic arrangement.

The initial concept was promoted in the late 1970s by two government-supported business organisations, the Pacific Business Economic Council (PBEC) and the Pacific Economic Cooperation Council (PECC). Both were committed to the regional expansion of trade, finance and productive capital. In the later 1980s, various governments became receptive to their proposals. The Cold War was ending, and the boundaries, institutions and alliances of the global economic order were being redrawn. The GATT negotiations were proving difficult. There were growing fears about aggressive US unilateralism, bilateral tensions between the US and Japan, and renewed protectionism. The European Community was expanding its membership and deepening its integration, and the Canada/US Free Trade Agreement (the precursor to NAFTA) signed in 1988 was expected to extend to Mexico and beyond. Commentators began predicting that the world would break into three defensive trading blocs. Other than ASEAN and CER, the Asian countries, Australia and New Zealand had no formal regional arrangement to fall back on.

By 1988, uncoordinated and often competing initiatives were being floated by academics, politicians and officials from various countries in Asia and the Pacific. In early 1989, baseline support emerged for proposals by Australia and Japan for some kind of ministerial-level cooperation on trade and economic issues in a forum that was outward-looking, promoted global liberalisation, was not a trade bloc, and was compatible with the GATT.

Australia saw the regional initiative as a counterweight to aggression by the US and the European Community, and a way to cement its own position in Asia; logically, the US – and by association Canada – would be excluded. Japan preferred a low-profile, OECD-style agency to assess regional economic trends and foster cooperation; the US was to be included in order to defuse fears of Japan's own dominance in the region, and to strengthen US commitment to Asia. The ASEAN countries (then Brunei Darussalam, Indonesia, Malaysia, the Philippines, Singapore and Thailand) were ambivalent. As frequent victims of aggression by the major powers, and major investors in the region themselves, they saw benefits in a forum where they could have a collective voice. But they also feared that a regional arrangement would undermine the cohesiveness and importance of ASEAN itself. Their support for APEC was conditional on a flexible and gradual approach, sensitive to the disparities of the region and its asymmetrical power relations. By contrast, the US saw APEC as a means of gaining freer access to the huge Asian market, strengthening links with the 'tiger' economies, and promoting liberalisation worldwide. The US eventually finessed its way into APEC by threatening to promote an alternative trade grouping in the region.

After a year of behind-the-scenes negotiations brokered by Australia, the first ministerial meeting of APEC was held in Canberra in November 1989. The twelve founding members were the ASEAN countries of Malaysia, Singapore, Thailand, the Philippines, Indonesia and Brunei, plus Australia, Canada, Japan, New Zealand, South Korea and the US. They agreed to establish a ministerial forum to discuss economic issues affecting the region, coordinated through consultations among senior officials. Member 'economies' were not seeking uniformity, just ways to promote regional economic cooperation and to liberalise trade and capital flows. A haphazard collection of collaborative projects was put forward and given ministerial support. A second ministerial meeting was held in Singapore in July 1990, where little was achieved.

Some focus emerged from the Seoul meeting of APEC ministers in 1991. The Uruguay Round of the GATT was effectively in stalemate at this time, and there were fears of 'introspective regionalism'. Some members challenged APEC's lack of progress, and questioned its value. To give APEC some substance, the meeting produced the Seoul Declaration; this endorsed a common commitment to sustained economic growth, built on interdependence and a spirit of partnership, openness and the free flow of goods and capital. The Declaration claimed that this would reduce economic disparities and enhance the social well-being of the region's peoples. The fourth APEC meeting, in Bangkok in 1992, decided to establish a small secretariat in Singapore, and an 'eminent persons group' to report to the 1993 meeting with a 'vision for trade in APEC to the year 2000'.

This was all very tentative. Much of APEC's early discussion centred on who could join.[7] By the time a moratorium on new members was imposed in 1993, APEC included Chile, China, Chinese Taipei, Hong Kong, Mexico and Papua New Guinea. That was also the year the US took its turn as chair, and began to move APEC down the path of free trade and investment.

▲ THE APEC CIRCUITRY

APEC's organisational form evolved. It was agreed from the start that formal structures should be minimal, and reflect the principles of voluntariness, consensus and diversity. So, unlike the European Union, APEC has no formal institutional structure, nor even a set of binding agreements, as with NAFTA. It functions through an annual cycle of meetings for standing committees, officials, ministers and leaders. Core activities are restricted to member 'economies' and official observers.[8] Membership is voluntary, and decisions are by consensus. A different member takes the chair each year, with ASEAN countries presiding in alternate years. Depending on which 'economy' it is, the host nation can wield considerable influence on the direction APEC takes.

APEC operates more like a network than an institution. The politicians and officials inside the network believe it is the most transparent intergovernmental process they have been involved in. Reports of meetings and official documents are published and posted on the Internet. Dialogue takes place with the myriad peripheral bodies that have clustered around APEC. Yet the member 'economies' are selective about whom they make privy to the process; 'transparency' for everyone else occurs only after decisions have been made. When viewed from outside, APEC's operations seem profoundly undemocratic. Journalist Bruce Ansley described the meeting of APEC trade ministers in Christchurch in July 1996 as follows:

> Little of it was reported. It met in secret, except for a few handouts, and the odd press conference where the idea was to say as little as possible and to stall questions with urbanities. No one outside the charmed circle knew what was going on, and those inside intended to keep it that way. ... What they were plotting, of course, was a brave new world where nations and their corporate alter egos could browse across one another's boundaries without impediment. A few elements of the new order presented themselves for inspection; there won't be nations – in Apec language ... nations become 'economies' without, apparently, irritating social philosophies. These economies aren't inhabited by people but by 'human resources'. They don't have elected representatives; doubtless to his gratification, Jim Bolger becomes an 'economic leader'. It is cold and grey and mechanical, and scary as hell.[9]

At the bottom of APEC's multi-layered process is a tier of working groups, ad hoc and formal committees and 'experts groups'. These feed into meetings of senior officials, who in turn service meetings of ministers. The summits of 'economic leaders' (or, in common parlance, presidents, premiers and prime ministers) are semi-detached from the process. All these operations are coordinated by a secretariat in Singapore. APEC relies for its research primarily on the Pacific Economic Cooperation Council. In the early 1990s it used the ad hoc Eminent Persons Group to help develop 'the APEC vision'; it then established an ad hoc Pacific Business Forum, reshaped in 1995 as a permanent APEC Business Advisory Council (ABAC), to advise on and monitor APEC's performance from a business perspective.

The key players in APEC are the trade (and sometimes finance) officials from member 'economies'. They drive the work programme, negotiate the wording of documents and pre-script the ministerial meetings. Officials from the same ministries – sometimes the same individuals – resurface regularly in different regional forums, ensuring consistency in negotiating positions and an almost seamless dialogue. The pre-requisites for APEC membership mean all share a commitment to the market economy. But there are tensions. Officials from different countries hold to varying cultural, economic and regulatory norms, and operate under political instructions. As international lawyer Pitman Potter observes: 'elites socialized in different cultures may behave in different ways and make different choices, even when placed in similar situations'.[10] Trade officials may also find that more powerful agencies within their own governments accord APEC a low priority, as New Zealand's Reserve Bank and Treasury appear to do.[11]

It is difficult for such a fluid entity to plan its future development, which is why the Eminent Persons Group was established in 1992. Initially it had only eleven members, nominated by their governments and approved by all the APEC 'economies'.[12] In 1994 the group had members from all the 'economies' except Chile, the New Zealand participant being the chair of the Dairy Board, Dryden Spring. Optimistically, members were expected to act as private individuals, not as government representatives. The group was chaired by Fred Bergsten, a former senior official of the US Treasury and head of the influential Institute for International Economics in Washington. Bergsten's strong personality and commitment to free trade and investment were reflected in the group's first report in October 1993. APEC's mission, it said, was to 'protect the forces of market-driven interdependence against governmental intrusion that could otherwise retard its natural evolution'.[13] This would be achieved by 'ratcheting up' the GATT process through trade liberalisation and coordination of domestic policy at regional level.[14] The report was highly rhetorical, offered no empirical evidence, and made little attempt to engage with the political economy or social and cultural context in which APEC operates.

At the request of ministers, the group's 1994 report was more specific. Now that the Uruguay Round had 'made the world safe' for outward-looking regionalism, the group advised APEC to commit itself to the goal of free trade and investment in the region by 2020. It anticipated that such a commitment would trigger a new GATT negotiating round.[15] The 1995 report was even more specific, recommending that APEC accelerate commitments to the Uruguay Round, secure a binding regional agreement on investment, and create a voluntary and non-binding mediation service for disputes between governments and the private sector. The report also urged deeper cooperation on monetary and macroeconomic issues, and that APEC work with the IMF to avert another financial crisis like the one that had recently struck Mexico.[16]

The reports of the Eminent Persons Group were 'think-pieces', with no official status. And although the group worked closely with officials, the

Pacific Economic Cooperation Council and later the Pacific Business Forum, its recommendations were viewed by many politicians and officials as too extreme. The group's mandate was not renewed by the APEC leaders in 1995. Yet the existence of the group and its reports made APEC seem more concrete, and it provided the momentum for promoting the 'free trade and investment' goal.

A more permanent source of advice to APEC is the Pacific Economic Cooperation Council, which has had formal observer status from the beginning. The Council operates through specific task groups, forums and sponsored studies, and produces most of the information, analysis and proposals on which APEC relies. It is described as a tripartite body of private sector representatives, academics and government officials, all acting 'in their private capacities'. This gives Council members access to inside information from APEC and its member governments, and allows officials to collaborate on developing proposals without compromising their government roles.[17] Less important is the Pacific Basin Economic Council, which aims to advance 'the economic and social development of the Pacific region as a whole by promoting free and open trade and investment by mutual cooperation between the business worlds in the countries of the region'.[18]

The role of the private sector was strengthened when the first meeting of 'economic leaders' approved the establishment of a Pacific Business Forum to 'specify problems for APEC to handle'. The forum produced a radical report to the ministerial meeting in Osaka in late 1995. Like the report of the Eminent Persons Group, it urged the accelerated implementation of Uruguay Round and APEC commitments, and the expansion of APEC's mandate. It also recommended that a permanent APEC Business Advisory Council be set up to provide APEC with a 'reality check' and economic advice. The leaders agreed.

The mandate of the Business Advisory Council is to advise APEC on the implementation of its commitments and the priorities of the business sector. Originally, each 'economy' was asked to nominate two representatives, one from big business and one from a small or medium-sized enterprise. The number later rose to three, with most representatives coming from big business. In 1998 New Zealand's members were Roseanne Meo (chair of TVNZ and AMP (NZ), and former president of the Employers' Federation); Kerry McDonald (managing director of Comalco, chair of the BNZ and the Japan New Zealand Business Council, and deputy chair of the New Zealand Institute of Economic Research); and Philip Burdon (millionaire mushroom-grower, former Minister for Overseas Trade, and chair of the Asia 2000 Foundation). Meo and McDonald were both members of the Business Roundtable. They were replaced for 1999 by

Douglas Myers (former chair of the Business Roundtable) and Fran Wilde (chair of Tradenz, and a former Labour MP, mayor of Wellington City and director of Brierley Investments Ltd).

Internally, APEC has four standing committees. The Committee on Trade and Investment is responsible for coordinating work on the liberalisation and facilitation of trade and investment, and has numerous subcommittees. The Economic Committee is charged with building APEC's capacity to analyse economic trends and specific issues, and promoting discussion among ministers on macro- and microeconomic issues that affect trade and investment flows. The Budget and Management Committee looks after the programming and operation of APEC activities. A subcommittee on economic and technical cooperation was established in 1998 to help coordinate the 'ecotech' part of the agenda. All standing committees report to the senior officials meetings (known as SOMs), where the main negotiations in APEC occur.

There is a proliferation of other informal committees and 'experts groups'.[19] Some in key areas enjoy the support of powerful APEC members and transnational enterprises. An Electricity Regulators Forum was established by the Energy Working Group. This operated alongside an Ad Hoc Business Forum for Regional Cooperation for Power Infrastructure, to discuss how to reduce the risks for businesses involved in independent or privatised power projects.[20] A working group on advancing the deregulation and privatisation of telecommunications similarly promoted private sector interests in securing infrastructure projects. The establishment of an APEC Financiers Group in 1996 was a significant indication of APEC's growing interest in capital markets.[21]

Nine working groups of officials, private sector representatives and academics also hold regional meetings on their particular subjects.[22] This interaction of technocrats, the private sector and the 'experts' forms the hub of APEC's practical work, although the intensity and quality of its output varies. Some groups are remnants from APEC's early directionless days; others have assumed greater prominence as APEC's priorities have become more focused. Specific governments promote and fund the groups closest to their interests. The working groups concentrate mainly on micro-level issues and the needs of business. Some have produced practical outcomes for large and small exporters, such as lower business transaction costs, the harmonisation of customs procedures, and the documentation of investment rules. Others, such as the telecommunications working group, actively promote deregulation and privatisation. Some governments, including New Zealand's, have complained that APEC's work programme has become too big and diffuse, and a review of these activities was approved in 1998.

Academics have played a marginal role in APEC. At the leaders' meeting in Seattle in 1993, the US proposed setting up an APEC study centre in every member 'economy'. These were intended to promote the APEC agenda through collaborative research, exchanges among like-minded academics, and training for current and future leaders in politics and business. The study centres were slow to get off the ground. Governments were reluctant to fund the project, and few academics were interested in APEC. After a push from Washington, the number of study centres grew, although they had no interface with the formal meetings. New Zealand's study centre was established at the University of Auckland in 1995. The first conference of study centres in Manila in May 1996 attempted to establish some coherence, and to connect the centres to that year's APEC agenda. The papers showed a divergence of positions which largely paralleled those of the presenters' governments, although none was actively critical of APEC. The centres have since met annually, but remain peripheral. The most committed academics tend also to be involved in the Pacific Economic Cooperation Council.

Politicians have played a relatively passive role in the APEC process. Except where contentious matters require resolution, they mainly approve the outcomes their officials have pre-scripted. For the first four years, only the ministers of trade or foreign affairs were involved. The programme then expanded to include meetings of ministers of finance, trade, environment, commerce and industry, education, human resources development, telecommunications, small and medium enterprises, energy, science and technology, and sustainable development. Some, notably finance ministers, became increasingly prominent; others, such as education or environment ministers, remained peripheral.

The presence of government leaders is mainly symbolic. The idea of a heads of government meeting was floated in late 1992. President Clinton agreed, somewhat reluctantly, to host a one-day gathering of APEC 'economic leaders' immediately following the 1993 ministerial meeting in Seattle. His advisors stressed that this would be an informal meeting, not a summit, and there would be no communiqué or pre-scripting of discussions. The 'non-summit' would signal the US administration's support for APEC, and give it the imprimatur of the region's leaders as a whole. As one senior APEC official put it, 'the meeting was the message'.[23]

The 'economic leaders' have since met annually. The formal declarations from their summits are brief, vague and exhortatory, and largely put the political seal on what ministers have already agreed. But the summits do serve other purposes. The leaders use the opportunity to hold collective and bilateral dialogue on diverse matters, often unrelated to APEC. The summits are also an important public relations exercise for the host and member governments. The lack of substantive outcomes from these meetings prompted the *Financial Times* in 1996 to report on the Manila summit under the headline: 'A Perfect Excuse to Chat', observing that the 'harsh truth facing leaders of the 18 countries who attended is that the expression is embarrassingly apt'.[24] By the Kuala Lumpur summit in 1998, the APEC acronym was being translated as 'Aging Politicians Enjoying Cocktails'. *New Zealand Herald* reporter John Armstrong was scathing: 'This year's declaration looked as fresh as week-old bread. And about as digestible. Most of it was drafted weeks ago and then watered down as officials haggled over every word, comma and full-stop. Are the politicians really there just to make up the numbers? Of course they are.'[25]

The attitudes of key leaders have also undermined APEC's credibility. President Clinton's decision to stay home in 1995 to deal with the US budget crisis was taken by many at Osaka to indicate that APEC was a low priority for the US. His absence again in 1998 was compounded by Vice-President Al Gore's calculated provocation of his Malaysian hosts by endorsing the local pro-democracy movement. Malaysian Prime Minister Mahathir had himself boycotted the initial Seattle meeting in 1993, alleging a US takeover of APEC, and maintained a consistently outspoken, independent line.

The scale and extravagance of the leaders' summits fuelled media and hence public criticism. A Manila newspaper reported Philippine officials as saying Japan had spent US$2 billion on the Osaka summit in 1995.[26] The Philippine government spent US$50 million on 21 villas where the APEC leaders spent around six hours (although the villas were expected to be sold at a premium).[27] The cost of the Vancouver meeting was estimated at C$57 million. The corresponding benefits predicted by a Vancouver Tourism study were C$13 million in visitor spending and C$10 million in economic spin-offs. Some C$13 million was spent on security.[28] The budgeted cost for hosting APEC in New Zealand in 1999 was NZ$46 million, including $18 million on security.[29]

The ministerial and leaders' meetings became a magnet for any business interest group or lobby with some connection to the region. Some received unofficial recognition. In 1997, for example, the first APEC meeting of chief executives was held parallel to the summit, and was addressed by six government leaders and twenty ministers. Most of the major transnationals and free-market think-tanks were represented, with a leading role played by the Business Council on National Issues (Canada's equivalent of the Business Roundtable).

APEC maintained close links with other inter-governmental economic agencies working in the region. The 1993 report of the Eminent Persons

Group saw one of APEC's roles as helping to bind the Asian tiger economies into the global economic policy framework:

> Current efforts to strengthen international macroeconomic policy cooperation are based in the G-7, the IMF and the OECD. The rapidly increasing importance of APEC economies, most of which are not represented in either the G-7 or the OECD, also suggests that there is scope for complementary efforts within APEC.[30]

As part of this process, people from the IMF, Asian Development Bank and similar agencies regularly attend and present papers at APEC-related meetings.[31]

The interface between APEC and the WTO is especially significant. It is a basic principle that all APEC activities must be consistent with the GATT, and a key objective is to give momentum to the WTO process. APEC's meeting of trade ministers in Montreal in May 1997 was attended by WTO Director-General Renato Ruggiero. Member 'economies' encouraged their officials in Geneva (the WTO headquarters) to meet regularly to ensure that APEC perspectives were heard within the WTO programme. APEC's ability to act as a catalyst was tested in 1996, when the leaders' meeting in Manila immediately preceded the first WTO ministerial meeting in Singapore. The US sought support from APEC ministers for zero tariffs on information technology, but initially failed, with Malaysia and Chile expressing concern over the speed of liberalisation and the need to protect certain areas of technology. At the leaders' meeting, President Clinton secured a much stronger (although not unconditional) endorsement of his proposal, with some provision for 'flexibility'.[32] This support proved significant in sealing the US-backed deal in Singapore. The APEC leaders also supported US-led efforts to complete outstanding WTO negotiations on basic telecommunications and financial services.[33]

APEC's role as a preparatory forum for the WTO is one of its most tangible outcomes. At the same time, however, some members have sidestepped pressure to make commitments within APEC by insisting that certain matters are dealt with at the WTO. Malaysia has consistently taken that line, as did Japan during the controversy over liberalisation of fisheries and forest products in 1998 (discussed below).

▲ COMPETING PARADIGMS

It is difficult enough to describe what APEC is; it is even harder to identify what APEC has achieved. Since 1993 there has been an internal tussle over the economic model APEC should adopt in promoting regional economic integration. This began in Seattle in 1993, when the US, as the APEC chair, began pushing hard for a binding regime of free trade and investment. This first meeting of APEC leaders made a broad commitment to reducing barriers to trade and investment. A flurry of activity followed.

The core document was a draft code for regional investment, prepared by the Trade Policy Forum of the Pacific Economic Cooperation Council.[34] This contained the standard commitments found in bilateral investment treaties – to national treatment, 'most favoured nation' status, transparency, and free and prompt transfers of currency, plus clauses protecting investors from nationalisation and expropriation. Members would commit themselves to reducing restrictions over time, and aim to harmonise their foreign investment policies, especially on tax legislation, incentives and subsidies. On the sensitive question of regulatory competition, the draft said it would not be 'appropriate to relax domestic health, safety and environmental measures for the *sole* purpose of encouraging investment'.[35] Although the code would be accepted voluntarily and not be enforceable, competitive disadvantage was expected to lead all APEC members to join eventually. The Council even suggested that the international financial institutions could assist by making compliance with the code a condition of loans to any APEC country.[36] In return, investors were 'expected' to act as 'good corporate citizens', recognise the rights of host governments, and contribute to the well-being of the host economy; they were also 'encouraged' to accept standards of corporate behaviour that were sensitive to local values and customs, and to comply with local laws and policies.[37]

The first report of the Eminent Persons Group in 1993 endorsed an Asia Pacific Investment Code, which 'should probably begin as a voluntary instrument but its conversion into a binding treaty should be considered over time'.[38] The 1994 report went further, supporting a commitment to free trade and investment in the region; the process would begin in 2000, and be completed by 2020. Having made that commitment, members should be bound to comply (which implies that APEC would also develop or endorse an enforcement mechanism). The report of the Pacific Business Forum suggested a tighter deadline of 2002 for 'developed' economies and 2010 for the rest.

▲ The Bogor Declaration 1994

Following an intense debate, the ministerial meeting in Jakarta in November 1994 adopted a set of 'non-binding investment principles' to achieve free trade and investment in the region by 2010 for 'developed member economies' and 2020 for 'developing economies'. Several days later, the leaders' meeting endorsed that goal. The preamble to their Bogor Declaration described the investment principles as 'consensual' and 'non-binding', and the wording was very loose. Even so, Malaysian Prime Minister Mahathir condemned the move as US-driven, and issued his own annex to the Declaration which made it even looser. Mahathir was ridiculed by the non-Asian media, politicians and officials, but his insistence on pragmatism was consistent with APEC's original objectives. And he was not alone. Among those who were more quietly concerned were the Japanese, who were about to assume the chair of APEC.

▴ *The Osaka Action Agenda 1995*

The liberalisation aspect of APEC had now gained ascendancy over economic cooperation. This threatened APEC's founding commitment to pragmatic compromise. The Japanese, in the chair in 1995, were expected to produce an agreed plan for implementing the 2010/2020 goal. Various interests, including both the Pacific Business Forum and the Eminent Persons Group, suggested ways to make these commitments binding and enforceable. The neo-liberal bloc went to Osaka demanding watertight commitments that could be monitored and compared. New Zealand ministers and officials deemed it their mission to eliminate any 'wriggle room'.[39] By contrast, the Malaysian member on the Eminent Persons Group had challenged the Bogor Declaration's standing, arguing that:

> ... the APEC economic leaders met for only a couple of hours, during which they read prepared texts. They did not debate the issues substantively ... It is a travesty to now use what is a political declaration to. ... imply that it is a legal 'agreement', legally binding the members to specific actions in specific areas, when the leaders did not even know they were addressing these specific issues, still less agreeing to them.[40]

Ministers eventually endorsed an Osaka Action Agenda that was exceedingly opaque and offered a vague list of guiding principles 'to achieve the long-term goal of free and open trade and investment'.[41] The accompanying text was full of phrases such as 'endeavor to ensure', 'endeavor to apply', 'endeavor to refrain from'. It reiterated the need for 'flexibility', given the different levels of economic development and diverse circumstances in each APEC economy. And it opted for 'concerted unilateral liberalisation', which meant that each member could determine its own plan for achieving the goal of the Bogor Declaration.[42]

At the ministerial press conference, the battle of interpretations began. Malaysia's trade minister insisted that 'voluntary and non-binding' meant that her country would meet the Bogor target date if it could:

First of all, there is no obligation on any APEC member to liberalize, whether it is 2010 or 2020. These are only indicative dates ... Malaysia fully supports this Action Agenda, and we are fully aware of the fact that where we can proceed and complete liberalization in some areas, we shall indeed do so. Where we have difficulties, we shall go according to the pace that we are comfortable with ... .[43]

South Korea and Japan took a similar position, although expressed somewhat more cryptically. Japanese officials described the commitments as only 'politically binding'; members 'should' liberalise by the deadlines, but 'when we say flexibility, it means flexibility'.[44] Similar ambiguity arose over whether *free* trade and investment meant *zero* tariffs and investment restrictions, or something less extreme. The Japanese claimed there was no consensus for zero tariffs.[45] Because this was not a free trade agreement, the terms did not have to be defined; such was the 'unique Asia-Pacific Way'.[46] The US responded to such obfuscation by accusing Japan of trying to protect its agricultural markets for domestic reasons.

The Australians offered their own variation, arguing that flexibility was 'not about whether the end dates are achieved, but about the process by which they are achieved'. Ultimately, the Bogor Declaration was 'a voluntary commitment to try very hard to achieve these objectives ... if someone can't or won't meet the commitments, then there's no particular sanctions available against them'. However, they were confident that the 'combination of self-interest and peer group pressure will produce the outcomes'.[47]

Members were also asked to present 'down-payments' or initial commitments at Osaka towards achieving the Bogor goal. These proved minimal, not least from the US, which claimed to be already more liberal than anyone else. Further concrete commitments, including timetables, were to be produced at the 1996 Manila meeting for implementation from January 1997. These would include individual action plans from each country, collective action plans negotiated among APEC members, and proposals linked to the WTO. Refining APEC's understanding of 'free and open investment' was relegated to a medium-term goal. Considering the merits of an APEC-wide investment agreement was an even more remote goal.[48]

The action plans sought commitments from APEC members on key areas of domestic policy. New Zealand was the so-called 'lead shepherd' on proposals dealing with deregulation and competition policy. Among the collective actions sought from APEC members were annual reports on steps taken to deregulate domestic regimes, including corporatisation and privatisation. Members were promised dialogue to help them identify 'best practice' experiences. Possibilities for the future work programme included the development of APEC guidelines on domestic deregulation, involving the business community.[49]

Although the process in the Osaka Action Agenda was structured to require commitments to both liberalisation and economic cooperation, the focus was on the former. To balance this, Japan announced a 10 billion yen initiative called 'Partners for Progress'. It was designed to promote market-friendly development cooperation in the region by encouraging common policy concepts, joint activities and policy dialogue.[50] Enabling each 'economy' to contribute information, knowledge, experience and expertise meant that members could move away from their outmoded donor/donee relationships. Preferred project areas included human resource development, industrial science and technology, economic infrastructure, energy, transport, and telecommunications. Consistent with the official APEC ethos, the projects would reflect genuine partnership, respect for diversity, mutual benefit, and consensus-building. By promoting this, Japan was clearly challenging the dominance of the free trade and investment goal.

▲ Manila Action Plan for APEC 1996

President Ramos used his turn as APEC's chair to showcase the Philippines to fellow governments and foreign investors, under the official slogan 'APEC means business'. The individual action plans of member countries were negotiated by officials throughout the year. They were meant to remain secret until signed at Manila; only those whom governments and officials chose to consult would know in advance what governments were promising to do. Much to the irritation of APEC governments, the second drafts of the plans were leaked to NGOs in Hong Kong and subsequently posted on the Internet. For the first time since APEC was formed, governments could be called to account for the promises they intended making, before they were made.

APEC became a domestic issue in New Zealand for the first time. The National government's draft plan promised to maintain the deregulatory changes of the previous twelve years. It also included commitments to:

- complete the existing tariff reduction programme, undertake another review in 1998, and consider binding these reductions at the WTO (so they could not be reversed)
- maintain and review the existing foreign and domestic investment regime
- continue to deregulate utility and essential facility markets
- continue to consider the scope for further privatisations of state-owned businesses and assets
- actively promote the removal of restrictions on provision of services by foreign suppliers through the GATS (for example, in tourism, advertising

and education) and consider extending the services covered (for example, to include broadcasting and health)
- keep open the market for government procurement (so that preference could not be given to local suppliers)
- complete law reforms and administrative changes to make it easier to register and enforce intellectual property rights.

The Customs Department schedules in New Zealand's plan prohibited the importation of goods manufactured by prison labour. Ironically, the Department of Corrections had just bought a recently closed shoe factory in Wanganui, which it was reopening using prison labour. Corrections Minister Paul East had announced the goal of turning 'every prison into a factory and every prisoner into a worker'.[51]

The leak caused some problems for the New Zealand government. During the November 1996 APEC meeting, negotiations were still under way to form a coalition government, and it was unclear whether New Zealand First, which held the balance of power, would join with Labour (and probably the Alliance) or National. Acting Prime Minister Jim Bolger and acting Foreign Affairs Minister Don McKinnon could attend the APEC meeting only in a caretaker capacity, and had no constitutional mandate to commit future governments to anything. They argued that New Zealand's plan was unobjectionable because it reflected existing law and policy. Yet the leaked draft conflicted with key election promises by Labour, the Alliance and New Zealand First. In an ironic twist, the New Zealand government now embraced the principle of voluntarism, although Bolger limited this to *how*, not *whether*, the Bogor goal was achieved. In a letter to Alliance leader Jim Anderton, he wrote: 'At its heart, APEC is a voluntary process', which leaves 'each economy with the flexibility to move toward the agreed APEC liberalisation goals at a pace, and in a manner, which is determined by them'. A future government could decide the manner and rate at which New Zealand met its commitments.[52] McKinnon went further, describing APEC as only morally binding. A future government could walk away from a commitment at any time – although this would probably mean the end of the country's participation in APEC.[53]

In Manila, old difficulties of interpretation and substance re-emerged. The Manila Action Plan for APEC (MAPA), which set out the individual and collective plans, was a non-event, although there was some attempt to talk it up.[54] The subsequent Business Advisory Council report was highly critical of APEC's progress.[55] Most economies had not moved significantly beyond their Uruguay Round commitments. There was some progress on tariffs, but almost half the countries just repeated their GATT offers, and only five out of eighteen indicated a zero tariff by 2010/2020. There were few commitments on finance and investment, and little on non-tariff measures or services. The Business Advisory Council noted, rather tartly, that databases and additional meetings might be useful, but were no substitute for liberalisation. Businesses wanted stronger, more standardised and specific commitments to the Bogor goal on both free trade and liberal investment flows.

The Philippine government was defensive, insisting that these were the first steps in an evolutionary process; the real gains of APEC could not be assessed until 2010/2020.[56] New Zealand's Don McKinnon was philosophical – while the specific content of plans was disappointing, domestic political pressures limited how far some members could go.[57]

▲ The Vancouver Year of Action 1997

Canada had, unwittingly, drawn the short straw as the chair for 1997. This was to have been APEC's Year of Action. At the time, challenges to the agenda of global free trade and investment were growing across the OECD. The stock-market crisis in Hong Kong was followed in July by the financial meltdown among the 'tiger cub' economies of Thailand and Indonesia, and to a lesser extent Malaysia and the Philippines. As the APEC ministers and leaders were meeting in Vancouver in November 1997, the Japanese banking sector suffered several major collapses, and the massive IMF bail-out of the South Korean economy was announced. This was especially embarrassing for APEC, whose leaders in Osaka in 1995 had attributed the region's successes to market-oriented policies.

> The Asia-Pacific is experiencing the most striking economic growth in the world and ever-increasing interdependence. It is a major contributor to global prosperity and stability. We believe our economic reforms based on market-oriented mechanisms have unleashed our peoples' creativity and energy and enhanced the prosperity and living standards of our citizens in the region and the world as a whole.[58]

APEC embarked on damage control. All efforts focused on reassuring the markets – an increasingly difficult task over the week. APEC leaders asserted their faith in the region's 'dynamism and resilience'; they believed that 'the prospects for economic growth in the region are strong', and that Asia-Pacific 'will continue to play a leading role in the global economy'. They remained convinced that open markets would bring significant benefits, and were determined to continue their liberalisation programme. It was inconceivable that their model might have failed. The former exemplars were now blamed for their lack of market discipline. They needed to adopt more 'prudent and transparent' structural adjustment and financial sector policies. Finance ministers were urged to work closely with central bankers to promote the development of financial and capital markets and support freer and more stable capital flows.[59]

The Japanese argued unsuccessfully for a specifically regional approach to the crisis. Pushed by the US, the 'economic leaders' in Vancouver opted instead to support an IMF-led package negotiated in Manila the week before.[60] This strengthened the arm of the US government, which had become impatient with APEC as a means of securing its liberalisation goals. APEC members committed themselves to work with the international financial institutions and cooperate with each other to strengthen their financial systems and markets.[61]

Some negotiators and commentators were concerned that the crisis would divert energy from APEC's free trade and investment goals. Others saw it as a window of opportunity. The hurriedly revised *Economic Outlook* report for 1997 from the Pacific Economic Cooperation Council insisted that 'sound' macroeconomic policies held the key to stability. It even claimed that, by hastening the resolution of unsustainable policy mixes and currency misalignments in the region, the recent turbulence might have enhanced the APEC region's longer-term prospects, though at the cost of somewhat reduced short-term growth. The Bogor goal could still be achieved, if policies of market deregulation, opening trade and capital markets, government spending cuts and privatisation were implemented. However, 'the pace of reforms may need to be accelerated to maintain the confidence of markets'.[62] In other words, the short-term pain of the crisis would force adjustments that produced long-term gain.

APEC's Year of Action did produce one major initiative. It had become clear that consensus was almost impossible on sensitive issues. Unilateral commitments would be slow. Collective commitments were also cautious and limited. Consequently, 'early voluntary sector liberalisation' was proposed, whereby member 'economies' would make commitments to liberalise in specific sectors which would later feed into the WTO. The idea had first been aired in 1995 in response to the unfinished business of the Uruguay Round, and by the Vancouver meeting officials had produced a list of fifteen possible sectors. These were reduced by negotiation to nine: fish and fish products; forest products; toys; jewellery; a mutual recognition agreement for telecommunication equipment; energy; chemicals; medical equipment; and environmental goods and services. Officials were set to work on detailed commitments during 1998 for implementation at the beginning of 1999. The remaining six sectors, plus others, would be addressed later. Chile and Mexico opted out of the process.[63]

New Zealand's trade minister, Lockwood Smith, repeatedly hailed the inclusion of forestry and fisheries as a significant gain. He predicted that the deal would 'be finalised this year, and will then go to the World Trade Organisation for possible global application'.[64] This optimistic statement treated the deal as done, and forgot to mention that voluntarism could see more countries opting out. Japan in particular, a major player in the process, had made it clear in Vancouver that it was not going to make commitments on forestry or fisheries.

▲ Malaysia 1998: APEC in Crisis

In 1998, Malaysia was in the chair. APEC seemed paralysed. Most of the Asian governments wanted to focus on its economic cooperation and trade facilitation role. They were in no mood for major moves on liberalisation, which they believed would leave the battered East Asian economies even more vulnerable. This signalled problems for the negotiations on early voluntary sector liberalisation. During the year Malaysia's trade minister, Rafidah Aziz, insisted that the principles of voluntarism and flexibility should be maintained and reflect each country's capacity.[65] Japan steadfastly maintained that it would not agree to tariff cuts on forest and fish products, although it was prepared to see those sectors included in broad-based negotiations at the WTO.[66] Japan's obstinacy threatened APEC's already shaky credibility. If other countries followed its example, the Bogor Declaration would be consigned to history.

At the ministerial meeting in November, after days of intense negotiation, it was decided to refer the package on to the WTO. Japan, having won, hailed APEC's principles of flexibility and voluntarism. Despite face-saving claims by various APEC ministers (including New Zealand's) that the negotiations at the WTO could be completed in 1999, they seemed much more likely to end up as part of the new 'millennium round', meaning that any firm commitments were years down the track. The US had demonised the Japanese for their protectionist attitudes and for threatening the future of APEC. Yet US Trade Representative Charlene Barshefsky admitted that she had no legal authority to commit the US to the kind of unilateral tariff cuts she had demanded of Japan, and that the US would negotiate each of these sectors at the WTO only if a critical mass of major traders was prepared to do so.[67] The Australians described the 'less-than-desirable compromise' as a 'fig leaf'.[68] Meanwhile, New Zealand's ever-optimistic ministers portrayed it as a victory snatched from the jaws of defeat.

APEC had survived, but to what tangible end? While officials and ministers were preoccupied with Japan's threat to the 2010/2020 goal, APEC member 'economies' were mired in an ongoing economic crisis that was devastating the lives of millions of people. Many had expected APEC, as the region's primary economic forum, to address the problem. An editorial in the *Weekend Australian* warned: 'If the forum cannot make progress on issues that promote recovery from the East Asian economic crisis, it must show cause why it should not be wound up'.[69] It did neither. APEC's Business Advisory Council was equally critical of the ministers' failure to grapple with the Asian crisis by taking decisive collective action to restore investor confidence and promote currency stability. In a straw poll at the parallel business forum, half the participants thought APEC's response to the crisis was 'poor'; the other half thought it was 'woeful'. They said that APEC was out of touch; that its structure was inappropriate to deal with these issues; that it had become irrelevant.

The gathering of 'economic leaders' added fuel to the fire. As mentioned earlier, President Clinton failed to show up, and Vice-President Gore made a provocative speech endorsing the Malaysian pro-democracy movement, known as *reformasi*.[70] Prime Minister Mahathir, as host, played down APEC's role relative to the WTO, and insisted that international financial reforms were needed to minimise exchange rate volatility and currency speculation. He received only polite support. The ministerial statement scripted by the Malaysians did express concern about the serious effects of the Asian crisis on prospects for growth and employment, and on poverty. Senior officials were instructed to intensify APEC's efforts to address the social impacts of the crisis as a high priority. But their solution was to strengthen international and domestic financial systems, develop capital markets, liberalise trade and investment, and formulate measures for social safety-nets.[71]

As the incoming chair, New Zealand Prime Minister Jenny Shipley said that no single economy had a 'monopoly on wisdom in the area of reform' – and then offered New Zealand as an exemplar:

> New Zealand has some experience in moving from a highly regulated to an open economy. There is much we can learn from each other about what has worked and what has not in terms of providing the stable and enduring conditions in which governments, business and investors can have confidence. New Zealand has not escaped the economic crisis in the region. Far from it. But without our economic reforms, New Zealand would have been much worse off. In that sense there is opportunity, as well as risk, in the current downturn.[72]

New Zealand journalists pulled no punches about the prospects for APEC in 1999. Even free market supporter Fran O'Sullivan wrote in the *New Zealand Herald* that no amount of 'spin-meistering' could obscure the reality that the APEC leaders had 'dropped the ball': 'While there is a great opportunity for New Zealand to put some spine back into Apec next year, the forum's very relevance is also being questioned by regional business leaders'.[73]

▲ The External Conflict

At the same time, APEC faced vigorous challenges to the market-centred model for regional economic development. The most visible opposition clustered around the annual APEC meetings, wherever they were held. In Seattle in 1993 there had been some localised opposition from NGOs (mainly American). From 1994 a counter-network of NGOs, unions, human rights and environmental groups began to emerge in the region. A meeting in Bangkok of the Working Group on APEC (part of the People's Project for the 21st Century) issued a statement urging discussion and debate on APEC's role. It proposed an alternative, people-centred approach to economic and social self-determination through a regional social charter, which would 'ensure that urban and rural workers, subsistence consumers, small scale and informal sector producers are effectively protected against the onslaught of economic globalization'.[74]

In Jakarta in 1994, the Suharto government banned meetings and the press conference called by representatives of NGOs from various Asian and Pacific countries, who had gathered to speak out against APEC. In preparation for the APEC summit, the streets had been cleared of itinerants and the poor. The military cracked down on dissident journalists, although they dealt more diplomatically with East Timorese students who had occupied the US Embassy compound. Meanwhile, APEC leaders in their batik shirts stood beside Suharto, smiling and waving to the cameras.

Prior to the APEC summit in Osaka a year later, a meeting was held of representatives from over one hundred NGOs and unions concerned with human rights, labour issues, the environment, and economic and social justice. Their Kyoto Declaration supported cooperation among the countries and peoples of the region, but condemned APEC's trade liberalisation agenda for negating the developmental and democratic aspirations of the people:

> Economic growth and promotion of trade are not ends in themselves. Genuine development must be centred on the needs of people and nature, and deliver real social and economic justice. The form of indiscriminate, unregulated economic growth and trade which APEC advocates delivers the opposite of this.[75]

The Japanese government did its own street-cleaning in preparation for the summit. The homeless people who lived in the square outside the conference venue were forcibly relocated to the other side of town. Local journalists reported that in the ensuing inter-group conflict at least one person died.[76]

In 1996 APEC came under particularly heavy attack at meetings, rallies and demonstrations across the Philippines. At least three different counter-APEC forums were held, several with a strong international presence. Two weeks before the summit, the Philippine government announced it had a black-list of at least one hundred people from eighteen countries who would be refused entry to attend the counter-APEC meetings. The list included Jose Ramos Horta, the East Timor independence leader and winner of the 1997 Nobel Peace Prize; Archbishop Desmond Tutu; and Danielle Mitterand, wife of the former French president.[77] President Ramos said the reason for the ban was 'not so much the threat to national security', but rather that the presence of such people at the counter-APEC forums was 'inimical to our national interest'.[78] The Indonesian government was already a major investor in the Philippines. One radio reporter portrayed Ramos as building a wall around APEC to keep his own people out.[79] A column in the *Philippine Daily Inquirer* asked: 'If you can allow goods to flow freely into countries, why can't you do the same thing for ideas?'[80]

As part of a US$1 million APEC 'beautification' programme, the Philippine government allegedly demolished the shanties of over 33,000 families to create an 'eye-sore-free' zone for foreign dignitaries.[81] Farmland in the Clark Special Economic Zone where the leaders would meet was cleared for extensions to the airport runway, despite farmers' protests that they were not allowed to harvest their crops first. A state of virtual martial law was declared in the surrounding area, with massive troop mobilisation and activation of paramilitary groups, curfews and checkpoints.[82] Limousines ferrying dignitaries sped up and down the APEC 'friendship lanes', fatally injuring two pedestrians in the process. Meanwhile, workers stuck in traffic jams had their pay docked for being late. Locals who knew nothing about trade liberalisation became instantly anti-APEC. The idea that removing national protections and extending the hold of transnational enterprises over the Philippine economy would solve their problems of endemic poverty seemed fanciful. Cardinal Sin cautioned the government 'not to cede the common good of the Filipinos, particularly the poor, by hastily committing itself to liberalization and abandoning its role to protect homegrown industries'.[83]

In Vancouver in 1997, there was yet another 'summit' of unions, human rights groups and NGOs. The gathering had become even bigger and was largely unproductive, prompting one New Zealand participant to dub it 'the NGO Olympics'.[84] Its role as an independent critical forum was also compromised by Canadian domestic politics, being part-funded by the federal and provincial governments. The 'People's Summit' posed no threat to APEC. But other opposition apparently did. Security documents identified 'long-standing native issues in British Columbia such as gaming, self-government, land claims, fishing rights and resource control over claimed lands' as a 'potential security risk', along with 'a collection of ad-hoc groups opposed to APEC'.[85] When students protested at the leaders' meeting being held at the University of British Columbia, their non-violent demonstration was broken up by Royal Canadian Mounted Police, who sprayed disabling pepper on them and members of the media. This, and other alleged excesses, became the subject of a formal inquiry and civil law suits. Official documents disclosed that the Prime Minister's Office had assured Indonesia's President Suharto that he would be shielded from politically embarrassing protests.[86]

During the Vancouver meeting, the voice of indigenous peoples on APEC was heard for the first time. The Union of British Columbia Indian Chiefs, marginalised from the People's Summit as well as the official event, issued its own challenge to the APEC process and agenda:

> The avoidance of dealing with our Peoples, on our terms, must cease. Treaty and non-treaty Indigenous Nations shall not surrender, cede our Aboriginal Title for an economic development agreement which deprives our future generations of benefits from their sacred homelands. We give notice to the APEC state leaders and their corporate elite that investment, especially in British Columbia, remains very uncertain.[87]

A conference of indigenous peoples from the South Pacific and APEC countries urged a different approach to Asia Pacific economic development using 'alternative trading networks based on our own traditional values and principles'. They gave examples of successful eco-timber projects that adopted an environmentally sensitive approach and shared the profits among resource- and land-owning communities.[88] These were not the only indigenous voices. On the other side of Vancouver, the Native Business Unit of the Canadian Ministry of Commerce was hosting a trade fair, in line with Aboriginal Business Canada's strategy of promoting development through trade and market expansion in the Pacific Rim.[89] Participants from New Zealand, Australia and Canada appeared on television to praise the opportunities offered by a deregulated global economy.

In Malaysia in 1998, the formal NGO 'summit' was part-funded by the federal Canadian government, and predictably did little to further action against APEC. But the gathering was an important opportunity for local unionists, women and other activists seeking democratic and social reforms in Malaysia to be heard in some safety. Ironically, the Americans' self-interested endorsement of the *reformasi* gave Prime Minister Mahathir ammunition to allege that the dissidents were part of a US-backed conspiracy. Several leaders, including a labour organiser of the People's Summit, were arrested within days.

Most APEC governments remained hostile to, or dismissive of, the NGOs and these annual meetings. But the international media, often bored with and increasingly sceptical of APEC, picked up the NGOs' concerns and activities. Some APEC members felt the need to respond to this pressure, especially the host governments. In 1996 the Philippine official in charge of the APEC meetings sought to defuse local opposition by suggesting that:

> ... the networks of civil society deserve attention in a participatory framework of markets corrected for failures due to externalities and non-provision of public goods. Viewed this way, *truly representative non-government organizations* must therefore be given chances to present their own agenda *for eventual incorporation* by the intergovernmental network of APEC in the implementation of action plans.[90]

This proposal raised more questions than it answered. Who would be considered a 'truly representative' NGO, by whom, and according to what criteria? Could NGOs, by their very nature, ever be 'truly representative'? To whom would they be accountable? On what terms might they be incorporated? Would only the well-resourced, well-connected organisations, approved by their governments or funded by major US or European foundations, be allowed in? How would such NGOs need to perform to maintain their credibility and credentials with APEC? Given that the Pacific Economic Cooperation Council defines itself as an NGO, could employers' organisations or neo-liberal think-tanks seek inclusion too? Which parts of the APEC network would mandated NGOs engage with – the working groups, ad hoc expert groups, standing committees, senior officials' meetings, ministerial meetings or leaders' meetings? The higher up the decision-making ladder, the less likely access would be. How could the democratic, social, cultural and environmental deficits attributed to APEC be remedied by NGOs taking part on the periphery, and on APEC's terms?

The Philippine government's solution was to offer the mildest critics a marginal role. In a highly publicised dialogue with a selected group of environmental NGOs, the government promised an APEC driven by principles of sustainable development and with a human face. The senior official claimed that the costs of structural adjustment would be a 'hot issue' in official discussions.[91] According to New Zealand's Don McKinnon, the subject was never discussed – nor, given APEC's economic parameters, would it have been appropriate or acceptable. Civil society and social costs were matters for each country to address domestically in its own way.[92] Similarly, Australian Prime Minister John Howard noted that there were 'lots of other forums to deal with those things', and that APEC should make further progress on the economic and trade front before becoming involved in 'other things'.[93]

Attempts to portray APEC with a human face continued when Canada took the chair in 1997. The Canadian government's *Results Report* noted that NGOs had participated in several 'high level' APEC meetings, mainly on environmental and human resource development issues.[94] Alongside the formal summit, the Canadian government had hosted an assembly of youth leaders. A second meeting of the Women Leaders' Network had addressed the concerns of women in business (with no attempt to explain how their proposals would alleviate the powerlessness and endemic poverty of hundreds of millions of women in the region).[95] Reflecting the Canadian position, the Vancouver leaders' statement observed that: 'Equity, poverty alleviation and quality of life are central considerations and must be addressed as integral to sustainable development'.[96] But there was no suggestion that these might require some rethinking of APEC's free trade and investment agenda. At Kuala Lumpur, Canada again proposed that APEC's programme be broadened to include social, human rights and environmental issues, and to provide a role for NGOs. Whatever Canada's motives, there was no remote chance of the proposal being accepted by a consensus of APEC 'economies'.

As in APEC itself, disparities emerged among its critics. Many Western NGOs and unions sought to engage APEC in dialogue over their concerns, mainly about labour standards and the environment.[97] APEC treated environmental issues as peripheral, and defined them in market-friendly terms. The first meeting of environment ministers, in March 1994, was initiated by Canada, whose proposal for a new body to promote environmental cooperation found no support. Moves by New Zealand's Simon Upton to promote economic environmental instruments, such as tradeable pollution rights, fell equally flat. A minimalist position emerged: a framework of principles for sustainable development would be 'fully integrated' into the programme of each working group and policy committee, and the senior officials would follow it up.[98] A ministerial meeting on sustainable development in June 1997 was again hosted by Canada, as APEC's chair. It had a narrow focus, framed by the leaders' call for a work programme on the sustainability of the marine environment, cleaner production, and sustainable cities.[99] This complemented ongoing work on a Japanese-initiated project to reconcile economic growth, energy requirements and environmental sustainability.[100] APEC's Economic Committee also began to prepare a database of environmental measures that impacted on trade liberalisation and facilitation. APEC had redefined environmental issues to fit its economic objectives.

Labour issues came under the rubric of human resource development. The main pressure for action came from the Asia Pacific Labour Network (APLN), the regional body of ICFTU-affiliated trade unions, whose position largely mirrored that of the parent body at the WTO. Meeting shortly before the Manila summit in 1996, the network prepared a 'trade union vision for APEC'. This asked President Ramos to promote the establishment of a Labour Advisory Forum within APEC to parallel the Business Advisory Council, and the APLN's acceptance on the Human Resource Development Working Group. The stated aim was 'to harness the APEC objective of the internationalization of markets to the improvement of the conditions of work and life of the citizens of our populous region. The reality of economic globalization requires a strategic response reaffirming the human-centred purpose of all growth and development.'[101]

Ramos apparently agreed. The New Zealand Council of Trade Unions (NZCTU), reporting from Manila, said it was 'surprising and refreshing to hear a Head of Government clearly articulate the view that Labour Standards were central to ensuring that the results of economic globalisation had to as a first priority alleviate poverty, improve living standards, and enhance workers' wellbeing'.[102] In 1998 it became official NZCTU policy to seek a 'social dimension in APEC', recognition of an APEC Labour Forum, and union participation in APEC committees, working groups and ministerial meetings.[103] The New Zealand Trade Union Federation (NZTUF), on the other hand, likened the APLN's request to 'urging the tiger to become a vegetarian', and said the proposal would never achieve consensus support among APEC's member 'economies'.[104]

Various APLN unions were subsequently included in national delegations to the Human Resource Development Working Group, a bottom-tier group that reported to senior officials and to periodic ministerial meetings. The first ministerial meeting on human resource development, in Manila in January 1996, initiated an action programme on the need for education and training to develop a flexible and adaptable workforce. When these ministers met again in September 1997, education and training remained the priorities. The working group was directed 'to develop a project in which representatives of labor, management, and government from member economies can exchange views on best practices on training, skills development, the use of technology, and other 'human resources' development related issues in the workplace'.[105]

The working group was concerned with the development of human resources. Union participation might improve some of its outcomes, but would not address the more fundamental issues of the rights of workers and unions. An Asian workers grouping called APEC Labour Monitor (ALARM), established in Hong Kong to coordinate action against the repression of workers in the region, condemned the APLN for legitimising what it saw as APEC's anti-worker agenda, and for delegitimising the voices of workers and unions who wanted to resist. For the NZTUF, whose members included clothing, textile and footwear workers, the APLN's actions also failed to challenge the impact on New Zealand workers of the APEC goals of trade liberalisation, market deregulation and labour market flexibility. During New Zealand's 1998 tariff review, ministers had repeatedly claimed that APEC *required* the removal of all tariffs between signatory countries by 2010 at the latest.[106] They failed to mention that APEC was non-binding and voluntary. The successful campaign to at least defer the elimination of tariffs on textiles, clothing and footwear by 2000 has already been discussed (see Chapter 6). To the NZTUF, opposing such policies at home meant opposing APEC, and any other international economic agreement with a free trade agenda.

Many Asian NGOs and workers' organisations also rejected 'engagement' with APEC, preferring to hasten its demise from outside. Despite some cultural sympathy for their governments' opposition to the US-led liberalisation of trade and investment, their target was not simply Western governments. They challenged the core APEC belief that integrated regional and global markets would improve the well-being of the mass of the region's people.

Their concerns were reinforced by regular documentation by human rights groups of the suffering of the region's poor under liberalisation. A report by Human Rights Watch Asia in 1994 agreed that rapid economic growth had benefited some, but for millions of others it meant low wages, the erosion of health and safety standards, and restrictions on workers' right to organise.[107] Indigenous peoples were dispossessed in brutal acts of cultural genocide. The traditional livelihoods of farmers were being destroyed, with no alternative jobs and incomes being provided. Trafficking of people, especially women and children, had increased. The natural resource base was being depleted, and the environmental degradation in some places was life-threatening. In many countries, free trade and investment regimes were accompanied by human rights abuses, as governments promoting favourable investment conditions silenced their political opponents and public critics, and suppressed attempts by workers or communities to organise collectively.[108] APEC meetings themselves had come to symbolise this repression, as hosts sought to shield themselves and their guests from embarrassment.

The APEC leaders' response to this lack of credibility was to convince people that APEC was good for them. Their 1997 statement noted that:

To underpin our efforts, support among the people of the region for continuing trade and investment liberalization is essential. We welcome the decision by Ministers to develop an APEC-wide work program to assess the full impacts of trade liberalization, including its positive effects on growth and employment, and to assist members [in] managing associated adjustments.[109]

In May 1998, the APEC Secretariat called for proposals from consultants to carry out this work programme, which would 'contribute to advancing community understanding of the benefits of trade and investment liberalisation, while acknowledging the associated adjustment costs'. There was no suggestion of any debate about APEC's goals. 'By raising understanding and support for liberalisation, this project directly contributes to APEC's core trade and investment liberalisation objectives'.[110] The first phase would use case studies to illustrate APEC's benefits; the second phase would develop communications strategies for member governments to use. As a third phase, New Zealand would host a seminar in June 1999 on how to communicate the benefits of trade liberalisation. The key question was not whether APEC's free market agenda was a good thing, but rather how to sell it.

▲ APEC 1999: AOTEAROA NEW ZEALAND

New Zealand's turn to host APEC came in 1999. Back in 1997, Prime Minister Jim Bolger hailed it as New Zealand's 'great opportunity to provide leadership to the Asia Pacific's most dynamic regional grouping'.[111] When 1999 arrived, the government took over what journalist Fran O'Sullivan called 'the poisoned chalice'.[112] The major meetings had been moved from November to September, before New Zealand's scheduled general election late in the year. But this was not the election year showcase that National had hoped for. The New Zealand government fervently believed that the liberalisation of trade and investment brought unquestioned benefits. As Bolger told the APEC trade ministers when opening their meeting in Christchurch in July 1996: 'There is no downside to opening up world trade. All you have to do is overcome political barriers, in other words, attitudinal barriers.'[113] National was not about to abandon that position when it took over the APEC chair in 1999.

One of the government's four goals for 1999 was 'to build broader support for APEC among the wider community'. The public relations machine was slow to crank up. In May 1998 the parliamentary select committee on foreign affairs, defence and trade made an unexpected call for submissions on the implications of New Zealand's participation in

APEC, with hearings scheduled for September. These were deferred until February 1999 – after the disastrous Kuala Lumpur meeting. The hearings were intended to provide a 'good news forum'. About 30 written submissions were lodged, most of which endorsed APEC. But even 'establishment' bodies such as Asia 2000 warned there was a 'real risk of divisions within APEC as a result of the Asian crisis and growing concerns about liberalisation'; it urged APEC to adopt a 'Bogor Plus' approach, which used broader tools than liberalisation to promote regional prosperity.[114] Terence O'Brien from the Centre for Strategic Studies likewise warned that the focus on liberalisation could see the '2010' richer countries become a semi-permanent division within APEC, and cause the grouping to decompose.

Meanwhile, Cabinet approved a public relations strategy to promote 'a broad-based and balanced understanding within APEC communities of the rationale for APEC's trade and investment goals'.[115] Officials advised that: 'Advertising and public relations activities will be required to get the APEC 1999 brand in the market place as quickly as possible, but will not focus on the complex substance of the APEC process such as trade liberalisation or facilitation'.[116] The Auckland City Council's marketing team planned an equally superficial approach: 'the message should state that APEC is good (and why)'.[117]

The government had hoped to reduce the scale of previous years' meetings,[118] but the conference calendar was soon littered with APEC acronyms. There were the three preparatory senior officials' meetings, two ministerial meetings and the leaders' summit. The regular sideshows would involve PECC, ABAC, PBEC and the APEC study centres. There was the peripheral 'social face' of APEC, reflected in meetings of women and youth, a business symposium and forum for CEOs and a meeting of the APLN unions. What participants expected to achieve from these events was unclear.

Discussion of APEC's substantive goals would be targeted to specific groupings. Documents secured under the Official Information Act showed that major business interests would be actively involved in setting APEC's goals for 1999. The government was less interested in small business. The APEC chair usually hosts a ministerial meeting on small and medium enterprises (SME), with a parallel private sector conference. Chile had originally offered to host the meeting for 1999, but withdrew. The New Zealand government then agreed to hold a meeting in Christchurch in April 1999; the cost of around $1 million would be met from existing business promotion funds. Commerce officials suggested that the meeting could be used to get APEC ministers to support microeconomic and regulatory changes to lower business costs to small and medium enterprises. Treasury was less convinced, and warned that: 'Hosting an SME Ministerial carries risks associated with the promotion of industry assistance policy outcomes which are at odds with existing policy settings'.[119] Prior to the conference, local industrialist and deputy director of the Export Institute, Gilbert Ullrich, commented caustically that APEC was being sold as the 'engine room for growth in the region', yet the New Zealand government had not sent anyone to similar conferences for the previous three years; it was clearly not a priority. Noting that unilateral tariff reductions – a key APEC policy – had destroyed many small businesses, Ullrich observed: 'If Apec turns out to have been an exercise in self-delusion, it won't bring back the industries or jobs we consigned to oblivion in our desire to lead the world.'[120] The well-scripted Christchurch business conference produced a communiqué that sat comfortably alongside the one from the ministers' meeting, and avoided any embarrassing suggestion that governments should intervene to support small business.[121]

The government was keen to get Maori on board, especially following the debacle on the MAI (see Chapter 9). Officials advised ministers that:

> A key domestic influence on the Government's success in executing our responsibilities as APEC Chair in 1999 will be the extent to which both partners under the Treaty of Waitangi are involved in the substance and the form of APEC events. The role of Maori in New Zealand society will be a critical part of the image of the country that is presented to the outside world. Maori will have a role in policy input, and in the broader activities in the outreach programmes with NGOs.[122]

Maori would be involved in the powhiri to welcome visiting dignitaries; the details would be 'signed off' before each event, presumably to protect both Maori and the government from embarrassment. Senior Maori figures would be 'positively engaged'. Maori businesses were to be 'mainstreamed' within general business events, although special briefings would be held. Beyond that, Maori groups and spokespeople would be treated according to the strategy of 'constructive engagement' with NGOs. Beyond that again, officials were aware that Maori nationalists would campaign actively against APEC as a symbol of ongoing colonisation.

Some Maori businesses had been involved on the periphery of APEC during 1997, attending the indigenous business meeting in Vancouver. A delegation was sponsored to participate in the business forum held alongside the formal meeting in Kuala Lumpur in 1998. Some Maori entrepreneurs, encouraged by officials within the ministries of Foreign Affairs and Trade and Commerce, were keen to support APEC's push for deregulation; others saw benefits from making business contacts, but otherwise maintained a watching brief.[123] In 1999 officials from Foreign Affairs and Trade and Te Puni Kokiri conducted a series of 'dialogues' around the country with invited Maori. One paper distributed to participants sought to reconcile APEC and the Treaty through the historical role of Maori as traders. Since the early days of trade among Maori and with settlers, the state had assumed more power, and Maori had lost some of their autonomy. A return to free trade would minimise the role of 'the governor', restore trade opportunities for Maori, and best support Maori aspirations for tino rangatiratanga.[124]

Those who attended the 'dialogue workshops' seemed to have their doubts. Key concerns from the Wellington workshop in May 1999 included the lack of voice in APEC for Maori small businesses, with the New Zealand representatives on the Business Advisory Council being drawn from the large corporates; the need for Maori input into policy-making *before* the government formulated its position; the need for honesty in portraying the position of Maori in the New Zealand economy; the need for a strategy to improve the position of Maori labour and Maori businesses in the mainstream economy; and the need to build domestic capacity and reduce disparities at home before attending to the rest of the Asia Pacific region. There were also real doubts about what APEC would deliver to Maori: 'If we accept that globalisation is irreversible we must position Maori for it. Is there a fall-back position if globalisation does not work? Can, for example, the Maori economy operate as an independent "economy" in the same way as APEC economies, not countries, operate in the APEC process?' The workshop participants also called for honesty in recognising that the potential benefits of liberalisation in natural resources like fisheries and forestry 'are subject to the influence of larger APEC member countries. If this is the reality, then should New Zealand be liberalising so quickly, when some of our APEC partners appear hesitant to do so?'[125]

From the officials' viewpoint, the attention NGOs were paying to APEC was both a risk and an opportunity. They warned that government should not become 'bogged down in long, resource-intensive consultation'.[126] Government strategy was to 'demonstrate to the international community New Zealand's ability to accommodate debate and dissent among a variety of NGOs', and to build broad support for APEC. 'Responsive' NGOs would be assisted to 'meet their own objectives of being seen to influence outcomes' – they would have input to policy processes, involvement in events, and 'controlled' access to politicians and officials.[127] This was all about managing dissent. There was no suggestion that politicians and officials might engage seriously with NGOs in debate over APEC's basic goals.

This image of tolerance was seriously dented when security issues surrounding APEC attracted unwelcome attention. In 1998 the Court of Appeal found that the Security Intelligence Service (SIS) had acted unlawfully in breaking and entering the house of Aziz Choudry in July 1996, when he was organising an anti-APEC conference during the trade ministers' meeting in Christchurch. Amendments to the SIS legislation to legalise the break-in caused a furore. The government was forced to revisit (albeit inadequately) the definition of 'security' introduced in 1996, which allowed the SIS to monitor people who were considered a risk to New Zealand's 'international or economic well-being'.[128] Other stories of overzealous security preparations included the harassment of students, Chilean exiles and other human rights activists.[129] New legislation that allowed the security guards of overseas leaders to be armed also drew criticism.[130]

APEC also proved hard to sell. In 1998 the government attempted to explain the economic benefits of APEC to New Zealanders in a statement headed: 'Ten Good Reasons Why APEC Matters'.[131] These included: APEC partners provided around 70 percent of New Zealand's imports, and bought a similar proportion of its exports; the value of external trade with APEC partners equalled about one-third of New Zealand's total economic activity, and was a major generator of jobs; and some 80 percent of New Zealand's foreign investment came from those sources. These figures are hardly surprising, given that New Zealand's 'APEC partners' include Australia, the US and Japan. But there was no indication of what specific added value APEC brought to this scenario; no reference to the paucity of concrete commitments to APEC's goals; and not even a passing mention of the impact of the Asian meltdown. The government was not required to provide a more detailed, let alone balanced, account. Because APEC is not a formally binding treaty, it is not subject even to the weak requirements for transparency and debate contained in the 1998 sessional orders relating to ratification of treaties. No 'national interest' analysis was required; even if it were, it would not have had to explain the downsides of APEC.

The government's assessment of the economic benefits of APEC relied primarily on a 1996 study by the Australian Bureau of Agricultural and Resource Economics (ABARE) of projected returns from APEC.[132] According to Minister of Foreign Affairs and Trade Don McKinnon, this showed that 'New Zealand stands to add 1.6 percent to its GDP and annual export volumes are likely to be about seven percent higher' than they would otherwise be. Transaction costs for businesses would also be reduced, as streamlining customs procedures 'could mean whopping savings' of around US$46 billion regionally per year.[133] However, economist David Steele noted that the Australian report showed the projected gain in New Zealand's real GNP after twenty years to be just 0.4 percent above the returns it expected to receive from the Uruguay Round (assessments that were themselves problematic). Pointing out that a poor monetary policy decision could change the level of GNP by 2 to 3 percent in a single year, Steele concluded that the projected gains from APEC 'seem trivial for something that has been raised to such a level of importance as a policy issue (underlining perhaps that APEC is really about politics, not economics)'. Further, the 0.4 percent gain included a 10 to 17 percent fall in manufacturing from the projected 2020 baseline, which was supposedly offset by major gains in agriculture – the area in which experience showed that gains were least likely to materialise.[134] Bob Edlin of the *Independent* subsequently described the Australian study as disclosing 'remarkably meagre' returns.[135]

The government also relied on the 1997 report of the APEC Economic Committee on the impacts of trade liberalisation in the region. According to economist Tim Hazledine, the committee's model predicted that liberalisation under the Manila Action Plan would increase members' GDP by about 0.1 percent by the year 2010:

> While this is quite large in dollar terms, in scientific terms it is insignificant – well within the likely range of modelling error. Sources of such error, as noted in the report itself, include the lack of 'dynamic' effects and the assumption of zero adjustment costs, including no change in unemployment as tariffs are cut.[136]

The report projected a larger gain (0.4 percent of GDP) by including hypothetical efficiencies stemming from trade facilitation. But Hazledine commented: 'there is no economics here – the numbers used in the study are just pulled out of the air without consideration of the costs of facilitation (eg in harmonising standards across countries) nor any account of why the gains will be achieved by [the Manila Action Plan] in particular'.[137]

These studies all assumed that APEC would achieve its stated goal. There was no suggestion that projected benefits might be reduced or outweighed by economic costs not factored into the model; nor that instabilities and systemic failures in the regional and global economy might derail the APEC process or negate the projected gains. Non-economic costs and benefits were simply ignored.

Initially, the government's claims for APEC received little critical scrutiny from New Zealand journalists. By 1999, however, the government could no longer rely on them. More articles, editorials and business commentaries began questioning the value of APEC and the costs of hosting it. The government tried to talk up the expected returns from the 1999 meeting. Minister of Foreign Affairs and Trade Don McKinnon claimed that hosting APEC would attract more than $65 million to the local economy, plus free international exposure.[138] That figure too seemed to have been plucked from the air. A subsequent Infometrics report for the Tourism Board and the government's APEC 1999 Taskforce estimated a

$27 million return from the government's reallocation of $29 million to fund APEC (comprising $44.5 million minus GST and spending on police equipment, which allegedly would have been purchased sometime anyway). Most of the benefits would go to Auckland, while regions not holding APEC-related events could experience a downturn.[139] The projections were again highly speculative. Figures in official speeches and documents had variously referred to between 7,000 and 10,000 visitors, assuming President Clinton and his entourage turned up. The government's tourism pitch faced another setback when Minister of Tourism Murray McCully was forced to resign during a controversy over the Tourism Board's alleged failure to capitalise on the big millennium events, including APEC.

As the officials had warned, there was a real risk that hosting APEC would misfire. The public might not understand why spending $45 million on lavish banquets and security was more important than health, education and pensions. Aucklanders might not think that APEC was worth the disruption to their lives and businesses. A scathing editorial in the *Sunday Star-Times* in October 1998 called APEC a 'monster out of control', and quoted former Prime Minister David Lange's description of it as 'a farcical waste of time'. It went on to observe:

> At a time when pensions are being cut and patients on hospital waiting lists are dying, it is also a scandalous waste of money. ... A few photo opportunities and some bland communiques which will do nothing to improve the economic conditions of the citizens of the countries involved [are] hardly worth the expense of this conference. Or most of its kind.[140]

▲ REFLECTIONS

Because APEC was non-binding it could not embed the government's neo-liberal agenda in the same way as the WTO. But it did have two other important roles. One was symbolic, promoting the orthodoxy of free trade and investment within the vision of a regional free market where New Zealand could prosper alongside the world's fastest-growing economies. The second was the potential leverage that APEC commitments gave the government to push through unpopular policies, so long as people did not realise the obligations were voluntary and non-binding. By 1999, both these benefits were evaporating. APEC was haemorrhaging internally. Its declarations and commitments seemed vacuous. Its credibility had been severely undermined, both with the businesses it existed to serve, and among the people whose interests its 'economic leaders' were supposed to represent. Once APEC came to New Zealand, these weaknesses were more publicly exposed.

APEC members faced a conundrum. If they maintained the goal of free trade and investment and forced each other to make concrete commitments, APEC would self-destruct. If they did not, APEC would have abandoned its virtual *raison d'être*, and the US especially would lose interest. It seemed more likely to limp on as an ineffectual shell.

9 ▲ The Multilateral Agreement on Investment

The World Trade Organisation was established as the vehicle for pursuing 'free trade'. Attempts to include negotiations on 'free investment' in its mandate proved too controversial. So work on a Multilateral Agreement on Investment (MAI) took place at the OECD in Paris instead. Formal negotiations started in May 1995 and were due to be completed in May 1997. The agreement had three main objectives: first, to make it easier for foreign investors to establish, operate and divest in countries that had signed the agreement; second, to protect those investments against government decisions that affected their operations and profitability; and third, to provide an international mechanism for investors and signatory governments to enforce the agreement. Once a government had signed the agreement, it could not withdraw for five years; if it did subsequently withdraw, its obligations to existing foreign investors would continue for another fifteen years. Investors' rights were not balanced by any responsibilities. The goal was to settle a 'high standard' agreement among the mainly capital-exporting rich countries of the OECD, which the capital-importing non-OECD countries would then be encouraged to sign.

A draft of the MAI was leaked and posted on the Internet in February 1997. The director of Canada's Polaris Institute, Tony Clarke, condemned it as a 'charter of rights and freedoms for corporations ... through this new global constitution, the rights of citizens and the powers of governments themselves will be largely superseded by those of the transnational corporations'.[1] By October 1998 opposition had spread across many countries of the OECD, while critical commentators in poorer countries condemned the OECD's plan to foist its MAI on the rest of the world. These were primarily national responses, but those involved drew on their overseas networks and used the Internet to build a highly successful international campaign.

Active opposition in New Zealand began around May 1997. Over the next eighteen months it extended to Maori, students, Grey Power, mayors and city councillors, farmers, small businesses, local community groups, environmental NGOs, talkback callers and hosts, activist unions, and MPs from the Alliance, New Zealand First and some in Labour. For Maori critics, the MAI represented a further denial of tino rangatiratanga, both by excluding Maori from international negotiations and by the Crown promising rights to overseas investors before settling its Treaty obligations at home. For many non-Maori, this was also an issue of sovereignty. Groups focused on the issues that most concerned them. For some it was privatisation, the environment, or education and health services. Others were concerned about labour practices, regional economic development, and the regulation of big business and foreign investment in New Zealand. All were outraged at the contempt shown for democracy.

Supporters of the MAI in the government and business were genuinely perplexed. There was nothing special about the MAI. It was a logical extension of similar rules in agreements such as NAFTA, GATS and CER, which sought to promote foreign investment by providing greater levels of certainty and security. Most of what it proposed was already law in New Zealand. As with other international agreements, the negotiations were conducted in confidence, as a matter of diplomatic necessity. Treaty of Waitangi interests had been protected by reserving the right to give Maori preferential treatment. Other international agreements and forums were the proper place to address issues such as labour and environmental standards. Over time, and after belated consultation with relevant government departments, officials and ministers reluctantly conceded that some of the concerns being raised might have some foundation, and had been recognised as problems in other OECD countries.

Governments across the OECD, faced with similar pressure, sought more clarification, carve-outs and exemptions in the agreement. The MAI text became complex and unworkable. The deadline was extended from May 1997 to April 1998. By then, negotiations had reached a standstill and the OECD ministers declared a six-month moratorium. Further informal discussions failed to resolve a number of core issues. These included environment and labour standards, exclusion of cultural industries, coverage of state and local government, the right to boycott investors because of their investments elsewhere, and special rules for regional economic integration agreements, such as the European Union. In October 1998, France announced it was withdrawing from negotiations on the MAI. The European Commission would not continue without France. Other OECD governments expressed their own reservations. In December 1998, negotiations on the MAI were formally abandoned (at least at the OECD).

▲ BACKGROUND TO THE MAI

The emergence of the MAI in the late 1990s did not reflect a lack of investment instruments. For nearly 40 years, a patchwork of bilateral and multilateral agreements had progressively opened up countries to foreign investors. But they were uneven in content, coverage and enforceability. In 1961 the OECD had developed codes to liberalise capital movements and 'invisible operations' (services), but these allowed only for consultation and had no dispute mechanism. An OECD Declaration on International Investment provided for 'national treatment' in 1979, but was exhortatory and non-binding.

The Uruguay Round negotiations were disappointing for investors. The General Agreement on Trade in Services (GATS) covered only those services a country opted to include. The agreement on trade-related intellectual property rights (TRIPS) gave too long a lead-time for implementation. Provisions for trade-related investment measures (TRIMS) that were included in the GATT banned trade-related measures that discriminated against foreign investors, imposed quantitative restrictions, or set conditions in return for their receiving an advantage.[2] Inconsistent measures had to be eliminated in two, five or seven years, depending on the country category. After that, governments could no longer use such measures to protect their local economies against foreign firms. The agreement, alongside more general issues of investment and competition law, was to be reviewed after five years. But the new disciplines did not include rights to establish investments. And because the agreement addressed only the trade impacts of investment rules, a complaint had to come from an exporter, rather than an investor, and the parent government had to be willing to pursue it.

Regional investment measures were also uneven. APEC's investment principles and supplementary declarations were voluntary and non-binding. The Treaty of Rome gave investors rights of establishment and 'national treatment', but these were limited to members of the European Union, and the treaty lacked a comprehensive coverage of investment issues. NAFTA applied only to the US, Canada and Mexico, although in the eyes of big business it offered 'an excellent example of the state-of-the-art standards that can be achieved by international investors'.[3]

There were also some 1,160 bilateral investment treaties, two-thirds of which had been completed in the 1990s. These took a broadly similar form, with a wide definition of 'investment', and standard 'national treatment' and 'most favoured nation' clauses. Investors were protected from expropriation and nationalisation, and given standing to enforce the agreement through special mechanisms for dispute settlement or adjudication. Most also provided for governments to reserve certain activities from coverage. Country-specific exceptions (also called 'reservations') were usually subject to 'standstill' and 'rollback' provisions, which meant they could not be added to, and were to be progressively reduced and eventually eliminated. The usual objective was not to change national laws, but to codify them so they could not be made more restrictive. Transnational corporations complained that the agreements lacked uniform provisions and coverage, and gave unequal access to different markets. Few countries had opted for the 'high standard' model of bilateral investment agreement designed by the US.

When the MAI burst into the public arena in 1997, it had been under preparation for almost a decade. In 1988, in the context of the Uruguay Round negotiations, OECD ministers had mandated the Committee on International Investment and Multinational Enterprises to examine ways to strengthen the existing OECD instruments on investment. In 1991 the committee recommended making these instruments binding, with governments making commitments to the 'standstill' and 'rollback' of existing restrictions. This did not go far enough for the US. The proposal was debated into the night at the 1991 OECD ministerial meeting, and came to what New Zealand officials called an 'ignominious end', without agreement.[4]

However, ministers did approve a feasibility study on a Wider Investment Instrument that would be binding, cover the right to establish investments, and provide for enforcement. In late 1992 the Business and Industry Advisory Committee of the OECD (which included the New Zealand Employers' Federation) presented ministers with a Statement on a Potential OECD Broader Investment Instrument. The 1993 ministerial meeting asked the Advisory Committee to pursue the initiative 'at a sustained pace'. The major powers continued to disagree about its objectives, especially the treatment of sub-national bodies, formal dispute settlement procedures, and forward-looking commitments to investment liberalisation. While most countries expressed support for a fairly ambitious approach, New Zealand officials noted that this 'was not fully consistent' with the actions of many of them at the Advisory Committee.[5] Some proposed a gradual consolidation of existing agreements. Others urged a 'maximalist' approach, from which some elements might later need to be dropped. The New Zealand officials noted the risk that, 'by aiming too high, no agreement at all is achieved'.[6] The Advisory Committee's report to the 1994 ministerial meeting concluded there was a strong case for a new multilateral agreement on investment, covering liberalisation, investment protection and dispute settlement, with the potential to extend coverage to non-OECD countries. Preparatory work continued, culminating in a two-day workshop for investment specialists and officials from OECD and non-OECD countries in Wellington in April 1995.

The transnationals lobbied hard for a comprehensive new agreement, working on their own governments and through the Business and Industry Advisory Committee at the OECD. The most powerful and insistent voice was the United States Council for International Business (USCIB), which officially represented major US business interests in the Advisory Committee.[7] In March 1995, the Council issued a policy statement setting out its recommendations for MAI negotiators. It wanted the highest possible liberalisation standards, based on the US model investment treaty and NAFTA. Firm commitments to the liberalisation and rolling-back of existing restrictions on investment should be a condition of entry, 'rather than a hollow package of standstill of existing restrictions combined with a commitment to future liberalization'.[8] 'Investment' had to be broadly defined. Privatisation, including any provision for golden shares,[9] should not discriminate against foreign investors at any stage. The granting of investment incentives or statutory monopolies, especially in telecommunications, should also be non-discriminatory.

The Council took an equally hard line on exceptions. Those written into the investment agreement must be narrowly drawn – they might include national security, but not public order. Temporary derogations for short-term balance of payments difficulties were rejected as 'ineffectual' and 'unjustified'. The European Union should not be allowed to maintain preferential treatment for its members. Nor should there be any carve-out to exempt cultural industries, as Canada enjoyed under NAFTA.[10] Any country reservations should be specific, listed, subject to phase-out wherever possible, and negotiated down to a minimum.

All signatories should be required to give unconditional consent to arbitration initiated by investors, and to abide by any award. This option would extend beyond the MAI to obligations arising from any other treaties where the dispute related to investment. However, disputes involving broad regulatory regimes or tax issues should be dealt with domestically. Remedies should cover breaches at both the pre- and post-establishment phase (including denial of permission to invest), and entitle investors to damages and specific relief. The Council's recommendations were largely, but not wholly, reflected in the draft MAI.

▲ THE EARLY NEGOTIATIONS

On 24 May 1995, trade ministers of the 25 OECD member countries formally launched negotiations on a multilateral investment agreement. A high-level negotiating group was established to meet monthly; five working groups were formed to prepare reports and options on existing liberalisation instruments, new issues, investor protection, dispute settlement, non-members and institutional issues. This was the first time the OECD had tried to negotiate this kind of binding international agreement. The decision to run the process through a separate negotiating group, rather than the OECD Investment Committee, was meant to distance the work from the troubled history of the Wider Investment Instrument. But it also meant that many of the technical problems and political difficulties with the agreement were not picked up until too late in the day.[11]

The transnationals maintained pressure on the negotiators. Six months into formal negotiations, the US Council for International Business issued *A Guide to the Multilateral Agreement on Investment*. It claimed to have already organised a core group of representatives from companies and business organisations to advise US government officials and to track the progress of MAI negotiations. It also formed a coalition of companies to lobby for grass-roots support from the business community, state and local government officials, and public opinion groups. Its *Guide* announced: 'There is no turning back the forces of global competition. When concluded, the MAI will become the next pillar in the global system of trade, finance and investment'.[12] It was important to restrict negotiations to OECD members to ensure a high-quality agreement. However, extending the MAI to non-OECD countries was a primary goal. 'Given the current competition for capital, accession to the MAI, particularly by developing countries, will serve as a "seal of approval", demonstrating commitment to the highest standards of investment liberalization, protection, and dispute settlement.'[13] This process should follow the informal practice of bilateral investment treaties, which required as a condition of accession some elements of liberalisation as a 'down payment', plus a schedule of commitments to liberalise non-conforming measures.

The OECD Secretariat organised a workshop in Hong Kong in March 1996 to explain the MAI to twelve selected 'dynamic developing countries', including China, India, Malaysia, South Korea and Singapore. Despite strong support for the MAI from Argentina and Hong Kong, the reception was described as 'cool and generally unfavourable', with objections to both the process and the substance. The Malaysian participant insisted that: 'If this MAI is intended for global accession, then it has to be a global process and all countries need to be more directly involved.'[14] Malaysia wanted a pragmatic, bottom-up process that was evolutionary, not regulatory. Others argued that each country's situation and stage of development was different. The OECD's approach was considered too one-sided, giving investors no responsibilities, while the domestic implications of foreign investment and the rights of host countries were ignored. Other seminars were held in Brazil, Egypt and South Korea. A select group of sympathetic non-OECD countries (Argentina, Chile, Brazil, Hong Kong-China and Slovakia) was included in the OECD negotiations in late 1997 as observers, a move cited as proof of wider support for the MAI.

The decision to negotiate the agreement in the OECD would remain controversial. The European Union and Japan wanted further work on investment liberalisation to be done at the (relatively) more inclusive WTO, and pushed this at the first WTO ministerial meeting in Singapore in December 1996. The US was not keen. The Uruguay Round experience suggested that the WTO would make only slow progress towards a low-quality agreement. The US believed that a high-standard multilateral agreement on investment had to be negotiated among the governments of OECD countries, who were the main capital exporters and thus had similar objectives. Non-OECD countries would then be encouraged to sign. When a critical mass had been reached, the document could be shifted across to the WTO. The New Zealand government confirmed that 'there has been a pattern in the past of work done in the OECD feeding in later to WTO negotiations. ... It can be expected that the experience OECD members have had in negotiating the MAI will inform their approach to the work in the WTO.'[15]

The US was correct in assuming that WTO negotiations would be slow and possibly unproductive. Many poorer countries, led by India, China and Malaysia, opposed any further negotiations on investment at the WTO. At an UNCTAD session in October 1996, the G-77 countries complained that they were already heavily burdened by their Uruguay Round commitments, and were suffering from 'negotiations fatigue'. They wanted the outcomes from the round evaluated before making further changes. They also asked for evidence that unregulated investment would benefit them. The investment debate, they said, had lacked balance, especially as negotiations on a UN code of conduct for transnational corporations had collapsed. The G-77 countries wanted the issue of investment rules addressed in a forum more sympathetic to development concerns, such as UNCTAD. The UN had already mandated UNCTAD to identify and analyse the implications of a possible multilateral framework on investment, as a way of bolstering the negotiating position of poor countries.[16]

After tense and selective discussions, the WTO's Ministerial Declaration in December 1996 produced an ambiguous compromise. A working group would examine the relationship between trade and investment, alongside UNCTAD, and without prejudging whether negotiations would be initiated. The working group was to report in December 1998, after the MAI negotiations were expected to end. Although UNCTAD became more proactive in promoting discussion,[17] it remained peripheral to work in the WTO and irrelevant to the OECD.

▲ THE MAI TEXT[18]

A progress report on the MAI was issued in December 1996, by which time an estimated 90 percent of the text had been concluded. Clauses on the contentious 'deal breaking' issues, such as regional economic integration agreements and secondary boycotts (see below), were presented in the text as alternatives, or were not yet tabled. The positions of individual governments were recorded in the footnotes to the text, although country names were removed from the official drafts that were later released.

The text drew heavily on two main sources: NAFTA, and the US model of bilateral investment treaty. Its definition of investment was extremely broad. It included an 'enterprise' (explicitly including research institutes and universities), stocks and shares, bonds, rights under contracts, intellectual property rights, rights under licence, and property that is moveable or immoveable, tangible or intangible. An investment could be controlled directly or indirectly by an investor that was legally constituted in a signatory country (including tax-haven subsidiaries whose parent was registered in a signatory country).

The agreement committed parties to the core rules of 'national treatment', 'most favoured nation' and transparency. This meant that foreign investors would have the same, *or better*, rights to establish, acquire, expand, operate, manage, maintain, use, enjoy, sell or otherwise dispose of their investments as domestic investors in similar situations. The best treatment a country gave to one domestic or foreign investor would have to be given to investors of all other MAI signatories – and of any other country to which it owed 'most favoured nation' obligations on investment. 'Transparency' required rules and procedures relating to investment to be public and easily monitored.

Governments would not be able to restrict the inflow or outflow of investors' funds and earnings. Many traditional performance requirements were prohibited. For example, investors could not be required to hire a certain proportion of local workers or achieve a specified level of employment. Governments could not demand the transfer of technology and knowledge to local companies. Nor could they impose levels of local investment, production or research and development, or require investment through joint ventures. Investors could not be required to use a specific level of domestic content or export a proportion of their production. However, governments that offered an 'advantage' to investors, such as subsidies, could still set certain conditions on location, employment, joint ventures, local shareholding, and spending on research and development. (New Zealand failed to get agreement to prohibit all investment incentives such as tax breaks and other financial supports, whether or not they discriminated against foreign investors.)

State-conferred monopolies would be allowed, but governments should not discriminate against foreign investors when awarding them; nor should they discriminate in deciding who to buy from.[19] Governments could not be required to privatise, but MAI disciplines would apply if they did. Some governments sought to limit this application to sales that followed an initial privatisation. They also wanted to retain the general right to use a golden share, management buy-out or share give-away, as long as it was non-discriminatory. The US argued that these measures should be addressed in a country's specific exceptions, annexed to the agreement.

Where an investor had committed, or was in the process of committing, 'a substantial amount of capital', they or their senior managers, plus their spouses and families, would have an automatic right to enter and reside in that country for one to three years. While this would be subject to national immigration laws and procedures, they could not be denied entry on the grounds of tests or quotas based on labour market or economic needs.

Governments were prohibited from acting in ways that nationalised or expropriated an investment, either directly or indirectly, or had an 'equivalent effect'. Exceptions were allowed for a 'public interest' purpose or in economic emergencies – provided they were non-discriminatory and full compensation was paid. Concerns were expressed that this wording, borrowed from NAFTA, could fetter a government's right to regulate in significant areas of foreign investment. The chair of the negotiating committee moved to address these concerns in March 1998.[20]

Although the MAI was a treaty between governments, it also gave enforcement rights to foreign investors. Governments and investors could seek, through international arbitration, a declaration that a host government was or would be in breach of the agreement for taking certain actions. Investors could also seek enforceable awards of compensation if those actions amounted to an expropriation of their investment. Disputes would be heard by panels of investment experts, preferably at the World Bank's International Centre for the Settlement of Investment Disputes, where only the investor and government parties would have legal standing. Governments were required to ensure that such awards were enforceable in domestic law.

The MAI was negotiated by national governments, but would also bind sub-national authorities such as state and local government. To give investors certainty, a government could not withdraw from the agreement for five years. It could then give six months' notice, but would be required to honour commitments to existing investors for a further fifteen years. That meant a minimum commitment of over twenty years.

Two kinds of exception were provided – general and country-specific. General exceptions carved out agreed areas of sensitivity from the agreement. One such exception covered transactions (not regulations) by central banks or other monetary authorities in pursuit of monetary and exchange rate policies. A second exempted taxation, although a tax could still be considered an expropriation if it was not 'generally within the bounds of internationally recognised tax policies and practices'.[21] The restructuring of sovereign (public) debt was also excluded. There was provision for governments to take actions to protect their 'essential security interests', comply with UN peace and security obligations, and (possibly) to maintain public order. Temporary restrictions could also be imposed on foreign exchange and capital movements during balance of payments emergencies, subject to certain constraints.[22]

The agreement applied to everything else that was not expressly set down in a country-specific exception. Originally these exceptions were to be subject to 'standstill' and 'rollback'. But governments became nervous. Some 600 pages of national-level exceptions were lodged in February 1997. Negotiators were sent away to prune them back. By then, governments were coming under public pressure to strengthen their protections in sensitive areas. To accommodate this, the last draft of the MAI proposed two categories of country-specific exception. Annex A would list existing laws or policies and the extent to which they were excluded. These exceptions would be subject to full 'standstill' disciplines, meaning they could not be added to, although changes could be made if that did not increase their non-conformity. Annex B would list specific sectors or activities where new measures could be adopted, provided they did not require existing investors to dispose of assets on the grounds of nationality. The terms for rollback, and whether this should involve periodic reviews, renegotiation or unilateral reductions, were never finalised.

The most controversial issues remained unresolved. The US sought to exclude sub-national levels of government (such as its own states) from coverage. The European Commission wanted to exempt regional economic integration organisations from 'most favoured nation' commitments, so that it could maintain preferences among its members. Disciplines were proposed to prevent 'secondary boycotts', where governments discriminated against companies because of their activities in another country. The main targets here were the Helms-Burton and d'Amato Acts, whereby the US imposed boycotts against investors who owned property confiscated from US owners in Cuba and Iran respectively. France and Canada insisted on a carve-out for cultural industries, or at least for the audio-visual industry, to protect cultural and linguistic diversity. Only the Nordic countries argued for a general exception in the agreement for indigenous peoples, although this was narrowly framed to protect the Saami people's exclusive right to husband reindeer.[23]

The other two main stumbling blocks were environment and labour standards. The OECD's Trade Union Advisory Committee (TUAC) – a parallel group to the Business and Industry Advisory Committee – and its affiliated unions were involved on the fringe of the MAI negotiations from the beginning. Like the ICFTU, the Trade Union Advisory Committee supported globalisation and the liberalisation of investment, but was concerned to secure the best possible treatment for labour issues.[24] Accordingly, it sought three related measures. First, the OECD's non-binding Guidelines for Multinational Enterprises, which set expected standards for their behaviour (see Chapter 5), should be incorporated into the MAI preamble and annexed to the text; in addition, signatories should become legally obliged to set up the public information 'contact points' referred to in the guidelines. Second, the preamble should include a commitment by governments to protect, enhance and enforce basic workers' rights. Third, the text itself should include a specific prohibition on attracting foreign investment by suppressing domestic labour standards or violating internationally recognised core workers' rights.

The first and second of these so-called 'anchors' were generally accepted by the negotiators, although there was ongoing discussion about the wording. New Zealand was one of three countries initially opposed. The third provision was more difficult. Over time, there was general, if somewhat reluctant, agreement among OECD members to some kind of clause on not lowering labour standards. By January 1998, only Australia, New Zealand, South Korea and Mexico were still holding out; Mexico threatened not to sign the agreement if the clause was included.

Just before the April 1998 meeting of OECD ministers, the chair of the negotiating committee produced a new compromise. The MAI preamble would recognise that 'investment, as an engine of growth, can play a key role in ensuring that economic growth is sustainable, when accompanied by appropriate environmental and labour policies'.[25] Parties would renew their commitment to observe internationally recognised core labour standards, the ILO being the competent body to set and deal with those standards. The clause on 'not lowering standards' stated that parties should not waive or otherwise derogate from their health, safety, environmental or labour measures, or offer to do so, as an encouragement to a specific investment. Two enforcement options were on the table. The first provided for consultation over an alleged breach. The second made no reference to enforcement. Also undecided was whether the clause should refer to the lowering of international or domestic labour standards.

The Trade Union Advisory Committee saw this outcome as a relative victory. Even so, there was a price. In concluding the consultation between the Advisory Committee and the OECD in January 1998, an official noted that the MAI had gone further than any other agreement on labour and the environment: 'Nowhere else would you find such an understanding of your issues, but in return we expect your support for this agreement out there in the big, wild world.'[26] The Advisory Committee later claimed that much of the blame for the breakdown in negotiations lay 'with OECD governments themselves, who believed that a small clique of investment experts could conclude a far-reaching liberalisation instrument away from the public gaze, and then communicate it to the outside world. In many respects this strategy has backfired.'[27] Yet its affiliated unions in most OECD countries had contributed little to exposing and debating the MAI since 1995.

References to the environment in the draft agreement followed a parallel path. As with the GATT, the draft MAI allowed a government to discriminate *where necessary* to protect human, animal or plant life, or conserve exhaustible natural resources (see Chapter 7). But, as Canadian trade lawyer Barry Appleton pointed out, many environmental regulations that reduced the value of an investment would still be prohibited – for example, changes to land use regulations, restrictions on resource extraction, or regulations requiring reparation for environmental damage. Governments also faced a heavy burden in showing that measures taken under the provision were necessary and the least investment-distorting option available. Appleton noted that, in every conflict between specific trade objectives contained in a treaty and a narrow environmental exception, the ability of governments to engage in environmental regulation had suffered. Further, the text would prevent the application of the precautionary principle in the Rio Declaration, that where threats of serious or irreversible damage exist, lack of full scientific certainty shall not be used as a reason for postponing cost-effective means to protect the environment. As a formal agreement, the MAI would take precedence over the Declaration as a general rule of international law. Appleton noted the irony that the agreement allowed a government to take prohibited measures with respect to financial services, and observed: 'It is difficult to comprehend why governments would be careful to ensure that they retained the ability to regulate financial institutions without retaining the ability to regulate public health, safety and the environment.'[28]

Unlike the unions, environmental NGOs were outside the OECD process. Leading the lobby, the World Wildlife Fund (WWF) produced the first of several discussion papers on the MAI in October 1996.[29] A year later, another paper outlined the major deficiencies of the agreement, and suggested ways to make any final agreement more consistent with environmental protection and sustainable development. By then the Fund was being criticised by some other NGOs for being too accommodating, so the paper noted its position 'should not be taken as an endorsement of the Agreement or its objectives. Indeed, the main conclusion of this analysis is that the negotiations on the MAI should not proceed until a comprehensive review of its potential impact on the environment and sustainable development has been undertaken.'[30] In late October 1997, OECD governments agreed to support national reviews of the MAI's environmental impact, to be produced by mid-January 1998.[31] But there was no opportunity for public participation. Delegations were 'invited' to communicate their findings to the negotiating committee; oral communication would be sufficient. There was no provision for public scrutiny of the reviews, or for any public response. The resulting document remained secret.

Environmentalists also focused on the MAI's expropriation clause. The US firm Ethyl Corporation had lodged a claim under the equivalent NAFTA provision for C$347 million in compensation after the Canadian government, on public health grounds, banned imports of a gasoline additive (MMT), which only that company produced.[32] In mid-1998, the government settled for nearly C$20 million in damages and a letter of apology, and promised to repeal the legislation. Another US company, Metalclad, was claiming US$97 million in damages after the Mexican government passed regulations designed to shut down its toxic waste dump.[33] The Business and Industry Advisory Committee warned that however much the negotiators tightened the definition of expropriation, they could not prevent investors from testing such measures in arbitration.[34] This reinforced environmentalists' fears about the chilling effect of the expropriation provisions, especially on poorer governments who could not afford the time and expense of fighting off constant assaults by transnational corporations. Mounting pressure on and from governments prompted the chair of the negotiating committee to issue an interpretive note in March 1998, saying that the exercise of a government's normal regulatory powers would not amount to expropriation.[35]

In the final draft, the approach to the environment mirrored that taken on labour issues – in the preamble, an affirmation of the goal of sustainable development and the Rio Declarations; non-binding reference to the OECD Guidelines for Multinational Enterprises (which contained a weak section on the environment); and an inconclusive 'not lowering standards' clause, which would leave any power to enforce the clause with governments and investors. NGOs were warned they would not get anything as favourable in the WTO.

▲ THE INTERNATIONAL CAMPAIGN

Many of the problems with the MAI arose in the course of fleshing out the details of the text. Others reflected the pressure from single-issue lobbies, notably on labour and the environment. But the most significant factor was the groundswell of opposition to the MAI in many OECD countries, which placed their governments under enormous pressure. By September 1998, the OECD Secretary-General was describing the agreement as a 'lightning-rod for anti-globalisation forces around the world'.[36]

A Canadian NGO received a leaked copy of the draft MAI text in February 1997. Drawing on their experiences and critique of NAFTA and led by the Council of Canadians,[37] a network including academics, unions, churches and environmental activists launched a concerted anti-MAI campaign. After intensive lobbying, provincial and local governments became involved. In April 1997 the British Columbia Legislative Assembly held a special debate in which 'all members stressed the need for a full public debate on the potentially far-reaching implications of the MAI while there was still time for Canadian negotiators to act on public concerns'.[38]

Public and political pressure forced the Canadian federal government to hold parliamentary committee hearings in Ottawa, which were broadcast on public television. The British Columbia government made a detailed submission. While it acknowledged the importance of foreign investment to Canada, and investors' need for enhanced security and stability, it also recognised significant public unease about the related economic and social dislocation and growing inequalities between and within countries. The proposed MAI 'tips the balance too far in favour of foreign investment protection. And it could significantly weaken the ability of governments to balance investor protection with other legitimate policy goals and interests, including protecting workers, consumers and the environment.' The submission concluded that the MAI provided no clear benefit to Canadians and entailed some significant risks: 'Based on our current analysis, the Government of British Columbia opposes the proposed MAI. Given the range and seriousness of our concerns ... the application of MAI disciplines to British Columbia's provincial and local governments should not be assumed.'[39]

The British Columbia legislature subsequently held its own select committee hearings on the MAI.[40] Several other provincial governments also voted to reject the agreement.[41] The Prince Edward Island legislature expressed particular concern about the effect on Island land, on access for foreign fishing fleets, and 'on many important areas of Island and Canadian life, including environmental protection, employment, wage levels, social programs and culture'. It resolved that the federal government 'impose a moratorium on ratification of the MAI until full public hearings on the proposed treaty are held in Prince Edward Island and across the country, so that all Islanders and Canadians may have an opportunity to express their opinions about it'.[42] The Premier of Saskatchewan condemned the MAI as a set of rules that would put Canada into a straitjacket in an unacceptable race to the bottom.[43] The Federation of Canadian Municipalities sought a permanent and explicit exemption to confine the agreement to federal jurisdiction. A number of leading Canadian cities passed strongly worded resolutions – the City of Toronto, for example, advised the government that it opposed the MAI, and requested that 'further negotiations cease and desist immediately'.[44]

Pressure mounted more slowly in the UK, France and Scandinavia. NGOs lobbied their governments, some of which, notably the French, took a strong stand. The European Parliament also became involved. A highly critical report from its Committee on External Economic Relations was tabled in March 1998, accompanied by legal opinions from various other committees.[45] European MPs adopted a resolution that recognised the importance of a multilateral agreement to improve clarity, certainty and security for investors. However, it said the proposed MAI failed to balance the rights of investors with their obligations to 'contribute to responsible development of the country of establishment by promoting technology, sustainable economic growth, employment, healthy social relations and protection of the environment'. The MPs wanted the social, environmental and development impacts of the MAI to be independently and thoroughly assessed. Non-OECD countries should not be pressured to accede to an agreement they had not negotiated. It was more appropriate to examine investment protection in a multilateral context that involved all the 'developing' countries, such as UNCTAD or the WTO. The MPs also regretted the 'utmost secrecy' of the MAI process, which excluded even national parliaments. Negotiations needed to be subjected to broader public debate and ongoing parliamentary monitoring.[46]

The resolution detailed substantive concerns relating to intellectual property, expropriation and dispute settlement provisions, and the rights of fishing communities. Several of its demands – for example, the exclusion of regional economic integration organisations such as the European Union from 'most favoured nation' commitments, and the coverage of secondary boycotts – were directed squarely at the US. So was the section of the resolution that 'regretted' the pressure being levied by 'certain' OECD members over the proposed derogation that would 'preserve and promote cultural and linguistic diversity'.[47]

Public interest groups in the US were preoccupied with fighting the renewal of presidential fast-track authority, and were slower than the

Canadians to respond. The State Department did not brief NGOs until July 1998. In October, some 99 civic groups presented the Clinton administration with a letter expressing opposition to the MAI and any move to take it into the WTO. *Inside US Trade* reported a lack of Treasury interest in the agreement, and only 'skin deep' support from business.[48]

The MAI also raised constitutional issues of US federal/state relations. The Harrison Institute for Public Law in Washington prepared a state-by-state assessment of the potential impact of the MAI on state and local law.[49] The Western Governors' Association protested that, under the principles of federalism, it should have been consulted during the negotiation process, and not be left trying to secure changes once decisions were made. The association commissioned a report on the implications of the MAI, which offered several hundred examples of adverse consequences for states in areas of economic regulation, land use and the environment, economic development, and enforcement of investor rights and state sovereignty. The governors were prepared to support the MAI in principle, but they wanted the federal government to ensure that states retained the authority to discriminate in favour of local residents, and that all current and future measures that potentially conflicted with the agreement were reserved. The right to use investment incentives and performance requirements for legitimate public purposes had to be protected. The governors also questioned whether claims of MAI breaches would be brought directly against state governments. If they were brought against the federal government, could states defend their laws? And would damages be recouped from states if they were found in breach?[50]

Reaction in Australia was surprisingly slow, with the MAI not gaining prominence there until early 1998.[51] For several weeks the Australian government refused to release the draft text, let alone the country's exceptions. Within a month, however, intense activity from local groups and unions, political pressure from the Democrats and some in Labor, academic analysis,[52] and extensive media coverage had forced the government to refer the MAI to the recently created select committee on treaties (see Chapter 1). The Senate asked the committee to examine the 'advantages and/or disadvantages for Australia arising from the MAI currently being negotiated in secret' by the Australian government at the OECD. Submissions were heard from all states. The committee's interim report in May 1998 recommended that 'Australia not sign the final text of the [MAI] unless and until a thorough assessment has been made of the national interest and a decision is made that it is in Australia's interest to do so'.[53] Meanwhile, the committee would continue its inquiry. This position reflected the acknowledgement at the Labor Party conference in January 1998 of growing concern about the MAI:

The capacity of an Australian government to develop strategic policy initiatives designed to ensure the future of Australia's economy, industries and jobs will not be emasculated or sacrificed by a failure to properly evaluate or protect the national interest. Labor therefore determines that the negotiation of any MAI must, in addition to ILO, social justice and environment issues, take into account government's need to regulate foreign investment according to socio-economic objectives consistent with the national interest.[54]

At the time of the November 1998 meeting in Paris, Trade Minister Tim Fischer announced that the government would not sign the MAI, conceding that there were 'legitimate concerns about Australia's sovereignty'.[55]

Public interest groups in the non-OECD countries, such as the Malaysian-based Third World Network, largely echoed the concerns expressed by their governments.[56] The economies of most colonised countries had been shaped to the advantage of foreign companies and financial institutions. Local people and enterprises needed time and protection before they could compete on more balanced terms with bigger foreign companies. Most governments now accepted the importance of foreign investment to help develop their services, infrastructure, export production and access to technology, and were trying to attract it. But because foreign investment was a double-edged sword, development policy needed to ensure that the benefits outweighed the costs. For foreign investment to play a positive role, the government must have the right and powers to determine the conditions for its expansion.[57] Control over the net outflow of foreign exchange was essential to protect the balance of payments. Legitimate responses included requiring foreign investors to export and to limit imports, and regulating the kinds of investment to discourage large firms from exploiting a market and displacing local firms. If national governments failed to maintain the rights and powers to regulate foreign investment, they risked serious economic and social consequences:

> Giving total freedom and rights to foreign investors may lead to the disappearance of many local enterprises, higher unemployment, greater outflow of financial resources, and therefore to balance of payments problems. It may also worsen social imbalances within society, thereby causing social instability which will offset economic prospects.[58]

These concerns were supported by development NGOs based in OECD countries. Oxfam, for example, argued that: 'Whether foreign investment has a positive or negative impact depends on a range of factors including the distribution of wealth and power, who controls production and distribution, the terms on which countries receive foreign investment and the nature of the regulatory framework.'[59] The MAI in its current form increased the rights of investors without imposing responsibilities, and seriously limited the ability of governments to regulate in the public interest. The beneficiaries would be investors and governments in richer countries; those who suffered would be poorer countries and their citizens.

In response to pressure from such NGOs, the Department for International Development in the UK commissioned a report on the development implications of the MAI, to be delivered within four weeks. The research involved no consultation with international bodies, NGOs working on the issue, or representatives of poorer countries themselves. The report concluded that poorer (especially very poor) countries would gain from membership of an MAI, primarily because it would improve their credibility in attracting investment. The concerns expressed by poorer countries about the loss of their 'economic sovereignty', and by NGOs about the lowering of labour and environmental standards, were considered unjustified:

> Although there are no specific provisions in the MAI for developing countries as such, the rules for country-specific exceptions leave sufficient scope in principle for developing country interests. Further, there is a real cost to developing countries of non-accession in terms of lower potential growth, and a significant danger of downward regulatory competition for foreign investment between those poor countries which are unable to join.[60]

The report's endorsement of the MAI was conditional. It emphasised the need to regulate short-term capital surges, and for OECD countries to provide the resources and technical assistance to make the accession of poor countries feasible: 'An accelerated programme of debt relief ... should also accompany accession, in order to reduce the macroeconomic uncertainty faced by potential investors.'[61] The UK-based World Development Movement expressed concern that the report had been circulated to other governments; it published a damning critique of the report, which concluded that the benefits of signing such an agreement had not been substantiated, while the future costs and risks were understated or ignored.[62]

▲ NEW ZEALAND'S RESPONSE

References to the MAI first appeared in the New Zealand media in April 1997.[63] By May a major campaign was under way, organised primarily by the GATT Watchdog group with support from the Trade Union Federation, other NGOs and individuals. A briefing paper by the author was circulated to MPs and journalists.[64] The Alliance adopted the issue and launched a sustained barrage of parliamentary questions. Over the next few months, newspapers published a series of articles and reported on the Alliance campaign. Magazines as diverse as *Grey Power* and *Canterbury Farmer* ran stories.[65] The MAI became the hot topic of talkback radio. Letters to the editor rolled in. Ministers, MPs and officials were deluged with demands for information and explanations. Emulating the earlier anti-nuclear campaign, a number of local councils declared themselves an 'MAI-free zone'. The most concerted and effective mobilisation was by Maori activists, media, MPs and even officials, who condemned the impact of the MAI on the Treaty of Waitangi, their right to control indigenous knowledge and resources, and their exclusion from international treaty negotiations that had major implications for them.

Opposition to the MAI was fuelled by the secrecy of the negotiations. Ministers and officials maintained that the text had to remain confidential until it was formally released by the OECD, and refused to discuss its provisions, even though it was on the Internet.[66] By October 1997 this position had become untenable. Indeed, officials began demanding greater openness from the OECD, including the public release of the draft text. The Secretary of Foreign Affairs and Trade, Richard Nottage, defended the general practice of closed-door negotiations, arguing that 'negotiating positions are compromised if they are widely known'. However, the 'New Zealand Government opposes confidentiality in the case of the [MAI] because it understands the level of public interest and concern about the issues it involves. We have been pressing the OECD to release the negotiating text.'[67] Yet public interest and concern arose only after people had access to the leaked text. Nottage's reasoning suggests that had the draft never been leaked, the MAI could have remained secret. Announcing that the draft would be made available in November 1997, Winston Peters even claimed that the government had always intended releasing it.[68] Ten months after the document was leaked, the OECD formally released the draft text. Updates were subsequently posted on the OECD website.[69]

The CTU was notably absent from the campaign. The OECD's Trade Union Advisory Committee adopted a position on labour issues, but left its affiliates to decide their general position on the MAI. The Canadian unions opposed it because of concerns about culture, not-for-profit activities and social services.[70] The European unions, which had more positive experiences of integration, supported the agreement. The CTU's president, Ken Douglas, had addressed the pre-negotiation seminar in Wellington in April 1995 on behalf of the Advisory Committee.[71] Nothing more was heard publicly from the CTU until its silence became an issue in late 1997. A number of unions were surprised to learn of the MAI, and expressed concern about its potential impacts, especially for state sector workers and universities.[72] In response to mounting pressure, the CTU informed its affiliates of the general TUAC line, and suggested that those who supported specific exemptions should either raise the issue directly with the government or channel their views through the CTU.[73] In March 1998, almost three years into negotiations, the CTU executive adopted an official position, which it then conveyed to the government. Under pressure, it had shifted from a singular focus on labour issues to say it would support an MAI only if it involved no further liberalisation of current restrictions on inward foreign investment, contained an enforceable labour standards clause, and the country-specific exceptions included 'delivery of public and social services and protection for New Zealand's cultural identity'.[74]

Some members of the CTU-affiliated unions were unhappy with its policy and strategy. Pat Martin, editor of the *PSA Journal*, was sacked for writing a report that gave prominence to opposition to the MAI at a meeting of Public Service International, and made only minor reference to the CTU's more supportive position. Although the PSA president stated publicly that the union was lobbying against the MAI because it believed the agreement was against the interests of all New Zealanders,[75] the union's general secretary told Martin that the 'PSA's position is decided by the CTU and this should be the main focus of the story'.[76] The next edition of the *Journal* headlined the CTU's policy on the MAI, and claimed that trade union efforts had secured wide support for a labour standards clause.[77]

The MAI controversy caught New Zealand politicians by surprise. International treaty negotiations were the exclusive domain of the Cabinet. When pre-negotiations on an investment agreement began in 1991, the National government was continuing the investment liberalisation policies of its Labour predecessor. The Cabinet Strategy Committee endorsed New Zealand's participation in formal negotiations in March 1995, and negotiations proceeded smoothly until early 1997.[78] There was no incentive to raise public awareness of, or seek support for, the MAI, especially given the level of public hostility to foreign investment (see Chapter 4).

The formation of the Coalition government in December 1996 posed a potential problem. New Zealand First's founding pledge was to 'put New Zealand First'. In its 1996 election campaign, it had promised to prevent further privatisation of state assets and to tighten the laws on foreign investment and immigration. The Coalition Agreement of December 1996 diluted this to a 'general principle that it is desirable that the control and ownership of important New Zealand assets and resources be held by New Zealanders'.[79] Even that loose wording conflicted with the core principles of the MAI. Most New Zealand First ministers would have first learned of the MAI in the eight-page briefing paper to the Cabinet in

March 1997, when officials sought authority to table New Zealand's country-specific exceptions.[80] The paper gave a bland summary of the content and presumed benefits of a model investment instrument. Ministers were assured that 'the proposals in this paper are consistent with the Coalition Agreement'.[81]

The short list of New Zealand's proposed reservations was appended. These preserved the existing foreign investment screening mechanism, overseen by the Overseas Investment Commission. (As discussed in Chapter 4, only foreign investments involving more than five hectares of land were required to satisfy a 'national interest' test; even then, the criteria were vague and the minister's powers discretionary.) They also preserved specific restrictions on foreign ownership that were imposed when Air New Zealand and Telecom were privatised,[82] and other limitations relating to optometry, New Zealand-registered ships, fishing quota (without ministerial consent), and the registration of fishing vessels. Eligibility for assistance for domestic and Maori broadcast programming and New Zealand films was protected. The monopoly powers of statutory producer boards were reserved. Notice was also given that some further protections might be entered on intellectual property rights, and the right to maintain higher levels of liberalisation under CER.

The briefing paper left ministers in no doubt about the effects of the MAI's 'standstill' and 'rollback' rules on country-specific exceptions:

> ... once a party has committed its regime ... it cannot at any time in the future move to make that regime more restrictive, unless it is able to obtain agreement of the other Parties. This would normally involve offering up some form of compensatory commitment in return. ... The objective, both in the first negotiation and over time, will be to reduce the overall level of reservations and in this way to achieve liberalisation. This is known as 'rollback'.[83]

The paper also showed that New Zealand's negotiators had taken a pure position on other issues:

> The New Zealand delegation has pressed hard, without much success, to have some disciplines on investment incentives included in the Agreement. There have been concerted efforts to work labour and environment references into the Agreement. This is contrary to New Zealand policy on what it is appropriate to address in an economic agreement of this type and we have stood out against these moves.[84]

Attached to the briefing paper was a certification by Minister for International Trade Lockwood Smith that there was no need to consult even the National and New Zealand First caucuses about the agreement, let alone the Opposition or outside groups.[85] It seems that the New Zealand First ministers did not object. This was consistent with a recent speech by Winston Peters to the Chinese government in Hong Kong, in which he embraced the MAI – although the mercurial Peters later asserted that: 'foreign investment should be for the economic and social interests of New Zealanders first and paramount. That is the consistent stand I took last year, and also take this year.'[86] Other New Zealand First ministers, notably Tau Henare and Tuariki John Delamere, who subsequently expressed reservations about the implications of the MAI for Maori, seemed unconcerned at the time.

As opposition to the MAI mounted during 1997, the government ran three main defences.[87] First, the MAI would be good for New Zealand investors overseas: '[It] will help us compete for markets against larger more powerful nations without being discriminated against. It will help us attract a share of the international investment pie without fear of being squeezed out by bigger players and it will allow us to invest overseas without barriers being placed in our path.'[88] Second, the MAI would benefit the small investor: 'Not signing the MAI would be depriving ourselves of the security the MAI will offer our $28 billion invested overseas'. Lockwood Smith claimed that these were not the investments of some nebulous concept like 'big business': 'According to its annual report, 28,175 people hold 1,000 or fewer shares in Carter Holt Harvey. ... The MAI will help protect the investment – the savings – of those 28,175 small shareholders.'[89] Third, the MAI would mean more jobs:

> If we don't sign, we'll be the only OECD country not to. We'll be sending a message that we don't want job-creating investment in New Zealand. We'll throw away the chance to get our unemployment rate down to one of the lowest in the world. It is ironic that the Alliance, which claims to stand for the disadvantaged, is opposing a treaty which helps create jobs and reduce unemployment.[90]

The validity of those arguments has been challenged in Chapter 4. They served as the basis for a dossier issued by the relevant ministers to National and New Zealand First MPs in January 1998 to help them deal with questions on foreign investment and the MAI.[91] It included various 'fact sheets' on overseas investment, the MAI, the sale of land, the Treaty of Waitangi, social services, the role of Parliament, and case studies on foreign companies. It also gave MPs a draft article for local newspapers, with accompanying graphics, and ministerial speeches. This was damage control in overdrive. Yet once it became clear that the MAI was falling apart, the agreement ceased being indispensable to New Zealand's interests. In February 1998, Lockwood Smith observed: 'Should the MAI not be concluded ... that would be disappointing but not the end of the world. New Zealand already has an open and competitive economy so we could expect to continue to be a preferred destination for job-creating overseas investment.'[92]

For the Alliance, the MAI was a ready-made issue. Having vied with New Zealand First for the 'economic sovereignty' platform for most of 1996, it now had the stage to itself. In May 1997 it launched an aggressive campaign against the MAI which Lockwood Smith labelled 'dishonest and despicable'.[93] Alliance MPs raised the issue at every opportunity and asked a constant stream of parliamentary questions. Winston Peters' responses were semi-coherent, usually avoiding the question, and repeating that everything was consistent with the Coalition Agreement. Other ministers were worryingly ill-informed. At one stage, Prime Minister Jim Bolger claimed that the procedures of the Overseas Investment Commission gave government the right to decline investment proposals not considered to be in the national interest, without noting that this applied only to certain lands.[94] The standard response from all parties was to belittle the Alliance rather than address the issues. Bolger, for example, attacked Alliance leader Jim Anderton, calling 'his antediluvian ideas on foreign investment and his strange belief [about] New Zealanders all becoming peasants and growing their own food and not exporting ... quite loopy and barmy'.[95]

The Labour Party was in a bind. While in government in the 1980s, it had liberalised investment laws and sold state assets to foreign companies. It was a strong supporter of the investment liberalisation agendas of APEC and the WTO. Maintaining this historical position, while differentiating it from both National's pro-liberalisation stance and the Alliance's opposition, was difficult. Some Labour backbenchers wanted to rethink the policy. But trade spokesperson Mike Moore remained fervently committed to the existing line. In November 1997 he urged the Labour caucus to support the MAI, using identical arguments and figures to those of the government. He accused MAI critics of 'incorrect interpretations, false assumptions, and to a certain degree ... deliberate misinterpretation of the facts'. Their opposition was based on 'misguided patriotism, mistrust of foreigners, a touch of xenophobia and conveyed in simplistic messages with little reference to objective fact. It is xenophobic, racist nonsense'.[96] His argument consisted of debunking a series of quotations allegedly from Jim Anderton, Bill Rosenberg and the author. These were unsourced and of dubious provenance. A correction and counter-analysis was sent to the Labour leader, but was never circulated to the caucus.[97]

There were electoral implications for Labour whatever stance it took on the MAI.[98] Not taking a strong public position was probably preferable to alarming the business community. But saying nothing was not an option. In

October 1997, finance spokesperson Michael Cullen issued a press release warning the Coalition government that it was 'in some danger of losing the public debate over the MAI, something which would not be in New Zealand's interests'.[99] He urged the government to hold select committee hearings and a parliamentary debate on the issue, and to extend the country-specific exceptions to protect future privatisations and to guarantee that Treaty of Waitangi rights would not be undermined. Given this general endorsement, his closing comment that the government 'should not be able to use the MAI as an excuse to restrict future governments' policy options' seemed to miss the central objective of the agreement.

Labour MPs, including Mike Moore, were more comfortable on the democracy issue. Moore blamed a lack of parliamentary debate for the 'level of misunderstanding', and proposed that the MAI should go to select committee for proper hearings – 'then I believe it would have the support of all members of this House except the terminally deranged'.[100] He had already put a paper to the foreign affairs select committee proposing that debates on international treaties be held once or twice a year, backed by a select committee process. Labour MP Ross Robertson promoted a similar position in a private member's bill.[101] The other parties also stuck safely to the process issues. ACT argued that treaties needed to be debated in Parliament, and MP Ken Shirley drafted a private member's bill to that effect. Peter Dunne of the United Party thought such agreements were inevitable, but supported a more transparent and democratic process involving at least some select committee scrutiny, a report back to Parliament, and debate.[102]

Ministry of Foreign Affairs and Trade officials met with the parliamentary parties to discuss Parliament's role in relation to international treaties. According to Bolger, it was accepted that 50-odd agreements could not be debated individually, so the officials would go away and think about what might be appropriate.[103] He would give no commitment to a debate on the MAI, let alone a vote or select committee hearings on it. Reluctantly and belatedly, the government announced that new sessional orders would allow Parliament to debate international treaties before they were signed, but not to vote on them. Final approval would remain the prerogative of Cabinet. This process would have seen the MAI tabled only after negotiations were complete and before it was ratified. A National Interest Analysis would have set out the benefits of the agreement as the Ministry of Foreign Affairs and Trade saw them. The select committee would have decided whether to examine the agreement and call for submissions. Its report may have been debated, but Parliament could not have voted the agreement down. Because the MAI negotiations were never completed, none of this occurred.

Despite public antagonism to foreign investment in the mid-1990s, Ministry of Foreign Affairs and Trade officials seemed just as surprised as their ministers by reactions to the MAI. Senior officials attending the high-level OECD meetings in Paris viewed the MAI as innocuous and routine. Yet back in 1994 they had anticipated problems with negotiations, noting a lack of political will among the major powers to settle differences, which 'does not augur well for future progress in the development of any [Wider Investment Instrument].'[104] Officials in New Zealand remained cautious about the prospects for the formal negotiations being proposed, canvassing options that ranged from a stalemate, as occurred with the Wider Investment Instrument, to a 'state of the art' agreement.[105] 'Multilateral investment negotiations have proven difficult in the past ... it would be rash to predict that an [MAI] will be successfully negotiated within the next two years.'[106] They were also lukewarm about the benefits, noting that the principal opportunities for New Zealand from an MAI would be 'using international pressure to exert additional leverage on the domestic liberalisation programme', and gains as an exporter of capital and a trading economy from securing binding liberalisation of international capital markets.[107]

When approving the original negotiating instructions on the MAI in April 1995, Cabinet directed officials to provide periodic progress reports and to seek specific direction when negotiations impacted on New Zealand's policies. Nothing was heard again until mid-January 1997, as officials prepared to table the initial list of reservations in February. The Ministry of Foreign Affairs and Trade began a rushed round of consultations with the ministries thought to be affected.[108] Sometimes they were given less than a day to respond, on the clear (and generally correct) assumption that comments would be confined to the detail. Some did ask questions. The Ministry of Transport raised the 'inappropriateness' of committing future governments to non-discrimination over the ownership of domestic airlines.[109] The officials in Paris did not share this concern, and were unwilling to reserve a right to discriminate where no legal barriers to foreign investors currently existed.[110]

▲ The Treaty of Waitangi

Ministers and officials proved especially ham-fisted in responding to Maori concern that the process and substance of the MAI were irreconcilable with tino rangatiratanga. The government was accused of excluding Maori yet again from international decisions that directly affected them. Having failed to honour the Treaty of Waitangi, it now proposed entering into a new treaty that would give foreign investors enforceable priority over resources and intellectual property that Maori were fighting to control. If Maori succeeded in their claim before the Waitangi Tribunal over indigenous knowledge and taonga, the price of compensating actual and prospective investors who were affected would give the government an excuse not to comply with the Tribunal's recommendations.[111] Nor would it be possible to strengthen the rules relating to foreign investment to better protect Maori interests. Some Maori entrepreneurs and corporations might benefit from the MAI by securing joint ventures or investing offshore; but past experience of foreign investment gave most Maori little cause to expect increased prosperity, secure jobs or greater control of their resources.

Many of these concerns were shared by officials in Te Puni Kokiri (formerly the Department of Maori Affairs). They were not consulted until February 1997 – despite Cabinet being told back in October 1995 that: 'Given the number of issues involved in the negotiations which may have implications for the Government's Treaty of Waitangi obligations, it will be appropriate for officials to conduct consultations with the Treaty partner'.[112] When consultation finally came, it was rushed and perfunctory. The government proposed a country-specific exception that preserved its ability to give preferential treatment to its Treaty partner in relation to commercial or industrial undertakings. In February the Ministry of Foreign Affairs and Trade had sent officials at Te Puni Kokiri the draft reservation, without the MAI text, seeking comment the same day. It allowed them three days to comment on the proposed Cabinet briefing paper on the MAI, due in March. Te Puni Kokiri responded ten days later, asking for an analysis of the implications for Maori of the proposed reservations on fisheries, broadcasting, sale of local body assets, sale of central government assets, producer boards, intellectual property and forestry.[113] No reply was ever received. In August 1997, Te Puni Kokiri officials told their minister, Tau Henare, they were concerned that any protection for Maori interests under the exception was temporary and hence insecure.

> The more fundamental issue from Te Puni Kokiri's point of view is the responsibility of MFAT as the Crown's expert advisor on national implications of international agreements to provide early-warning signals to departments of pending negotiations, to manage public consultation and acknowledge their responsibility to provide advice and a pro-forma Treaty of Waitangi analysis of risks and benefits of international agreements and activities which New Zealand is party to or currently engaged in negotiating.[114]

Te Puni Kokiri's advice that the government consult widely with Maori had been ignored. This was a costly mistake. During August 1997,

Alliance MP Sandra Lee asked a series of embarrassing parliamentary questions about consultation with Maori over the MAI, observing that Foreign Affairs and Trade officials seemed to interpret 'consultation with Maori' as consultation with Maori officials.[115] She reminded Henare that he had said in opposition that Maori wanted to be part of and fully involved in the decision-making process of the nation.[116] Henare later replied: 'I strongly favour consultation with the Maori treaty partner before an official position on the multilateral agreement is finalised. I have also received advice from my ministry to that effect.'[117] Given the awkward political situation, consultation also bought him time before having to take a firm position.

Exercising its new powers under MMP, the Maori Affairs select committee summoned the various officials to discuss the MAI. Te Puni Kokiri reported on the process to date, including the lack of early warning to ministries, the failure to provide the assessment of Treaty implications, and the unwillingness of the Ministry of Foreign Affairs and Trade to consult with iwi, hapu, Maori business and other Maori organisations.[118] The ministry complained publicly that these comments were wrong on a number of points. This drew a strong but diplomatic rebuke from the chief executive of Te Puni Kokiri, Ngatata Love. He went on to note that any consultation exercise with Maori would be difficult and challenging, and require clear protocols about appropriate behaviour.[119]

The appearance of the Foreign Affairs and Trade and Treasury officials before the select committee proved disastrous. They insisted there was not a problem. The exception relating to the Treaty allowed the government to give Maori any preferential treatment that might otherwise breach the MAI; a decision on whether intellectual or cultural property would be included in the agreement had yet to be made.[120] Maori MPs from all parties came away from the select committee unconvinced of the robustness of the exceptions, and highly offended by the officials' arrogance. As Rana Waitai observed: 'We were screwed in the last treaty we got mixed up in, so you will appreciate there are a lot of misgivings about this one.'[121]

Eventually, the government bowed to pressure. Henare announced a consultation process of public meetings and 'focus workshops' with Maori, beginning in mid-December and running until late March 1998. He reserved his position on the MAI until then. The Maori Congress condemned the consultations as an after-thought, noting that Maori had been left to force their way into the MAI process, as they had with the GATT.[122] Ministry of Foreign Affairs and Trade officials interpreted the consultations as an opportunity to convey information, and to 'reassure both the Crown and the Treaty partner that the proposed ... reservation is adequate'. The reservation would remain in draft form until the consultation process was complete. The officials did not intend to debate the merits of the agreement itself.[123]

Seven separate hui were held around the country. Trade officials later described them as 'robust and spirited', and the concerns expressed as 'heartfelt and genuine'. Their own assurances that globalisation meant 'the sovereignty of all nations was being eroded all the time', and that all New Zealanders were 'giving up a little bit of sovereignty to gain greater benefits for the people as a whole', failed to convince.[124] The MAI was overwhelmingly rejected at all seven hui. As a result, the government agreed to a joint Treaty Impact Analysis by the Ministry of Foreign Affairs and Trade and Te Puni Kokiri, and promised to review the proposed exception.[125] As the April 1998 deadline for the completion of MAI negotiations approached, a hikoi opposing the MAI set out from Te Hapua in Northland, attracting Maori and non-Maori support along the way. Henare maintained 'a cautionary approach because I am not sure that agreements of this nature will bring about the changes necessary for the socio-economic conditions of Maori to improve'.[126] When the MAI negotiations collapsed in October, the Treaty Impact Analysis had still not been completed.

▲ Privatisation

The government also came unstuck on privatisation. Given the uncertainty over the final MAI text, most governments reserved the right to restrict foreign investment if they privatised state assets. The New Zealand government's initial list of reservations covered only the existing 'Kiwi share' provisions in the Articles of Association of privatised Telecom and Air New Zealand. There was no attempt to preserve the right of future governments to impose similar or other constraints on privatisations by central or local government. This was deliberate. The first draft of the March 1997 Cabinet briefing paper on the MAI referred to areas of possible risk to the government's objectives.[127] The final draft confirmed:

> The provisions in the Coalition Agreement regarding privatisation do not require reservation however because they deal only with the decision to privatise or not and the [MAI] will impose no obligation to privatise. Should a privatisation take place, National Treatment disciplines would apply, ie equal opportunities must be provided to both foreign and domestic investors in the privatisation process.[128]

Ministers repeatedly stated, quite correctly, that the MAI did not require governments to privatise. The issue was what they could do if something was privatised. The government insisted that the Coalition Agreement promised not to sell specified strategic assets, such as TVNZ, ECNZ and Transpower, so there was no need to make any provision covering their sale. There were no restrictions in the Coalition Agreement on selling anything else, so no reservation was required there either. The effect of this was highlighted in October 1997, when the *New Zealand Herald* reported on speculation that 'New Zealand First may agree to renegotiate the coalition agreement to allow the sale of TVNZ, with the proviso that it stays under New Zealand owned control and that New Zealand – including Maori – content on screens is guaranteed'.[129] The MAI would not have allowed any such proviso, and 'standstill' rules (as then proposed) would have prevented a government from adding such an exception unless all other signatories agreed, which seemed unlikely. The only options would be to withdraw from the MAI (provided the government had been a signatory for five years) or pay massive compensation to an actual or potential investor who was disadvantaged.

The officials were called before the foreign affairs select committee to explain the government's position. Several of the exchanges that took place were followed up by Alliance MPs in writing.[130] The Alliance was told there was currently nothing to prevent the government from selling assets to foreign buyers, so nothing would change under the MAI. This ignored the fact that the government could currently *refuse* to sell to a foreign buyer, and that such discrimination would not be allowed under the MAI. At times the responses were wrong on basic facts – for example, in claiming that applications to purchase land under five hectares or assets over $10 million attracted a 'national interest' test. They were also told that the Overseas Investment Commission's screening mechanism 'is not intended actively to assist the sale or entry of an investor' – yet the Commission operates under an explicit presumption that applications should be granted (see Chapter 4).

The government moved to defuse concerns about privatisation in November 1997. Prime Minister Jenny Shipley and her deputy, Winston Peters, made a carefully worded announcement that they were 'committed to reserving New Zealand's position on NZ Post, ECNZ, Contact, Transpower, TV1, Radio NZ, National Programme and Concert FM, Ports, Airports, Electricity and Gas Utilities, and that the Government will examine how it might best do this in the MAI negotiations'.[131] This was not, however, the same as pledging to include these assets in the New Zealand government's exceptions. Subsequently, officials indicated that the exceptions on privatisation would be revisited, but this was never formally done.[132]

◆ Environment and labour standards

It seems extraordinary that the Ministry for the Environment was not officially consulted until late August 1997. Indeed, environment officials were barred from electronic access to the official MAI document until July 1997.[133] The New Zealand branch of WWF raised the organisation's concerns about the environmental implications of the MAI with Lockwood Smith in March 1997, prior to the negotiators' meeting in Paris, and asked for much wider public consultation on the issues.[134] The minister was dismissive. He saw no reason why the MAI should undermine international or domestic environmental regimes. The environment, like labour, was best addressed in another venue: 'We doubt that an agreement of this sort would be the most appropriate or effective instrument for dealing with environmental issues which are different in character and require different types of disciplines from those governing investment to which the Agreement is primarily devoted.'[135] Smith's position had been determined without consulting the Ministry for the Environment.

In July 1997, environment officials expressed concern to their minister, Simon Upton, that the MAI should not conflict with existing domestic and international environmental measures. If 'expropriation' was taken to include a loss of profit from tighter environmental regulations, the MAI might limit the government's ability to set new national standards for environmental quality, and provoke demands for compensation. The officials suggested that the agreement should 'explicitly recognise states' sovereignty to set their own standards for environmental management, subject to certain disciplines, and implicitly recognise the need to safeguard states' actions to promote global environmental protection and sustainable development'.[136] Trade officials maintained that the link between environment and investment was undesirable; that environmental matters were dealt with elsewhere; and that any reference to environmental issues in the agreement would deter non-OECD countries from signing up.[137] Their original negotiating position was to oppose any such references, other than a non-binding preamble or a reference to the Guidelines on Multinational Enterprises.[138]

Environment officials remained concerned about the right to regulate. Their internal legal advice warned that:

> If the MAI is signed without reference to environmental matters ... this could have very serious consequences for New Zealand's ability to pursue the goal of sustainable management. If environmental standards are going to be seen as impediments to investment then New Zealand may as well forget trying to maintain its 'clean, green' image.[139]

The officials eventually referred the matter to the Crown Law Office, which concluded there was probably no problem, but suggested strengthening New Zealand's environmental exceptions to the MAI, just in case.[140]

Concern that investors could complain if government regulation reduced the value of their investments was not confined to environmental issues. Both the Ministry of Foreign Affairs and Trade and the Commerce Commission were convinced that the MAI's expropriation provisions would not impede the government's right to regulate.

> In the specific case of New Zealand an explicit and integral part of light-handed regulation in essential facility industries is ... the introduction of more heavy-handed regulation, for example price control, should the need arise. The view that foreign companies investing in New Zealand essential facility companies were buying the right to earn monopoly rights is not acceptable.[141]

New Zealand investors seemed to disagree. When Minister of Energy Max Bradford indicated in September 1997 that he would force the electricity supply companies to split their line and energy business, and to cap the earnings from line charges of companies that did not split, power companies complained that this would increase their costs and diminish their value.[142] Major shareholders, including foreign investors, threatened to sue the government. It was doubtful whether they had sufficient grounds under domestic law; under the MAI, however, they could have challenged the move as having 'equivalent effect' to an expropriation.

The final package on the environment presented by New Zealand negotiators to the April 1998 meeting in Paris addressed only some of these concerns. It contained a commitment in the preamble to sustainable development; a non-binding 'not lowering standards' clause; a binding clause affirming the government's right to regulate on the environment; a binding interpretative note that normal exercise of regulatory powers would not amount to expropriation; and the annexation of the voluntary OECD Guidelines for Multinational Enterprises.[143]

The government took an even harder line on labour standards. Cabinet was told in February 1998 that 'New Zealand has accepted non-binding language on the environment and continues to strongly oppose any language on labour at all'.[144] Department of Labour officials were perfectly comfortable with this, noting:

> The Government has consistently argued that labour standards are more effectively dealt with in organisations like the International Labour Organisation and have no place in economic agreements dealing with commodities or, like the MAI, invisibles. Furthermore the Government considers that using

trade measures to promote labour standards is ineffective and open to protectionist abuse. This approach is consistent with our approach to the linkages between trade and labour in the WTO.[145]

This was not surprising, given that the chief executive was a former senior Treasury official and the department administered the Employment Contracts Act. Under attack in Paris, the New Zealand negotiators reportedly said that the government could not ratify all ILO conventions because of 'idiosyncrasies' in domestic law. This presumably referred to its acknowledged breaches of a number of ILO conventions,[146] and the 1994 ILO report which found that the Employment Contracts Act was incompatible with the core ILO principle to promote collective bargaining.[147] Asked by Labour's Michael Cullen whether the government would support references to the right to organise and bargain collectively in the (non-binding) preamble to the MAI, Lockwood Smith replied: 'New Zealand would not be impressed by any requirement for collective bargaining'.[148]

▲ Local government

The MAI was intended to bind local authorities and cover the privatisation of local authority trading enterprises (LATEs) and other council assets or operations. Minister of Finance Bill Birch told Parliament, quite correctly, that: 'Nothing in the draft [MAI] will prevent local authorities from selling their assets to locally owned consumer trusts. The Government has therefore not lodged any reservations on the matter.'[149] The government insisted that its position was consistent with the Coalition Agreement, which said that any local authority or consumer trust wanting to sell 25 percent or more of its shares in port, airport or gas assets would need prior approval from the local community. Consultation was required only about the decision to sell, not how the asset was sold or to whom. Hence, there was no need to reserve the right to discriminate against foreign buyers.[150] But this was not the issue – it was whether any local authority could decide to sell *only* to New Zealand buyers.

The agreement would have prevented councils from discriminating in favour of local purchasers when selling a bus company, airport or sea-port – so the debate over whether to sell government shares in Wellington airport to foreigners, which triggered the collapse of the Coalition government, would have been a non-starter. The MAI would also have allowed foreign investors to seek compensation if local governments barred them from acquiring rights under contract or gave preference to domestic bidders. This would have ruled out the suggestion in 1997 from Minister of Transport Jenny Shipley that some mandatory local shareholding might be required if the building and operation of roads was contracted out.[151]

Depending on the final wording, the MAI might even have prohibited management buy-outs, share give-aways to local residents, and requirements for joint ventures or a 'golden share', which were considered discriminatory, unless they were included in a government's exceptions.

Despite this, the New Zealand Local Government Association initially declined even to keep a watching brief on developments.[152] Some mayors and local councils, residents and the Alliance pressed the issue. Their concerns centred on privatisation, resource management, and subsidies for local businesses. In April 1998, the Christchurch City Council sought a deferral of the signing of the agreement, and asked Local Government New Zealand to formulate a position on the issue for presentation to government. Should the MAI be signed in the mean time, it wanted an exemption for all current and future measures in relation to local government.[153] The mixture of local pressure and concern from the International Union of Local Authorities prompted the New Zealand body into action. On 30 March 1998 its officials wrote to Prime Minister Jenny Shipley expressing concern at the lack of information and consultation with them, and seeking answers to nine specific questions about the implications of the agreement for local government. It also raised a wider concern, 'the extent to which it is possible, and appropriate, for agreements between national governments to bind sub-national governments within the countries concerned', noting that these were internal constitutional matters for each country. Further, it seemed 'wholly inappropriate that these jurisdictions should be constrained by an agreement to which local government is not a party and which has not been debated or sanctioned by Parliament'.[154] Shipley acknowledged the letter two weeks later. Despite prompting from Local Government New Zealand, she took another three months to reply with a bland assurance that the government would act in the best interests of all New Zealanders.[155] The nine questions were ignored. A further letter in August seeking consultation drew a reply in October. Shipley agreed that consultation was important, but uncertainty surrounding the agreement made it hard to know what to consult about. If the MAI did proceed, she promised that the government would consult local authorities fully.[156]

▲ *Procurement and social services*

On numerous occasions, the New Zealand government dismissed concerns which other countries had taken on board. For example, Lockwood Smith accused Jim Anderton of 'having a screw loose' and being 'deluded' for insisting that the MAI had implications for social services and procurement.[157] Smith insisted that the MAI 'would have no impact on, and specifically excludes contracts for, the provision of social services'.[158] Other countries clearly believed that it would. Canada, for example, entered exceptions to cover health care and social services. Even so, the British Columbia government expressed deep concern that the limited and temporary nature of the exceptions meant 'the integrity of Canada's existing health care system and social services will not be adequately protected'.[159]

New Zealand officials insisted that the government could still invite private bids for health services, and exclude foreign bidders.[160] This assertion was based on a clause which, according to Smith, 'makes it absolutely clear that it does not apply to procurement of services by a Government or a State agency'.[161] That was only partly true. The government could still grant a monopoly; however, it was not meant to discriminate against foreign investors in doing so. In addition, if a public or private sector agency was providing goods or services for government purposes, but did so for commercial resale, it could not discriminate in whom it purchased from. This effectively limited the 'procurement' exception to situations where the government provided a full subsidy (in other words, the public received the goods or services free of charge). Most social services in New Zealand involved a mixture of public and private funding, and had some commercial element, such as part-charges or fees charged on a cost-plus basis. Further, procuring these services would also be considered 'rights under contract', which were defined as investments. That meant the government could not discriminate against foreign investors in awarding them. Having sought clarification in Paris, officials advised Cabinet in April 1998 that there were 'varying interpretations' of the issue, and that a reservation might be needed to protect New Zealand's position.[162]

The situation with preferential subsidies was also unclear. The MAI stated that governments could not discriminate against foreign investors in their right to enjoy, expand and operate their investment. This could include an equal right to subsidies. Several OECD countries proposed a clause that would still allow 'advantages', including government grants or regional assistance subsidies, to be offered to foreign investors, subject to a limited range of performance conditions (including the transfer of technology and spending on research). The issue was never settled.

▲ THE END OF THE MAI?

The MAI began as a state-of-the-art agreement to promote the interests of foreign investors and transnational corporations. By 1998 it had become sufficiently diluted that big business was losing interest. When the Business and Industry Advisory Committee met with OECD officials in

January 1998, it raised a long list of concerns. US business representatives were especially frustrated. One observed:

> When [the MAI] started out, the plan was to use it to raise protections for investment (among developed countries) and then get some developing countries to sign on to these higher standards. Somewhere along the way, the major OECD members decided that, for whatever reason, they weren't ready to get rid of their restrictions, and that they wanted a lot of exceptions.[163]

Another concluded that the MAI was not worth the effort: 'With all the opposition ... why expend all this energy if it doesn't raise investment protections very much?'[164] Their government could still negotiate high-standard bilateral investment treaties, and resort to unilateralism where necessary. OECD officials actively sought to keep them on board:

> It was useful to get some pressure from you. We need you to blow in our sails or the MAI will never reach the shore. [We] need your support in newspapers and electronic media, where you are barely present by comparison with the NGOs. Talk to your governments in the capitals too, if you want to influence the negotiations.[165]

Such comments confirmed the huge impact of the international campaign against the MAI. Complacent governments, the OECD and some of the ICFTU unions had received a major wake-up call. Claims in the *Financial Times* and elsewhere that the MAI was defeated by 'vigilantes whose decisive weapon is the internet' and who were 'operating from around the world via websites', misunderstood the nature of the opposition.[166] The campaigns were mainly national-based and loosely coordinated through existing networks, including via the Internet. Activists made connections at various forums, notably the Vancouver meetings of APEC and the WTO ministerial meeting in Geneva. There were occasional meetings in Paris, where campaigners hotly debated the terms and extent of any dialogue with the OECD. For example, in October 1997, representatives from numerous NGOs met in Paris just before the negotiators' meeting. Some wanted to present the OECD with an impossible set of demands. Others wanted to reject the MAI outright. OECD officials found the compromise statement presented to them at an informal meeting almost totally unacceptable. For many key activists, that was the end of dialogue. Subsequently, a statement to the OECD was circulated via the Internet, and was signed by some 565 organisations in 68 countries.[167] Those who did not sign believed it contained too many concessions. They insisted that this time around, the MAI could be beaten. They were right.

As the April 1998 deadline approached, the US and the European Commission were locked in a battle reminiscent of the Uruguay Round.

The US attacked the lack of commitment of other OECD members, while seeking to carve out areas of sensitivity to itself. President Clinton's failure to secure fast-track negotiating authority in 1997 meant that Congress would have to approve the detail of any MAI. That, in turn, meant appeasing the diverse and often conflicting interests of big business, small business, organised labour, environmental NGOs, and supporters of secondary investment boycotts of Cuba and Iran. The US federal structure was a further complication, as states vigorously opposed being bound by the MAI. In February 1998 there was some excitement when US Trade Representative Charlene Barshefsky announced that the US would not sign the agreement in April. Some interpreted this, prematurely, as the defeat of the MAI.[168] But by then, it seemed clear there would be no agreement to sign in April anyway. The US was playing hardball – a negotiating tactic it had used to secure a more favourable outcome during the closing stages of NAFTA and the Uruguay Round of the GATT.

Western European governments faced different dilemmas. The 'national treatment' and 'most favoured nation' rules, as well as those on expropriations, would directly impact on the ability of the European Commission to give preference to its own investors and to impose more restrictive regulatory regimes in the future. There were also jurisdictional complications with both national governments and the European Parliament being involved. France remained resolute in its demands for a carve-out of cultural industries, which Canada supported but the US again opposed.

When France threatened to withdraw in April, citing concerns about culture, labour and the environment, the ministerial meeting declared a six-month moratorium. Bill Birch supported the break in negotiations, telling the meeting that the agreement fell short of the high standards sought. Maintaining New Zealand's hard-line position, he expressed special concern at the reference to labour and the lack of disciplines on investment incentives.[169] This was a rather different line from the one produced for home consumption. Trade officials told the foreign affairs select committee in September 1998 that the government now recognised the need to balance a high-standard agreement with 'commitments that take full account of economic concerns and political, social and cultural sensitivities'.[170]

'Informal chats' continued between the US and the European Commission; New Zealand had ongoing discussions with Australian and Canadian officials.[171] Several forums involving UNCTAD, the WTO and NGOs were held. But there were too many outstanding issues.[172] When France withdrew altogether in October, just before the negotiating group reconvened, the European Commission's position became untenable. Other governments had less power, but their positions and objections further complicated matters, especially as the list of country-specific exceptions to be negotiated grew. The OECD ministers confirmed in December 1998 that the negotiations were dead. About half of those present supported moving the MAI into the WTO – but not the US.[173]

Negotiations were effectively called off in November 1998. But the MAI was far from dead. Pressure from the transnationals for a high-quality multilateral agreement on investment would continue, supported pragmatically by their home governments and ideologically by their allies in countries such as New Zealand. WTO Director-General Ruggiero was already on record as saying: 'We are no longer writing the rules of interaction among separate national economies. We are writing the constitution of a single global economy. ... The question is where – not whether – work on trade and investment should take place.'[174] Some lessons had been learned. A less ambitious approach, perhaps modelled on the 'bottom up' approach of the GATS, might emerge in the WTO negotiations as an entry point to begin a more comprehensive negotiations. But success was far from assured. The rich OECD countries would face more resistance in the WTO from poor countries who opposed any such deal, and the NGOs, as the *Financial Times* observed, had 'tasted blood'.[175] There was also the risk that any attempt to revive the investment issue might see the NGOs' active opposition flow into other areas of the WTO.

▲ REFLECTIONS

Had the MAI been signed, it would have effectively embedded New Zealand's policies on investment liberalisation and deregulation for the next twenty years. The 'standstill' requirement (depending on how it was framed) would have constrained future New Zealand governments from tightening the rules on foreign investors, while commitments to 'rollback' would have required existing restrictions to be reduced over time. An international arbitration process would have ruled on breaches of the agreement and compensation, but its awards would have been enforceable in New Zealand courts. A future government could have withdrawn from the agreement after five years, but its provisions would have applied to existing investors for another fifteen. Alternatively, a future government could have refused to comply with the agreement, but the retaliatory sanctions and diplomatic costs of doing so were potentially enormous. Despite these ramifications, Parliament would not have been entitled to vote on whether New Zealand should sign the agreement. This was an exercise in external sovereignty. Defeat of the MAI was therefore critical to maintaining the independent capacity of the state to act.

Stopping the MAI was important for another reason – it sent a strong signal that New Zealanders were not prepared to see the government abdicate the country's right to make rules to control the activities of foreign investors and give preference to their own. The disparate, and generally uncoordinated, collection of people and groups who opposed the MAI reflected a spontaneous reaction to a proposal that paid no heed to New Zealand's political, social and cultural life, or to the Crown's obligations under the Treaty of Waitangi. In a small country, that many voices had an impact, especially against the backdrop of similar ferment in other countries. Perhaps most significantly for the future, it also showed that the interests of Maori and non-Maori can coincide on what is for both a matter of sovereignty.

10 ▲ Reclaiming the Future

For fifteen years, the twin images of prosperity in a global free market and of New Zealand leading the world went largely unchallenged. Globalisation was represented as linear, evolutionary and irreversible. Even if the results were disappointing or unfair, there was no alternative. At the cusp of the millennium, such claims are not tenable and New Zealanders from diverse walks of life are saying so.

This book has revealed the beginnings of a backlash against New Zealand's free market revolution. Moves to eliminate tariffs on clothing and textiles brought together local mayors, unions and small manufacturers in 1998 to defend their towns and their industry in a campaign that enjoyed widespread public sympathy. At the same time, dairy farmers and fruit-growers, supported by the local communities, took to the streets as well as the political lobbies to defend the producer and marketing boards against deregulation. In 1999 sheep farmers protested against the hypocrisy of the US over free trade, while pig farmers sought temporary protection from subsidised international competition. Even strong free market supporters, such as Michael Barnett from the Auckland Chamber of Commerce, urged the government in June 1999 to adopt a more middle-of-the-road approach: 'By promoting a free-trade economy, we bared our soul to the world. But the reality is that while we went down the road first, the rest of the world is slower and this is turning to a disadvantage for New Zealand'.[1]

In 1997 and 1998, negotiations for a Multilateral Agreement on Investment at the OECD, which would have given foreign investors powerful new rights, met concerted opposition from such diverse quarters as Maori, Grey Power, radio talkback callers, the Alliance, city councils and Local Government New Zealand. The government was forced to release an unprecedented amount of information and eventually to endorse a moratorium, before negotiations on the agreement broke down completely. The Royal

New Zealand College of General Practitioners objected to Australian authorities deciding whether New Zealanders should know if their food is genetically modified. Coromandel Watchdog forced mining companies to accept some responsibility for their tailings dams, while the government proposed (but failed to introduce) legislation to require those companies to meet the cost of the hazards they created. Commercial and public criticism succeeded in forcing the government to concede the need for price regulation of the electricity industry and more rigorous constraints on the abuse of market power and natural monopolies. Proposals to replace traditional trade remedies (for dumping and to safeguard local industry) with domestic competition law were deferred as being too controversial; the introduction of 'more market' amendments to the resource management laws was delayed until just before the 1999 election.[2]

In parallel, Maori asserted their tino rangatiratanga (self-determination) in ways that reflected their common experience of colonisation and class, although strategies and objectives varied among the nationalists, entrepreneurs and pragmatists. They achieved mixed success. Iwi and Maori nationalists insisted on a constitutional voice in both domestic governance and international policy arenas. They forced the government to hold nation-wide hui on the MAI, which caused real problems for government and negotiators, but more selective dialogue on APEC had no apparent impact on the government's position. Attempts to defend indigenous knowledge and natural resources from becoming the intellectual property of transnationals enjoyed wide-ranging Maori support, but with minimal results; Maori objections to genetic engineering on cultural grounds had more potential allies, and hence prospect of success. Maori with large landholdings campaigned actively but unsuccessfully alongside the Business Roundtable for deregulation of the producer and marketing boards, although the voice of Maori small farmers was not heard. Maori workers and their local communities were part of the broad alliance that failed to stop the removal of tariffs on motor vehicles, but won a reprieve for textiles, clothing and footwear.

These challenges from such diverse groups of New Zealanders were mostly ad hoc attempts to defend the status quo – the belated drawing of a line in the sand – although some proposed positive alternatives. They drew together pragmatic and shifting coalitions of business people, unions, farmers, local communities, the elderly and Maori – reflecting a residue of the historic compromises of the Keynesian welfare state, combined with Maori aspirations for economic survival and self-determination.

The major political parties responded by moderating their positions in the name of the 'knowledge economy', while maintaining a basic free trade and investment line. Ideologues in the Business Roundtable berated their allies in government for their weakness of resolve, but failed to understand the more subtle rearguard action that was underway. Key ministers and officials had not abandoned their programme. Some proposals, such as producer board deregulation, were repackaged with a legislative timetable that was designed to limit the opportunity to mobilise dissent. Cosmetic moves were made to placate discontent over international treaty-making, such as the belated consultation over the government's WTO negotiating position. Other legislative amendments, especially to the resource management law, were introduced mainly for electioneering purposes. Those measures which government had reluctantly conceded were necessary to address market failures – notably the Commerce Act amendment on the abuse of monopoly powers and the regulation of electricity pricing – became deadlocked after aggressive lobbying of senior politicians by Telecom, and the minority government's inability to design a package that secured multi-party support, respectively. Despite these clawbacks, however, there was no doubt that the policy climate had changed.

The backlash was not unique to New Zealand. At a seminar on the future of the multilateral trading system in Geneva in May 1998, a panel of prominent free-marketeers conceded that their 'bicycle was getting wobbly'.[3] In the past year, the Asian tiger economies had collapsed. President Clinton had lost his 'fast-track' authority to conclude trade treaties, meaning that Congress could pick and choose which parts to accept. Negotiations on the controversial MAI had been suspended. People in many countries were challenging the erosion of national democracy and state sovereignty by the onset of globalisation. There was pressure to reintroduce regulation of capital flows and protectionist approaches to trade. It could have been noted too that the IMF was being blamed for making the Asian crisis worse, and that the chief economist at the World Bank had challenged the 'Washington consensus' on structural adjustment, which both institutions had been implementing for fifteen years.

The Geneva panel's solution was to pedal faster so the bicycle stayed upright. They warned that any moves to regulate short-term financial flows must not hinder progress in freeing up international trade and investment. Meanwhile, governments had to educate their people better about the benefits of global free markets. The international institutions of the WTO, IMF and World Bank could boost public confidence by making their documents and decisions more transparent. They might even show a social face, and invite responsible members of 'civil society' to participate on the fringe. But there was no hint of recognition that their economic model needed to be debated and rethought, and it was inconceivable that it might have failed.

The analysis presented in this book suggests there are three main causes of the current fractures in the globalisation process. The first is internal, as disagreements between states threaten the image of international consensus and make it difficult to maintain, let alone advance, the global free market agenda. Far from being a coherent body of global economic policy-making, the major international institutions and economic agreements are fragile. Internal tensions always exist in inter-governmental bodies. But when the goal is to produce an integrated global market-place, run according to uniform rules agreed in these international forums, there is a point at which dissension makes them dysfunctional. The second cause is systemic, reflected most graphically in the 1997 meltdown of East Asian financial markets – that most integrated and self-regulating element of the global economy. The third is the opposition of people and communities at local, national and international levels to the political processes and substantive policies adopted by states and international institutions in the name of globalisation.

Examining these trends in the New Zealand context, this book has focused on the two fundamentals of a truly global economy – 'free' trade and 'free' investment – and the international institutions and agreements dedicated to advancing them. To question these fundamentals is not anti-trade; nor does it view foreign investment as evil per se. Rather, it asks whether there are better ways to engage realistically with a turbulent international environment while addressing the urgent questions that face New Zealanders at home – social well-being, economic viability, democratically accountable government, and responsibilities under the Treaty of Waitangi.

Such sentiments became unfashionable during the free market era, being dismissed as inherently undesirable or impractical in the global environment. Desirability is a matter of informed popular choice. Practicality is more a question of fact. The previous chapters have sought to open up discussion on both the desirability and practicality of the current economic agenda, and to identify options for New Zealand governments in the years ahead. They show that there are alternatives. In promoting debate about these and other possibilities, this book does not suggest that New Zealand should retreat within its island borders as if immune from what is happening in the rest of the world, nor does it deny the future opportunities and challenges posed by the information technology revolution and strategic economic integration. Nor is there any attempt to offer a blueprint for the future. The goal is to provide an impetus for New Zealanders to engage in a rigorous and open debate.

For this, a fresh perspective is needed, one that jettisons the ideology of globalisation and concentrates on what is happening in practice.

It is important to move beyond the search for evidence of what has been and may become globalised, and to identify what power remains in, or can be restored to, local hands. This conclusion therefore examines two key questions: is the global free market agenda pursued in New Zealand since 1984 sustainable in the longer term? If not, has the market-driven paradigm been so effectively embedded that even the kind of moderate alternatives identified throughout this book are truly inconceivable?

▲ THE SUSTAINABILITY OF THE GLOBAL VISION

After fifteen years of radical free market policies, the contradictions Karl Polanyi identified with nineteenth century laissez-faire are clearly visible in New Zealand today – a dysfunctional domestic economy, an unacceptable social cost, and a stubborn survival of values that are irreconcilable with the self-regulating global market-place. In addition, the collision between the universalising goal of globalisation and people's deep-seated notions of sovereignty, democratic government and tino rangatiratanga has created tensions that seem impossible to reconcile.

▲ *A dysfunctional domestic economy*

Minister of Foreign Affairs Don McKinnon observed in 1996 that: 'increasing interdependence must give people results, if not they find an external force to blame and the events of the past twenty years will be reversed'.[4] Talking up the economic returns of the free market project has been essential for its survival. This meant focusing on the positive indicators: low inflation since 1991, successive budget surpluses since 1994, repayment of government debt, and significant reductions in government expenditure in relation to GDP. But structurally the economy was in serious trouble. In 1999 the economic picture looks bleak. Growing criticism of the failure to deliver sustained economic growth, improved international competitiveness and better living standards for all New Zealanders suggests that a contest of ideas about the future direction of the economy has begun to emerge.

This is a significant development. As academic economist Paul Dalziel observes, most New Zealand economists have consistently praised the results of the neo-liberal programme. He quotes a survey by Lewis Evans and others in the prestigious *Journal of Economic Literature* in 1996, which concludes:

The success of the reforms to date has strengthened support for free-trade policies within New Zealand's business community, perhaps to an unusual degree by OECD standards. Many of the lessons from the New Zealand experiences are worthy of emulation by other countries. Others, like its tardy labor market deregulation, provide a cautionary note. After decades of policy errors and investment blunders, New Zealand appears to have finally diagnosed its predicament appropriately and is on a trajectory to maintain its economy as a consistent high performer among the OECD. New Zealand once again appears to be emerging as a laboratory from which results will animate economic debate and policy throughout the world.[5]

Dalziel challenges this conclusion in a paper entitled 'New Zealand's Economic Reform Programme was a Failure', written in 1999. He examines two key indicators of success: whether New Zealand's real gross domestic product is higher after fifteen years of 'reform' than it would have been under likely alternative policies, and whether all households are better off than they were before 1984.

Matching the growth rate of New Zealand from 1978 to 1998 against that of Australia (which he takes as the most appropriate comparator), Dalziel notes a striking similarity between the two countries' GDP paths up until 1984, and a striking divergence after that. He concludes that:

> ... if New Zealand had continued to grow at approximately the same rate as Australia (as it did between 1978 and 1984), it would have produced extra output between 1985 and 1998 amounting to more than NZ$210 billion in 1995/96 prices, or well over *twice* New Zealand's total GDP in 1998. ... It would be unreasonable to lay all the blame for this dismal performance at the door of the reforms – but even if only half this lost production was due to 'the special character of New Zealand's reform programme', it still amounts to more than a year's worth of income having been sacrificed.[6]

Australia's more pragmatic market policies, while similar in intent to New Zealand's, avoided much of the social and political upheaval experienced in New Zealand, and sustained the long-term productive capacity of the economy (although it too had balance of payments problems). By contrast, extensive industrial restructuring in New Zealand saw the large-scale destruction of capital, such as freezing works and car assembly plants, which had few alternative uses. The economy was starved: high unemployment meant low consumption expenditure; high interest rates reduced investment expenditure; large cutbacks in government spending meant less public consumption expenditure; and the high value of the New Zealand dollar caused new export expenditure to slow down. The sacrifice of economic output in the late 1980s as a result of Labour's 'big bang' economic programme showed no sign of being compensated for by higher growth in the 1990s. The costs of this failure were high, and were generally borne by those who could least afford to do so. Dalziel concludes that Australia and the rest of the OECD were well-advised not to follow New Zealand's example – a very different 'lesson' from that drawn by Evans et al.

In a separate assessment in 1997, Dalziel took issue with another claim by the same authors, namely that the real per capita income of New Zealanders in 1995 was 6.8 percent higher than the pre-1984 average growth rate would have predicted. Dalziel tested this claim against three periods that began and ended at comparable stages of the economic cycle. He calculated that New Zealand's real per capita output in the year ending March 1995 was still 1.5 percent *below* the level that would have resulted if the economy had continued to grow at the trend level between 1966/67 and 1981/82 (years in which the economic cycle peaked). The income sacrificed between 1987/88 and 1993/94 as a result of that lower trend was $11,625 per working-age person, or 32.5 percent of annual GDP. Dalziel concluded that: 'there is still no clear-cut improvement in the sustainable growth performance of the New Zealand economy ten to twelve years after the beginning of the reform programme, but substantial income sacrifices were incurred'.[7]

In 1997 Brian Easton, another economist critical of the 'reform' programme, reviewed the overall performance of the economy from 1985 to 1996. He found that: 'on all other measures [apart from the low inflation figure] – rising unemployment, employment growth, GDP volume growth, labour productivity growth, export volume growth, and the current account deficit – New Zealand has had a poorer performance than the OECD [average]'; and in all but the external current account it had performed worse than Australia.[8] Export growth fell relative to the rest of the world, while the rise in imports continued. The tradeable sector showed no growth in productivity after 1985. The removal of domestic support was not the whole reason. There was also a 'spectacular reduction in the level of competitiveness in the mid-1980s', mainly as a result of the Reserve Bank's manipulation of the real exchange rate. New Zealand's GDP growth rate since Easton's study was 1.5 percent in the year ended March 1998, and minus 0.2 percent in the year ended March 1999 (although growth in the March 1999 quarter was 0.7 percent). (See Appendix: Figure 1.)

These analyses of the domestic economy contrast starkly with the image of international orthodoxy and success on which the champions of New Zealand's experiment depend. As the Introduction to this book showed, by the later 1990s similar assessments were being voiced by leading members of the business community and the business media.

Concerns about growth and productivity were reinforced by the dire state of the key international economic indicators, particularly the external current account of the balance of payments (see Chapter 4, and Appendix: Figure 2). The current account deficit for the year to March 1999 was $6.4 billion (up from $6 billion in December 1998), or around 6.4 percent of GDP. Reducing the deficit would require greatly increased overseas earnings and/or reduced imports and returns to foreign investors. Meanwhile, the gap between the country's income and expenditure had to be bridged through asset sales, more overseas borrowing, or using up government reserves. Bob Edlin of *The Independent* estimates that half of the deficit has been met by $3.4 billion from asset sales, while the rest has been added to the foreign debt.[9]

By March 1999, New Zealand's total foreign debt had reached $101.9 billion, or 103.6 percent of GDP, up from 101.4 percent in March 1998 (see Appendix: Figure 3). This was equivalent to about three years and five months' worth of exports of goods and services. The country's net external liability was estimated at 95 percent of GDP.[10] The private sector had been responsible for all increases in foreign debt in recent years, while the government had reduced its overseas borrowings significantly, largely through the proceeds from asset sales. Approximately half the foreign debt was in New Zealand dollars.

Interest and debt repayments impose a massive drag on the productive economy. Long-term servicing of the debt poses a major problem, because little of the borrowing has gone into building New Zealand's productive capacity. Investment analyst Brian Gaynor points out that much of the country's offshore borrowing, especially by the registered banks, has been short-term.[11] Forty percent of the debt at March 1998 (equivalent to 1.5 times the annual export of goods and services) fell due within twelve months. The majority of those funds were invested in property. Reserve Bank figures show that, in the year to 31 March 1998, bank lending rose by $9.4 billion, with $6.7 billion (71 percent) of that going to construction, property and residential housing, and only $0.8 billion (9 percent) to the productive sector. Registered banks had total loans of $61 billion to the property sector and less than $20 billion to export-related industries. Property investment does not generate the foreign exchange earnings needed to service the offshore debt. Part of the problem has been the low level of household savings. In a 1998 OECD survey of annual household savings rates, New Zealand ranked 21st out of 22 countries, with an average savings rate of 1.7 percent of household income. Half the OECD countries surveyed had rates exceeding 10 percent. But increased household savings alone would not provide an alternative pool of finance; the country also needed local corporate and government investment.

Two main factors accounted for the external current account deficit: the net outflow of investment earnings, and the country's poor international trade performance. The serious imbalance between the earnings of foreign investors in New Zealand and from New Zealand investments offshore, and the recent failure of foreign investors to reinvest their profits, were discussed in Chapter 4. In addition to its effect on the balance of payments, the export of earnings by foreign investors has reduced the amount of finance available to fuel the New Zealand economy.[12] Statistics New Zealand reported in 1999 that the proportion of income from domestic production that remained available to New Zealanders, after adjusting for net profits, interest and dividends remitted abroad, was stable from 1950 until the mid-1970s. It began falling after the effects of the oil shocks were felt in 1974, and declined rapidly through to 1986. After a slight recovery between 1990 and 1993, it fell dramatically again. In 1997 the ratio was the lowest recorded in the post-war period (see Appendix: Figure 4).[13]

Nor could New Zealand's international trade provide sufficient foreign exchange earnings to bridge the current account deficit. The free-traders assumed that unilateral trade liberalisation and domestic deregulation would increase efficiency and make the country's exporters more competitive in a deregulated global trading environment. But international markets have proved far from 'free'. Indeed, during the 1990s trade barriers, especially non-tariff barriers, rose in many rich countries, while they came down in the poorer ones. Robert Wade interprets foreign investment trends within the OECD as evidence that many companies expect trade restrictions to continue: 'Overall, the trade data on both flows and policies do not support any simple idea that the world economy is operating in a new, more internationalized, or less nationally or regionally segmented way'.[14] Expanding New Zealand's market share would be difficult under such conditions, even if its economic policies had worked.

New Zealand's trade profile has shown some change. The trading base has broadened. Services, notably tourism, emerged as an important export earner, although projections were highly inflated.[15] Exports of niche manufactures and forest products also grew. However, natural resource products (agriculture, horticulture, fish and forestry) continued to account for over half the commodity exports. Dairy dominated, with its share rising from 13.3 percent in 1992 to 16.8 percent in 1997. Export markets also diversified. Between 1960 and 1997, exports to the UK fell from half New Zealand's total export revenue to 6.5 percent. Exports to Australia increased to over 20 percent by 1997, probably reflecting the impact of CER. Exports to Asian countries grew most dramatically, from 2.9 percent of total export revenue in 1960 to 31.1 percent in 1980 and just over 39 percent in 1997 (40 percent of which went to Japan). However, New Zealand was also the only non-Asian OECD country to go into recession after the Asian crisis; the impact was felt heavily in tourism from South Korea and in exports to Japan and South Korea, especially of wool and forest products. The merchandise trade deficit for the year ended April 1999 was $1.29 billion; the provisional merchandise trade balance for that month was in deficit by $38 million – the first time for thirteen years that an April trade balance had not been in surplus.[16]

The terms of trade (the volume of merchandise imports that can be funded by a fixed volume of merchandise exports) had deteriorated seriously in the 1990s. A drop in the terms of trade index shows that the purchasing power of exports has fallen. After a significant improvement in the late 1980s, the index remained in a trough for most of the 1990s. Figures for the June 1997/98 year were the worst for fifteen years. In the December 1998 quarter, the index fell another one percent. Export volume had grown, and the trade-weighted exchange rate remained relatively low; but depressed international markets meant that export prices still declined, while imports remained flat. In the March 1999 quarter, the terms of trade index fell another 2.1 percent, putting it at the lowest point since the September 1987 quarter. This meant that 2.1 percent fewer imports could be funded by a fixed amount of exports. Meanwhile, imports continued to rise, partly due to a significant increase in the number of imported motor vehicles following the closure of the domestic car assembly industry. In June 1999, despite the slowing trend in the growth of exports, and the excess of import costs over export earnings, International Trade Minister Lockwood Smith hailed a 'steady upward trend in exports', which showed that 'New Zealand exporters continue to expand their business in competitive world markets'.[17]

In fact, the international trade comparisons were far from impressive. The 'openness' of an economy is often measured by how much of the country's total economic activity involves imports and exports – that is, the ratio of imports and exports to GDP. This indicator rose strongly in New Zealand after 1984, but was still several percent below the average for small OECD countries in 1993/94. Other countries' trade was expanding faster. In 1998 a survey of 45 countries showed that New Zealand was one of five to have lost market share over the past six years, a trend that was predicted to continue for another two years.[18] In the same year, New Zealand was ranked twentieth out of 25 OECD countries on export growth performance indicators.[19]

Many structural problems contributed to New Zealand's poor trade performance, including distance, size and access to heavily protected agricultural markets. External shocks (global recessions, the Asian crisis) and natural disasters (drought, electricity outages) were beyond the government's control. The poor export performance also reflected New Zealand's continued dependence on basic agricultural commodities and manufactures with little value added. But a large share of the blame was laid on the huge fluctuations in the value of New Zealand's currency as the Reserve Bank relied on interest and exchange rates to achieve price stability, irrespective of the impact on the real economy. In the mid-1980s, the newly floated dollar appreciated rapidly as speculators cashed in on high real interest rates, neutralising the benefits for exporters of the 20 percent devaluation in 1984. This stopped after the 1987 crash. Exports began to recover, although recession also stepped in. The situation recurred in the mid-1990s. As the Reserve Bank sought to contain the inflationary potential of the 1992 recovery, speculators took advantage of its strategy of high interest and exchange rates. The rapid rise in the trade-weighted exchange rate index (TWI), from 53.2 in December 1992 to 67.2 in December 1996, led exporters to complain that the currency was overvalued by 10 to 15 percent.[20] The Reserve Bank had responded to an inflationary blow-out in the property sector with high exchange rate policies which punished the tradeable sector (that is, exporting and import-competing firms) where inflation was already low. Speculators continued to take advantage of the highest real interest rates in the OECD, and a virtually guaranteed exchange rate. The TWI rose to 68.6 in April 1997.

The combination of deteriorating economic conditions, an easing of monetary policy, and the onset of the Asian crisis sent the dollar into free-fall (see Appendix: Figure 5). The TWI fell 13.9 percent between the June 1997 and June 1998 quarters. In October 1998 it was down to 55.8. In late 1998 the New Zealand dollar began to rise slowly against the major currencies except Australia, but not against the Asian currencies, which remained weak. Exporters struggled in the face of dead Asian markets, competition from Asian products made cheaper by their exchange rates, and fears of a global recession on top of the domestic one. The Reserve Bank's Monetary Conditions Index,[21] introduced in 1997 to indicate the acceptable level of interest and exchange rates, was challenged as 'idiosyncratic', 'eccentric' and 'bizarre'.[22] In early 1999 the Bank adopted the approach of simply nominating an official interest rate, as used by central banks with inflation records at least as good as New Zealand's (including Australia). However, the Bank continued to rely on making public statements to indicate what monetary conditions should be.

After being treated as sacrosanct for over a decade, the Reserve Bank's approach to monetary policy was now being questioned. Exporters, who were feeling the dual impact of competition from lower-cost (and often protected) foreign producers and the Reserve Bank's exchange rate strategy, demanded a monetary policy that served the real economy. Their calls were supported by international commentators, who questioned the monetarist obsession with near-zero inflation. Paul Krugman observed that:

> [It is] one of the dirty little secrets of economic analysis that even though inflation is universally regarded as a terrible scourge, most efforts to measure its costs come up with embarrassingly small numbers. ... As far as economic analysis can tell us, a steady inflation rate of 3 or 4 percent does very little harm – and even a rate of 10 percent has only small costs.[23]

World Bank chief economist Joseph Stiglitz went further, citing recent studies which found that 'when countries cross the threshold of 40 percent annual inflation, they fall into a high-inflation/low-growth trap. Below that level, however, there is little evidence that inflation is costly'. Respected researchers had suggested that 'low levels of inflation may even improve economic performance relative to what it would have been with zero inflation'.[24] The most substantial contribution to such thinking in New Zealand came in a paper from the Alliance in 1998 on alternative monetary policy.[25] This provoked discussion at the time, which fell away once the exchange and interest rates stabilised in 1999.

In other countries, these economic indicators would have caused grave concern. But New Zealand officials insisted there was no problem because of the quality of the current account deficit. New debt was being incurred by the private sector while the government was repaying public debt. If private debt became too high, the market would lose confidence and make firms 'adjust' (as happened in Asia). According to Reserve Bank Governor Don Brash, the best the government could do to assist the balance of payments was to maintain fiscal surpluses as a contribution to domestic saving.[26] Price stability remained a paramount objective for government, alongside lowering international barriers to trade, attracting foreign investment, reducing domestic constraints on competitive markets and improving efficiency.

Prominent business leaders such as Hugh Fletcher, Gilbert Ullrich and Jim Scott urged the government to abandon its hands-off approach and take positive action to rebuild the country's productive and export base. Their suggestions included balancing the objectives of price stability and economic growth, introducing compulsory superannuation to provide a domestic investment pool, and promoting strategic investment in promising export industries.[27] This would require some rethinking of the 'fundamentals', although they remained committed to an export-oriented economy that was integrated into global markets. Visiting US economist Michael Porter, the author of a 1991 study of New Zealand's competitiveness, also argued that free market ideology had been taken too far, and advocated investment in high-tech industry 'clusters'.[28] Ireland emerged as the favoured model of an open, export-based economy with little import protection, extensive foreign investment, falling government debt, and firm fiscal and monetary policies. The differences lay in Ireland's positive incentives for new investment in high-tech 'sunrise' industries, combined with active labour market policies, the removal of tertiary education fees, and higher direct tax rates, social security and government spending. From a worse starting point, Ireland's GDP had grown 80 percent more than New Zealand's since 1984, albeit with the help of substantial subsidies from the European Union.[29]

Significantly, a number of these commentators also stressed the importance of New Zealand's 'social capital'. As noted in the Introduction, Hugh Fletcher insisted that a vibrant New Zealand economy required a healthy social fabric, including recognition of the central place of Maori in New Zealand society. Gilbert Ullrich, general manager of Ullrich Aluminium, expressed discomfort with the relentless pursuit of corporate profit, which since 1984 had come to exemplify 'successful business'; he argued instead for an 'enterprise culture' that valued its workers, consumers and local community. Ullrich's own company had consciously shifted away from an 'aggressive and confrontational' approach to suppliers, customers and workers, after the company concluded that 'our drive for efficiency could be defeating itself. The first lesson was that the company should focus on its most valuable asset – *the people who work for it*'. In 1998 he reported that the signs were looking good, and suggested that other industries could benefit from doing the same: 'There's a new mood emerging in NZ. People no longer want to think of themselves as just economic units, mere cogs in some company machine. They want to be valued, listened to, made to feel they have a genuine part to play. That is not just the decent way for business to behave, it is also the most efficient.'[30]

Other successful local business leaders echoed his call. Dick Hubbard, founder of a company producing quality breakfast cereals, challenged the Business Roundtable's view that the sole purpose of business is to maximise shareholders' wealth, and that social issues are the responsibility of government and voluntary agencies. In Hubbard's view, a company has 'a moral obligation to look at the way its business decisions impact on all the stakeholders that have a direct or indirect stake in the business'.[31] That includes a social contract to provide as many jobs as possible, while recognising the need for efficiency: 'Part of our criterion for success is how many jobs we have created.' If other companies made the same effort, 'we could make a big dent in unemployment'.[32] In 1998 Hubbard spearheaded the creation of Businesses for Social Responsibility, claiming support from 100 companies that ranged from two-person businesses to large New

Zealand corporations. Although not established specifically to oppose the Business Roundtable, it was intended to offer a strong and credible alternative voice.[33]

This shift in business values reflected a desire to preserve New Zealand's autonomy, and a belief that communities and businesses could benefit from being committed to each other. For economists like Tim Hazledine, restoring the value of 'social capital' also requires a shift in emphasis from the export sector – always problematic for a remote country like New Zealand which is dependent on primary exports – to servicing more of its economic needs from within.[34] His suggestion of import substitution, although unfashionable, resonates strongly with the research of Canadian economist John Helliwell, who concludes that national borders do still matter:

> The striking size and pervasiveness of border effects reveal that the global economy of the 1990s is really a patchwork of national economies, stitched together by threads of trade and investment that are much weaker than the economic fabric of nations. This makes untenable many of the central assumptions of international economics, and requires a major rethinking about how best to model international flows of goods and capital.[35]

Helliwell observes with refreshing frankness that researchers have been unable to verify the main empirical projections of international trade theory (based on notions of general equilibrium, full information and global technology) because too much trade is missing. Basically, even though OECD countries operate in a relatively deregulated economic environment they have not traded with each other to their full potential because companies still tend to rely on familiar institutions, networks and tastes. These, in turn, draw on broadly common values and expectations that are developed through families, social groups and nations.

Such factors are important, even for those who insist that New Zealand's future rests with the so-called 'knowledge economy'. There is no doubt that the information technology revolution is changing the nature of personal and commercial transactions for those who have access to them. But cyberspace will never displace the need for human interaction and social relationships – and the benefits these provide. As Ireland's experience shows, the knowledge-based society also depends on public investment and planning to ensure a broad base of education, technical skills and analytical abilities in a vibrant intellectual environment where new ideas can be generated, tested and debated.[36] Successful interaction with the international economy requires not just technicians, scientists and engineers, but lateral thinkers and people with knowledge of language, literature, politics, history and culture. So too does a confident nation that knows who it is and where it is going.

Helliwell concludes that most poorer countries with relatively closed economies would, on balance, benefit from reducing border constraints. However, 'for the industrial countries already tightly bound into the global trading system, there are likely to be fewer gains from further globalization'.[37] Such conclusions, especially when echoed by local business leaders and intellectuals, provide the basis for exploring genuine alternatives for New Zealand.

However, a well-grounded debate on a new economic direction needs to learn from the failure of the free market approach. First, it needs to restore a link between economic policy and New Zealanders' economic needs, social values and cultural identities. There will be no consensus on what these are; but some understanding can be reached through a vigorously contested debate. Second, it needs to take into account the lessons of history. That includes the benefits and pitfalls of the compromise between national capital, paid (mainly male) and unpaid (mainly women) workers that underpinned the Keynesian welfare state. Third, it needs to address the place of Maori in the national economy. That requires debate amongst Maori over the economic development model they wish to pursue: the kind Mike Smith described in the Introduction, where traditional values bind together people's economic, spiritual, social and political life; or self-determination sourced in entrepreneurial activities, with the proceeds distributed to tribal and/or urban beneficiaries through cash, services or cultural development programmes. It equally requires non-Maori to reflect on ways that the future might address long-standing Maori grievances over resources and power, and locate points of common interest and values, as well as difference. A forward-looking debate would also take a more sophisticated approach to the concept of economic wellbeing, which currently focuses on GDP and and its simplistic treatment of activities such as growing organic apples and creating a toxic waste dump as equally valuable in the country's economy. Unpaid work, ecological sustainability, and social impact need to be treated as significant features of the real economic life of any country, as many economists of the future are beginning to recognise. New Zealand's responsibility to poorer countries in the vicinity of the South Pacific, and in other parts of the world, would inevitably form another part of such a debate.

▲ An unacceptable social cost

The nascent debate about New Zealand's economic future has emerged in response to the damage caused to the real economy by free market theories. The social costs have also become unsustainable. Over a decade and a half, many urban and rural communities have been shattered by government policies imposed with little or no warning, and with callous disregard for their effects on people's lives. In single-industry towns, the closure of the major employer – a timber mill, car assembly plant, freezing works or clothing factory – was devastating. As jobs went, shops and banks closed. Schools and emergency services that no longer had a critical mass were shut down. Some former employees became self-employed contractors, carrying all the risk for an often small and uncertain income. Many young people left town, or opted for gangs, drugs or suicide. Small businesses that serviced the local community maintained a marginal existence or went bankrupt. Towns such as Thames struggled to survive; smaller ones withered away. In the cities, rich suburbs prospered as a result of policies that made a virtue of self-interest and greed. Property values rose, along with executive salaries and professional fees; new wealth was spent on a wide range of consumer luxuries, often imported into New Zealand or bought overseas. The urban poor – Maori and Pacific Islands people, the elderly, women alone, single parents, young unemployed, working class families, new immigrants, the mentally ill, among others – were trapped in enclaves of unemployment, homelessness and poverty.

Since the mid-1980s, New Zealand society has visibly polarised along intersecting lines of race, gender, age and economic class. By 1993, studies of poverty based on different methodologies were producing consistent findings: around one in five New Zealanders, and one-third of the country's children, were living in poverty – more than double the numbers in 1988. Maori families were two and a half times (and Pacific Islands families three and a half times) more likely to live in poverty than Pakeha families.[38]

A major redistribution of wealth has taken place in a very short time. Srikanta Chatterjee and Nripesh Podder report that between 1984 and 1996, the richest 5 percent of New Zealanders increased their share of national income by 25 percent, and the top 10 percent of the population by 15 percent (see Appendix: Figure 6).[39] The share of national income received by the bottom four-fifths of New Zealanders fell, with the poorest proportionately losing most. The general findings of previous research were confirmed in early 1999 by a Statistics New Zealand report on long-term trends in national income from 1982 to 1996. The chief statistician called the results 'striking' and 'unequivocal': 'income inequality has increased substantially'.[40]

Minister of Finance Bill English welcomed the Statistics New Zealand report, implying that it exonerated National because 'income disparities were stable in the 1980s, then increased significantly between 1986 and 1991, and appear to have stabilised again since 1991'.[41] English overstated the case: the data showed that the average household market income for the richest 10 percent rose from $121,500 in 1991 to $134,100 in 1996.[42] He also ignored the impact of National's $1.3 billion benefit cuts which took effect in 1991. Since then, two more rounds of tax cuts (in 1996 and 1998) had increased inequality by disproportionately benefiting the rich, just as Labour's 1987 tax cuts had done.[43] The figures also took no account of added costs, such as user charges for formerly subsidised services in health, education, housing and public transport; these impacted most harshly on low- and middle-income families, who had limited discretionary income.

Despite clear evidence that the rich had benefited most under Labour, its social welfare spokesperson Steve Maharey was unwilling to condemn Rogernomics and accept responsibility for the cost: 'Given what occurred in this country at that time we would expect that there would be huge changes in the distribution of income. No one disagrees that those changes were necessary.'[44] ACT interpreted the Statistics New Zealand report as evidence that taxes and intrusive governments continued to impose burdens on the middle class. The Alliance's Jim Anderton saw it as 'an official declaration that the free market experiment had failed. They were wrong. Roger Douglas, Richard Prebble, Ruth Richardson and Bill Birch owe New Zealanders an apology'.[45]

The reality of what poverty meant for hundreds of thousands of New Zealanders seemed to escape most of the politicians. A 1996 study of 100 households living on benefits in Wellington showed that a large majority had problems paying for food and housing, had gone without meals, could not pay their electricity bills on time, and went without necessary clothes or shoes. A quarter had sold household items to pay bills. Some 14 percent had no washing machine, 33 percent had no carpet, 9 percent had no electric jug, and 6 percent had no heater. During the previous six months, at least one household member could not afford a doctor (43 percent), a dentist (53 percent) or a prescription (32 percent).[46] Community organisations and charities could not hope to bridge the gap. By 1994, some 365 foodbanks around the country were providing $25 million in support to the poor (whereas the 1991 benefit cuts had been $1.3 billion). In 1999 the foodbanks reported that demand had continued to rise, and over 70 percent of those seeking help in the previous year were doing so for the first time.[47]

Despite the mantra that free markets were the key to prosperity for all, the median personal income of all New Zealand adults declined by 13.4 percent between 1986 and 1996.[48] The gap between Maori and non-Maori had widened. Official statistics showed that the average personal market income of Maori fell from $16,800 in 1982 to $11,900 in 1991, and recovered only to $14,400 by 1996. The comparable figures for Pakeha were $20,700 in 1982, $19,500 in 1991, and $21,000 in 1996. A special report to the Minister of Maori Affairs in 1998 showed that over one-third of Maori (compared to 14.3 percent of non-Maori) were now primarily dependent on (constantly eroded) government benefits. Maori rental housing had become less affordable. Maori were almost twice as likely as non-Maori to be admitted to hospital. The health gap widened on key poverty-related illnesses such as glue ear, youth suicide, diabetes, pneumonia and mental health. After some improvement in education disparities in the 1980s, the situation had remained static.[49] There was also a stark increase in the feminisation of poverty, especially for elderly women and sole parents, who were hardest hit by user charges, cuts to public services, and reductions in the value of pensions and benefits.

Promises of a high-employment, high-earnings economy were just as illusory. In November 1998 there were still 34,400 (or 3.2 percent) fewer full-time filled jobs than in February 1987, when the household labour force surveys began, but 243,900 (or over 100 percent) more part-time filled jobs.[50] In the year to March 1999, permanent part-time jobs increased by 7.7 percent while full-time jobs fell another 1.4 percent. The constant shift from full-time employment in the tradeable sector, especially manufacturing, to part-time work in the services sector meant that the quality of jobs had deteriorated. Brian Easton described the emergence of a dual employment market – a top tier of high-status, high-income earners in relatively secure employment, and a bottom tier of people who fluctuated between low-quality, low-paid and part-time or insecure jobs and unemployment.[51] Many of the bottom-tier workers were now servicing the personal and household needs of the élite, either as self-employed or on minimal individual contracts with firms.[52] Those for whom there was no work available, or who could not work, became dependent on declining government support, which left many with minimal means to survive. For others, the punitive abatement rates for benefits and potential loss of benefit top-ups and supplements created a poverty trap; some simply could not afford to take paid employment on the current minimum wage.

Unemployment reinforced the polarisation of New Zealand society and set worrying trends for the future. Over a third of the unemployed in March 1999 were under 25. The unemployment rate in areas such as Northland and Bay of Plenty was nearing twice the national average. Again, Maori had been hit hardest. Until 1987, Maori were more likely than non-Maori to be participating in the labour force. But massive job losses in the state sector and in industry in the later 1980s had a huge impact on Maori. Long-term unemployment (26 weeks or more) grew from one percent of the Maori labour force in 1986 to over 15 percent in March 1992, compared to just 3.9 percent of the non-Maori labour force. In early 1992, almost half of all Maori aged 16 to 19 were unemployed; the non-Maori figure was 19.1 percent.[53] Maori unemployment was still 19 percent in March 1999, while for Pakeha the rate was 5.6 percent, Pacific Islands people 14.5 percent, and 'other' ethnic groups 11.5 percent.

Changes in employment patterns flowed through to families and social roles. The number of women in paid work increased, while men's participation rates declined. Between 1986 and 1991, the total number of people employed fell by some 100,000, of whom 96 percent were men.[54] But most of the new work for women was of low quality. As of 1996, women made up 70 percent of those in part-time work, and were clustered in the services sector. Statistics New Zealand commented that: 'women's dominance in part-time positions has often meant casual jobs with comparatively low rates of pay, minimum employment conditions and little employment security'.[55] Women in full-time jobs still earned only 85 percent of what men earned. Graduate women faced greater discrepancies: the median income of women with a post-graduate degree in 1996 was $39,800; her male counterpart earned $54,700.[56]

That such outcomes resulted from New Zealand's free market experiment is no accident. Increased inequality between and within countries is an intrinsic feature of that economic model. In 1994 *The Economist* said it was 'no coincidence that the biggest increases in income inequalities have occurred in economies such as those of America, Britain and New Zealand, where free-market economic policies have been pursued most zealously'.[57] Not only were such results expected; those responsible positively welcomed them. Finance Minister Bill Birch was reported in March 1995 as saying that income disparities were widening 'and they will widen much more. That doesn't worry me'.[58] And again in July 1998: 'The fact that incomes at the top of the ladder have grown more than those at the bottom is not a bad thing. I think it's an inevitable part of increasing rewards for effort. ... You've got to send the right signal.'[59]

Such clinical detachment from the struggle of many New Zealanders to live decent lives implies that the globalisation project could be sustained irrespective of the social dislocation and human pain it caused, that self-regulating markets could dictate the terms of social existence for the long term, and that those people, iwi (tribes) and communities who suffered in the process would adapt to their new reality.

▲ *A stubborn survival of values*

The studies of structural adjustment discussed in Chapter 1 stressed the need for 'social learning' that combined strong support from an élite with an adjustment of expectations by the rest. By the mid-1990s, there were some signs this was happening in New Zealand. There was a solid support base for the country's market-driven economy in the international arena, and from the local entrepreneurial élite, senior officials in the market-focused bureaucracy and both major political parties. Inequality, poverty, even crime and social unrest seemed containable, so long as the victims believed there was nothing they could do, and others were content to blame them for their misfortune or accept that there was no alternative.

For most of the period from 1984, there was no concerted resistance to the policy regime. Those who objected early on were discredited as vested interests who put their own concerns before the needs of the nation; critical commentators were generally derided and sometimes punished. There were small-scale local rebellions over the years: elderly people refusing to pay asset-tested charges for hospital care; rental strikes by state housing tenants; the campaign to stop the sale of Auckland's port. Some national campaigns focused on specific proposals, such as the sale of Trustbank and the state forests, or on particular issues through the Coalition for Public Health, the Coalition on Accident Compensation or Power for Our Future. Individuals took risks as whistle-blowers over unsafe practices in public and psychiatric hospitals, or exposing unethical practices by the corporate élite. Maori interventions repeatedly delayed, although they largely failed to stop, the corporatisation and privatisation programme.[60] Yet few of these efforts were coordinated or sustained. For more than a decade, most New Zealanders offered little more than a grumbling acquiescence. People focused their discontent on changing the government in 1990, and changing the electoral system in 1993. But the economic agenda remained the same.

The crucial question is whether that situation can be sustained. There are already signs of cracks in the consensus of the élite. Given the increased inequality and hardship facing many families and communities, it also seems likely that the current rumblings of discontent will grow. That has the potential to become something more substantial, if the only political choices on offer are variations on the market-centred paradigm, while the majority of those affected retain a very different set of values.

Social values are notoriously difficult to assess, but the studies available suggest that the conservative values of the welfare state still prevail in New Zealand in the late 1990s. Systematic surveys of New Zealanders' social attitudes have been conducted by Massey University researchers Paul

Perry and Alan Webster in 1989, 1993 and 1998.[61] These surveys show a remarkable consistency across the decade. Asked in 1998 whether they would be prepared to pay more tax to increase government spending on health and education, around 90 percent of respondents said yes, a majority strongly so. Over 60 percent wanted more taxpayer assistance for the unemployed. Pensions and environmental protection were also major concerns. Support for government redistribution of wealth was slightly down, at 45 percent. So was support for government ownership of big industries, at around 30 percent. A majority still wanted tighter regulation of big business and multinationals, although the percentage had fallen. Two-thirds supported stricter limits on selling foreign goods in New Zealand, in order to protect local jobs. Almost 70 percent felt that the country was 'run by a few big interests looking out for themselves'; less than 20 percent believed it was run for the benefit of all the people.

In 1998 there were new questions about poverty: three-quarters of those surveyed believed that poverty had increased over the decade, 58.7 percent said the government was not doing enough in response to it, and 40 percent believed that some people had no chance to escape poverty. Yet despite poverty having the deepest impact on Maori, Pacific Islands people and beneficiaries, there was weak support for more taxpayer assistance to these groups. Support for more government action to address Treaty of Waitangi grievances remained low, and had fallen: only 5.5 percent were strongly in favour, and 10.8 percent somewhat so.

Surveys like these are not a scientific description of the values of New Zealanders. But they present a picture of a country whose dominant values are poles apart from the philosophy pursued by its governments since 1984. There is little indication that people have shifted their values to accommodate the free market regime; given the consistency of the survey results, there is no indication that they will, although the values of the new generation of 'children of the market' remain largely unknown.

The fact that the majority of voters continue to support parties whose policies do not reflect their values suggests a popular perception that only the major parties can influence decisions. (The experience of MMP to date does not tend to support this view.) It also suggests a belief that, although alternatives are desirable, they are no longer possible. A continuation of the free market agenda seems likely to leave the mass of citizens deeply alienated from the market-centred world in which they live and work – an outcome those who value 'social capital' would see as dysfunctional for both the economy and the society.

Yet, as Polanyi observed, people are not bystanders in the society in which they live. Their sense of identity and values shape their view of the world, their responses to adverse situations, and their political positions.

These factors have come to the fore in response to the most visible manifestations of globalisation – foreign investment and immigration. Social anthropologist Eve Darian-Smith has observed the 'seemingly contradictory relations between a global economy which is diminishing "spatial barriers" and the rising tension amongst peoples who cling to "neighborhood and nation, region, ethnic grouping, or religious belief as specific marks of identity"'.[62] Groups of 'Us', claiming a united identity against the foreign and threatening 'Them', try to erect barricades against the rapid and radical transformation of economic, political, cultural and social life. Sometimes this is expressed in a racist nationalism that coincides with the territorial state, as with the hostility of many Pakeha to Asian immigration and, ironically, to Maori. At other times, it challenges the nation-state's assertion of a homogeneous national identity and national interest, as with Maori opposition to foreign investment and immigration from the standpoint of tino rangatiratanga.

As this book has described, these tensions surfaced as New Zealanders rejected policies they saw as threatening their identity and control over their lives. Among Pakeha, this nationalism was often a poorly articulated, defensive position which avoided the hard questions of what being a New Zealander means. If economic alternatives are to draw on strong local and national communities or groups based on common interests, a clearer and more confident sense of those relationships and identities needs to emerge. The sense of nationalism that drove Maori responses was also rather messy: a common core of values, a shared history of colonisation, and a tribally-centred identity was confused by urbanisation and the costs, attractions and imperatives of a Western capitalist democracy. Positions taken on issues often reflected the unequal distribution of power amongst Maori, and unresolved tensions between those wanting to embrace the market and those committed to traditional values. This conflict, and the overwhelming rejection in the Massey surveys of any government obligation to break the poverty trap experienced by many Maori (and Pacific Islands people), and to address Treaty of Waitangi grievances – let alone confront the vexed question of Maori political authority – does not bode well for developing a more sophisticated, just and enduring national identity in the near future.

▲ THE STATE'S CAPACITY TO ACT

People's sense that they are losing control is encapsulated in the collision between globalisation and sovereignty, democracy and tino rangatiratanga. Despite popular concerns about national sovereignty, that is not really the issue, for reasons explained in Chapter 1. Technically, the government can withdraw from all the international agreements, nationalise the privatised enterprises and assets, impose a strict 'national interest' test on foreign investors, re-regulate the financial sector, tighten environmental laws, commit itself to full employment, raise income taxes for big companies and the rich, return all disputed resources to iwi, and recognise their independent authority. The real question is how far the state retains the practical capacity to do so.

In Chapter 1, it was argued that OECD countries have a significant degree of autonomy, despite the power of transnational enterprise, global finance and the information technology industry. Their autonomy reduces as governments open their doors to foreign direct investment, deregulate their financial markets, privatise, and loosen their regulatory regimes. This creates practical problems of control, and increases the risk and cost of reversing the changes. But it does not eliminate the ability of the state to re-regulate. Such decisions require sober assessment of the costs and benefits, not just rhetorical hype about capital flight, credit rating downgrades and loss of investor confidence.

Chapter 1 also recognised that there are ways of embedding changes to increase the cost (and hence reduce the likelihood) of reversing them. Three main factors were identified in this process: technical barriers of law and policy, penetration by international capital of New Zealand's economy, and lack of political will. According to the globalisers, future New Zealand governments have little room to re-regulate financial markets, capital movements and investment rules, to increase taxes, or to provide support for domestic producers. By the same reasoning, any government policies that impact on international competitiveness and profitability would also be fettered, including those relating to the Treaty of Waitangi, labour, the environment, and social policy. But the durability of the market-driven system can be overplayed. Despite the ideological coherence and practical integration of current policies, individual elements can still be changed, as moves to regulate electricity prices have shown. Over time, what initially appear as anomalies can become a new orthodoxy; alternatives once deemed not to exist are seen as feasible and appropriate.

The colonisation of key ministries by former Treasury officials as chief executives, the hiring of like-minded middle managers, and the creation of numerous state-owned enterprises and other 'fire alarm' bodies are intended to minimise this risk. But just as governments retain the power to determine the direction of their policies, they can require the bureaucracy to implement them. Trade negotiators in the Ministry of Foreign Affairs and Trade can be expected to warn the government of serious damage to its integrity if it were to change tack radically. But major policy shifts occur in many countries. Implementing a new government's policies is the task of a professional public service, after offering informed and balanced advice. Unwillingness or inability to perform that role would indicate the need for a sweeping review of the state sector. The pre-1984 public service could not be restored, even if that were desired; but a career public service with an institutional memory, which offers impartial and non-ideological advice with broad-based public input, is still quite possible.

Key domestic legislation, such as the Fiscal Responsibility Act and the Reserve Bank Act, have been treated as sacrosanct in order to maintain the confidence of 'the markets'. Yet benefits to the real economy from a more balanced monetary policy may mean incurring the disapproval of the markets is a risk worth taking. These Acts can be amended by a simple parliamentary majority. Other options exist. Both Acts allow the government to deviate temporarily from the legislated 'fiscal responsibility' or 'price stability' norms, provided that Parliament is informed. Repeated exceptions can become norms. Paul Krugman describes how the brief era of pure monetarism in US monetary policy from 1979 to 1982 was replaced by pragmatism, after the Federal Reserve repeatedly set aside its monetary targets for the year. Over time, he notes, the targets attracted less attention. 'So the Fed, if it was ever monetarist, was monetarist for less than three years. ... There are still monetarists, but they almost seem like relics now. Milton Friedman's forecasts of doom were at first taken seriously, then ridiculed, then ignored.'[63] Re-regulation of the labour market and raising of progressive income tax levels might attract even more vigorous resistance from vested interests; but such changes also remain perfectly possible.

It is far more difficult to re-regulate international banking and finance flows, especially given New Zealand's position as a passive recipient of developments in the global financial market-place. Major initiatives to reduce the risk of systemic collapse will largely depend on international regulatory regimes, such as those developed by the Bank of International Settlements. However, complementary national options, such as currency controls, which were until recently deemed irreconcilable with free market orthodoxy, are now being canvassed in various countries. The results will not be perfect. But New Zealand's vulnerability to short-term speculative capital flows suggests it is irresponsible for its government not to be actively examining these options. In banking, much will depend on the policies adopted by the home governments of banks that control the New Zealand industry. However, some restraints on bank lending are still possible. A capital gains tax could deter borrowing for speculative investment. The voluntary powers of the Banking Ombudsman could be extended, and if necessary formalised. Government will also need to find some way to ensure access to personal banking services for poor and isolated communities, if the big commercial banks abandon them. Likewise, it will face intense pressure to reconsider calls for more active regulation of the share-market, an enforceable takeovers code that protects small shareholders, and a Securities Commission that has resources and teeth.

In trade policy, it is possible to repeal the legislation requiring zero tariffs for textiles, clothing and footwear; it is also possible, where appropriate after broad-based empirical assessment, to restore tariffs selectively in agriculture and industry to the (still low) levels allowed under New Zealand's GATT commitments. The government could shift its attention from meeting the needs of big business to supporting small local enterprises (some 86 percent of New Zealand businesses have fewer than six employees). Strategic support, including venture capital, could be provided for growth industries and adding value to agricultural production. (Even sources of minimal support, such as the Business Development Boards, were shut down at the end of 1998 after nine years, without any comprehensive monitoring or evaluation.) New Zealand consumers could be encouraged to 'buy New Zealand first', as a commitment to local industry and fellow workers as well as helping to cut the country's import bill.

New Zealand's level of exposure to foreign direct investment is unlikely to reduce significantly in the near future, unless a severe crisis provokes a wholesale withdrawal. To date, the selling-down of shares in major (especially privatised) companies has further diffused shareholdings offshore. It is possible that some foreign investors might sell out to New Zealand companies, but any significant buyers would need to be New Zealand transnationals or the government. Some foreign-owned operations might also close down, creating a void for New Zealand businesses (public or private) to fill. For the future, it is certainly possible to limit foreign investment, although such moves would need to be complemented by the creation of an alternative pool of local capital, most probably through compulsory superannuation savings. An effective screening mechanism could give priority to job-creating 'greenfield' investment, backed by a broad-based 'national interest' test consistent with the Treaty of Waitangi, environmental ethics and regional development objectives.

The large-scale nationalisation of privatised strategic assets is not a realistic option, except in dire situations of corporate collapse. However, in cases of privatisation through the introduction of competition it is possible to restore the preference to state providers where activities have a public good dimension, such as accident compensation, public housing and tertiary education. The contracting out of services can also be reconsidered, provided that government agencies have not become irretrievably dependent on systems or plant owned by private companies. The cost of doing this is intended to be prohibitive, politically as well as financially, as evidenced by the prolonged battle over whether the Auckland City Council should resume control of the corporatised Metrowater company, at a time when ratepayers already faced large increases to cover deferred expenditure. Local authority trading enterprises and state-owned enterprises have shown that they can remain publicly owned and be highly profitable – yet their employment policies have often been as anti-union and hard-line as those in the private sector, and the government has absorbed the profits without exercising its statutory power to subsidise unprofitable services. Bruce Jesson's first-hand account of the commercial success of the Auckland Regional Services Trust in *Only Their Purpose is Mad* provides compelling grounds for reconsidering the potential of such publicly-owned enterprises both to succeed commercially and be socially responsible.[64]

Local and central governments could place a moratorium on privatisation and undertake an independent audit, followed by public debate, on the costs and benefits so far. Any further asset sales could be conditional on an independent assessment and full select committee scrutiny to show that the economic and social gains from the sale would outweigh the economic benefits of retaining the asset and its income stream, and the social gains from delivering the relevant public goods. Official regulators could be established for privatised operations to monitor their price, quality and equity of access, in line with privatisation practice in most other countries. Activities affecting people's physical liberty, such as prisons, policing and justice, could be ring-fenced as core areas of government responsibility not to be contracted out. Where new investment in areas of strategic importance is beyond the government's capacity, alliances could be sought that would maintain an effective government role and responsibility (which the 'Kiwi share' does not). The government could be required to develop an integrated information technology strategy for computerisation of government operations and enforceable codes of accountability, with proper transparency.

Where transnationals are the major investors, the government still has the power to regulate. It could introduce a capital gains tax, along with stronger laws on transfer pricing and 'thin' capitalisation. Competition laws could be strengthened, even selectively, to prohibit anti-competitive practices in strategic areas (such as utilities) and to balance efficiency with other economic and social objectives. Other problems, such as the excessive commercialisation of the media and the lack of a social dimension to local transport, could be addressed through quotas, subsidies or more active state or local government provision, as other countries do.

The government could use its power to intervene under the Commerce

Act to prevent profiteering by private or state monopolies, through price regulation of public goods. A more rigorous consumer protection and food safety regime could be backed by well-resourced enforcement authorities with real teeth. Labour laws could once again provide protection for vulnerable workers, including a presumption in favour of collective bargaining, legalising strikes in support of multi-employer contracts, and restoring statutory support for the role of unions. Environmental regulations could reflect a much more balanced and realistic assessment of costs and benefits to the community of proposals for resource use, and impose effective responsibility on developers for any adverse consequences. These domestic options could be supplemented by binding and voluntary codes of corporate ethics, enforced by worker and consumer alliances within New Zealand and internationally.

New Zealand's commitments under various international economic agreements seek to constrain the form and extent of these options. Each agreement needs to be examined separately to determine its effect and the extent to which future governments retain room to make independent policy choices. The WTO is the most potent of these arrangements, given the range of sectors it covers and the sanctions it can impose. Yet governments can deviate temporarily from WTO rules, for example if their balance of payments continues to deteriorate, if their exhaustible natural resources are under threat, or to alleviate unfair pressures on l ocal producers. Other countries use these provisions as and when necessary; the fact that some abuse them is not a reason to condemn their use altogether. As New Zealand has lowered its national barriers much further than most countries, future governments can justifiably impose a moratorium on further commitments on trade, agriculture, services and other deals. Within the WTO, New Zealand governments could go further and support moves by poorer countries for a reconsideration of the Uruguay Round agreements; refocus on the traditional issues of trade in goods (including agriculture) by rejecting the WTO's expansion into any new areas; and promote a shift from the globalisation agenda to securing a balance between international trade rules and domestic economic, social and cultural objectives. New Zealand's Treaty of Waitangi commitments place an obligation on the government to sponsor a genuine dialogue with indigenous peoples on the recognition of their voice in an equitable international trading system which is based on more holistic values.

APEC is a much more vacuous entity, built on inconclusive dialogue and abundant rhetoric. Formal APEC commitments are voluntary, non-binding and (to date) minimal. Its main effect is to provide leverage to member governments wanting to introduce and maintain unpopular policies. Even big business, which it is supposed to empower, has questioned its value. With its free trade and investment goal discredited, APEC could be left to wither away. New dialogue could begin on a form of regional economic cooperation that reflects the economic reality and human needs of the people of the region.

Binding international constraints on the regulation of foreign investment are mainly contained in bilateral treaties and WTO agreements on services and trade-related investment measures. Their impact on New Zealand is limited, yet significant. Any expansion of those commitments requires rigorous examination. The Multilateral Agreement on Investment at the OECD had much greater potential to act as an embedding device, but fell victim to the arrogance and naked self-interest of transnational enterprises and major capital-exporting countries. The success of the public campaign against that initiative, in New Zealand and elsewhere, suggests that parallel negotiations at the WTO or any other forum would face equally vigorous opposition.

CER has the most direct impact of any of these agreements, cementing in the open economy, through trans-Tasman economic integration, cross-investment and trade inter-dependency, backed by enforcement through international arbitration. For economic and political reasons, the pace of trans-Tasman integration is slowing. Controversial elements of CER, such as the Australia New Zealand joint food standards agreement, are open to periodic review; New Zealand governments can seek to amend them, or even withdraw. The imminent debate on a single currency will provide the opportunity for a sophisticated cost and benefit assessment of the Treaty, social, cultural and regional development issues which further economic integration with Australia would raise.

Future New Zealand governments therefore have many practical options. Whether those options are *desirable* is a matter for debate. A critical element in that discussion will be whether deregulation, privatisation and internationalisation of the New Zealand economy have made such changes too costly to pursue. There has been a great deal of scaremongering about the risk of capital strike, credit rating downgrades, declining international credibility, and a collapse in the confidence and viability of the domestic economy. It is often assumed that significant changes to current policies will have such an effect, yet extremely high levels of foreign debt and the balance of payments deficit will not. The fear that credit rating downgrades, negative OECD, WTO and IMF reports, and lower World Competitiveness ratings would follow a major policy shift needs to be put in perspective, and the ideological hype separated from real economic consequences. Truly independent economic commentators might well see the prospect of better economic returns, lower foreign debt and an improved balance of payments as preferable to the country's prevailing economic malaise.

The likely reaction of the international cheer-leaders should also not be conflated with the attitude of investors themselves. Despite assertions of New Zealand's international orthodoxy, regulations and protections of the kind suggested above continue to exist in many countries that attract foreign and local investment. New Zealand may well be less attractive because of its location, size, weak economy and deteriorating infrastructure. But it should not be assumed that all foreign investors will be deterred by government policies that are designed to restore the country's physical and intellectual infrastructure and a healthy social environment. Given the questionable contribution of foreign direct investment to the New Zealand economy in the 1990s, it is also worth asking whether, if investors did find such policies unattractive and chose not to come, or decided to disinvest, that would necessarily be a disaster for the New Zealand economy? In the short term it could cause real hardship, and the risks and costs would need to be weighed carefully. Domestic industry would need assistance to develop innovative responses; but that could provide valuable spillover benefits to local workers, suppliers and communities. If areas of strategic importance were at risk, the government could offer specific incentives to overseas investors – or provide some public goods itself. Taking back control from the rentiers would not be painless, but continuing to strengthen their hold on the country might be more painful still.

▲ POLITICAL WILL

The remaining obstacle to even considering such possibilities is the lack of political will. A huge paradigm shift has taken place in New Zealand politics since 1984. The 'political market' is now dominated by those who support the globalisation agenda. By the turn of the century, both Labour and National were committed to a more sophisticated version of the global economy, founded on free trade and investment, as the way ahead. A significant shift in their party positions may only occur when popular pressure makes it not just safe, but necessary for political survival. The political dynamics of MMP could increase the pressure for change in a coalition of the centre-left. Minor parties can influence debate as the Alliance and some Maori MPs have shown. Yet MMP could also be a barrier to any significant shift in direction. MMP means that, provided no party secures an outright majority, the blitzkrieg approach to policy-making of the later 1980s and early 1990s cannot occur without the complicity of a second party (or more). While that has tended to constrain further major deregulation, it is equally a fetter on a party that seeks to promote an alternative agenda. The other wild card is Maori politics which by the end of the century was being taken much more seriously. While Maori MPs were often as opportunist as Pakeha MPs and the nuances of their more principled positions were poorly understood, continued pressure for recognition of independent Maori authority would keep Maori demands in the political foreground.

Parliament has been the traditional focus for debate on law and policy-making. The expansion of international economic policy-making has placed strains on traditional modes of democratic oversight. The international economic institutions – the WTO, IMF, World Bank, NAFTA, APEC – sought to deflect criticisms of a democratic deficit at the institutional level by offering an opportunity for dialogue to selected representatives of 'civil society', on the institutions' terms. Little has been achieved from such engagement.

Governments involved in these arrangements have faced consistent pressure to increase their accountability at the domestic level. Their responses have varied. New Zealand's has been minimalist. The introduction of weak sessional orders and provision for a one-sided 'national interest analysis' of international treaties did nothing to increase the transparency of international negotiations, or to promote debate on the issues. Consultation on the WTO, 'dialogue workshops' with Maori and the select committee hearing on APEC, and various public information campaigns have been more about containment and propaganda than democracy. Yet, even these gestures show the government has become aware that it can no longer hide behind the notion of 'external sovereignty'.

The watershed in New Zealand and internationally was the MAI. Complacent negotiators, OECD officials and the transnational lobby miscalculated badly, creating precedents that will be hard to roll back. Drafts of the text were released as the negotiations proceeded. In the Australian and Canadian legislatures, full select committee inquiries on the MAI were held *during* the negotiations; the European Parliament received numerous committee reports and passed a detailed resolution on what the European Commission's negotiating position should be; even the New Zealand government held hui with Maori around the country, although it never allowed the select committee to call for submissions.

In future negotiations, the WTO will need to decide whether draft texts will be released regularly and governments will face demands to tell their people what their negotiating position is and what offers they are preparing to make. In New Zealand, officials will need to decide whether Cabinet papers will be made available to MPs, and to the public via the Official Information Act. All these things happened with the MAI. As New Zealand officials admitted, there was nothing exceptional about that set of negotiations, except that the draft text had been leaked and people had sufficient information to force the government's hand. There is no logical reason why the WTO negotiations – or those relating to a single currency under CER, or any other international economic treaty – should be treated any differently.

Yet for those committed to globalisation, secrecy is vital. As the MAI showed, public debate can help to sink an international agreement. The objective of such treaties is to tie the hands of future governments; secrecy enables negotiators to circumvent domestic pressure groups who oppose that goal. Opening the process to sustained debate, based on informed empirical assessments and evidence of the benefits and downsides, would impede the negotiating process. Governments that were truly accountable might never support an international deal that was profoundly unpopular at home. Small countries would find it more difficult to sacrifice the interests of some of their citizens in order to secure important concessions from more powerful countries.

Yet, if what negotiators propose is so good for the country, it must be able to withstand rigorous scrutiny. The benefits of globalisation are not an unquestioned economic truth – the failure of the New Zealand experiment provides a compelling counter-factual. Incumbent governments have no monopoly on wisdom that gives them the right to determine the national interest beyond their term in office. A domestic law that sought to entrench current positions for the future would face complex requirements for a two-thirds or three-quarters majority in Parliament and/or a referendum; yet international treaties seek to achieve this without any parliamentary involvement at all.

The government will also face strong demands from Maori for a say in the international treaty-making process – in part because it is their constitutional right to participate as equal partners with the Crown in the international arena, and also because globalisation poses substantive risks to the Maori life-world. The first rationale is advanced by iwi entrepreneurs and Maori nationalists alike. The second is held sufficiently strongly by diverse Maori interests that it cannot be ignored. As any government will know, addressing either element has much wider ramifications than the negotiation of international treaties.

▲ A MODERN TRANSFORMATION

In conclusion, it in appropriate to return to the book that provided the starting point for this analysis – Karl Polanyi's *Great Transformation*. Reflecting on the demise of the laissez-faire economy, Polanyi insisted that the self-regulating market of the nineteenth century was radically different from what had gone before, 'in that it relied for its regulation on economic self-interest'.[65] Organising a whole society on the principle of gain and profit had far-reaching consequences when the harms it produced were not checked by social goals. It crushed people's sense of self, family and neighbourhood, in which their economic existence had previously been embedded. This, in turn, destroyed the social fabric on which the market economy depended. While shifting to something new seemed for many 'a task too desperate to contemplate',[66] Polanyi observed that:

> Much of the massive suffering inseparable from a period of transition is already behind us. In the social and economic dislocation of our age, in the tragic vicissitudes of the depression, fluctuations of currency, mass unemployment, shiftings of social status, spectacular destruction of historical states, we have experienced the worst. Unwittingly we have been paying the price of change.[67]

Although restoration of the past was not possible, the collapse of the self-regulating market system did not leave people in a void: 'Not for the first time in history may makeshifts contain the germs of great and permanent institutions. Within the nations we are witnessing a development under which the economic system ceases to lay down the law to society and the primacy of society over that system is secured.'[68]

The Great Depression may seem light years away from New Zealand at the cusp of the 21st century. But the parallels are there. New Zealand governments that sought to put the ideology of globalisation into practice believed they could reshape the country's economic, social and cultural existence to fit an economic theory. Market failures, Treaty rights, economic decline, social distress and public opposition were all swept aside by the free market evangelists, supported by élites eager to defend the gains and opportunities they had secured. Yet those human realities did not disappear. New Zealanders, faced with governance by the market, began to demand an effective say in the decisions that directly affected them, and new forms of intervention, regulation and support to address the problems they encountered.

Without overstating the case, the stories that emerge throughout this book show that New Zealanders are beginning to resist, and sometimes they are succeeding. They are mainly seeking to hold the line or minimise change, rather than promote alternatives. Broad-based alliances have given them strength of voice, diverse skills and different targets to influence. As single-issue campaigns, however, they lack any ongoing commitment to work together, and any guiding set of principles or long-term common vision.

Once people believe that collectively they can influence the major decisions that affect their lives and can shift the political will, it is a small step to believing that greater change is possible. Deciding what those changes might involve requires a vigorous and open contest of ideas that is rooted in social reality, not economic dogma. It means having to rethink the role of the nation-state in a constantly changing international environment, confront the recognition of tino rangatiratanga, articulate core social, cultural and ethical values, and debate what it is that makes us New Zealanders. Achieving that requires people from all walks of life – from iwi, churches, unions, media, universities, local communities, business, NGOs, and many more – to show leadership, to provide quality information and analysis, to organise and to provide avenues for the voices of ordinary people to be heard.

It is time to cast the myths of globalisation aside. The tide is turning against the global free market in New Zealand, and around the world. The lessons of history, and the message of this book, are that *nothing is inevitable*. The state of the future still rests largely in our hands.

▲ Appendix: *Figures 1-6*

FIGURE 1. **REAL GROSS DOMESTIC PRODUCT**[1] **1997-98**

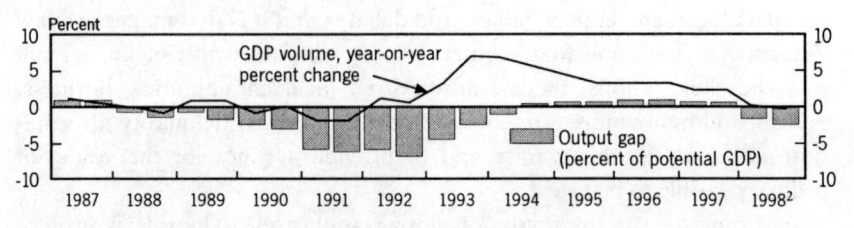

1. Output measure.
2. Estimates for the second half of 1998.

Source: OECD Economic Surveys: New Zealand, *OECD, Paris, 1999, p.18. figure 1.A.*

FIGURE 2. **EXTERNAL CURRENT ACCOUNT 1988-1998**

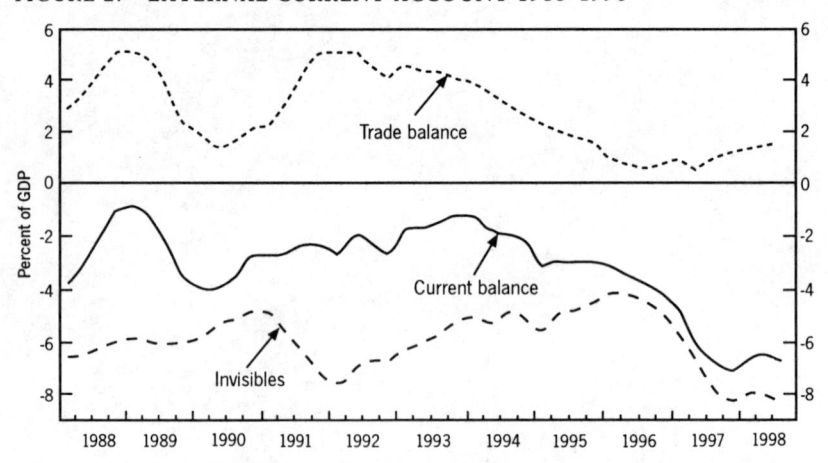

Source: Statistics New Zealand, in OECD Economic Surveys: New Zealand, *OECD, Paris, 1999, p.30, figure 6.*

INTRODUCTION ▲ 387

FIGURE 3: TOTAL NEW ZEALAND OVERSEAS DEBT 1990-1999

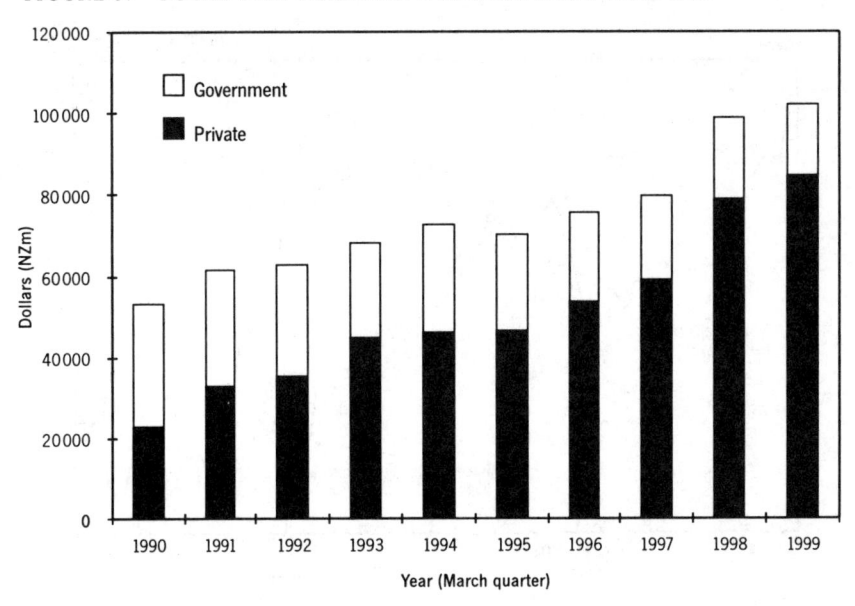

Source: Statistics New Zealand: Total New Zealand Overseas Debt

FIGURE 4: RATIO OF GROSS NATIONAL INCOME TO GROSS DOMESTIC PRODUCT 1947-1997

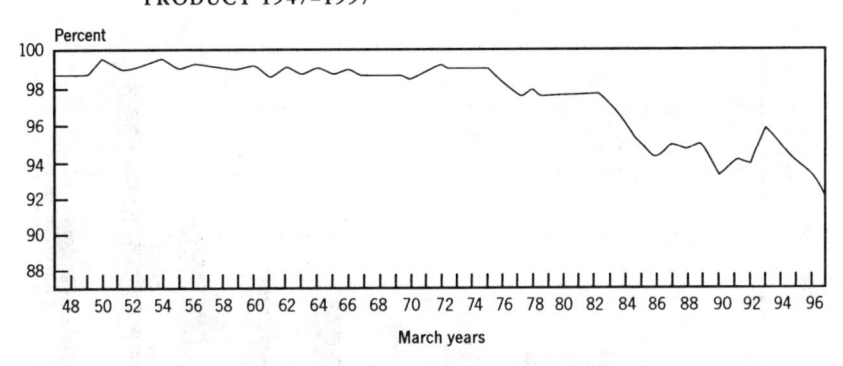

Source: Statistics New Zealand, in New Zealand Now: Incomes, Wellington, 1999, p.14, figure 1.4.

FIGURE 5: INTEREST RATE AND EXCHANGE RATE 1996–1999

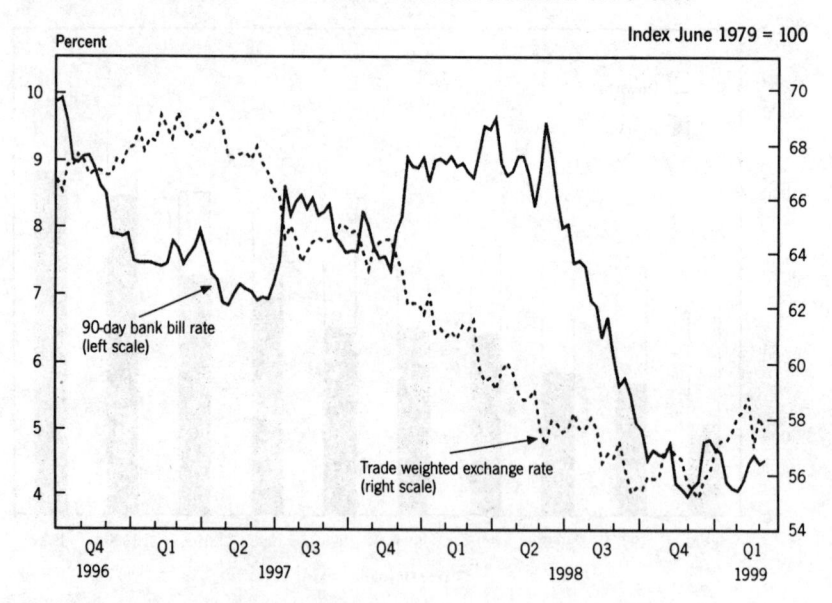

Source: Reserve Bank of New Zealand, in OECD Economic Surveys: New Zealand, OECD, Paris, 1999, p.43, figure 8.B.

FIGURE 6: TRENDS IN INCOME INEQUALITY IN NEW ZEALAND 1983–84/1995–96

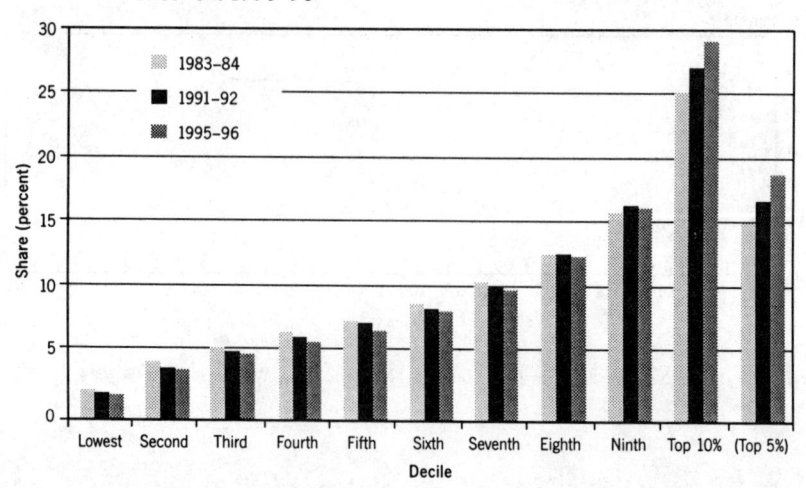

Source: S. Chatterjee and N. Podder, 'Sharing the National Cake in Post Reform New Zealand: Income Inequality Trends in Terms of Income Sources', paper to the Annual Conference of the New Zealand Association of Economists, Wellington, 2–4 September 1998.

▲ References

INTRODUCTION

1. K. Ohmae, *The End of the Nation State: The Rise of Regional Economies*, The Free Press, New York, 1995; see also *The Borderless World: Power and Strategy in the Interlinked Economy*, Harper, New York, 1991.
2. F. Fukuyama, *The End of History and the Last Man*, Avon Books, New York, 1992, p.xiv.
3. D. Korten, *When Corporations Rule the World*, Kumarian Press, West Hartford, 1995.
4. Korten, p.78.
5. R. Reich, *The Work of Nations: Preparing Ourselves for 21st-Century Capitalism*, Simon & Schuster, London, 1991, p.3.
6. E.g. 1999 Nobel economics prize winner Amartya Sen in A. Sen and S. Anand, *Sustainable Human Development: Concepts and Priorities*, UNDP, New York, 1996; former World Bank economist Herman Daly in *Beyond Growth: the Economics of Sustainable Development*, Beacon Press, Boston, 1996; feminist economists Marilyn Waring, *Counting for Nothing: What Men Value and Women are Worth*, Allen & Unwin/Port Nicholson Press, Wellington, 1988, and Prue Hyman, *Women and Economics: A New Zealand Feminist Perspective*, Bridget Williams Books, Wellington, 1994.
7. K. Polanyi, *The Great Transformation: The Political and Economic Origins of our Times*, Beacon Press, Boston, 1957, p.71.
8. Polanyi, p.201.
9. Polanyi, p.130.
10. Polanyi, p.132.
11. Polanyi, p.143.
12. Polanyi, p.143.
13. See C. Offe, 'Legitimacy Through Majority Rule', in J. Keane (ed.), *Claus Offe: Disorganised Capitalism*, Polity Press, Oxford, 1985.
14. J.G. Ruggie, *Constructing the World Polity: Essays on International Institutionalization*, Routledge, London, 1998, p.84.
15. See J. Kelsey, *The New Zealand Experiment: A World Model for Structural Adjustment?*, 2nd edn, Auckland University Press/Bridget Williams Books, Auckland, 1997.
16. Polanyi, pp.111–12.
17. NZ Treasury, *Economic Management*, Treasury, Wellington, 1984, p.103.
18. *Economic Management*, pp.107–8.
19. NZ Treasury, *Government Management: Brief to the Incoming Government 1987*, Volume 1, Treasury, Wellington, 1987. Volume 2 dealt exclusively with education.
20. NZ Treasury, *1990 Briefing Papers*, Treasury, Wellington, 1990, p.31.
21. *1990 Briefing Papers*, p.38 (emphasis added).
22. 'Globalisation: What's it all about?', Discussion Paper no.2, NZTUF Conference, 1–2 May 1997.
23. 'APEC & Globalisation: A Trade Union Response', unpublished paper, NZTUF, July 1997.
24. Notably David Steele in the Alliance office and John Lepper from Integrated Economic Services.
25. W. Rosenberg, *New Zealand Can be Different – and Better*, New Zealand Monthly Review Society, Christchurch, 1993.
26. E.g. J. Kelsey, 'Democratisation and Participation of Domestic and Regional Economic Policy-Making', paper to the New Zealand Asia Institute consultation on Regional Economic Policy-Making and Cultural Identity, Auckland, August 1997; 'Social and Political Impacts of Globalisation', keynote paper to seminar on Globalisation and Local Cultures: Emerging Issues for the 21st Century, Social Sciences Committee of Royal Society of New Zealand/FoRST/UNESCO, June 1997; 'Selling off New Zealand – and Claiming it Back', Stout Research Centre seminar series on 'The New Zealand Revolution', February 1997.
27. J. Kelsey, 'Selling off New Zealand'.
28. See Te Puni Kokiri, *Progress Towards Closing Social and Economic Gaps Between Maori and non-Maori*, Te Puni Kokiri, Wellington, 1998.
29. M. Moore, speech to University of Canterbury Seminar on 'International Liberalisation', 25 August 1997.
30. Moore, 'International Liberalisation', 1997.
31. *Press*, 15 July 1996.
32. *NZ Herald*, 13 June 1998.
33. Reich, p.9.
34. K. Douglas, speech to the New Zealand Labour Party Conference, 18 November 1995.
35. D. McKinnon, 'New Zealand Sovereignty in an Interdependent World', in G. Wood & L. Leland (eds), *State and Sovereignty: Is the State in Retreat?*, Otago University Press, Dunedin, 1997, p.7 at p.12.
36. A. Meehan, 'Viewpoint: "Globalisation" – New Zealand's Choice', *Asia 2000 Foundation of New Zealand*, no.4 (June/July 1995), p.3.
37. B. Matthew, 'Globalisation: Facts and Fallacies', speech to the Institute of Chartered Accountants, Auckland, 22 August 1997.
38. Matthew, 'Globalisation: Facts and Fallacies'.
39. *NZ Herald*, 24–25 October 1998.
40. *NZ Herald*, 22–23 May 1999.
41. *NZ Herald*, 25 March 1999.
42. *Independent*, 12 August 1998.
43. *Manukau Courier*, 18 June 1998.
44. T. Hazledine, *Taking New Zealand Seriously:*

The Economics of Decency, HarperCollins, Auckland, 1998, p.218.
45 See J. Kelsey, A Question of Honour? Labour and the Treaty 1984-1989, Allen & Unwin, Wellington, 1990.
46 Government Management, Ch.5.
47 T. O'Regan, speech to the opening of the NZ Asia Institute Conference on Cultural and Economic Diversity in Asia, August 1997.
48 'Sir Tipene O'Regan', in H. Melbourne, Maori Sovereignty: The Maori Perspective, Hodder Moa Beckett, Auckland, 1995, p.153 at pp.158-59.
49 'Bob Mahuta', in Melbourne, p.143 at p.146.
50 'Bob Mahuta', p.150.
51 'Bob Mahuta', p.149.
52 'Bob Mahuta', p.152.
53 'John Tamihere', in Melbourne, p.109 at pp.112-13.
54 'John Tamihere', p.116.
55 'Mike Smith', in Melbourne, p.97 at pp.101-2.
56 'Mike Smith', p.106.
57 'Mike Smith', p.105.
58 H. Clark, speech to Labour's Election Year Congress, Wellington, 8 May 1999.
59 NZ Herald, 22 May 1999.

CHAPTER 1

1 S. Haggard and R. Kaufman, 'Institution and Economic Adjustment', in S. Haggard and R. Kaufman (eds), The Politics of Economic Adjustment, Princeton University Press, New Jersey, 1992, p.19.
2 J. Kelsey, The New Zealand Experiment: A World Model for Structural Adjustment?, 2nd edn, Auckland University Press/Bridget Williams Books, Auckland, 1997.
3 B. Easton, 'How Did the Health Reforms Blitzkrieg Fail?', Political Science, vol.4, no.2 (1994), p.215.
4 A. Bollard, 'New Zealand', in J. Williamson (ed.), The Political Economy of Policy Reform, Institute for International Economics, Washington, 1993, p.89 at p.97.
5 J. Williamson and S. Haggard, 'The Political Conditions for Economic Reform', in Williamson (ed.), p.527 at p.574.
6 R. Douglas, Unfinished Business, Random House, Auckland, 1993, p.218.
7 Haggard and Kaufman, pp.19-20.
8 M. McCubbins, R. Noll and B. Weingast, 'Administrative Procedures as Instruments of Political Control', Journal of Law, Economics and Organization, no.6 (1990), p.243 at p.261.
9 P. Evans, 'The State,' in Haggard and Kaufman (eds), pp.178-79.
10 Haggard and Kaufman, p.36.
11 S. Haggard and R. Kaufman, 'The Prospects for Democracy', in Haggard and Kaufman (eds), p.349.
12 J. Nelson, 'Poverty, Equity and the Politics of Adjustment', in Haggard and Kaufman (eds), p.221 at p.260.
13 D. Harper and G. Karacaoglu, 'Financial Policy Reform in New Zealand', in A. Bollard and R. Buckle (eds), Economic Liberalization in New Zealand, Allen & Unwin, Wellington, 1987, p.206 at p.235.
14 A. Bollard, 'More Market: The Deregulation of Industry', in Bollard and Buckle (eds), p.25 at p.40.
15 P. Krugman, Pop Internationalism, MIT Press, Cambridge, Mass., 1997, p.133.
16 Krugman, p.130.
17 J. Toye, 'Comments', in Williamson (ed.), p.40.
18 Toye, p.35 at p.39.
19 See Kelsey, The New Zealand Experiment, especially Chapter 1.
20 Krugman, p.140.
21 J. Stiglitz, 'More Instruments and Broader Goals: Moving Toward the Post-Washington Consensus', Helsinki, Finland, 7 January 1998, www.worldbank.org. The World Bank's president publicly endorsed the IMF's approach a week later (see Chapter 3).
22 In 1994 transnational enterprises controlled over one-third of the world's productive assets, accounted for over one-third of international trade, yet employed only 5 percent of the world's workforce; see UNDP, World Investment Report 1994, United Nations, New York, 1994.
23 See N. Woods, 'Editorial Introduction: Globalization: Definitions, Debates and Implications', Oxford Development Studies, vol.26, no.1 (1998), pp.5-6.
24 N. Angell, The Great Illusion, Heinemann, London, 1912, p.50, quoted in Woods, p.5.
25 J. Helliwell, How Much Do National Borders Matter?, Brookings Institution, Washington, 1998, p.122.
26 T. Hazledine, Taking New Zealand Seriously: The Economics of Decency, HarperCollins, Auckland, 1998, p.15.
27 R. Wade, 'Globalization and Its Limits: Reports of the Death of the National Economy are Greatly Exaggerated', in S. Berger and R. Dore (eds), National Diversity and Global Capitalism, Cornell University Press, New York, 1996, p.60 at p.81.
28 The Economist, 7 October 1995, p.15.
29 G. Garrett, 'Shrinking States? Globalization and National Autonomy in the OECD', Oxford Development Studies, vol.26, no.1 (1998), p.71 at p.93.
30 G. Teubner, '"Global Bukowina": Legal Pluralism in the World Society', in G. Teubner (ed.), Global Law Without a State, Aldershot, Dartmouth, 1997.
31 J.G. Ruggie, 'Territoriality and Beyond: Problematizing Modernity in International Relations', International Organization, vol.47, no.1 (1993), p.139 at p.143.
32 R. Sally, 'Multinational Enterprises, Political Economic and Institutional Theory: Domestic Embeddedness in the Context of Internationalization', Review of International Political Economy, vol.1, no.1 (1994), p.161 at p.162.
33 J. Rosenau, 'Governance, Order and Change in World Politics', in J. Rosenau and E-O Czempiel (eds), Governance Without Government: Order and Change in World Politics, Cambridge University Press, Cambridge, 1992, p.1 at p.4.
34 Rosenau, p.8.
35 S. Picciotto, 'The Regulatory Criss-Cross: Interaction between Jurisdictions and the

Construction of Global Regulatory Networks', in W. Bratton et al. (eds), *Regulatory Competition and Co-ordination*, Oxford University Press, Oxford, 1996, p.89 at p.118.
36 R. Bates and A. Krueger, *Political and Economic Interactions in Economic Policy Reform*, Blackwell, Oxford, 1993, pp.462–63; and generally, Haggard and Kaufman (eds), pp.462-63.
37 R. Cox, 'Critical Political Economy', in B. Hettje (ed.), *International Political Economy: Understanding Global Disorder*, Zed Books, London, 1995, p.31 at p.39.
38 This can be limited to the parties to that specific agreement or be unconditional and apply to the parties to other agreements where the signatory has comparable MFN obligations.
39 Most commonly, agreements provide for reference of disputes to an existing international settlement mechanism such as the International Centre for the Settlement of Investment Disputes (ICSID), established by the World Bank in 1965.
40 D. Schneiderman, 'Investment Rules and the New Constitutionalism: Interlinkages and Disciplinary Effects', paper to the Consortium on Globalisation, Law and Social Science, New York, April 1997.
41 J. Kelsey, 'Global Economic Policy-Making: A New Constitutionalism?', *Otago Law Review*, vol.9, no.3 (1999), p.535 at pp.548–49.
42 This refers to the inability of government to secure the desired policy outcomes because of the democratic and constitutional barriers that exist in the 'political market-place'.
43 B. Hoekman and M. Kostecki, *The Political Economy of the World Trading System: From GATT to WTO*, Oxford University Press, Oxford, 1995, p.24.
44 Hoekman and Kostecki, p.24.
45 Hoekman and Kostecki, p.28.
46 R. Putnam, 'Diplomacy and Domestic Politics: The Logic of Two-Level Games', in P. Evans et al. (eds), *Double-Edged Diplomacy: International Bargaining and Domestic Politics*, University of California Press, Berkeley, 1993, p.431 at p.446.
47 A. Hurrell and N.Woods, 'Globalisation and Inequality', *Millennium: Journal of International Studies*, vol.24, no.3 (1995), p.447 at p.460.
48 Arbitration (International Investment Disputes) Act 1979.
49 See especially *Tavita v Minister of Immigration* [1994] 2 NZLR p.257 (CA); *Puli'uva v Removal Review Authority*, CA 236/95, 24 May 1996; *Rajan v Minister of Immigration*, CA 177/95, 30 July 1996; *Wellington District Legal Services Committee v Tangiora* [1998] 1 NZLR p.129.
50 *Black's Law Dictionary*, 6th edn, West Publishing Co, Minnesota, 1990, p.1396.
51 Eg. Minister of Health Simon Upton, reported in *Dominion*, 1 May 1995.
52 D. Held, 'Democracy, the Nation-State and the Global System', in D. Held (ed.), *Political Theory Today*, Polity Press, Cambridge, 1991. Sometimes this capacity is misleadingly referred to as *economic* sovereignty.

53 D. Brash, 'Foreign Investment in New Zealand: Does it Threaten our Prosperity or Our Security?', Address to Wellington Rotary Club, November 1995.
54 Brash, 1995.
55 W. Rosenberg, 'A Critical Perspective on Foreign Investment', in P. Endelwick (ed.), *Foreign Investment: The New Zealand Experience*, Dunmore Press, Palmerston North, 1998, p.199 at p.208.
56 US Trade Act 1974, §2151 and 2153.
57 US Trade Act 1974, §2155.
58 US Trade Act 1974, §2155.
59 For a discussion of the basis for 'executive act of state' or 'exercise of Crown prerogative', see M. Gobbi and M. Barsi, 'New Zealand's Treaty-Making Process: Understanding the Pressures and Proposals for Reform', Ministry of Justice, Draft no.3, June 1997, pp.7–8.
60 D. McKinnon, 'New Zealand Sovereignty in an Interdependent World', in G.A. Wood and L.S. Leland (eds), *State and Sovereignty: Is the State in Retreat?*, Otago University Press, Dunedin, 1997, p.7 at pp.8 and 11. The orthodox position was also argued by the international legal adviser in the Ministry of Foreign Affairs and Trade, in D. MacKay, 'Treaties – A Greater Role for Parliament?', *Public Sector*, vol.20, no.1 (1997), p.6.
61 See M. Zacher, 'The Decaying Pillars of the Westphalian Temple: Implications for International Order and Governance', in Rosenau and Czempiel (eds), p.58 at p.59.
62 See A. Twomey, 'Treaty Making and Implementation in Australia', and D. Williams, 'Treaties and the Parliamentary Process', *Public Law Review*, vol.7 (1996), pp.4, 199.
63 *Trick or Treaty? Commonwealth Power to Make and Implement Treaties*, Commonwealth Parliament, Canberra, November 1995.
64 Ministry of Justice, Briefing Paper for the Minister of Justice, Oct. 1996, p.51. See also Twomey, p.4.
65 www.austlii.edu.au/dfat.
66 New Zealand Law Commission, 'The Making, Acceptance and Implementation of Treaties: Three Issues for Consideration', draft paper, July 1995; *A New Zealand Guide to International Law and its Sources*, New Zealand Law Commission, Wellington, 1996, p.3. See also K.J. Keith, 'New Zealand Treaty Practice: The Executive and the Legislature', *New Zealand Universities Law Review*, vol.1, 1964, p.272.
67 See D. McGee, 'Treaties – A Role for Parliament?', *Public Sector*, vol.20, no.1 (1997), p.1; 'Treaties and the House of Representatives', Annex D to *Report of the Standing Orders Committee on its Review of the Operation of the Standing Orders*, 1996, I.18B.
68 Ministry of Justice, *Briefing Paper for the Minister of Justice*, Oct. 1996, p.51.
69 *A NZ Guide to International Law*, pp.2–3.
70 *A NZ Guide to International Law*, p.3.
71 Matt Robson MP (Alliance) and Ken Shirley MP (Act) both placed private member's bills in the ballot which would subject treaties to formal parliamentary process. Mike Moore (Labour) presented a paper to the foreign

affairs select committee proposing new rules to increase parliamentary and select committee scrutiny.
72 *Inquiry into Parliament's Role in the International Treaty Process: Report of the Foreign Affairs, Defence and Trade Select Committee*, Wellington, 1997.
73 Notices of Motion, 28 May 1998.
74 *Government Response to the Report of the Foreign Affairs, Defence and Trade Select Committee Inquiry into Parliament's Role in the International Treaty Process*, Wellington, undated.
75 Official Information Act 1982, s.6(b).
76 Official Information Act 1982, s.6(e)(vi).
77 See S. Ramphal, *Our Global Neighbourhood: Report of the Commission on Global Governance*, Oxford University Press, Oxford, 1995; U. Baxi, '"Global Neighbourhood" and "Universal Otherhood": Notes on the Report of the Commission on Global Governance', *Alternatives*, vol.21 (1996), p.525.
78 ILO Conventions 29 and 105 on abolition of forced labour; 87 and 98 on rights to freedom of association and collective bargaining; 111 and 100 on prevention of discrimination in employment and equal pay for work of equal value; and 138 on minimum age for employment.
79 S. Pursey, 'Implementation of Labour Standards in the Multilateral System', in *Labour Standards in the Global Trade and Investment System*, TUAC-OECD, Paris, November 1996, p.73 at p.74
80 Pursey, p.75.
81 R. Falk, 'Global Civil Society: Perspectives, Initiatives, Movements', *Oxford Development Studies*, vol.26, no.1 (1998), p.99 at p.105.
82 E. Durie, 'United Nations or United Peoples', in C. Arup and L. Marks (eds), *Cross Currents: Internationalism, National Identity and Law*, special edn of *Law in Context*, vol.14, no.1 (1996), p.1.
83 E. Durie, p.7.
84 See M. Durie, *Te Mana, Te Kawanatanga: The Politics of Maori Self-Determination*, Oxford University Press, Auckland, 1998, especially Chapter 1.
85 M. Durie, pp.238–39.
86 Claim WAI-262 to the Waitangi Tribunal by members of Te Rarawa, Ngati Kuri, Ngati Koata, Whanau a Rua, Ngati Porou, Ngati Kahungunu, Ngati Wai Iwi and others relating to 'the Protection, Control, Conservation, Management, Treatment, Propagation, Sale, Dispersal, Utilisation and Restriction on the use of and transmission of the knowledge of New Zealand Flora and Fauna and the general resource contained therein'. See also N. Tomas, 'Tangata Whenua Issues', *New Zealand Environmental Law Reporter*, October 1995, p.144.

CHAPTER 2

1 A. Gramsci, *Prison Notebooks*, Lawrence & Wishart, London, 1978, p.10.
2 Gramsci, p.195.
3 B. Gustafson, *The First 50 Years: A History of the New Zealand National Party*, Reed Methuen, Auckland, 1986, p.180.
4 D. Korten, *When Corporations Rule the World*, Kumarian Press, West Hartford, 1995, p.133.
5 P. Marchak, *The Integrated Circus: The New Right and the Restructuring of Global Markets*, McGill-Queens University Press, Montreal, 1991, p.104.
6 M. Crozier et al., *The Crisis of Democracy: Report on the Governability of Democracies to the Trilateral Commission*, New York University Press, New York, 1975, pp.6–7, cited in Marchak, p.106.
7 Marchak, pp.110–11.
8 World Economic Forum, 'Confidential Notes', 1997, note 1.
9 *Building the Network Society: The Report on the World Economic Forum 1997 Annual Meeting in Davos*, WEF, Geneva, 1997, pp.114–17.
10 Interview, Geneva, May 1997.
11 World Economic Forum, 'Confidential Notes', note 5.
12 The New Zealand Business Roundtable is different from other Roundtables found internationally. Elsewhere, although their membership is similar, they operate more as Chambers of Commerce. Some 200 chief executives of the major transnationals formed the first Roundtable in the US in 1972.
13 P. Harris and L. Twiname, *First Knights: An Investigation of the New Zealand Business Roundtable*, Howling at the Moon, Auckland, 1998.
14 *Fraser Forum*, Fraser Institute, Vancouver, June 1993, p.2.
15 *Fraser Forum*, p.5.
16 'Toward the New Millennium: A Five Year Plan for the Fraser Institute', Fraser Institute, Vancouver, January 1997.
17 S. George, 'How to Win the War of Ideas: Lessons from the Gramscian Right', *Dissent*, vol.44, no.3 (1997), p.3.
18 *1997 Index of Economic Freedom*, Heritage Foundation, Washington, 1997.
19 F.A. Hayek, *The Road to Serfdom*, University of Chicago Press, Chicago, 1944. The Institute published two of Hayek's later books: *A Tiger by the Tail*, Institute of Economic Affairs, London, 1972; and *Economic Freedom and Representative Government*, Institute of Economic Affairs, London, 1973.
20 Harris and Twiname, p.53.
21 R. Douglas, *Unfinished Business*, Random House, Auckland, 1993, Ch.10.
22 S. Sexton, *New Zealand Schools: An Evaluation of Recent Reforms and Future Directions*, Business Roundtable, Wellington, 1990.
23 D. Green, *From Welfare State to Civil Society*, Business Roundtable, Wellington, 1996.
24 *Unshackling the Hospitals: Report of the Hospital and Related Services Taskforce*, Ministry of Health, Wellington, 1988.
25 This and following quotations are all from an interview with Michael Porter in Melbourne, 19 March 1998.
26 NZ Treasury, *Economic Management*, Treasury, Wellington, 1984.

27 Tasman University, 'Confidential Information Memorandum: Private Offering of Equity in Tasman University', 12 July 1988, pp.4, 17.
28 See A. Molloy, *Thirty Pieces of Silver*, Howling at the Moon, Auckland, 1998, for an account of the controversy surrounding Russell McVeagh's activities during this period.
29 W. Kasper, *Populate or Languish?*, Business Roundtable, Wellington, 1990.
30 M. Porter, 'Getting on Top Internationally – The Centrality of Labour Market Reform', in *Economic and Social Policy*, Business Roundtable, Wellington, 1989, p.105.
31 The collapse of the electricity supply to the Auckland Central Business District in March 1998 was blamed largely on decisions taken by Mercury Energy. See *Auckland Power Supply Failure 1998: The Report of the Ministerial Inquiry into the Auckland Power Supply Failure*, Ministry of Commerce, Wellington, 1998.
32 *Sunday Age*, 7 April 1996.
33 John Fernyhough retired from the board of the Tasman Institute in February 1999, but remained a director of Tasman Asia-Pacific.
34 On paper, Myers was worth $325 million in 1997.
35 *NZ Herald*, 15 November 1997.
36 OECD, *Economic Survey: New Zealand*, OECD, Paris, 1998, p.ii.
37 Interview, OECD, Paris, May 1997.
38 Interview, OECD, Paris, May 1997.
39 *Reuter*, 23 June 1988.
40 *NZ Herald*, 22 December 1988.
41 *Reuter*, 1 May 1989.
42 *Reuter*, 1 May 1989.
43 *Reuter*, 2 June 1989.
44 *NZ Herald*, 22 December 1989.
45 *NZ Herald*, 30 June 1990.
46 *NBR*, 21 December 1990.
47 NZ Treasury, *1990 Treasury Briefing Papers*, Treasury, Wellington, 1990.
48 *NZ Herald*, 31 March 1991.
49 *NZ Herald*, 21 February 1992.
50 *Reuter*, 7 June 1994.
51 *Evening Post*, 25 May 1996.
52 *Dominion*, 30 May 1996.
53 *NBR*, 19 May 1989.
54 OECD, *Thematic Review of the First Years of Tertiary Education: New Zealand*, OECD Directorate for Education, Employment, Labour and Social Affairs, Paris, 1997, p.12.
55 Ministry of Education, *A Future Tertiary Education Policy for New Zealand: Tertiary Education Review: Green Paper*, Ministry of Education, Wellington, 1997.
56 Interview, OECD, Paris, May 1997.
57 'Understanding on Notification, Consultation, Dispute Settlement and Surveillance 1979', negotiated during the Tokyo Round. B. Hoekman and M. Kostecki, *The Political Economy of the World Trading System: From GATT to WTO*, Oxford University Press, Oxford, 1995, p.45.
58 *GATT Trade Policy Review: New Zealand*, GATT, Geneva, November 1990.
59 WTO, *Trade Policy Review: New Zealand*, WTO, Geneva, 1996, p.143.
60 *Trade Policy Review*, 1996, pp.143–44.
61 *Trade Policy Review*, 1996, pp.2–3.
62 E.g. P. Massey, *New Zealand: Market Liberalization in a Developed Economy*, St Martin's Press, New York, 1995.
63 E.g. B. Easton and R. Gerritsen, 'Economic Reform: Parallels and Divergences', in F. Castles et al. (eds), *The Great Experiment: Labour Parties and Public Policy Transformation in Australia and New Zealand*, Auckland University Press, Auckland, 1996, p.22.
64 E.g. J. Francois et al., 'Assessing the Uruguay Round', in W. Martin and L.A. Winters (eds), *The Uruguay Round and Developing Countries*, World Bank Discussion Paper no.307, World Bank, Washington, 1995; G. Harrison et al., 'Quantifying the Uruguay Round', in Martin and Winters (eds); and the overview of model results in *Trading Ahead: The GATT Uruguay Round: Results for New Zealand*, Ministry of Foreign Affairs and Trade, Wellington, 1994, p.16.
65 *Trade Policy Review*, 1996, p.1.
66 *Trade Policy Review*, 1996, p.14.
67 NZ Treasury, *Economic and Fiscal Update: December 1998*, Treasury, Wellington, 1998, Table 1.1, p.10.
68 *Trade Policy Review*, 1996, p.64.
69 *Reuter*, 23 December 1996.
70 *NZ Herald*, 11 July 1984; *Press*, 12 July 1984.
71 *Reuter*, 27 May 1988.
72 *NZ Herald*, 17 July 1992.
73 R. Kronenberg et al., 'New Zealand: Recent Economic Developments', IMF Staff Country Report No.96/14, February 1996.
74 *Evening Post*, 3 January 1997, with reference to M. Cangiano, 'Accountability and Transparency in the Public Sector: The New Zealand Experience', IMF Working Paper No.96/122.
75 'New Zealand – Selected Issues and Statistical Appendix', IMF Country Report No.96/144, December 1996.
76 'IMF Concludes Article IV Consultation with New Zealand', 12 January 1998, www.imf.org.
77 This was blamed on exchange rate appreciation and declining competitiveness of exports; more liabilities were owed to foreign investors than foreign investment income earned; and migrant transfers had fallen under tighter immigration laws.
78 E.g. *NZ Herald*, 4 September 1997; *Dominion*, 26 September 1997.
79 *NBR*, 24 February 1990.
80 Bancorp economist Roger Kerr, *NBR*, 18 January 1991.
81 D. Hayward and M. Salvaris, 'Rating the States: Credit Rating Agencies and the Australian State Governments', paper presented to the Social Policy Conference, University of New South Wales, July 1993. See also D. Hayward and M. Salvaris, 'Rating the States: Credit Rating Agencies and the Australian State Governments', *Journal of Australian Political Economy*, no.34 (December 1994), p.1.
82 Hayward and Salvaris, 1993.
83 Interview, Standard and Poor's, London, June 1998.
84 *Reuter*, 5 May 1988.

85 *NZ Herald*, 12 June 1989.
86 *NZ Herald*, 30 September 1989.
87 *NZ Herald*, 6 November 1991.
88 *Reuter*, 9 April 1991.
89 *Business Review Weekly*, 9 August 1991.
90 *Reuter*, 8 November 1991.
91 *NBR*, 6 September 1991.
92 *Reuter*, 3 June 1993.
93 *NBR*, 2 April 1993.
94 *Press*, 8 October 1993.
95 *Reuter*, 30 November 1993.
96 *Reuter*, 17 February 1994.
97 *Dominion*, 5 January 1996.
98 *Sunday Star Times*, 4 February 1996.
99 *Evening Post*, 7 February 1996.
100 *NBR*, 14 June 1996.
101 *Waikato Times*, 26 June 1998.
102 *Dominion*, 14 August 1998.
103 *Evening Standard*, 12 September 1998.
104 World Economic Forum, *The Global Competitiveness Report 1996*, WEF, Geneva, 1996, p.8.
105 *Global Competitiveness Report 1996*, p.11.
106 *Global Competitiveness Report 1996*, p.12 (emphasis added).
107 L. Smith, speech to Orewa Rotary Club, Silverdale, 20 January 1998; L. Smith, speech to investment forum, Taipei, 15 June 1998; Budget speech, NZPD, vol.568, 14 May 1998, per Peters, p.8545.
108 Ministry of Foreign Affairs and Trade, *Invest in New Zealand: The Right Choice*, MFAT, Wellington, 1999.
109 *Global Competitiveness Report 1996*, p.17.
110 *Global Competitiveness Report 1997*, p.20.
111 *Invest in New Zealand*, pp.2, 6 (emphasis added).
112 *1997 Index of Economic Freedom*, p.333.
113 B. Johnson, 'Factors of the Index of Economic Freedom', in *1997 Index of Economic Freedom*, p.33.
114 Johnson, pp.33–45. The Fraser Institute's 1997 plan suggested including freedom of commercial speech (e.g. tobacco advertising), free choice in education (privatisation of state education), and freedom in the labour market (individual contracts); see fn.16.
115 See also J. Wood, New Zealand Ambassador to the US, speech, Wisconsin Forum, Wisconsin, 18 February 1997.
116 D. Henderson, *New Zealand in an International Perspective*, Business Roundtable, Wellington, 1996, p.13.
117 Some political reporters took a more critical stance, for example Bruce Jesson, Simon Collins, Alistair Morrison, Gordon Campbell and Anthony Hubbard.
118 Personal communication. There have also been some notable exceptions among business journalists, such as Terry Hall, *Dominion* business editor in the late 1980s, and Bob Edlin in the *National Business Review*, *Independent* and *Rural News*.
119 *The Economist*, 1 June 1985, p.19.
120 *The Economist*, 8 August 1988, p.45; 15 June 1991, p.72; 13 November 1993, p.155; 13 October 1993, p.128; 10 July 1993, p.75.
121 *The Economist*, 16 October 1993, p.20.
122 *The Economist*, 19 October 1996, p.19.
123 *The Economist*, 14 June 1997, pp.44–45.
124 *The Economist*, 5 November 1994, p.19.
125 *The Economist*, 5 October 1996, p.39.
126 *The Economist*, 2 May 1998, p.70.
127 'New Zealand strides down the hard road to economic recovery', *The Times*, 22 June 1992; 'Blueprint for a shrinking state', *Financial Times*, 24 July 1992; 'Radically sensible New Zealand', *Globe & Mail*, August 1994, reported in *NZ Herald*, 20 September 1994; 'Kiwi School of Economics', *Wall Street Journal*, 14 December 1994.
128 E.g. *Toronto Star*, 29 March 1993; *Canadian Forum*, April 1995, p.10; *Globe & Mail*, 11 September 1995.
129 Notably 'The Remaking of New Zealand', *Ideas*, CBC, 12 October 1994.
130 *Independent on Sunday*, 13 March 1994.
131 *Le Monde Diplomatique*, April 1997.

CHAPTER 3

1 L. Smith, speech to Orewa Rotary Club, 20 January 1998.
2 M. Camdessus, 'The IMF: Looking to the Future: Address to the Plenary Meeting of the Bretton Woods Commission on the Future of the Bretton Woods Institutions', Washington, 21 July 1994.
3 See, for example, J. Head, 'Suspension of Debtor Countries' Voting Rights in the IMF: An Assessment of the Third Amendment to the Charter', *Virginia Journal of International Law*, vol.33 (1993), p.591 at pp.599–600; Testimony of Walden Bello before the Banking Oversight Subcommittee, Banking and Financial Services Committee, US House of Representatives, 21 April 1998, www.igc.org/dgap
4 Camdessus, 'The IMF: Looking to the Future'.
5 The International Bank for Reconstruction and Development provides loans to 'developing' and 'emerging' countries at near-market rates, and is funded by selling bonds. The International Development Association draws on voluntary contributions from 30 richer countries to fund long-term loans to 'least developed' countries, largely interest-free. The International Finance Corporation borrows money from international money markets to lend directly to the private sector, at market rates, for projects that would not otherwise attract commercial funding. It also 'helps governments privatize state-owned enterprises ... and advises on legal and regulatory issues' ('The World Bank's Role', www.worldbank.org). The Multilateral Investment Guarantee Agency provides a guarantee of up to 80 percent for private investors against non-commercial risks, such as expropriation or war. The International Centre for Settlement of Investment Disputes offers facilities to resolve disputes between governments and investors.
6 'The World Bank's Role'.
7 M. Sato, speech to the ADB Annual Meeting, Auckland, 1995.
8 See, for example, P. Chatterjee, 'World Bank Failures Soar to 37.5% of Completed Projects in 1991', in K. Danaher (ed.), *50 Years is*

Enough: The Case Against the World Bank and the International Monetary Fund, South End Press, Boston, 1994, p.137 at p.138; B. Rich, 'World Bank/IMF: 50 Years is Enough', in Danaher (ed.), p.10; *ADB Annual Report 1997*, ADB, Manila, 1997, p.23; K. Hansen-Kuhn and D. Hellinger, 'Conditioning Debt Relief on Adjustment: Creating the Conditions for More Indebtedness', http://www.igc.org/dgap/debtpa/html.
9 See generally Development Gap, http://www.igc.org/dgap/debtpa/html.
10 D. Korten, *When Corporations Rule the World*, Kumarian Press, West Hartford, 1995, Ch.12.
11 J. Stiglitz, 'More Instruments and Broader Goals: Moving Toward the Post-Washington Consensus', Helsinki, 7 January 1998; see also J. Stiglitz, 'Responding to Economic Crisis: Policy Alternatives for Equitable Recovery and Development', Ottawa, 29 September 1998, www.worldbank.org.
12 M. Kahler, 'Bargaining with the IMF: Two-Level Strategies and Developing Countries', in P. Evans et al. (eds), *Double-Edged Diplomacy: International Bargaining and Domestic Politics*, University of California Press, Berkeley, 1993, p.363 at p.377.
13 G. Scott, 'Government Reform in New Zealand', IMF Occasional Paper No.140, 1996.
14 Interview, IMF, Washington, April 1997.
15 'The New Strategic Compact', www.worldbank.org.
16 Interviews and informal discussions with World Bank staff, April 1997.
17 Interview, World Bank, Washington, April 1997.
18 See A. Hurrell and N. Woods, 'Globalisation and Inequality', *Millennium: Journal of International Studies*, vol.24, no.3 (1995), p.447 at pp.461–63.
19 World Bank, *The State in a Changing World: World Development Report 1997*, Oxford University Press, Oxford, 1997, p.83.
20 S. Nishimoto, 'The Bank's Governance Policy', in *Governance: Promoting Sound Development Management*, ADB, Manila, 1997, p.9.
21 Nishimoto, pp.10–11.
22 World Bank, *From Plan to Market: World Development Report 1996*, Oxford University Press, Oxford, 1996.
23 *The State in a Changing World*, p.4.
24 *The State in a Changing World*, p.4.
25 *The State in a Changing World*, p.6.
26 *The State in a Changing World*, p.12.
27 *The State in a Changing World*, pp.14–15.
28 *The State in a Changing World*, p.7.
29 *The State in a Changing World*, p.2.
30 *The State in a Changing World*, p.13.
31 *The State in a Changing World*, p.14; see also Chs 13–15.
32 See J. Kelsey, *The New Zealand Experiment: A World Model for Structural Adjustment?*, Auckland University Press/Bridget Williams Books, 2nd edn, 1997, Chs 1–3; A. Bollard, 'New Zealand', in J. Williamson (ed.), *The Political Economy of Policy Reform*, Institute for International Economics, Washington, 1993, p.73.
33 *The State in a Changing World*, p.6.
34 R. Douglas, *Unfinished Business*, Random House, Auckland, 1993, Ch.10.
35 *The State in a Changing World*, pp.1, 87, 91, 94, 117, 153.
36 *The State in a Changing World*, p.1.
37 *The State in a Changing World*, p.87.
38 Interview, World Bank, Washington, April 1997.
39 Interview, World Bank, Washington, April 1997.
40 Interview, World Bank, Washington, April 1997.
41 Interview, World Bank, Washington, April 1997.
42 Interview, World Bank, Washington, April 1997.
43 'The Remaking of New Zealand', *Ideas*, CBC, 12 October 1994.
44 See D. Cooper and D. Neu, 'The Politics of Debt and Deficit in Alberta', in T. Harrison and G. Laxer (eds), *The Trojan Horse: Alberta and the Future of Canada*, Black Rose Books, Montreal, 1995, p.163; K. Taft, *Shredding the Public Interest: Ralph Klein and 25 Years of One-Party Government*, University of Alberta Press, Edmonton, 1997.
45 Interview, Calgary, November 1997.
46 Interview, Calgary, November 1997.
47 Interview, Calgary, November 1997.
48 See Kelsey, pp.299–303.
49 E-mail communication, March, 1997.
50 Interview, OECD, Paris, May 1997.
51 *NZ Herald*, 17 March 1998.
52 Interview, IMF, Washington, April 1997.
53 Tradenz exists to assist New Zealand businesses in the international market-place. Interview, Washington, April 1997.
54 Interview, World Bank, Washington, April 1997.
55 *ADB Annual Report 1998*, p.283, Table 33.
56 *ADB Annual Report 1998*, p.283, Table 33. The cumulative value of ADB technical assistance projects awarded to New Zealand by December 1998 was US$64.7 million: *ADB Annual Report 1998*, p.282, Table 32.
57 Human Resources International (NZ).
58 New Zealand Qualifications Authority.
59 Hume Management Consultants (NZ).
60 Fuels & Energy Management Group (NZ).
61 Vinstar Consulting (NZ), Buddle Findlay (NZ), Unitech (NZ).
62 Deloitte Touche Tohmatsu (NZ).
63 Fuels & Energy Management Group (NZ), Worley International (NZ), NZIER.
64 PA Consulting Group, Tonkin and Taylor International, Chapman Tripp Sheffield Young (NZ).
65 M. Rossabi, 'Mongolia in the 1990s: From Commissars to Capitalists?', www.soros.org/mongolia.html.
66 *ADB Annual Report 1997*, ADB, Manila, 1997, p.25.
67 'NZODA Programme Annual Review 1998', MFAT, Wellington, 1998, p.59.
68 *Education International Asia Pacific Newsletter*, vol.1 (April 1998), p.6.
69 *ADB Annual Report 1997*, p.95 (emphasis added).

70 'NZODA Programme Profiles 1998: Mongolia', MFAT, Wellington, 1998.
71 'NZODA Programme Annual Review 1998', p.22.
72 'Going Private: Public Enterprise Reform in New Zealand', 8–12 December 1996, Agenda.
73 Speakers, in addition to numerous Bank representatives (mainly New Zealanders), included Douglas, Richardson, Scott, Kerr, Deane, Prebble, Shipley, Williamson, Butcher, representatives of Ernst & Young, CCMAU, Tranzrail, Transport, Transit New Zealand, NZ Post, Capital Power, several other senior executives and consultants. Presumably offering 'balance' were Labour's Steve Maharey and the Engineers' Union.
74 Commonwealth Secretariat, 'Towards a New Public Administration' (pamphlet).
75 *Current Good Practices and New Developments in Public Service Management: A Profile of the Public Service of New Zealand*, Country Profile Series No. 5, Commonwealth Secretariat, London, 1995, p.14.
76 *Current Good Practices*, p.14.
77 *Current Good Practices*, p.13.
78 *Current Good Practices*, p.13.
79 *Current Good Practices*, p.16.
80 *Current Good Practices*, p.17.
81 Director Rob Laking was a former senior official in the SSC and chief executive of the Housing Ministry.
82 They included Richardson and former Prime Minister Geoffrey Palmer plus current or former officials: Graham Scott (Treasury), Mark Prebble (Treasury), Doug Martin (SSC), Rob Laking (SSC), Margaret Bazley (Transport, then Social Welfare) and John Chetwin (Treasury, then Labour). Academic Jonathan Boston was the neutral voice.
83 Interview, Commonwealth Secretariat, London, May 1998.
84 'Background Briefing Paper: Costa Rica', World Bank, Washington, 11 July 1995.
85 A tour by Bank staff in early 1997, for example, was treated to Graham Scott (former Treasury), Ruth Richardson (former Finance Minister), Don Hunn (former SSC), Ian Ball and Tony Dale (former Treasury), Roger Kerr (Business Roundtable), Rod Deane (Telecom, former Reserve Bank, SSC, Electricorp), Doug Martin (former SSC, later Fire Service Commission), Doug Andrew (Treasury), Peter Bushnell (Treasury), Margaret Bazley (Social Welfare), Richard Prebble (ACT), Brian Elwood (Ombudsman), Alan Bollard (Commerce Commission, later Treasury), Sue Wood (former National Party president) and Neil Gordon (MetService). Only Pat Walsh (Public Policy, Victoria University) and a last-minute meeting with the author offered any diversity.
86 'Background Briefing Paper: Costa Rica'.
87 Interview, World Bank, Washington, 1997.
88 Interview, World Bank, Washington, 1997.
89 A. Schick, *The Spirit of Reform: Managing the New Zealand State Sector in a Time of Change*, State Services Commission, Wellington, 1996.
90 *Mekong Connection*, vol.1, no.4 (Oct–Dec 1997), p.6.
91 *Mekong Connection*, p.6.
92 *Mekong Connection*, p.6.
93 J. Bolger, speech to Board of Governors, ADB Meeting, Auckland, 3 May 1995.
94 Transcript of press conference, 4 May 1995; see also *Press*, 4 May 1995.
95 *NZ Herald*, 5 May 1995.
96 Speech to the Wisconsin Forum, 18 February 1997 (original emphasis).
97 NZ Treasury, *The December Economic and Fiscal Update*, Wellington, 9 December 1997, Table 1.1, p.22.
98 *Reserve Bank of New Zealand Monetary Policy Statement*, RBNZ, Wellington, August 1998, Table I, p.41.
99 *December Economic and Fiscal Update*, 1997, Table 1.1, p.22.
100 *New Straits Times*, 25 June 1998.
101 S. Henriksson and A. Svenson, *New Zealand: What is the Outlook for Welfare?*, Ministry of Health and Social Affairs, Stockholm, 1998.
102 R. Gilpin, *The Political Economy of International Relations*, Princeton University Press, Princeton, 1987, pp.391–92.
103 World Bank, *The East Asian Economic Miracle: Economic Growth and Public Policy*, Oxford University Press, Oxford, 1993.
104 R. Wade, 'Japan, the World Bank and the Art of Paradigm Maintenance: The East Asian Miracle in Political Perspective', *New Left Review*, vol.217 (1996), p.3 at p.5.
105 R. Richardson, 'Governance: Promoting Sound Development: Management Lessons from New Zealand', in Asia Development Bank, *Governance: Promoting Sound Development Management*, ADB, Manila, 1997, p.21.
106 I. Kubota, 'The Role of the Government in Dynamic Economic Development Process', in *Governance*, p.45 at p.50.
107 Kubota, pp.54–55. The new Japanese-funded ADB Institute, created in 1997 to act as a development 'think-tank' and provide high-level management training for policy-makers from public and private sector development institutions, was a staging-post for Japan's model of 'development'.
108 Reported in *NZ Herald*, 16 July 1998.
109 Opening Statement of Chair Spencer Bachus to the Subcommittee on General Oversight and Investigations, Committee on Banking and Financial Services, and Rep. Bernie Sanders, US House of Representatives, April 21 1998.
110 Projections for GDP growth in Thailand in 1998 went from 2.5 percent when the package was announced in August 1997 to 0.6 percent during the December 1997 review and -3.5 percent at the next review in February 1998; *Focus on Trade*, no.25 (May 1998).
111 *New York Times*, 14 January 1998.
112 *NZ Herald*, 21 January 1999.
113 E.g. the US$17.2 billion loan to Thailand was designed to cover debt servicing while loans were restructured.
114 *Focus on Trade*, no.25 (May 1998).
115 *NZ Herald*, 16 December 1998.

116 *Focus on Trade*, no.25 (May 1998).
117 *NZ Herald*, 14 July 1998.
118 *NZ Herald*, 21 January 1999.
119 'The IMF's Response to the Asian Crisis', 1 September 1998, www.imf.org.
120 *Financial Times*, 20 February 1998.
121 Economic Planning Agency, 'Outline of Emergency Economic Package', Ministry of Finance, Tokyo, 16 November 1998.
122 *Business Time on Line*, Singapore, 31 May 1999.
123 E.g. J. Stiglitz, 'More Instruments and Broader Goals: Moving Toward the Post-Washington Consensus', Helsinki, 7 January 1998, www.worldbank.org.
124 J. Wolfensohn, 'World Bank Commends Indonesian Reforms', news release, 15 January 1998.
125 *Press*, 16 January 1999.
126 M. McCubbins, R. Noll and B. Weingast, 'Administrative Procedures as Instruments of Political Control', *Journal of Law, Economics and Organization*, no.6 (1990), p.243 at p.261.

CHAPTER 4

1 The Multilateral Agreement on Investment: Frequently Asked Questions and Answers, May 1998, www.oecd.org/daf/cmis/mai/faqmai.htm#2; 'The MAI: Presentation by the Ministry of Foreign Affairs and Trade', undated [1997].
2 While UNCTAD puts the threshold for FDI at 10 percent, the level adopted by Statistics NZ and the OIC is a 25 percent equity stake.
3 This was the first time an inventory of private foreign investment in New Zealand had been made. W. Rosenberg, 'Capital Imports and Growth: The Case of New Zealand: Foreign Investment in New Zealand, 1840–1958', *The Economic Journal*, vol.LXXI (1961), p.93 at p.97. I am grateful to Bill Rosenberg for alerting me to this material.
4 W. Rosenberg, pp.100–1.
5 W.B. Sutch, *Takeover New Zealand*, A.H. & A.W. Reed, Wellington, 1971, p.128.
6 See B. Jesson, *Behind the Mirror Glass*, Penguin Books, Auckland, 1987.
7 TVNZ, *Frontline: New Zealand Commercial Involvement in Chile*, 1 May 1988.
8 NZ Treasury, *Government Management: Brief to the Incoming Government 1987*, Volume 1, Treasury, Wellington, 1987, p.248.
9 NZ Steel, Petrocorp, Development Finance Corporation, Post Office Bank, Shipping Corporation, Air New Zealand, Rural Bank, State Insurance Office, Tourist Hotel Corporation, Government Printing Office, Maui Gas and Synfuels, and Telecom, alongside the sale of Landcorp's mortgages and cutting rights to the state's plantation forests.
10 Cabinet Strategy Committee, 'The Government's Role in the Promotion of Foreign Direct Investment in New Zealand', CSC (91) 61, 16 July 1991.
11 *NZ Herald*, 19 November 1991.
12 'Briefing Notes: Meeting between the Foreign Direct Investment Advisory Group and the Prime Minister', 20 August 1992.
13 *NBR*, 10 April 1992; 15 March 1996.
14 D. McKinnon, speech at launch of Asia 2000 Seminar, July 1993.
15 J. Bolger, speech in Tokyo, May 1993.
16 R. Walker, 'The Government's Economic Mantra of BIP Immigration', unpublished paper, September 1991; R. Walker, 'Immigration Policy and the Political Economy of New Zealand', in S. Greif (ed.), *Immigration and National Identity in New Zealand*, Dunmore Press, Palmerston North, 1995, p.282.
17 *NBR*, 3 April 1992. See similar results in *NBR*, 11 November 1994, 13 September 1996.
18 D. McKinnon, speech at International Conference on Asian Studies, Wellington, July 1993.
19 T. Brooking and R. Rabel, 'Neither British nor Polynesian: A Brief History of New Zealand's Other Immigrants', in Greif (ed.), p.23.
20 R. Chung, 'Foreign Investment in New Zealand Commercial Property', Ernst & Young, Auckland, August 1994.
21 *NBR*, 10 June 1994.
22 *Financial Times*, 27 August 1993.
23 *OECD Economic Surveys: New Zealand*, OECD, Paris, 1999, p.122, Table A2.
24 *Foreign Control Watchdog*, no.76 (September 1994), pp.24–30.
25 Statistics NZ subsequently developed a regular update on New Zealand's International Investment Position, which is somewhat more informative than (and sometimes diverges from) the OIC's reports.
26 Report of the Ombudsman for the year ended June 1993, p.135.
27 Figures supplied by Bill Rosenberg, based on annual listing in *Management* magazine, December 1994, pp.4, 68.
28 *Foreign Control Watchdog*, no.77 (December 1994), pp.1–2.
29 *NBR*, 26 May 1995. Note: The figures opposing foreign land ownership and seeking a ban seem contradictory.
30 *Dominion*, 4 May 1995. There are suspicions that the latter prediction may have proved true with reference to several forestry fires in the central North Island.
31 *Sunday Star Times*, 30 April 1995.
32 *Report of the Winebox Inquiry: Commission of Inquiry into Certain Matters Relating to Taxation*, GP Publications, Wellington, 1997; *Peters v Davison* (No.2), (1998), *New Zealand Administrative Reports* 309; *Peters v Davison* (No.3), (1998), vol.18, *New Zealand Tax Cases* 14,027.
33 American Chamber of Commerce, 'The Contribution of Foreign Direct Investment to the New Zealand Economy', October 1995.
34 American Chamber of Commerce, 'New Zealand Foreign Investment Conditions: A Review of Government Policy and the Current Barriers to Increased Foreign Investment', September 1995.
35 *NBR*, 15 March 1996.
36 *NZ Herald*, 3 December 1996.
37 *NZ Herald*, 8 May 1996.
38 *NZ Herald*, 3 August 1996.

39 *The Coalition Agreement*, 10 December 1996, p.32.
40 This could have proved interesting, given that Brierley Investments, which co-owns Sealord with the Treaty of Waitangi Fisheries Commission, is now defined as an overseas company by the OIC.
41 *NZ Herald*, 23 January 1997; 24 January 1997; 28 January 1997.
42 M. Moore, speech to University of Canterbury Seminar on 'International Liberalisation', August 1997.
43 Ministry of Foreign Affairs and Trade, *Invest in New Zealand: The Right Choice*, MFAT, Wellington, 1999.
44 *NZ Herald*, 18 November 1997.
45 *NZ Herald*, 17 November 1997.
46 CAB (92) M24/7f, June 1992.
47 Chair, Foreign Direct Investment Advisory Group, to Prime Minister, 25 May 1995.
48 Cabinet Strategy Committee, 'Foreign Direct Investment Advisory Group', CSC (95) 90M22/1, 20 June 1995.
49 Treasury, 'Disestablishment of the Foreign Direct Investment Advisory Group', 22 December 1997.
50 The OIC's figures can only indicate investment trends, as they deal with applications rather than actual investments, and are limited to those with a value of more than $10 million (except for land) and a 25 percent overseas interest.
51 *OIC Update*, 24 November 1998. The actual inflow of US direct investment was minimal in 1997 and 1998, with most of the investment flow coming from Australia and the UK. Statistics NZ, 'Direct Investment Statistics by Country and Country Groupings', March 1998 year.
52 *OIC Update*, 24 November 1998.
53 Kirin actually bought only 45 percent of Lion.
54 Expansion of existing shareholdings also meant that some investment moved from the 'portfolio' category to FDI.
55 'Direct Investment Statistics by Country'.
56 Statistics NZ, 'International Investment Position', 31 March 1998.
57 This data is drawn primarily from Bill Rosenberg, 'Critique of MFAT presentation on foreign investment in New Zealand in its slide show on the MAI', *Foreign Control Watchdog*, no.86 (December 1997), pp.9–10.
58 L. Smith, speech to Orewa Rotary Club, 20 January 1998; Moore, speech to University of Canterbury Seminar.
59 *Independent*, 18 February 1998.
60 *Independent*, 12 August 1998.
61 'The MAI: Presentation by MFAT'.
62 *NZ Herald*, 18 October 1997.
63 *NZ Herald*, 26 March 1999.
64 'The MAI: Presentation by MFAT'.
65 M. Moore, 'Multilateral Agreement on Investment: Proposed Caucus Position', 17 November 1997.
66 L. Smith, speech to the Orewa Rotary Club.
67 See *Foreign Control Watchdog*, no.82 (August 1996), p.39; no.83 (December 1996), p.8; no.84 (May 1997), p.34; no.86 (December 1997), p.66; no.87 (June 1998), p.23.
68 *NZ Herald*, 13 August 1998.
69 *NZ Herald*, 12 August 1998.
70 *NZ Herald*, 14 August 1998.
71 *NZ Herald*, 5 February 1999.
72 'The MAI: Presentation by MFAT'.
73 'The MAI: Presentation by MFAT'.
74 M. Moore, 'MAI: Proposed Caucus Position'; 'The MAI: Presentation by MFAT'.
75 *NZ Herald*, 18 October 1997.
76 B. Rosenberg cites Securities Commission and AGB McNair surveys, reported in *NZ Herald*, 21 August 1996 and *Christchurch Mail*, 14 July 1997 respectively.
77 *NBR*, 16 August 1996.
78 *Foreign Control Watchdog*, no.83 (December 1996), p.9.
79 *NZ Herald*, 16 June 1999.
80 *Foreign Control Watchdog*, no. 86 (December 1997), p.36.
81 Statistics NZ, 'Balance of Payments', 27 January 1997.
82 *NZ Herald*, 18 October 1997.
83 *NZ Herald*, 26–27 December 1998.
84 D. Brash, 'New Zealand's Economic Reforms: A Model for Change?', Chatham House, London, 3 June 1998; *NZ Herald*, 11 June 1998.
85 J.M. Keynes, *The General Theory of Employment, Interest and Money*, Harcourt Brace & Co, New York, 1936, pp.150–51.
86 Keynes, p.154.
87 Keynes, p.159.
88 Keynes, p.164.
89 K. Polanyi, *The Great Transformation: The Political and Economic Origins of our Times*, Beacon Press, Boston, 1957, p.142.
90 See J. Hogan, *Break the Dollar Deadlock: The Failure of the Bretton Woods Plan*, Technical Books, Wellington, 1952.
91 W. Rosenberg, 'New Zealand on a New Road: After the IMF – What?', *New Zealand Monthly Review*, Christchurch, 1961, p.4.
92 A borrowing country is authorised, under certain conditions, to buy a specified amount of hard currency from the IMF using its own currency. The transaction must be reversed within a specified time. New Zealand originally deposited gold valued at US$28 million, which gave it access to a possible US$140 million in credit. *NZPD*, vol.352, 11 July 1967, p.1738.
93 H. Lake, *International Monetary Fund and World Bank: Implications of New Zealand Membership*, Government Printer, Wellington, 1961.
94 See W. Rosenberg, 'New Zealand's Relations with the International Monetary Fund', *New Zealand Company Director*, vol.1, no.1 (April 1967); *NZPD*, vol.353, 31 October 1967, pp.3773–96.
95 *NZPD*, vol.353, 31 October 1967, p.3777.
96 E. Kapstein, *Governing the Global Economy: International Finance and the State*, Harvard University Press, Cambridge, 1994, p.56.
97 P. Krugman, *The Age of Diminished Expectations: US Economic Policy in the 1990s*, MIT Press, Cambridge, 1994, p.174.
98 For a New Zealand account, see *Independent*, 12 August 1998.

REFERENCES TO PAGES 147 TO 164 ▲ 399

99 This is what George Soros's Quantum Fund did with the Thai Baht in 1997.
100 US fund Long-Term Capital Management, which collapsed in late 1998, was leveraged to at least 30 times its original investment.
101 D. Korten, *When Corporations Rule the World*, Kumarian Press, West Hartford, 1995, p.198.
102 'What Really Happened to Long-Term Capital Management', posted on www.slate.com on 1 October 1998.
103 Korten, p.205.
104 D. Harper and G. Karacaoglu, 'Financial Policy Reform in New Zealand', in A. Bollard and R. Buckle (eds), *Economic Liberalisation in New Zealand*, Allen & Unwin, Wellington, 1987, p.206.
105 Reserve Bank of New Zealand, *Financial Policy Reform*, RBNZ, Wellington, 1986, pp.39–40.
106 Figures from D.K. Sheppard, 'The 1989 Reserve Bank Bill as a Charter for Price and Financial Sector Stability: A Review of its Defacto Performance', 1989, p.4 (Submission on Reserve Bank Bill, 1989).
107 *Report of the Winebox Inquiry; Peters v Davison (No.2)* (1998), NZAR 309; *Peters v Davison (No.3)* (1998), 18 NZTC 14,027.
108 P. Fitzsimons, 'The New Zealand Securities Commission: The Rise and Fall of a Law Reform Body', *Waikato Law Review*, vol.2 (1994), pp.87, 104.
109 D. Brash, speech to the Southland Federated Farmers, Invercargill, 11 November 1996.
110 *NZ Herald*, 13 January 1997; 19 June 1998.
111 M. Fox and G. Walker, 'Evidence on the Corporate Governance of New Zealand Listed Companies', *Otago Law Review*, vol.8, no.3 (1995), p.317; G. Walker and A. Borrowdale, 'Overseas Notes: New Zealand', *Company and Securities Law Journal*, vol.12 (1994), p.529.
112 *NZ Herald*, 23–24 January 1999.
113 *NZ Herald*, 11–12 July 1998.
114 *NBR*, 15 March 1996.
115 *NZ Herald*, 22 January 1998.
116 *NZ Herald*, 26 April 1997.
117 *NZ Herald*, 9–10 January 1999.
118 *NZ Herald*, 26 November 1998.
119 *NZ Herald*, 19–20 December 1998; 1–2 August 1998.
120 *NZ Herald*, 13 May 1998.
121 Some practical changes were made to Stock Exchange listing requirements affecting takeovers in February 1999. *NZ Herald*, 22 February 1999.
122 *NZ Herald*, 29 September 1995.
123 *Sunday Star Times*, 25 October 1998; see also *Australian Financial Review*, 26 November 1998; *Listener*, 21 November 1998.
124 *Listener*, 24 April 1999.
125 *NZ Herald*, 25 August 1997; 15 December 1997.
126 G. Soros, 'The Capitalist Threat', *Atlantic Monthly*, vol.279, no.2 (1997), p.45.
127 B. Easton, 'Constant Crises', *Listener*, 10 April 1999.
128 Kapstein, p.83.
129 The collapse of this scheme for linking the value of European Union currencies is blamed on speculation by the Quantum Fund on the British pound.
130 Krugman, Ch.12; Kapstein, pp.108–9.
131 D. Rodrik, 'Who Needs Capital-Account Convertibility?', *Essays in International Finance*, no.207 (May 1998), p.55.
132 N. Bullard et al., *Taming the Tigers: The IMF and the Asian Crisis*, CAFOD, London, March 1998.
133 Mahathir, speech to APEC-CEO Summit, Vancouver, 23 November 1997.
134 *NZ Herald*, 28 October 1998.
135 *New Straits Times*, 17 November 1998.
136 *Australian Financial Review*, 26 November 1998.
137 Hong Kong did the same in August 1998 and ultimately profited from it. *Financial Times*, 27 March 1999.
138 *Globe and Mail*, 25 March 1999.
139 *Wall Street Journal*, 18 September 1998; *Review and Outlook (Wall Street Journal)*, 5 April 1999.
140 *Financial Times*, 13 April 1999.
141 *Wall Street Journal*, 11 December 1998.
142 G. Soros, *The Crisis of Global Capitalism*, Public Affairs, Washington, 1998.
143 *NZ Herald*, 5 January 1999.
144 IMF Annual Meeting, Hong Kong, 1997.
145 Testimony of Walden Bello before the Banking Oversight Subcommittee, Banking and Financial Services Committee, US House of Representatives, 21 April 1998.
146 D. Brash, speech hosted by Chatham House, London, June 1998.
147 D. Brash, A Presentation to Small and Medium Enterprises, November/December 1998.
148 Quoted in A. Van Dormael, *Bretton Woods: Birth of a Monetary System*, Macmillan, London, 1978, p.32.
149 B. Jesson, *Only Their Purpose is Mad*, Dunmore Press, Palmerston North, 1999, p.39.

CHAPTER 5

1 UNCTAD, *World Investment Report 1997: Transnational Corporations, Market Structures and Competition Policy: Overview*, United Nations, New York, 1997, p.9.
2 *World Investment Report 1997*, p.12.
3 K. Ohmae, 'Putting Global Logic First', *Harvard Business Review*, vol.73, no.1 (1995), p.119; see also K. Ohmae, *The End of the Nation State: The Rise of Regional Economies*, The Free Press, New York, 1995.
4 R. Barnet and R. Muller, quoted in D. Korten, *When Corporations Rule the World*, Kumarian Press, West Hartford, 1995, p.121.
5 *World Investment Report 1997*, p.2.
6 *Report of the Permanent People's Tribunal Session on Workers and Consumers Rights in the Garment Industry*, Permanent People's Tribunal, Rome, 1998. See also *NZ Herald*, 15 January 1999.
7 S. Picciotto, 'International Business and Global Development', in S. Adelman and A. Paliwala (eds), *Law and Crisis in the Third World*, Hans Zell, London, 1993, p.149.

8 *World Investment Report 1997*, p.18.
9 R. Wade, 'Globalization and Its Limits: Reports of the Death of the National Economy are Greatly Exaggerated', in S. Berger and R. Dore (eds), *National Diversity and Global Capitalism*, Cornell University Press, New York, 1996, pp.60, 72–73.
10 In 1996, foreign direct investment into 'developing' countries was US$129 billion, although US$42 billion of that went to China. The 48 'very poor' countries received around US$1.8 billion. *World Investment Report 1997*, p.26.
11 Korten, p.76.
12 *World Investment Report 1997*, p.7.
13 *NZ Herald*, 9–10 January 1999.
14 D. Hayward and R. Bell, *1994 Kaikohe Business Survey: Summary of Survey Findings*, Working Paper No.6, Department of Geography, Auckland University, 1997; see also R. Le Heron and E. Pawson (eds), *Changing Places: New Zealand in the Nineties*, Longman Paul, Auckland, 1996, p.77.
15 J. Cassels, *The Uncertain Promise of Law: Lessons from Bhopal*, Toronto University Press, Toronto, 1993; ARENA, *Bhopal: Industrial Genocide?*, Arena Press, Hong Kong, 1985.
16 Tuwharetoa ki Kawerau end submission to the 9th hearing of Te Runanga o Tuwharetoa ki Kawerau, Claim to the Waitangi Tribunal, 16–19 October 1995 (WAI-62).
17 *NZ Herald*, 25 November 1997.
18 Interview with Tame Iti, July 1992.
19 E.g. *Vancouver Sun*, 29 April 1991. Opposition in 1999 was focused on Fletchers' major competitor MacMillan Bloedel after the BC government granted the company rights to mill on Crown-owned land that was under First Nations claims, and exempted it from compliance with the Forest Practices Code. *Globe & Mail*, 18 March 1999.
20 'Statement in Support of the Restitution of Lands Usurped by Forestry Companies and for Respect for the Rights of the Mapuche People', Arauco, April 1998.
21 *Foreign Control Watchdog*, no.85 (August 1997), p.47.
22 *Foreign Control Watchdog*, no.84 (May 1997), p.32.
23 P. Muchlinski, *Multinational Enterprises and the Law*, Blackwell, Oxford, 1995, pp.575–97.
24 *OECD Guidelines for Multinational Enterprises*, OECD, Paris, 1994, pp.32–33; see also OECD Declaration on International Investment and Multinational Enterprises, *International Legal Materials*, vol.15 (1976), p.967.
25 This largely reflects the non-binding ILO Tripartite Declaration of Principles concerning Multinationals and Social Policy 1977.
26 These are contained in the 'clarifications' of the text in the commentary on Guideline 2.
27 OECD Guideline 8.
28 'Ethical Trading Initiative: Information Pack', Department for International Development, London, 1998.
29 *The Economist*, 20 March 1999, p.63.
30 R. Sally, 'Multinational Enterprises, Political Economy and Institutional Theory: Domestic Embeddedness in the Context of Internationalization', *Review of International Political Economy*, vol.1, no.1 (1994), pp.161, 162.
31 The Global Climate Coalition, which included companies like Dow Chemical, claims the US can wait at least 20 years before taking action to limit gas emissions. *The Nation*, 16 December 1996, pp.21–24.
32 'A Guide to the Multilateral Agreement on Investment (MAI)', USCIB, Washington, January 1996.
33 M. Vander Stichele, *Towards a World Transnationals' Organisation?*, Transnational Institute, Amsterdam, 1998, p.6.
34 American Chamber of Commerce, 'New Zealand Foreign Investment Conditions: A Review of Government Policy and the Current Barriers to Increased Foreign Investment', September 1995; 'The Contribution of Foreign Direct Investment to the New Zealand Economy', October 1995; P. Enderwick, 'The Foreign Investment Climate in New Zealand 1998', October 1998.
35 P. Harris and L. Twiname, *First Knights: An Investigation of the New Zealand Business Roundtable*, Howling at the Moon, Auckland, 1998.
36 *NZ Herald*, 7 May 1993.
37 *NZ Herald*, 21 September 1996.
38 *NBR*, 12 April 1996.
39 *NZ Herald*, 6 January 1999.
40 Wade, p.85.
41 *NZ Herald*, 4 August 1998.
42 Submission to the Taxation (International Taxation) Bill, 9 October 1995; *NBR*, 26 January 1996.
43 There were also changes to the withholding tax on fully imputed dividends.
44 The government's guidelines for business on the transfer pricing regime were not released until 22 months later. *NZ Herald*, 30 October 1997.
45 *NZPD*, 17 August 1995, pp.8758–60.
46 *NZPD*, 5 December 1995, Sutton.
47 *NZ Herald*, 2 July 1998.
48 *The Economist*, 8 February 1992, p.62; see also 15 February 1992, p.16.
49 X. Vasquez, 'The North American Free Trade Agreement and Environmental Racism', *Harvard International Law Journal*, vol.34, no.2 (1993), p.357 at pp.368–69.
50 *The 1997 People's Annual Report*, INFACT, Boston, 1997, p.44.
51 *NZ Herald*, 28 May 1999.
52 American Chamber of Commerce, 'The Resource Management Act: Survey on the Act's Administration and its Impact on Investment', 1997.
53 Minister for the Environment, *Land Use Controls under the Resource Management Act: A Think Piece*, Ministry for the Environment, Wellington, 1998.
54 Action for Community and the Environment, 'A Guide to the Proposals for Amendment to the Resource Management Act', November 1998.
55 'Proposals for Amendment to the Resource Management Act', Ministry for the Environ-

ment, Wellington, 1998, p.5; *Independent*, 30 September 1998.
56 For an account sympathetic to the company, see *Independent*, 3 February 1999.
57 The company puts the cost at $27 million; *NZ Herald*, 24 September 1997. *Geo Resource Forum*, 24 April 1997, puts it at $21 million.
58 Quoted in Coromandel Watchdog, MPs Information Pack, 'The Burden of Gilt – Taxpayer Liability for Toxic Waste at Golden Cross Mine', undated.
59 *Geo Resource Forum*, 24 April 1997.
60 *NZ Herald*, 24 September 1997.
61 *Coromandel Watchdog News*, March 1997.
62 Coromandel Watchdog, MPs Information Pack.
63 The company gives the figure of $15 million; *NZ Herald*, 24 September 1997.
64 Coromandel Watchdog, MPs Information Pack.
65 *Geo Resource Forum*, 24 April 1997.
66 *Waihi Leader*, 29 July 1997.
67 Parliamentary Commissioner for the Environment, 'Golden Cross Mining Project Environmental Impact Audit 1988', preface.
68 Parliamentary Commissioner for the Environment, *Long-term Management of the Environmental Effects of Tailings Dams*, Wellington, 1997, p.65.
69 *Long-term Management*, pp.60–61.
70 *Long-term Management*, p.87; see also *Foreign Control Watchdog*, no.84 (May 1997), p.30.
71 E.g. Golden Cross, *Rehab News*, April 1999, edition 4.
72 See J. Kelsey, *The New Zealand Experiment: A World Model for Structural Adjustment?*, 2nd edn, Auckland University Press/Bridget Williams Books, Auckland, 1997, Ch.6.
73 *NZ Herald*, 7 May 1999; www.cyberuni.ac.nz.
74 R. Birchfield and I. Grant, *Out of the Woods: The Restructuring and Sale of New Zealand's State Forests*, GP Books, Wellington, 1993, p.228.
75 *Dominion*, 16 June 1999; 17 June 1999.
76 These were transactions worth more than $10 million; *Privatisation International*, April 1997, p.26.
77 See Kelsey, pp.132–35.
78 'Government Administration Committee on the Inquiry into the Sale of the Government Printing Office', *AJHR*, 1.6A, Vol.XXIII (1991–93).
79 *NZ Herald*, 30 August 1997.
80 *NZ Herald*, 30 August 1997.
81 See *Foreign Control Watchdog*, no.85 (August 1997), p.11.
82 *Foreign Control Watchdog*, no.77 (December 1994), p.3.
83 *NZ Herald*, 20 December 1996; see also *NBR*, 24 March 1995.
84 *NBR*, 22 November 1996; see also *NZ Herald*, 27 December 1997.
85 *NZ Herald*, 5 January 1999; *Press*, 29 June 1999.
86 TUANZ media statement, 17 May 1999; *Independent*, 18 November 1998, 5 May 1999; *NZ Herald*, 1 June 1999.
87 *Foreign Control Watchdog*, no.88 (September 1998), pp.29–30.

88 Ministry of Commerce, 'Review of the Competition Thresholds in the Commerce Act 1986 and Related Issues: A Discussion Document', April 1999.
89 'Review of Competition Thresholds', p.3.
90 Between January 1991 and December 1996, market dominance was found only where the merged parties' share was over 70 percent of the market, and not always then; of 211 applications for business acquisitions, only 15 were declined. 'Review of Competition Thresholds', pp.11, 21.
91 *NZ Herald*, 5–6 June 1999.
92 B. Spicer et al., *The Power to Manage: Restructuring the New Zealand Electricity Department as a State-Owned Enterprise*, Oxford University Press, Auckland, 1991; I. Duncan and A. Bollard, *Corporatization and Privatization: Lessons from New Zealand*, Oxford University Press, Auckland, 1992, Ch.8.
93 *NZPD*, 22 April 1999, per Hodgson.
94 *NZPD*, 22 April 1999, per Shirley.
95 *Foreign Control Watchdog*, no.90 (April 1999), p.4.
96 *Wall Street Journal*, 23 December 1998; *NZ Herald*, 21 April 1999.
97 *NZ Herald*, 15–16 May 1999.
98 *NZ Herald*, 27–28 March 1998.
99 *NZPD*, weekly No.70, 22 April 1999, pp.16034–36; *NZ Herald*, 21 April 1999.
100 Ministry of Commerce, 'Electricity Reform: Enhancing the Credibility of the Threat of Price Control on Electricity Line Businesses', information brief, 16 December 1998; *Independent*, 3 May 1999; *NZ Herald*, 2 April 1999.
101 Commerce (Controlled Goods or Services) Amendment Bill 1999. The formula was based on methods including the consumer price index minus a set amount.
102 Minister for Enterprise and Commerce, media release, 25 May 1999.
103 'Review of Competition Thresholds', p.43.
104 *NZPD*, weekly No.70, 22 April 1999, p.16042, per Shirley.
105 *NZPD*, weekly No.70, 22 April 1999, p.16031, per Hodgson.
106 *Foreign Control Watchdog*, no.76 (September 1994), p.44.
107 *Foreign Control Watchdog*, no.83 (December 1996), p.55.
108 *Foreign Control Watchdog*, no.73 (August 1993), p.18.
109 *NZ Herald*, 17 November 1994.
110 *NZ Herald*, 14 June 1996.
111 *NBR*, 31 May 1996.
112 R. Miles, *Fay Richwhite's Railway*, Robert Miles, Timaru, 1998, p.3.
113 *Press*, 10 September 1997.
114 *Press*, 5 February 1999; see also Kelsey, p.123, Table 6.1.
115 *NZ Herald*, 7 March 1997.
116 *Department of Labour v Tranz Rail*, District Court, Wellington, per P.J. Evans, 22 November 1996; *Listener*, 14 December 1996.
117 *NZ Herald*, 30 January 1997; *Press*, 1 May 1997.
118 *Dominion*, 5 July 1997.
119 *Press*, 10 November 1997.

120 Listener, 9 March 1996, p.20.
121 Independent, 28 February 1997, based on the US Journal of Commerce.
122 Management Today, July 1997, p.28.
123 'Financial highlights, year ended 30 April 1998', Hl/Companies/stagecoach2.htm.
124 Management Today, July 1997, p.28.
125 NZ Herald, 15 June 1999.
126 NZ Herald, 27 August 1998.
127 Independent, 17 March 1999.
128 NZ Herald, 8 January 1999.
129 Foreign Control Watchdog, no.90 (April 1999), p.17.
130 City Voice, 20 August 1998.
131 Hosking v Wellington City Transport (1995) 1 HRNZ 542.
132 Media release, Human Rights Commission, 31 March 1998.
133 NZ Herald, 27 November 1998.
134 KPMG 1998 Financial Institutions Performance Survey, updated for 1998 mergers.
135 NZ Herald, 27 November 1998.
136 See J. Kelsey, Rolling Back the State: The Privatisation of Power in Aotearoa New Zealand, Bridget Williams Books, Wellington, 1993, pp.37–39.
137 See E. Carew, Westpac: The Bank that Broke the Bank, Doubleday, Sydney, 1997; B. Rosenberg, 'The Skeletons in Westpac's Cupboards', Foreign Control Watchdog, no.82 (August 1996), p.10.
138 Press, 30 August 1993; Westpac Banking Corporation v Ancell (1993) NZBLC 103,259; NZLR 218; Cigna Life Insurance NZ v Westpac Securities [1996] 1 NZLR 81.
139 Press, 22 November 1997.
140 NZ Herald, 27 November 1998.
141 D. Tripe, 'Mergers on the Cards: Should We Have More Bank Mergers in New Zealand?', FinSec, Wellington, April 1999.
142 'The Best Banks', Consumer, no.364 (October 1997), p.16 at p.21; see also Consumer, no.327 (June 1994), p.6.
143 Press, 5 October 1995.
144 NZ Herald, 4 November 1998.
145 NZ Herald, 3 August 1998; 11 November 1998.
146 NZ Herald, 1 June 1999.
147 NZ Herald, 1 June 1999.
148 World Investment Report 1997, p.10, Table 3.
149 See e.g. NZ Herald, 27 October 1998.
150 NZ Herald, 25 May 1999.
151 Hl/Companies/eds_defense.htm.
152 Evening Post, 15 November 1997; Dominion, 24 December 1997; Evening Post, 17 February 1998; Press, 14 October 1998; see also Dominion, 11 January 1996; Press, 3 September 1998.
153 NZ Herald, 4 November 1997.
154 NZ Herald, 6 May 1999.
155 NZ Herald, 11 March 1999.
156 Public Service International's Research Network Newsletter, no.12 (April 1997), p.3.
157 Public Sector Research Centre Contract Monitor, no.7, p.4.
158 Hl/Companies/nz_ministry_seeks_shtml.
159 Hl/Companies/nz_ministry_seeks_shtml.
160 The initial code expired in July 1996; a new code was issued in May 1997. Privacy Commissioner, EDS Information Privacy Code 1997.
161 This section draws heavily on B. Rosenberg, 'News Media Ownership in New Zealand', unpublished paper, 1998.
162 The privatisation of broadcasting has been challenged by Maori in numerous court cases; e.g. Attorney-General v. New Zealand Maori Council, [1991] 2 NZLR 129; New Zealand Maori Council v. Attorney-General, [1992] 2 NZLR 576; New Zealand Maori Council v Attorney-General, [1994] 1 NZLR 513; Waitangi Tribunal, Radio Spectrum Management and Development: Interim report, (WAI-776), Waitangi Tribunal, Wellington, March 1999.
163 NZ Herald, 1 July 1999.
164 Press, 14 January 1999.
165 NZ Herald, 11 March 1998.
166 Press, 20 December 1996.
167 Listener, 11 November 1995; Dominion, 19 October 1995.
168 NZ Herald, 20 March 1998.
169 NZ Herald, 1 July 1999.
170 Press, 11 December 1995; see also NZ Herald, 2 March 1998.
171 Pursuant to the Radiocommunications Act 1989.
172 ANP later reduced its holding to 19 percent.
173 T. Frewen, 'Who Sets the Agenda?', paper to a seminar on Who Owns the News?, Christchurch, August 1996.
174 Defamation action following TVNZ's screening of 'For the Public Good' in 1990 had a long-term chilling effect; see more recently Lange v Atkinson, [1998] 3 NZLR 424.
175 R. Kerr, speech to the Christchurch Rotary Club, 2 May 1995.

CHAPTER 6

1 L. Smith, speech to the Warkworth Rotary Club, 11 June 1998.
2 P. Krugman, 'Does the New Trade Theory Require a New Trade Policy?', The World Economy, vol.15, no.4 (1992), p.423 at p.432.
3 Krugman, 1992, p.438.
4 'Special 301' and 'super 301' were legislated through the Omnibus Trade and Competitiveness Act 1988; section 335 et seq. of the US Tariff Act also allows investigations to determine whether foreign goods are supported by unfair trade practices.
5 NZ Herald, 18 September 1998; 19 November 1998.
6 P. Krugman, Pop Internationalism, MIT Press, Cambridge, 1997, p.120.
7 P. Krugman, The Age of Diminished Expectations: US Economic Policy in the 1990s, MIT Press, Cambridge, 1994, pp.126–28.
8 Krugman, 1994, p.125.
9 Krugman, 1994, p.134.
10 M. Kahler, 'Trade and Domestic Differences', in S. Berger and R. Dore (eds), National Diversity and Global Capitalism, Cornell University Press, New York, 1996, p.298 at p.302.
11 Krugman, 1994, pp.134–35.
12 R. Howse and M. Trebilcock, 'The Fair Trade – Free Trade Debate: Trade, Labor, and the Environment', International Review of Law and Economics , vol.16 (1996), p.61.

13 P. Streeten, 'Free and Managed Trade', in Berger and Dore (eds), p.353 at pp.356–57.
14 J. Ruggie, *Constructing the World Polity: Essays on International Institutionalization*, Routledge, London, 1998, Ch.2; see also 'International Regimes, Transactions and Change: Embedded Liberalism in the Postwar Economic Order', *International Organization*, vol.36, no.12 (1982), p.195.
15 Streeten, p.357.
16 Ministry of Foreign Affairs and Trade, *Trade Policy Briefing 1993*, MFAT, Wellington, 1993, pp.23–24.
17 NZ Treasury, *Economic Management*, Treasury, Wellington, 1984, pp.313–14.
18 Howard Fancy, 1995–96; Paul Carpinter, 1996– .
19 For a detailed account, see P. Wooding, 'Liberalising the International Trade Regime', in A. Bollard and R. Buckle (eds), *Economic Liberalisation in New Zealand*, Allen & Unwin, Wellington, 1987, pp.86, 98.
20 A. Bollard, 'More Market: The Deregulation of Industry', in Bollard and Buckle (eds), p.25 at p.45.
21 NZ Treasury, *Government Management: Brief to the Incoming Government 1987, Volume 1*, Treasury, Wellington, p.242.
22 *Government Management*, pp.250–51.
23 *Government Management*, p.250.
24 *Government Management*, p.243.
25 *Government Management*, p.250.
26 A. Bollard and B. Easton (eds), *Markets, Regulation and Pricing: Six Case Studies*, Research Paper 31, NZIER, Wellington, 1985.
27 Bollard, p.45.
28 *Manufacturer*, May 1990.
29 *NZ Herald*, 23 June 1992.
30 *NZ Herald*, 17 December 1994.
31 Minister of Finance, *Finance Focus*, Wellington, December 1994.
32 *The Coalition Agreement 1996*, Wellington, December 1996, p.29 (emphasis added).
33 *NZ Herald*, 28 March 1996.
34 *Business Review Weekly*, 3 July 1995, p.21.
35 *Australian Financial Review*, 8 September 1997.
36 *TUF Times*, September 1997.
37 *NZPD*, vol.561, 26 June 1997, p.2764.
38 Office of the Minister of Commerce, 'General Tariff Review: Implications for Tariff Policy Post-2000', July 1998.
39 Ministry of Commerce, *Review of Post-2000 Tariff Policy*, Wellington, 1997.
40 J. Luxton, 'Budget Announcement', 26 June 1997.
41 The Alliance, 'Cost/Benefit Analysis of Motor Vehicle Assembly Industry', October 1997.
42 *Press*, 18 December 1997.
43 Automotive Component Manufacturers' Federation, quoted in *NZ Herald*, 19 December 1997.
44 *NZ Herald*, 19 December 1997.
45 *NBR*, 12 September 1997.
46 *Press*, 18 December 1997.
47 *NZ Herald*, 19 December 1997.
48 *NZ Herald*, 15 May 1998.
49 *NZ Herald*, 16 April 1998.
50 *NZ Herald*, 19 December 1997.
51 Based on an interview with John Robinson, Thames Business Enterprise Project, June 1999; see also *NZ Herald*, 17 July 1998.
52 E.g. Retail Merchants Association.
53 Submission, NZ Footwear Industry Association, October 1997.
54 Submission on behalf of Apparel and Textile Federation, New Zealand Footwear Industry Association, New Zealand Carpet Manufacturers Association, New Zealand Textile and Woollen Mills Association on the 1998 Tariff Review of Post 2000 Tariff Policy, November 1997.
55 Submission, NZ Footwear Industry Association, October 1997.
56 *NZ Herald*, 3 June 1998.
57 Submission, Apparel and Textile Federation, November 1997.
58 W. Creech MP to constituent, 28 May 1998.
59 Submission, NZ Carpet Manufacturers Association, October 1997.
60 Submission, LWR Industries, November 1997.
61 Submission, Employers and Manufacturers Association (Northern), November 1997.
62 T. Hazledine, 'Tariffs in the New Zealand Textiles, Clothing and Footwear Industries: A Report for the NZ Trade Union Federation', 14 October 1997.
63 Hazledine, 'Tariffs'.
64 NZIER and R. Lattimore, 'Tariff Reduction Post-2000: Costs and Benefits of Alternative Paths', March 1998.
65 Infometrics Consulting, 'Report to the Apparel and Textile Manufacturers', 18 September 1998.
66 *NZ Herald*, 20 April 1998.
67 *NZ Herald*, 17 April 1998.
68 Office of the Minister for Enterprise and Commerce, 'General Tariffs Review: Tariff Policy Post-2000', undated.
69 *Independent*, 30 June 1999.
70 Hills Headwear Ltd, press release, 18 December 1997; *Evening Post*, 25 March 1998; *TUF Times*, June 1998.
71 L. Evans, 'Farming in a Changing Economic Environment', in Bollard and Buckle (eds), p.102; *1990 New Zealand Official Yearbook*, Government Printer, Wellington, 1990, pp.682–83.
72 R. Bremer and T. Brooking, 'Federated Farmers and the State', in B. Roper and C. Rudd (eds), *State and Economy in New Zealand*, Oxford University Press, Auckland, 1993, p.108 at p.121.
73 Evans, p.120.
74 Personal communication, November 1998.
75 Apple Fields held some 227 hectares in orchard partnerships and land-owning companies, and 957 hectares of rural land.
76 *NBR*, 12 February 1999.
77 W. Moran et al., 'Family Farmers, Real Regulation, and the Experience of Food Regimes', *Journal of Rural Studies*, vol.12, no.3 (1996), p.245.
78 Bremer and Brooking, p.116.
79 See D. Williams, *'Te kooti tango whenua': The Native Land Court 1864–1909*, Huia Publishers, Wellington, 1999.

80 *NZ Herald*, 15 October 1998.
81 For a concise description of their development and functions, see W. Moran et al., 'Empowering Family Farms Through Cooperatives and Producer Marketing Boards', *Economic Geography*, vol.72, no.2 (1996), p.161.
82 *Management*, December 1998, p.74.
83 *Economic Management*, pp.303–4, and Ch.12.
84 *New Zealand Apple and Pear Marketing Board v Apple Fields Ltd* [1991] 1 NZLR 257.
85 Apple and Pear Marketing Amendment Act 1993, section 4.
86 G. Crocombe et al., *Upgrading New Zealand's Competitive Advantage*, Oxford University Press, Auckland, 1991, pp.59–70.
87 See ACIL, *Agricultural Marketing Regulation: Reality Versus Doctrine*, NZBR, Wellington, 1992; see also W. Bates, *The Dairy Board's Export Monopoly*, NZBR, Wellington, October 1997; W. Bates, *Farmer Control: Does it Serve the Interests of Farmers?*, NZBR, Wellington, 1998; NZBR Submission on the Producer Board Acts Reform Bill, 1997.
88 R. Kerr, speech to the Agricultural and Resource Economics Society 1998 Conference, Blenheim, 4 July 1998.
89 R. Douglas and B. Burgess, *Options for Kiwifruit: An Industry in Crisis. An Independent Review*, Wellington, 1992.
90 E.g. *NBR*, 15 December 1995.
91 See www.dairytrade.com/dtcnzdb.htm. In 1996 the Board had 15 percent of the world market for cheese, over 40 percent for butter/butter-oil, 18 percent for nonfat dry milk and over 30 percent for milk powder.
92 *NBR*, 7 March 1997.
93 *NZ Herald*, 4 November 1997.
94 E.g. *NBR*, 18 April 1997, 9 May 1997, 23 May 1997, 13 June 1997, 14 November 1997; *NZ Herald*, 4 November 1997.
95 Waitangi Tribunal, *Kiwifruit Marketing Report 1995*, (WAI-449), Wellington, p.15.
96 NZ Treasury, 'Kiwifruit Initiatives and the Coalition Agreement', 8 January 1998.
97 NZ Treasury, 'Regulatory Arrangements for Export Marketing of Kiwifruit', 14 January 1997.
98 NZ Treasury, 'Maori Support for New Zealand Kiwifruit Marketing Board', 21 March 1997.
99 NZ Treasury, 'Policy Strategy and Process around the Kiwifruit Summit', 24 September 1997.
100 *Foreign Control Watchdog*, no.75 (1993), p.9.
101 *Press*, 5 October 1993.
102 Notably from the Meat and Wool Levypayers, based in Northland; e.g. *NZ Herald*, 9 June 1997.
103 *NZPD*, vol.565, 9 December 1997, p.6297, per Jennings.
104 *NZPD*, vol.558, 6 March 1997, pp.686–87, per Marshall.
105 *NZPD*, vol.565, 9 December 1997, p.6295, per Wylie.
106 NZ Treasury, 'Producer Board Reform', 20 March 1998.
107 'Producer Board Reform', Memorandum for Cabinet from Treasurer, 24 April 1998.
108 Minister of Agriculture, 'Producer Board Reform: Comment on Paper for Cabinet', 29 April 1998.
109 NZ Treasury, Aide Memoire for Producer Board Reform Paper to Cabinet on 4 May 1998, 1 May 1998.
110 *NZPD*, vol.568, 14 May 1998, p.8545.
111 R. Kerr, speech to Agricultural and Resource Economics Society.
112 *NZ Herald*, 15 October 1998.
113 Speech to Massey University 50th Dairy Conference, 21 May 1998.
114 *NZ Herald*, 24 September 1998.
115 *NZ Herald*, 14 October 1998.
116 *NZ Herald*, 17–18 April 1999; 19 April 1999.
117 United Kiwi, *Analysing Industry: Community Viability and Risks for the Kiwifruit Industry*, YAF Consulting, Palmerston North, 1998, p.8.
118 The Tesco chain in the UK has turnover of NZ$45 billion, while America's largest chain, Albertson's, covers 2,470 stores and NZ$72 billion in annual sales; United Kiwi, p.15.
119 United Kiwi; and United Fruit, *Supporting the Single Desk: A Preliminary Review of Economic and Community Issues*, YAF Consulting, Palmerston North, September 1998.
120 United Fruit, p.30.
121 *NZ Herald*, 16 November 1998.
122 *NZ Herald*, 13 October 1998.
123 *NZ Herald*, 25 May 1998; 13 November 1998.
124 G. Allen, 'The Deal on Services: A Necessary Step to Integration', in K. Vautier et al. (eds), *CER and Business Competition: Australia and New Zealand in a Global Economy*, Commerce Clearing House, Auckland, 1990, pp.165, 171.
125 Allen, p.175.
126 J. Farmer, 'The Harmonisation of Australian and New Zealand Business Laws', in Vautier et al. (eds), p.48.
127 *NZ Herald*, 27 May 1999.
128 *NZ Herald*, 19 August 1998.
129 *NZ Herald*, 11 September 1996.
130 *NBR*, 9 December 1994.
131 *Sunday Star Times*, 27 November 1994.
132 *NBR*, 13 September 1996; *NZ Herald*, 27 March 1998.
133 *NZ Herald*, 25 June 1998.
134 *NBR*, 16 February 1999.
135 *Australian Financial Review*, 23 February 1999.
136 *NZ Herald*, 4 November 1996; *Australian Broadcasting Authority v Project Blue Sky Inc*, [1996] 1087 FCA 1 (12 December 1996).
137 *NZ Herald*, 17 July 1998; *Project Blue Sky v Australian Broadcasting Authority* [1998] HCA 28 (28 April 1998).
138 *NZ Herald*, 19 March 1999.
139 Limited exemptions included firearms, fireworks, gaming machines, pornographic material, and agricultural and veterinary chemicals.
140 'Agreement Between the Government of Australia and the Government of New Zealand Establishing a System for the Development of

Joint Food Standards', *Australian Treaty Series*, 1996, No.12.
141 Australia New Zealand Food Authority Act 1991.
142 Food Amendment Act 1996; *NZPD*, vol.556, 19 June 1996, p.13229.
143 'Agreement Between the Government of Australia and the Government of New Zealand Establishing a System for the Development of Joint Food Standards', Wellington, 5 December 1995; *Australian Treaty Series*, 1996, No.12.
144 *NZ Herald*, 21 July 1998.
145 *Dominion*, 1 December 1998.
146 *NZ Herald*, 31 July 1998.
147 *NZ Herald*, 31 July 1998.
148 *NZ Herald*, 18 December 1998.
149 *NZ Herald*, 31 March 1999; 3 April 1999.
150 *NZ Herald*, 22 February 1999.
151 Food (Genetic Modification Information) Amendment Bill 1997; Genetic Engineering Moratorium and Commission of Inquiry Bill 1999.
152 *NZPD*, 19 May 1999, pp.16551-67.
153 *NZ Herald*, 11 December 1998; 16 March 1999.
154 For subsequent discussion, see *Independent*, 31 March 1999; 5 May 1999.
155 A. Coleman, 'Economic Integration and Monetary Union', Treasury Working Paper 99/6, 1999.
156 'Economic Integration', p.30.
157 'Economic Integration', p.15.
158 'Economic Integration', p.15.
159 'Economic Integration', p.15, fn28.

CHAPTER 7

1 J. Ruggie, *Constructing the World Polity: Essays on International Institutionalization*, Routledge, London, 1998, p.75.
2 'The General Agreement on Tariffs and Trade: Preamble', *United Nations Treaty Series*, vol.55 (1948), p.194.
3 J. Viner, 'Conflicts of Principle in Drafting a Trade Charter', *Foreign Affairs*, vol.25, no.4, p.612 at p.613, quoted in Ruggie, p.75.
4 'Declaration on the Contribution of the [World] Trade Organisation to Achieving Greater Coherence in Global Economic Policymaking', Uruguay Round Act 1994, Part III.2. Cooperative agreements with the World Bank and IMF were signed in 1996.
5 R. Ruggiero, speech to the WTO Ministerial Meeting, Singapore, December 1996.
6 Ministry of Foreign Affairs and Trade, *Trading Ahead: The GATT Uruguay Round: Results for New Zealand*, MFAT, Wellington, 1994, p.3.
7 *NZ Herald*, 15 July 1996.
8 Ultimate authority rested with the annual Session of Contracting Parties, where governments were represented by officials. In between, the GATT was administered through regular meetings of its Council of Representatives, again comprising officials. Trade ministers met infrequently, usually to authorise or close a round.
9 M. Karns, 'Multilateral Diplomacy and Trade Policy: The United States and the GATT', in M. Karns and K. Mingst (eds), *The US and Multilateral Institutions: Patterns of Changing Instrumentality and Influence*, Routledge, London, 1990, p.141 at pp.143, 151.
10 Geneva Round, 1947; Annecy Round, 1949; Torquay Round, 1951; Geneva Round, 1956; Dillon Round, 1960-61; Kennedy Round, 1964-67.
11 These imposed disciplines on so-called non-tariff barriers (NTBs), including subsidies and countervailing measures, technical barriers to trade and revisions to the 1967 Anti-dumping Code.
12 By 1985 Dunkel had got the G-7, their new counterpart known as 'Quad' (trade ministers from the EC, US, Canada and Japan), the OECD ministers and the EC on board. An expert group on problems with the trading system (known as the Luetwiler Group) produced fifteen recommendations, including one for a new round. See J. Croome, *Reshaping the World Trading System: A History of the Uruguay Round*, World Trade Organization, Geneva, 1995, pp.18-20.
13 These covered tariffs, non-tariff measures, tropical products, natural resource-based products, textiles and clothing, agriculture, safeguards, subsidies and countervailing measures.
14 Personal communications, GATT meeting, Brussels, October 1990. See also speech of Luis Fernando Jaramillo (Colombia), outgoing chair of the G-77, New York, January 1994.
15 Comprising Argentina, Australia, Brazil, Canada, Chile, Colombia, Hungary, Indonesia, Malaysia, the Philippines, Thailand, Uruguay and New Zealand.
16 See generally R. Higgott and A. Cooper, 'Middle Power Leadership and Coalition Building: Australia, the Cairns Group, and the Uruguay Round of Trade Negotiations', *International Organization*, vol.44, no.4 (1990), p.589.
17 The seven years of negotiations have been officially chronicled by a former GATT official, John Croome; see Croome, 1995.
18 *Assessing the Effects of the Uruguay Round*, OECD, Paris, 1993; see also *The Times*, 16 December 1993.
19 By 1996 there were more than 30 councils and standing committees; the WTO averaged 46 meetings a week. Governments were represented by officials attached to diplomatic posts in Geneva (or elsewhere on the Continent) and from home. Only ten of the 29 very poor countries in the WTO had permanent offices in Geneva, with one or two employees. New Zealand's ambassador in Geneva served as the representative at the WTO; several staff were seconded from MFAT to work on GATT issues virtually full time.
20 'Declaration on the Contribution of the [World] Trade Organisation'.
21 B. Hoekman and M. Kostecki, *The Political Economy of the World Trading System: From GATT to WTO*, Oxford University Press, Oxford, 1995, p.24.

22 'Interdepartmental Report on Submissions Received on the GATT (Uruguay Round) Bill', undated, p.12.
23 Personal communications.
24 *Foreign Control Watchdog*, no.83 (December 1996), p.8.
25 *Trading Ahead*, p.6.
26 *Trading Ahead*, p.8.
27 *Trading Ahead*, p.12.
28 *Trading Ahead*, pp.34, 36, 46, 53, 50.
29 Personal communication from MFAT official, recorded in B. Rosenberg, 'Mad Cow Disease and Rogernomics on a global scale', speech to Pacific Institute of Resource Management conference, Wellington, September 1994.
30 B. Philpott and G. Nana, 'The Implications of Global Trade Reform on the New Zealand Economy', NZIER, July 1993, p.11.
31 B. Philpott and G. Nana, 'The GATT Agreement: A General Equilibrium Analysis of its Impact on the New Zealand Economy by the End of the Century', NZIER, Wellington, August 1994.
32 A. Rae and C. Nixon, 'The GATT Settlement: Analysis of its Impact on New Zealand Agriculture', NZIER, Wellington, June 1994, p.1.
33 Rae and Nixon, p.1.
34 R. Sandrey, 'The GATT Uruguay Round in Perspective: Implications for New Zealand', *New Zealand Journal of Business*, vol.16, no.1 (1994), p.51 at p.57.
35 Ministry of External Relations and Trade, 'The Uruguay Round and New Zealand', 2 December 1992.
36 Minister of Agriculture to L. Cookson, 8 September 1993.
37 'Interdepartmental Report on Submissions'.
38 Official Information Act 1982, s.9(2)(j); also, s.9(2)(d), to 'avoid prejudice to the substantial economic interests of New Zealand'.
39 W. Rosenberg, *New Zealand Can be Different – and Better*, New Zealand Monthly Review Society, Christchurch, 1993, p.166.
40 Minister for Trade Negotiations to D. Small, 13 October 1993.
41 The Association of University Staff secured details of the GATS offer relating to education only weeks before the final signing in Marrakein in 1994.
42 D. McGee, 'Treaties – A Role for Parliament?', *Public Sector*, vol.20, no.1 (1997), p.3.
43 *NZPD*, vol.545, 29 November 1994, p.5162, per Sandra Lee.
44 Press release, 29 November 1994.
45 Office of Minister for International Trade to Cabinet Economic Committee, 'World Trade Organisation: Financial Services', Appendix One, undated.
46 Investment issues are addressed in Chapter 9.
47 M. Ritchie, 'Free Trade versus Sustainable Agriculture', *The Ecologist*, vol.22, no.5 (Sep/Oct 1992), p.221 at p.222.
48 Higgott and Cooper, p.598.
49 Cairns Group, 'Declaration of the Ministerial Meeting of Fair Traders in Agriculture', Cairns, Australia, 26 August 1986; 'Cairns Group Proposal for a Multilateral Reform Programme for Agriculture', 1989; see also Hoekman and Kostecki, pp.202–4.
50 'Cairns Group Proposal for a Multilateral Reform Program for Agriculture', undated.
51 W. Bello, 'The GATT Agricultural Accord and Food Security: The Philippines Case', *Focus on Trade*, no.24, part 2 (April 1998).
52 A. Kwa, 'WTO May Ministerial Conference: A Time for Celebration or Mourning?', *Focus on Trade*, no.24, part 1 (April 1998).
53 See M. Khor, 'The WTO and the South: Implications and Recent Developments', Third World Network, Malaysia, 1998.
54 By 36 percent in value terms, and 21 percent by volume.
55 *Trading Ahead*, p.12.
56 M. Ingco, 'Agricultural Trade Liberalization in the Uruguay Round: One Step Forward, One Step Back?', International Economics Department, World Bank, Policy Research Working Paper no.1500, August 1995.
57 Ingco, p.22.
58 Ingco, p.51.
59 Quoted in Bello.
60 *Wall Street Journal*, 25 March 1998.
61 *Bridges Weekly Trade News Digest*, 31 March 1998.
62 'Completing the Task', vision statement from the 18th Cairns Group Meeting, Sydney, Australia, 3 April 1998.
63 Tim Fischer, press conference, WTO ministerial meeting, Geneva, May 1998.
64 E.g. *NZ Herald*, 15 October 1998.
65 *NZ Herald*, 29 March 1999.
66 *NZ Herald*, 2 June 1999, 4 June 1999.
67 *NZ Herald*, 7 June 1999.
68 *NZ Herald*, 10 June 1999.
69 Dumping and Countervailing Duties Act 1988.
70 Ministry of Commerce, *Trade Remedies in New Zealand: A Discussion Paper*, February 1998.
71 Ministry of Commerce, 'Review of Trade Remedies Policy: Analysis of Issues', 30 June 1998.
72 *Trade Remedies*, p.5.
73 E.g. WTO Working Group on the Interaction between Trade and Competition Policy.
74 World Bank figures suggest that global trade in services had grown from 18.8 percent of world trade in the 1980s to 22.2 percent in 1993. OECD dominance had increased slightly in the same period, from 79 percent of global exports of commercial services to 81 percent.
75 W. Drake and K. Nicolaidis, 'Ideas, Interests and Institutionalization: "Trade in Services" and the Uruguay Round', *International Organization*, vol.46, no.1 (1992), p.37 at p.45.
76 Drake and Nicolaidis, p.63.
77 Drake and Nicolaidis, p.47. The implications of this are well illustrated in 'Report on the Export of Educational Services', prepared for the Marketing Development Board by Hugo Consulting Group (1987).
78 Drake and Nicolaidis, p.47.
79 The French were implacably opposed to the inclusion of cultural services, especially audio-visual.

80 See Chapter 1.
81 Fourth Protocol to the General Agreement on Trade in Services (on Basic Telecommunications Services).
82 Fifth Protocol to the General Agreement on Trade in Services (on Financial Services).
83 The policy was announced in the May 1998 Budget, and confirmed in Minister of Education, *Tertiary Education in New Zealand: Policy Directions for the 21st Century: White Paper*, Ministry of Education, Wellington, November 1998. Such concerns apply to all private providers, but are intensified when they are based offshore.
84 R. Wiessman, 'Patent Plunder: TRIPping the Third World', *Multinational Monitor*, November 1990, p.8. The companies argued that, because individual governments set their own intellectual property laws, rules vary. Some give strong protection. Others provide minimal protection, or impose conditions for knowledge and technology transfer to host governments or local companies. Existing rules are often poorly enforced, which encourages unauthorised copying or counterfeiting. Some laws are outdated, and inappropriate to deal with new developments such as computer software. The transaction cost of meeting different standards in different countries is high.
85 RONGEAD, *GATT Briefing No.2*, Brussels, July 1990.
86 Croome, p.376.
87 The term for copyright is 50 years, and seven years for trade marks, renewable indefinitely. Patents are protected for a minimum of 20 years.
88 Article 8, TRIPS.
89 Article 27(3), TRIPS. The TNEs complained that the lead time was too long.
90 *Press*, 1 July 1992.
91 The Patents Amendment Act, Trade Marks Amendment Act, Animal Remedies Amendment Act, Pesticides Amendment Act, Medicines Amendment Act, Copyright Act, Geographical Indications Act, Layout Designs Act (all in 1994).
92 'Scoping Paper on the Protection of Maori Intellectual Property Rights', Nga Kaiwhakamarama I Nga Ture, February 1994. See also V. Shiva, 'Biodiversity and Intellectual Property Rights', in R. Nader et al. (eds), *The Case Against Free Trade: GATT, NAFTA and the Globalization of Corporate Power*, Earth Island Press, San Francisco, 1993, p.108.
93 The Mataatua Declaration on Cultural and Intellectual Property Rights of Indigenous Peoples, 5 June 1993, presented to the session of the Working Group on Indigenous Peoples, Commission on Human Rights, United Nations, 19–30 July 1993 (original emphasis).
94 Claim WAI-262 to the Waitangi Tribunal by members of Te Rarawa and others, relating to 'the Protection, Control, Conservation, Management, Treatment, Propagation, Sale, Dispersal, Utilisation and Restriction on the use of and transmission of the knowledge of New Zealand Flora and Fauna and the general resource contained therein'.
95 C. Roberts, 'Prospects of Success of the National Institute of Health's Human Genome Application', *European Intellectual Property Review*, vol.1 (1994), p.30 at p.32.
96 Intellectual Property Rights Workshop, Geneva, August 1994, cited in *Whose Genes Are They Anyway?*, Report of the Health Research Council Conference on Human Genetic Information, Wellington, 1995.
97 *Bridges Weekly Trade News Digest*, vol.3, no.13 (April 1999).
98 D. Korten, *When Corporations Rule the World*, Kumarian Press, West Hartford, 1995.
99 Agreement Establishing the World Trade Organization, Article XVI, para 4.
100 Of 120 complaints considered between 1948 and 1990, half were settled before a panel report was produced. Of the remainder, only four reports were not adopted. These were settled bilaterally. Hoekman and Kostecki, p.49.
101 *Third World Economics*, no.169 (16–30 September 1997), p.4.
102 Complaint by the US on Patent Protection for Pharmaceutical and Agricultural Chemical Products: Violation of TRIPS articles 27, 65, 70, WT/DS50, July 1996, with a dispute settlement panel established in November 1996; Complaint by the EC on Patent Protection for Pharmaceutical and Agricultural Chemical Products: Violation of TRIPS article 70, paras 8 and 9, WT/DS79/1, April 1997.
103 *Bridges Weekly Trade News Digest*, 15 March 1999.
104 However, the Appellate Body overruled the panel's finding that environmental policies designed to protect the global commons fell outside the GATT provision.
105 *Inside US Trade*, 2 April 1999. For a discussion of these cases, see J. Kelsey, 'Global Economic Policy-Making: A New Constitutionalism?', *Otago Law Review*, vol.9, no.3 (1999), p.535, and 'International Economic Agreements and Environmental Justice', in B. Richardson and K. Bosselmann (eds), *Environmental Justice and Market Mechanisms*, Kluwer International, The Hague, 1999.
106 Complaint numbers WT/DS26/2 and WT/DS26/5.
107 *Bridges Weekly Trade News Digest*, 29 March 1999.
108 *Third World Economics*, no.205 (16–31 March 1999), p.3.
109 *Third World Economics*, no.207/208 (16 April–15 May 1999), p.5.
110 'WTO Ministerial Conference: Sustainable Developments', International Institute for Sustainable Development, December 1996.
111 All customs and other duties for all information technology products defined in the agreement would be eliminated by 2000. See also *Wall Street Journal*, 13 December 1996.
112 *Third World Economics*, no.209 (16–31 May 1999), p.3.
113 United Nations Secretary-General, speech to the WTO Conference, Geneva, 19 May 1998.

114 *Tanada and others v. Angara and others*, Republic of the Philippines Supreme Court, Manila, 2 May 1997, per Panganiban J.
115 R. Howse and M. Trebilcock, 'The Fair Trade – Free Trade Debate: Trade, Labor and the Environment', *International Review of Law and Economics*, vol.16 (1996), p.61. See also M. Trebilcock and R. Howse, *The Regulation of International Trade*, Routledge, London, 1995, Ch.13.
116 Howse and Trebilcock, p.79.
117 See generally C. Raghavan, *Recolonization: GATT, the Uruguay Round and the Third World*, Third World Network, Penang, 1990.
118 The US position was ironic, as it had accepted less than one-fifth of the then 170 ILO conventions.
119 ICFTU, 'Looking Ahead to the WTO Ministerial Council – An ICFTU View', in *Labour Standards in the Global Trade and Investment System*, TUAC/OECD, Paris, November 1996, p.93.
120 OECD, 'Joint Report on Trade, Employment and Labour Standards by the OECD Employment, Labour and Social Affairs Committee and the OECD Trade Committee', in *Labour Standards*, p.77 at p.81.
121 'Singapore Ministerial Declaration', Singapore, 13 December 1996, www.wto.org/govt/mindec.html.
122 ICFTU Submission for the Second Ministerial Meeting of the WTO, 18 May 1998.
123 Minister of Labour, speech to the ILO Plenary Session, June 1994.
124 *Reuter*, 15 May 1998.
125 International Chamber of Commerce, 'World Business Priorities for the Second Ministerial Conference of the WTO', May 1998.
126 Ministry of Foreign Affairs and Trade, 'Trade and the Environment: GATT', 36/1/5, undated.
127 Submission by New Zealand to Committee on Trade and Environment, 15 February 1996; 'New Zealand's Proposal Before the WTO on Trade and the Environment', 20 August 1997. See also WWF, 'Trade Measures and Multilateral Environmental Agreements: Backwards or Forwards in the WTO?', September 1996.
128 *Third World Economics*, no.206 (1–15 April 1999), p.9.
129 Oral comments, press briefing, WTO Ministerial Conference, Geneva, 18 May 1998.
130 President Clinton, speech to the WTO Ministerial Conference, Geneva, 18 May 1998.
131 ICFTU press dispatch, Geneva, 18 May 1998.
132 R. Ruggiero, speech to the WTO Ministerial Conference, Geneva, 18 May 1998.
133 *Financial Times*, 30 April 1998.
134 See *Third World Economics*, no.206 (1–15 April 1999).

CHAPTER 8

1 W. Bello and J. Chavez-Malalulan, *APEC: Four Adjectives in Search of a Noun*, Manila People's Forum on APEC, Manila, 1996. The phrase was originally used by Australia's former Foreign Affairs Minister, Gareth Evans.
2 C. Butler, 'APEC: Pathway to Prosperity', talking notes for chair of APEC Committee on Trade and Industry, Vancouver, 1997.
3 J. Spero, Undersecretary of State for Economic, Business and Cultural Affairs, statement to US Congress Committee, Washington, July 1995.
4 *The Age*, quoted in *The Nation*, 6 November 1995.
5 This historical analysis is based on a review of MFAT's APEC files dated 1988 to 1993. For more detailed accounts of the evolution of APEC see W. Bello, 'APEC and the Conflict of Capitalisms', and J. Kelsey, 'APEC: Catching a Tiger by the Tail', in E. Tadem and L. Daniel (eds), *Challenging the Mainstream: APEC and the Asia-Pacific Development Debate*, Arena Press, Hong Kong, 1995.
6 This was carried through to the ASEAN/EU dialogue, where other Asian members of APEC were granted observer status, but not the US, Canada, Australia and New Zealand. See *European Union News*, vol.14, no.2 (Feb/Mar 1996), p.1. Australian (and hence New Zealand) participation was again deferred at the ASEAN European Union Ministerial (ASEM) Summit in April 1998, until 2000.
7 Formal membership criteria were determined only in 1997. These were primarily: location within the region; substantial economic linkages with existing APEC members; and pursuit of externally oriented, market-driven economic policies.
8 As at 1998, official observers were the Pacific Economic Cooperation Council, APEC's Business Advisory Council and the South Pacific Forum.
9 *NZ Listener*, 3 August 1996.
10 P. Potter, 'Cultural Aspects of Trade Dispute Resolution', paper to the APEC Study Centre Meeting, Manila, May 1996.
11 File notes on the report from the meeting of finance and central bank officials in 1994 indicate 'zero interest' from the Reserve Bank and Treasury.
12 New Zealand provided the Secretary.
13 This included competition policy, dispute settlement, environmental issues, export credits, financial services, foreign investment, government procurement, intellectual property rights, state trading, tariff reductions and tariff matching in particular sectors. *A Vision for APEC: Towards an Asia Pacific Economic Community: Report of the Eminent Persons Group*, APEC, Singapore, 1993, p.27 at p.36.
14 *A Vision for APEC*, p.31.
15 *Achieving the APEC Vision: Free and Open Trade in the Asia Pacific: Second Report of the Eminent Persons Group*, APEC, Singapore, 1994.
16 *Implementing the APEC Vision: Third Report of the Eminent Persons Group*, APEC, Singapore, 1995.
17 M. Yamaoka, 'PBEC, PECC and APEC', Institute of Development Studies, Discussion paper series no.5, March 1996, p.23.

REFERENCES TO PAGES 286 TO 297 ▲ 409

18 PBEC began operation in 1968 as a voice for the advanced economies of the Pacific – Australia, Japan, the US, Canada and New Zealand – alongside a business grouping drawn from its 'developing' countries. In 1997 it claimed representation from 17 countries and over 1,000 important companies, and worked closely with members' governments.
19 Expert groups deal, for example, with harmonisation of customs procedures, dispute mediation, energy and competition policy. 'Competition policy' is defined broadly to include deregulation, competition law, trade liberalisation, corporatisation, privatisation, anti-dumping and industrial policy.
20 E.g. a Manual of Business Practice Principles for Independent Power Producers, aimed at mobilising capital for private sector investment in power infrastructure, was approved by energy ministers in 1997.
21 Predictably, they recommended the development of domestic bond markets and better access to equity markets by reducing listing requirements, plus strong investor protections. An effective, credible rating agency was a medium-term priority for each 'economy'. APEC Financiers Group Meeting, 8 August 1997.
22 Energy, Fisheries, Human Resources Development, Industrial Science and Technology, Marine Resource Conservation, Telecommunications, Tourism, Trade Promotion and Transportation.
23 Personal communication.
24 *Financial Times*, 27 November 1996.
25 *NZ Herald*, 21 November 1998.
26 *Philippine Daily Inquirer*, 26 November 1996.
27 *Philippine Daily Inquirer*, 26 November 1996.
28 *Vancouver Sun*, 26 November 1997.
29 *Dominion*, 17 March 1998.
30 *A Vision for APEC*, pp.40–41.
31 The 1994 EPG Report, *Achieving the APEC Vision*, noted it 'is especially valuable that the Finance Ministers are bringing some of the major existing institutions – the IMF, the World Bank, the International Finance Corporation (IFC) and the ADB – into the process of regional cooperation in a more formal way'. This occurred during the ADB meeting in Auckland in May 1995. The 1996 Finance Ministers Meeting in Kyoto in March 1996 included the Managing Director of the IMF, with the ADB, IMF, IFC and APEC Financiers Group involved in preliminary work. The ADB collaborated with APEC in producing the voluntary guidelines for infrastructure and promoting financial and capital market development, approved by the APEC Finance Ministers Meeting in Cebu, 5 April 1997. Heads of the World Bank, IMF and ADB attended the Finance Ministers Meeting in Alberta in May 1998.
32 'Leaders' Declaration: From Vision to Action', Subic, 25 November 1996.
33 Statement of the Chair, Trade Ministers Meeting, Montreal, May 1997.
34 PECC, *A Draft Asia Pacific Investment Code*, Singapore, undated.
35 *A Draft Asia Pacific Investment Code*, p.17 (emphasis added).
36 *A Draft Asia Pacific Investment Code*, p.12.
37 *A Draft Asia Pacific Investment Code*, pp.13, 17.
38 *A Vision for APEC*, pp.38–39.
39 MFAT officials' pre-APEC briefing to media, circa 9 November 1995; NZ Trade Minister's media briefing, Osaka, 16 November 1995.
40 *Third World Economics*, no.123 (October 1995), p.9.
41 The nine principles for action were: comprehensiveness of measures; WTO-consistency; comparability of commitments; non-discrimination; transparency; standstill; simultaneous start, continuous process and differentiated timetables; flexibility; and cooperation.
42 'Osaka Action Agenda: Implementation of the Bogor Declaration', Osaka, 19 November 1995.
43 Joint Press Conference by the APEC Ministers, Osaka, 17 November 1995.
44 Briefing by Press Secretary, Japan Ministry of Foreign Affairs, Osaka, 15 November 1995.
45 Briefing by Press Secretary, Japan Ministry of Foreign Affairs, Osaka, 16 November 1995.
46 Briefing by Press Secretary, Japan Ministry of Foreign Affairs, Osaka, 15 November 1995.
47 Senators Gareth Evans and Robert McMullan, Osaka, 17 November 1995.
48 The investment liberalisation aspects would be guided initially by existing WTO agreements, APEC's non-binding investment principles, other relevant international agreements, and any commonly agreed guidelines developed by APEC.
49 'Osaka Action Agenda'.
50 For a contemporaneous discussion, see A. Elek, 'An Asia-Pacific Model of Development Cooperation', Foundation for Development Cooperation, April 1996, presented to APEC Study Centre Conference, Manila, May 1996.
51 Minister of Corrections, Media Release, 14 August 1996.
52 Prime Minister Bolger to Jim Anderton, 12 November 1996.
53 Personal interview, 23 November 1996.
54 PECC had commissioned a report, co-sponsored by the Asia Foundation and the Philippines Institute for Development Studies, which heralded the achievements of MAPA: the enhanced reduction of tariffs beyond Uruguay Round commitments; reinforcement of many non-tariff WTO commitments; explicit support for WTO negotiations; increased transparency; and reduced transaction costs. PECC, 'Perspectives on the Manila Action Plan for APEC', December 1996.
55 APEC Business Advisory Council, *ABAC's Call to Action*, Vancouver, November 1997.
56 Secretary Macaranos, press briefing, Manila, 19 November 1996.
57 Personal interview, 23 November 1996.
58 'APEC Leaders' Declaration of Common Resolve', Osaka, 19 November 1995.
59 'APEC Economic Leaders' Declaration: Connecting the APEC Community', Vancouver, 25 November 1997.
60 New Framework for Enhanced Asian Regional Cooperation to Promote Financial

Stability, endorsed at meetings of Finance and Central Bank Deputies of several APEC countries in Manila, 18–19 November 1997.
61 The leaders also endorsed a Framework for Enhanced Public-Private Partnerships for Infrastructure Development. This was designed to support privately financed megaprojects that required cross-country integration of regulation, mobility of specialist personnel and capital movements.
62 Economic Committee, *Economic Outlook: Economic Performance and Prospects in the APEC Region*, APEC, Singapore, 1997, pp.12–13.
63 They objected to APEC's deviation from the consensus approach, and Chile had a technical problem with selectively reducing tariffs. APEC press advisory briefing, 21 November 1997.
64 E.g. speech to the Gore Branch, New Zealand National Party, 12 February 1998.
65 *Xinhua English Newswire*, 22 June 1998.
66 Briefing by the Japanese Delegation, Kuala Lumpur, 13 and 14 November 1998.
67 US State Department, Excerpts from the APEC Joint Ministerial Press Conference, Kuala Lumpur, 15 November 1998; Press briefing, C. Barshefsky, Kuala Lumpur, 15 November 1998.
68 Notes from Joint Ministerial Press Conference, Kuala Lumpur, 15 November 1998.
69 *Weekend Australian*, 14 November 1998.
70 US Vice-President Al Gore, APEC Business Summit, Kuala Lumpur, 16 November 1998.
71 'APEC Economic Leaders Declaration: Strengthening the Foundations for Growth', Kuala Lumpur, 18 November 1998.
72 J. Shipley, speech to Malaysian APEC Business Summit, Kuala Lumpur, 16 November 1998.
73 *NZ Herald*, 19 November 1998.
74 Statement of the PP21 Working Group on APEC, Bangkok, July 1994.
75 'Kyoto Declaration: Statement from the 1995 NGO Forum on APEC', November 1995.
76 Oral report from several Japanese journalists, Osaka, October 1995.
77 *Philippine Daily Inquirer*, 26 October 1996.
78 Agence France-Presse, Manila, 23 October 1996.
79 Unidentified Manila radio station, 24 November 1996.
80 *Philippine Daily Inquirer*, 25 October 1996.
81 *Philippine Daily Inquirer*, 18 September 1996.
82 *Manila Times*, 10 November 1996.
83 *Philippine Daily Inquirer*, 19 November 1996.
84 Robert Reid, comments from the floor, People's Summit, Vancouver, 24 November 1997.
85 'The Terrorist Threat to APEC', Canadian Security Intelligence Service Presentation to ICSI, 29 October 1997.
86 *Globe & Mail*, 10 December 1997; *Times Higher Education Supplement*, 16 October 1998.
87 Union of British Columbia Indian Chiefs Statement on APEC, Vancouver, 21 November 1997.
88 'The Pacific Peoples' Declaration on APEC', 14–16 November 1997, Saanich, British Columbia.
89 Native Investment and Trade Association of Vancouver, press release, 21 November 1997.
90 Secretary Macaranos, press briefing, Manila, May 1996 (emphasis added).
91 Secretary Macaranos, press briefing, Manila, 19 November 1996.
92 Personal interview, Manila, 23 November 1996.
93 John Howard, press conference, 25 November 1996; also discussed in *The Australian*, 26 February 1997.
94 *APEC in Action: 1997 Results Report*, APEC, Vancouver, 1997, pp.37–40.
95 An ad hoc group on science and technology would examine best gender practices in education, while the HRD working group would examine all its projects for the extent to which they involve women. The APEC Transport Ministerial would identify training and development initiatives to ensure women were well prepared for career opportunities in the sector. Ministers were asked to integrate a gender perspective at all levels of work on small and medium enterprises.
96 'APEC Economic Leaders' Declaration: Connecting the APEC Community', Vancouver, 25 November 1997.
97 See e.g. Nautilus Institute for Security and Sustainable Development, http://www.nautilus.org/aprenet, and Asia Pacific Labour Network, discussed below.
98 First Meeting of Ministers Responsible for the Environment, Vancouver, March 1994.
99 *1997 Results Report*, p.26.
100 Known as Food, Energy, Economic, Environment and Population (FEEEP).
101 APLN, 'A Trade Union Vision for APEC', Manila, 31 October 1996.
102 NZCTU Memorandum from President to National Executive, 'Overseas Activities: APEC-APLN', 11 November 1996.
103 NZCTU National Executive Statement on APEC, 3 July 1998.
104 NZTUF, 'APEC and Globalisation: A Trade Union Response', June 1997.
105 Report of the Second Meeting of APEC HRD Ministers, Seoul, 26 September 1997.
106 E.g. Minister of Education to constituent, 28 May 1998.
107 'Human Rights in the APEC Region: 1993', Human Rights Watch, New York; see also 1994 and 1995 reports.
108 See also R. d'Souza, 'Workers' Rights in a Global World: Trade and Workers' Human Rights in the Asia Pacific', Asia Pacific Workers Solidarity Links, Thailand, November 1995; Bello, 'APEC and the Conflict of Capitalisms'.
109 'APEC Economic Leaders' Declaration: Connecting the APEC Community', Vancouver, 25 November 1997; www.apecsec.org.sg.
110 Statement of the Chair, Meeting of APEC Ministers Responsible for Trade, Kuching, 22–23 June 1998; 'Communicating with APEC Communities on the Impact of Liberalisation', May 1998, www.apecsec.org.sg.
111 J. Bolger, press release, 11 August 1997.

112 Fran O'Sullivan, *NZ Herald*, 19 November 1998.
113 J. Bolger, speech to APEC Meeting of Ministers in Charge of Trade, Christchurch, 15 July 1996.
114 Asia 2000, submission to the select committee on APEC, August 1998.
115 MFAT to Cabinet Strategy Committee, 'APEC 1999: Overview', STR(98)198, 24 August 1998.
116 'APEC 1999: Overview'.
117 Millennium Activity Coordination, Auckland City to APEC Taskforce, 3 September 1998.
118 *Dominion*, 17 March 1998.
119 Cabinet Strategy Committee, 'APEC 1999: SME meeting', undated; 'APEC 1999: Small and Medium Enterprises Ministerial Meeting', STR(98)206, 25 August 1998.
120 *Dominion*, 25 November 1998.
121 See *Independent*, 5 May 1998.
122 Cabinet Strategy Committee, 'APEC 1999: Maori Participation', undated.
123 *Mana Magazine*, December 1998.
124 P. Ammunson, 'Reconciling APEC, Trade Liberalisation and the Treaty Relationship', background paper to the CTU Maori Standing Committee, March 1999. This paper was tagged as not stating an official MFAT position.
125 'Key Themes', APEC Maori Policy Dialogue Workshop, Wellington, 11 March 1999.
126 'APEC 1999: Engagement with NGOs', STR (98)203, 24 August 1998; Cabinet Strategy Committee Minutes, 'APEC 1999: Organisational Issues', STR(98)M27/3af, 26 August 1998.
127 'APEC 1999: Organisational Issues'.
128 E.g. J. Kelsey, submission to the select committee on the New Zealand Security Intelligence Bill 1999.
129 *NZ Herald*, 5 December 1998; 9 December 1998.
130 Arms Amendment Act 1999.
131 MFAT, 'Ten Good Reasons Why APEC Matters', undated.
132 'ABARE Modelling of APEC Trade Liberalisation: A Summary', prepared for Australian Ministry of Foreign Affairs and Trade, Research Report 96/7, March 1996.
133 D. McKinnon, speech to the Queenstown Rotary Club, 23 June 1998.
134 D. Steele, 'ABARE Modelling of APEC Outcomes', analysis for APEC Monitoring Group, 1998, referring especially to ABARE, p.12, section 2.
135 *Independent*, 11 November 1998.
136 T. Hazledine, comments to APEC Monitoring Group, 20 August 1998, on APEC Economic Committee, *The Impact of Trade Liberalization in APEC*, Singapore, November 1997.
137 Hazledine, comments.
138 *Press*, 5 November 1998.
139 *Independent*, 2 December 1998; *Dominion*, 15 December 1998.
140 *Sunday Star Times*, 25 October 1998.

CHAPTER 9

1 T. Clarke, 'The Corporate Rule Treaty: A Preliminary Analysis', Canadian Centre for Policy Alternatives, April 1997, p.2.
2 An illustrative list mainly targeted requirements for local content and export performance. Other requirements related to product mandating, trade-balancing, domestic sales, exchange restrictions, technology transfer, local equity, licensing requirements, and remittance restrictions. These were not discussed in Chapter 7 because of the coverage of investment issues in this chapter.
3 'Statement of the USCIB on the Multilateral Investment Agreement (MIA)', New York, March 1995.
4 Referred to in MFAT Briefing Cable, 1 September 1995; MFAT to J. Kelsey, 11 June 1999.
5 MFAT Briefing Cable, 13 January 1994.
6 MFAT Briefing Cable, 13 January 1994.
7 The US transnationals had a lot at stake. The USCIB said it was not unusual for a US company to have half or more of its annual revenue produced by sales, profits, royalties and returns on overseas investments. In 1994, royalties, fees and profits from overseas affiliates yielded US$86 billion, US$33 billion of which was reinvested abroad and US$53 billion remitted to the US. USCIB, *A Guide to the Multilateral Agreement on Investment (MAI)*, New York, January 1996, p.11.
8 'Statement of the USCIB on the MIA', p.6.
9 A 'golden share' is a residual shareholding retained by government and written into the articles of association to enable government intervention in company decision-making on specified major issues. Also known in New Zealand as a 'Kiwi share'.
10 The EU's 'TV Without Frontiers' directive also required, where practicable, at least 51% of TV broadcasting to be European programming.
11 S. Picciotto, 'A Critical Assessment of the MAI', paper to seminar on International Economic Regulation and the Multilateral Agreement on Investment (MAI), London, March 1998.
12 USCIB, *A Guide to the MAI*, p.13.
13 USCIB, *A Guide to the MAI*, p.13.
14 *Third World Economics*, 1–15 April 1996, p.3.
15 Multilateral Agreement on Investment: Questions Posed by Dr Jane Kelsey, MFAT response, August 1997.
16 UNCTAD, 'A Partnership for Growth and Development', Geneva, 24 May 1996 (TD/377), para 89(b); UNCTAD, 'Existing Regional and Multilateral Investment Agreements and their Relevance to a Possible Multilateral Framework on Investment: Issues and Questions', Geneva, 21 January 1998, TD/B/COM.2/EM.3/2. UNCTAD's own position was shifting towards investment liberalisation, partly due to US pressure on the UN.
17 Rapporteur on MAI, 'European Parliament: Special Briefing on the Status of the OECD MAI Negotiations: Expert Meeting on

Existing Regional and Multilateral Investment Agreements and their Development Dimensions', Geneva, 1 April 1998.
18 This analysis is based on the last text released by the OECD during negotiations. OECD, 'The MAI Negotiating Text (as of 24 April 1998)', Directorate for Financial, Fiscal and Enterprise Affairs, OECD, Paris, 1998.
19 An exception exists for non-commercial government procureignt, in MAI, Part III: Monopolies, cl.A3(b).
20 'Chairman's Note on Environment and Related Matters and on Labour', 9 March 1998, DAFFE/MAI (98)10, OECD, Paris.
21 MAI, Part VIII.
22 Following the Asian currency crisis, a more extensive provision was drafted to allow the imposition of non-conforming prudential requirements on financial service, although this was uncertain in scope. Picciotto has queried whether 'prudential measures' would for example allow controls on short-term international capital flows.
23 Most governments' exceptions reserved some ability to offer preferential treatment to indigenous communities.
24 R. Jones, 'The OECD MAI: Key Concepts and the Trade Union Response: Discussion Paper', TUAC, Paris, January 1998.
25 'Chairman's Note on Environment and Related Matters'.
26 WWF, 'Report of Observation of TUAC and BIAC Consultations with the MAI Negotiators, 15 January 1998', Paris, 23 January 1998 (email).
27 Jones, 'The OECD MAI'.
28 B. Appleton, 'The Environment and the MAI', presentation to the Canadian House of Commons Sub-committee on International Trade, Trade Disputes and Investment, 18 November 1997.
29 See also WWF, 'The OECD Multilateral Agreement on Investment', WWF Briefing Paper, Surrey, March 1997.
30 WWF, 'Is the MAI Sustainable?', WWF Briefing Paper, Surrey, October 1997.
31 These addressed conflicts with national environmental laws; potential investor abuse of the MAI dispute settlement system; conflicts with multilateral environmental agreements; weakness of current MAI environmental clauses; and investor guidelines on environmental responsibility.
32 Manganese-Based Fuel Additive Act 1996 (Canada).
33 *Toronto Star*, 29 July 1998.
34 WWF, 'Report of Observation of TUAC and BIAC Consultations with the MAI Negotiators, 15 January 1998', Paris, 23 January 1998 (email).
35 'Chairman's Note on Environment and Related Matters'.
36 *Guardian*, 10 September 1998.
37 T. Clarke and M. Barlow, *MAI and the Threat to Canadian Sovereignty*, Stoddart Publishing, Toronto, 1997.
38 I. Waddell, MP and N. Schacter, Ministry of Employment and Investment, 'Submission to the Sub-Committee on International Trade,

Trade Disputes and Investment of the House of Commons Standing Committee on Foreign Affairs and International Trade regarding the Proposed Multilateral Agreement on Investment by the Government of British Columbia', 26 November 1997, p.2.
39 Waddell and Schacter, 'Submission by Government of British Columbia', pp.3, 12.
40 These began on 29 September 1998; www.legis.gov.bc.ca/cmt.
41 E.g. Prince Edward Island and Yukon.
42 Resolution 47 of the Prince Edward Island Legislature, 18 December 1997.
43 Press statement, 31 January 1998.
44 Toronto City Council, Strategic Policies and Priorities Committee, Report no.4, February 1998, Clause 28.
45 Committees on Economic and Monetary Affairs and Industrial Policy; Legal Affairs and Citizens' Rights; Culture, Youth, Education and the Media; Development and Cooperation; and Fisheries, referred to in 'Resolution Containing Parliament's Recommendations to the Commission on Negotiations in the Framework of the OECD on a Multilateral Agreement on Investments (MAI)', adopted 10 March 1998, Brussels, A4-0073/98.
46 'Resolution', 10 March 1998.
47 'Resolution', 10 March 1998.
48 *Inside US Trade*, 30 October 1998.
49 Preamble Center for Public Policy, 'The MAI and the States: A Preliminary and Non-Exhaustive State by State Analysis of the Potential Impact of the MAI on State and Local Law', excerpted from materials prepared by the Harrison Institute for Public Law, Georgetown University, Washington, 25 August 1997.
50 Western Governors' Association, 'Multilateral Agreement on Investment: Potential Effects on State and Local Government', Denver, 1997. Because the association had no security clearance to access confidential documents, the report drew solely on publicly available documents.
51 A story on Australian National Radio's 'Background Briefing', 30 November 1997, went largely unnoticed.
52 P. Ranald, *Disciplining Governments? What the MAI Would Mean for Australia*, UNSW Public Sector Research Centre & Evatt Foundation, Sydney, 1998.
53 Joint Standing Committee on Treaties, 'Multilateral Agreement on Investment: Interim Report', Canberra, May 1998.
54 Australian Labor Party Platform Conference, Hobart, 20 January 1998.
55 *Bloomberg News*, Canberra, 3 November 1998.
56 Third World Network, 'The Multilateral Agreement on Investment (MAI): Policy Implications for Developing Countries', Penang, undated, p.7.
57 Third World Network, 'The MAI', p.7.
58 Third World Network, 'The MAI', p.7.
59 Oxfam, 'The OECD Multilateral Agreement on Investment', Oxford, September 1997, p.1. See also World Development Movement,

'A Dangerous Leap into the Dark: Implications of the MAI', Oxford, November 1997.
60 E. Fitzgerald, 'The Development Implications of the Multilateral Agreement on Investment, prepared for the Department for International Development', DFID, London, 21 March 1998, p.4.
61 Fitzgerald, 'Development Implications', p.5.
62 World Development Movement, 'Developmental Implications of the MAI: WDM Critique of the Fitzgerald Report to DFID', Executive Summary, Oxford, July 1998.
63 *Independent*, 4 April 1997, 11 April 1997; *Sunday Star Times*, 13 April 1997; *Rural News*, 21 April 1997.
64 MFAT to J. Kelsey, 5 August 1997.
65 Grey Power, *Lifestyle Quarterly*, September 1997; *Canterbury Farmer*, August 1997.
66 Officials were willing, however, to answer general hypothetical questions; e.g. MFAT to J. Kelsey, 5 August 1997.
67 *NZ Herald*, 21 October 1997; also *Mana News*, 2 October 1997.
68 *Evening Post*, 23 October 1997.
69 www.oecd.org/mai.
70 Canadian Trade Union Congress, 'MAI Fact Sheet: What the MAI Means for Workers and All Canadians', Ottawa, September 1997.
71 K. Douglas, 'Multilateral Investment Rules: A View from the Trade Union Perspective', Wellington, 6 April 1995.
72 E.g. J. Kelsey, 'The Draft OECD Multilateral Agreement on Investment: Some Implications for the Universities', paper presented to the International Conference of University Teachers Organisations, Melbourne, January 1998.
73 *CTU Work*, January 1998, p.4.
74 *CTU Work*, March 1998, p.3.
75 *Mana News*, 27 January 1998.
76 See *Evening Post*, 25 February 1998; *Dominion*, 4 March 1998.
77 *PSA Journal*, vol.85, no.1 (4 March 1998).
78 Cabinet Strategy Committee, 'OECD MIA: Negotiating Mandate', CSC (95) 27, 21 March 1995; see subsequent authority to negotiate in CAB (95) M38/11, October 1995.
79 *The Coalition Agreement 1996*, Wellington, December 1996, p.32.
80 Minister for International Trade to Committee for Enterprise, Industry and the Environment, 'Multilateral Agreement on Investment: Mandate for Negotiation of Reservations', undated.
81 'MAI: Mandate for Negotiation of Reservations'. It was apparently assumed that subsequent amendments to foreign investment laws which would be incorporated into the reservations were consistent with the Coalition Agreement.
82 No single foreign investor could hold more than 49.9% of total voting shares in Telecom without Crown approval, and at least half the board members had to be New Zealand citizens. Foreign ownership in Air New Zealand was restricted to 49%, without Crown approval; class A shares were reserved for New Zealand nationals.
83 'MAI: Mandate for Negotiation of Reservations'.
84 'MAI: Mandate for Negotiation of Reservations'.
85 'Consultation on Cabinet and Cabinet Committee Submissions', 13 March 1997.
86 *NZPD*, vol.565, 25 November 1997, p.5621.
87 MFAT, 'The MAI: Presentation by the Ministry of Foreign Affairs and Trade', undated.
88 'Article by the Minister of Foreign Affairs and Trade', 12 November 1997.
89 Minister of Forestry and International Trade, speech to NZ Forest Owners Association, Auckland, 12 November 1997.
90 'Draft article', in package prepared by Minister of Foreign Affairs and Trade and Minister for International Trade, 'Overseas Investment and the MAI', 12 January 1998.
91 'Overseas Investment and the MAI', 12 January 1998.
92 Minister for International Trade, press release, 15 February 1998.
93 Minister for International Trade, press release, 12 November 1997.
94 *NZPD*, vol.560, 21 May 1997, p.2025.
95 *NZPD*, vol.560, 21 May 1997, p.2026.
96 M. Moore, 'Multilateral Agreement on Investment: Proposed Caucus Position', 17 November 1997.
97 A detailed response was sent by Rosenberg to Moore and Helen Clark, demanding its circulation around the caucus; this was never acknowledged by Moore or circulated by Clark.
98 *NBR*, 24 October 1997.
99 M. Cullen, press release, 22 October 1997.
100 *NZPD*, vol.565, 25 November 1997, p.5616.
101 Called the Multilateral Agreement on Investment (Parliamentary Approval) Bill.
102 P. Dunne MP to A. Choudry, 3 September 1997.
103 *NZPD*, vol.560, 12 June 1997, p.2324.
104 MFAT Briefing Cable, 13 January 1994.
105 MFAT Briefing Cable, 18 August 1995.
106 MFAT File note, 'Multilateral Investment Agreement: Background and New Zealand Objectives', 22 February 1995.
107 MFAT Briefing Cable, 18 August 1995.
108 Treasury, OIC, Commerce, IRD, Reserve Bank, Justice, MAF, Transport, Health, Immigration, Fisheries, Te Puni Kokiri and Department of the Prime Minister and Cabinet.
109 New Zealand was the only country that allowed 100% foreign ownership of domestic airlines. This was not set down in legislation, and Transport officials 'felt it was inappropriate to bind future governments on this matter'. Transport to MFAT, 'OECD MAI', 13 February 1997.
110 MFAT to MOT, 'MAI Reservations: Air Transport', 24 March 1997.
111 Maori Claims to Indigenous Flora and Fauna (WAI-262), Waitangi Tribunal, October 1991.
112 MFAT to Cabinet Strategy Committee, 'OECD: Multilateral Agreement on Investment: Negotiating Mandate', 4 October 1995.

113 Te Puni Kokiri to MFAT, 10 February 1997.
114 Te Puni Kokiri to Minister of Maori Affairs, 12 August 1997.
115 *NZPD*, 6 August 1997, p.3623.
116 Referring to *NZPD*, vol.549, 3 August 1995, p.8467.
117 *NZPD*, vol.563, 16 September 1997, p.4294.
118 *Gisborne Herald*, 10 October 1997.
119 CEO of Te Puni Kokiri to Secretary of MFAT, 13 October 1997.
120 D. Quigley to M. Robson, 1 December 1997.
121 *NZ Herald*, 20 October 1997.
122 NZPA, 24 October 1997.
123 Quigley to Robson.
124 Minister for Overseas Trade to Cabinet Economic Committee, 'Multilateral Agreement on Investment (MAI): Report on Hui', undated.
125 'MAI: Report on Hui'.
126 Minister of Maori Affairs to A. Choudry, 14 September 1998.
127 There was some consideration also of government sale and procurement reservations for producer boards.
128 MFAT, 'Multilateral Agreement on Investment: Mandate for Negotiation of Reservations', paper to Committee for Enterprise, Industry and the Environment, March 1997.
129 *NZ Herald*, 4 October 1997.
130 Quigley to Robson.
131 Coalition Partners Memorandum, 18 November 1997.
132 MFAT to Cabinet Economic Committee, 'OECD: Ministerial Council Meeting: Multilateral Agreement on Investment (MAI)', 3 April 1998.
133 Ministry for the Environment, 'OECD Multilateral Agreement on Investment', 25 July 1997.
134 Chris Laidlaw, Executive Director, WWF to Lockwood Smith, 19 March 1997.
135 L. Smith to C. Laidlaw, 24 April 1997.
136 Ministry for the Environment to Minister for the Environment, 25 July 1997.
137 MFAT to Ministry for the Environment, 25 July 1997.
138 MFAT briefing note to Minister for the Environment, 26 August 1997.
139 Legal Division to Environment Policy Directorate, Ministry for the Environment, 26 August 1997.
140 Crown Law Office, 'Expropriation in the Multilateral Agreement on Investment and the Resource Management Act 1991', 4 June 1998.
141 Chairman, Commerce Commission to Laila Harre MP, 2 December 1997, said (wrongly) that reservations would cover NZ Post.
142 *NBR*, 26 September 1997; see also *NBR*, 24 April 1998.
143 Ministry for the Environment to A. Choudry, 20 November 1998.
144 MFAT, 'Talking points for Cabinet Oral Item on the MAI', 23 February 1998.
145 Secretary of Labour to R. Reid, 16 September 1998.
146 In December 1993 the Minister of Labour acknowledged that the government was in breach of Article 9 of ILO Convention no.17, relating to medical treatment costs for work injuries. The CTU has complained to the ILO of additional breaches relating to Conventions 12, 17 and 42. The TUF has complained to the ILO of breaches of Convention 29 (relating to forced labour) and Conventions 87 and 98 (relating to freedom of association).
147 Case no.1698, Complaint against the Government of New Zealand presented by the New Zealand Council of Trade Unions (NZCTU), International Labour Organisation, No.1994 (ILO Final Report).
148 *NZPD*, vol.565, 20 November 1997, p.5570.
149 *NZPD*, vol.563, 17 September 1997, p.4331.
150 *NZPD*, vol.563, 17 September 1997, p.4331.
151 *NZ Herald*, 17 July 1997.
152 Minutes of National Council, Local Government New Zealand, 21 October 1997.
153 Report of the Christchurch City Council Strategy and Resources Committee, 14 April 1998.
154 Local Government New Zealand to Prime Minister, 30 March 1998.
155 Prime Minister to Local Government New Zealand, 23 July 1998.
156 Prime Minister to Local Government New Zealand, 6 October 1998.
157 *NZPD*, vol.565, 20 November 1997, p.3570.
158 *NZPD*, vol.564, 13 November 1997, p.5375.
159 Waddell and Schacter, 'Submission by Government of British Columbia', p.8.
160 Based on a briefing by MFAT officials, J. Anderton to Minister for International Trade, 5 December 1997.
161 *NZPD*, vol.565, 20 November 1997, p.5569.
162 MFAT to Cabinet, 'OECD: Ministerial Council Meeting: MAI', 3 April 1998.
163 'OECD Advisory Panel Slams Proposed Investment Treaty', *Journal of Commerce*, 16 January 1998.
164 *Journal of Commerce*, 16 January 1998; see also *Financial Times*, 15 January 1998, 19 January 1998.
165 WWF, 'Report of Observation of TUAC and BIAC Consultations with the MAI Negotiators, 15 January 1998', Paris, 23 January 1998 (email).
166 *Financial Times*, 30 April 1998.
167 'Joint NGO Statement on the MAI to the OECD', Paris, February 1998.
168 Minister for Overseas Trade, press releases, 14 February 1998, 15 February 1998; Jim Anderton, press release, 14 February 1998.
169 MFAT, 'Draft speaking points' for Minister of Finance at OECD Ministerial Meeting in Paris, 27 April 1998.
170 MFAT, Briefing to Foreign Affairs, Defence and Trade Select Committee, 22 September 1998.
171 Minister of Finance to A. Choudry, 15 September 1998.
172 *Labour Left Briefing*, London, October 1998.
173 *Globe & Mail*, 21 October 1998.
174 R. Ruggiero, addressing UNCTAD Trade and Development Board, 8 October 1996, www.unicc.org/unctad/en/special/TB43Pro5.htm.
175 *Financial Times*, 30 April 1998.

CHAPTER 10

1. Press release, 17 June 1999.
2. Other examples not discussed in this book include a user-pays system for the country's roads, and the corporatisation of its public universities.
3. 'Seminar on the Future of the Multilateral Trading System', Asian Development Bank Meeting, Geneva, May 1998. Panelists were Renato Ruggiero (Director-General of the WTO), Supachai Panitchpakdi (Deputy Prime Minister of Thailand), Jagdish Bhagwati (a leading trade economist), Fred Bergsten (Director of the Institute for International Economics, Washington), and Martin Wolfe (deputy editor of the *Financial Times*).
4. D. McKinnon, 'New Zealand Sovereignty in an Interdependent World', in G. Wood and L. Leland (eds), *State and Sovereignty: Is the State in Retreat?*, Otago University Press, Dunedin, 1997, pp.7, 12.
5. L. Evans et al., 'Economic Reform in New Zealand: 1984–95: The Pursuit of Efficiency', *Journal of Economic Literature*, vol.34, no.4 (1996), p.1856 at p.1895, quoted in P. Dalziel, 'New Zealand's Economic Reform Programme was a Failure', unpublished paper, 21 April 1999.
6. Dalziel, 'New Zealand's Economic Reform Programme was a Failure'.
7. P. Dalziel, 'Evaluating New Zealand's Economic Reforms, 1984–95: Comment', *Victoria Economic Commentaries*, vol.15, no.1 (1998), p.1.
8. B. Easton, 'Why has New Zealand's Economic Performance been so Disappointing?', paper for the Economic and Social Research Trust of New Zealand, Wellington, 1997. See also B. Easton, *In Stormy Seas: The Post-War New Zealand Economy*, Otago University Press, Dunedin, 1997, especially Ch.1.
9. *Independent*, 16 June 1999.
10. *NZ Herald*, 16 June 1999.
11. *NZ Herald*, 20–21 June 1998.
12. The March 1999 quarter was the first for two years in which a majority of foreign investors' profits were retained rather than paid out as dividend; all but $133 million of the $2.89 billion that foreign direct investors made in profits in the year to March 1999 was paid out in dividend. *NZ Herald*, 19–20 July 1999.
13. Statistics New Zealand, *New Zealand Now: Incomes*, Wellington, 1999, p.14, Figure 1.4.
14. R. Wade, 'Globalization and Its Limits: Reports of the Death of the National Economy are Greatly Exaggerated', in S. Berger and R. Dore (eds), *National Diversity and Global Capitalism*, Cornell University Press, New York, 1996, pp.60, 69.
15. The Tourism Board's projections in 1996 for the year 2000 of $9 billion in foreign exchange earnings and 180,000 tourism-related jobs were twice what was achieved; *NZ Herald*, 2 January 1999.
16. Statistics New Zealand, *Hot off the Press: Merchandise Trade Balance*, Wellington, May 1999.
17. *Independent*, 16 June 1999.
18. *NZ Herald*, 3 February 1998.
19. *NZ Herald*, 20–21 June 1998.
20. *Sunday Star Times*, 8 December 1996.
21. The index combined the ninety-day bill rate and the exchange rate in a manner that implied a fall in the exchange rate should be offset by a rise in interest rates, and vice versa.
22. *NZ Herald*, 5–6 December 1998; 9 February 1999.
23. P. Krugman, *The Age of Diminished Expectations: US Economic Policy in the 1990s*, MIT Press, Cambridge, 1994, pp.60, 62.
24. J. Stiglitz, 'More Instruments and Broader Goals: Moving Toward the Post-Washington Consensus', Helsinki, Finland, 7 January 1998, www.worldbank.org.
25. The Alliance, 'Towards a New Monetary Policy', Wellington, 1998.
26. D. Brash, 'New Zealand's Economic Reforms: A Model for Change?', Chatham House, London, 3 June 1998; *NZ Herald*, 11 June 1998.
27. E.g. *NBR*, 19 September 1997; *NZ Herald*, 3 December 1997; *Manukau Courier*, 18 June 1998; *Independent*, 12 August 1998.
28. *NZ Herald*, 10 November 1998.
29. See *Independent*, 16 April 1999; *NZ Herald*, 17–18 April 1999; *Listener*, 19 June 1999.
30. G. Ullrich, 'Company Personnel in Battle Zones until Peace was Established', undated.
31. Ansett NZ, *Southern Skies*, November 1998, p.26.
32. Ansett NZ, *Southern Skies*, November 1998, p.26.
33. D. Hubbard, 'The Business of Business is Not Just Business', Hubbard Foods, Auckland, undated.
34. T. Hazledine, *Taking New Zealand Seriously: The Economics of Decency*, HarperCollins, Auckland, 1998, p.15. See also *NZ Herald*, 26 March 1998; 3 June 1999.
35. J. Helliwell, *How Much Do National Borders Matter?*, Brookings Institution, Washington, 1998, p.118.
36. *NZ Herald*, 23 July 1999.
37. Helliwell, p.133.
38. B. Easton, 'Poverty in New Zealand 1981–1993', paper for the Economic and Social Research Trust of New Zealand, Wellington, 1994; C. Waldegrave, R. Stephen and P. Frater, 'Most Recent Findings in the New Zealand Poverty Measurement Project', *Social Work Review*, vol.8 (1996), p.3.
39. S. Chatterjee and N. Podder, 'Sharing the National Cake in Post Reform New Zealand: Income Inequality Trends in Terms of Income Sources', paper to the Annual Conference of the New Zealand Association of Economists, Wellington, 2–4 September 1998.
40. Statistics New Zealand, *New Zealand Now: Incomes*, p.9.
41. *The Jobs Letter*, no.95 (19 February 1999).
42. Statistics New Zealand, *New Zealand Now: Incomes*, p.58.
43. Economist Paul Dalziel assessed the share of the 1996 tax cuts that went to poor and middle-income families at just 29 percent. P. Dalziel, 'Poor Policy: A Report for the New Zealand Council of Christian Social Services

on the 1991 Benefit Cuts and the 1996 Tax Cuts', April 1996.
44 *The Jobs Letter*, no.95 (19 February 1999).
45 *The Jobs Letter*, no.95 (19 February 1999).
46 C. Waldegrave and S. Stuart, 'An Analysis of the Consumer Behaviour of Beneficiaries', Report to the Social Transformation Council, Anglican Diocese of Wellington, 1996.
47 *NZ Herald*, 23 April 1999.
48 Statistics New Zealand, *New Zealand Now: Women*, Wellington, 1999, p.108.
49 Te Puni Kokiri, *Progress Towards Closing the Social and Economic Gaps Between Maori and non-Maori*, Wellington, 1998.
50 Statistics New Zealand, *Key Statistics: May 1999*, Wellington, p.34, Table 3.05.
51 B. Easton, 'The Maori in the Labour Force', in P. Morrison (ed.), *Labour, Employment and Work in New Zealand*, Victoria University of Wellington, Wellington, 1994, p.206.
52 *NZ Herald*, 20 May 1999.
53 Te Puni Kokiri, *Closing the Gaps*, p.15.
54 Statistics New Zealand, *New Zealand Now: Women*, p.87.
55 Statistics New Zealand, *New Zealand Now: Women*, p.89.
56 Statistics New Zealand, *New Zealand Now: Women*, p.121.
57 *The Economist*, 5 November 1994, p.19.
58 *NZ Herald*, 16 March 1995.
59 Birch, 28 July 1998, quoted in Joint Methodist Presbyterian Public Questions Committee and Council of Christian Social Services, 'Myths About Poverty in Aotearoa New Zealand', October 1998, Wellington, sheet 7.
60 The exceptions were the sale of the Coal Corporation and aspects of the airwaves.
61 P. Perry and A. Webster, 'The New Zealand Study of Values', Massey University, 1999. See also J. Kelsey, *The New Zealand Experiment: A World Model for Structural Adjustment?*, 2nd edn, Auckland University Press/Bridget Williams Books, Auckland, 1997, pp.324–25, Tables 13.1 and 13.2.
62 E. Darian-Smith, 'Law in Place: Legal Mediations of National Identity and State Territory in Europe', in P. Fitzpatrick (ed.), *Nationalism, Racism and the Rule of Law*, Dartmouth, Aldershot, 1995, p.27 at p.33.
63 Krugman, pp.105–6, 107.
64 B. Jesson, *Only Their Purpose is Mad*, Dunmore Press, Palmerston North, 1999.
65 K. Polanyi, *The Great Transformation: The Political and Economic Origins of Our Times*, Beacon Press, Boston, 1957, p.125.
66 Polanyi, p.250.
67 Polanyi, p.250.
68 Polanyi, p.251.

▲ Select Bibliography

A Vision for APEC: Towards an Asia Pacific Economic Community: Report of the Eminent Persons Group, APEC, Singapore, 1993.
Achieving the APEC Vision: Free and Open Trade in the Asia Pacific: Second Report of the Eminent Persons Group, APEC, Singapore, 1994.
ACIL, *Agricultural Marketing Regulation: Reality Versus Doctrine*, Business Roundtable, Wellington, 1992.
Allen, G., 'The Deal on Services: A Necessary Step to Integration', in K. Vautier, J. Farmer and R. Baxt (eds), *CER and Business Competition: Australia and New Zealand in a Global Economy*, Commerce Clearing House, Auckland, 1990, p.165.
APEC Business Advisory Council, *ABAC's Call to Action*, Vancouver, November 1997.
APEC Economic Committee, *Economic Outlook: Economic Performance and Prospects in the APEC Region*, APEC, Singapore, 1997.
ARENA, *Bhopal: Industrial Genocide?*, Arena Press, Hong Kong, 1985.
Asian Development Bank, *Governance: Promoting Sound Development Management*, ADB, Manila, 1997.
Auckland Power Supply Failure 1998: The Report of the Ministerial Inquiry into the Auckland Power Supply Failure, Ministry of Commerce, Wellington, 1998.
Bates, R. and A. Krueger, *Political and Economic Interactions in Economic Policy Reform*, Blackwell, Oxford, 1993.
Bates, W., *Farmer Control: Does it Serve the Interests of Farmers?*, NZBR, Wellington, 1998.
Bates, W., *The Dairy Board's Export Monopoly*, NZBR, Wellington, October 1997.
Baxi, U., '"Global Neighbourhood" and "Universal Otherhood": Notes on the Report of the Commission on Global Governance', *Alternatives*, vol.21 (1996), p.525.
Bello, W., 'APEC and the Conflict of Capitalisms', in E. Tadem and L. Daniel (eds), *Challenging the Mainstream: APEC and the Asia-Pacific Development Debate*, Arena Press, Hong Kong, 1995.
Bello, W. and J. Chavez-Malalulan, *APEC: Four Adjectives in Search of a Noun*, Manila People's Forum on APEC, Manila, 1996.
Berger, S. and R. Dore (eds), *National Diversity and Global Capitalism*, Cornell University Press, New York, 1996.
Birchfield, R. and I. Grant, *Out of the Woods: The Restructuring and Sale of New Zealand's State Forests*, GP Books, Wellington, 1993.
Black's Law Dictionary, 6th edn, West Publishing Co, Minnesota, 1990.
Bollard, A. and B. Easton (eds), *Markets, Regulation and Pricing: Six Case Studies*, Research Paper 31, NZIER, Wellington, 1985.
Bollard, A., 'More Market: The Deregulation of Industry', in A. Bollard and R. Buckle (eds), *Economic Liberalisation in New Zealand*, Allen & Unwin, Wellington, 1987.
Bollard, A., 'New Zealand', in J. Williamson (ed.), *The Political Economy of Policy Reform*, Institute for International Economics, Washington, 1993.
Bremer, R. and T. Brooking, 'Federated Farmers and the State', in B. Roper and C. Rudd (eds), *State and Economy in New Zealand*, Oxford University Press, Auckland, 1993, p.108.
Brooking, T. and R. Rabel, 'Neither British nor Polynesian: A Brief History of New Zealand's Other Immigrants', in S. Greif (ed.), *Immigration and National Identity in New Zealand*, Dunmore Press, Palmerston North, 1995, p.23.
Bullard, N., W. Bello and K. Malhotra, *Taming the Tigers: The IMF and the Asian Crisis*, CAFOD, London, March 1998.
Carew, E., *Westpac: The Bank that Broke the Bank*, Doubleday, Sydney, 1997.

Cassels, J., *The Uncertain Promise of Law: Lessons from Bhopal*, Toronto University Press, Toronto, 1993.
Chatterjee, P., 'World Bank Failures Soar to 37.5% of Completed Projects in 1991', in K. Danaher (ed.), *50 Years is Enough: The Case Against the World Bank and the International Monetary Fund*, South End Press, Boston, 1994, p.137.
Clarke, T. and M. Barlow, *MAI and the Threat to Canadian Sovereignty*, Stoddart Publishing, Toronto, 1997.
Commonwealth Secretariat, *Current Good Practices and New Developments in Public Service Management: A Profile of the Public Service of New Zealand*, Country Profile Series No. 5, Commonwealth Secretariat, London, 1995.
Cooper, D. and D. Neu, 'The Politics of Debt and Deficit in Alberta', in T. Harrison and G. Laxer (eds), *The Trojan Horse: Alberta and the Future of Canada*, Black Rose Books, Montreal, 1995, p.163.
Cox, R., 'Critical Political Economy', in B. Hettje (ed.), *International Political Economy: Understanding Global Disorder*, Zed Books, London, 1995.
Crocombe, G., M. Enright and M. Porter, *Upgrading New Zealand's Competitive Advantage*, Oxford University Press, Auckland, 1991.
Croome, J., *Reshaping the World Trading System: A History of the Uruguay Round*, World Trade Organisation, Geneva, 1995.
Daly, H., *Beyond Growth: The Economics of Sustainable Development*, Beacon Press, Boston, 1996.
Dalziel, P., 'Evaluating New Zealand's Economic Reforms, 1984–95: Comment', *Victoria Economic Commentaries*, vol.15, no.1 (1998), p.1.
Darian-Smith, E., 'Law in Place: Legal Mediations of National Identity and State Territory in Europe', in P. Fitzpatrick (ed.), *Nationalism, Racism and the Rule of Law*, Dartmouth, Aldershot, 1995, p.27.
Douglas, R. and B. Burgess, *Options for Kiwifruit: An Industry in Crisis: An Independent Review*, Wellington, 1992.
Douglas, R., *Unfinished Business*, Random House, Auckland, 1993.
Drake, W. and K. Nicolaidis, 'Ideas, Interests and Institutionalization: "Trade in Services" and the Uruguay Round', *International Organizations*, vol.46, no.1 (1992), p.37.
Duncan, I. and A. Bollard, *Corporatization and Privatization: Lessons from New Zealand*, Oxford University Press, Auckland, 1992.
Durie, E., 'United Nations or United Peoples', in C. Arup and L. Marks (eds), *Cross Currents: Internationalism, National Identity and Law*, special edn of *Law in Context*, vol.14, no.1 (1996), p.1.
Durie, M., *Te Mana, Te Kawanatanga: The Politics of Maori Self-Determination*, Oxford University Press, Auckland, 1998.
Easton, B. and R. Gerritsen, 'Economic Reform: Parallels and Divergences', in F. Castles, R. Gerritsen and J. Vowles (eds), *The Great Experiment: Labour Parties and Public Policy Transformation in Australia and New Zealand*, Auckland University Press, Auckland, 1996.
Easton, B., 'How Did the Health Reforms Blitzkrieg Fail?', *Political Science*, vol.4, no.2 (1994), p.215.
Easton, B., *In Stormy Seas: The Post-War New Zealand Economy*, Otago University Press, Dunedin, 1997.
Easton, B., 'The Maori in the Labour Force', in P. Morrison (ed.), *Labour, Employment and Work in New Zealand*, Victoria University of Wellington, Wellington, 1994, p.206.
Evans, L., A. Grimes and B. Wilkinson, with D. Teece, 'Economic Reform in New Zealand: 1984–95: The Pursuit of Efficiency', *Journal of Economic Literature*, vol.34, no.4 (1996), p.1856.
Evans, L., 'Farming in a Changing Economic Environment', in A. Bollard and R. Buckle (eds), *Economic Liberalisation in New Zealand*, Allen & Unwin, Wellington, 1987, p.102.
Evans, P., 'The State', in S. Haggard and R. Kaufman (eds), *The Politics of Economic Adjustment*, Princeton University Press, New Jersey, 1992.

SELECT BIBLIOGRAPHY ▲ 419

Falk, R., 'Global Civil Society: Perspectives, Initiatives, Movements', *Oxford Development Studies*, vol.26, no.1 (1998), p.99.
Farmer, J., 'The Harmonisation of Australian and New Zealand Business Laws', in K. Vautier, J. Farmer and R. Baxt (eds), *CER and Business Competition: Australia and New Zealand in a Global Economy*, Commerce Clearing House, Auckland, 1990, p.48.
Fitzsimons, P., 'The New Zealand Securities Commission: The Rise and Fall of a Law Reform Body', *Waikato Law Review*, vol.2 (1994), p.87.
Fox, M. and G. Walker, 'Evidence on the Corporate Governance of New Zealand Listed Companies', *Otago Law Review*, vol.8, no.3 (1995), p.317.
Fraser Forum, Fraser Institute, Vancouver, June 1993.
Fukuyama, F., *The End of History and the Last Man*, Avon Books, New York, 1992.
Garrett, G., 'Shrinking States? Globalization and National Autonomy in the OECD', *Oxford Development Studies*, vol.26, no.1 (1998), p.71.
George, S., 'How to Win the War of Ideas: Lessons from the Gramscian Right', *Dissent*, vol.44, no.3 (1997), p.3.
Gilpin, R., *The Political Economy of International Relations*, Princeton University Press, Princeton, 1987.
Gramsci, A., *Prison Notebooks*, Lawrence & Wishart, London, 1978.
Green, D., *From Welfare State to Civil Society*, Business Roundtable, Wellington, 1996.
Gustafson, B., *The First 50 Years: A History of the New Zealand National Party*, Reed Methuen, Auckland, 1986.
Haggard, S. and R. Kaufman, 'Institution and Economic Adjustment', in S. Haggard and R. Kaufman (eds), *The Politics of Economic Adjustment*, Princeton University Press, New Jersey, 1992.
Harper, D. and G. Karacaoglu, 'Financial Policy Reform in New Zealand', in A. Bollard and R. Buckle (eds), *Economic Liberalisation in New Zealand*, Allen & Unwin, Wellington, 1987.
Harris, P. and L. Twiname, *First Knights: An Investigation of the New Zealand Business Roundtable*, Howling at the Moon, Auckland, 1998.
Hayward, D. and R. Bell, *1994 Kaikohe Business Survey: Summary of Survey Findings*, Working Paper No.6, Department of Geography, Auckland University, 1997.
Hayward, D. and M. Salvaris, 'Rating the States: Credit Rating Agencies and the Australian State Governments', *Journal of Australian Political Economy*, no.34 (December 1994), p.1.
Hazledine, T., *Taking New Zealand Seriously: The Economics of Decency*, Harper-Collins, Auckland, 1998.
Head, J., 'Suspension of Debtor Countries' Voting Rights in the IMF: An Assessment of the Third Amendment to the Charter', *Virginia Journal of International Law*, vol.33 (1993), p.591.
Held, D., 'Democracy, the Nation-State and the Global System', in D. Held (ed.), *Political Theory Today*, Polity Press, Cambridge, 1991.
Helliwell, J., *How Much Do National Borders Matter?*, Brookings Institution, Washington, 1998.
Henderson, D., *New Zealand in an International Perspective*, Business Roundtable, Wellington, 1996.
Henriksson, S. and A. Svenson, *New Zealand: What is the Outlook for Welfare?*, Ministry of Health and Social Affairs, Stockholm, 1998.
Higgott, R. and A. Cooper, 'Middle Power Leadership and Coalition Building: Australia, the Cairns Group, and the Uruguay Round of Trade Negotiations', *International Organization*, vol.44, no.4 (1990), p.589.
Hoekman, B. and M. Kostecki, *The Political Economy of the World Trading System: From GATT to WTO*, Oxford University Press, Oxford, 1995.
Hogan, J., *Break the Dollar Deadlock: The Failure of the Bretton Woods Plan*, Technical Books, Wellington, 1952.
Howse, R. and M. Trebilcock, 'The Fair Trade – Free Trade Debate: Trade, Labor, and the Environment', *International Review of Law and Economics*, vol.16 (1996), p.61.

Hurrell, A. and N. Woods, 'Globalisation and Inequality', *Millennium: Journal of International Studies*, vol.24, no.3 (1995), p.447.
Hyman, P., *Women and Economics: A New Zealand Feminist Perspective*, Bridget Williams Books, Wellington, 1994.
ICFTU, 'Looking Ahead to the WTO Ministerial Council – An ICFTU View', in *Labour Standards in the Global Trade and Investment System*, TUAC/OECD, Paris, November 1996, p.93.
Implementing the APEC Vision: Third Report of the Eminent Persons Group, APEC, Singapore, 1995.
Inquiry into Parliament's Role in the International Treaty Process: Report of the Foreign Affairs, Defence and Trade Select Committee, Wellington, 1997.
Jesson, B., *Behind the Mirror Glass*, Penguin Books, Auckland, 1987.
Jesson, B., *Only Their Purpose is Mad*, Dunmore Press, Palmerston North, 1999.
Johnson, B., 'Factors of the Index of Economic Freedom', in *1997 Index of Economic Freedom*, Heritage Foundation, Washington, 1997.
Kahler, M., 'Bargaining with the IMF: Two-Level Strategies and Developing Countries', in P. Evans, H. Jacobson and R. Putnam (eds), *Double-Edged Diplomacy: International Bargaining and Domestic Politics*, University of California Press, Berkeley, 1993, p.363.
Kahler, M., 'Trade and Domestic Differences', in S. Berger and R. Dore (eds), *National Diversity and Global Capitalism*, Cornell University Press, New York, 1996, p.298.
Kapstein, E., *Governing the Global Economy: International Finance and the State*, Harvard University Press, Cambridge, 1994.
Karns, M., 'Multilateral Diplomacy and Trade Policy: The United States and the GATT', in M. Karns and K. Mingst (eds), *The US and Multilateral Institutions: Patterns of Changing Instrumentality and Influence*, Routledge, London, 1990, p.141.
Kasper, W., *Populate or Languish?*, Business Roundtable, Wellington, 1990.
Keane, J. (ed.), *Claus Offe: Disorganised Capitalism*, Polity Press, Oxford, 1985.
Keith, K., 'New Zealand Treaty Practice: The Executive and the Legislature', *New Zealand Universities Law Review*, vol.1 (1964), p.272.
Kelsey, J., 'APEC: Catching a Tiger by the Tail', in E. Tadem and L. Daniel (eds), *Challenging the Mainstream: APEC and the Asia-Pacific Development Debate*, Arena Press, Hong Kong, 1995.
Kelsey, J., 'Global Economic Policy-Making: A New Constitutionalism?', *Otago Law Review*, vol.9, no.3 (1999), p.535.
Kelsey, J., 'International Economic Agreements and Environmental Justice', in B. Richardson and K. Bosselmann (eds), *Environmental Justice and Market Mechanisms*, Kluwer International, The Hague, 1999.
Kelsey, J., *A Question of Honour? Labour and the Treaty 1984–1989*, Allen & Unwin, Wellington, 1990.
Kelsey, J., *Rolling Back the State: The Privatisation of Power in Aotearoa New Zealand*, Bridget Williams Books, Wellington, 1993.
Kelsey, J., *The New Zealand Experiment: A World Model for Structural Adjustment?*, 2nd edn, Auckland University Press/Bridget Williams Books, Auckland, 1997.
Keynes, J.M., *The General Theory of Employment, Interest and Money*, Harcourt Brace & Co, New York, 1936.
Korten, D., *When Corporations Rule the World*, Kumarian Press, West Hartford, 1995.
Krugman, P., 'Does the New Trade Theory Require a New Trade Policy?', *The World Economy*, vol.15, no.4 (1992), p.423.
Krugman, P., *Pop Internationalism*, MIT Press, Cambridge, 1997.
Krugman, P., *The Age of Diminished Expectations: US Economic Policy in the 1990s*, MIT Press, Cambridge, 1994.
Kubota, I., 'The Role of the Government in Dynamic Economic Development Process', in *Governance: Promoting Sound Development Management*, ADB, Manila, 1997, p.45.
Lake, H., *International Monetary Fund and World Bank: Implications of New Zealand Membership*, Government Printer, Wellington, 1961.

Le Heron, R. and E. Pawson (eds), *Changing Places: New Zealand in the Nineties*, Longman Paul, Auckland, 1996.
Marchak, P., *The Integrated Circus: The New Right and the Restructuring of Global Markets*, McGill-Queens University Press, Montreal, 1991.
Massey, P., *New Zealand: Market Liberalization in a Developed Economy*, St Martin's Press, New York, 1995.
McCubbins, M., R. Noll and B. Weingast, 'Administrative Procedures as Instruments of Political Control', *Journal of Law, Economics and Organization*, no.6 (1990), p.243.
McGee, D., 'Treaties – A Role for Parliament?', *Public Sector*, vol.20, no.1 (1997), p.3.
McKinnon, D., 'New Zealand Sovereignty in an Interdependent World', in G. Wood and L. Leland (eds), *State and Sovereignty: Is the State in Retreat?*, Otago University Press, Dunedin, 1997.
Meehan, A., 'Viewpoint: "Globalisation" – New Zealand's Choice', *Asia 2000 Foundation of New Zealand*, no.4 (June/July 1995).
Melbourne, H., *Maori Sovereignty: The Maori Perspective*, Hodder Moa Beckett, Auckland, 1995.
Minister of Education, *Tertiary Education in New Zealand: Policy Directions for the 21st Century: White Paper*, Ministry of Education, Wellington, November 1998.
Ministry of Commerce, *Review of Post-2000 Tariff Policy*, Ministry of Commerce, Wellington, 1997.
Ministry of Education, *A Future Tertiary Education Policy for New Zealand: Tertiary Education Review: Green Paper*, Ministry of Education, Wellington, 1997.
Ministry of Foreign Affairs and Trade, *Invest in New Zealand: The Right Choice*, Ministry of Foreign Affairs and Trade, Wellington, 1998 and 1999.
Ministry of Foreign Affairs and Trade, *Trade Policy Briefing 1993*, Ministry of Foreign Affairs and Trade, Wellington, 1993.
Ministry of Foreign Affairs and Trade, *Trading Ahead: The GATT Uruguay Round: Results for New Zealand*, Ministry of Foreign Affairs and Trade, Wellington, 1994.
Ministry of Justice, *Briefing Paper for the Minister of Justice*, Ministry of Justice, Wellington, October 1996.
Molloy, A., *Thirty Pieces of Silver*, Howling at the Moon, Auckland, 1998.
Moran, W., G. Blunden and A. Bradly, 'Empowering Family Farms Through Cooperatives and Producer Marketing Boards', *Economic Geography*, vol.72, no.2 (1996), p.161.
Moran, W., G. Blunden, M. Workman and A. Bradly, 'Family Farmers, Real Regulation, and the Experience of Food Regimes', *Journal of Rural Studies*, vol.12, no.3 (1996), p.245.
Muchlinski, P., *Multinational Enterprises and the Law*, Blackwell, Oxford, 1995.
Nader, R. and others (eds), *The Case Against Free Trade: GATT, NAFTA and the Globalization of Corporate Power*, Earth Island Press, San Francisco, 1993.
Nelson, J., 'Poverty, Equity and the Politics of Adjustment', in S. Haggard and R. Kaufman (eds), *The Politics of Economic Adjustment*, Princeton University Press, New Jersey, 1992.
New Zealand Law Commission, *A New Zealand Guide to International Law and its Sources*, New Zealand Law Commission, Wellington, 1996.
New Zealand Treasury, *1990 Briefing Papers*, Treasury, Wellington, 1990.
New Zealand Treasury, *Economic and Fiscal Update: December 1998*, Treasury, Wellington, 1998.
New Zealand Treasury, *Economic Management*, Treasury, Wellington, 1984.
New Zealand Treasury, *Government Management: Brief to the Incoming Government 1987, Volume 1*, Treasury, Wellington, 1987.
Nishimoto, S., 'The Bank's Governance Policy', in *Governance: Promoting Sound Development Management*, ADB, Manila, 1997, p.9.
OECD Declaration on International Investment and Multinational Enterprises, *International Legal Materials*, vol.15 (1976), p.967.
OECD, 'Joint Report on Trade, Employment and Labour Standards by the OECD Employment, Labour and Social Affairs Committee and the OECD Trade Commit-

tee', in *Labour Standards in the Global Trade and Investment System*, TUAC/OECD, Paris, November 1996, p.77.

OECD, *Thematic Review of the First Years of Tertiary Education: New Zealand*, OECD Directorate for Education, Employment, Labour and Social Affairs, Paris, 1997.

Offe, C., 'Legitimacy Through Majority Rule', in J. Keane (ed.), *Claus Offe: Disorganised Capitalism*, Polity Press, Oxford, 1985.

Ohmae, K., 'Putting Global Logic First', *Harvard Business Review*, vol.73, no.1 (1995), p.119.

Ohmae, K., *The Borderless World: Power and Strategy in the Interlinked Economy*, Harper, New York, 1991.

Ohmae, K., *The End of the Nation State: The Rise of Regional Economies*, The Free Press, New York, 1995.

Parliamentary Commissioner for the Environment, *Long-term Management of the Environmental Effects of Tailings Dams*, Parliamentary Commissioner for the Environment, Wellington, 1997.

Picciotto, S., 'International Business and Global Development', in S. Adelman and A. Paliwala (eds), *Law and Crisis in the Third World*, Hans Zell, London, 1993, p.149.

Picciotto, S., 'The Regulatory Criss-Cross: Interaction Between Jurisdictions and the Construction of Global Regulatory Networks', in W. Bratton, J. McCahery, S. Picciotto and C. Scott (eds), *International Regulatory Competition and Coordination*, Oxford University Press, Oxford, 1996.

Polanyi, K., *The Great Transformation: The Political and Economic Origins of Our Times*, Beacon Press, Boston, 1957.

Porter, M., 'Getting on Top Internationally – The Centrality of Labour Market Reform', in *Economic and Social Policy*, Business Roundtable, Wellington, 1989.

Pursey, S., 'Implementation of Labour Standards in the Multilateral System', in *Labour Standards in the Global Trade and Investment System*, TUAC/OECD, Paris, November 1996.

Putnam, R., 'Diplomacy and Domestic Politics: The Logic of Two-Level Games', in P. Evans, H. Jacobson and R. Putnam (eds), *Double-Edged Diplomacy: International Bargaining and Domestic Politics*, University of California Press, Berkeley, 1993.

Raghavan, C., *Recolonization: GATT, the Uruguay Round and the Third World*, Third World Network, Penang, 1990.

Ramphal, S., *Our Global Neighbourhood: Report of the Commission on Global Governance*, Oxford University Press, Oxford, 1995.

Ranald, P., *Disciplining Governments? What the MAI Would Mean for Australia*, UNSW Public Sector Research Centre & Evatt Foundation, Sydney, 1998.

Reich, R., *The Work of Nations: Preparing Ourselves for 21st-Century Capitalism*, Simon & Schuster, London, 1991.

Report of the Permanent People's Tribunal Session on Workers and Consumers Rights in the Garment Industry in Brussels (April–May 1998), Permanent People's Tribunal, Rome, 1998.

Report of the Winebox Inquiry: Commission of Inquiry into Certain Matters Relating to Taxation, GP Publications, Wellington, 1997.

Reserve Bank of New Zealand, *Financial Policy Reform*, RBNZ, Wellington, 1986.

Rich, B., 'World Bank/IMF: 50 Years is Enough', in K. Danaher (ed.), *50 Years is Enough: The Case Against the World Bank and the International Monetary Fund*, South End Press, Boston, 1994, p.10.

Richardson, R., 'Governance: Promoting Sound Development: Management Lessons from New Zealand', in *Governance: Promoting Sound Development Management*, ADB, Manila, 1997.

Ritchie, M., 'Free Trade versus Sustainable Agriculture', *The Ecologist*, vol.22, no.5 (September/October 1992), p.221.

Roberts, C., 'Prospects of Success of the National Institute of Health's Human Genome Application', *European Intellectual Property Review*, vol.1 (1994), p.30.

Rodrik, D., 'Who Needs Capital-Account Convertibility?', *Essays in International Finance*, no.207 (May 1998), p.55.

Rosenau, J., 'Governance, Order and Change in World Politics', in J. Rosenau and E-O Czempiel (eds), *Governance Without Government: Order and Change in World Politics*, Cambridge University Press, Cambridge, 1992.
Rosenberg, B., 'A Critical Perspective on Foreign Investment', in P. Endelwick (ed.), *Foreign Investment: The New Zealand Experience*, Dunmore Press, Palmerston North, 1998.
Rosenberg, W., 'Capital Imports and Growth: The Case of New Zealand: Foreign Investment in New Zealand, 1840–1958', *The Economic Journal*, vol.LXXI (1961), p.93.
Rosenberg, W., *New Zealand Can be Different – and Better*, New Zealand Monthly Review Society, Christchurch, 1993.
Rosenberg, W., 'New Zealand on a New Road: After the IMF – What?', *New Zealand Monthly Review*, Christchurch, 1961, p.4.
Rosenberg, W., 'New Zealand's Relations with the International Monetary Fund', *New Zealand Company Director*, vol.1, no.1 (April 1967).
Ruggie, J.G., *Constructing the World Polity: Essays on International Institutionalization*, Routledge, London, 1998.
Ruggie, J.G., 'International Regimes, Transactions and Change: Embedded Liberalism in the Post-war Economic Order', *International Organization*, vol.36, no.12 (1982), p.195.
Ruggie, J.G., 'Territoriality and Beyond: Problematizing Modernity in International Relations', *International Organization*, vol.47, no.1 (1993), p.139.
Sally, R., 'Multinational Enterprises, Political Economic and Institutional Theory: Domestic Embeddedness in the Context of Internationalization', *Review of International Political Economy*, vol.1, no.1 (1994), p.161.
Sandrey, R., 'The GATT Uruguay Round in Perspective: Implications for New Zealand', *New Zealand Journal of Business*, vol.16, no.1 (1994), p.51.
Schick, A., *The Spirit of Reform: Managing the New Zealand State Sector in a Time of Change. A Report Prepared for the State Services Commission and the Treasury*, State Services Commission, Wellington, 1996.
Sen, A. and S. Anand, *Sustainable Human Development: Concepts and Priorities*, UNDP, New York, 1996.
Sexton, S., *New Zealand Schools: An Evaluation of Recent Reforms and Future Directions*, Business Roundtable, Wellington, 1990.
Soros, G., 'The Capitalist Threat', *Atlantic Monthly*, vol.279, no.2 (1997), p.45.
Soros, G., *The Crisis of Capitalism*, Public Affairs, Washington, 1998.
Spicer, B., R. Bowman, D. Emanuel and A. Hunt, *The Power to Manage: Restructuring the New Zealand Electricity Department as a State-Owned Enterprise*, Oxford University Press, Auckland, 1991.
Statistics New Zealand, *New Zealand Now: Incomes*, Wellington, 1999.
Statistics New Zealand, *New Zealand Now: Women*, Wellington, 1999.
Streeten, P., 'Free and Managed Trade', in S. Berger and R. Dore (eds), *National Diversity and Global Capitalism*, Cornell University Press, New York, 1996, p.353.
Sutch, W.B., *Takeover New Zealand*, A.H. & A.W. Reed, Wellington, 1971.
Taft, K., *Shredding the Public Interest: Ralph Klein and 25 Years of One-Party Government*, University of Alberta Press, Edmonton, 1997.
Te Puni Kokiri, *Progress Towards Closing the Social and Economic Gaps Between Maori and non-Maori*, Te Puni Kokiri, Wellington, 1998.
Teubner, G., '"Global Bukowina": Legal Pluralism in the World Society', in G. Teubner (ed.), *Global Law Without a State*, Aldershot, Dartmouth, 1997.
Tomas, N., 'Tangata Whenua Issues', *New Zealand Environmental Law Reporter*, October 1995, p.144.
Toye, J., 'Comments', in J. Williamson (ed.), *The Political Economy of Policy Reform*, Institute for International Economics, Washington, 1993.
Trebilcock, M. and R. Howse, *The Regulation of International Trade*, Routledge, London, 1995.
Trick or Treaty?: Commonwealth Power to Make and Implement Treaties, Commonwealth Parliament, Canberra, November 1995.
Twomey, A., 'Treaty Making and Implementation in Australia', *Public Law Review*, vol.7 (1996), p.4.

UNCTAD, *World Investment Report 1997: Transnational Corporations, Market Structures and Competition Policy: Overview*, United Nations, New York, 1997.
United Fruit, *Supporting the Single Desk: A Preliminary Review of Economic and Community Issues*, YAF Consulting, Palmerston North, September 1998.
United Kiwi, *Analysing Industry: Community Viability and Risks for the Kiwifruit Industry*, YAF Consulting, Palmerston North, 1998.
USCIB, *A Guide to the Multilateral Agreement on Investment (MAI)*, New York, January 1996.
Van Dormael, A., *Bretton Woods: Birth of a Monetary System*, Macmillan, London, 1978, p.32.
Vasquez, X., 'The North American Free Trade Agreement and Environmental Racism', *Harvard International Law Journal*, vol.34, no.2 (1993), p.357.
Wade, R., 'Globalization and Its Limits: Reports of the Death of the National Economy are Greatly Exaggerated', in S. Berger and R. Dore (eds), *National Diversity and Global Capitalism*, Cornell University Press, New York, 1996.
Wade, R., 'Japan, the World Bank and the Art of Paradigm Maintenance: The East Asian Miracle in Political Perspective', *New Left Review*, vol.217 (1996), p.3.
Waitangi Tribunal, *Kiwifruit Marketing Report 1995*, WAI 449, Waitangi Tribunal, Wellington, 1995.
Waldegrave, C., R. Stephen and P. Frater, 'Most Recent Findings in the New Zealand Poverty Measurement Project', *Social Work Review*, vol.8 (1996), p.3.
Walker, G. and A. Borrowdale, 'Overseas Notes: New Zealand', *Company and Securities Law Journal*, vol.12 (1994), p.529.
Walker, R., 'Immigration Policy and the Political Economy of New Zealand', in S. Greif (ed.), *Immigration and National Identity in New Zealand*, Dunmore Press, Palmerston North, 1995, p.282.
Waring, M., *Counting for Nothing: What Men Value and Women are Worth*, Allen & Unwin/Port Nicholson Press, Wellington, 1988.
Whose Genes Are They Anyway?, Report of the Health Research Council Conference on Human Genetic Information, Wellington, 1995.
Wiessman, R., 'Patent Plunder: TRIPping the Third World', *Multinational Monitor*, November 1990, p.8.
Williams, D., *'Te kooti tango whenua': The Native Land Court 1864–1909*, Huia Publishers, Wellington, 1999.
Williams, D., 'Treaties and the Parliamentary Process', *Public Law Review*, vol.7 (1996), p.199.
Williamson, J. and S. Haggard, 'The Political Conditions for Economic Reform', in J. Williamson (ed.), *The Political Economy of Policy Reform*, Institute for International Economics, Washington, 1993.
Williamson, J. (ed.), *The Political Economy of Policy Reform*, Institute for International Economics, Washington, 1993.
Wooding, P., 'Liberalising the International Trade Regime', in A. Bollard and R. Buckle (eds), *Economic Liberalisation in New Zealand*, Allen & Unwin, Wellington, 1987, p.86.
Woods, N., 'Editorial Introduction: Globalization: Definitions, Debates and Implications', *Oxford Development Studies*, vol.26, no.1 (1998), p.5.
World Bank, *From Plan to Market: World Development Report 1996*, Oxford University Press, Oxford, 1996.
World Bank, *The East Asian Economic Miracle: Economic Growth and Public Policy*, Oxford University Press, Oxford, 1993.
World Bank, *The State in a Changing World: World Development Report 1997*, Oxford University Press, Oxford, 1997.
Zacher, M., 'The Decaying Pillars of the Westphalian Temple: Implications for International Order and Governance', in J. Rosenau and E-O Czempiel (eds), *Governance Without Government: Order and Change in World Politics*, Cambridge University Press, Cambridge, 1992.

▲ Index

ACT, 24, 27, 185, 196, 197, 224, 369
Agreement on Trade-related Aspects of Intellectual Property Rights (TRIPS), 263–6, 317
agriculture, 218–29, 252–9
Air New Zealand, 127, 342
Alberta, 101–2, 104
Alliance, parliamentary opposition to: foreign investment in NZ, 129, 130–1; globalisation, 12; MAI, 332–3, 337, 343, 347; producer boards reform, 224; tariff cuts, 210, 216; Uruguay Round Bill, 251
American Chamber of Commerce, New Zealand Branch (AMCHAM), 129–30, 170–1, 172, 173, 175
Ameritech, 127, 178, 180–1
Anderton, Jim, 295, 337, 347, 369
Annan, Kofi, 272
Ansley, Bruce, 284
anti-dumping and safeguard laws, 257–8
APEC, 279–314, 379–80; commitments voluntary and non-binding, 214, 317, 379–80; competing paradigms, 290–307; historical background, 281–3; Labour Advisory Forum, 305; Manila Action Plan 1996, 294–6; opposition to, 300–7; organisation of, 283–90
APEC Business Advisory Council (ABAC), 284, 286, 295, 296, 299, 308, 310
APEC Labour Monitor (ALARM), 306
APEC meetings: (Jakarta, 1994), 291–2, 300; (Osaka, 1995), 292–4, 300–1; (trade ministers; Christchurch, 1996), 284; (Manila, 1996), 294–6, 301, 303–4, 305; (Vancouver, 1997), 296–8, 301–2; (Kuala Lumpur, 1998), 298–300, 302–3, 305; (Auckland, 1999), 217, 307–13
Apple and Pear Marketing Board, 219, 220, 221, 224, 228, 229
Apple Fields, 218–19, 221
Appleton, Barry, 326
Armstrong, John, 289
ASEAN, 274, 281, 282, 283
Asia 2000, 126, 308
Asia Pacific Economic Cooperation. *See* APEC
Asia Pacific Investment Code, 291
Asia Pacific Labour Network, 305
Asian Development Bank (ADB): annual meeting (Auckland, 1995), 94, 111–12, 129; anti-democratic leverage over governments, 38; and APEC, 290; and Asian financial crisis, 117; market-based approach, 92; policy and debate on governance, 97, 116–17; promotes New Zealand model, 90, 91, 94, 96, 100, 102; supports privatisation, 66; technical assistance project in Mongolia, 105–6
Asian Development Bank Institute, 119
Asian financial crisis, 117–19, 154, 296–7, 299
Asian immigration, 126
Asian investment (in New Zealand), 126–7
Asian Monetary Fund, Japanese proposal for, 119
Association of South East Asian Nations (ASEAN), 274, 281, 282, 283
Atlas Foundation, 62
Auckland Regional Services Trust, 378
Australia: and APEC, 280, 281, 283, 293, 298, 311–12; economic performance of, 358–9; leader of Cairns Group, 245; and MAI, 325, 330–1, 382; parliamentary oversight of treaty-making, 47–8, 330–1; tariff policy (1996), 209; taxation, 173–4. *See also* CER
Australia New Zealand Food Standards Authority, 233–5, 380
Australia New Zealand Food Standards Council, 233–5, 380
Australian Bureau of Agricultural and Resource Economics (ABARE), 311
Awatere Huata, Donna, 63

Aziz, Rafidah, 298
balance of payments, 141–2
Bank of International Settlements, 152, 157, 376
Bank of New Zealand, 126, 152, 180, 189, 190, 191
banks, 148–9, 152–3, 189–91
Barshefsky, Charlene, 276, 298, 350
Belgrave, John, 264
Bell Atlantic, 127, 178, 180–1
Bello, Walden, 117, 118, 155–6
Bergsten, Fred, 285
Berryman, Warren, 197
Bhopal disaster, 165–6
Bilderberg Group, 58
Birch, Bill, 82, 130, 140, 174, 346, 350, 371
Blair House Accord, 254–5
blitzkrieg strategy, 27, 63, 100–4, 108–9
Blue Star, 180
Bogor Declaration 1994, 291–2
Bolger, Jim: and APEC, 295, 307; attacks Anderton over MAI, 337; calls NZ an 'Asian nation', 126; cites OECD report, 72; dines with Rupert Murdoch, 196; praises Thai horticultural plant, 186; receives advice on investment incentives, 130; scaremongering before 1996 election, 125; speaker at Davos, 60
Bollard, Alan, 27, 31, 207, 208
Bougainville, 167
Bradford, Max, 184–5, 217, 345
Brash, Don, 45–6, 60, 107, 142, 158, 364
Brazil, 100, 118, 154, 244, 320, 321
Bretton Woods conference, 6, 91–2, 144
Brierley Investments, 130, 161, 186, 196
Brunei, 244, 282, 283
Bunkle, Phillida, 235
Burdon, Philip, 208, 251, 286
Business and Industry Advisory Committee (OECD), 170, 318, 319, 327, 348–9
Business Council of Australia, 209
Business Council on National Issues (Canada), 289
Business Roundtable: cited in WTO review, 74–5; dominant neo-liberal think-tank and corporate transnational lobby, 60, 171, 172; faith in free market policies, 27; and food standards, 234; influence waning, 17, 24, 67; and international treaty-making, 42; links with IEA, 62, 63; and producer boards, 221, 222, 224; reports, 60, 86, 222; and Resource Management Act, 175; and sharemarket regulation, 151–2; views challenged, 365–6; and zero tariffs, 212; mentioned, 64, 258, 286

Cairns Group of Free Trading Nations, 245, 254, 256, 271
Camdessus, Michel, 75, 92, 119
Campaign Against Foreign Control of Aotearoa (CAFCA), 11
Canada, 101–2, 280, 281, 283, 317, 324–5, 327, 328–9, 382
Canadian Broadcasting Corporation, 88
Canadian Taxpayers Federation, 101
Canterbury Farmer, 333
Canterbury Regional Council, 189
'capacity building', 96
capital flows, 153–8, 171, 172, 376
Capital Properties, 134
Car Owners' Association, 66
Carter Holt Harvey, 124, 127, 128, 138–9, 161, 166
Carter, Richard, 124
Castro, Fidel, 272
Caygill, David, 70, 80
Centre for Independent Studies (Australia), 62, 63
Centre for Independent Studies (New Zealand), 62, 64
Centre for Policy Studies (Monash), 64

CER, 10, 30, 38, 206, 229–37, 238, 380, 383
Chile, 124, 157, 166–7, 244, 283, 290, 297, 321
China, 281, 283, 320, 321
Choudry, Aziz, 310–11
Christchurch City Council, 184, 347
'civil society', involvement of, in treaty-making process, 50, 382
Clark, Helen, 337
Clear Communications, 181–2
Clinton, President: and APEC, 288, 289, 290, 313; 'fast-track' authority, 350, 355; at GATT's 50th birthday celebrations, 271; at WTO, 276–7; mentioned, 254
Closer Economic Relations trade agreement with Australia. *See* CER
clothing industry, 212–17
Coalition Agreement (1996), 131, 209, 334, 335, 343, 346
Coalition for Better Government, 82, 171
Coalition government (1996–98), 49, 83, 87, 131–2, 171, 208–17, 223, 334–5
Code of Social Responsibility, 63
Codex Alimentarius, 269
Coeur d'Alene Mines Corp, 176, 177
Coeur Gold (NZ), 176–7, 178
Colman, Barry, 196–7
Comalco NZ Ltd, 185–6
Commerce Act 1973, 182
Commerce Act 1986, 29, 182, 221, 355, 378–9; review of (1999), 182
Commerce Commission, 175, 182–3, 184, 185, 197, 229, 258, 345
Committee on Trade and the Environment, 275
Commodity Levies Act 1990, 221, 223
Common Agricultural Policy, 253
Commonwealth Secretariat, 90, 102, 107–9
comparative advantage, 202
competitiveness rankings, 83–6, 114, 116
consensus formation, 56–67
Consumers' Institute, 191
Contact Energy, 183–4
Cook Islands tax schemes, 129, 149, 179
Coromandel Watchdog, 176, 178, 354
CORSO, 11
Costello, Peter, 66
Council of Trade Unions (CTU), 14, 215, 258, 305, 333–4
credit rating agencies, 77–83, 114
Crossroads, 65–6
CS First Boston, 179, 234
Cullen, Michael, 82, 338, 346
current account deficit, 141–2, 360

Dairy Board, 124, 161, 220, 221, 226, 228
Dairy Brands New Zealand, 218–19
Dairy Industry Restructuring Bill, 229
Dairy Trade Coalition (US), 222
Dalziel, Paul, 357–9
Databank, 193
Davos, 59, 60
Deane, Rod, 63, 64, 65, 67, 94, 181, 182
Declaration on International Investment and Multinational Enterprises, 167, 317
Delamere, Tuariki, 223, 225, 336
democratic scrutiny, of treaty-making process, 43–52, 338, 355
Department for International Development (UK), 332
Department of Labour, 345–6
Department of Trade and Industry, 206
Development Finance Corporation, 125, 152, 179
Dewes, Whaimutu, 60
Dinning, Jim, 102
diplomacy (on behalf of structural adjustment), 112–15
Donovan, Peter, 212–13
Douglas, Ken, 15, 333
Douglas, Roger: approves sale of state assets to foreign companies, 125; has contacts with neo-liberal think-tanks, 60–1, 65, 67; promotes blitzkrieg strategies, 63, 100–1, 102; recommends privatisation of producer boards, 221, 222
Dunkel, Arthur, 243, 251
Dunne, Peter, 338
Durie, Eddie, 52
Durie, Mason, 52–3

The East Asian Miracle: Economic Growth and Public Policy (World Bank, 1993), 116
East, Paul, 295
Easton, Brian, 27, 74, 86, 153, 359, 370
ECNZ/Electricorp, 65, 183
Economic Management, 8–9, 20, 64, 206, 220
Economic Outlook, 69, 70, 71, 297
Economist, 77, 86–8, 116
Edison Mission Energy, 183–4
Edlin, Bob, 136, 312, 360
electoral reform, 13, 82
electricity industry, 183–6
Electricorp/ECNZ, 65, 183
Electronic Data Systems (EDS), 178, 193–5
electronic media, 197–9
Eminent Persons Group (APEC), 284, 285–6, 289–90, 291, 292
Employers and Manufacturers Association (Northern), 214, 258
Employers' Federation, 42, 212
employment, 203–4
Employment Contracts Act 1991, 29, 30, 186, 346
Engineers' Union, 258
English, Bill, 24, 368–9
environment, 174–8, 273–4, 275–7, 326–7, 344–5
Epstein, Richard, 65
Ernst & Young, 179
Ethical Trading Initiative, 169
Ethyl Corporation, 327
European Commission, 349, 350–1
European Common Market, 162
European Community, 244, 245, 253, 254
European Exchange Rate Mechanism, 154, 155
European Parliament, 329, 382
European Union, 11, 38, 51, 202, 269–70, 276, 321
Evans, Lewis, 357–8
Evening Post, 72, 76
exchange rate, 146, 148
Export Enhancement Program, 253
exporting the New Zealand model, 90–120
expropriation, 317, 323, 327, 344, 345

Farmer, Jim, 230
Fay, Michael, 65, 67, 180
Fay Richwhite, 179, 180, 181, 186
Federated Farmers, 42, 212, 218, 220, 224, 228
Federation of Maori Authorities, 224
Fernyhough, John, 64, 67
Fernz Corporation, 161, 172–3
'financial arbitrage', 147
financial crises, 153–8
financial markets, 142–58
Financial Times, 116, 119, 126–7, 277, 289, 349
Fiscal Responsibility Act 1993, 30, 82, 376
Fischer, Tim, 256
Fisher, Antony, 62
fisheries, 298
Fletcher Challenge, 124, 128, 130, 138, 161, 166
Fletcher Construction, 60
Fletcher, Hugh, 18, 19, 136, 364, 365
Food and Beverage Exporters' Council, 234
food standards, 233–5, 353–4, 380
footwear industry, 212–17
Foreign Control Watchdog, 128, 136, 181
foreign debt, 140–1, 360
foreign direct investment (FDI), 123–42, 150, 377
foreign-owned companies: earnings remitted overseas, 137; employment record, 138–9; tax paid, 137
forestry, 125, 127, 128, 178, 298
Forestry Corporation, 130, 140
France, 324–5, 350
Fraser Institute, 61
'free' investment regime, 121–58, 361
free market model: politically unsustainable, 3–4, 12–13, 357–74
free trade, 200–38; and agriculture, 218–29, 252–9; and industry, 206–17; social costs of, 203–4; theory and reality, 201–6. *See also* CER
Friedman, Milton, 57, 146
From Welfare State to Civil Society (Green), 63
'fundamentals', 29–30, 82, 112, 121, 125, 132, 154, 364

INDEX ▲ 427

GATT, 6, 220, 241–5, 271–2, 282, 290. *See also* Uruguay Round; WTO
GATT Watchdog, 11, 332, 250
Gaynor, Brian, 137, 139, 141, 151, 180, 184, 186–7, 360
GCS (Government Computing Service), 193, 195
General Agreement on Tariffs and Trade. *See* GATT
General Agreement on Trade in Services (GATS), 41, 259–63, 317
genetically modified food, 234–5, 353–4
Gibbs, Alan, 62–3, 64, 65, 67, 179, 197
Gilbert, Wayne, 66
Global Competitiveness Report, 83–5, 86
Global Forum on Reinventing Government (Washington, 1999), 120
globalisation: historical background, 4–7; as ideology, 2, 8, 55, 56; myths of, 31–43; in practice, 2, 55, 56; sustainability of, 357–74
'good governance', 96–100, 107, 155
Gore, Al, 120, 289, 299
Gould, Bryan, 82–3
Government Computing Service (GCS), 193, 195
government intervention, in New Zealand economy, 8
Government Management, 9, 20, 207
Government Printing Office, 180
government procurement and social services, 347–8
Government Property Services, 134
The Great Transformation (Polanyi), 4, 383–4. *See also* Polanyi, Karl
Green, David, 62, 63
'greenfield' investment, 136, 377
Grey Power, 132, 333
Group of Seven (G-7), 38
Group of 24 (G-24), 244
Group of 77 (G-77), 243, 244, 321
Guidelines for Multinational Enterprises (OECD, 1976), 168–9, 325, 327, 344, 345

Haggard, Stephen, 26–8
Hart, Graeme, 180
Hayek, Friedrich von, 57, 62
Hazledine, Tim, 19, 36, 215, 312, 366
health care services, 178
health information initiative, 194–5
'hedge funds', 147, 156–7
Heeren, Alex van, 186
Heinz, 196
Helliwell, John, 35–6, 366–7
Henare, Tau, 336, 340, 341
Heritage Foundation, 61–2, 85, 114, 117
Hide, Rodney, 63
Hong Kong, 210, 283, 296, 320, 321
Hood, John, 60
Hop Marketing Board, 220, 224, 228
Housing Corporation mortgages, 179
Howard, John, 190, 232, 235, 303
HR Nicholls Society, 63, 66
Hubbard, Dick, 365–6
Human Genome Diversity Project, 266
Human Genome Project, 266
Human Rights Act 1993, 189
Human Rights Commission, 189
Human Rights Watch Asia, 306

IBM, 192
Iceland, 103, 104
IMF: anti-democratic leverage over governments, 38; and APEC, 285, 290; approach to Asian financial crisis, 117–18; criticism of, 93, 117–18; established, 6, 91, 144; and floating exchange rates, 145–6; and globalisation agenda, 57, 92; Malaysia's independence from, 156; and monetary stability, 6, 91, 144–5, 145–6, 240; new powers proposed, 158; and New Zealand, 75–7, 93–5, 104–5, 145; mentioned, 157, 167–8, 246, 382
import licensing, 206, 208
INCIS (police computer system), 192
Independent (NZ), 89, 136, 197, 360
Independent (UK), 88
Independent Newspapers Ltd (INL), 132, 195, 197
Independent Newspapers Plc (INP), 196
Index of Economic Freedom, 85–6, 114
India, 157, 243, 244, 247, 267–8, 273, 320, 321
indigenous peoples, 166–7, 247, 272–3, 302, 306

Indonesia, 117, 154, 156, 184, 244, 282, 283, 296
industry, 206–17
Infometrics, 216, 312
information processing, 178
Information Technology Agreement (ITA), 271
Inland Revenue Department, 193
insider trading laws, 151
Institute of Economic Affairs (IEA), 62, 63
intellectual property, 202, 263–6, 317
interest rates, 148
International Centre for the Settlement of Investment Disputes, 43, 323
International Centre for Trade and Sustainable Development, 277
International Chamber of Commerce, 168, 170, 275
International Confederation of Free Trade Unions (ICFTU), 14, 50–1, 273, 274, 277, 305
International Credit Insurance Corporation, 157
International Democratic Union, 57
International Finance Agreements Act 1961, 145
International Labour Organisation (ILO), 274–5, 325
International Monetary Fund. *See* IMF
International Organization of Employers, 170
International Paper, 127, 138
International Trade Commission (US), 257
international treaties. *See* treaty-making process
Internet, 179, 315, 333
Invest in New Zealand (MFAT booklet), 85, 86, 132
investment, 121–58, 361. *See also* MAI
Ireland, 365, 366

Jackson, Moana, 265
Japan: and APEC, 281, 282, 283, 289, 292–4, 293, 297, 298; competing paradigm, 115–17, 119; investment liberalisation, 321; prefers bilateral approach to trade negotiations, 243; and Uruguay Round, 244, 254; mentioned, 202, 203, 210, 362
Jennings, Owen, 229
Jesson, Bruce, 378
Jones, Morgan, 187

Kaikohe, 165
Karns, Margaret, 242
Kaufman, Robert, 26–8
Kawerau pulp and paper mill, 124, 166
Keating, Paul, 231
Keith, Kenneth, 48
Kelsey, Jane, 96, 110–11, 115, 337
Kennedy Round, 253
Kennett, Jeff, 66
Kerr, Roger, 17, 60, 62–3, 64, 65, 66, 67, 198, 225–6
Keynes, John Maynard, 143–4
Kinleith pulp and paper mill, 139
Kirin Brewery, 134, 151
Kirk, Norman, 145
'Kiwi share', 342, 378
Kiwifruit Marketing Board, 220, 222, 223, 224–5, 226–7, 228, 228–9
'knowledge economy', 366
knowledge industries, 192–9
Korten, David, 1, 58, 93, 147, 164
KPMG survey, 137, 139
Krugman, Paul, 32, 33, 146, 147, 200, 202–3, 364, 376
Kubota, Isao, 116–17
Kwa, Aileen, 254

Labour government (1984–90): BNZ bail-out, 152; committed to 'opening up' economy, 10, 124; deregulates financial sector, 148; favourable treatment of Fay Richwhite, 180; free trade agenda, 200, 201–2, 206–8; and producer boards, 221; removes restrictions on investment, 124, 124–5; and Uruguay Round, 250
Labour party (in opposition): and food standards, 235; and MAI, 332, 337–8; opposes electricity reforms, 183, 185; and producer boards, 224; sits on fence over foreign investment, 129, 132; softens policies, 14; supports tax relief for transnationals, 173–4; supports Uruguay Round Bill, 251; and tariff reduction, 216–17
labour standards, 273–5, 325–6, 345–6
Lake, Harry, 145
Laking, Rob, 104
lamb exports to US, 257

Lange, David, 65, 313
Latvia, 110-11
Law Commission, 48-9
Learning Leadership Centre (World Bank), 109
least developed countries (LDCs), 175, 270
Lee, Sandra, 341
Liberty Press, 196
Lindsay, Greg, 62, 64
Lion Nathan, 134, 151
Listener (NZ), 89
local government, 346-7
Long-Term Capital Management, 152
Love, Ngatata, 341
Luxton, John, 184, 210, 211, 224, 226, 228

McCully, Murray, 313
McDonald, Kerry, 185, 286
McGee, David, 48, 251
McKinnon, Don: and APEC, 295, 296, 303, 311, 312; on external sovereignty, 47; on Mekong Institute, 111; on NZ in Asia Pacific region, 126; on reform programme, 15, 125, 357
McShane, Owen, 175
Maharey, Steve, 369
Mahathir bin Mohamed, 156, 281, 289, 292, 299, 303
Mahuta, Robert, 21
MAI, 315-52, 382, 383; background to, 317-19; early negotiations, 319-21; New Zealand government's response, 332-48; opposition to, 328-32; text of, 322-7; mentioned, 6, 16, 43, 170, 382, 383. See also investment
Major Electricity Users Group, 185
Malaysia: and APEC, 183, 281, 290, 292-3, 298-300, 302-3; ASEAN member, 244, 282; and Asian financial crisis, 154, 156, 296; G-77 member, 243; and IMF, 156; and MAI, 320, 321; WTO upholds 'Shrimp Turtle' complaint, 268
Malaysia New Zealand Business Council (Sarawak Chapter), 114
'managed' trade, 203, 206
Manila Action Plan for APEC 1996 (MAPA), 294-6
Manufacturers' Federation, 42, 206, 207, 208, 216, 258
manufacturing, 127
Maori, actual or potential concerns of: APEC, 309-10; Asian immigration, 126; average incomes, 369-70; biodiversity, 266; decolonisation, 19-23, 52-4; farming, 219, 259; forestry transnationals, 166; free trade, 241; globalisation, 19-23, 52-4; GM foods, 235; health status, 370; intellectual property rights, 265-6; international treaty-making, 278, 383; MAI, 132,,339-42; MMP, 382; national currency, 237; producer boards, 222-3, 224, 238; tino rangatiratanga, 44-5, 52-4, 265, 339, 354, 374; Treaty of Waitangi, 339-42; unemployment, 370-1; Waitangi Tribunal claims, 130
Mapuche, 166-7
Market Surveillance Panel, 151
Martin, Pat, 334
Mataatua Declaration on Cultural and Intellectual Property, 265
Matthew, Bob, 16-17
Maungatoroto, 191
Meat Board, 220, 221, 224, 228
media, 86-9, 195-9
Mekong Institute, 111
Meo, Roseanne, 286
Mercury Energy, 66
Metalclad, 327
Mexico, 154, 282, 283, 297, 317, 325, 327
mining, 176-8
Ministry of Commerce, 181, 206, 212, 216, 257-8, 266
Ministry of Consumer Affairs, 184
Ministry of Foreign Affairs and Trade: consultations with Maori, 266, 309-10, 341; established, 206; and international treaty-making, 338; likely response to major policy shift, 375; and MAI, 338-9, 341, 342, 345
Ministry of Justice, 48
Mitterand, Danielle, 301
mixed member proportional representation (MMP), 13, 82, 171, 381
Miyazawa Plan, 119
Monash University, 64
monetary policy, 148, 149, 363-5

Mongolia, 103, 105-6
Monopolies and Mergers Commission (UK), 188
Monsanto, 235
Mont Pelerin society, 62-3
Moody's. *See* credit rating agencies
Moore, Mike: dismisses critics of GATT, MAI, 240, 337; in favour of MAI, 132, 138, 337, 338; as Leader of the Opposition supports the public's right to know, 81; seeks post of WTO Director-General, 272; supports 'internationalism', 14
'moral hazard', 146, 190
'most favoured nation', 241, 264, 317, 350
Muldoon government, 64, 75, 80, 124, 206
Multilateral Agreement on Investment. *See* MAI
Murdoch, Rupert, 65, 67, 170, 195, 195-6
Myers, Douglas, 63, 64, 65, 66, 67, 151, 287

Nader, Ralph, 117
National Business Review: on credit-rating agencies, 77; generally sympathetic to reform programme, 60, 71; locally owned, 196; misinterprets 'foreign currency debt', 140; on MMP and forthcoming 1996 election, 171; myopic, 89; on NZ's poor economic performance, 83; and OECD, 71, 72; polls, 126, 129, 130
National Council of Women, 212
National Distribution Union, 213, 215, 216
National government (1990-96): 1995 amendment to Overseas Investment Act, 128-9; BNZ bail-out, 152; continues Labour's reform programme, 10; favourable treatment of Fay Richwhite, 180; free trade agenda, 200, 201; opposes 'social clause' in economic treaties, 51; policy initiatives come unstuck, 15-16; tariff reduction policy, 208; and Uruguay Round, 250, 251
National government (1998-99), 235
National Maori Congress, 251-2, 265, 341
National Priorities Project, 66
'national treatment', 241, 260, 264, 317, 350
nationalisation, 317, 323, 377
Neha, Jack, 187
Neilson, Peter, 70
networking, 58-60
New Zealand: and APEC, 280, 281, 283, 307-13; Cairns Group member, 245; free trade negotiations, 273; GATT negotiations, 244-5; and ILO, 275; and MAI, 322-3, 325, 332-48; position in Uruguay Round, 248-52
New Zealand Business Roundtable. *See* Business Roundtable
New Zealand Businesses for Social Responsibility, 18, 36, 365-6
New Zealand economy: dysfunctional, 357-67; government intervention in, 8; IMF annual reviews, 75-7; OECD surveys, 69-72; WTO trade policy reviews, 73-5
New Zealand First: 1996 election results, 131, 295; campaigns on 'economic sovereignty', 12, 337; founding pledge, 334; and MAI, 132; opposes 1995 amendment to Overseas Investment Act, 129; and producer boards, 223, 224, 225; and sale of Forestry Corporation, 130; tariff policy, 209; mentioned, 130. *See also* Coalition Agreement (1996); Coalition government (1996-98)
New Zealand Herald, 70, 71, 80, 103, 171, 195, 196, 211, 289, 299-300
New Zealand Institute of Economic Research (NZIER), 217, 249-50
New Zealand Rail, 126
New Zealand Trade Union Federation (TUF), 11-12, 51, 216, 305, 306, 332
'New Zealand's Economic Reform Programme was a Failure' (Dalziel), 358-9
Ngai Tahu, 20-1
non-government organisations (NGOs), 50, 270, 273, 277, 300-4, 349
North American Free Trade Agreement (NAFTA), 6, 11, 38, 162, 282, 317, 327, 382
Nottage, Richard, 333
Nozick, Robert, 57

O'Brien, Terence, 308
Occupational Safety and Health Service, 188
OECD, 68-73; Business and Industry Advisory Committee, 170, 318, 319, 327, 348-9; Committee on International Investment and Multinational Enterprises,

318; Declaration on International Investment and Multinational Enterprises, 167, 317; economic policies of member countries, 36–7; Guidelines for Multinational Enterprises, 168–9, 325, 327, 344, 345; surveys of economic performance, 69–72; Trade Union Advisory Committee (TUAC), 325, 326, 333–4; mentioned, 10, 38, 50, 57. *See also* MAI
Official Information Act 1982, 49, 129
Only Their Purpose is Mad (Jesson), 378
Oram, Rod, 17, 211
O'Regan, Tipene, 20–1
O'Reilly, Tony, 132–3, 196
Organisation for Economic Cooperation and Development. *See* OECD
Orion, 184
Osaka Action Agenda 1995, 292–4
O'Sullivan, Fran, 299–300, 307
Otago Daily Times, 195
overseas borrowing, 140–1, 360
overseas development assistance, 106
Overseas Investment Act 1986, 29; 1995 amendment, 128–9, 130; 1997 amendment, 131–2
Overseas Investment Commission, 124–5, 127, 128–9, 133–5, 136, 150, 219, 343
Oxfam, 331–2

Pacific Basin Economic Council, 286
Pacific Business Economic Council (PBEC), 282, 308
Pacific Business Forum, 284, 286, 292
Pacific Economic Cooperation Council (PECC), 282, 284, 286, 288, 291, 297, 308
Palmer, Geoffrey, 222
Papua New Guinea, 283
Parker, Selwyn, 165
Perot, Ross, 193
Perry, Paul, 372–3
Peru, 100–1, 281
Peters, Winston: as Deputy Prime Minister, 49, 333, 336, 337, 343; and deregulation of Kiwifruit Marketing Board, 223, 225; pre-election promises, 12, 130, 131; as Treasurer, 83, 209
Philippines, 40, 156, 244, 272–3, 282, 283, 289, 296, 301
Philpott, Bryan, 217
Polanyi, Karl, 4–5, 7, 144, 357, 373, 383–4
police computer system (INCIS), 192
policy consultancies, 104–12
pork imports from US, 257
Pork Industry Board, 220, 221, 224, 228, 257
Porter, Michael (co-author of *New Zealand's International Competitiveness*), 63, 221, 364–5
Porter, Michael (founder of Tasman Institute), 63–7
Press, 190, 198
Price Waterhouse, 179
print media, 195–7
Privacy Commissioner, 195
privatisation, 125, 178–86, 342–3, 377–8
procurement and social services, 347–8
producer boards, 220–9, 237–8
Producer Boards Act Reform Bill, 224
Programme on Good Governance, 107
PSA Journal, 334
Public Finance Act 1989, 29, 30
Punta del Este Declaration (1986), 245, 274

radio, 197–8
Raghavan, Chakravarthi, 272
Ramos Horta, Jose, 301
Ramos, President, 301, 305
Rank Group, 180
Rankin, Keith, 257
Raspberry Marketing Committee, 220, 228
re-regulation: political will for, 381–5; possibility of, 374–81
Reagan, Ronald, 7, 33, 163
Reich, Robert, 1, 14
Reserve Bank Act 1989, 29–30, 82, 376
Reserve Bank of Australia, 157
Reserve Bank of New Zealand, 64, 148, 149, 152, 236, 285, 359, 363
Resource Management Act 1991, 175–6
Richardson, Ruth: dogmatism, 103; international consultancy and speaking engagements, 95, 96, 100, 101,

102–3, 116; Minister of Finance, 27, 81, 125; mentioned, 63, 65, 222
Richwhite, David, 64, 67, 180
Rio Declaration (1992), 326
Rio Tinto, 167, 185
The Road to Serfdom (Hayek), 62
Robertson, Ross, 338
Rockefeller, David, 58
'rollback' provisions, 318, 324, 351
Rosenberg, Bill, 136, 137, 140, 196, 218, 337
Rosenberg, Wolfgang, 12, 45–6, 141, 145
Ruggie, John Gerard, 6, 37
Ruggiero, Renato, 240, 275, 276, 277, 290, 351
Russia, 154, 281

Sachs, Jeffrey, 84
safeguard and anti-dumping laws, 257–8
Sally, Razeen, 170
Sato, Mitsuo, 92
Saturn Communications, 182
Schick, Allen, 96, 110
Schneiderman, David, 40
Scott, Graham, 95, 96, 104, 106, 106–7
Scott, Jim, 364
Sealord purchase, 21
'secondary boycotts', 324
Securities Commission, 151, 218, 377
Security Intelligence Service (SIS), 310–11
Seoul Declaration (1991), 283
share-market, 148–52
Shipley, Jenny, 120, 228, 234, 235, 299, 343, 346, 347
Shirley, Ken, 338
Shirtcliffe, Peter, 82, 171
'Shrimp Turtle' case, 268
Sin, Cardinal, 301
Singapore, 210, 244, 282, 283, 320
Singapore Declaration (1996), 274
single currency, 235–7, 383
Slovakia, 321
Smith, Lockwood: and APEC, 297–8; on exports, 362; on free trade, 200; and MAI, 336–7, 344, 346, 347, 348; opposes fast-track approach on kiwifruit, 225, 226; optimistic about forestry earnings, 138; on success of reform programme, 90, 114
Smith, Mike, 22–3, 112, 367
'social capital', 365, 373
social cost (of government's free market policies), 367–71
social services and procurement, 347–8
Soros, George, 147, 153, 157–8
South Korea, 117, 154, 156, 244, 281, 283, 293, 320, 325, 362
sovereignty: external, 43–4, 47, 240–1; internal, 43–4, 47; legal, distinguished from state's capacity to act, 45–6; state's capacity to act, 374–81
Spencer, Grant, 94
Spring, Dryden, 226, 257, 285
Stagecoach, 187–9
Standard and Poor's. *See* credit rating agencies
'standstill' provisions, 318, 324, 343, 351
The State in a Changing World (World Bank, 1997), 97–100
State-owned Enterprises Act 1986, 29
State Sector Act 1988, 29
steel industry, 178
Steele, David, 311–12
Stiglitz, Joseph, 33, 119, 355, 364
'strategic trade policy', 203–4
structural adjustment: exporting the New Zealand model, 90–120; politics of embedding new regime, 26–31
study tours of New Zealand, 109–11
Suez Lyonnaise des Eaux, 175
Summers, Larry, 174
Sundakov, Alexander, 94, 110
Sunday Star-Times, 313
Supachai Panitchpakdi, 272
Sutch, Bill, 123
Sutch, Helen, 110
Switzerland, 103
Sykes, Annette, 112

Taiarahia mountain, 166
Tainui, 21

430 ▲ INDEX

Taipei, 283
Takeover New Zealand (Sutch), 123
takeovers code, 151–2
Tamihere, John, 22
Tanzania, 243
Tariff (Zero Duty) Amendment Bill, 217
tariff reduction, 208–17, 237, 377; for cars and light commercial vehicles, 210–12; for textiles, clothing and footwear, 212–17
'tariffication', 224, 255, 256
Tasman Asia-Pacific, 66, 66–7
Tasman Institute, 63, 65, 67
Tasman University (proposal for), 65
taxation, 137, 173–4
te Heuheu, Hepi, 54
Te Puni Kokiri, 309, 340, 341, 342
Telecom, 125, 127, 128, 137, 178, 179, 180–2, 342
television, 197
terms of trade, 362
textiles industry, 212–17
Thailand, 106–7, 117, 154, 156, 186, 244, 268, 282, 283, 296
Thames, 211–12
Thatcher, Margaret, 33, 57, 163
Thatcher, Mark, 194
'there is no alternative' (TINA), 10, 12, 24, 31, 32
think-tanks, 60–7
Third World Network, 331
tino rangatiratanga, 44–5, 52–4, 265, 339, 354, 374
Tobin tax, 157
Tokyo Round, 242–3, 253, 260
Tourism Board, 312, 313
Trade Act (US), 202
trade sector, performance of, 361–3
Trade-related Aspects of Intellectual Property Rights (TRIPS), 263–6, 317
trade-related investment measures (TRIMS), 317
Trade Union Advisory Committee (TUAC), 325, 326
Trade Union Federation. *See* New Zealand Trade Union Federation (TUF)
Tradenz, 104, 133
Trading Ahead, 249, 255
Trans-Tasman investment, 231
Trans-Tasman Mutual Recognition Agreement, 232
TransAlta, 183, 183–4
transnational enterprises (TNEs), 34, 35, 36, 161–99; nature of, 162–7; as political actors, 169–86; rights and responsibilities of, 167–9
Transparency International surveys, 114, 116
Tranz Rail, 127, 128, 132, 179, 186–8
Treasury: and APEC, 285; briefing papers (1984, 1987, 1990), 8–9, 20, 64, 206–8, 220; colonisation of key ministries, 375; and producer boards, 220–1, 223, 227; mentioned, 64, 125, 133, 216
treaty-making process, democratic scrutiny of, 43–52, 338, 355
Treaty of Rome, 317
Treaty of Waitangi, 20, 44, 50, 53, 129, 167, 251, 265, 339–42, 379
Trilateral Commission, 58
TRIPS, 263–6, 317
Trotter, Ron, 64, 65, 67, 124
Troughton, Peter, 63, 66
Tuhoe, 23, 166
Tutu, Desmond, 301
Tuwharetoa, 166

Ullrich, Gilbert, 18, 309, 364, 365
Unfinished Business (Douglas), 101, 102
Union Carbide, 166
United Fruit, 227
United Kiwi, 227
United Nations Conference on Trade and Development (UNCTAD), 161, 192, 243, 321, 329

United States: and APEC, 280, 281, 283, 293; and European Union, 254, 269–70; and free trade, 202, 203; and GATT, 244, 245; and MAI, 329–30, 349–50; political scrutiny of treaty-making, 46–7; supports ICFTU's demands, 51; and Uruguay Round, 254; and WTO, 276. *See also* North American Free Trade Agreement
United States Council for International Business (USCIB), 57, 170, 319, 320
Upton, Simon, 63, 75, 175–6, 303, 344
Uruguay Round, 239–41, 244–5; agreement on agriculture, 252–9; GATS, 259–63; New Zealand's position in, 248–52; projected benefits of, 220, 249–50, 311; TRIPS, 263–6; mentioned, 10, 11, 206, 248, 278, 283, 285, 286, 295, 297, 317, 321. *See also* GATT; WTO
Uruguay Round Bill, 251
Uruguay Round Trade Agreements Act 1994 (US), 246
Utilicorp, 183

'value added', 137
values, survival of, 372–4
Vancouver Year of Action 1997, 296–8
Vietnam, 66, 281
Viner, Jacob, 239

Wade, Robert, 36, 115–16, 164, 361
Waikato Regional Council, 176, 177
Waipareira Trust, 22
Waitai, Rana, 341
Waitangi Tribunal, 130, 166, 222, 266, 340
Washington consensus, 32–3, 93, 94, 98, 109, 117, 119, 204, 355
waste disposal, 175–6, 178
water supply, 178
Watson, Eric, 151
Webster, Alan, 373
WELCOM (World Economic Community), 59–60
welfare state values, survival of, 372–4
Whanganui (iwi), 23
Wilde, Fran, 287
Williamson, Maurice, 192, 196
Wilson and Horton, 195, 196
'Winebox inquiry', 149, 179
Wisconsin Central, 127, 128, 178, 186
Wisconsin Forum (February 1997), 113–14
Wishart, Ian, 249
Wolfensohn, James, 92, 119
Wood, John, 113–14
Woods, Sue, 65
Wool Board, 220, 221, 224, 228
World Bank: anti-democratic leverage over governments, 38, 382; and Asian financial crisis, 117, 119; assessment of agreement on agriculture, 255–6; background, 91–6, 167–8; export of New Zealand model, 90, 100–1, 104, 104, 106, 107, 110–11; International Centre for the Settlement of Investment Disputes, 40, 323; Learning Leadership Centre, 109; World Development Report (1997), 97–100; mentioned, 6, 50, 57, 66, 240, 246
World Competitiveness Yearbook, 85
World Development Movement, 332
World Economic Forum (WEF), 58–60, 83, 170
World Intellectual Property Organisation (WIPO), 263
World Trade Organisation. *See* WTO
World Wildlife Fund (WWF), 326–7, 344
WTO, 239–78; dispute settlement process, 267–70; establishment of, 246–8; interface with APEC, 290, 293, 298; and MAI, 315, 321, 329; ministerial meetings, 270–2; most powerful of multilateral bodies, 38, 379; need for democratic scrutiny of negotiations, 382–3; trade policy reviews on New Zealand, 73–5; mentioned, 6, 10, 30, 50, 54, 57, 167, 279. *See also* GATT; Uruguay Round
Wyllie, Tu, 224

Zespri Group Ltd, 228–9